1991

Leftism
From de Sade and Marx
to Hitler and Marcuse

LEFTISM

From de Sade and Marx
to Hitler and Marcuse

ERIK von KUEHNELT-LEDDIHN

ARLINGTON HOUSE·PUBLISHERS

NEW ROCHELLE, NEW YORK

To the Noble Memory of Armand Tuffin, Marquis de la Rouërie

Courageous Fighter for Liberty
Ardent Admirer of America
Bitter Foe of the Jacobins
Friend of George Washington
Member of the Order of the Cincinnati

Copyright © 1974 Arlington House

Library of Congress Cataloging in Publication Data

Kuehnelt-Leddihn, Erik Maria, Ritter von, 1909-
    Leftism: from de Sade and Marx to Hitler and
Marcuse.

    Includes bibliographical references.
    1. Liberalism--History. 2. Democracy--
History. 3. Conservation--History. 4. Political
science--History. I. Title.
JC571.K79   320.5'1'09   73-78656
ISBN 0-87000-143-4

Manufactured in the United States of America

Contents

Part III   Liberalism

Part IV   The Left and U.S. Foreign Policy

Part V   Leftism Today

Preface

The author of this tome thinks that he owes it to his readers to declare his baggage, to say a few words about the purpose of this book as well as about himself.

I am an Austrian with a rather varied background and a good share of unusual experiences. Born in 1909 as the son of a scientist (radium and X-ray) who died as a victim of his research work, I traveled quite a bit as a young boy and acquired a knowledge of several tongues. Today I read twenty languages with widely varying skill and speak eight. At the age of sixteen I was the Vienna correspondent of the *Spectator* (London), a distinguished weekly founded by Addison and Steele. Engaged in the study of law and Eastern European history at Vienna University at the age of eighteen, I transferred a year later to the University of Budapest (M.A. in Economics, Doctorate in Political Science). Subsequently I embarked on the study of theology in Vienna, but went to England in 1935 to become Master at Beaumont College and thereafter professor at the Georgetown Graduate School of Foreign Service from 1937 to 1938. I was appointed head of the History Department in St. Peter's College, Jersey City (1938-1943) and lecturer in Japanese at Fordham University. Until 1947 I taught at Chestnut Hill College, Philadelphia. These studies and appointments were interspersed with extensive travels and research projects, including the USSR as early as 1930-1931.

During my years in America I traveled in every state: Only southeastern Oregon and northern Michigan alone are still my "blank spots." In 1947 I returned to Europe and settled in the Tyrol, halfway between Paris and Vienna, and between Rome and Berlin, convinced that I had to choose between teaching and research. From 1949 onward I revisited the United States on annual lecture tours. Since 1957 I have traveled every year either around the world or south of the Equator.

One of my ambitions is to know the world; another one is to do research in arbitrarily chosen domains serving the coordination of the various branches of the humanities: theology, political science, psychology, sociology, human geography, history, ethnology, philosophy, art. I have a real horror of one-sided, permanent specialization. I am also active as a novelist and painter. My books, essays, and articles have been published on five continents and in twenty-one countries.

Introduction

So much about myself. The purpose of this book is to show the character of leftism and to what extent and in what way the vast majority
of the leftist ideologies now dominating or threatening most of the modern world are *competitors* rather than *enemies*. This, we think, is an
important distinction. Shoe factory A is a *competitor* of shoe factory
B, but a movement promoting the abolition of footwear for the sake
of health is the *enemy* of both.

In the political field today this distinction, unfortunately, is less obvious and largely obscured by a confusion in semantics. This particular
situation is bad enough in Europe, but it is even worse in the United
States. This state of affairs, in turn, has adversely influenced the foreign
policy of the United States which in the past and in the present not
only has been determined by what—really or only seemingly—is
America's self-interest, but also by ideological prejudices. Very often
these ideological convictions coloring the outlook, the aims, the policies
of those Americans responsible for the course of foreign affairs (not
only Presidents, cabinet members, or congressmen, but also professors,
radio commentators and journalists), have actually run counter to
America's best interest as well as to the very interest of mankind.

There is no reason to believe that ideologies—i.e., coherent political-
social philosophies, with or without a religious background—have come
into play in America only during this century when America was

engaged in two crusades under two Democratic administrations. Nor do we subscribe to the opinion so dear to certain "conservatives" that simply equates leftism and ideology.[1] I think that the nascent United States of the late eighteenth century was already in the throes of warring political philosophies showing positive and negative aspects. Even then the ideological impact of these ideas was keenly felt in Europe where, I must sadly admit, their inner content was often promptly misunderstood and perverted. The American War of Independence had an undeniable influence on the French Revolution and the latter, in the course of the years, had a deplorable impact on America.

Still, it is only in the twentieth century, in our lifetime, that the United States *decisively* intervened in world affairs and that Europe suddenly found herself on the "receiving end" of American foreign policy. Decisions made in Washington (with or without the advice or the prodding of refugees) affected Central Europe—which I consider my home—deeply and often adversely. The long years which I more or less accidentally spent in the United States made me realize the origins, the reasons, the psychological roots of the Great Euramerican Misunderstanding which, as one might expect, has *several* aspects: (1) the lacking self-knowledge of America, (paralleled by the nonexistence of self-knowledge of Europe); (2) the American *misinformation* about Europe (plus the European *ignorance* of America); and (3) the totally deficient realization of where we all now stand historically, what the big, dynamic ideologies truly represent, and how they are related to each other. And let us not overlook the fact that these three points are all somewhat interconnected, since both America (or, better still, the English-speaking world) and Europe (or, more concretely, the Continent) cannot be properly understood without an excursion into the field of ideology. Even the folklores are deeply affected by "philosophies." A sentence such as "One man is as good as any other man if not a little bit better" reminds one automatically of a certain sector of American sentiment. It smacks of Sandburgian folkloric romanticism. On the other hand the words *suum cuique* (to everybody his due) are still inscribed at Innsbruck's law school. Yet it is equally true that Ulpian's great legal principle also makes sense to a number of Americans while egalitarian notions today are rampant in Europe. The Atlantic Ocean, no less than the Channel, is shrinking and, slowly but surely, our confusions are fusing. To make matters worse, our respective semantics are still far apart.

The positive and constructive understanding between America and Free Europe is no less necessary than the realization of what political and economic order is good, right, fruitful. Therefore, this book tries to serve a double purpose: the reduction, if not the elimination of the Great Intercontinental Misunderstanding as well as the Quest for Truth which entails an exposé of the multifaced, multiheaded enemy which is *leftism*.

I think, however, that in all fairness I owe it to the reader to inform him of my starting point, the premises from which I work. I am a Christian: I am emphatically not a democrat but a devotee to the cause of personal liberty. I would thoroughly subscribe to the words of Alexis de Tocqueville when he wrote, "Despotism appears to me particularly to be dreaded in democratic ages. I think that I would have loved liberty at all times, but in the present age I am ready to worship it."[2]

There are, of course, selfish "European" reasons for my writing this book replete with views often not properly represented or understood in America. It is precisely the unwarranted identification of democracy with liberty which has caused a great many of the recurrent tragedies of American foreign policy (as well as a number of internal American woes!). We have to remember all the wars, all the propaganda, all the pressure campaigns for the cause of democracy, how every hailed and applauded victory of democracy has ended in terrible defeat for *personal liberty*, the one cause really dear to American hearts.

This is by no means a new story. Even Burke welcomed the French Revolution in the beginning. Eminent Americans praised it. But it all ended in a forest of guillotines. Mr. Woodrow Wilson enthusiastically welcomed Alexander Kerensky's government which was to make Russia "fit for a league of honor."[3] But how long did it last? The Weimar Republic, the near-republican Italian monarchy, the Spanish republic, the "decolonized" free nations from Haiti to Tanzania, from North Vietnam to Indonesia, Latin America from Santo Domingo to Buenos Aires—all have been grievous disappointments to "progressive" Americans, all terminating in dictatorships, civil wars, crowded jails, confiscated newspapers, gallows and firing squads, one-party tyrannies, sequestrations, nationalizations, "social engineering."

Yet beyond these obvious failures, besides the brutal and open elimination of liberty and decency, there is also—so clearly foreseen by de Tocqueville —the democratic evolution towards nonviolent slavery due to a turn of mind and outlook basically like the one leading to the more obvious forms of tyranny. One should not be surprised about this, because the roots of the evil are historically-genetically the same all over the Western World. The fatal year is 1789, and the symbol of iniquity is the Jacobin Cap. Its heresy is the denial of personality and of personal liberty. Its concrete realizations are Jacobin mass democracy, all forms of national collectivism and statism, Marxism producing socialism and communism, fascism, and national socialism, leftism in all its modern guises and manifestations to which in America the good term "liberalism," perversely enough, is being applied. The issue is between man created in the image of God and the termite in a human guise. It is in defense of man and in opposition to the false teachings which want to lower man to the status of an insect that this book has been written.

Part I

The Leftist Mind

Chapter 1

Identity and Diversity

Let us state at the outset of our investigation that, viewed from a certain angle, we all are subject to two basic drives: one toward *identity*, the other toward *diversity*. Neither in ourselves as persons, nor in the nations through the course of history are these drives always the same in their intensity and in their balance.

How do they manifest themselves? We can all experience a mood during which we feel the desire to be in the company of people of our own age, our own class, our own sex, conviction, religion or taste. It is quite possible that this drive toward conformity, this herd instinct, is something we share with the animal world. This strong identitarian feeling can rest squarely on a real herd instinct, a strong feeling of commonness and community directed in a hostile sense toward another group. In race riots and demonstrations of ethnic groups this collective sentiment can manifest itself with great strength. This sort of conformist herd instinct was the driving motor of the nationalistic gymnastic organizations of the Germans and the Slavs,[1] so potent in the first half of this century and engaging in enormous, carefully synchronized gymnastic performances. When five or ten thousand identically dressed men or women are carrying out identical movements, the onlooker gets an overpowering impression of homogeneity, synchronization, symmetry, uniformity.

Identity and identitarian drives tend towards an effacement of self, towards a nostrism ("usness") in which the ego becomes submerged. Of course, nostrism (a term created by the Austrian Nazi Walter Pembaur) can be and usually is a clever multiplication of egoisms. Whoever praises and extols a collective unit in which he participates (a nation, a race, a class, a party) only praises himself. And therefore all identitarian drives not only take a stand for sameness and oppose otherness, but also are self-seeking. There is an identitarian (and nonsexual) aspect to homosexuality ("homoeroticism") coupled with the refusal to establish the sometimes difficult intellectual, spiritual, psychological bridge to the other sex. And in this respect homosexuality is a form of narcissism, of immaturity and implies the limitations of the "simpleton."[2]

Luckily man in his maturity and in the fullness of his qualifications has not only identitarian but also diversitarian drives, not only a *herd instinct* but also a *romantic sentiment*. More often than not we have the yearning to meet people of the other sex, another age group, another mentality, another class, even of another faith and another political conviction. All varieties of the *novarum rerum cupiditas* (curiosity for the new)—our eagerness to travel and to eat other food, hear another music, see a different landscape, to get in touch with another culture and civilization are derived from this diversitarian tendency in us. A dog neither wants to travel, nor does he particularly mind getting the same food day in and day out, if it is healthy fare. Man, however, wants change. The ant state, the termite state, might remain the same all through the centuries, but man's desire for change results in "history" as we know it. There is something in us that cannot stand repetition, and this hunger for the new *can* be quite fatal if it is not blended with an element of permanence —and prudence.

All higher theist religions rest squarely on this longing, this love for otherness. Though I would not subscribe to Karl Barth's formula of *Gott als der ganz andere* (God as the totally different One), no theist will deny God's otherness. We are created in His image, though we are not a facsimile of God. This is one of the reasons why the Incarnation moves man so profoundly, why over its exact nature the first Ecumenical Council raged with such bitterness and led to tragic heresies and schisms.

Viewing these two tendencies, these two drives, both with *psychological* foundations, but only the romantic sentiment with an *intellectual* character, we inevitably come to the conclusion that modern times are more favorable to the herd instinct than to the enthusiasm for diversity. This is perhaps not immediately evident, because in a few ways the opposite seems to be the case: The craving for travel can now more

16

easily be satisfied, and in the domain of art a greater variety of tastes and schools exists today than in the past. In other, more important realms, however, identity has been pushed in every way, partly by passions (mostly of an animal order), partly by modern technology and procedures forming part and parcel of modern civilization. In another book we have dealt with the dishonesty in the use of the fashionable term "pluralism." As a matter of fact all modern trends point to the specter of a terrifying, bigger and more pitiless conformity.

In this connection we must never forget that identity is a cousin of equality. Everything which is identical is automatically equal. Two fifty-cent coins of the same issue are not only identical but also equal. Two quarters are equal to a fifty-cent coin, but they are not identical with it. Identity *is* equality: It is equality-at-first-sight, an equality which takes no lengthy reasoning or painstaking investigation to discover. Therefore all political or social forms which are inspired by the ideal of equality will almost inevitably point into the direction of identitarianism and foster the herd instinct (with subsequent suspicion, if not hatred, for those who dare to be different or have a claim to superiority).

There exists a dull, animalistic leaning toward identitarian gregariousness, but we encounter also a programmatic, passionate, fanatical drive in that direction. Nietzsche[3] knew of it, so did Jacob Burckhardt.[4] It has fear as its driving motor in the form of an inferiority complex engendering hatred and envy as its blood brother. Fear implies a feeling of being inferior to another person (or to a situation): Hatred is possible *only* if one feels helpless in the face of a person considered to be stronger or more powerful. A feeble and cowardly slave can fear and hate his master; his master in return will not hate, but will have mere contempt for the slave. Haters all through history have committed horrible acts of *cruelty* (which is the inferior's revenge),[5] whereas contempt —always coupled with a feeling of superiority—has rarely produced cruelty. In order to avoid that fear, that feeling of inferiority, the demand for equality and identity arises. Nobody is better, nobody superior, all can relax, all can be at ease, nobody feels challenged, everybody is "safe." And if identity, if sameness has been achieved, then the other person's actions and reactions can be forecast. No (disagreeable) surprise can be expected, everybody can read thoughts and feelings in everybody else's face. And thus a warm herd feeling of brotherhood will emerge. These sentiments, these emotions, this rejection of quality (which can never be the same with everybody!) explain much of the spirit of the mass movements of the last 200 years.

The other factor is *envy*. Envy has complex psychological roots

. . . several, not just one. There exists, first of all, the curious feeling that whatever the other person possesses has in some (roundabout) way been taken away from me. "I am poor because he is rich." This inner, often unspoken argument rests on the assumption that all goods and good things in this world are finite. In the case of money or, even more so, of landed property, such argument might have some substance. (Hence the enormous envy of peasants as to each other's real estate.) Yet this argument is often unconsciously extended to values which are not finite. Isabel is beautiful; Eloise is ugly. Yet Isabel's beauty is not the result of Eloise's plainness, nor Bob's brightness of Tim's stupidity. Again envy *might* subconsciously use a statistical argument. ("Not all of us brothers can be bright, not all of us sisters pretty. Fate handed it to her, to him, and discriminated against me!")

The second aspect of envy lies in the superiority of another person in an important respect. The mere suspicion that the other person *feels* superior on account of looks, of brain-power, of brawn, of cash, etc., can create a burning feeling of envy. The only way to find a compensation lies in a successful search for inferior qualities in the person who figures as the object of envy. "He is rich, but he is evil," "He is successful, but he has a miserable family life," "He is well born and well connected, but, oh, so stupid." Sometimes these shortcomings of an envied person serve as a consolation: sometimes they also serve as a "moral" excuse for an attack, especially if the object of real or imagined envy has moral shortcomings.

In the last 200 years the exploitation of envy, its mobilization among the masses, coupled with the denigration of individuals, but more frequently of classes, races, nations or religious communities has been the very key to political success. The history of the Western World since the end of the eighteenth century cannot be written without this fact constantly in mind. All leftist "isms" harp on this theme, i.e., on the privilege of groups, minority groups, to be sure, who are objects of envy and at the same time subjects of intellectual-moral inferiorities. They have no right to their exalted positions. They ought to conform to the rest, become identical with "the people," renounce their privileges, *conform.* If they speak another language, they ought to drop it and talk the lingo of the majority. If they are wealthy their riches should be taxed away or confiscated. If they adhere to an unpopular ideology, they ought to forget it.[6] Everything special, everything esoteric and not easily understood by the many becomes suspect and evil (as for instance the increasingly "undemocratic" modern art and

18

poetry). Of course there is one type of unpopular minority that cannot conform and therefore is always in danger of being exiled, suppressed or slaughtered: the *racial* minority.

As always hypocrisy is the compliment which vice pays to virtue, and in inciting envy, this ugly feeling will never be openly invoked. The nonconforming person or group sinning against the sacred principle of sameness will always be treated as a *traitor*, and if he is not a traitor the envious majority will push him in that direction. (As late as 1934 there were German Jews who tried to form a Nazi group of their own: naively enough they considered anti-Semitism a "passing phase." Yet can one imagine a German Jew in 1943 *not* praying in his heart for an Allied victory? He was pushed in that direction.) Thus to be different will be treated as or made into treason. And even if the formula Nonconformist-Traitor will not always be promulgated with such clarity, it lurks at the back of modern man's mind only too often, whether he openly embraces totalitarianism or not. One wonders how many people who sincerely reject all totalitarian creeds today would subscribe to the famous dictum of St. Stephen, King of Hungary, who wrote in his will to his heir presumptive, St. Emmeric: "A Kingdom of only one language and one custom is a fragile and stupid thing."[7] Unity and uniformity have been blended in our minds.

The modern magic of sameness has been enhanced not only by a technology producing identical objects (e.g., one type of car owned "commonly" by half-a-million people), but also by the subconscious realization that sameness is related to cheapness and that sameness makes for greater intelligibility, especially to simpler minds. Identical laws, identical measurements, an identical language, an identical currency, an identical education, an intellectual level, an identical political power ("one-man-one-vote"), identical pay rates, identical or near-rency, an identical education, an identical intellectual level, an identical political power ("one-man-one-vote"), identical pay rates, identical or near-identical clothes (the blue denim of Communist China!)—all this seems highly desirable. It simplifies matters. It is cheaper. It saves thinking. To certain minds it even seems "more just."

These identical tendencies run into two obstacles; nature and man (who is part nature). Still, nature is more easily pressed into identical patterns by human endeavor, as witness certain types of gardening. Hills can be "leveled." Geometry can be impressed upon the landscape. To make man more identitarian is a more difficult task, yet not such a hopeless one to the dolt who "optimistically" declares, "All men are equal" and then "All people are more alike than unlike." Here one has to remember Procrustes, the legendary Greek robber and sadist who flung his victim onto a bed: Those who were too short were stretched and hammered until they filled it, those who were too long were "cut to size." Procrustes is the forerunner of modern tyranny.

Here, however, the identitarian comes up against the mystery of personality. Human beings are different: They are of different ages, different sexes, they vary according to their physical strength, their intellect, their education, their ambitions. They have different character and different kinds of memory, different dispositions. They react differently to the same treatment. All this enervates and antagonizes the identitarian. The shoemaker takes it for granted; it is a headache for the shoe manufacturer. It is natural to the governess and no mystery to parents, but it can become an insoluble problem to the teacher of a large class. Along with this goes the proclivity among large groups to give up at least part of the personality. Mass-man in a mass has the tendency to think, act, and react in synchro-mesh with the crowd, a phenomenon that might have a scientific explanation.

And precisely because *human* identity is difficult to achieve, a poor substitute often has to be brought in. This equally unworkable substitute is equality.

Chapter 2

Equality and Liberty

Since this book is written by a Christian let us first deal with the well-known cliché according to which, even though we are neither identical nor equal physically or intellectually, we are at least "equal in the eyes of God." This, however, is by no means the case. None of the Christian faiths teaches that we are all equally loved by God. We have it from Scriptures that Christ loved some of his disciples more than others. Nor does any Christian religion maintain that grace is given in equal amount to all men. Catholic doctrine, which takes a more optimistic view than either Luther or Calvin, merely says that everybody is given sufficient grace to *be able* to save himself, though not to the same extent. The Reformers who were determinists did not even grant that minimum. It is obvious that the Marquis de Sade and, let us say, St. Jean Vianney or Pastor von Bodelschwingh were not "equals in the eyes of God." If they had been, Christianity no longer would make any sense, because then the sinner would equal the saint and to be bad would be the same as to be good.

It is, however, interesting to observe what inroads secular "democratic" thinking has made among the theologians. Obviously equality does not figure in Holy Scripture. Freedom is mentioned several times, but not equality. Yet there are far too many minds among religious thinkers who would like to bridge the gap between religion, i.e., their Christian faith and certain current political notions. Hence they talk about *adverbial* equality—and are not really aware that they are playing a trick. They will start out saying that all men have souls *equally*, that they are *equally* called upon to save their souls, that they are equally created in the image of God, and so forth. But two persons who equally have noses or banking accounts, do not have equal noses or equal banking accounts. While our physical and intellectual differences, inferiorities, and superiorities can be fairly obvious, our spiritual status is much more difficult to determine. *We* do not know who among us is nearer to God, and because we do not know this very important fact, we should *treat* each other as equals. This, however, is merely procedural. We are in a similar position to the postman who delivers two sealed letters indiscriminately, the one that carries a worthless ad and the other that brings great joy. He does not know what is inside. The comparison is far from perfect, because all human beings have the same Father and we are therefore brothers—even if we are spiritually on different levels and have different functions in human society. (From a social viewpoint one person obviously can be more important than another; however, since everybody is unique, *everybody is indispensable*. To state the contrary is democratic nihilism.)

This is also the place to say a few words about the other equality mentioned by so many people in a most affirmative way: equality before the law. At times, equality before the law might be an administrative expedient, saving money and the strain of lengthy investigations. In other words, equality before the law is "practical." The question remains whether it is really desirable, whether it always should be adhered to, and, finally, whether it is just. It is obvious that a child of four having committed manslaughter (it does happen!) should be dealt with differently from a child of twelve, an adolescent of seventeen, or a mature man of thirty. The egalitarian will accept this but will add that all men or women at the age of thirty should be punished the same way. Yet most (not all) courts in the civilized world take "circumstance" into consideration. St. Thomas, for instance, insisted that stealing in a real emergency is no sin—for instance: a desperate beggar having received no alms and thereupon stealing a loaf of bread for his family. The Austrian law practice, under such circumstances, would invoke *unwiderstehlicher Zwang* (irresistible urge) and the "criminal" would get either a suspended sentence or go free. When the Germans were freezing in the winter of 1945-1946 Cardinal Frings of Cologne told the faithful that, under the circumstances, to steal coal was no sin, no crime in the eyes of God. (Hence the phrase: *Kohle fringsen*, to fringsize coal). In certain situations the difference between the sexes will put obstacles on the path of equality before the law. Women, for instance, can *decide* to conceive and thereby get pregnancy leave with pay, while a man *cannot* do this. When the topless bikini became a fad in 1964 a German paper humorously protested against police interference because it was a violation of the highly democratic and egalitarian *Staatsgrundgesetz* ("Basic Law" of the Federal Republic) which forbids all discrimination between the sexes; Why should women be compelled to cover the upper part of their bodies while men are not? Has not God discriminated physically between the sexes? Equality before the law might be highly unjust: witness the outcry, *Summum ius, summa iniuria*. Indeed, justice is better served by Ulpian's principle which we have already quoted, *Suum cuique,* to everybody his due.

A third kind of equality is invoked by a great many: *equality of opportunity.* In the narrow sense of the term it can never be achieved and should not even be attempted. It would be much wiser to demand the abolition of *unjust* discrimination, arbitrary discrimination without a solid "factual" foundation. In employing labor we must discriminate between the skilled and the inexperienced, the industrious and the lazy, the dull and the smart, etc. It is interesting to see, however, that there is a trend in many trade unions to protest against such just discrimination and insist on "indiscriminate" wage rates and employment security. (On the other hand, trade unions have an ugly record of racial discrimination which is patently unjust—especially so in the Union of South Africa where the "common man" tends to be a racist while capital and big business are "color-blind"!![1]

"Just discrimination," in other words, "preference based on merit" is conspicuously absent in a process which, in our society, has a deep and wide influence as a sanctified example—political elections. Whether it is a genuinely democratic election in the West or a plebiscitarian comedy in the East, the one-man-one-vote principle is now taken for granted. The knowledge, the experience, the merits, the standing in the community, the sex, the wealth, the taxes, the military record of the voter do not count, only the vegetable principle of age—he must be 18, 21, 24 years old and still "on the hoof." The 21-year-old semiliterate prostitute and the 65-year-old professor of political science who has lost an arm in the war, has a large family, carries a considerable tax burden, and has a real understanding of the political problems on which he is expected to cast his ballot—they are politically equal as citizens. Compared with a 20-year-old student of political science our friendly little prostitute actually rates higher as a voter. One should therefore not be surprised if in the "emerging nations"—and even in others—literacy is not required for voting. It is this egalitarianism of the voters which has psychologically fathered (as we shall see later) other egalitarian notions and which has been so severely criticized by Pope Pius XII.[2] And not only by him.[3]

Let us return to "Equality of opportunity." In a concrete sense, not even a totalitarian tyranny could bring this about, because no country could decree that a child upon entering this world should have "equal parents." They might be equal to all other parents in the nation as far as wealth is concerned, but will they have equal pedagogical qualifications? Will they provide equal heredity? Will they give their child the same nutrition as other parents? The cry for an identical and equal education has been raised again and again in democracies, totalitarian or otherwise, and the existence of various types of schools has been deemed "undemocratic." Just because parents are so different (every marriage offers another "constellation") egalitarians have advocated not only intensive schooling, but boarding schools for all. Children should be taken out of their homes and collectively educated twenty-four hours a day. This, at present, is the tendency in the Soviet Union where (if everything really goes according to plan) more than 90 percent of all children after the age of six will be in boarding schools after 1980. (How this will affect the birthrate is quite another matter).[4] Yet even all these measures will never result in complete equality of opportunity unless one also totally disregards idoneity (capacity, skills, etc.). If this should happen, a general decline of all levels would set in.

However, as Friedrich August von Hayek has pointed out, a certain equality of treatment is necessary in a free society.[5] Only by treating people equally do we find out who is *superior* to whom. We must give the same test to a group in order to classify its members. We have to see that the horses in a race all start from the same line. By treating people equally (we are back at the adverb) we are not making them equal. Naturally, in a free and open society the timocratic principle will prevail: Those more qualified than others will get ahead faster. "Honor to whom honor is due." There can be no doubt that from the point of view of the common good, the commonweal, the open society is best, because talents have a better chance to be developed in it than in societies divided by castes or estates.[6] It is in the nature of class barriers that they can be transcended. It would, however, be a great mistake to think that the absence of fixed social handicaps increases personal happiness. The gifted bourgeois who failed in pre-Revolutionary French society always had the consolation that an iniquitous system prevented his rise to the top. The man in a free society must either blame himself (which leads to the melancholia of those plagued by inferiority complexes) or will be bound to accuse imaginary conspiracies of ill-wishers and downright enemies.

Psychologically his stand is now a far more difficult one. A society with great mobility naturally will bring a great many fulfillments but, as it is in the nature of things, even more disappointments. In fact, we would not be surprised to find that the number of psychological disturbances, "nervous breakdowns," and suicides among males increases with social mobility (as well as with something quite different, loss of religious convictions). This, however, does not cancel the intrinsic superiority of an open society over a closed one.

Egalitarianism, as we have already intimated, cannot make much progress without the use of force: Perfect equality, naturally, is only possible in total slavery. Since nature (and naturalness, implying also freedom from artificial constraints) has no bias against even gross inequalities, *force* must be used to establish equality. Imagine the average class of students in a boarding school, endowed with the normal variety of talents, interests, and inclinations for hard work. The powerful and dictatorial principal of the school insists that all students of the class should score Bs in a given subject. This would mean that those who earned C, D, or E would be made to work harder, some so hard that they would collapse. Then there would be the problem of the A students whom one would have to restrain, giving them intoxicating drinks or locking them up every day with copies of *Playboy* or *The New Masses*. The simplest way would probably be to hit them over the head. *Force would have to be used,* as Procrustes used it. But the use of force limits and in most cases destroys freedom.

A "free" landscape has hills and valleys. To make an "egalitarian" landscape one would have to blow off the tops of the mountains and fill the valleys with rubble. To get an even hedge, one has to clip it regularly. To equalize wealth (which so many "progressive" countries on either side of the Iron Curtain are now doing) one would have to pay "equal wages and salaries," or tax the surplus away—to the extent that those earning above the average would refuse additional work. Since these are usually gifted people with stamina and ideas, their refusal has a paralyzing effect on the commonweal.

In other words, there is a real antagonism, an incompatibility, a mutual exclusiveness between liberty and enforced equality. This is a curious situation if we remember that in the popular mind these two concepts are closely linked. Is this only due to the fact that the French Revolution chose as its slogan "Liberty, Equality, Fraternity"—or is there another reason?

Apart from this formulation there is in fact no basis for this state of affairs except for the psychological nexus we mentioned earlier. If A is superior to B—more powerful, more handsome, more intelligent, more influential, wealthier—then B will feel inferior, ill at ease, and probably even afraid of A. If we subscribe to the famous "Four Freedoms" and accept the formulation of "Freedom from Fear," then we can see how inequalities actually engender fear—and envy, though envy is rarely mentioned in this connection. Fear and envy, needless to say, are twin brothers, yet we really should speak of triplets, because hate keeps them good company.

This psychological tie notwithstanding, equality on one side and freedom on the other are mutually hostile. Since equality is the dynamic element in democracy, while liberty lies at the base of true liberalism, these two political concepts do not really mix.

Chapter 3

Democracy and Liberalism

Democracy is a political form, a system of government. It has no social content, although it is frequently misused in that sense. It is wrong to say, "Mr. Green is very democratic; on his trips he sits down for lunch with his chauffeur." He is, rather, a friend of simple people, and so is appropriately called *demophile,* not *democratic.*

"Democracy" is a Greek word composed of *demos* (the people) and *krátos* (power in a strong, almost brutal sense). The milder form would be *arché* which implies leadership rather than rule. Hence "monarchy" is the fatherlike rule of a man in the interest of the common good, whereas "monocracy" is a one-man tyranny. Aristotle and the early and the late Scholastics divided the forms of government according to the table on page 28.

Here it must be remembered that, later on, aristocracy also came to mean not a form of government but the highest social layer. The term republic came to mean every (external) form of government that is non-monarchical and "public." *Rzeczpospolita* was a term used for the Polish State prior to 1795 and after 1918, while American and British scholars speak about the "Polish Commonwealth" for the elective kingdom after 1572. Yet the term republic covers indeed a multitude of forms of government if we think not only of the Polish Kingdom prior to 1795, but also of the highly aristocratic Republic of Venice (the *Christanissima Res Publica*), the Soviet Republic (USSR), the present

GOOD FORMS:	BAD FORMS:
Monarchy, the rule of one man in the interest of the common good.	*Tyranny*, the rule of one man to his own advantage.
Aristocracy, the rule of a group in the interest of the common good.	*Oligarchy*, the rule of a group for their own benefit.
Republic or Polity, the rule of the better part of the people in the interest of the common good.	*Democracy*, the rule of the worse part of the people for their own benefit.

(presidential) French Republic, and the presidentless Republic of San Marino with five *capitani reggenti*. The United States is *de facto* a republic, but is not called one in the Constitution. Only the states of the Union are required to have a "Republican Form of Government" (Article IV.4).

Given these semantics in an historical perspective, the question arises how to define in modern terms a democracy (once a pejorative label). Democracy's answer to the question, "Who should rule?" is: "The majority of the politically equal citizens, either in person or through their representatives." This latter qualification refers to direct and indirect democracy. Still, this formulation raises a number of subsidiary questions.

One school insists that only direct democracy is real democracy, whereas elected delegates form an oligarchy with a time limit. There exists a so-called "oligarchic school" of this interpretation of democracy and its foremost opponents were Vilfredo Pareto, Gaëtano Mosca and Roberto Michels (an Italianized former German Socialist). All three might conceivably be called fascist sympathizers, but it is probably the intellectual and realistic climate of Italy, so hostile to all forms of illusions, which influenced their critical thinking.[1] Another school maintains that the election of representatives, bound in conscience to voice the views of their electors, is a *democratic* performance, while representatives who during their period of legislation let themselves be guided by their own lights, their own knowledge, their own conscience, should be considered the executors of a *republican* spirit.[2] Many ancient commentators presuppose that the republic no less than democracy is ruled by majorities, but that in the case of the republic, the majority is not only the *pars maior,* but also *sanior,* whereas in a democracy the majority happens to be the worse part of the nation. It will indeed be the case in every nation that the lower "half" of the social pyramid (if this expression is permitted) is by far the "bigger half," which means that the people of quality *can* always be outvoted. We do not say that they inevitably will be. One *can* imagine that the "natural aristoi" be largely included in the party that wins the elections. They are out of luck, however, if a demagogue (in ancient Greece a "leader of the people" in a democratic state) successfully mobilizes the masses against them.

When we speak of the "politically equal citizens" we must confess that the definition of the "full citizen" (participating in the rule of the country) is *always* arbitrary. In Switzerland and Haiti, for instance, women are excluded from the suffrage. Yet it is hard to argue that Switzerland, therefore, is not a democracy. It could be done, though. The main Swiss counterargument, and one that is typical of this highly militarized nation, is to the effect that women do not serve in the armed forces. They do not have equal duties and, for this good reason, do not have equal rights. Educational or intellectual reasons for this discrimination are never given, because this would be too plainly "undemocratic."[3]

Even more arbitrary are the age limits which are set in order to get "mature voters." But one man (or woman) can achieve maturity early, another one at the "voting age," a third one late and a fourth, never. There is maturity without knowledge, and knowledge without wisdom, but these analyses could lead us too far away from our subject. For those who insist that all human beings are not only *animalia socialia,* but also *zoa politika,* the arbitrarily set voting ages are a serious and also insoluble matter: *If* we accept the reasoning of these theories, then some people are being deprived of their "God-given right" (inherent in their God-given nature). In many a country the voting age was lowered to the age of military service, clearly the result of using the Swiss argument concerning rights and duties. It was this argument also, which led—applied in reverse—to the conscription and to the *levée en masse* in the First French Republic.

Yet, whatever our marginal remarks, the fact remains that *democracy* rests on two pillars: *majority rule and political equality;* and this although certain constitutions make it possible that (with or without gerrymandering) a minority of citizens can vote in a majority of deputies. Proportional representation (P.R.) eliminates this possibility. The many disadvantages of Proportional Representation are frequently pointed out and the idea pilloried,[4] but there can be no doubt that P.R. is more "democratic" than the majority system as it exists in the United States and Britain—but not necessarily better.

Freedom, however, has nothing to do with democracy as such—nor has the republic. The repression of 49 percent by 51 percent or of 1 percent by 99 percent is most regrettable, but it is not "undemocratic." We have to bear in mind that only democracy has made the concepts of majority and minority an absolute political reality:[5] naturally the whole people is never the ruler, but a majority (usually) through its representatives. If this majority is lenient towards those it defeated in the last election, it will be motivated not by democratic principles but by tolerance. And if this tolerance is ideologically systemized, we can speak of *liberalism* in the genuine sense, not in the totally perverted American sense. (See Chapter VIII.)

Thus we see in the democratic order that the phrase "rule of the people" is misleading. The majority rules over the minority, which reminds one of George Orwell's famous phrase from *Animal Farm*: "All animals are equal, but some are more equal than others." This notion of one part lording it over another displeases the "democratist," i.e., the supporter of democrat *ism* which is democracy erected into an ideology. He will argue that those who have been beaten in an election have actually (by their cooperation in the process) helped the majority to carry out their plan just as the man who bought a lottery ticket that did not win has contributed to the jackpot won by somebody else. The real democrat, so the argument goes, when casting his vote, thereby inwardly accepts and anticipates the fact that the majority is the winner. This, however, will certainly not be the case where only a part of the population believes in democracy as an article of faith. (In the German elections in July and November 1932, a very small part of the electorate genuinely believed in democratic processes.) Yet even if the entire electorate is convinced of the dogmas of democratism, the "yes" of the disappointed voter is a very qualified and sometimes even a most unhappy one. In an existential sense democracy is not self-government at all, and self-government (unless we stand for unanimity in a democratic procedure) is and remains an illusion. Herman Melville expressed this view when he said, "Better to be secure under one king, than exposed to violence from twenty millions of monarchs, though oneself be one of them."[6] Actually the voter never knows precisely what effect his vote will have—whether it will make him a winner or a loser. The morning after the election he will buy a newspaper and, having ascertained whether he won in the lottery or not, how he fared in the horse races, what trends prevailed in the stock exchange, will finally come to page one and see whether he is among the winners or losers. In many a country he will even have to wait because it can happen that none of the parties has an absolute majority and a government will be formed only after lengthy negotiations on which the voter has no influence whatsoever. He can only watch joyfully or angrily how his vote is utilized. As a matter of fact, "existentially" he is always "confronted" by a preestablished situation: He has to choose between candidates he rarely *helped* to pick (and never picked himself, singlehanded) and thus he is usually choosing the least objectionable among undesirables. In large nations the voter is, needless to say, a microscopic unit. If the electorate of the United States were equal to a thick black line as high as the Empire State Building in New York, graphically a single vote would be about 4mu which is four times the thousandth part of a millimeter (and a millimeter is the 28th part of an inch). The formula "self-government," under these circumstances, makes hardly any sense.

Yet "self-government" is an understandable dream. Convinced that government (The State) would not exist without Original Sin,[7] we have to see in democratism a "Paradisiacal" movement—and several other items which promise us an Edenlike utopia, more often than not depicted as a *return* to a lost Golden Age. (This Golden Age, in secular vistas, was not lost owing to the rebellious sin of our ancestors but as a result of a wicked conspiracy of evil minorities.) The notion of self-government implies that we will not be ruled by somebody else: We'll do it ourselves and thereby we'll be "free." Thus rule, force, and subservience will come to an end. Nudism wants to solve the sexual problem by disposing with clothes. Yet the result is only that people get used to nudity while their real sexual problems remain (as in the case of Japan). There is just no return to Paradise by the back door or by political legerdemain. The hardship of being ruled by somebody else remains, and this hardship can be alleviated only if we love those who rule us. Servitude can only be dissolved in love,[8] but how can there be love for those who rule us when we hire and fire them like obnoxious menials? Have not the words *politics* and *politician* assumed pejorative meanings in democracies? Do they not express contempt, suspicion, sarcasm, and irony?

When we spoke about tolerance as the essence of liberalism which might or might not enter the democratic scene, we meant thereby the readiness to "carry" (*tolerare*), to "put up with" the presence, the propagation, the presentation of views, ideas, and notions we reject or oppose. We suppress our explosive indignation, we marshal our charity, we give our fellowmen the opportunity for open dissent although our feelings are contrary. There is a real virtue in tolerance because it entails self-control and an "ascetic" attitude.

At the same time we have to admit that there are certain limits to tolerance. One cannot tolerate all behaviors, all political ideologies at all times: The United States, for instance, severely restricted the immigration of anarchists, and prospective immigrants had to swear that they were neither anarchists nor bigamists. Anarchists believed in the "Propaganda of Deeds" which meant assassination, destruction, and open revolution. Nor could one be tolerant towards all faiths. There are religions encouraging murder, as, for instance, the East Indian Thugs who assassinated travelers for the greater glory of Kali. (Whether religious polygamy should be outlawed is a moot question. When I was born about half a million of my fellow citizens were Muslims; and Mormon fundamentalism is certainly an authentic American religion. And almost all American states permit polygamy on the instalment plan.[9]) Western Germany, for instance, for better or worse, outlawed for years the Communist party. Yet it is legal in Austria where the brown-clad supporters of the gas chamber cannot have a political party, whereas the red executioners, who practice the shot through the nape of the neck, can. In these matters, again, a certain arbitrariness prevails.

Those who have no principles, no grounded convictions, no dogmas, cannot be tolerant—they can only be *indifferent*, which is quite another matter. From an agnostic one expects indifference, not tolerance, because he has no good reason to *suffer* from another person's opinions. To him truth is either nonexistent or humanly unattainable. A strict agnostic makes no value judgments and thus there is for him neither "good" nor "bad," while "right" and "wrong" have only practical, circumstantial meanings. To to a person like Oliver Wendell Holmes, Jr., man was no better than a baboon or a grain of sand. He also wrote, "Man at present is a predatory animal. I think that the sacredness of human life is a purely municipal idea of no validity outside the jurisdiction."[10] An agnostic, a philosophic relativist can only say to his adversary, "I *think* that I am right in *my own way,* and although you differ from me, you may be right in your own way. So let's make it fifty-fifty." All of which reminds one of that delightful conversation between Franklin D. Roosevelt and Stalin at the Teheran Conference when Stalin wanted to execute 50,000 "Junkers and Militarists" and Roosevelt first proposed 49,000 and then offered as a compromise 49,500. The conversation was facetious and, in a way, not so facetious. It disgusted even such an immoralist as Winston Churchill.[11]

Yet, whether out of tolerance or indifference, the readiness to yield and to compromise is the quintessence of parliamentary life in a democracy. It does not belong *per se* to democracy. (No stump orator will promise to be a compromiser *par excellence* once he is elected, but rather the contrary!) Yet it is the lubricant and the *conditio sine qua non* of democracy. Let us also agree at this point that the majority of people inspired by liberal principles in the Western World when talking about democracy usually refer to a *liberal* democracy. Thus such errors arise as when the confiscation of a newspaper is called "undemocratic." If the majority of the people approve of it, such an act is highly democratic, but surely it is not liberal.

When then is liberalism *correctly understood?* Liberalism is not an exclusively political term. It can be applied to a prison reform, to an economic order, to a theology. Within the political framework, however, it does not *answer* the question (as democracy does), *"Who* should rule?" but *"How* should rule be exercised?" The reply is, *"Regardless of who rules, a monarch, an elite, or a majority, government should be exercised in such a way that each citizen enjoys the greatest possible amount of personal liberty."* The limit of liberty is obviously the common good. At the same time it must be admitted that the common good (material as well as immaterial) is not easily defined, that it rests on value judgments, and that its definition never escapes a certain arbitrariness. Speed limits curtail freedom in the interest of the common good. Yet there is arbitrariness in setting these limits. Can one make a watertight rational case for 40, 45, or 50 miles per hour? Certainly not. Nevertheless, it is obvious that liberty is only relative, that the true liberal merely wants to push it to its feasible limits and that it cannot be identical at all times, in all places, under all circumstances, for the same persons. (One might, for instance, permit an 18-year-old to drive a car but not a 13-year-old, and so forth). Not man, only God is absolutely and perfectly free. But freedom does pertain to man (Wust's *animal insecurum*)[12] because man is created in the image of God. Liberty belongs neither to the animal world nor to the sphere of inanimate matter.

Freedom, as we see, is the only postulate of liberalism—of all the four phases of genuine liberalism. If, therefore, democracy is liberal, the life, the whims, the interests of the minority will be just as much respected as those of the majority. Yet it is obvious that not only a democracy but even a monarchy (absolute or otherwise) or an aristocratic (elitarian) regime *can* be liberal. As a matter of fact, the affinity between democracy and liberalism is not at all greater than between, let us say, monarchy and liberalism or a mixed government and liberalism. (People under the Greek monarchy, which was an *effective* and not only symbolic mixed government, were not less free than in Costa Rica, to name only one example.)

Viewed in the light of the terminology we are using in accordance with the leading political scientists,[13] it seems that—to quote a few instances—monarchs such as Louis XIV, Frederick II, or George II are genuine liberals *by modern standards*. None of the aforementioned could have issued a decree whereby he drafted all male subjects into his army, a decree regulating the diet of his citizens, or one demanding a general confession of all his economic activities from the head of each household in the form of an income tax declaration. We had to wait for the democratic age to see conscription, prohibition, and modern taxation made into laws by the people's representatives who have much greater power than even the absolute monarchs of old dreamed of. (It must be noted further that in Western and Central Europe the "absolute" monarchs—thanks to the *corps intermédiaires*—never were really absolute: the local *parlements* in France and the regional *Landtage* and *Stände* in the Germanies never failed to convene.) Modern parliaments can be more peremptory in all their demands because they operate with the magic democratic formula. "We are the people, and the people—that's us."

The monarchs, in a way, always stood on thin ice. They desperately tried to bequeath their countries to their heirs. If they failed utterly, they sometimes had their heads chopped off. They could not conveniently retire to a quiet law office like deputies or presidents failing to get reelected. *There are certain totalitarian and monolithic tendencies inherent in democracy* that are not even present in the "absolute" monarchy, and even less so in mixed government which, without exaggeration, can be called *the* great Western political tradition.

From the foregoing we can see that democracy and totalitarianism are not mutually exclusive terms. Professor J. L. Talmon has rightly entitled one of his books (on the French Revolution) *The Origins of Totalitarian Democracy,*[14] and it is no accident that the isms which menaced liberty from the eighteenth century to our days called themselves "democratic." It was always claimed that the majority, nay, the vast majority of the people supported this "wave of the future." At times this claim has had a solid statistical foundation. *Genuine* liberalism, on the other hand, rarely became a real mass movement —conservatism never. The marriage between democracy and liberalism (again we add: in the etymological sense of the term) came late in history and had the seeds of divorce in it. De Tocqueville saw only too clearly that while democracy could founder into chaos, the greater danger was its gradual evolution into oppressive totalitarianism, a type of tyranny the world had never seen before and for which it was partly conditioned by modern administrative methods and technological inventions. [15]

Chapter 4

Right and Left

Until now, we have cleared up a great deal of semantic rubble in the vocabulary commonly used in the Western World (though sometimes not in the United States). But we have now come to a very necessary, not universally accepted definition, the definition of the terms "right" and "left."

If a workable definition existed, our task would be superfluous. This would also be the case if we could dispense altogether with these two magic words. They can, however, be put to very good use and often—as handy labels— truly simplify matters.

Right and left have been used in Western civilization from times immemorial with certain meanings; right (German: *rechts*) had a positive, left a negative connotation. In all European languages (including the Slavic idioms and Hungarian) right is connected with "right" (ius), rightly, rightful, in German *gerecht* (just), the Russian *pravo* (law), *pravda* (truth), whereas in French *gauche* also means "awkward, clumsy," (in Bulgar: *levitsharstvo*). The Italian *sinistro* can mean left, unfortunate, or calamitous. The English *sinister* can mean *left* or *dark*. The Hungarian word for "right" is *jobb* which also means "better," while *bal* (left) is used in composite nouns in a negative sense: *balsors* is misfortune.[1]

In Biblical language the just on the Day of Judgment are to be on the right[2] and the damned on the left. Christ sits *ad dexteram Patris* (on the right hand of the Father) as the Nicene Creed asserts. In Britain it became the custom to allocate seats to the supporters of the government on the right and to the opposition on the left side. And when a vote is taken in the House of Commons the "ayes" pass into the *right* lobby behind the Speaker's chair while the "noes" go to the *left* lobby. They are counted by four members who then inform the Speaker of the outcome. Thus in the Mother of Parliaments right and left imply affirmation or negation.

On the Continent, beginning in France, where most parliaments have a horseshoe shape (and not rows of benches facing each other) the most conservative parties have been seated to the right, usually flanked by liberals; then came the parties of the center (who frequently held key positions in the formation of government coalitions); then the "radicals" and finally the Socialists, Independent Socialists, and Communists. In Germany after World War I, most unfortunately, the National Socialists were seated on the extreme right because to simple-minded people nationalists were rightists, if not conservatives—a grotesque idea when one remembers how antinationalistic Metternich, the monarchical families, and Europe's ultraconservatives had been in the past. Nationalism, indeed, has been a by-product of the French Revolution (no less so than militarism). After all, nationalism (as the term is understood in Europe, though not in America) is identitarian, whereas patriotism is not. In Central Europe nationalism has a *purely ethnic connotation* and implies an exaggerated enthusiasm about culture, language, folklore, ways of life. Patriotism, on the other hand, puts emphasis on the *country*. A patriot will be happy if there are many nationalities living in his Fatherland, whose keynote ought to be variety, not uniformity. The nationalist is hostile toward all those who do not ethnically conform. Thus nationalism (as understood on the Continent) is the blood brother of racialism.[3]

The misplacing of the Nazis in the *Reichstag* has thus hardened a confusion in semantics and logical thinking that had started some time earlier. The Communists, the Socialists, and the Anarchists were identified with the left, and the Fascists and the National Socialists with the right. At the same time one discovered a number of similarities between the Nazis on the one side and the Communists on the other. Thus the famous and perfectly idiotic formula arose: "We are opposed to all extremism, be it from the left or the right. And, anyhow, Red and Brown are practically the same: extremes always meet."

All this is the result of very sloppy thinking, because *extremes never meet*. Extreme cold and extreme heat, extreme distance and extreme nearness, extreme strength and extreme weakness, extreme speed and extreme slowness, none of them ever "meet." They do not become identical or even alike. The moment one counterattacks and inquires from the good man who just pontificated about the meeting of extremes what precisely he understands by right and left, he proves unable to give any coherent analysis of these terms. Lamely he will hint that on the extreme are the reactionaries—the Fascists, for instance. Asked whether Mussolini's *Repubblica Sociale Italiana* was a reactionary or a leftist establishment, he will again mumble something about those paradoxical extremes. Certainly the left is collectivist and progressive; the Communists are "extreme progressivists." If he sticks to this piece of nonsense, one should point out to him that certain primitive African societies with a tribal collectivism are not really so "extremely progressive." This is usually the moment when the conversation expires.

The first fault with this loose reasoning lies in the aforementioned belief that "extremes meet"; the second in the almost total absence of clear definitions of left and right. In other words, there is a deficiency of logic as well as an absence of semantic clarity. Logic stands independent of our whims, but we can provide clear definitions.

Let us then agree that right is what is truly right for man, above all his *freedom*. Because man has a personality, because he is a riddle, a "puzzle," a piece of a puzzle which *never completely* fits into any preestablished social or political picture, he needs "elbowroom." He needs a certain *Lebensraum* in which he can develop, expand, in which he has a tiny personal kingdom. *L'enfer, c'est les autres.* "Hell, that's the others," has been said by Sartre, a pagan existentialist, towards the end of his play *Huis Clos*. The Great Menace is all around us. It is vertical because it comes from above, but it is also horizontal because it attacks us from all sides. In a state-insured, government-prescribed, and—to make matters worse—socially endorsed collectivism, our liberty, our "Western" personality, our spiritual growth, our true happiness is at stake. And all the great dynamic isms of the last 200 years have been mass movements attacking—even when they had the word "freedom" on their lips—the liberty, the independence of the person. Programmatically this was done in the name of all sorts of high- and even low-sounding ideals: Nationality, race, better living standards, "social justice," "security," ideological conviction, restoration of ancient rights, struggle for a happier world for us all. But in reality the driving motor of these movements was always the mad ambition of *oratorically or at least literarily gifted intellectuals* and the successful mobilization of masses filled with envy and a thirst for "revenge."

The right has to be identified with *personal freedom,* with the absence of utopian visions whose realization—even if it were possible—would need tremendous collective efforts; it stands for free, organically grown forms of life. And this in turn implies a respect for tradition. The right is truly progressive, whereas there is no real advance in utopianism which almost always demands—as in the *Internationale*—to "make a clean sweep" of the past, *du passé faisons table rase: dyelayem gladkuyu dosku iz proshlago!* If we return to point zero, we are again at the bottom of the ladder, we have to start from scratch again.[4] Bernard of Chartres said that generations were "like dwarfs seated on the shoulders of giants, thereby capable of seeing more things than their forebears and in a greater distance."[5] As a matter of fact, almost all utopias, though "futuristic" in temperament, have always preached a *return* to an assumed Golden Age, glowing in the most attractive colors of a falsely romanticized version. The true rightist is not a man who wants to go back to this or that institution for the sake of a return; he wants first to find out what is eternally true, eternally valid, and then either to restore or reinstall it, regardless of whether it seems obsolete, whether it is ancient, contemporary, or even without precedent, brand new, "ultramodern." Old truths can be rediscovered, entirely new ones found. The Man of the Right does not have a time-bound, but a sovereign mind. In case he is a Christian he is, in the words of the Apostle Peter, the steward of a *Basîleion Hierateuma*, a Royal Priesthood.[6]

The right stands for liberty, a free, unprejudiced form of thinking, a readiness to preserve traditional values (provided they are true values), a balanced view of the nature of man, seeing in him neither beast nor angel, insisting also on the uniqueness of human beings who cannot be transformed into or treated as mere numbers or ciphers; but the left is the advocate of the opposite principles. It is the enemy of diversity and the fanatical promoter of identity. Uniformity is stressed in all leftist utopias, a paradise in which everybody should be the "same," where envy is dead, where the "enemy" either no longer exists, lives outside the gates, or is utterly humiliated. Leftism loathes differences, deviation, stratifications. Any hierarchy it accepts is only "functional." The term "one" is the keynote: There should be only one language, one race, one class, one ideology, one religion, one type of school, one law for everybody, one flag, one coat of arms and one centralized world state.

Left and right tendencies can be observed not only in the political domain but in many areas of human interest and endeavor. Let us take the structure of the state, for instance. The leftists believe in strong centralization. The rightists are "federalists" (*in the European sense*), "states' righters" since they believe in local rights and privileges, they stand for the principle of subsidiarity. Decisions, in other words, should be made and carried out on the lowest level—by the person, the family, the village, the borough, the city, the county, the federated state, and only finally at the top, by the government in the nation's capital. The breakup of the glorious old French provinces with their local *parlements* and their replacement with small *départements*, named after some geographic feature and totally dependent upon the Paris government, was a typically leftist "reform." Or let us look at education. *The leftist is always a statist*. He has all sorts of grievances and animosities against personal initiative and private enterprise. The notion of the state doing everything (until, finally, it replaces all private existence) is the Great Leftist Dream. Thus it is a leftist tendency to have city or state schools —or to have a ministry of education controlling all aspects of education. For example, there is the famous story of the French Minister of Education who pulls out his watch and, glancing at its face, says to his visitor, "At this moment in 5,431 public elementary schools they are writing an essay on the joys of winter." Church schools, parochial schools, private schools, or personal tutors are not at all in keeping with leftist sentiments. The reasons for this attitude are manifold. Here not only is the delight in statism involved, but the idea of uniformity and equality is also decisive; i.e., the notion that social differences in education should be eliminated and all pupils should be given a chance to acquire the same knowledge, the same type of information in the same fashion and to the same degree. This should help them to think in identical or at least in similar ways. It is only natural that this should be especially true of countries where "democratism" as an ism is being pushed. There efforts will be made to ignore the differences in IQs and in personal efforts. Sometimes marks and report cards will be eliminated and promotion from one grade to the next be made automatic. It is obvious that from a scholastic viewpoint this has disastrous results, but to a true ideologist this hardly matters. When informed that the facts did not tally with his ideas, Hegel once severely replied, "*Um so schlimmer für die Tatsachen*"—all the worse for the facts.

Leftism does not like religion for a variety of causes. Its ideologies, its omnipotent, all-permeating state wants undivided allegiance. With religion at least one other allegiance (to God), if not also allegiance to a Church, is interposed. In dealing with organized religion, leftism knows of two widely divergent procedures. One is a form of separation of Church and State which eliminates religion from the marketplace and tries to atrophy it by not permitting it to exist anywhere outside the sacred precincts. The other is the transformation of the Church into a fully state-controlled establishment. Under these circumstances the Church is asphyxiated, not starved to death. The Nazis and the Soviets used the former method; Czechoslovakia still employs the latter.

The antireligious bias of leftism rests, however, not solely on anti-clericalism, antiecclesiasticism, and the antagonism against the existence of another body, another organization within the boundaries of the State: It gets its impetus not only from jealousy but, above all, from the rejection of the idea of a supernatural, a spiritual order. *Leftism is basically materialistic.*

The Provident State, Hilaire Belloc's *Servile State,* is obviously a creation of the leftist mentality. We will not call it the Welfare State because every state exists for the welfare of its citizens; here a good name has been misused for a bad thing. In the final prophecy of Alexis de Tocqueville in *Democracy in America* the possibility, nay, the probability of the democratic state's totalitarian evolution toward the Provident State has been foretold with great accuracy. Here again *two* wishes of the leftist find their fulfillment, the extension of government *and* the dependence of the person upon the state which controls his destiny from the cradle to the grave. Every movement of the citizen, his birth and his death, his marriage and his income, his illness and his education, his military training and his transportation, his real estate and his travels abroad—everything is to be a matter of knowledge to the state.

One could continue this list *ad nauseam.* Naturally, we must add that in the practical order of things there are exceptions to the rule because leftism is a disease that does *not necessarily* spread as a coherent, systematic ideology. Here and there an isolated manifestation can appear in the ''opposite camp.'' Sometimes, to quote an example, the stamp of rightism has been applied to Spain's present government. Yet it is obvious that certain features of the Franco government have a leftist character as, for instance, the strong centralizing tendencies, the restrictions placed on languages other than Castilian, the censorship, the monopoly of the state-directed syndicates. As for the first two failings —leftist tendencies *are* failings—one has to remember the effects of the immediate historic past.

Nationalism (in the European sense) *is* leftism; and Catalonian, Basque, and Gallegan (Galician) nationalism naturally assumed a radically leftist character opposing ''Castilian'' centralization. Hence, in Madrid, almost all movements promoting local rights and privileges, be they political or ethnic, are suspect as leftist, as automatically opposed to the present regime as well as to the unity of Spain. (Spain is *"Una, Grande, Libre"*!) Oddly enough—but understandable to anybody with a real knowledge of Spanish history—the extreme right in Spain, represented, naturally, by the Carlists and not at all by the Falangists, is federalistic ("localistic," anticentralistic) in the European sense. The Carlists are opposed to the centralizing tendencies of Madrid and when late in 1964 the central government made an effort to cancel the privileges of Navarra, the *fueros*, the Carlists of Navarra, nearly issued a call to rebellion—at which point the government quickly declared its own preparatory steps as a "mistake" and backed down.

All conservative movements in Europe are federalistic and opposed to centralization. Thus we encounter in Catalonia, for instance, a desire for autonomy and the cultivation of the Catalan language among the supporters of the extreme right as well as the left. The notorious Catalonian Anarchists always have been supporters of autonomy, but formal anarchism has always been a curious *mixtum compositum*. Its ultimate vistas were leftist, socialistic in essence, but its temper was rightist. Much of present-day "communism" in Italy and Spain is merely "popularly misunderstood anarchism." But, on the other hand, it is also significant that in 1937 open war broke out in Barcelona between the Communists and the Anarchists. And it was the Anarchists who resisted the Communists in Russia longer than any other group, until in 1924 they were literally exterminated in all Soviet jails and camps. Hope of "taming" them had been abandoned.

Or let us take the Metternich regime in Central Europe. Basically it had a rightist character, but having been born in conscious opposition to the French Revolution it had—as so often tragically happens—learned too much from the enemy. True, it never became totalitarian, but it assumed authoritarian features and aspects which must be called leftist, as for instance the elaborate police system based on espionage, informers, censorship, and controls in every direction.

Something similar is true of Maurrasism, which was also a curious blend of rightist and leftist notions, characterized by deep inner contradictions. Charles Maurras was a monarchist and a nationalist at the same time. Yet monarchy is a basically supranational institution. Usually the monarch's wife, his mother, and the spouses of his children are foreigners. With two exceptions (Serbia and Montenegro)[7] all the sovereign ruling houses of Europe in the year 1910 were foreign by origin. Nationalism is "populist" by contrast, and the typical republican constitution insists that the president be a *native* of the country. Maurras undoubtedly had brilliant insights and many a European conservative

42

has borrowed from him. But it was by no means accidental that he collaborated when the Nazis occupied his country. Nor was he a Christian during most of his lifetime. He returned to the Faith, however, some time before his death.[8]

If we then identify, in a rough way, the right with freedom, personality, and variety, and the left with slavery, collectivism, and uniformity, we are employing semantics that make *sense*. Then the stupid explanation that communism and Nazism are alike because "extremes always meet" need not trouble us any longer. In the same camp with socialism, fascism, and that particularly vague leftism which in the United States is known perversely enough as liberalism, there is a phenomenon to be explained in Chapter XIV. This, however, is not the case with European liberalism. It is significant that the Italian Liberal party (The PLI) is seated to the right of the *Democristiani*, next to the monarchists. Right and left will always be used in this book in the sense we have outlined here, and we are convinced that this distinction in semantics is indeed a vital one in discussing the political scene of our age.

Part II

Leftism In History

Chapter 5

The Historic Origins of Leftism

The Earliest Roots

Leftism in the Western World has roots reaching way back into the dim past. Leftist ideas and notions made themselves felt again and again in late medieval and modern history, but for its first *concrete* and, in a way, fateful outbreak and concretization we have to look to the French Revolution.

Leftist tendencies, according to the terminology outlined above, existed in ancient Greece. Hellenic (Athenian) democracy not only insisted on the rule of the many, it also had a strong egalitarian slant. Naturally the notion of equality only applied to the full citizens, not to women, slaves, and foreigners (*metoikoi*), so that the electorate in Greek democracies always constituted a minority. We must add that Greek democracies, while frequently most oppressive, had certain liberal aspects; respect for men in elevated positions was not stressed and the absence of a strongly concretized ruling class as well as the total lack of anything resembling a "presidency" weakened authority. In the descriptions of democracy by Plato and also by Aristotle we perceive the elements of equality and social, though not necessarily political liberty. Envy was written large and excellence was suspect. The fear of a monarchical restoration was a permanent feature and thus all concentration of power was dreaded. If anybody excelled in merits and prestige, exile through ostracism menaced him. Yet, while social liberties were perhaps marked, political liberties were few, though here we have to bear in mind that the concept of the person as we know it did not exist in antiquity. It makes its appearance in the Western World—and solely in the Western World—only with the advent of Christianity. When Aristotle called man a *zoon politikon* he meant a creature practically absorbed by the city or by the state.

The hostility of Plato toward democracy (more apparent in the *Politeia* than in the *Nomoi*) was similar to that of Aristotle, who finally fled the democratic rule of Athens and went to Chalcis on Euboea admittedly in order to avoid the fate of Socrates. Plato's antidemocratic bias was not only the automatic reaction of the intellectual against a form of government which puts no premium on reason or knowledge; it was also the result of the deeply felt experience of his master's death. The average educated American or European, though aware that Socrates had been put to death on account of his "impiety" in introducing strange gods and for "corrupting" the young, rarely knows the full story. The last charge (far from having anything to do with sex) was subdivided (according to Xenophon) into several accusations: (1) that he taught his disciples to treat the institutions of the state with contempt; (2) that he had associated with Critias and Alcibiades; (3) that he had taught the young to disobey their parents; and (4) that he constantly quoted Homer and Hesiod against morality and democracy (especially *Iliad, II*, 198-206). Not only the democratic government, but the "dear people" were opposed to Socrates and he can, without exaggeration, be called a victim of democracy, of the *vox populi*.[1]

Salvador de Madariaga has said that Western civilization rests on two deaths —the death of Socrates and the death of Christ. And indeed the Crucifixion was also a democratic event. When our Lord was brought before Pilate and told him that He had come as a witness to the Truth, the governor, as a true agnostic, asked Him, "What is Truth?" And without waiting for an answer, he passed Him by and consulted "the people." The *vox populi* condemned our Lord to death as it had Socrates more than three centuries earlier. But if we despair of truth, if we believe that truth either does not exist or can humanly not be attained, we either have to leave things to chance or look for mere preferences—personal preferences or "preferences statistically arrived at" (which often means accepting the "verdict of the majority"). This is a handy means to settle differences of opinion, yet it neither tells us the truth nor does it offer *rational* solutions to burning problems.

Greek democracy was buried under the power drive of Macedonia,

48

but this was applauded by Isocrates.[2] Rome was never a real democracy, not even in the broad sense of the term used by antiquity. Yet Marius represents most certainly the Roman left and his wife's nephew, Caesar, actually became a leftist dictator, thereby figuring as a fulfillment of the *anakyklosis* as defined by Polybius[3] and foreseen by Plato, that is, the evolution of monarchy into aristocracy, aristocracy into democracy, democracy into tyranny, and tyranny again into monarchy. We have to ask, however, whether Roman Caesarism was ever genuine monarchy or only, as Metternich argued,[4] a form of "Bonapartism" —military dictatorship. Until the days of Diocletian the Romans were hardly aware of the fact that their *Res Publica* no longer existed, since it still bore that label. "Emperor" (*Imperator*), after all, only meant "general," "prince" (*princeps*)—"First Man." ("First Lady" is the unofficial title of the American President's wife.) With Diocletian the situation at long last became clear: He had himself crowned with a golden crown and demanded *proskynesis* in the best oriental fashion; the Senate lost all its importance. At that point even the simplest Romans presumably realized that the Republic had gone the way of all flesh and that Rome now had a fundamentally different constitution, a fact that Tacitus already had strongly suspected.[5]

During the Middle Ages "democracy" had a bad connotation among intellectuals who alone knew its meaning. It existed, however, in small private societies as, for instance, in the high villages of the Alps and the Pyrenees, in Iceland and Norway, and in Slavic villages in the form of the *vyetche*. The larger and more developed political societies had for the most part mixed governments with a monarch at the top who owed his status either to birth or to election by a small elite. The *Regimen Mixtum* normally had a diet (or even two "Houses") composed of representatives of the three or four estates. (Originally only the nobility and clergy were represented. Then came a new element, the "Third Estate," i.e., the burghers, and in many cases the peasantry as a Fourth Estate, as in Sweden and the Tyrol.) The mixed governments are balanced ones. The king was not at all powerful. *Rex sub Lege*[6] was the standard formula. He had no right to levy taxes and the penury of monarchs is a permanent feature of medieval and post-medieval society. The king's power was curtailed by powerful vassals, the Church, the diet in which the Estates were represented, and the free municipalities who had great privileges. Absolutism and totalitarianism were unknown in the Middle Ages.[7]

All during that period the word "democracy" appeared only in learned treatises, but it is important to remember that insidious religious sects with leftist social and political programs were active over, or rather under, the larger part of Europe. The Albigenses (Bogumilians, *Catharoi*) were not egalitarians, but a strong leftist character can be discerned among the earlier Waldensians (founded by Peter Waldo). The object of their scorn is not only the "rich, sinful Church" but also all the high and mighty, luxury, ostentation, and power. The dualistic sects with their Manichaean roots made their way from the Near East into the Balkans and from there to northern Italy, southern France, Belgium, Bohemia, and England (in other words, a geographic migration roughly from the southeast to the northwest). They had apocalyptical visions of the wickedness of wealth, the punishment of the arrogant, the destruction of the two great organizations, Church and State. Naturally these visions were not uniform. The accents changed and compromises with reality were frequent. But there is a red thread that is very distinct: As far as their ideas went, the sects did have certain influence on the origins of the Reformation.[8]

What distinguished them from the Reformers was the cult of poverty as we find it, for instance, among the "Poor of Lyons," an early Waldensian group. The Waldensians from Lombardy (as distinct from those of France) insisted that their faithful live from the fruits of manual labor. Especially as weavers they lived together, worked together, were hostile to military service, rejected oaths, and hated sumptuous churches. They also seem to have had an anti-intellectual bent. From Lombardy they spread as far as Bohemia.

The English Forerunners

In northern France we encounter the *Turlupins,* a Christian sect preaching human equality. They had apparently been somehow connected with the ideas of the monk Joachim de Floris, who preached a pantheistic chiliasm, and they may have been behind that big peasant rising, the *Jacquerie.* The revolt of the farmers in England, led by John Ball and Wat Tyler, also had a certain religious motivation. (John Ball was a priest and his revolutionary sermons were frequently on the theme, "When Adam delved and Eve span, who was then the gentleman?")[9] These risings were connected with the teaching of Wyclif, whose new doctrines had far-reaching political effects: Naturally, every infringement of the precept that one should let sleeping dogs lie starts off a series of questions, movements, and criticisms.

Wyclif began by first denouncing papal supremacy, thus earning the sympathies of his king. He then proceeded to question transubstantiation and the prerogatives of the clergy for which he received the support of the nobility. Finally he advanced democratic theories and denounced wealth altogether, and so gave impetus to the agrarian revolt. An analogous development took place when Luther (who knew the writings of Wyclif) declared the Pope to be antichrist and received the protection of the princes against the Emperor; and then, when he denounced the clergy and the monastic institutions, he won the applause of the nobility. Luther never went further. When the enormous wave of criticism of the existing order reached the peasantry and resulted in violent rebellion, and the lower middle classes in certain regions embraced Anabaptism (Münster, for example), or engaged in iconoclastic orgies, Luther applied the brakes and denounced this extremism. Wyclif also once halfheartedly protested against Ball and Tyler (who insisted they were followers of Wyclif), but he died before the full development of Lollardy. Wyclif's "Poor Preachers" are definitely an effort toward a "democratization" of religion, a "populism" along semiecclesiastical lines. The Poor Preachers were often pastmasters in exploiting the envy of the masses.

Wyclif, however, does not stand at the beginning of a new development. He was a reader of Marsilius of Padua and, much later, so was Luther. Marsilius, in support of Emperor Ludwig I and trying to undermine the political claims of the papacy, also attacked its hierarchical status and finally developed a democratic theory of government.[10] He declared that original political power resides in the people collectively or at least in its better (*valentior*) part. Another source of Wyclif's inspiration came from extreme factions of the Franciscan order with their emphasis on poverty. It is significant that the mendicant orders strongly supported Wyclif at the beginning of his activities.[11] As we shall see later in this book, there is a curious relationship between a misconceived notion of the monastic idea and the leftist currents in every age. It reminds one of the outcry of St. Thomas, *Corruptio optimi pessima* ("When the best is corrupted, it becomes the worst").

Lollardy, which survived Wyclif for generations and could still be observed at the beginning of the sixteenth century,[12] was not solely a poor people's religious attitude, it also had a good deal of support from the landed gentry. Its basic psychological drive was material and intellectual envy. The wealth of the Church was heavily criticized as inconsistent with the teachings of Christ. Nor was this attack confined to the Church. By that time the legend already seems to have been firmly embedded that Christ was the indigent son of a poor carpenter and that His Apostles were a bunch of paupers anxious to avoid any contamination by the rich.[13]

The other type of envy was nonmaterial: Theology was looked at askance as something complicated, not necessarily comprehended by the uneducated, and as the "private property" of the intellectually *beati possidentes*. As a matter of fact, even in the Franciscan Order, soon after its founding, there had been a bitter struggle between an intellectual and a nonintellectual faction ending in the victory of the former. Thanks to it we have in St. Bonaventure, Alexander Hales, Occam, and Duns Scotus outstanding representatives of Christian theology.

And, last, a third kind of envy made its appearance, an envy that had a spiritual cause: The clergy reserved the Chalice for itself.

Thus the demand for equality, the rebellion against differences and privileges was mounting. It is no coincidence that the cry first went up in England, one of the most class-conscious countries in Western civilization. It was repeated there in similar forms during the seventeenth century when egalitarian sects arose again in great numbers and when, for the first time in Christian European history, a king was formally put to death.

The first truly concrete, "systematized" identitarian revolution in Europe is Taboritism, the radical form of Hussitism. Hus was not only the translator and commentator of Wyclif, he was his most faithful copyist. And here again we see how automatically and inevitably all religions change, how new religious doctrines affect political ideas. All the new currents were hostile to hierarchies and differentiations; they stood for brotherhood and assailed fatherhood. The attack on the Pope (Pápa) was directed against the father image. Psychologically this invited a revision of the concept of God as father and, therefore, of the Trinity. (Several attempts were made in the sixteenth, seventeenth, and eighteenth centuries to found antitrinitarian, i.e., unitarian faiths; in Transylvania, in Poland, in England, in Scotland, and in New England.) Descending to the political sphere, this meant a questioning of monarchy as well as of mixed government with a monarchic head. Finally this development inevitably shook the position of the father in the family, which is not surprising since the patriarchal[14] order forms a coherent unity; man's mind, after all, is an organic whole.[15]

It is obvious that psychological sequiturs are not necessarily of a *logical* order. It is possible for one to be a Lutheran monarchist or a tyrannical *paterfamilias* belonging to the Unitarian religion. We have Catholic republicans who think (erroneously) that every papal encyclical is an infallible document, and we have agnostic monarchists who are not enthusiastic about physical fatherhood and reject the papacy as they reject the Father-in-Heaven. Yet psychological affinities should never be overlooked. The New Englanders at the end of the eighteenth century who were convinced that George III had secretly become a Catholic were factually in error[16] as far as the person of the British monarch was concerned, but in regard to the institution their suspicion, though wrong, was not grotesque. Kierkegaard (to quote just one example) thought that all genuine royalists lean towards the Catholic faith.[17]

Like Wyclif, Hus is not really the champion of the "common people." Like Wyclif he got support largely from the lower nobility, and like Wyclif he was a nationalist. Wyclif was an "English Firster" while Hus became the spokesman of the Czech people against the German element in Bohemia-Moravia. And there, in the lands of the Crown of St. Wenceslas, we see for the first time in European history outbreaks of national hatred, clashes at the university between national student organizations, and that type of collective fury which brought ruin to Europe in the nineteenth and twentieth centuries. The stage for leftist mass movements was set. On top of it there existed in Bohemia for some time a fairly strong late-Waldensian underground movement supplemented by the Beghards (Pickarts), the male counterpart of the Béguine Order, but disorganized and riddled with heretical ideas.[18]

The martyr-death of Hus, who was burned at the stake in Constance, led to a fiery outbreak of popular wrath in the Czech parts of Bohemia. John XXIII was then counter-pope and the responsibility for the ignoble death of Hus was partly his.[19] Even more responsible, however, was the Emperor who had given Hus safe conduct which was not honored by the Council.

The death of Hus resulted in the establishment of two groups: A more moderate one, the Utraquists, content with administration of communion under both species, bread and wine, and a radical one, the Taborites, which found its center in the newly established city of Tábor. (*Tábor* in Czech means camp.) The Taborites were extreme fanatics, and they were organized militarily. Their leader at the beginning was Jan Žižka, scion of a recently nobilitated family of German origin. Their ideology was chiliastic, nationalistic, puritanical, democratic, and socialistic. *Here we have a real and concrete prefiguration of all the isms of our times* in a dynamic synthesis. By filiation perhaps more than by analogy the mass movements of our days are related to Taboritism.

Taboritism, however, was more deeply influenced by the Waldensians and the Beghards than by pure Hussite theology. In its earlier phase the socialist and puritanical ideas were more in the foreground and the ultra-extremists, the nudist Adamites, were severely persecuted by Žižka. Still, the Taborites believed in the coming of a millennium in the form of a Third Kingdom (taken from the prophecies of Daniel). A radically socialist program regarding property was adopted in the first years, but after the death of Žižka of Trocnov the egalitarian spirit weakened under the leadership of Prokop Holý (who apparently also was of German origin). Hussite armies invaded the surrounding German areas and a crusade was preached against the Taborites. The army of the crusaders was routed near Domažlice (Taus) and only then did the old leading classes become fully aware of the danger. In alliance with the Utraquists, who had kept the original moderate Hussite spirit, the Taborites were finally defeated in the battle of Lipan, and Prokop was killed. This furious explosion of a synthetic mixture of nationalism, socialism, and radical democracy with communist innuendos not only had devastated large parts of Bohemia, Moravia, and Upper Hungary, but also had deeply shaken the social and spiritual fabric of Europe. In their perennial ramifications the shadows of this profound revolution are still with us and will continue to be for some time.

Proudhon said that it is surprising how at the bottom of politics one always finds theology.[20] The reader might feel inclined to believe that our emphasis on theological ("religious") ideas, movements, and arguments so far are merely due to the profoundly religious character of the Middle Ages. This is by no means the case. Looking way back at the tragedy of Socrates we see clearly how it was largely conditioned by an intermingling of political, philosophical, and religious sentiments and concepts. This interconnection persisted during the first 1,700 years of Christian history whereas in the last 200 years it has become evident that the isms cannot coexist peacefully with theistic religions, but have to fight them with all the means at their disposal. And vice versa. It is precisely this fact that the modern totalitarian ideologies— from simple leftism to national socialism, international socialism, and communism —have not only a pseudomonastic but also a "heretical" aspect that make them so unacceptable and so incompatible with the great religions of the West: Christianity, Islam, and Judaism. They derive most of their strength, as we shall see later on, from the secularized version of a few Christian tenets. Therefore they are all *Religionsersatz* (substitutes for religion) and the parties representing them are secular "churches" with hierarchies, rituals amounting to a real liturgy, secular equivalents to the sacraments, "orders," (general) confessions, ministries of propaganda,[21] a system of worldwide missions, etc. The efforts to draw comparisons between the Vatican and the Kremlin are usually made in a spirit of hostility, but they are not without substance if we bear in mind that the various isms, as fundamental heresies, are indeed evil caricatures of fragments of Christian doctrine, of Christian institutions. Our isms could not have grown, in the first instance, on non-Christian soil even if they can be transferred to such areas where Christianity is not indigenous. The reason for the latter phenomenon is twofold: All human beings have a "naturally Christian soul" (*anima naturaliter Christiana*) and the entire globe is in a process of Westernization, i.e., of accepting secular forms of Christianity.

It is not our task here to investigate the influence of Hus, Wyclif, and Marsilius on Luther and the first stage of the sixteenth-century Reformation. We have done this elsewhere.[22] It is important, however, to remember that the Reformation, contrary to an obsolete concept still surviving in English-speaking countries and finding its way into textbooks and films,[23] was by no means the "beginning of liberalism" (genuine or fake), nor anything like the fulfillment of the Renaissance, but a late medieval and "monastic" reaction[24] against humanism and the spirit of the Renaissance. To Luther the Renaissance (no less than Humanism) was a foul compromise between Christianity and paganism. After all, Plato, Socrates, and Aristotle, according to him, all were broiling in the eternal fires of Hell.[25]

Unfortunately the picture of Luther, a true wrestler with Christ as presented in American Catholic and Evangelical[26] education on a popular level, is mostly a radically false one. He was neither a neurotic who wanted to marry a nun; nor was he a libertarian subjectivist who wanted to promote "private interpretation" of the Bible; nor did he yearn for "personal freedom." He was most decidedly a *rigorist* who wanted to go *back* to what he considered the original purity of the Church. That he was shocked in Rome by the depravity of the hierarchy is pedagogical nonsense. The moral situation in Germany was not a whit better. And in scholastic theology the moral virtues had a very low rating.[27] (In this respect too, Luther was a typical medievalist.) Far from advocating anything like classic liberalism, Luther taught the omnipotence of the state and opposed all forms of rationalism, Christian or otherwise, as well as the "worship of man." *Soli Deo Gloria* was Calvin's battle-cry, but it also could have been Luther's who was convinced that man could not really contribute anything substantial to his salvation; only the blood of the Lamb could wash away his sins, and good works were of no avail.

Because the Reformation was a reaction *against* Humanism and the Renaissance, we should not be surprised that the Middle Ages in a certain sense continued in the Reformed world. Until very recently the Gothic style was the accepted one for churches and colleges even in the United States. Whoever wants to advertise candles, organs, or clerical vestments in America uses Gothic script even today. In the Catholic world, however, the Renaissance style slowly evolved into Baroque and later into Rococo. And while the world of the Reformation evolved in the direction of discipline, commercialism, industry and hard work, of some sort of secular monasticism, the monastic and medieval ideas in the Catholic world remained restricted to real monasteries and convents;[28] Catholic life continued to be artistic, intellectual, and anarchical.

From then on, the "wild sects" continued to exist almost solely in the *Mundus Reformatus*. The sixteenth century saw a furious outbreak of sectarian chiliasm in various parts of Germany—in the southwest along the Rhine and, above all, in Münster. It was Thomas Münster, a German Anabaptist who, after visiting Prague in 1521 to get in touch with Hussite circles, started a series of popular uprisings in the name of religion. He attacked the Reformers for having done halfhearted work, for not having gone far enough in the domain of religion, and for having neglected to change state and society. He preached and wrote in favor of a communistic theocracy he wanted to see established. He was completely opposed by Luther who wanted to have no truck with him. After having taken up contact with the Swiss Anabaptists he (together with the former monk Pfeifer) seized the Upper Alsatian town of Mühlhausen where he succeeded in deposing the local government and plundered the convents as well as the houses of the rich. In 1525 he joined the Peasant Revolt, but his warfare against the "godless princes and priests" ended in failure. Beaten in battle, he and Pfeifer were taken prisoner and decapitated.

Jan van Leyden, also called Jan Bokelszoon, was born in Holland but became the master of Münster after the Anabaptists had taken hold of the town and Jan Matthys, his predecessor and a fanatical preacher, had been killed in a military action. He established a communist "Kingdom of Zion," based on a weird mixture of socialist and Old Testament notions, and terrorized the entire population. Everybody was given goods "according to his needs."[29] The sexual corruption of his "court" knew no limits. Finally the city was taken back by Bishop Count Bernhard von Galen, and Jan van Leyden was put to death.

It was in Münster that the Anabaptists had set up the most famous model of their political order, but their settlements in southern Moravia in the late 1520s and early 1530s were more concretely communist. Their religious principles in this area were set down in the "Nikolsburg Articles" which feature prominently the opposition to organized government as well as all forms of learning, especially theology. (The Scriptures, admittedly not easy for the common man to understand, are necessary only for the wicked and the heathen. The children of God do not need them. And Christ, obviously, is not the Son of God, but merely a prophet.)[30]

More interesting than their religious faith was their social organization in that part of the Holy Roman Empire. Carl A. Cornelius gives us a short but vivid description:

> The Zürich Doctrines were obeyed in their most uncompromising and radical form. Government offices, oaths and the use of arms were strictly outlawed. Nobody owned property. The stranger who asked for Baptism had to surrender all his earthly goods to the community but in the case of excommunication or banishment nothing was returned to him. Family life, which cannot be imagined without property, was replaced with a different order. The marriages, without consultation of the partners, were decreed and blessed by the Servants of the Word. The children soon after their birth were handed over to wet nurses and later placed in the common school house. Dressed and fed in an identical way, the adults lived according to their occupation in larger households under the supervision of a Servant of the Necessity. The whole life moved, day in day out, within the narrowest limits. Any manifestation of personal independence or freedom led to banishment, which meant to bottomless misery.[31]

Yet, as in the case of the Low-German Anabaptists (finally centred in Münster), the expectation of an imminent Day of Judgment, dooming the wicked and exalting the faithful, was very strong. In our time, though in a more secular version, the extreme left has also invariably believed in either a millennium or (sometimes anticipating this chiliastic fulfillment) in a very earthly Day of Judgment crowned by the triumph of the chosen race, be they the pure-blooded "Aryans" or the "proletarians" or just the "progressive forces of mankind," over the Jews, the idle rich, or the dark forces of reaction—to use the Nazi expression, in a "Night of the Long Knives."

The collapse of Anabaptism in northeastern Germany under the joint blows of the Catholics and the Lutherans terminated in the great leftist wave on the Continent for well over 200 years. This wave was essentially medieval in character, and we have mentioned its pseudomonastic traits. Even the Waldensians have given the impression to their contemporaries that they were "manqués" friars.[32] Only in the north of Europe do we see a true continuation of the medieval spirit (owing to the "medieval" and "Gothic" character of the Reformation), and therefore we encounter in England in the mid-seventeenth century another explosion of religious Leftism.

With the downfall of the first Stuart monarchy and the execution of Charles I (a truly world-shaking event), a new outbreak of populism emerged from the lower social layers and even endangered Cromwell's regime. The movement of the Levellers under John Lilburne threatened army discipline. Lilburne saw clearly that Cromwell's and Ireton's leadership led to oligarchic rule and thus he strongly emphasized the prerogatives of the Parliament. Cromwell rejected egalitarianism outright, and even Lilburne defended private property and protested against the "Leveler" label. But the most radical Levellers, the "Diggers," went even further to the Left.

England in the seventeenth century thus proved a breeding ground of leftist heresies, and certain religious-political notions born there at that time found their way to the United States. It is not easy to put them into right focus, i.e., neither to underestimate nor to exaggerate their impact on the Thirteen Colonies and, later, on the young American Republic. Up till the War of Independence, however, they were hardly articulate. Still, it would be a great mistake to think that there was any specifically leftist or "progressivist" element in New England Puritanism. The anti-Episcopalian (and also anti-Catholic and antimonarchical) attitude of the Pilgrim Fathers and their more immediate descendants had no egalitarian overtones.[33] There is no egalitarianism inherent in Calvinist theology: very much the contrary. Predestination brutally separates mankind into those who are damned and those who are saved, and in the best Old Testament tradition the saved already partake of Divine favor. A dim reflection of their eternal bliss already descends upon them on this earth. (Hence the concerted efforts of individuals to prove by deeds and facts that they are saved, which resulted in the tremendous economic upsurge of the Calvinist countries, according to the thesis of Max Weber and Müller-Armack.)[34] Paul Kecskemeti said rightly: " . . . the basic idea upon which the Puritan political system was founded was that Church members alone could have political rights. This ensured that the Puritan commonwealth could be nothing but an oligarchy. As wealth was one of the criteria (though by no means the only one) on the basis of which it was determined whether one belonged to the 'elect,' the commonwealth was necessarily controlled by the wealthy."[35]

Chapter 6

Nascent America

The Pilgrim Fathers and the Puritans were certainly neither democrats nor liberals. John Winthrop declared that democracy was "the meanest and worst of all forms of government." The best part of the people he considered always the least, and of the best part the wiser again always the lesser. John Cotton was equally blunt: "Democracy, I do not conceyve that God did ever ordeyne as a fitt government either for the church or commonwealth. If the people be governors, who shall be governed? As for the monarchy and aristocracy, they are both of them clearly approved and directed in scripture."

The Dutch establishment in New Amsterdam (New York) had no democratic character either. The Constitution of Pennsylvania (William Penn's *Concessions*) had a somewhat democratic character, but freemen and proprietors alone could vote. On the other hand, only the Constitution of Pennsylvania could be called liberal, and it remained so. (Religious tolerance in Maryland, shaken in 1692, came to an end in 1715 when Catholics were disenfranchised.) Democracy certainly had no appeal south of the Potomac, and after Independence was achieved by the Thirteen Colonies there was only one state which had an egalitarian franchise—Vermont, a state admitted to the Union only in 1791.

And yet it is undoubtedly the American War of Independence (which was not a revolution!) that provided the main psychological momentum for the French Revolution. Of course there were also other intellectual and political currents contributing to the French Revolution. First of all, there was the "example" of England, frequently and tirelessly cited by Voltaire, who owed so much to this northern neighbor of France. Then there was the example of Switzerland, which fitted in so well with the romantic temper of the time: the beautiful, rustic, well-regulated, republican, progressive community on the doorstep of France. There were the Encyclopedists. There was Rousseau (from Geneva!), and last but not least, the Marquis de Sade, the Grandfather of modern democracy.

Yet we must remember that the picture of England, as seen and understood by Voltaire, and the sentimental portrait of Switzerland, had very little to do with the reality of these two countries. The Swiss Federation became a democracy only thanks to her Constitution of 1878, and it can be argued that certain Swiss cantons remained oligarchic-aristocratic units until the dawn of this century. No wonder, therefore, the third *Image d'Epinal*, the United States, is the most fascinating temptation of them all, because, due to its geographical remoteness, it is even more of a lure to the revolutionists than France's immediate neighbors. The interpreting of a foreign country, a foreign culture and civilization, and, above all, of a foreign political movement, is always full of pitfalls.

In other words, the filiation between the American War of Independence and the French Revolution exists in a technical sense, *but as far as ideas and content are concerned, we are faced with a tremendous and catastrophic misunderstanding.*

The United States, it must be remembered, owes its political structure and its Constitution to the fact that it was the primary wish of the Thirteen Colonies to escape the tutelage and the domination of "London," of two institutions in a remote city: Parliament and the Crown. At the time there was probably no practical possibility for a genuine representation in the "Mother of Parliaments." The ruler (who happened to be intermittently insane) had obviously little sympathy for the just grievances of his subjects beyond the seas. As a matter of fact, the people of Britain as a whole, with the exception of certain radical Whigs and a few Irish (Burke among them), neither understood the Americans nor particularly cared for them. In their quarrel with the Colonies the British failed in public relations and did little to present their certainly not exaggerated financial claims in the light of reason and equity. The situation became really critical when the cry "No taxation without representation!" was raised. Both demands were probably just: the British desire to recover some of the expenses for the war which led to the annexation of Canada, and the insistence of the Americans on being full citizens of the realm. These conflicting wishes *almost* but not quite inevitably had to lead to secession. Yet, looking at the issue more closely, one discovers other factors as well. Naturally, one can argue that if an area wants to secede from another which happens to have monarchical rule and there is no local family to claim a not yet existent throne, the establishment of a republican government is the only solution.[1] This seemingly stands to reason, but the history of the last 150 years teaches us that it is by no means necessarily the case. During the nineteenth and early twentieth centuries the republican-democratic forms of government were generally considered to be so intrinsically inferior—the murder of Socrates and the chaotic end of the Roman Republic stood before the eyes of the classically educated Europeans as vividly as the horrors of the French Revolution and the sanguinary anarchy of Latin America!—that secessions ended in monarchical instaurations. When the Belgians broke away from the Dutch they called in a Lutheran prince of the Saxe-Coburg family (and this in spite of the fact that secession had been largely motivated by denominational animosities). This new king, Leopold I, played an important part in European politics. (All of which shows that the Christian monarchy is an international, interracial, "diversitarian" institution, not a national institution, as the republic is by its very nature.[2] When the Norwegians terminated their "personal union" with Sweden in 1905, they called in the Danish Prince Charles who as Haakon VII ruled the country until 1957. Throwing off the Turkish yoke in the nineteenth century the Balkan countries in two cases established local dynasties (the Petrović-Njegoš in Montenegro and the Karagjorgjević in Serbia), but the Greeks, Bulgars, and Rumanians sent for foreign princes. The Rumanians tried it with a native at first but then imported the Catholic Hohenzollerns. As we said before, the dynasties of Serbia and Montenegro were the only sovereign *native* dynasties in Europe in 1910.[3]

In other words, the establishment of an American *republic* (in fact, though not in name) was not inevitable. As late as 1787 Nathan Gorham, President of the Congress under the old Constitution, and Baron von Steuben "conspired" to persuade Prince Henry of Prussia, brother of Frederick II (the "Great") to come to the United States to assume the office of "hereditary stadholder." It is obvious that the Dutch Republic (officially transformed into a kingdom in 1815) served as a pattern. The *stadhouders* belonging to the House of Oranje-Nassau served in a hereditary capacity and had the title of "prince" . . . a true *regimen mixtum*. Prince Henry, however, declined: He probably feared that such an American "adventure" might prove to be abortive.[4] When about forty years later General San Martín met Simón Bolívar in Guayaquil, the former beseeched *El Libertador* to find a European prince willing to become the ruler of Spanish America, but Bolívar flatly refused, San Martín went into exile with a broken heart. The Latin American tragedy that began then has not yet ended.[5] Monarchical solutions after successful secession have not been rare or were, at least, attempted. The *New York Gazette and Weekly Mercury* wrote on April 23, 1770: "God forbid that we should ever be so miserable as to sink into a Republic."[6]

One of the Founding Fathers, Alexander Hamilton, perhaps the most gifted of them all, regretted that the United States could not become a monarchy. Van Buren saw in Hamilton a monarchist,[7] certainly a conviction well grounded in facts[8] in view of Hamilton's speeches at the Federal Convention in 1787 and 1788 in New York. And Francis Lieber very rightly pointed out that the Declaration of Independence is not really an antimonarchical document.[9] The sentence, "A prince whose character is thus marked by every act which may define a tyrant, is unfit to be the ruler of a free people" merely condemns George III but, at the same time, voices great respect for the royal office. The average American today would be surprised to hear the term "ruler of a free people" in which he sees a *contradictio in adjecto*. But in formulations like these we perceive a few aspects of Jefferson's highly contradictory character and mind. He does stand near the mainstream of American leftist thought and deserved Hamilton's severe strictures.[10] But then he was also the man who, in a letter to Mann Page, spoke about the "swinish multitudes."[11] And Gouverneur Morris, on the extreme right, wrote to Nathanael Green in 1781, "I will go farther, I have no hope that our Union can subsist except in the form of an absolute monarchy."[12]

So far, so good. Yet we would delude ourselves if we were to assume that there existed no strong antimonarchical or even leftist sentiment in the Thirteen Colonies. Earlier we mentioned religious and political traditions in the colonies which clearly stem from British independentism. The civil war in Britain and the Jacobite-Hanoverian antagonism also left their imprint on North America. And so did the political crystallization of British parliamentary life with its two factions: the Tories and the Whigs. The term Whig had originally a Scottish and Presbyterian connotation with republican undertones and also implied toleration of the Dissenters. The word Tory was Irish and denoted loyalty to the Stuarts as well as "Popish" inclinations. These were originally nicknames and they underwent a certain evolution. The Whigs, moreover, were related to the Roundheads and the Tories to the Cavaliers.

By the middle of the eighteenth century, however, it was evident that the Tories were the party of royal privileges, of the small nobility with aulic leanings, of the clergy of the Established Church; while the Whigs stood for the big, independent-minded, rich, landed nobility. Thus the Whigs, not the Tories, represented the aristocratic spirit. The French Revolution has somewhat obscured the real state of affairs by creating a curious alliance between the Crown and the nobility, who were opponents and competitors throughout most of European history. It is evident that a genuine aristocracy is never in favor of an absolute or an excessively strong monarchy unless the monarch, as a *primus inter pares*, is merely the executor of the will of the nobility. *Und der König àbsolut, wenn er unsren Willen tut!''* (The king may be absolute as long as he does our will!) Aristocrats are often downright republican in spirit: In a monarchy the nobility can only play second fiddle to the king's first, while republics often have been exclusively aristocratic in character. This is especially true of ancient Venice and Genoa as well as of a number of Swiss city-cantons. In this connection remember that monarchs, by their power to *nobilitate*, are (or rather were) constantly able to foster the process of social mobility and, in fact, were acting against aristocratic exclusiveness. The aristocratic republics (sometimes dominated by a patriciate without titles and even more exclusive than many a titled aristocracy!) were therefore often highly static and conservative states. Old Geneva was, needless to say, a far more hidebound city than, let us say, Munich, Berlin, or even St. Petersburg.

Toward the end of the eighteenth century we witness in Britain the split between the New Whigs and the Old Whigs, an evolution that did not take place in North America. It is obvious that in the Western Hemisphere the Whigs were the ones who were critical of the Crown and, therefore, of the tie with Britain. The Tories were again the "Loyalists" as they were in seventeenth- and early eighteenth-century Ireland. The Whigs are those frequently inspired by certain republican notions: they felt that they were "just as good as the King" and they were the ones who made the War of Independence against Britain, against the Tories . . . against the Tories abroad and at home.

We owe it to the pen of Kenneth Roberts, who not only was a good novelist but also a first-rate amateur historian, that we have in his *Oliver Wiswell* a very "live" picture of the civil war aspect of the American

War of Independence—a civil war between Whigs and Tories. This struggle as was to be expected, also had its analogies and repercussions in England where Whigs, quite unpatriotically, could not suppress a feeling of elation over the victory of their political coreligionists in America.

And since the Whig was the true aristocrat,[13] the American War of Independence, which did not have the character of a real revolution, found a friendly if not enthusiastic echo among Europe's noblemen. They soon flocked to North America as volunteers, among them primarily the French who had never forgotten the years of the *Fronde* and who were now imbued with liberal ideas. And, indeed, if one visits the capital of the United States one finds in the center of Jackson Square, right in front of the White House, the equestrian statue of Andrew Jackson, "Old Hickory," the first President of the United States who dared to call himself a democrat. In the four corners of the square, however, are four statues dedicated to European noblemen who had come to fight in America for freedom, but certainly not for democracy: Tadeusz Kościuszko, von Steuben, the Comte de Rochambeau, and the Marquis de Lafayette. The Polish nobleman Kazimierz Pulaski, the only General of the Union killed in action, has his monument in Savannah, Georgia, but the most valiant and characteristic of them all, Charles-Armand Tuffin, Marquis de la Rouërie, to whom we shall refer later, has not been commemorated in any way. Jean de Kalb ("Baron de Kalb") has been honored in various parts of America, but his nobility is of rather spurious origin.[14]

Thus the foundations of the American republic are aristocratic and whiggish. As we have pointed out, this does not stand in contradiction to an antimonarchic sentiment, however. The antimonarchical tradition of the United States, moreover, has long roots. It has probably increased rather than decreased over the years and has affected American foreign policy in the most fatal way—fatal to those on the receiving end, fatal also for American self-interest. Antimonarchism, as we shall see, has cost untold billions of dollars and, what is far more depressing, thousands upon thousands of American lives, victims of a piece of American folklore activated and accentuated by leftist prejudices and propaganda.

Whiggery, nevertheless, has not been the only source of the republican sentiment in the Thirteen Colonies prior to 1776. We find it as a latent feeling nourished by religions other than the Church of England —especially among Congregationalists, Presbyterians, perhaps even the Dutch Reformed, the Quakers, the Unitarians. The whole tradition of the Independents (connected with the Cromwellian Commonwealth) was not only violently anti-Catholic (and moderately anti-Anglican) but antihierarchical and therefore also antimonarchical. John C. Miller has emphasized the effectiveness of this interconnected anti-Catholic-antimonarchical animosity which was particularly strong in New England in the years preceding the War of Independence,[15] and even more interesting material can be culled from Ray Allen Billington's *The Protestant Crusade 1800-1860.* Billington quotes Daniel Barber's *History of My Own Time* on the anti-Catholic sentiment: "This feeling remained so strong through the early part of the Revolution that the President of Princetown University [John Witherspoon] believed the common hatred of Popery caused by the Quebec Act the only thing that cemented the divergent religious groups in the colonies together sufficiently to allow them to make war, an opinion which was shared by British observers."[16] As a matter of fact, the Quebec Act, granting religious tolerance to the French Canadians, by a curious twist of reasoning, was considered a major menace to freedom. As a result the following ditty was sung during the Revolution:

If Gallic Papists have the right
To worship their own way,
Then farewell to the liberties
Of poor Americay.

The suspicion arose that George III (who had so stoutly resisted the emancipation of Catholics) had secretly become a Catholic: kings, after all, must admire popes, and popes will support kings. John Trumbull in his satirical poem *McFingal* accused the King in these terms:

Struck bargains with the Romish churches
Infallibility to purchase.
Set wide for popery the door,
Made friends with Babel's scarlet whore.

These accusations, though unfounded, were psychologically not base-less since the Catholic tradition is one of mixed government with a monarchical head. Yet even today, in spite of the fact that the majority of "Protestant" nations are at least symbolically ruled by monarchs, the Catholic-monarchic equation continues to survive magically in the United States. It is an argument used by professional anti-Catholics, very much to the annoyance of *certain* American Catholics who, wanting to be taken for 200 percent Americans,[17] are determined to prove that every good Catholic ought to be a democratic republican.[18] Rarely do they realize that these desperate efforts earn them little intellectual respect from intelligent people. Those engaged in "political theology" almost always try to prove too much.[19]

While we have to bear in mind that there existed in the Thirteen Colonies an antimonarchical sentiment and occasionally feelings which even might be styled egalitarian, we have to see in the young American Republic a polity which was deeply whiggish or, in other words, aristocratic in character. One should never forget the term "democratic" appears neither in the Declaration of Independence nor in the Constitution, and that even the noun "republic" can be found in neither of these two documents. The Constitution merely insists that the member states of the Union should have a "republican" form of government. And actually, if we analyze the Constitution of the United States, we find that, *in its original form,* it can be considered a serious attempt to establish a mixed government with democratic, aristocratic, and monarchical elements, a government of checks and balances. If these three elements would derive their power from different sources, the attempt could be called successful. As it was, the Constitution provided for a republic (polity) rather than for a *regimen mixtum,* but ever since its inception the American Republic has been exposed constitutionally to democratizing influences, the dependence of the electors upon the voters, the direct election of senators, even the two-term amendment, the impending direct election of the President, etc. The older republican (and more strongly democratic) constitutions do not provide for a president—neither for a head of state nor for a head of the government. The Swiss "President," for instance, is merely the chairman of the council of cabinet ministers, (the seven Federal Councillors) elected by both Houses of Parliament. He is elected for one year only. His portrait is not found in public buildings, but that of the commanding colonel's. (Only in times of mobilization does Switzerland have a general).

The Founding Fathers, as educated men of their period, rejected democracy outright and this even more intensely when totalitarian repression became the dominating feature of the French Revolution. (Modern Americans also forget too easily that the French Revolution, and later the Napoleonic regime, murdered or exiled the three godfathers of the American republic—the kings of France and Spain and the *Stadhouder* of the Netherlands.[20] George Washington, the Master of Mount Vernon, was anything but a democrat.[21] And John Adams, the second President of the United States, though he formulated democracy rather strictly, had nothing but hatred and contempt for this form of government. Only remotely related to Samuel Adams of Boston who had been a bit of a rabble rouser if not an early leftist, John Adams was a real patrician with a strongly aristocratic outlook. The near-mystical fascination exercized by royal blood he saw founded on the general attention it drew. "Noble blood," he wrote in his *Discourses on Davila* which created an enormous outcry in the budding American left, "whether the nobility be hereditary or elective, and indeed, *more in republican governments than in monarchies, least of all in despotisms,* is held in estimation for the same reason.[22] (Italics mine.) As a matter of fact, he considered a democratic conviction with egalitarian undertones a sign of immaturity. Jefferson tells us about a conversation between Dr. Ewen and John Adams during which the doctor informed the President that he had a younger son who was a "democrat" and an older one who was an "aristocrat." "Well," said the President, "a boy of fifteen who is not a democrat is good for nothing, and he is no better who is a democrat at twenty."[23] Yet when John Adams came to judge democracy as such, his criticism became much stronger.

In a letter to John Taylor, Adams insisted that democracy would inevitably evolve into oligarchy and oligarchy into despotism[24]a notion he obviously shared with Plato and Aristotle. He flatly equated democracy with ignorance and maintained that "the moment you give knowledge to a democrat, you make him an aristocrat."[25] In his *A Defence of the Constitution of the Government of the United States* he said, "Democracy, simple democracy, never had a patron among men of letters. The people have almost always expected to be served gratis, and to be paid for the honor of serving them, and their applause and adoration are bestowed too often on artifice and tricks, on hypocrisy and superstition, on flattery, bribes and largesses."

In the same work he wrote that "we may appeal to every page of history . . . for proofs irrefragable that the people, when they have been unchecked have been as unjust, tyrannical, brutal, barbarous and cruel as any king or senate possessed by an uncontrollable power. The majority has eternally and without any one exception usurped over the rights of the minority." And he added in another passage, "All projects of government formed upon a supposition of continual vigilance, sagacity, virtue, and firmness of the people, when possessed of the exercise of supreme power, are cheats and delusions." This tallies with his remark, "The proposition that the people are the best keepers of their own liberties is not true. They are the worst conceivable, they are no keepers at all: they can neither judge, act, think, or will, as a political body. Individuals have conquered themselves: nations and large bodies never." Adams fired his heaviest artillery at democracy in the same work when he advanced twelve points, of which we quote only a few:

1. No democracy ever did or ever can exist. . . .[26]
4. That no love of equality, at least since Adam's fall, ever existed.
5. That no love of frugality ever existed as a passion, but always as a virtue.
6. That therefore the democracy of Montesquieu . . . [is] all mere fragments of the brain, a delusive imagination.
7. That his passion of love for democracy would be in the members of the majority only a love of the majority. . . .
11. That in reality, the word democracy signifies nothing more nor less than a nation or people without any government at all. . . .

And in a letter to Jefferson he stated that "Democracy will envy all, contend with all, endeavor to pull down all, and when by chance it happens to get the upper hand for a short time, it will be revengeful, bloody and cruel."[27] John Adams saw clearly that private property was basically endangered by democracy which would almost always be in the hands of the lower and far more numerous part of the social pyramid. In his letter to John Taylor he added, "If you give more than a share in the sovereignty to the democrats, that is, if you give them the command or the preponderance in the sovereignty, that is, the legislature, they will vote all property out of the hands of you aristocrats, and it will let you escape with your lives, it will be more humanity, consideration and generosity than any triumphant democracy ever displayed since the creation."[28]

Madison, fourth President of the United States, had the same fears concerning democracy, which is evident in his letter to Jared Sparks where he says that laws must be "capable of protecting the rights of property against the spirit of democracy."[29] Of course, Madison distinguished between pure democracy and the spirit of democracy. Pure democracy to him was direct democracy, as can be gleaned from his definitions in the *Federalist*, No. 10 and No. 14. Yet E. M. Burns is right when he says that "instead of defending the absolute sovereignty of the majority, Madison detested it so strongly that he sought in almost every conceivable way to prevent its exercise."[30] Nor was Madison an egalitarian. In a letter to Edmund Randolph he admitted that "there are subjects to which the capacity of the bulk of mankind are unequal and on which they must and will be governed by those with whom they happen to have acquaintance and confidence."[31] This is a far cry from the views of Andrew Jackson who said in his first annual message that "the duties of all public offices are . . . so plain and simple that men of intelligence may readily qualify themselves for their performance."[32]

Until the end of the nineteenth century an American Republican (with a capital "R") would never have termed his country a "Democracy" but rather a "representative republic."[33] Madison, however, in his basic political views seems to have been more influenced by Jefferson than by Hamilton. Yet if we take into account the way in which Madison refers to Hamilton's monarchical views and the latter's reservation concerning the republic during the Philadelphia Convention, we might suspect that Madison had certain sympathies for them.[34]

Frequently one hears Americans comparing "Jeffersonian democracy" with "Jacksonian democracy." But the question remains as to whether the third President of the United States was actually a convinced democrat. Dr. Mortimer Adler is more right than wrong when he says that "the dawn of American democracy really begins with Jackson."[35] And, perusing carefully the Washington and Ford editions of Jefferson's *Works,* one finds only one positive allusion to the terms "democrat" and "democracy."[36] Actually, in a letter written to Lafayette, Jefferson insisted that the Constitution of 1791 would work out in France, provided it was kept within the framework of a constitutional monarchy.[37] Still, Jefferson had an exaggerated notion of the qualities of the American people (only somewhat modified in his declining years) when he wrote that "if all the sovereigns of Europe were to set themselves to work to emancipate the minds of their subjects from their present ignorance and prejudice . . . a thousand years would not place them on that high ground on which our people are now setting out."[38]

But in order to understand Jefferson more fully—by no means an easy task—we have to remember that he was an agrarian romantic who believed in the high virtues and qualities of a free yeomanry. The language of one of his relatives, John Randolph of Roanoke (who told the Virginia Constitutional Convention, "I am an aristocrat: I love liberty, I hate equality.") certainly was not Jefferson's.[39]

"Those who labor in the earth," Jefferson wrote, "are the chosen people of God if ever he had a chosen people."[40] To Madison he wrote, "I think that our government will remain virtuous for many centuries, as long as they are chiefly agricultural, and this will be as long as there are vacant lands in any part of America. When they get piled upon one another as in the large cities of Europe, they will become corrupt as in Europe."[41] Since Jefferson figures in the folklore of the American left—in the 1930s and 1940s there was a Jefferson School run by Communists in New York—it is rather interesting to remember what the slave-owning master of Monticello thought about the urban working class. "The mobs of the great cities add just so much to the support of pure government, as sores do to the strength of the human body," he wrote to John Jay in 1785.[42] And then he confessed, "I consider the class of artificers as the panders of vice, and the instruments by which the liberties of the country are generally perverted."[43] In a letter to John Adams, speaking about the United States and using the same "reactionary" language, he insisted that "everyone by his property, or by his satisfactory situation is interested in the support of law and order. And such men may safely and advantageously reserve to themselves wholesome control over their public affairs, and a degree of freedom, which in the hands of the *canaille* of the cities of Europe, would be instantly perverted to the demolition and destruction of everything public."[44]

What then did he hope for? Who really should govern? In the same letter Jefferson proves himself a true timocrat: "The natural aristocracy I consider as the most precious gift of nature, for the instruction, the trusts and governments of society. And indeed, it would have been inconsistent in creation to have formed men for the social state, and not to have provided virtue and wisdom enough to manage the concerns of society. May we not even say that that form of government is the best, which provides most effectually for a pure selection of these natural *aristoi* into the offices of government?"[45]

As we can see quite clearly, the Founding Fathers of the United States were not professed democrats, and the United States was not established as a "democracy." Albert Jay Nock wrote: "One sometimes wonders how our Revolutionary forefathers would take it if they could hear some flatulent political thimblerigger charge them with having founded 'the great and glorious democracy of the West.' "[46] Senator Arthur H. Vandenberg once remarked that "the government of the United States is a representative republic and not a pure democracy. The difference is as profound today as it was when the foundations of the Constitution were set in the ages. . . . We are a representative republic. We are not a pure democracy. . . . Yet we are constantly trying to graft the latter on the former, and every effort we make in this direction, with but few exceptions, is a blow aimed at the heart of the Constitution."[47]

So much about the alleged intrinsically leftist nature of nascent America.

Chapter 7

The French Revolution

Looking now at the background of the French Revolution—historically the mother of most of the ideological evils besetting not only Western civilization but also the rest of the world—we have to make an inventory of the roots of this iniquity. We find misinterpretation and distortion of events in America, but there were also other factors leading to the French Revolution and we will consider them later.

In dealing with the first phase of the Great Euramerican Misunderstanding we have to admit that there probably were more Frenchmen misinterpreting what they saw and experienced in America than Americans (and Englishmen!) propagating ideas in France, all bound to produce unhappy results. We have mentioned the English in this connection because ideologically their impact on the Continent was very similar to that of the United States. England is not physically part of Europe (though it naturally belongs to Western civilization) and there is a relatively large minority of Britishers (Winston Churchill and Evelyn Waugh among them) who refer to the Continent as "Europe," as if their island did not really belong to this western peninsula of Eurasia. This does not mean that eminent Britishers and Americans have not enjoyed life on the Continent time and again. As a matter of fact, the Continent is dotted with graves of outstanding British non-conformists who preferred to escape the control of British society. They range from Keats, Shelley, and Kemble to Oscar Wilde and D. H. Lawrence.

(Byron's body was brought back to Britain.) The reactions of Americans to Europe naturally showed great variety and more often than not they had political implications. Philip Rahv's *Discovery of Europe*[1] provides a broad spectrum of positive judgments, of delight and enthusiasm, though much more for the Continent than for Britain. Certainly the notion expressed by Adet, a French agent for the *Directoire* in the United States, that all Americans are "born enemies of all the people of Europe"[2] was and still is untrue. Yet there are some voices of dissent in Rahv's book: John Adams, who was too unbending, and Jefferson and Mark Twain, who were too provincial and too agnostic (each in his own way, though).

Hamilton was convinced that Jefferson, while American Minister in Paris, had played a rather negative part. Hamilton said that "in France he [Jefferson] saw government only on the side of its abuses. He drank freely of the French philosophy, in religion, in science, in politics. He came from France in the moment of fermentation, which he had a share in exciting, and in the passions and feelings of which he shared both from temperament and situation."[3]

Jefferson's eventual successor, Gouverneur Morris, was certainly of another breed. He spent several years in Paris and Western Europe before being appointed United States Minister to France. He wrote in his diary, "At dinner I sit next to M. de Lafayette who tells me I injure the cause, for that my sentiments are continually quoted against the good party. I seize this opportunity to tell him that I am opposed to the democracy from regard to liberty."[4] Yet Morris was a voice crying in the wilderness. As an American aristocrat he moved in the highest French circles and was nauseated by the leftist sentiments he encountered everywhere, not only among the nobility but also among the clergy. The Bishop of Arras who thought it would make Morris happy to hear the American Constitution praised as the best in the world, found that he pleased him not at all, although he had helped to draft this document. As a matter of fact, Morris was always haunted by the specter of dictatorship in America.[5] His eulogies of aristocracy did not please the republican countesses and princesses.[6] Probably Lafayette irritated him more than anybody else. Talking to him, he "pointed out for the hundredth time, that each country needed to have its own form of government, that an American Constitution could not do for France and that, above all, France needed stability. He gave the reasons for his advice clearly and forcibly, but poor Lafayette flinched from it, and could not be persuaded to make any effectual step."[7] This was the same Gouverneur Morris who at a banquet he gave in New England in 1815 exclaimed, "The long agony is over. The Bourbons are restored. France reposes in the arms of the legitimate prince. We may now express our attachments to her consistently with the respect we owe to ourselves. . . . Thank God, we can, at length, avow the sentiments of gratitude to that august family under whose sway the fleets and armies of France and Spain were arrayed in defence of American liberty. . . . The Bourbons are restored. Rejoice France! Spain! You are governed by your legitimate kings! Europe! Rejoice!"[8] One can imagine the outcry of the early American left when the full text of this address became known.

Yet that there exists a "technical" filiation between 1776 and 1789 can hardly be denied, and it is precisely this "factual" connection which effectively masks the misunderstanding. First of all one has to bear in mind that 1789 did not lead *necessarily and inevitably* to 1792 and to the rise of totalitarianism in Europe and later in all other quarters of the globe. Georges Bernanos always emphasized the difference between the initial stage of the French Revolution which had the almost unanimous support of the French nobility[9] (and a very large sector of the clergy) and the terror regime of the lower middle class which was later followed by a proletarian-agrarian movement under Gracchus Babeuf. In other words, the aristocratic character of the American Revolution and of the initial stage of the French Revolution were very similar. But in the latter we see, from the beginning on, the active collaboration and interference of bloodthirsty mobs which gained in strength and dynamism until the fall of the Robespierre regime.[10] The nobility, as de Tocqueville pointed out, nursed their old grievances against all forms of royal absolutism and it was the nobility which really forced the issue by insisting that the King convoke the Estates General. The *noblesse de la robe* spearheaded that movement. The historian A. Mathiez has coined the phrase *révolte nobiliaire*[11] and this development merely shows how dangerous it can be to tamper radically with a political structure in a period of transition when prosperity is increasing considerably, when an era of reforms has been inaugurated already.

Yet besides the old aristocratic tendency to oppose the monarch in the best whiggish fashion,[12] there were, naturally, other interior factors at work. One was the ancient hatred of the Jansenists for the Crown, which now again made itself felt in various ways.[13] Bishop Henri Grégoire belonged to that faction: He headed the Constitutionalist priests (who were in a real schism with Rome) and received, before his death in 1831, the absolution of a Jansenist priest. He had played an eminent part during the Revolution, had voted against the monarchy ("kings are in the political order what monsters are in the natural") and was one of the first in the National Convention to demand a trial of the King. The other religious opposition came from the Huguenots who were equally unforgiving. Edmund Burke who, as an Anglican, belonged to a faith not much unlike theirs, had to acknowledge, ''I am sorry to say that they behaved shockingly since the very beginning of the rebellion, and have been uniformly concerned in its worst and most atrocious acts. Their clergy are just the same atheists with those Constitutional Catholics, but still more wicked and daring. Three of their number have met from their republican associates the rewards of their crimes.''[14] This attitude of the rebels could be understood in view of the intolerance of the French Kings in the past. Yet Brienne, Bishop of Toulouse, had already proposed the emancipation of the Calvinists in 1787, and by 1788 their emancipation was a fact. André Siegfried, himself a Protestant, had to confess that the French Protestant even today ''has naturally, almost necessarily to be a partisan of the French Revolution, which means in other words that he is congenitally an enemy of the *Ancien Régime* and of anything that might be styled 'reaction.' ''[15]

The President of the Constitutional Assembly, Jean Paul Rabaut St. Etienne, was the son of a distinguished Reformed minister and, belonging to the more moderate Girondins, met with a tragic fate. In the popular mind, however, the Huguenots became so identified with support of the French Revolution (and not without cause, as we have seen) that after the Restoration anti-Huguenot riots took place, notably the so-called *massacres de Nîmes* (a reaction against the *bagarres de Nîmes*).[16]

Among the foreign ''influences'' (mostly ''misinterpretations'' of foreign countries and their institutions) we should again mention the ''images'' of Switzerland and of England. Voltaire was truly bewitched by England and we have to see him as the man who spearheaded Anglomania in France.[17] Metternich was always haunted by the idea that copying England had been the undoing of France, if not of the entire Continent, was also certain that England would eventually be ruined by imitating French patterns, by submitting to the *école francaise*.[18] In a secret memorandum to Alexander I, written circa December 1820, Metternich said, ''It is difficult to overlook the influence which England for a long time has exercised on France. England, however, is in such a unique situation that we can maintain without exaggeration that one of the forms congenial to that State, none of its habits or institutions can be adopted by any of the states of the Continent, and when these are actually taken for models, the result is nothing but troubles and dangers without any accompanying advantages."[19] Alfred Müller-Armack also sees this very decisive English influence on the ideology of the French Revolution.[20] Charles Seignobos insists that a sketchy forerunner of the *Déclaration des Droits de l'Homme* had been shown to the rebelling citizens of Bordeaux by the English Colonel Sexby. This outline was the preamble of a constitutional draft proposed by the British Army to the Parliament in 1648.[21]

The English and Swiss examples, needless to say, were effective thanks to the emphasis on personal liberty in these two nations and to the economic wellbeing of their respective upper classes. (The *general* prosperity of Switzerland is the product of a much later period. Emigration and military service in foreign countries characterizes the Swiss economy until the early part of the nineteenth century.[22] The "Patricians," however, always lived in great comfort.) The American example, because of its great distance from the English and Swiss examples was less concrete but had a highly romantic halo. At first there were the French volunteers who had arrived prior to the break between Paris and London. Then there were the regular army men who had fought shoulder to shoulder with the Americans. Finally, there was a Roussellian aura about America: virgin forests, noble savages, free men, simple lives, log cabins, manors, and town halls in Grecian style. The Americans in Paris—Jefferson, Benjamin Franklin, Silas Deane—excited the French imagination beyond belief. In fathering the French Revolution naively and unknowingly, these Americans were perhaps less instrumental, however, than the Frenchmen, volunteers and regular officers, who had fought in the New World and had come home imbued with notions they had picked up at random and had not well digested.

It took me many years in the United States to understand what makes that country "tick," what is the inner meaning of certain words, what is the mind and thought of both the average and the extraordinary American. The confusion among the French (and other volunteers) must have been considerable in many ways.

The evidence of this misunderstanding, to which so many Frenchmen succumbed and which helped to bring about the French Revolution, receives documentation in a number of works. Among these I would like to mention merely the writings of Lafayette,[23] of Count Louis Philippe de Ségur,[24] of Madame de Staël,[25] of Madame Campan,[26] of Lamartine,[27] of Taine,[28] Chateaubriand,[29] and many others. Later Lord Acton,[30] Alexis de Tocqueville,[31] Philippe Sagnac,[32] Georg Jellinek,[33] and Felix Somary[34] have emphasized the American roots of the French

Revolution but also insisted that the ideas prevailing in America at the time of the War of Independence had been grossly misinterpreted by the French: They assumed a new meaning and, when transplanted in French soil, degenerated rapidly.

Hamilton was certain that Jefferson had not been innocent concerning the evolution in France after 1789 (p. 73) and John Adams was tortured by the thought that the United States and he himself had to take a large share of the blame for the horrors that followed the storming of the Bastille. The former President of the United States wrote to Dr. Benjamin Rush in a letter dated August 28, 1811: "Have I not been employed in mischief all my days? Did not the American Revolution produce all the calamities and desolation to the human race and the whole globe ever since? I meant well, however. My conscience was clear as a crystal glass, without scruple or doubt. I was borne by an irresistible sense of duty. God prospered our labors, and, awful, dreadful, and deplorable as the consequences have been, I cannot but hope that the ultimate good of the world, of the human race, and of our beloved country, is intended and will be accomplished by it."[35]

Yet the ultimate good had not been achieved so far, and Adams himself knew that the crowned dictator who followed the French Revolution had been its offspring. "Napoleon and all his generals were but creatures of democracy," he wrote to John Taylor of Caroline, Virginia.[36] But other men were infinitely more responsible than John Adams in pushing the ideas of the French Revolution, men like the Anglo-American Thomas Paine who much later became the hero of the Nazi playwright Johst.[37] Other Nazis, for instance a certain Dr. Friedrich Schönemann, praised Jefferson and damned Hamilton, seeing in the former a precursor of the historic evolution leading to the victory of the Common Man—and of German National Socialism.[38] Earlier European authors dealing with the United States have extolled George Washington and Alexander Hamilton, and criticized Jefferson as well as, later, the American Democratic Party in which they saw a helpmate to the "party of revolution"[39] in Europe. Then as now, to be sure, only a few recognized the United States for what it really was and, temperamentally, still is: an aristocratic state.[40]

Charles-Armand Tuffin, Marquis de la Rouërie, was a Frenchman who participated in the War of Independence and who clearly perceived the difference between that noble struggle and the French Revolution, a man who should be much better known to Americans than the immensely vain and morbidly ambitious Lafayette,[41] a man who should inspire young Americans, young Frenchmen, and lovers of liberty everywhere, as well as defenders of all human values. He came to America before Lafayette, left after Lafayette, and fought bravely *for* freedom and *against* democracy. No monument, no street name, no stamp, no memorial whatsoever to commemorate his name or his deeds can be found in the United States. His life is briefly described in an Appendix (see pp. 435-443).

This aristocrat differed radically from other noblemen who, each in his own way, contributed to the French Revolution. We have already mentioned Lafayette, still so popular in America, and we also referred to Maximilien de Robespierre.[42] But above all we should discuss the "grandfather of modern democracy," the Comte de Sade, sometimes called "the Divine Marquis." He is better known for his sexual aberrations than for his philosophy—sadism is named after him—but his real importance lies in the domain of politics, in his one historic intervention and, later, in the spreading of his political ideas.

Research on de Sade started slowly only half a century ago: The first serious efforts were made by Dr. Eugen Dühren (a pseudonym for Iwan Bloch) who, however, was interested in Sade only from the point of view of sexual pathology. After World War I there was Maurice Heine, originally a member of the French Socialist party which, like the Russian one, underwent a profound schism and split into the old-fashioned Socialists and the Communists. Heine joined the radical group and soon became editor of *L'Humanité*, the Communist daily. He made a mistake that is not rare in the Latin countries: He confused communism with anarchical libertinism. Upon orders from Moscow he was fired by his paper in 1922 and the year after was thrown out of the Parts, the P.C.F. He then concentrated largely on de Sade and sadism[43] and came to admire de Sade as a totally free, unfettered, and diabolical spirit.

The events of World War II have increased public interest in de Sade, who emerges from a number of essays as a "fellow like you and me." Refer to the book by M. Pierre Klossowski, called significantly *Sade, notre prochain*. A private edition of de Sade's collected works has been published as well as a serious but, in my opinion, still not definitive biography by Gilbert Lely.[44] By and large the crimes of the Divine Marquis had been exaggerated: His deeds were neither so numerous nor so ferocious as reputed, since he spent most of his time in jails and hospitals for the criminally insane. However, he was not *mentally* ill. As a fanatical and confirmed atheist he more or less acted in accordance with his views, and apart from the aid of skilled theologians and philosophers, he might have needed the attention of a competent psychiatrist. Still he was neither schizophrenic, nor a paranoiac, and he was fully responsible for his actions.

What has *not* been done so far is a systematization of his political and philosophical thought which is to be found in a few pamphlets and minor essays while the larger part is dispersed among his pornographic works. One would have to wade through an ocean of smut (shocking, perhaps, in the beginning, but merely tiring in the long run) in order to get a coherent whole. As far as one can see without having undertaken this Herculean task, we have here a real system of thought waiting to be expounded. There was method and logic to this man. His books were widely read but, naturally, rarely quoted because even for the end of the eighteenth century they were far from respectable. And precisely because these were volumes one did not like to boast of knowing, it will always be very difficult to prove *unequivocally* how influential they were at the time of their publication—and after. One would have to look for their oblique reflection in the sayings, writings, and actions of others.

It is probable that de Sade's ideology-philosophy was the outflow of his inclinations and aberrations—and not the other way round. It is quite possible that we all have sadistic drives but that in normal, in average persons they exist only within certain limits. It can be argued that de Sade in this respect was not an exception but that, being able to justify his yielding to these instincts, he finally became their slave. They certainly dominate his imagination, his daydreams, his writings, his whole intellect.

Donatien Alphonse Francois Comte de Sade was born on June 2, 1740 in Paris as scion of an ancient southern French, Provençal family. He served in the army and in 1763 married Mademoiselle de Montreuil whose wealthy family belonged to the *noblesse de la robe*. A few months after the wedding he engaged in sadistic torture of a prostitute and was jailed for fifteen days as a consequence. A similar though graver case occurred in 1768 when he cruelly flogged a girl and was again committed to prison. Released, he engaged in an orgy in a brothel in Marseille which resulted in a more severe sentence in 1772. Imprisoned in Miolans, he succeeded in escaping but was again arrested in Paris in 1777 and brought back to the south of France where, thanks to another escape, he enjoyed thirty-nine days of liberty. Arrested once more, he spent five and a half years in Vincennes followed by another five and a half years in the Bastille and after that a year in the hospital for the criminally insane in Charenton. This long imprisonment was not due to a jail sentence but to a *lettre de cachet* from the King, issued upon the request of de Sade's mother-in-law, the Présidente de Montreuil.

When the government had decided to liquidate the prison tract of the fortress of Vincennes, de Sade was transferred to the Bastille, which also was "doomed" during the reform year 1788. The government wanted to raze this state prison and to sell the ground for a real estate development. History only precipitated events. During his imprisonment de Sade wrote assiduously, expressing his libertine, atheistic, materialistic, and leftist views. Knowing about the unrest in Paris, he began to harangue the people from his window, saying that the prisoners were tortured and assassinated in the dark dungeons of the Bastille. He used a funnel to give greater strength to his voice. We have a letter from M. de Launay, Governor of the prison, to M. de Villedeuil, Minister of State, dated July 2, 1789, in which the former insists that under the circumstances his prisoner ought to be transferred to the hospital for the criminally insane[45] in Charenton. Actually, after the prisoner had repeated his performance on July 3, his transfer was carried out in the morning of July 4. The documentation concerning de Sade's noisy appeals is fairly complete[46] and when, much later, he was arrested at the height of the Terror, he boasted of his contribution to the fall of the Bastille. He spoke of the "ardor with which I called the people on the third of July to destroy the Bastille where the despots had me imprisoned: thus I possess the most glittering civic record of which a republican can pride himself."[47]

Was de Sade then really the main culprit in this sordid affair? He well might have been because the forthcoming destruction of the Bastille was well known and political prisoners were rarely, if ever, locked up behind its walls.

The Governor of the Bastille, M. de Launay, an enlightened liberal, had a tiny garrison of Swiss and some invalid veterans at his disposal when the mob finally gathered around the building on July 14: He offered only token resistance. The delegates of the Town Hall and two appointees of the mob were received and were invited to join the governor at his meals. In the meantime the drawbridge of the outer court was let down and guns were directed at the inner court. The soldiers, sensing that they had no commander willing to take the responsibility, surrendered. The governor was killed after having been atrociously tortured. He implored the monsters to finish him off and when, at last, he had been given the *coup de grace*, a young cook "who knew how to handle meat" cut off his head with a small kitchen knife. The head was carried around in triumph until the late evening hours. Three of the officers were also murdered fiendishly and two of the invalids who once had heroically fought for France were hanged by the howling mob, which also cut off the hands of a Swiss guard. The surprise came when the "victors" found only seven prisoners. Four were forgers who quickly decamped, two were insane (they had been there only for observation), and one was a dissolute young man of noble descent who considered himself the real hero of the day: he harangued the people with revolutionary phrases. All in all, a nauseating and disgraceful performance, certainly not fit to serve as the basis for a national holiday—and inspired in every way by the "Divine Marquis."

Donatien de Sade stayed at Charenton only until April 2, 1790, when he was released, thanks to a decree of the National Assembly, which declared all *lettres de cachet* of the King null and void. It was Good Friday. His wife sued for separation from the monstrous man and got it. De Sade felt "betrayed." Yet he soon engaged in local politics and became a leader of the Place Vendôme section of Paris. After the September massacres in 1792 he was even appointed its secretary. It is evident that he was somewhat torn between a certain snobbery—after all, the de Sades belonged to the highest nobility—and his materialistic and atheistic convictions which drew him toward the left. The mere fact that he was of noble origin proved to be no obstacle either in his case or in others to a "career" in Republican circles. Yet at the height of the Terror, in spite of the fact that his section had been directed by Robespierre, de Sade was in danger of being guillotined. The 9th Thermidor, the day of Robespierre's fall, saved his life.

However, de Sade's writings are of even greater interest. In 1791 he published his first great pornographic novel *Justine, ou les malheurs de la vertu.* Here philosophical remarks and debates are wedged in between scenes of sexual debauchery. His *Addresse d'un citoyen de Paris au roi des Francais,* issued in the same year, is purely political and shows not the extreme leftist materialist views which we encounter in later writings, as for instance in *Aline et Valcour, ou le Roman Philosophique,* a "novel" in four volumes that was printed three times between 1793 and 1795. With its total of more than 1,700 pages, it had an enormous impact on the French Revolution which was, in so many ways, a sanguinary sex orgy.

Even worse, from a purely moral-esthetic as well as from an ideological point of view, were *La philosophie dans le boudoir* (1795) and *La Nouvelle Justine, suivi de l'histoire de Juliette ou les prospérités du vice* (1797). De Sade, especially during his jail terms and his sojourn in Charenton, must have had a prodigious capacity for work and a truly limitless imagination, because the abovementioned works by no means exhaust the list of his *opera omnia*. Some of his manuscripts were destroyed by his son or by the police. Others were published post-humously—for instance the very important *Dialogue entre un prêtre et un moribond* which contains the quintessence of de Sade's atheistic, materialistic outlook, while the more scandalous *Les 120 Jours de Sodome ou l'Ecole du libertinage* is onesidedly pornographic.

Lost is the manuscript of *Projet de création de lieux de prostitution, organisés, entretenus et dirigés par l'Etat* which contains an interesting plan for totalitarian sex control. Altogether thirty-one published books and pamphlets are listed in Lely's biography of de Sade,[48] twenty-three unpublished ones and thirty-five lost manuscripts. Among all these are only seven smaller (published) political pamphlets (between four and eight pages), seven of which were issued by the *Section des Piques* (Vendôme) during the time "Citizen Sade" was politically active. Among the unpublished manuscripts there is a large number of plays. One of these, *Le Comte Oxtiern ou les Effets du Libertinage*, was performed for the public in the Théatre Molière (October 1791).

De Sade's outlook was materialistic-atheistic-totalitarian, with a curiously contradictory anarchical bent. He believed that human beings were not superior to animals: The whole "animal kingdom" as well as the plants (he drew the line at minerals) admitted no hierarchic superiorities and inferiorities,[49] all were "equal." His determinism was complete. "Pedantic louts, hangmen, scribblers, legislators, tonsured scum, what are you going to do once we prevail? What will happen to your laws, your morality, your religion, your powers, your paradise, your gods, your hell, when it will be proved that such and such a flow of humor, a certain type of fibres, a specific degree of acidity in the blood or in the animal spirits will make a man the object of your punishment or your rewards?"[50] According to him the idea that murder, destruction, annihilation could be "bad" completely contradicts the workings of nature: As a matter of fact, there can be no creation without preliminary destruction,[51] an idea which we also find expressed in Oliver Wendell Holmes's writings (p. 180).

The nihilism of de Sade went so far that he contemplated with a certain satisfaction the possibility that mankind could annihilate itself. "This total self-destruction would merely return to nature the opportunity of creation which we have taken from her by propagating ourselves."[52]

Needless to say, children should belong to the state, a demand that will always be raised by leftists who have an innate hatred for the family as an "individualistic" group that tries to separate itself as an independent cell within the state and society.[53] Yet de Sade's hatred of the family also took other forms. He insisted that any society based on fraternity should make incest mandatory between brothers and sisters. (Interestingly enough, this theme recurs in the writings of Thomas Mann, a leftist of great literary talent.)[54] Promiscuity will naturally end the concept of fatherhood which rests on man's ability to identify children as his own by an act of faith and conviction, but that does not matter. Motherhood will survive and man has a fatherland, a *patria*, and this is sufficient.[55] Just as creation-propagation loses its value, so also murder loses its horror.[56]

The French Revolution truly lived up to de Sade's visions, and there can be little doubt that, in a certain way, the "Divine Marquis" is the patron saint of all leftist *movements*. In making this statement, however, one must bear in mind that only leftists produce *movements*, whereas, at best, the right can "organize" in a relatively hierarchic fashion. It has been well said by Spengler that the concept of the "party" in itself is leftish.[57] Yet if movements and parties have no affinities for a genuinely rightist outlook, we must come to the conclusion that the principles of the right within the parliamentary-democratic framework can only prevail after a catastrophic default or collapse of leftism. The right cannot normally win by its own virtue, its truth, its values because it will never fascinate the masses. It will attract extraordinary and superior people but hardly ever the average man.

It is obvious that de Sade was by no means solely responsible for the French Revolution—nor were the confused veterans of the American war. Nor even Voltaire, who was instrumental in undermining, eroding, and corroding the principles of religion and order on which the *ancien régime* rested. His part was very similar to that of the German Leftist pseudoliberal intellectuals and artists who can be called collectively the spiritual Kerenskys of the decaying Weimar Republic.[58] Voltaire was certainly *not* an ardent republican, nor was he a democrat. His ideal was a constitutional monarchy headed by a *roi sage*, Plato's philosopher-king.[59] So was Diderot's. Voltaire wrote of the republic that it represented a social order leading to tyranny.[60] "Independent of my love for freedom," he wrote, "I still would prefer to live under a lion's paw than under the teeth of a thousand rats who are my fellow citizens."[61] In a letter to d'Alembert he said that the canaille was not made for reason. In another letter he insisted that "we never intended to enlighten shoemakers and servants, that is up to the apostles."[62] A democracy, he said in the *Dictionnaire de Philosophie*, "would only be feasible in a very small country which also must have a most fortunate geographical location. And in spite of its smallness it will commit many mistakes because it will consist of human beings, which means that discord will rule in it as in a monastery."[63] Yet he forgot his geographic reservations when he sang his usual praises of the British Constitution. Once when he embarked again on his panegyric, the Prince de Ligne interrupted him, saying, "Add to it the protection of Britain by the Ocean without which she would not last a year."[64]

Rousseau too was convinced that the democratic republic fitted only small states while large ones ought to have monarchical governments.[65] However, it is not this particular theory that gave Rousseau his importance as a political theorist but rather his notions of the social contract which opened an era of totalitarianism in whose midst we are still living. As one can easily imagine, the French Revolution was deeply indebted to Rousseau, who died in 1778. His memory was honored at every possible (or impossible) opportunity. At the Feast of Reason in Notre Dame the busts of Voltaire, Rousseau, and Franklin were objects of veneration.[66] In 1794 Rousseau's remains were solemnly buried in the Pantheon but removed again in 1814.

A vain person, a shabby immoralist burdened with an unbalanced mind (especially during the last years of his life when his neuroses left him on the verge of insanity), Rousseau helped to father the French Revolution and subsequent developments. He also had an impact on the American scene—from a folkloric as well as from an intellectual point of view. We can see this reflected in George D. Herron's enthusiasm for Rousseau and Calvin.[67] Jacques Maritain is convinced that Rousseau influenced the rise of democracy and democratism in the United States, although he admits that this was less the case than in France.[68] Walter Lippmann, on the other hand, states unequivocally that "Jacobinism became the creed of American democracy"[69] and that Rousseau's ideas (as well as those of two other Swiss, Fröbel and Pestalozzi)[70] made themselves felt in American education. Alfred Müller-Armack, on the contrary, insists that neither Montesquieu nor Rousseau, but *seventeenth-century* England[71] originally provided the French Revolution with its ideological foundations. We should not forget, however, that Rousseau hailed from Geneva, that his original faith was Calvinism, and that there are various analogies as well as dialectic contradictions between his thought and Calvin's. A certain emotional trait pervades the thinking of both, a fact well brought out by a Dutch author.[72] To Rousseau's *sentiment intérieur*, his avowal that he "never

84

thought out anything," that he had felt everything, stands Calvin's remark about the "inner gifts of the spirit, the *autópiston,* which one should never subject to demonstration or reason,"[73] certainly a language very different from that of the scholastics.

Yet one should distinguish clearly between analogy and dialectic contradictions, and the antinomian reaction of Rousseau to Calvin and Calvinism is undoubtedly stronger than his readiness to copy from the Reformers.[74] Temperamentally, too, these two men were poles apart: Maître Jean, the man from Noyon was, after all, a cold spirit and a methodical thinker; Jean-Jacques, the native Genevan, was a confused emotionalist.

Still, both Genevans[75] stood for absolutes and Jellinek is quite right when he also sees Hobbes as a forerunner of Rousseau. "It was obviously the concept of the sovereign king in his own glory, which engendered the demand for a free, sovereign people. The omnipotent king became the ancestor of the omnipotent people and Thomas Hobbes found a master in a pupil surpassing him—in J. J. Rousseau."[76] However, Jellinek also recognized the emotionalist in Rousseau, the man who has to experience everything before formulating a theory.[77] And there is possibly in Rousseau even a deist with pantheistic inclinations, a sort of mystic—the term taken in a general sense—more so than in the theocentric Calvin.[78]

We have to admit, however, that both Calvin and Rousseau were not only "absolutistic" in their thinking but also totalitarian, which is by no means the same. Benjamin Constant, a genuine liberal, rightly called Rousseau's theory of the social contract "the most terrible aid to all types of despotism."[79] In a way Rousseau's notion of the people reminds one of the totality of the Greek city-state, but it is also the precursor of modern nationalism. Irving Babbitt knew very well that nationalism and internationalism (as opposed to genuine patriotism or a feeling of universality) are different in degree, not in essence, and rightly accused Rousseau of having given a new impetus to both collectivist drives. At the same time he admitted that Rousseau "in his final phase is an emotional nationalist, and that is because he saw that the patriotic virtue is a more potent intoxicant than the love of humanity."[80] If this emotional nationalism is exploited by an able imperialistic leader who, spurning all ethical discipline, not only is dominated by the lust for knowledge and for feeling, but even more so by the lust for power, we have to expect the "most sinister of all types, the efficient megalomaniac. The final use of science that has thus become a tool of the lust for power is, in Burke's phrase, to 'improve the mystery of murder.' ''[81] Indeed these were prophetic words published in 1919 by Babbitt, one of the most brilliant minds among American conservative thinkers.

It would be wrong to think in this connection only of the obvious mass assassins, of Hitler and Stalin. One has to add the butchers of Hamburg, Dresden, Hiroshima, and Nagasaki. "The leadership of the Occident is no longer here," Babbitt wrote scathingly. "The leaders have succumbed in greater or lesser degree to naturalism, (the Church, so far as it has become humanitarian, has itself succumbed to naturalism) and so have been tampering with the moral law. That the brutal imperialist who brooks no obstacle to his lust for domination has been tampering with this law goes without saying, but the humanitarian, all adrip with brotherhood and profoundly convinced of the loveliness of his own soul, has been tampering with it also, *and in a more dangerous way*, for the very reason that it is less obvious."[82] (Italics mine.)

To what extent Rousseau not only laid the foundations of the French Revolution but also of the modern totalitarian state can be gleaned even better from Werner Kägi's fascinating essay, "The Constitutional State and Democracy."

"Rousseau," he says, "might be a representative of the idea of local rights, but within the state he had denied all manifestations of pluralism as a menace to democracy. This monistic—unitary-centralistic —thinking has determined the very character of the French Revolution's ideology. The *république une et indivisible* became the great postulate of constitutional evolution and 'simplification' was equated with 'progress.' Thus the unitary centralistic state became the prevailing form of state structure,"[83] and we are finally faced with a "democratic Leviathan."[84] No wonder, since the "massively absolutistic democratism of the twentieth century is not dominated by the notion of representation, but by identity, because the representatives do not have a well grounded position of constitutional power, but have merely the unstable status of 'agents' as defined by Rousseau,"[85] whose seminal ideas matured only in our age.[86]

Rousseau had chosen between uniformity, equality, and freedom—although he cagily used the latter term. "Whoever refuses to pay obedience to the general will," he wrote, "shall be liable to be compelled to it by the force of the whole body. And this is in effect nothing more than that he may be compelled to be free."[87] This formulation, on the other hand, is not surprising if we remember that Rousseau, entirely in keeping with much of democratic thought, insisted on an *a priori* consent of every citizen to all laws, including those against which he voted and to which he objected.[88] Naturally "the most generally expressed will, the will of the majority [*la volonté la plus générale*] is most just because the voice of the people is the voice of God."[89] (Nor is this emphasis on majority rule alien to Jefferson.)[90]

Starting with the individualism of eighteenth-century romanticism, with antiroyalism and the concept of the noble savage ("people born free are now in chains"),[91] Rousseau's programmatic switch from the rule by one to the rule by all paved the way to totalitarianism. The glorified individual in his ideology reappears as a cipher. The foundations of socialism were laid thereby. Naturally the old individualistic man who had grown up in the *ancien régime* was hardly ideal material for this new society of obedient nonentities ready to be submerged in the mass: Man had to be created anew. "He who dares to legislate to a people," Rousseau wrote, "has to be capable, so to say, of changing human nature . . . he must transform human nature in order to strengthen it."[92]

In a statement like this we can sense that absolute contempt for personality, for the character of individuals as well as of entire nations, that mixture of ignorance and arrogance which is typical of the entire modern left bent upon putting mankind into a strait jacket. A Girondist like Condorcet manifested the same outlook when he wrote, "One law is good for all the nations just as a theorem in geometry is good for all minds."[93] Of course there is in Rousseau not only the sloppy, contradictory thinker, but also the sentimentalist with exhibitionist tendencies and, above all, the visionary, the prophet.[94]

Ideas have consequences. Jean-Jacques died eleven years before the outbreak of the French Revolution, but the great revolutionary leaders thought and acted in his spirit. His totalitarian attitude is well exemplified by the speech of Saint-Just on October 10, 1793. "You have to punish not only the traitors" he shouted, "but even those who are indifferent: You have to punish whoever behaves in the Republic in a passive spirit and does nothing for her, because ever since the French people has manifested their will, everything outside of the sovereign is an enemy."[95] This is the same man who declared on February 26, 1794: "You wanted a republic . . . what constitutes a republic is the total destruction of everything which places itself in its way."[96] And Maximilien de Robespierre, with a contradictory Roussellian concept of "collective liberty," stated on February 7, 1794, "The government of the Revolution is the despotism of liberty against tyranny."[97] The same phraseology reappears under the Nazis, who were ideologically nurtured by Fichte, the great defender of the French Revolution.

The French Revolution is still with us in every way. Not only are its ideas everpresent, but there is much in its historic evolution that can teach us—in North America no less than in Europe. Its initial period began with the undermining of traditional values and ideas, coupled with the demand for moderate reforms. With Voltaire a whole series of scoffers, facile critics, and agnostics in the literal sense of the term made their appearance. They subverted religion, convictions, traditions, and the loyalties on which state and society rested. The process of decomposition and putrefaction always starts at the top—in the royal palace, the presidential mansion, among the intellectuals, the aristocracy, the wealthy, the clergy—and then gradually enmeshes the lower social layers. In this process it is interesting to notice *how the high and mighty develop a sense of guilt and with it a readiness to abdicate,* to yield to expropriation, to submit to the loss of privileges, in other words, *to commit suicide politically and economically.* For this masochist act, however, they are well prepared by the ideological propaganda coming from their own ranks. In the case of the French Revolution we had in Louis XVI not a representative of either "reaction" or "conservatism" but an avid reader of the *Encyclopédie* and (not so improbably) perhaps a Freemason. The members of the nobility who took active part in the intellectual or political undermining of the *ancien régime* and then participated in the Revolution are very numerous; without their support the French Revolution is well-nigh unimaginable. Among its forerunners we encounter Holbach, Grimm, and Madame d'Epernay, and later Mirabeau, Noailles, Malesherbes, Victor Claude de Broglie,[98] Clootz, Condorcet, Robespierre, Custine, St. Just, Clermont-Tonnerre, de Séchelles, Boissy d'Anglas, Barras, Collot d'Herbois, Corday d'Armont, Rouget de Lisle, Sade, Lafayette, Lanjuinais, the brothers Lameth, Barère de Vieuzac, and the Duc d'Orléans. In compiling such an inventory one is inevitably reminded of the fact that, statistically speaking, the natural death of states and nations as well as of classes and estates, is not murder but *suicide.* However, this act of suicide is usually preceded by a period of delusions and follies. *Quem deus vult perdidi prius dementat.*

The first president of the Jacobin Society in 1790 was the Duc d'Auguillon, and even the man who, in moderation, spread the Revolution over the map of Europe, Napoleon, came from a noble family. The pioneers of the Revolution also belonged frequently to the clergy. The "philosophizing abbés" could be found everywhere, men such as Sieyès, Raynal, (Bishop) Grégoire, Mably, de St. Pierre and Barthélmy. Voltaire owed his deism to the Abbé de Châteauneuf and not without reason did Rousseau put the summary of his sentimental-deistic philosophy into the mouth of his *Vicaire Savoyard*. Enlightenment and the Revolution had little to fear from the more intellectual clergy. Voltaire and Diderot both had been educated by the Jesuits (who are by no means the mind molders a certain type of propaganda makes them out to be). And since the totalitarian movements of the last hundred years are in parts or even predominantly Christian heresies if not caricatures of the monastery, it is not so surprising that men and women with a distinctly Christian background fall for them. Neither the clerical state nor seminary training are by any means prophylactics against such deviations. Who could imagine the French Revolution without the participation of clerics and exclerics, Russian Bolshevism without Stalin and Mikoyan, both former seminarians? Nor could one conceive of the earlier leftist currents without Arnaldo di Brescia, Joachim de Floris, John Ball, John Wyclif, or Campanella. *Corruptio optimi pessima*. We will revert to this theme some time later.

The second lesson to be learned from the French Revolution concerns the danger inherent in reforms that are not carried out by a very firm hand.[99] The majority of human beings do not respond to generosity with gratitude and frequently the loosening of reins becomes a signal for general unrest and mutiny.[100] The Reformation gave to extremist illiterate groups a feeling that there were no fixed laws, no eternal rules, no set standards, no permanent authority—all this in spite of the fact that the Reformation was by no means a liberal revolution but a rigoristic movement, a spiritual revolt against the rationalism of Rome, in other words, the very reverse of the Enlightenment (which, in turn, was the grandchild of the Renaissance).

Still, the fact that radical *changes* took place completely upset the inner balance of the masses. Anarchical peasant risings occurred and mad, weird sects made their ubiquitous appearance. Luther strongly invoked the secular arm, and since secular authority had not been shaken by this purely religious evolution, order was preserved and restored. In the French Revolution, however, secular authority was undermined and attacked after religious loyalties had been gravely weakened. Only *outside* military intervention could help the Old Order, but the energies let loose by the revolutionary volcano were too strong. For twenty years Continental Europe was at the mercy of the French Revolution and its Bonapartist aftermath, with the United States a virtual ally of Napoleon in the War of 1812.

The Kerenskys usually appear on the scene in a time of reform. They take over and pretend to be the originators of all improvements. In fact they not only continue the reforming-liberalizing policy of their "reactionary" forerunners, but soon they lose hold and are defeated by a combination of wild demagogues and frantic mobs. The Lafayettes, Lameths, Mirabeaus, in precisely this fashion, failed to stem the mounting tide of radicalism. As in a Greek tragedy, events had to run their course. The anarchical tyranny of the many had to evolve into the despotism of a single man. Civilian chaos became military order. *Skytalismos,* the rule of the club, yielded to the rule of the sword. Tyranny "settled down" to becoming a monarchy, as foreseen by Plato, Aristotle, and Polybius. However, the "royalization" of tyranny, unfortunately, is no longer possible. Totalitarian tyrannies no longer evolve because *Big Brother* cannot become a *father.* Thus we get endless intrigues, palace revolts, and assassinations. Only total military defeat breaks the evil chain.

We saw that during the years 1789-1815 France was a classic example of political revolution-evolution, but the classic does not always prevail just as diseases do not always follow the pattern laid down in medical textbooks. In history we can never talk prophetically about certainties, only about likelihoods, about lesser or greater possibilities. Nothing is inevitable, yet only a fool would disregard the lessons of history which individuals sometimes learn, but nations (as Hegel remarked) *never.* There is personal memory and there is personal learning: Collective memory is very problematic and the masses never study. The real historian, however, beyond his task of finding facts, is neither a determinist nor a pure pragmatist. Still, Friedrich Schlegel was right when he called the historian a backward-looking prophet.[101]

The horrors of the French Revolution were the direct and logical outcome of the philosophy or philosophies underlying it. The atrocities surprised only the British and American observers (as did the nightmarish deeds of Communists and Nazis a century and a half later) because, owing to the relativistic post-Protestant mind of the English-speaking world, extremism and absolutism in thought and deed became "unimaginable." By the end of the eighteenth century the American and British intellectuals were beginning to veer from deism to agnosticism. The recession of Catholic (and Eastern) religiousness on the Continent, however, did not give way to agnosticism but, rather, to atheism and antitheism. Absolutism in thinking was not replaced with polite doubt, but with other radical and extreme attitudes, with secular faiths of a sentimental or pseudorational character. Anatole France, who was certainly not a convinced Christian nor a hidebound secular dogmatist, once remarked that "only extremes are bearable."[102]

This was the same Anatole France who in his novel, *Les Dieux ont soif*, described the blood orgies of the French Revolution, a revolution that pleased and inspired the budding American left more than 170 years ago. Although the delirious horrors committed by the National Socialists and the international Communists in our century were even worse, the French Revolution, marking the rebirth of democracy after its foundering in antiquity, laid down a pattern of inhumanity which set a lasting example. It can be argued, on the other hand, that the French Revolution, much more even than its Russian counterpart and quite differently from its Nazi imitators, engaged in "unauthorized" tortures and massacres, that it had a truly popular *élan*, whereas National Socialism, for instance, perpetrated its crimes in a purely bureaucratic and almost always clandestine way. The tortures to which the officers of the Bastille were submitted were carried out by the "dear people" in full daylight. The fiendish dissection of the Princesse de Lamballe and the delirious work of sadists and sex maniacs can be ascribed to "ignoble savages," to our deified friend, the Common Man. The reader may forgive—or thank—me for not serving him details.[103] Still, I would think that the ghoulish procession in which the private parts of this unfortunate woman were carried on a pike through the streets was a fitting symbolic overture to the democratic tragedy which, until our day, became the nightmare of Europe.

Metternich's reactions to the French Revolution led him to the remark, "When I saw what people did in the name of fraternity, I resolved if I had a brother to call him cousin."[104] And, indeed, the history of the Revolution is a nauseating mixture of idealistic verbiage, of treachery and intrigue, of sentimental incantations and senseless butcheries, of envy and outbursts of sadism. The *colonnes infernales* of the revolutionary army under General Turreau[105] massacred the population of entire villages in the Vendée and eastern Brittany. As during the Soviet occupation of Eastern Germany and Austria, women and girls of all ages were raped, from three- and four-year-olds to tottering matrons. The republican regional governor, Président Cholet, wrote to Turreau that his soldiers committed horrors of which not even cannibals would be capable.[106] Some of the worst cruelties were committed after Le Mans fell into the hands of the Republicans, who murdered all the wounded counterrevolutionaries in the military hospitals. Almost everyone who had not fled was butchered. The women and girls were undressed, raped, slain, and finally placed together with naked male corpses in obscene positions—scenes which General Turreau perhaps failed to notice in his official *promenades* (as he called them). These slaughters were also designed to reduce the *grande armée de bouches inutiles*.[107] The *Noyades* in the Loire were nauseating beyond description and had a homosexual character.[108]

These nightmarish horrors were repeated in Arras, where the guillotine was placed in front of the theater from whose balcony the revolutionary leader Lebon and his dear wife could watch the spectacle. After a very arduous day with a big crop, the executioners amused themselves by imitating the *batteries nationales* of Le Mans, they denuded the decapitated corpses of both sexes, mixing the macabre with the lascivious. Another time the hangman fastened a *ci-devant* marquis on the board and then proceeded for ten minutes to read aloud the last issue of the local newspaper. Finally he exhorted the wretched marquis to inform his friends and relatives in the beyond about the victories of the French armies.[109] During the September Massacres, which took place in the Paris jails (1792) the butcher-volunteers were paid six francs each and received as much wine as they could drink. But not only the *aristos* were made to suffer, even the children in the reformatories and temporarily arrested prostitutes in the Bicêtre and La Salpêtrière jails were not spared. There indescribable scenes of bestiality took place. Big butcheries among prostitutes were also organized by the left during the Spanish Civil War in Barcelona and by SS units in Eastern Poland —not perhaps out of moral indignation but for "hygienic" reasons. For the genuine materialist there is no fundamental, but only a gradual, an "evolutionary" difference, between man and a pest, a noxious insect.

The revolutionary fervor spared nobody. When Lavoisier, the great mathematician, physicist, and chemist, was accused of counterrevolutionary activities and the tribunal condemned him to death, his lawyer cried out that he was a great scientist. But to a convinced democrat one man is as good as any other, and Coffinhal, the president of the Law Court, replied quite truthfully, *"La République n'a pas besoin de savants."*[110] In spite of the cult of reason, true intellectuality soon became suspect. The envy for titles and honors rapidly evolved into envy for knowledge and it was naturally only a question of time for the strongest form of this vice to appear, envy for material possessions, which played such a potent part in the radical democratic movements in seventeenth-century England.

The *Enragés*, the left wing of the *Montagne,* with men such as Roux, Varlet, and Leclèrc, increased their protest against the inequality of wealth. The equality of civil rights, they insisted, was senseless without financial equality. Hébert spoke in the same way and Saint-Just declared war on the rich. It was Joseph Lebon, the butcher of Arras, who started the methodic warfare against the "rich" in the North: 392 were guillotined in Arras, 149 in Cambrai. In a famous speech before the National Convention Jacques Roux had demanded equal incomes for everybody. Identitarianism wanted to go all the way, and it was only the fall of Robespierre and later the defeat of Gracchus Babeuf, the first modern Communist leader (in 1797) which prevented a further development in this direction. In the course of the French Revolution, however, the inner connection between democratism and socialism again had become clearly visible.

It would be wrong to believe, as "sensible" but badly informed people like to do, that the French Revolution (as any other one) represented the "swinging of the pendulum in the other direction" or the "just reaction to earlier abuse." In American high schools and colleges such interpretations of history are quite popular and are often given with the best intentions, to provide the students with a story that "makes sense" and at the same time suggests that reason and justice, though not always effective, are forces to be reckoned with in the gradual evolution of mankind. The alternative seems merely an endless enumeration of names, places, and dates, all amounting to the inventory of a madhouse or a vale of tears, the Beyond remaining the only consolation. The average teacher is afraid to tell young people who want to "establish" themselves cosily on this globe that Luther was only too right in calling the world *des Teufels Wirtshaus,* the "Devil's Inn." The deeper meaning of history is theological and he who flees theology can only try to solve the riddles of history by offering banalities of a moralizing nature, such as an optimistic Old Liberalism and Marxism (related to each other in certain ways) have tried to provide. This world, however, is a vale of tears and man, from a purely terrestrial viewpoint, a tragic creature. The trouble is that America and Europe, after a long process of de-Christianization, are no longer capable of assimilating a philosophy of the tragic or a theology of the Cross.[111] Besides the facile spiritual-moral explanation of history we have the rationalizations, the abovementioned pendulum theory, the conviction that "where there's smoke there's fire." This theory forgets, however that there can be an enormous fire with little smoke and a tiny fire, maybe only a glow, enveloping a whole area in dark fumes. We shall encounter these phenomena again and again in our study. There was no more reasonable sequitur between "provocation" and "reaction" in the case of the French Revolution than in the case of the Jews and the Nazis, the Armenians and the young Turks, the old Russian regime, the Kerensky interlude and bolshevism, Portuguese colonial rule in Angola and the horrors perpetrated by savage monsters of Holden Roberto's "Liberation Front," the Belgian administration in the Congo and the delirious atrocities of Gbenye and Mulele, British colonialism in Kenya and the Mau-Mau. We have to face the fact that man is not "good"—only the extraordinary man is, only the heroic saint or the saintly hero, while the noble savage belongs to the world of fairy tales.

If we look at the French Revolution from a social viewpoint we will make the discovery that it took place in a period of general wellbeing and increasing prosperity. External trade had quadrupled since the death of Louis XIV: The value of exchanged goods exceeded a billion francs in 1788, a sum that was reached again only in 1848.[112] Not the poorest but the richest regions of France were the most revolutionary, those where the mirage of limitless wealth had driven cupidity to new heights.[113] The same phenomenon could be observed in Spain during the Civil War (1936-1939) or in Italy after the last war, when communism was (and is) strongest in areas where equitable social conditions exist and where there are no latifundia: the *huerta* of Valencia and the Emilia with its rich soil. Another example is the strong Communist or agrarian-Socialist movement in pre-Communist Bulgaria, a country without an upper crust and with only a small middle class, a nation where the factor of envy should hardly have come into play.

In France the relationship between the old nobility and the peasantry ranged from fair to good. (The largely fake nobility of the newly rich,[114] however, did not have the demophile-patriarchal qualities of the ancient *noblesse de l'épée.*) Serfdom survived only in a few remote corners of the extreme East and in the Bourbonnais. Louis XVI himself had eliminated the last vestiges of serfdom on his own domain. About half of the land in France was owned by the peasantry and peasants, as a rule, even though they were proprietors, also rented land from those who had large estates. In addition there were numerous home industries. Yet there were endless minor frictions and troubles about rents, over borders and title deeds: This will not surprise those who know something about French rural mentality.[115] There was, of course, no slavery.

Edmund Burke, who had traveled in France fairly widely before the Revolution, gives a good picture of the character of the classes and their mutual relationships.[116] He noted that the nobility showed "something more nearly approaching familiarity than is generally practiced with us,"[117] toward the lower classes. And he added that the aristocracy had no "manner of power in the cities" and very little in the country. Still, he berated them for their foolish Anglomania which (politically at least) contributed to their downfall. They were morally lax and hesitant to take in the new moneyed class. "All this violent outcry against the nobility I take to be a mere work of art," he wrote. As to the Catholic hierarchy of France, Burke remarked that they were "liberal and open, with the hearts of gentlemen and men of humour, neither insolent nor servile. They seemed to me a rather superior class."

It is, however, legitimate to ask whether the French Revolution would have taken place without an ideological preparation in which as we said before, large sectors of the nobility and a not insignificant number of the clergy had an appreciable share. Even when the mask was off and the face of the beast clearly recognizable, some silly priests and stupid friars of the "constitutional" type, as well as formally unfrocked clerics enthusiastically supported the Revolution. It was, in fact, Claude Royer, a pastor from Chalon-sur-Saone and member of the Paris Jacobin Club in the Rue Saint-Honoré, who made the first great appeal for a regime of sheer terror. "Let us stop talking," he shouted, "yet let our silence be terrible. It should be the signal for combat, putting fear into the hearts of the conspirators and acting as a call to men hesitating to support liberty. . . . Yes, my friends, let us be terrible but save liberty!" Royer repeated this speech before the Convention and demanded that the *Levée en Masse* and the jailing of all suspects should be decreed. Danton and Robespierre seconded this proposition. Mass arrests were voted immediately and Royer had a pamphlet printed carrying the headline, "Let us make terror the order of the day!"[118] One of the shrillest propagandists for the execution of the royal couple was the ex-Capuchin monk Chabot who supported Moras in his bloodcurdling attacks.[119] The perversion of basic Christian sentiments comes easily to silly priests who have neglected their spiritual life, and secularizing theology, become real mobmasters, as it now so frequently happens in Latin America.[120]

Royalist authors later intimated that the "Jacobin Fathers" of the Rue Saint-Honoré (who were Dominicans) were imbued with an antiroyalist spirit from the time of the *Ligue*, but this is an exaggeration. Still, they actively invited the Jacobins to install themselves in their monastery and they undoubtedly had leftist leanings—unlike the monks of the same order domiciled in the Rue Saint-Jacques.[121]

The tragedy of the intellectual leftist nobleman is best personified by Chrétien de Lamoignon de Malesherbes, a liberal of somewhat sectarian cast and a pillar of the Enlightenment. In 1750, at the age of 29, he became President of the *Cour des Aides* of the Paris *parlement* while his father was made Chancellor (but left all the work to his son).

He used his position to promote the Enlightenment and, trying desperately to appear "tolerant," "progressive," "broadminded," he not only gave every imaginable aid to those who undermined the old order but even persecuted opponents of the Enlightenment. This was easy for him because his office entailed the censorship of all printed matter published in France. As one can see, the Holy Illiberal Inquisition in the literary field already worked effectively even in those days. In all these "establishments" of the left, then as now, the pink intellectual, fearing to be out of tune with the times, is not only the most contemptible, but also the most ridiculous creature.

Baron Grimm said without exaggeration that "without the assistance of Malesherbes the *Encyclopédie* would probably never have been published."[122] Pierre Gaxotte calls him *'le type achevé du libéral qui a toujours peur de passer pour en réactionnaire.'* Elie Fréron, the enemy of Voltaire, d'Alembert, and Marmontel, published a relatively conservative journal, *L'Année Littéraire,* which was again and again confiscated and in 1758 he was almost jailed for having discussed in his paper a book opposed to the *Encyclopédie*. Although he was constantly attacked by the men of the Enlightenment, he was actively prevented by Malesherbes from defending himself. In 1752 Malesherbes forbade the publication of a work by Father Julien Louis Geoffroy because it was critical of Diderot. Father Thomolas from Lyons, who had dared to reply to the article *Collège*[123] in the *Encyclopédie*, was warned not to be impudent. Father Charles Palissot de Montenoy, an Oratorian, was persecuted by Malesherbes and so was the gifted Nicholas Laurent Gilbert who died young. "The philosophers shouted that they were being tyrannized," Gaxotte remarks, "yet they were the ones who exercised a tyrannical rule over the literary world."

Malesherbes, we can be sure, finally saw the light, but then it was too late. He returned from Switzerland, where he had been given asylum, in order to defend the King before his judges, and it was his bitter task to tell the monarch that he had been sentenced to death. He then retired to the country but was arrested in December 1793 together with his daughter, his son-in-law, and his grandchildren. They were all condemned to death and, with the great delicacy that always distinguishes convinced leftists, the executioner had all the family beheaded in the presence of the old man (the grandfather of Alexis de Tocqueville) before his turn came (April 23, 1794). Certainly he expiated all his sins. The road leading to the hell of leftist radicalism is not only broad, it is also fast and steep. Under such circumstances the brakes rarely work.

The significance of the French Revolution lies not only in the revival of democracy, and it represented not only the adoption of political patterns prevailing in antiquity and among primitives, but it also gave a new impetus to state worship and to ethnic nationalism. The all-powerful *polis*-state again made its appearance. In other words, the identitarian drives culminated not only in a frantic demand for equality (which went so far that only Robespierre's fall prevented the destruction of all steeples and towers),[124] but also of ethnic sameness. In the chapter dealing with National Socialism we shall see how much the Nazis owe, directly and indirectly, to the French Revolution and also to what extent "well-meaning," "moderate," "enlightened," and "progressive" leftists had contributed to the rise of the brown scourge. Here, however, we would like to draw the reader's attention to *The Jacobins*, Professor Crane Brinton's excellent book on the radical clubs during the French Revolution. The volume was published in New York in 1930, three years before Hitler came to power. It reads exactly like the work of an author who tries methodically to prove that the Nazis knowingly adopted and imitated the notions, plans, and actions of the Jacobins —who were by no means internationalists.

"When the war went wrong," Brinton writes about the first defeats inflicted by the Prussian-Austrian alliance, "and the peoples refused to rise, Frenchmen were almost obliged to consider themselves the only virtuous people. The society of Guéret waited nobly until January 1794, and then removed the American and English flags from the tree of liberty. The tricolor flew alone."[125]

Yet Professor Brinton argued rightly that, even without a foreign war, the *patriote* would have evolved from a lover of mankind into a nationalist because equality could not remain an abstraction: It had to find concrete expression. All other qualities were accidental, but Frenchness now became the touchstone of equality.[126] All Frenchmen should have a common language and soon the Jacobin clubs began a minor crusade against all other languages—Provençal, Breton, German, Flemish, Basque. The Jacobin Club of Strasbourg even suggested that all Alsatians who refused to learn French be deported and in their stead *sans-culottes* imported.[127] French was *la langue républicaine*[128] and the French people the historically predestined bearer of truth, of a messianic message. Thus we get a hint of the extent to which the French Revolution is not only a forerunner but an ideological stepping-stone to the slow growth of Nazi ideas, which finally found their concrete expression only in our time.

The reader might object that, as far as fanaticism, extremism, and savagery are concerned, the National Socialists far outdid their precursors. In a purely quantitative way this is surely the case. Yet *la terreur* was far more programmatic with the French Revolution (to which the uncommitted, non-Marxian left always assented the world over) than the system inaugurated by Hitler. It is difficult for outsiders to believe how effectively the truth about systematic murder was kept from the Germans, who certainly knew about the concentration camps and even about the killing of the insane, but not about the extermination camps.[129] *Schrecklichkeit*—terribleness—was used as a means for paralyzing resistance and creating fear—but it was used quite sparingly. Anybody who would have dared to tell openly and publicly the truth about Auschwitz, Tremblinka, Majdanek, and the other horror chambers would have risked his life. Those Jews who were still at liberty did not know what was in store for them. Here and there rumors leaked out, but since they were vague it is understandable that people's minds shied away from accepting the tales of horror. We were all still too much conditioned by the centuries of Christianity.[130]

In the French Revolution this was quite different. In spite of the Roussellian fancies, it soon became obvious what a depraved individual the average man can be. One literally danced around the guillotines. Various military and civil commanders openly and officially boasted about their bestial deeds, which in all their nauseating horror were perpetrated above all against the "internal enemy." Thus General Westermann in his message to the Committee of Public Welfare, after the defeat of the *Chouans* near Savenay, could declare:

> The Vendée, republican fellow citizens, no longer exists. She is dead under our sabres, together with her women and children. I have just buried her in the swamps and forests of Savenay. Following the orders you gave me, I have trampled the children to death with our horses, I have massacred the women, and they are no longer going to give birth to any more brigands. I am not guilty of taking a single prisoner, I have exterminated them all. . . . The roads are covered with corpses. There are so many of them at several places they form pyramids. The firing squads work incessantly at Savenay since every moment brigands arrive who pretend that they will surrender as prisoners . . . but we are not taking any. One would be forced to feed them with the bread of liberty, but compassion is not a revolutionary virtue.[131]

The unspeakable Westermann, an Alsatian, belonged to the faction around Danton. He was later arrested and guillotined on April 5, 1794. But his spirit continues to live. An official report reaching Paris from Avranches said, "The Hospital was also filled with wounded and they too were subjected to the national vengeance. They have been finished off." Among them was a woman who "simulated a disease." Doctor Gainou, a friend of Robespierre, wrote him from Fougères that "the soldiers have killed all the wounded and the sick in the hospital. Several wives of brigands were there in a state of illness. They were raped and their throats cut." Marceau-Desgraviers, a real soldier who participated in the war against the Vendée, was tormented for the rest of his life—he was killed in action in 1796—by nightmares about the horrors perpetrated by this renascent democracy. At Le Mans he had rescued a royalist girl and thereupon barely escaped the guillotine. Meanwhile the commissioner of Angers wrote triumphantly to the mayor of Paris, "Our Holy Mother Guillotine is working full time. . . ." And it was in Angers that the Republicans issued an order to have the heads of the "brigands" (the *Chouans*) scalped and dissected and then exposed on small pikes on the ramparts of the city. The doctors who had to do this appetizing job, however, were too slow. Since the Republicans needed quick demonstrations of democratic fervor, they guillotined whatever civilian prisoners they had, among them the 82-year old Abbess of Fontevault. She was blind but, as the chronicler tells us, "*pleine de vertus et de charité.*"[132]

One ought to read not only the reports by the minions of the victorious Revolution on this war, but also the accounts of other eyewitnesses. There are the descriptions of the Le Mans massacre, where Bourbotte and Prieux watched not only the raping of naked women and girls whose throats were subsequently slit, but the raping of corpses—real orgies of necrophilia. Beauvais, writing about the event after the retreat from Fougères, relates that "all the wounded in the hospital were massacred in the most fiendish way. Incisions were made on their footsoles and all their members without exception were cut off bit by bit. The women were treated in exactly the same way until, finally, cartridges were inserted in their private parts in order to terminate their lives and their sufferings with an explosion."[133] Tortures of this sort were also perpetrated by the admirable Loyalists in the Spanish Civil War, but instead of hospitals they selected churches for their expressions of sexual democracy.

Mass murder had become the order of the day. If the Nazis succeeded in slaughtering millions, thanks to the development of technology, the French revolutionaries were prevented from doing just that only because they did not have the means. They certainly tried very hard. The chemical engineer Fourcroy invented a poison gas which, however, did not prove really effective. He had acted on the command of Robespierre, Collot d'Herbois, Barère, and Fouché. Carrier then proposed to poison the rivers and lakes with arsenic. What Renan later called the "zoological wars" had already begun.[134]

The spirit of the *Marseillaise* was already Nazi and racist: "To arms, citizens, form your battalions, let us march, march, so that impure blood will drench our furrows." A clever inversion of the blood-soil complex, *Blut und Boden*, seems to be contained in these lines.

Chapter 8

From Democracy to Romantic Socialism

The concept of socialism and communism is a great deal older than St. Thomas More's *Utopia*, generally considered to be the first "Communist Manifesto." *Utopia* is a half serious, half humorous, profound, yet satirical effort to visualize a state and a society based purely on the four natural virtues—prudence, fortitude, temperance, and justice. Faith, hope, and charity, the three theological virtues, naturally do not figure in this imaginary non-Christian part of the world. Platonic notions play a certain part in this highly rational polity which has far-reaching equality among its citizens (women must also serve in the army) for instance. There is no private property. The scholars, however, enjoy privileges, and there are monasteries.

Utopia also has an ironic aspect. It tries to show a perfect pagan society and indirectly reminds the reader that the Christian nations, in spite of being favored by God, often fall below pagan levels. Freedom, though not totally lacking, is rather limited in Utopia and state controls are ubiquitous and severe.

The basic ideas of the Communist order—lack of private property, equality, a nonhereditary government, common work, and common social life—can be found not only in Western civilization but also in the most diverse parts of the world. We find it concretely expressed in monasticism. This way of life, however, presupposes a *vocation*, the *sacrifice* of innate rights, and a *voluntary* act of surrender. Although it must be admitted that monastic life normally provides for certain non-spiritual advantages, such as regulated work, free medical care, and material security, it represents basically a *sacrificial* form of existence —even if outsiders, at the sight of the thick walls of some monastery, might sigh enviously: "It's easy for them!" (But they don't join.)

The purpose of the monastery is spiritual. Nobody is going to measure the success of a monastic order by its economic record (which, more often than not, is modest to say the least). Yet historically certain purely external features of the monastery are precursors of more or less modern institutions: the prison, the barracks and, above all, the *factory*, all practicing a more or less far-reaching separation of the sexes. Naturally this does not mean that these collective institutions have been consciously patterned after the monastery. But practical circumstances enforced the analogy.

The monastic spirit in the West seems to have made its first appearance in the Holy Land in the Essene communities. The earliest Christian monks were—as their name indicates—*monachoi*, men living singly, anchorites, hermits. Only somewhat later the *monachoi* began to live together in groups as *coenobites*. At a still later period St. Benedict established an order with formal vows of obedience, chastity, and poverty, the three "councils of perfection." The Middle Ages were the great period of monasticism and we must not forget that for centuries the monasteries and convents were the fortresses of religious life, learning, the arts, and the higher crafts. Many of the intellectual treasures of antiquity were saved by the monks who copied and recopied ancient texts.

With the decline of the Middle Ages, in the fifteenth century, the monasteries too began to decline and the orders founded after the Reformation lack the monastic character. Jesuits, Redemptorists, and Salesians are not monks. They are not cloistered. The Oratorians (founded by St. Philip Neri) are not even an order but simply a congregation of priests. And with the twentieth century we get the "secular institutes" and finally "associations of the faithful" as, for instance, the *Opus Dei*.

On the other hand we have to bear in mind that the Reformation was started by a monk, an Augustinian hermit, and that it was, as we said before, essentially a reaction against the spirit of the Renaissance and of Humanism. In Rome Luther (understandably, one might say) received the impression that Christianity under the Popes had sold out to paganism. Luther was aghast when he saw that the medieval concept of the universe, the circle with God as its center, had been exchanged for an elliptical concept with two focal points, God *and* man. Luther decried worship (the saints elevated to the honor of the altars!) and protested against the enthusiasm for the cultural and intellectual treasures of antiquity. These were pagan in origin and everything pagan was damned for all eternity.[1] The entire theological and philosophical intellectualism and "rationalism," which started even before St. Thomas and had finally fused with the new learning, was odious to him. Reason did not lead to God[2] and man could be saved *by faith alone*.

This fideism was one of the many aspects of Luther's teachings alienating the leading humanists—Erasmus, Pirckheimer, Adelmann, and even the very anticlerical Reuchlin—and resulted in a real enmity of the universities toward the new teaching.[3] Luther, of course, never taught the doctrine of "private interpretation";[4] he was not a precursor of liberalism.[5] He was basically a rigorist and a disciplinarian[6] and a conservative by inclination. The term "freedom" as used by him had no personal meaning.[7] He was a predestinarian as much as Calvin, but thanks to Melanchthon's intervention his notion of the enslaved will[8] was not inserted in the *Confessio Augustana*. Melanchthon thought, quite rightly, that such teaching would prove an important obstacle to eventual reunion. Calvin's reforms had a far stricter character than Luther's[9] and Geneva under Calvin and later under Besa and Farel actually became the first totalitarian state in Europe.[10] Calvin's *Soli Deo Gloria!* certainly did not make for any "polycentrism."

It would be a great error to believe that the Reformation swept the European Continent as a torrential new surge of freedom.[11] In certain areas the changes were dictated by the secular authorities (as in Scandinavia), but in others they were adopted with great popular enthusiasm.The Reformation was riding the wave of greater religious awareness, of an increased religious *Innerlichkeit* (inner-directedness) and popular piety. The feeling was quite general, however, that greater asceticism and greater strictness were needed: Luther's monastic severity descended on Central Europe like a second coming of the Irish monks.[12] Sebastian Franck, an ex-Dominican who could speak from experience, declared: "Now we think we have escaped the monastery, but actually we have to be monks all our life."[13] And while the Catholic world, continuing in the spirit of the Renaissance, the Baroque and the Rococo, remained individualistic and anarchical, revolutionary and torn between holy and unholy passions, the areas converted by the Reformation settled down to law and order and a strong community spirit.

In these parts the community, the congregation, the group dominated religious life to a large extent. The monarchical-patriarchal idea was badly shaken in the Calvinist world where republican ideas were soon on the march. It is no accident that strongly egalitarian and communistic notions made themselves felt in England during the time of the Commonwealth (Levelers, Diggers) and, later on, in the northern part of the American Colonies. Puritanism, after all, is a half-religious, half-secular kind of monasticism.

At the same time it remains true that the monastery served (very much against its own intentions) as a prefiguration of the *big communities behind real or symbolic walls,* not only of the seminary but also of the boarding school, the barracks, the hospital, the jail, or the factory—communities consisting usually (or predominantly) of one sex only. And what do we find in monasteries? The habit (uniform), mental and physical discipline, order, conformity, regulated work, community spirit, common meals, equality in hierarchy, cells (as in jails) or dormitories (as in barracks), self-control, subordination, mental concentration, an ascetic way of life, simplicity, and sobriety, altogether an autonomous but collective existence. There is no place in the monastery for sloth and individualism.

What would be the very opposite of the monastery? The bohemian family of a wild but prosperous artist in an isolated home where everybody dressed, acted, created, loafed, came and went according to his whims and inclinations. Now we do not insinuate that this is necessarily an ideal form of existence. The monastery has a positive value because, as we said, it rests on *voluntary* sacrifice which immediately would become odious if it assumed a coercive character, as is more or less the case with barracks, jails, boarding schools, hospitals, or factories. (This is equally true of their "hybrids": the military hospital, the reformatory, etc.).

We have, however, oversimplified the issue because the monastery is not always pure sacrifice. Athough weakly developed, there is a monastic instinct in most of us. Don't we sometimes envy the monks and nuns their settled, their "secure" life? The curious dilemma in this complexity of feelings is illustrated by the well-known question: "Who is sure of all his basic needs? Who has work, spiritual care, medical care, housing, food, occasional entertainment, free clothing, free burial, free everything?" The answer might be "the monks," but the standard answer is: "the jailbirds." And inevitably this makes us think of the citizens of the provider state, having material protection from "the womb to the tomb." But here again, to sacrifice an eye for a dear friend is one thing; to be blinded by an executioner is quite another.

To marry a woman one pities is one thing; a shotgun wedding is quite another.

Yet the monastic yearning, as we have said, is also *in us* and therefore some of us will readily respond to the appeal of a false monasticism. The security element most certainly motivates this fascination. On the other hand, the person with the *genuine* monastic vocation will desire such security in his heroic struggle merely in order not to be detracted by material problems and to be able to lead a life of complete spiritual devotion. (All of which does not eliminate the fact that in bygone ages there have been men and women attracted to the monastic life by purely material considerations. In our oversexed, overeroticized and highly materialistic age such a "temptation" hardly exists.)

The situation is quite different in the "world," where we find millions who crave security, who dread responsibility, who long for the gregarious life, who find happiness not in external but even in internal conformity. Oddly enough, the two historic epochs which in the secular domain were most inclined towards monasticism, were the Reformation and the French Revolution, two periods in which monasteries and convents were confiscated and dissolved by the thousands. (In Russia the same thing happened after 1917.) The smaller the number of monasteries, the stronger is perverted secular monasticism. The most extreme form of secular monasticism, however, is communism, and the communist movement's strength in a given area often can be measured by the number of empty or ruined monasteries. This is also true of countries outside Western Europe and North America: It is true not only of Russia, but also of China, Southeast Asia, and Mexico.

The eccentric or ex-monk often is an ardent advocate of secular monasticism in one form or another. A typical representative of this type of mind and outlook was Tomaso Campanella, a rather odd Dominican who lived between 1568 and 1639. He is an even better example than Joachim de Floris (1145-1202), a radical Cistercian. Both were of noble birth and both came from Oalabria. The ideas of Joachim later profoundly affected the "spiritual" wing of the Franciscans and created grave theological and monastic disturbances. His vistas, considered quite orthodox during his lifetime, had an apocalyptic and eschatological character. Like Fourier and other visionary socialists he quite arbitrarily divided history into "ages" of the past and the future. In Joachim's case they were: the Age of the Father, characterized by obedience; the Age of the Son (the "present time"), guided by reading; and the coming Age of the Spirit, devoted to prayer and song. The last and final age was supposed to be entirely monastic in character:

Humanity will consist only of monks and nuns in preparation for the Day of Judgment. These quite "gnostic" Joachimite ideas were widely spread; they also influenced Wyclif and Roger Bacon and had a certain bearing on the Reformation.

Enjoying the protection of Frederick II, the *stupor mundi*, Joachim de Floris had as little trouble in his lifetime as Jansenius, Bishop of Ypres, who unknowingly stated the Jansenist heresy. Tomaso Campanella, on the other hand, had grave political difficulties and spent many years in jail because he opposed Spanish rule in Naples. He wrote several philosophical treatises but owed his fame to his *Civitas Solis*, the "Sun State" published in 1602. This interesting and intellectually contradictory man was also one of the first "one-worlders," but F. Meinecke, the great German historian, has called his outlook "one of the greatest psychological riddles in the new history of ideas." *Civitas Solis* may or may not represent a mere intellectual exercise such as Thomas More's *Utopia*. It was published as a part of his *Realis Philosophiae Partes Quattuor*.

In this essay Campanella envisaged an idealist state which has no Christian characteristics nor a political-social aura reminiscent of Catholic concepts. (This dichotomy, however, is typical of all Campanella's intellectual efforts: His philosophy does not tally with his theology, nor his theology with his political theory, nor his basic political views with his practical notions.) In his "Sun State," with a monarchical head there is intellectual-elitarian leadership, no private property and no lasting marriage. Sterile women automatically become public harlots. Pregnant women can have sexual intercourse with everyone. Yet women who use makeup, wear high heels, or long skirts to conceal their feet will be condemned to death as "liars." Incest, except between mothers and sons, is encouraged. Have we here a forerunner of de Sade?

Campanella was liberated from his Spanish jail in Naples by Pope Urban VIII through a ruse. He later fled to Rome and then settled in Paris. There he enjoyed the favors of Cardinal Richelieu who saw in him an *esprit fort*, an emancipated spirit. (This controversial friar, with the vivid sexual imagination, preceded Morelly by only a century.) He surely was a political agent, a theoretical libertine, a socialist thinker, a defender of absolute monarchy and papalism, and an enemy of Machiavelli's teachings. Indeed there was nobody like him. He died, oddly enough, in the Dominican monastery of the Rue Jacob in Paris which spawned the smaller monastery in the Rue St. Honoré. The Dominicans in Paris were nicknamed *Les Jacobins* after the first monastery and the name also stuck to the radically leftist club established in the smaller house across the Seine. So even today, in a purely historic sense, Jacobin means Dominican.[14]

Nevertheless, it was obvious that religious monasticism had to shed its Christian roots in order to evolve perversely into secular socialism. True, this was not always the case, as witness the monastic bent in the younger William Morris, who later developed socialistic tendencies. A man quite divorced from the traditional values, however, was Morelly, of whom we know very little. Even his first name is a matter of conjecture, and it is not certain that he did hail from Vitry-le-Francois as some suppose. He is the author of several dull epics but also of a very important utopian socialistic treatise, the *Code de la Nature,* published 1755 in Amsterdam. It has been reprinted a few times, last by a Communist publishing house in Paris, and its influence on later socialist thinking cannot be underestimated. (Alexis de Tocqueville dealt with it very seriously in his *L'Ancien Régime et La Révolution.)* At first Diderot was thought to be its author, but this theory was exploded in the 1820s. In 1846 a German translation was published in Berlin. V. P. Volgin, a Soviet "politologist" who wrote the preface for the Paris edition in 1953, called Morelly "the purest interpreter of Socialism" (p. 8).

The most important part of this small book is the fourth giving a "Model of Legislation in Conformity with Nature." Law No. I.2 stipulates that "every citizen will be fed, housed, and employed at public expense." No goods were to be exchanged, bartered, bought, or sold. Every transaction in this ideal order was to go through the hands of the state. "All non-perishable products shall be stored in public warehouses in order to be distributed" (II.6). There were to be jails for those with short sentences, but penitentiaries were to hold those serving long terms (IV.2). And in the midst of the cemeteries those dangerous maniacs and enemies of humanity who attempted to abolish the sacred laws and tried to introduce detestable property were to be jailed for life. They were to die a "civil death" and be separated from the rest of mankind in perpetuity by thick walls and iron grills (XII.2). The size of all cities was to be about the same and also the quality of the houses (IV.2-3). Everybody between the ages of 10 and 30 was to wear a uniform, one for work and one for holidays. Vanity was to be repressed by the "chiefs." The laws, needless to say, could never be changed. There was to be uniform education for all children and the most severe censures taken against anybody teaching metaphysics or trying to define the Divinity in human terms (X.9). Freedom of teaching was allowed only as far as the natural sciences were concerned —not in the humanities. (XI.5). Private property was strictly outlawed; there were severe marriage laws relating to obligatory marriage; and equally strict sanctions against adultery (XII.3). Children were to be taken from their parents at the age of five, but occasional contacts through the schools were to be permitted (X.4). The political structure of this socialist utopia is in essence a hierarchic system of councils, of *Soviets*. [15]

Gracchus Babeuf knew the nightmarish works of Morelly, a precursor of Orwell, and so in all probability, did Comte Henri de Saint-Simon, the first nineteenth-century socialist in Europe and another French Leftist aristocrat.

Henri de Saint-Simon belonged to a junior branch of the Ducs de Saint-Simon. Born in 1760, he owed a great deal of his education and intellectual inspiration to d'Alembert, while he himself profoundly influenced Auguste Comte, the founder of Positivism. [16] An enthusiastic young man, he and a host of aristocratic friends volunteered to fight for the young American Republic. Endowed with a great deal of imagination, he then offered the Viceroy of New Spain (Mexico) a plan for a canal between the two oceans. Back in France his great interest in economics prompted him a tidy little sum. He did not participate in the Revolution but was temporarily imprisoned during the Terror as a *ci-devant*. He then contracted an unfortunate marriage, got a divorce, was completely ruined, and took a menial position providing him with $200 a year. He later gave up this job when a former valet, who had become well-to-do in these turbulent times, gave him food and shelter.

Saint-Simon's earlier works dealt with scientific, political, and social problems and brought him neither fame nor fortune. His ideas were not taken seriously. But, after the fall of Napoleon and the restoration of the Bourbon monarchy, Saint-Simon became more aggressive. His writings now dealt intensively with the growing class of workers, a new social element and the product of the Industrial Revolution. The working class developed largely on the outskirts of the bigger cities and was neither intellectually nor spiritually taken care of. (For this reason, incidentally, it cannot be said that the Church ''lost'' the working class —it had never been properly inside.) It recruited itself partly from urban layers, but in its majority it consisted of uprooted sons and daughters of the peasantry, young people unwilling to work for years as apprentices and journeymen in order to acquire skills. They wanted to leave their dull villages and earn money immediately. Nor did they like the controls and the discipline of life in other families to which young craftsmen were subjected. Thus we see not only in France but everywhere in Western Europe (just as in England at an earlier period) the rise of a propertyless, ill-paid class, the industrial proletariat. Whether wages could have been substantially higher at that stage of technological development is not an easy question to answer. A good deal of historical, sociological, and economic research will have to be done first, but it is highly probable that the factory hands working on the new, rather primitive, yet quite expensive machines could not really have achieved substantially better living standards. At this stage of industrial development figures indicate that the manufacturers lived rather spartan lives and the reinvestments were enormous.[17] But whatever the reason for their misery, the fact remains that an entire race of melancholic, desperate, destitute paupers was growing up, "wild animals" who became a potential menace to society.[18]

Saint-Simon's compassion for these victims of an economic-social transformation may have been partly influenced by his own financial misery, the indifference of his relatives, his intellectual background conditioned by the Encyclopedists, and the kindness of his former butler, which strengthened his conviction that the lower classes were morally superior to the upper ones.[19] Since, in a book published in 1820, he insisted that the death of 10,000 workers would be a much greater loss to France than that of 10,000 noblemen and members of the royal family, he was dragged into the courts but not condemned. (The judges, after all, were more independent then than in 1945-1946.) In 1821-1822 he published *l'Industriel, a work dedicated to the industrialists, pro*claiming that he wrote for the managers and against the courtiers, for the bees and against the hornets.

In vain, and quite naively, he appealed to Louis XVIII for support. The public reaction to his work, however, was weak. A few idealistic young men admired him, but he despaired of the success of his ideas. The butler who had supported him died and he had to live practically from alms. In a fit of depression he tried to commit suicide (1823) but only managed to hurt one of his eyes. He lived two more years, just long enough to see the publication of his *Nouveau Christianisme*. In his last work he proposed the creation of a social-sentimental religion with a global hierarchic organization based on brotherly love.

It is this particular book which influenced the "Saint-Simonists" most strongly, above all a man called Barthélémy Prosper Enfantin who, on the basis of the ideas of Saint-Simon, founded together with Amand Bazard, an organization of modified Saint-Simonists which published *Le Producteur* and later controlled *Le Globe*. Now the rather odd ideas of Saint-Simon developed in the direction of real madness. The crazy radicalism which characterized the French Revolution, beginning with Roussellian nature worship and ending in a utopianism totally alien to nature, now demonstrated its full dynamism. Whoever wanted to establish utopia had to change, to reform, to rebuild, to smash existing forms.

Barthélémy Enfantin did not intend to prescribe total equality of wealth. His goal was the destruction of the family and therefore he wanted to do away with inheritance. Only the state should inherit. The Steering Committee of the Neo-Saint-Simonists which met in Paris and published *l'Organisateur* did not divulge the entire program of the New Theocracy, which was to be administrated by a brand new type of priest. These priests were to run a control agency which would turn over the means of production to those most capable of handling them. Christianity was accused of having retarded humanity by its dualism of flesh and spirit. The new "theology" pushed by Enfantin preached the "Emancipation of the Flesh."

The revolution of 1830 gave new impetus to these weird teachings and Enfantin's *Economie Politique* created a minor sensation among the more literate representatives of the working class. *Le Globe* was now published under the title *Journal de la doctrine de Saint-Simon*, and since the organization was represented in most leading cities of France, Enfantin now had himself declared *Le Pére*, "The Father," head of the Saint-Simonist Church of Tomorrow. He now openly preached total promiscuity (his version of the "Emancipation of the Flesh"), but Bazard disagreed with him and a schism was the result. In the summer of 1832 Enfantin established some sort of monastery at Menilmontant with forty-odd members who donned weird-looking habits and worked collectively in the fields of the estate. The police, however, intervened. Enfantin was brought to court and the "family" dissolved. The provincial centers were also liquidated. Thus the first phase of ideological-practical French socialism had come to an end.

We have mentioned Morelly and Babeuf as forerunners. One should add J. P. Brissott de Warville, later the leader of the Girondists, who already in the early 1780s expressed the idea that the owning of property can be theft. He thought that people should merely have an income sufficient to cover normal living expenses, and no more.[20] Brissott is one of the many genuine links between democracy and socialism. The Abbé de Mably, whose real name was Gabriel de Bonnot and who was the brother of the philosopher Etienne Bonnot de Condillac, must also be considered a precursor of socialism and communism. The Abbé was invited in 1771 to visit Poland with Rousseau in order to draft a new constitution for the Polish Commonwealth. He was born in 1709 in Grenoble and died in 1785 after having written a number of works in which he enthusiastically advocated the cause of democracy and socialism.

It is true that Gabriel Bonnot de Mably was a priest merely for the sake of convenience (as was his more famous younger brother), but Spengler is more right than wrong with his remark about the frequency of priests in leftist movements. It is not monasticism only which "suggests" socialism but also, to a more naive mind, Christianity itself. Let us agree that socialism and Communism (the fulfillment of socialism) take their *initial* inspiration from basic Christian tenets. Universal brotherhood, altruism, mutual aid, social justice, all-pervading charity, humility-in-equality—all these notions have Christian roots, a Christian background. But, remember, *Corruptio optimi pessima!* Due to this common source and to the ensuing confusions, we also have a "left Catholicism" and a "left Protestantism," fanatical isms whose errors, deviations, and transgressions must be understood in the light of this Christian root.

The temptation to inject Christian precepts into the practical order in such a naive way that they become self-defeating is especially great in a society where Christian trends have a sentimental and historic basis. Socialism and communism, though able to invade areas without a Christian tradition, could have been born only of civilizations with a strong Christian background. And not only the ethical content of Christianity fosters and promotes the temptation toward socialism, but also much of Christian imagery and doctrine. Along the path of the socialist utopia lies a day of judgment when the humble will be exalted and the rich and mighty brutally dispossessed.[21] And from the Socialist-Communist utopia itself can be gleaned the picture of paradise lost—and regained: a new age of innocence, of peace and brotherly love, with envy, crime, and hatred banished forever.[22]

Of course this "Edenism" is already present in democracy which is a conscious-subconscious effort—no more and no less so than nudism —to recreate Paradise. Democracy uses the magic formula, "We are not ruled, we rule ourselves" to relativize the State, the painful result of original sin,[23] just as nudism tries to solve the sexual problem by shedding clothes. (As if nude people had no sexual problems!) Neither in our political nor in our sexual life does it make sense to pretend that we are like Adam and Eve.

In the Socialist-Communist vision, with its accent on the salvation of the world through the proletariat, not only is Christian imagery important but also the gross misinterpretation of Christ and early Christianity. Unfortunately the Christian churches are not entirely innocent in this respect. In Christian folklore the Savior appears as the Son of the humble carpenter, the poor Boy from a lowly family, born in the stable and venerated by the Magi as He lies among domestic animals. He is the simple Man who talked to uneducated fishermen and associated primarily with the indigent. Early Christianity, furthermore, is presented as a movement of the outcasts of the Roman Empire, of slaves, paupers and illiterates, a proletarian movement which—according to Communist doctrine—has been taken over eventually by the high and mighty. These exploited and lulled the masses into subservience by offering them salvation in the hereafter. Hence the formula of Marx that "Religion is the opium of the people."

It is amazing how often the romantic notions about Christ and early Christianity are repeated by well-meaning Christians of all denominations. This, unfortunately, only proves that the New Testament is rarely read intelligently, that knowledge of Jewish history and sociology is nil even among the better educated Christians, that our schools teach almost nothing about the Church in antiquity.

The most obvious mistake concerns the beloved picture of the Magi in front of the manger. Scripture tells us clearly (Math. 2:11) that they entered a house, probably the house of Joseph and Mary. As for the "Son of the carpenter," we should know that *tektôn* in Greek means carpenter as well as house-builder, architect, contractor. Joseph, moreover, is not an "ordinary Jew" but as a descendant of David he is of royal blood and therefore, in the eyes of his compatriots, a potential heir to the Throne of Judea. The angel characteristically addresses him as "son of David," but Christ too was addressed as "Son of David" (for instance, in Matt. 20:31; Mark 10:48; Luke 18:38) and had to flee in order not to be proclaimed king (John 6:15). "My kingdom is not of this world," however, makes his position clear. Yet when Pilate asked him whether he was a king, Christ answered in the affirmative. And since the Virgin Mary is the niece or grandniece of Zacharias and Elizabeth, both Aaronites and therefore of the priestly caste, she also belongs to the highest Jewish social layer. Although Joseph and Mary were *probably* not rich, they still rated very high socially. Joseph must also have been a landowner in Bethlehem, the Davidic village, which explains why he had to be there for the census.[24]

Our Lord certainly did not concentrate on the proletariat or on the illiterate in His teaching years. Peter seems to have been the boss of a group of fishermen. John, the most beloved disciple, obviously was an intellectual of the first order (and so, later, was Paul). The other Evangelists certainly belonged to the educated classes. Nor did Our Lord shun the company of rich people.[25]

The notion that Christianity was a religion of outcasts in the Roman Empire is totally erroneous. One need only peruse the Roman Missal and observe the social background of the early Martyrs to see that Christians could be found in all layers of society—among the patricians, the families of senators, the emperor's family, among actors and intellectuals. Nobody can maintain that the early Fathers of the Church were mostly simpleminded illiterates. Ignatius of Antioch, Tatian, Justin, Origen, Tertullian, Cyprian, Clement of Rome, Lactantius, Minucius Felix, Clement of Alexandria, Polycarp of Smyrna, Irenaeus, and Novatian were first rate intellectuals, spiritual men—and certainly not "social reformers." A religion of slaves undermining an aristocratic-heroic commonwealth: This picture is totally unhistorical.[26] But there always will be a certain breed of "conservatives" with a pagan-heroic outlook who are prone to see in Christianity a weak, unmanly faith of crybabies—as did Winston S. Churchill. Maurras, too, was not far from this position. The antics of certain Christian leftists confirm them in this view.

Yet it has a powerful effect as a myth. There are good Christians who believe that the rich man is bound to be bad, whereas his real problem is not to become enslaved by his wealth, to be "poor in spirit," *ptochos to pneumati*. Rarely pondered is the possibility that a wealthy man might not serve Mammon while a man less endowed with material goods may struggle and toil desperately to achieve them, thereby neglecting his spiritual life. Nobody will deny that the rich man who gives away his possessions liberally in a spirit of charity is acting virtuously. But is poverty *in itself* sanctifying? Is laziness with resulting poverty more admirable than the industriousness and thrift that produce material wellbeing? This is hardly the case. However, in the Christian world of today, replete with romanticism among Catholics as well as among Evangelical Christians, there is not only a perfectly wholesome readiness to live a life of poverty, but also a tendency to worship the poor: the agrarian pauper and above all the "proletarian." Curiously enough the pro-Socialist and Socialist sentiment in Christendom is nourished by this weird romantic enthusiasm—an oddity, because socialism and communism *hate* poverty. Socialism is opposed to it. It copies from monasticism the idea of collective work, of a regulated life, of obedience and sobriety, of "mutualism" and equality. It *hopes*, however, to eliminate poverty, to achieve general material wellbeing. (It will probably never achieve this goal, at least not as speedily and effectively as the free world whose economics is based on a far more realistic evaluation of the average man's character; but here this is not the point.)

The grim fact remains that there always will be Christians casting longing glances at the Socialist camp, sincerely regretting that Marxism is by its very nature atheistic.[27] They dream of a "Christian communism," of the possibility of transforming dialectic materialism by "baptizing" the concept of a collective society. Communism operates on the notion of the "dictatorship of the proletariat" (i.e., of the party), and what is called "democratic socialism"[28] wants to achieve the same end by peaceful, by democratic means. If 51 (or 99) percent vote for socialism, the rest (49 or only 1 percent) will have to knuckle under. The genuine democrat will have no difficulty in underwriting this; we are here faced with Locke's thesis that "Right is what the majority wills—what the majority wills is right."[29]

In our ecumenical age the tendency prevails to build bridges not only between the Christian faiths but in every direction, to open up dialogues with every imaginable body of thought, to show a readiness to learn from everybody and to compromise wherever and whenever compromise is possible—or impossible. (So far nobody has offered to start a fruitful dialogue with the Nazis and other advocates of genocide—yet let us be patient!)

If there is a strong trend in our age to use Christian tenets, knowingly or unknowingly, to justify a reconciliation with leftism, why should we be surprised to encounter the same tendency in bygone centuries? We mentioned Saint-Simon and his *Nouveau Christianisme*. Auguste Comte, the founder of Positivism, who dreamed of a completely secular Catholic Church was, after all, Saint-Simon's secretary for many years.

A distinctly non-Christian competitor of Saint-Simon in the ancestral gallery of early Socialist thought was another Frenchman, François Charles Marie Fourier. Born in 1772, son of a small manufacturer, he survived Saint-Simon by twelve years. Fourier surprised the public with his first work in 1808, his *Théorie des quatres mouvements*. His vision was rather different from Saint-Simon's. The blueprint he proposes for a Socialist society is based on his monomaniacal notion of *harmony*, in which he sees a crucial human drive. Numbers and geometric notions play a decisive part in his utopia where the arbitrary is curiously mingled with the prophetic, and odd rationalizations alternate with dreams of utter unreality—tendencies and propensities which increased in him as he got older.

Fourier wanted to divide humanity into groups of 1,600 people, the *phalanges* which were to live in monasterylike buildings called *phalanstères* (reminiscent of Morelly's jointly housed "tribes"). Economically each of these units was to be self-sufficient. Each was to have its fields and workshops. As in the case of Saint-Simon's utopian reveries, the visionary elements combined with pure rationalism to form weird blueprints. Since madness is very often a combination of cold reason with a fantasy severed from all reality, we are faced here with madness in a pure form. Surprisingly, or perhaps not so surprisingly, the response to Fourier's ideas was considerable.[30] Even if all efforts failed to make his dreams work—there have been repeated attempts on both sides of the Atlantic—followers of Fourier appeared in all countries, in Russia no less than in the United States.

The study of Fourier's writings is interesting because we encounter here a truly sick mind, much further from sanity than Saint-Simon's. Fourier's utopianism worked both ways: "constructively" in planning for the future, retrospectively in explaining and expounding a totally unreal past. His descriptions of the earth's past are entirely imaginary. For instance, he assumes that the earth had another satellite named Phoebe which in the dim past fell on our globe. The ensuing general destruction and confusion helped to bring 150 new species of snakes and forty-three new races of bedbugs into existence. His views of life on the planets were equally interesting. He insisted that the inhabitants of the planets and the *solariens* who existed on or around the sun had a physical organ which the *terriens*, the inhabitants of the earth, did not have. This member had the following properties: protection in falling, powerful defense, splendid ornament, gigantic strength, remarkable dexterity, and cooperation and support in all bodily movements. From his description this sounded like a sort of trunk or tail, and his enemies used his own words to lampoon the *solariens* in delightful cartoons.

As to our history, he divided it in the following way:
A. Periods anterior to history
   1. Bastards, no human beings
   2. Primitive, called Paradise
   3. Savagery or inertia
B. Divided Industry: repulsive
   1. Patriarchalism with small industry
   2. Barbarism with middle-sized industry
   3. Civilization with big industry
C. United industry: attractive

1. Guaranteeism: half-association
2. Sociantism: simple association
3. Harmonism: full association

The final goal is "harmony," the earth being divided into a number of completely peaceful empires with monarchical rather than republican constitutions,[31] without total equality and with a slight difference in income (according to a key granting percentages for capital investment, work, and "talent"). These sixty-odd empires have small "armies" working together in large economic and technological projects. Sexual life is at last freed from all shackles; free unions are formed and abandoned every day.

The true social unit is the phalanster, in which the most intensive social life takes place. People sleep from ten P.M. to three A.M. From three to four in the morning they wash and dress to make the assembly at four. There the chronicle of the night is read so that everybody can satisfy his or her curiosity as to who shared the bed with whom. Half an hour later the *"délite,"* the first meal is eaten, followed by the "industrial parade." A shooting and hunting party is organized for five A.M. At seven fishing begins. From eight to nine is breakfast, at nine the newspapers are distributed and read and at ten there is divine service. Then comes a break when people watch the pheasants until eleven, which is library time. Dinner is at one P.M., after which people repair to the hothouses, then to the exotic plants, then to the fish ponds and at six P.M. they enjoy a champagne party, followed by a visit to the merino sheep. At eight the phalansterians march to the stock exchange, supper is at nine. Music and dancing follows till bedtime at ten P.M.

This sort of daily timetable tells a story in itself. We see the unrealism of a man who believes that five hours of sleep is a good average and that work—as fun!—could be done in between. Two hours a day, wedged in here and there, seemed to him sufficient. Religion is not eliminated: Fourier believed in God who had endowed man with passions but not with reason, which is a purely human and ungodly inclination. In spite of his socialism, he was not an egalitarian. He would not even have objected to titles in his *phalanstères* as long as they were not a handicap to brotherliness and human harmony resting on free interplay of the passions which should not be resisted, merely "harnessed." (The influence of Saint-Simon is not certain but that of Rousseau is obvious.)

Unlike the later "scientific" Socialists, Fourier was a real Epicurean. He not only envisioned sexual libertinism (as we find it in Campanella and Saint-Simon) but had a marked penchant for the joys of the palate and stomach—joys which somehow would not impair the health of the *Harmoniens* scheduled to live at least 150 years. Fourier planned for semiculinary, semimedical specialists, the *gastrosophes*, whose task it would be to watch over alimentation. "The gastrosophers thus become inofficial doctors for each individual, protectors of his health by means of pleasure. It should be their ambition to see to it that each phalanster become well known for its appetite and the enormity of its food consumption."[32] Altogether a rather French vision.

Of course there was to be a uniform type of school with an identical basic education for everybody, avoiding at the same time any overeducation of those children who preferred to develop their bodies. (And, obviously, instincts and passions are better guides than idle ratiocinations.) On the other hand, children also like to band together and this penchant should be fostered assiduously. Fourier proposed the establishment of delightful organizations such as the *petites bandes* (consisting of two-thirds little girls and one-third boys) and the *petites hordes* with an inverse ratio of the sexes. The predominantly masculine *petites hordes* were to be dressed in Tartar costumes, all of different colors so that from a distance they would look like a "well-mixed field of tulips."

For the *petites bandes* our great visionary reserved the task of controlling the language. People with bad accents and bad grammar were to be persecuted by this largely female horde. If anybody fell below the standard set for the universal language, he was to receive from the chancellery of the *petites bandes* a list of the errors he committed and was to be exhorted not to repeat them.

Smaller children would be trained as scavengers (because of their natural inclination to play with dirt), and this would keep the *phalanstère* in perfect order. Adolescents, according to their sexual activity, were to be divided into *vestels* and *vestales*, leading a continent life, and *damoiseaux* and *damoiselles* opting for a more tantalizing way of sexual behavior.

For all this, life in the *phalanstères* was only a part of Fourier's grandiose view of the future. The enormous work-armies of the age of Harmony would engage in huge enterprises. They would pierce the Isthmus of Suez and the one of Panama, they would transform the Sahara into fertile land, they would see to it that the Arctic Ocean was perfumed. (All in a two-hour workday?) Most interesting would have been the creation (through careful cross-breeding) of such animals as the "antilion," a superb, docile, "elastic" quadruped which could transport its rider in almost no time from one corner of France to the other. Starting in the morning from Calais, one might have lunch in Paris and dine in Marseilles. The animal would be about three times the size of our own miserable lions and with every step he would cover eight yards. "It would be a pleasure to live in this world if one could enjoy such wonderful service,"[33] observed Fourier wistfully.

Indeed it would, since even the hardest work would be sheer delight. Take, for instance, farming. "We would see all these active groups well distributed over a beautiful valley, well-housed in colored tents, working in separate groups, moving about with flags and instruments, and singing hymns in chorus. Then we would behold the whole canton spotted with castles and rural palaces with columns and turrets instead of huts covered with straw. Would we not believe that this is an enchanted landscape, a country of fairies, an olympic dwelling place?"[34]

The pleasure of these visions overpowered Fourier. "He who has seen the interior galleries of a *phalanstère* will consider the most beautiful palace to be merely a place of exile, a manor for idiots who after three thousand years of experimenting with architecture have still not learned to house themselves in a healthy and comfortable way."[35]

These visions—most of them quite detailed—fill hundreds of pages. The reader might ask whether the musings of a certainly not well-balanced man are of any interest except to the psychologist or the psychiatrist. The fact is that they are of considerable importance. Fourierism is a crucial stage not only in the gradually unfolding history of socialism and communism, but also in the development of leftist thought in the United States. The chasm between the utopian Socialists and the scientific Socialists of a later period is not so great as the latter would like us to believe. The psychological foundations are practically the same; only the intellectual "superstructure" is different.

Friedrich Engels in his *Anti-Dühring* praised Fourier very highly, especially for his attitude toward women but also for the skill with which he "manages" dialectics. In this, Engels likens him to Hegel, Fourier's contemporary. In the revolutionary movements of 1848-1849 Victor Considérant, Fourier's leading disciple, played a key part as an aide to the great demagogue Ledru-Rollin. Considérant was a former student of the *Ecole Polytechnique* and became editor of *La Phalange* after Fourier's death. He finally persuaded a rich Englishman to finance a *phalanstère* in Condé-sur-Vègre in central France. It collapsed and with it *La Phalange*. The paper, however, was replaced with another one, *La démocratie pacifique*. During these years Considérant published a number of books, the majority of them almost as fantastic and as remote from reality as those of his mentor. He was elected to the Assemblée Nationale in 1848 and again in 1849. Since he sided with what was then called *La Montagne*, he had to flee to Belgium.[36] From there he went to Texas where he founded another *phalanstère*, called *La Réunion*, near San Antonio.[37] This project also failed, but Considérant was permitted to return to France in 1869 where he died at the age of 85 in 1893.

It is not from Texas, though, that Fourierism affected American intellectuals but rather via George Ripley and Brook Farm, originally started as an experiment of the New England Transcendentalists. The purpose of the enterprise in the beginning was to combine manual labor and intellectual life into an ideal example of collective living. The Transcendentalists, moreover, had a certain antirational bent and leaned toward "intuitivism." All in all the influence of monastic ideals (in spite of the Unitarian background) was very obvious, the secular-sentimental imitation of the monastery quite apparent. It was probably not accidental that the founder of the Paulists, Father Isaac Hecker, was connected with Brook Farm in his pre-Catholic days: a rare example of an evolution back to the original (and healthy) sources of a concept. (The evolution in the opposite direction is far more frequent.)[38]

In 1845, under the influence of Fourierism, George Ripley transformed Brook Farm into a phalanster, but a year later the not-yet-finished main building burned down and by the end of 1847 the whole experiment had come to an end. Still, Brook Farm had many friends and supporters, inmates, and sympathizers: Ralph Waldo Emerson (who favored it from a distance), Francis J. Barlow, Nathaniel Hawthorne (who was there for a short while), Arthur Brisbane, Charles A. Dana, James Russell Lowell, William H. Channing, Elizabeth Palmer Peabody, Margaret Fuller, and Horace Greeley. George Ripley wrote a column (mainly about Fourierism) in Horace Greeley's *New York Tribune*, a most respectable daily and the forerunner of the *New York Herald Tribune*. After Greeley and Ripley, Arthur Brisbane[39] was most active on behalf of Fourierist ideas. He organized the North American Phalanx in New Jersey which failed. (A Wisconsin Phalanx met the same fate.)

While Fourierism entered the American Olympus (even if on the sly and with a number of modifications), it had—as one can see from *The Possessed* by Dostoyevski—a marked influence on the Russian left, the precursors of Bolshevism. Even Alexander I in his earlier, leftist period (prior to 1812) was a reader of Fourier. Byelinski was profoundly impressed by Fourier[40] and so was, as one might expect, Alexander

Herzen who, however, saw in him and in Saint-Simon merely a forerunner of the real Socialist ideology of tomorrow.[41]

Fourier also made a deep impression on Nikolay Gavrilovitch Chernyshevski, son of a priest whose novel *What to do?*[42] stands at the very beginning of the intellectual and emotional trends that led almost directly to Bolshevism in Russia. There is only one cleverly masked reference to Victor Considérant's *La destinée sociale* in this highly programmatic novel, but Fourierism makes itself felt all through. (The attitude toward female emancipation, the theory of the delight in work rendered disagreeable only by "circumstances" are typical takeoffs from Fourier.) Another avid reader of Fourier was Peter Lavrov, a nobleman and revolutionary living mostly in exile, who made France his home. Thus, as we can see, raving madness stands at the cradle of a revolutionary movement which led to the Red October and to the crisis in which we all are; its weird, dark specter has never left us since.[43]

Chapter 9

From Romantic to Scientific

and International Socialism

A. Proudhon

Fourierism in France became eclipsed by the rise of a man with a clearer and deeper socialist mind who, unfortunately for us, was overshadowed in turn by Karl Marx—Pierre Joseph Proudhon, like Fourier a native of Besançon. Fourier's father was a shopkeeper of certain means, whereas Proudhon's father came from a "proletarian" milieu. Pierre Joseph nevertheless succeeded in getting a good education in a *collège*[1] where he was taught Latin and Greek which was later supplemented with Hebrew. He soon lost his Faith, became influenced by socialistic ideas, but revolted against the mad speculations and prophecies of Fourier and his disciple Considérant whom he attacked in pamphlets. He became the first truly methodical and scientific socialist thinker, yet unlike his bitter opponent, Karl Marx, he always kept—even in his "atheism"—a certain human and metaphysical outlook.[2] He was, in a way, an atheist tormented by doubts, and toward the end of his life he fought bitterly against the fanaticism of antireligious haters. His socialism was "distributist" rather than collectivistic; the keyword of his economic thinking is "mutualism." He was strongly opposed to economic liberalism because he feared bigness, the concentration of wealth, mammoth enterprises, yet he was equally an enemy of the omnipotent centralized state which figures as the keystone in all leftist thinking.

In Proudhon's numerous books and pamphlets one finds notions and ideas which any true lover of liberty or any true conservative could underwrite, but which really are part and parcel of the "arsenal" of rightist thought. He did belong to that not so very rare category of theorists who, given the right contacts, the right friends, and the right ambiance, could have overcome the magnetism of the left.

In his *Confessions of a Revolutionary* Proudhon says that it "is surprising to observe how constantly we find all our political questions complicated with theology"[3] and indeed he never entirely divorced himself from a theological outlook. He always remained a healthy antistatist and naturally a convinced antidemocrat. It is significant that one of the leading contemporary Catholic theologians, Henri de Lubac S. J. devoted a profound study to him: *Proudhon et le christianisme.*[4] Constantin Frantz, the great German conservative, could not hide his admiration for Proudhon, but regretted that he had to cite a "French radical" because Germany, the classic country of thinkers, had become intellectually sterile.[5] Proudhon, however, remained convinced that France was the nation of "golden mediocrity."[6]

Let us just cite a few passages to give at least a vague idea of the part of Proudhon's mind that was bound to conflict with the later socialist outlook which was dictatorial, centralizing and "democratic."

"The February Revolution replaced the system of voting by 'classes':[7] democratic puritanism still was not satisfied. Some wanted the vote given to children and women. Others protested against the exclusion of financial defaulters, released jailbirds, and prisoners. One wonders that they did not demand the inclusion of horses and donkeys.[8]

"Democracy is the idea of the state without limits.[9]

"Money, money, always money—this is the crux (*le nerf*) of democracy.[10]

"Democracy is more expensive than monarchy, it is incompatible with liberty.[11]

"Democracy is nothing but the tyranny of the majorities, the most execrable tyranny of all because it rests neither on the authority of a religion, nor on the nobility of race nor on the prerogatives of talent or property. Its foundation is numbers and its mask is the name of the people.[12]

"Democracy is an aristocracy of mediocrities.[13]

"Authority, which in monarchy is the principle of the governing activity, is in democracy the aim of the government.[14]

"The people, thanks to its inferiority and its misery, will always form the army of liberty and progress—but due to its ignorance and the primitiveness of its instincts, as a result of the urgency of its needs and the impatience of its desires, it inclines towards simple forms of authority. What it is looking for are by no means legal guarantees of which it has no concrete notions nor any realization of their power . . . it has faith in a leader whose intentions are known to them. . . . To such a leader it accords authority without limits and irresistible power. . . . The people does not believe in principles which alone could save it: it lacks the 'religion of ideas.'[15]

"Democracy is, in fact, essentially militaristic.[16]

"Every state is by its very nature 'annexationist.'[17]

"Left to themselves or led by a tribune, the masses will never accomplish anything. They have their faces turned to the past. No tradition is formed among them . . . about politics they understand nothing but intrigues, about the government only waste and sheer force; of justice only the accusations; of liberty only the erection of idols which are destroyed the next day. The rise of democracy starts an era of backwardness which will lead nation and state to their death.[18]

"Accept in a manly way the situation in which you are and convince yourself once and for all that the happiest of men is the one who knows best how to be poor.[19]

"My views on the family are not unlike those of the ancient Roman law. The father of the family is to me a sovereign . . . I consider all our dreams about the emancipation of women as destructive and stupid.[20]

"When we say 'the People' we always mean unavoidably the least progressive part of society, the most ignorant, the most cowardly, the most ungrateful.[21]

"If democracy is reason, then it ought to represent above all *demopedy,* 'education of the people.'[22]

"The twentieth century is going to open up a period of federation or humanity will enter a purgatory of a thousand years."[23]

Thus one should not be surprised that this man of the people, largely self-educated but possessed of a certain earthy wisdom, was bound to conflict with another man whose mind was strangely divorced from reality, a fervent hater, an illusionist, but at the same time a skilled demagogue—Karl Marx. These two men, even if both had a genuine claim to the label "socialist," were temperamentally poles apart.

123

Proudhon, in spite of his anticlericalism (which abated toward the end of his life) was deeply imbued with Christian moral principles.[24] He led an exemplary pure and studious life and made every sacrifice for his ideas,[25] always guided by deep and lasting affections.

A book he published in 1846, *Système des contradictions economiques ou Philosophie de la misère,* was the reason for the clash with Marx. The bourgeois from Trier furiously assailed Proudhon in a savage writ, *La Misère de la philosophie.* Although Proudhon and Marx dreamed of a "withering away of the state," Marx sought the fulfillment of his ideas by revolutionary means, by the use of brute force, by the "dictatorship of the proletariat." Proudhon, on the other hand, was an "evolutionist": The right order of things should be *discovered,* not arbitrarily blueprinted. Socialism should come gradually, in stages, without upheavals, by persuasion: It should encompass the globe through voluntary adherence and finally unite mankind not under one centralistic superstate but in a federal system, by federations deeply rooted in local customs, institutions, and traditions. Father de Lubac notes Proudhon's sentimental attachment to the part of France in which he was born and reared—the Franche Comtè which had been under Spanish rule for a long time and where the feeling for *personal liberty* was particularly strong.

When the savage and perhaps unexpected attack from Marx came, Proudhon did not reply. This sensitive and noble man probably considered it below his dignity to react to that boorish piece of writing. Although Proudhon could rise to great heights of enthusiasm, although he was the man who had coined the term "scientific socialism," he was devoid of the bitter unbending dogmatism of Karl Marx. Had Proudhon retained leadership of the Socialist movement, he would have given it a more anarchical, "personalistic" character, a greater plasticity and humaneness. The Western world would have coped with it more easily. Instead Karl Marx prevailed with his rigid, secular monasticism destined to plunge civilization into abysmal misery. Daniel Halévy wrote quite rightly that, "There was a place for a great dialogue between the two men: Marx, the protagonist of the revolution of the proletarian masses, and Proudhon, the champion of the personalist revolution. The dialogue foundered and Marx is to blame for it, because the tone he gave to it right in the beginning rendered the expected discussions impossible."[26]

B. Marx and Lassalle

Who was this Karl Marx, source of so much evil in the past two generations? He was born in 1818 into the family of a Jewish lawyer in the old bishopric of Trier as a subject of King Frederick William III, the Congress of Vienna having allotted the Rhenish bishoprics to Prussia. When he was six years old his father embraced the Lutheran faith of the new Prussian master and not the Catholic religion of the areas. It is difficult to find out whether this step was taken for religious or social reasons. The entire family gradually followed suit, but it is significant that as soon as little Karl was able to read he studied, together with his father, the works of Voltaire—not precisely an atheist but certainly a scoffer at orthodox Christianity. Having finished his *Gymnasium* (the classical high school and college), he studied law and philosophy at the Universities of Bonn and Berlin. He wrote a dissertation on Epicurus, whose philosophy has a decidedly materialistic flavor, for the University of Jena which gave him a Ph.D. In Berlin young Marx became strongly influenced by Hegel and his school. It is interesting to analyze not only the intellectual but also the emotional development of young Marx. His relation with his mother was bad; however, his relation with his father was intimate, and it is significant that he always carried with him a picture of his father which Engels placed in his coffin. Nevertheless, his father understood very well the weaknesses of his son, who spent considerable sums of money (for purposes never elucidated by research). When he wrote to his father that he was a "torn" (*zerrissene*) person, his father replied to him, "To be quite candid, my dear Karl, I do not like this modern word which serves as a cloak to weaklings who are at odds with the world because they do not own without effort and toil beautifully furnished palaces, vast fortunes and elegant carriages. This "tornness" [*Zerrissenheit*] to me is disgusting, and I expect it least of all from you. What reasons can you have for it?"[27] The reasons were the precocious young man's mad ambitions as well as the sometimes unwholesome influence of German romanticism. Professor Ernst Kux has reminded us that Marx, by no means a "scientific mind" in his younger years, belongs to the *mainstream of German Romanticism*. He always "felt" first and then looked for a "scientific proof of his emotions."[28]

Young Marx who has a considerable appeal for the New Left, knew Bettina von Arnim and Arnold Ruge and was a close friend of Heinrich Heine who soon found him intolerable. He called Marx a *docteur en révolution,* and a "godless self-god."[29] Yet young Marx was basically an artist or at least a would-be artist who wrote mediocre poetry and also planned to publish a theatrical review. The nonfulfillment of his dreams made him a revolutionary, and here we have a strong analogy with Hitler. The frustrated artist wants to destroy the world which does not appreciate him. No wonder, because art is creation and a man not permitted to create is thoroughly thwarted. For Marx artistic activity was the very essence of human activity.[30] His great dream was a Communist society where the "rich and profound all-round person is not restricted to an exclusive domain of action, but can develop himself in every branch, where society regulates general production and makes it possible for him to do this today and that tomorrow, to hunt in the morning, to fish at noon, to do some stock-farming in the evening, to engage in criticisms after the meals, just as he feels inclined—without ever becoming a hunter, a fisher, a shepherd, or a critic."[31] As one can easily see, the ideas of Fourier, the utopianism of an earthly paradise profoundly colored his thinking. At the same time Marx became increasingly more and more Promethean in his visions. He put man in the place of God, the notion of the *Übermensch*, superman, appears in his writings.[32] Needless to say, all this is a far cry from Leninism and far more akin to the New Left. Yet the purely artistic vein, his interest in art (as in the case of Hitler) never disappeared entirely. Marx always remained an estheticist.[33] On the other hand, one does not find any preoccupation with ethics in Marx's thinking or writing. A person cannot be made responsible for historical processes which happen automatically as the result of scientific laws. (Such reflections are typical for a later period of his life.[34]) "The Communists preach no morality."[35] Any morality leads to ideology, and ideology leads not to tragedy but to comedy. Any philosopher who preaches a system of ethics is childish enough to believe that a different conscience could change the order of things.[36] How could this be if the historic process is preordained and immutable?

Originally Marx thought to enter upon an academic career and applied for an extraordinary professorship at the University of Bonn. His friends, however, dissuaded him and in 1842 (at the age of 24) he became editor-in-chief of the *Rheinische Zeitung* in Cologne. A year later the daily was stopped by government order and Marx, undaunted by this failure, married Jenny von Westphalen. (Ladies of noble blood play a major role in almost all Socialist movements: There is probably a deeper psychological reason for this phenomenon.)[37] There is no doubt that Marx, initially at least, loved his wife and his daughters dearly, but he was basically not only a critic and a scoffer, but also a hater. We have seen how he treated Proudhon. Arnold Ruge with whom he collaborated (but soon fell out in Paris) wrote to Fröbel that "gnashing his teeth and with a grin Marx would slaughter all those who got in the way of this new Babeuf. He always *thinks* about this

126

feast which he cannot *celebrate.*"[38] The best description of Marx in his thirtieth year we have from Carl Schurz, American Senator and German-born forty-eighter who met him in Cologne at a public session of democratic leagues and wrote in his *Lebenserinnerungen:* "The stocky, heavily built man with his broad forehead, with pitchblack hair and full beard, attracted general attention. . . . What Marx said was indeed substantial, logical and clear. But never did I meet a man of such offensive arrogance in his demeanor. No opinion deviating in principle from his own would he give the slightest consideration. Anybody who contradicted him was treated with hardly veiled contempt. Every argument which he happened to dislike was answered either with biting mockery about the pitiful display of ignorance or with defamatory suspicions as to the motives of the interpellant. I still well remember the sneering tone with which he spat out the word *bourgeois.* And as *bourgeois,* that is to say, as an example of a profound intellectual and moral depravity he denounced anybody who dared to contradict his views."[39]

Marx, who as an educated German was fully conversant with French, transferred his residence late in 1843 to Paris. He expected greater liberty under the regime of Louis-Philippe than in the Rhineland dominated by the Prussians. With Arnold Ruge he started to publish the *German-French Yearbooks,* but after the printing of the first issue the editors quarreled and the periodical never again appeared. It was in France that Marx broke with orthodox Hegelianism, retaining only Hegel's concept of the dialectic process of history. Here too he met with Proudhon, received his first communications from Engels, and wrote his first bitterly hostile essay about the Jews. We have to bear in mind that Marx nurtured a real hatred for the Jews in whom he saw the very embodiment of bourgeois capitalism.[40] Yet his prejudice had not only a sociological but also, as we will see, a racist character. It might be that his anti-Semitism was partly due to Bruno Bauer, a Lutheran theologian and a friend of his younger years, who had been one of the originators of Biblical criticism. Bauer's views showed a marked anti-Jewish bias. A Hegelian in his philosophical outlook, he incurred the hatred of Marx after the latter's break with Hegel's philosophy and thus, together with Engels, Marx wrote one of his most venomous pamphlets: *The Holy Family Against Bruno Bauer and Company.* Engels, as a matter of fact, was one of the very few people with whom Marx was able to maintain a lasting friendship. This wealthy manufacturer from the Ruhr Valley also had sufficient funds to support the penurious cofounder of international socialism and communism. Lenin's "useful idiots" thus existed long before Lenin.

The materialism of Ludwig Feuerbach made the deepest and most lasting impression not only upon Marx but also upon Engels, and it hastened their break with German idealism. Feuerbach's criticism of religion in general and of Christianity in particular, combined with a violent materialism, (*Der Mensch ist, was er isst*—"Man is what he eats") laid the foundations for Marx's unwavering rejection and hatred of all religions. Feuerbach's notion that culture and education can and should supplant religion has a rather German and romantic tinge, but his idea that one has to replace the readiness to "believe" with the readiness to "will" shows the direction in which Marx and Engels were also moving. Morality, Feuerbach insisted, will never be sustained by religion, but only by an *improvement in living conditions*—in other words, by "social betterment." This of course is a notion which not only became typically Marxist but which is shared by the American moderate left, if not by American folklore. After all, the great consolation to so many in this valley of tears is the childlike belief in the automatic character of progress. Here we find the fulfillment of Dostoyevski's prophecy (through the mouth of his "Grand Inquisitor" in *The Brothers Karamazov*) that the time shall come in which science and the sages will proclaim the nonexistence of criminals and sinners—there are only hungry people. In popular terms this means, "Poverty. . . . Poverty breeds socialism: If people have not enough to eat, they will develop a 'communism of the stomach.' " This, however, is just another fallacy. And while Marx learned from Feuerbach only through books and articles, he established direct contact in Paris with disciples of Saint-Simon and also with the count's former secretary, Auguste Comte, the father of Positivism. Comte's effort to explain social laws by the laws of nature (which are not the "natural law") also left a permanent imprint on Marx's thinking.

In 1845 the Prussian government asked the French to expel Marx as a dangerous agitator, and the French complied. Thus he went to Brussels where he published his pamphlet against Proudhon in 1847. In 1848 together with Engels he issued the *Communist Manifesto*. A month later he was asked by the Belgian authorities to leave Brussels, whereupon he returned with Engels to a Paris seething with revolution. Louis-Philippe was then overthrown. From Paris they went to the Rhineland, to Cologne, where the revolutionary fervor reached a high pitch. There Marx published a daily paper, *Die Neue Rheinische Zeitung* with the subtitle *Demokratisches Organ*. In November of that year the paper incited its readers not to pay taxes and to engage in armed resistance against the Prussian government which had dissolved the National

Assembly. Thereupon the newspaper was confiscated, Marx was arrested and tried, but acquitted by a middle-class jury. To avoid another arrest he went back to France where the government had become less radical in temper. He was thus given the choice either to leave France or to settle somewhere outside of Paris. Yet Marx had to be near big libraries—he was a real bookworm—so he went to a country which already had its own socialist movement—Britain. He found an abode in London and stayed there, working ceaselessly in the reading room of the British Museum until his dying days. His financial support came mainly from Engels, whose Calvinist-Pietist family had "paid him out," and from the *New York Tribune*. Without the dollars and the marks of capitalism, there probably would have been no Socialist and Communist movements.

Let us return, however, to the *Manifesto of the Communist Party*. In Brussels Marx had joined a "League of the Just" which later changed its name into *Bund der Kommunisten*, "League of Communists"—now, by the way, the official name of the former Communist party of Yugoslavia: *Savez komunista*. The *Manifesto*, a short pamphlet of about 12,000 words, gives a vivid if unmethodical insight into the basic notions of Marxism. It was written jointly with Engels in a forceful, pungent style, yet its (German) vocabulary is such that it could scarcely be understood by the average worker and only by a minority of the working class elite. My edition, published in 1921[41] when education had substantially increased, contains a glossary of twelve closely printed pages—all of which proves that socialism (no less than communism) was emphatically a movement of intellectuals with complex psychological motives, intellectuals capable of mobilizing the masses, either through their writings, their oratorical gifts, or both. International socialism and communism were *not* born among the "toiling masses." Nor were they invented, planned, and organized by men with overflowing affection for the downtrodden but—with few exceptions—by venomous haters. Neither love nor pity nor compassion plays a role in Marx's heart or mind.

The *Communist Manifesto*, written in Brussels but first published in London, starts with the famous words: "A specter haunts Europe—the specter of Communism."[42] After a preamble it sets out to explain all of history as the history of class struggle, but the authors of the *Manifesto* also disclosed their conviction that prehistoric society had known no classes and that property was held in common. In other words, they adopted the Roussellian notion of a paradisiacal situation, a Golden Age, a secular version of the Biblical record.

The *Manifesto* then goes on to praise the "bourgeoisie" (a term, by the way, without any real equivalent in other European languages) for having overthrown feudalism and its culture, but berates it for creating an iron rule of its own. A violent critique of bourgeois civilization follows which, when all is said and done, brings out the dominant characteristic of Marx: self-hatred. Marx, the typical product of bourgeois culture, is antibourgeois; Marx, of Jewish origin, is anti-Jewish; Marx, a permanent resident of capitalist Britain, is anticapitalist; Marx having married an aristocrat is anti-aristocratic. In the third part of his *Manifesto* Marx even becomes boiling mad about "aristocratic socialism," about the proworker attitude of aristocratic opponents of the bourgeois outlook. The self-hater typically wants no allies, no help from anybody.

Still, Marx praises the bourgeoisie for having established the firm domination of the city over the countryside, for having effected mass migrations of persons to the cities, "tearing them away from the idiocy of the rural life." Here is the voice of the rootless intellectual.

Marx also extolled the bourgeoisie for its antifeudal, antiaristocratic trend toward centralization by promotion of "one nation, one government, one law, one national class interest, one customs area." He raves about all these achievements. But then he tries to prove that technology is in complete opposition to the then prevailing ways of production. The bourgeoisie is in the midst of a terrible crisis. Wars, general starvation, and economic chaos are menacing bourgeois society from every corner. Production is too high. The only way out is the conquest of new markets and the further brutal exploitation of the old markets. The bourgeoisie have to create new crises to survive. On the other hand they have created the working class of the proletariat that will eliminate them as they themselves have eclipsed the old ruling aristocracy.

What now follows is surprising in a way—not so surprising, however, if we remember German romanticism. It is a furious and not entirely unjust critique of modern industry, of the entire machine age, of the servitude imposed on the worker by the precursors of the assembly line. The worker, Marx says, is enslaved by the machine and by the overseers in the service of the exploiting bourgeoisie. And here he comes to the other evil: The worker receives only a fraction of the wages due to him.

But there is one consolation. The big bourgeoisie pressed everybody down to the level of the proletariat. Bigness is seemingly victorious all along the line. There are petty bourgeoisie who join the ranks of the proletariat willy-nilly. And within the proletariat a new civilization already exists: the relationship of the proletariat to wife and child, to state and nation is already radically different from the older patterns. He has no fatherland, no bourgeois morality, no religion. And whereas in the past only minorities fought for their interests, the proletarian movement is an "independent movement of the vast majority in the interest of a vast majority." Since, in addition, the proletariat is the lowest layer, the basis of society, it cannot rise without blowing up the rest of society.

While in the past small social segments could rise socially, the worker cannot do this. He gets poorer and poorer under the iron heel of the bourgeoisie. Yet, with the proletariat the bourgeoisie creates its own gravediggers. Its downfall and the victory of the proletariat are equally unavoidable. (But if history works "automatically" why then organize a movement, one might ask.)

The ensuing critique of "bourgeois" property, education, morality, and sentiment is filled with weasel words, little insincerities, and wisecracks. An oblique attack is made by declaring all these values to be already nonexistent for the vast majority of the people. Nine-tenths of the population, Marx and Engels claimed, have no property anyhow. "Bourgeois marriage" is bankrupt. The *Manifesto* goes on to say that the Communists would not abolish the right to own individual objects, but then again it insists that private property would come to an end in the Communist order.

"The first step in the Revolution of the Workers is the transformation of the proletariat into the ruling class which is to enforce democracy."[43]

Yet unlike later developments in Russia there was to be step by step transformation. "The proletariat is going to use its political domination to deprive the bourgeois gradually of its capital, to place all the instruments of production into the hands of the state which means to centralize it in the hands of the proletariat organized into a ruling class, and to increase as fast as possible the mass productive energies.

"This, of course, can only be achieved by despotic interventions against property rights . . . measures which might seem economically insufficient and untenable, but which in the course of the development achieve a wider scope and are unavoidable as the means for the transformation of the entire system of production."

As one sees, the economic aspects are subordinate to the messianic vision.[44] "The measures," the authors add, "will be different in the various countries, but for the nations which have progressed furthest, the following ones could be enacted:

1. Expropriation of real estate, the rent being used for the expenses of the government.

2. A highly progressive taxation.

3. Abolition of the right to inherit.

4. Confiscation of all property of emigrants and rebels.

5. Centralization of all credit in the hands of the state through the agency of a National Bank with state capital and an exclusive monopoly.

6. Centralization of all means of transport under state control.

7. Increase of national factories and the means of production. Improvement of lands based on a common plan.

8. Universal conscription of labor. Organization of industrial armies, especially for agricultural purposes.

9. Unification of industrial and agrarian production. Efforts to eliminate gradually the differences between town and country.

10. Public and free education for all children. Abolition of factory work for children in its present form. Amalgamation of education with material production.

Then comes a large section which criticizes and ridicules with bitter remarks all the other Socialist and leftist trends and parties. The *Manifesto* ends with the declaration that Communists are ready everywhere to support the despised bourgeois in their struggle against the remnants of feudalism and monarchism. "The Communists foster the cooperation and mutual understanding of democratic parties of all countries. The Communists disdain to keep their views and plans secret. They openly declare that their aims can only be achieved through a violent overturn of the present social order. Let the ruling classes tremble before the Communist Revolution. The proletarians have nothing to lose but their chains. They have a world to win. *Proletarians of all countries, unite!"*

This document is interesting not only because it reveals the mentality of its authors, their quasireligious vistas, their petty insincerities, their romantic outlook, their dogmatism, and the inconsistencies of their views. (For instance, even granting the deadening character of modern industrial work "alienating" the laborer from his toil, the situation in this respect would not be different in a "progressive" Communist world state.)[45] The most interesting aspect of the *Manifesto*, however, not only lies in its vision of a secular "Day of Judgment," but in the relation of the "Preparatory Program" just cited to the existing trends in the free world of today. In other words, we can use this program as a measuring rod to see to what extent we and our contemporaries have become Marxists and, especially, to what extent the perverted scions of old liberalism in the United States and in Britain have fallen for Marxist notions. Anybody condemned to listen to the loose talk in drawing rooms or political meetings where socialism is not the official creed is always astonished to observe how much headway the "false but clear ideas" of Marxism have made and have become common property. ("Vietnam? But that's only Wall Street wanting to profit from the rice paddies!")

Point One has been carried out by a number of highly "bourgeois" states such as Czechoslovakia, Estonia, Latvia, and Rumania between the two wars, and by Italy after World War II. (Hungary, Spain, and Poland enforced minor agrarian reforms.) Yet it must be admitted that in the free world the confiscation and redistribution of agricultural lands was enacted to benefit the farming class and not the state. (The most radical agrarian reforms before World War I were carried out by Imperial Russia—in the nineteenth century in conjunction with the liberation of the serfs and fifty years later under Stolypin.) Agrarian reforms, nevertheless, constitute a far-reaching and doubtfully legitimate intervention in the domain of private property.[46]

Point Two has become the rule in the vast majority of Western nations. From the governments' point of view it brings in amazingly little revenue:[47] The "soaking the rich" formula serves primarily to satisfy the envy of the masses.[48] Yet sometimes there is also another reason for progressive taxation, the state's instinctive fear of the rich and therefore *independent* person.

Point Three is practiced in the West in another form. In certain countries death duties have reached a level which renders them confiscatory. As a result fortunes are frequently amassed in such a manner that they can easily be transferred invisibly or be smuggled abroad. The millionaire dying in a hotel room with three suits in his closet after having gradually given away everything is a symbol of our times. (Here again the "wicked reactionary Fascist aristocratic landowner" who cannot escond his property pays the full penalty.)

Point Four is academic in the free world, but it is all the more fervently practiced east of the Iron Curtain.

Point Five menaces all of free Europe. The "exclusive monopoly" does not yet exist in a general manner, but there is a strong tendency to nationalize the banks. Thus all the big banks of France and Austria are fully nationalized and as a result the smaller banks literally have to compete with the state.

Point Six, the centralization and nationalization of transport, is a hard fact all over Western Europe. The same is true of the means of communication. Only in the United States do we find private railroads competing against each other[49]—and also against an efficient network of bus companies and airlines. The American telephone system, still privately owned, is one of the best in the world.

Point Seven is far advanced in free Europe and elsewhere in the world—in India, in Africa, Latin America. In 1945-1946, in the shadow of the Red hysteria that affected even "Christian Democratic" parties from the Channel to Vienna, nationalizations were enacted right and left —partly in order to please the Socialists, partly as a manifestation of "Christian social consciousness."

Point Eight, to tell the truth, has been more to the liking of National Socialist and other similar regimes which introduced a compulsory labor service. "Labor armies" on a voluntary basis, however, also were seen in the United States during the New Deal.

Point Nine has to be understood in the light of the Marxian notion of the "idiocy of rural life." The farmer was always and still remains the stumbling block to Socialist experiments everywhere. Since he raises his own food and usually lives in his own house, he can be less "controlled" than anybody else. The urbanization of our civilization is a worldwide phenomenon needing no aid or planning. Whether it is a blessing is quite a different question. Yet in Russia the dream of the *Agrogorod*, the "Agrarian City," is always reappearing in leading Communist circles.

Point Ten is already a largely fulfilled demand of all leftist parties. Its underlying notion is the expectation that intellectual-social leveling and standardization of knowledge at a tender age will bolster and foster equality and uniformity.[50]

The *Manifesto* by no means gives us the full Marxist theory. Still, the list of steps to be taken immediately after the proletarian victory clearly reflects the mind of the allegedly "non-Marxist" left which, partly knowingly but largely unknowingly, is imbibing ideas and notions from Marxist sources.

Marx's further work is largely based on the *Manifesto*. He merely went on to intellectualizing and rationalizing his emotions. Positivism and a concomitant atheism are the foundations of his thinking. Auguste Comte and Feuerbach were his initial guiding stars. To them must be added the Hegelian dialectic.[51] And as further stimuli French Socialism (Proudhon), English Socialism (Robert Owen), certain tenets of Ricardo and the personally experienced misery of the British working class whose horrors should not be underestimated.[52] And since Britain was the industrial leader in the world, Marx was convinced that all the other Continental nations would have to go through the same stages of debasement—which, like almost all his other prophecies, proved untrue. The distance of a bookworm from reality can be considerable.

From his books, letters, and essays we get a more complete and fuller view of his ideas. Only the first volume of *Das Kapital* was published during his lifetime. The other two (in certain editions, three) volumes were compiled and edited by Engels and Kautsky from the material left by Marx after his death. A further concretization of the utopia to come cannot clearly be found in those pages. The critical side in Marx was stronger than his prophetic gifts. Hatred was stronger in him than the creative urge which needs love as a driving motor. Of all his theories as to the iniquities, dangers, and pitfalls of capitalism today, only *one* can still be taken seriously. That is the theory of concentration and monopolization which our classic Old Liberals consider to be as inane as the rest of Marxist doctrine. (They have a point if they bring a worldwide free trade into their calculations.) Neo-Liberalism, on the other hand, which is profoundly interested in continued competition as the life blood of a free economy, has a strict antitrust and anticartel attitude. (This, however, does not mean that every Neo-Liberal would subscribe to every bit of American antitrust legislation which, at times, is animated not by a sincere devotion to the cause of economic liberty but by anticapitalist prejudices.[53]) Yet, as history shows, the trend toward concentration is a problem which free enterprise in a free society can cope with. Concentration and mammothism, on the other hand, is the life principle of socialism, which *is* state capitalism.

None of Marx's other prophecies relating to the evolution of "capitalism" (an unhappy term) came true. Marx lived too early: He wrote about free economy like a young man writing about life while knowing only his own age group. What a youngster writes about older persons is fatally bound to be erroneous; it can only be sheer guesswork. Later in his life Marx was fully convinced of the importance of technology and it strongly figures in his calculations, but it was then much too new an element in our civilization and too rapidly evolving for us to use it as a fixed cipher in our equations. (Nor can we really assess the coming impact of computers and automation today.) There seems to be some indication, though, that Marx was emotionally so deeply immersed in his theories that he consciously-subconsciously overlooked a number of new phenomena which must have come to his attention in the years between the publication of the *Communist Manifesto* and his death in 1883. Torn between his fanaticism and his burning intellectuality, he also had a quasireligious vision patterned after Biblical notions. It conceived history as starting with an innocent, paradisiacal prehistory, followed by the evil rise of classes, the family, religions, the government, and iniquitous exploiting systems of production, until he (a real prophet) and his friends were to arrive on the stage to preach the new Gospel of Salvation by writing the new Holy Scriptures. The millennium of the Dictatorship of the Proletariat was not far off and it would lead to the old Paradise Lost in a better, more progressive, and more modern version. Marx, however, was too clever and also too cautious to paint that picture of a redeemed humanity with the ridiculous precision of the utopian Socialists. He wanted to be a "scientific Socialist," a logician, rationalist, scholar, researcher—even if his daydreams led him completely astray.

Marx's monumental hatreds gravely conflicted with his Biblical patterns. It is difficult to say whom he loathed more, the "deviationists" in his own camp—men such as Proudhon, Bakunin, Lassalle—or the faceless, impersonal enemy, the *Grande Bourgeoisie Capitaliste* whom he attacked more impersonally, in a far more general way than his fellow leftists. In all this he was supported by a very facile pen, by a brilliant style enlivening even such a basically dry work as *Das Kapital* with purple passages. The real Marx, however, comes to life in his letters, especially when he vents his hatred on former friends, collaborators, or sympathizers. Marx actually vied with Engels in heaping anti-Jewish invectives upon the head of Lassalle, insults of a descriptive physical nature, reminding us literally of the smutty Nazi weekly *Der Stürmer* edited by Julius Streicher. Marx saw in Lassalle a "niggerlike Jew," but Engels' invectives were not more moderate either.[54] In a way these attitudes are not so surprising because socialism and the Jewish outlook, the Jewish mind, the Jewish character do not easily mix.[55] Belonging to a religious minority within Christendom (with which they remain mysteriously connected), the Jews are apt to have the critical bent of small religious bodies everywhere. Questioning a great deal of the intellectual-spiritual foundations on which the majority lives, these minorities will often be emphatic in their negations and thus easily become unpopular, because the Philistine hates the critic. Let such minorities rise financially and opposition against them will increase: Envy will be added to discomfort and suspicion. The situation is by no means unique, as in the case of the Calvinists in France, of the Germans in old Russia, of the Greeks and Armenians in Turkey, of the Copts in Egypt, the Parsees in India, the Indians in Africa, the Viets in Cambodia, or the Chinese in Indonesia.

Yet, although Jews might be attracted by the *critical* aspect of Socialist theory and even play important parts in nascent Socialist movements—the names of Trotsky, Kamenev, Zinovyev, Kún, Bernstein, Eisner, Blum, Bauer come to mind—they are constitutionally averse to its conformism, its anti-individualism, its moralizing cant, its intellectual controls.[56] This may be less evident to an American or East European observer and for the same reason: In Eastern Europe there lived the most indigent part of the Continent's Jewry and this was precisely the element which in the last three decades before the World War I largely immigrated into America. For sociological reasons they were most likely to embrace leftist ideas.[57] This was by no means the case with the old established American Jewry.

Yet even in Eastern Europe a break between the forces of socialism and communism and the Jews had to come. (For a while this was obscured by the fact that the Nazis literally drove Jews in that area into the arms of organized Leftism.) There was a latent, sometimes even an open, anti-Jewish sentiment in the ranks of Europe's Socialist parties[58] and anti-Semitism did not spare Red Russia either.[59] By the time World War II had broken out, Stalin had killed many more Jews than Hitler.[60] Needless to say, Jewish *haute finance* was never really pro-Communist: Even if Jewish bankers did business with the Soviet Union, the guilt of gentile manufacturers and financiers (not to forget German generals of the Ludendorff and Seeckt type) is even more impressive.[61] Antonio Machado, the great Spanish poet who died in exile, had predicted the inevitable turn toward anti-Judaism that Marxism would take.[62] Marx himself had started it: "What is the secular basis of Judaism?" he asked. "Practical needs, egoism. What is the secular cult of the Jew? Huckstery. What is his secular God? Money."[63] No wonder Goebbels declared eighty years later that *all* socialism is anti-Semitism.[64]

Marxism is not only non-Jewish, it is also nonproletarian. It is absolutely bourgeois and therefore strongly appeals to the left-of-center middle-class mind with its commercial background. Waldemar Gurian was very much to the point when he wrote, "Marxism and therefore Russian Bolshevism does not voice the secret and unavowed philosophy of bourgeois society when it regards society and economics as absolute. It is faithful, likewise, to its morality when it seeks to order this absolute, the economic society, in such a way that justice, equality, and freedom, the original war cries of the bourgeois advance, may be the lot of all. The rise of the bourgeoisie and the evolution of bourgeois society have made economics the lot of all."[65] It was the late Ben Hecht who admonished his readers not to believe in the picture of the Communist as a man with a bomb in one hand and a dagger in the other. To Hecht bolshevism was a movement logically evolving from nice middle-class democracy. "Democracy," he wrote, "was the most atrocious insult leveled at the intelligence of the race by its inferiors.

Bolshevism goes one better, however." He thought that it would be fostered in the United States one day by "our lowest types"—politicians, thinkers, and writers.[66]

Yet the partial victories of Marxism—which, *as a doctrine*, found a resonance only among the partly educated, the "lowest types"—are due to the religious crisis which is a moral, a philosophical, and a theological one at the same time. As E.F.W. Tomlinson said, "Because men cannot do without a philosophy, and if they reject the good one they must do with the dregs of all the rest. Dialectical materialism is an agglomeration of all the dregs of the wayward metaphysics of the nineteenth century."[67] Alongside this, as we have said before, there is in Marxism a curious eschatological vision, consciously-subconsciously copied from Christianity, an ecstatic waiting for the Second Coming of the Pan-Proletarian Christ, oddly counterbalanced by the antinomy of a purely mechanical predetermined notion of history with loud if not hysterical appeals to sanguinary revolutions and sacrifices. This dogmatism and orthodoxy jointly create the bad conscience among the watered-down Marxists, the "Social Democrats" Western style and the Laborites when they are confronted with the Communists. This bad conscience is the reason why so many Social Democrats or Socialists in the satellite world let themselves be bossed, forced, and coaxed into unitary Socialist (*de facto* completely Moscow-controlled) parties of which the Socialist Unitary Party (*Sozialistische Einheitspartei Deutschlands,* S. E. D.) of the so-called German Democratic Republic (D. D. R.) is the most typical. This is also the reason why Western Socialist parties, when hearing the "call of the wild," suddenly get weak in their knees.

In England Marx had contacts with the English Socialists who were, in a way, the forerunners of the Labor party. The founder of British Socialism was Robert Owen, the son of a shopkeeper. At the age of twenty this gifted man was the director of a textile factory and soon succeeded in making himself independent. In New Lanark, in Scotland, he established a model factory which can be regarded as a social rather than a socialistic experiment.[68] Yet Owen did not stop at the realization of social ideas. Soon he began to show an interest for socialistic dreams. In 1824 he went to the United States where he bought the lands, property, and livestock of Georg Rapp, leader of a German Communist sect, who had established a settlement in New Harmony, Indiana, not far from Evansville. The "Rappites" went to Pennsylvania and in 1826 New Harmony was revived with a fresh crop of immigrants under Owen's guidance. Some of them were men of intelligence, education, and high moral qualities; others were eccentrics and "marginal characters" who disturbed the whole order. Thus the experiment failed totally within two years.

Owen returned to England in 1829. He, the man of mere reforms, had now become a radical Socialist. Because of his attacks on "organized religion" and on the basic tenets of Christianity he lost much of the general respect as well as the public support he had received in earlier years. Although he was one of the cofounders of the first trade unions in 1833, Owen's interest lay rather in the guilds and cooperatives than in modern type trade unions. With advancing years his crotchety and cranky ideas multiplied. Actually he founded a new ethical system (rather than a religion) which his supporters spread all over England in "Halls of Science." The essence of this teaching was that man is *essentially a product of his environment*, an idea which profoundly influenced Marx and can be considered today an almost essential part of the folklore of Western half-education. For Marx it was the system of production that formed man and created the super-structure of all thinking: Marx attacked free will no less than Owen, who was convinced that through environment anyone's character could be formed, made to order. His strong belief in education found a power-ful echo in Northern Europe and North America. Yet in spite of his determinism, his attitude toward ethics was a far more positive one than that of Marx. Before his death Owen turned toward spiritualism.

Marx founded his International Workers' Association in 1864, six years after Owen's death. This was the First International whose history is marked by the bitter struggle between the real Socialists and the Anarchists under Bakunin's leadership.[69] Marx's strong dislike for Russia and the Russians[70] was partly colored by his hatred for Bakunin, the Russian anarchist nobleman who in turn converted Prince Kropotkin to his ideas.[71] Marx had Bakunin expelled in 1872 and the seat of the First International was transferred to New York where the organization died a lingering death. The antagonism between the professorial, petty stickler, Marx, and the dashing ex-officer of the Imperial Russian Army had been ruinous.

Nor did Marx get along with another dashing person, Ferdinand Lassalle. Son of a Jewish merchant in Breslau and the first organizer of the German workers, Lassalle was an immensely colorful character. Again and again accused of this or that political misdemeanor, he was frequently acquitted. Courageous, witty, a lover of the fair sex, and a playwright, he was liked neither by Marx nor by Engels. Long con-nected with Countess Sophie Hatzfeld, whose lawyer he was, he was finally killed in a duel with a Rumanian near Geneva over the hand and heart of Helene von Dönniges, the daughter of a Bavarian diplomat.

Lassalle was intellectually not unique, but he had an excellent mind and published several essays on a variety of political and social questions as well as a volume on Heraclitus from a Hegelian viewpoint. He dreamed of the emancipation of the German worker through the aid of the state and made a passionate appeal to William I to transform the Kingdom of Prussia into a "social monarchy." Bismarck, who knew him well and respected him, said in his eulogy in the Diet that Lassalle had been a thorough royalist, though not quite sure whether Prussia should be ruled by the Hohenzollerns or the Lassalles. A brilliant conversationalist, impeccably dressed, a gourmet, this high-living man who was the idol of the German working class unavoidably became the object of Marx's intense hatred. Had he lived longer—he was only thirty-nine years old when he died—he would in all likelihood have given an entirely different turn to the development of socialism in the heart of Europe and thus to the world. Marx must have breathed more freely when his competitor died in 1864. Three years later the first volume of *Das Kapital* was published.

The weaknesses of Marxian thought are manifold. The "mature" Marx became less interested in philosophical quests. His general disillusionment due to political disappointments (above all the failure of the Paris *Commune*) increased his bitterness heightened by constant financial worries.[72] His character drove all his friends away with the exception of Engels. He sought forgetfulness in the arms of his housekeeper, Helene Demuth (which means "humility"), who bore him a son whom Engels loyally claimed to have begotten. (The true story leaked out much later.[73]) Bitterness perhaps also acted as a brake on his mind and work, which made very slow progress. His solitude and isolation caused him to make grave errors precisely concerning the human character, errors which subsequently affected the entire Marxist landscape, primarily in countries where Marxism became the state religion. Marx seems to have been unaware of the dictum of Pascal that man is neither beast nor angel, and he who wants to turn him into an angel will inevitably degrade him to the level of a beast—a thought also expressed in our thesis of the enforced monastic life. Indeed the coercive "Paradise" becomes a Hell. Another short-circuit in his line of thought is due to his rejection of ideology, while he himself created one.[74] He could point out that what he preached was not an ideology which, naturally, rests on mere ideas, but that it represented an outline of facts and laws which were active in this world. He just told the shape of things to come against which resistance was vain—just as one could not fight an exact meteorological forecast. Yet if this really *were* the case, why then the movements, the parties, the intrigues, the secret police, the concentration camps, the armies, the wars, the propaganda, the broadcasts? Only to speed up a "natural evolution"? In that case shouldn't a little patience be called for? Questions like these have remained unanswered now for some time. Yet Marx had and still has a fairly universal appeal. He appeals to the "left" in us, he personifies a temptation which we have to overcome. Jean Paul in his *Quintus Fixlein* says that in every century the Almighty sends us an evil genius to tempt us. In the nineteenth century this spirit was Karl Marx.

C. The Fabians

Marx died in 1883. German socialism, which means the German Social Democratic party, went through a very difficult period. It became more and more evident that many of the ideas and theories of Marx were not true to fact, true to life. Revisionism loomed around the corner. In 1889 the Second International was established. Engels died in 1895. By this time only fanatics still insisted that the "forces of reaction" were hell-bent on destroying, exploiting, and humiliating the working class, which had friends, supporters, defenders in all social layers and camps. One of the major reasons for the break between William II and Bismarck was the difference in their attitudes toward organized labor and social legislation. The young emperor was prolabor. Bismarck had to remind him that the owners and the directors of the factories were also his subjects, expecting loyalty from him as he expected loyalty from them.[75]

Revisionism or rather a more elastic version of socialism was also born in Britain. In 1883 an ethical discussion club in London fathered a special group which slowly assumed a Socialist character. George Bernard Shaw, Sidney and Beatrice Webb (later Lord and Lady Passfield), and William Morris belonged to it. By 1887 the "Fabian Society" ("Society of the Fabians") had a definite profile. Soon the *Fabian Tracts* began rolling from the printer's press. The society took its name from Quintus Fabius Maximus Cunctator, the Roman general famous for his hesitant and cautious way of waging the Second Punic War. In other words, the society adopted a manner of investigating and promoting Socialist ideas entirely at variance with Continental dogmatism and very much in keeping with the trend toward understatement, compromise, and halfway measures so characteristic of the English (and, one might add, the Austrians, who have their own version for the word "muddling through.")

Much of the economic theory of the Fabians was supplied by George Bernard Shaw, whose persuasive arguments and dashing literary style were the talk of the British intellectual world. (Still, the Irish in him often made him talk with his tongue in his cheek, and he could be extremely nonconformist among these neoconformists, for instance, by praising Mussolini which evoked shrieks of indignation.) Sidney Webb criticized the Marxist theories concerning the increasing misery of the working class and the inevitable collapse of the entire capitalist system. Orthodox Marxism was rejected as much as the theory of class war. These ideas just did not appeal to the English character. Yet there was considerable enthusiasm for the nationalization of the means of production, which included the *soil*. This reflected the potent influence of the American Henry George and his single tax.

It was only after 1890 that the Fabians (in this respect strongly animated by Beatrice Webb) tried to hitch their wagon to the rising star of the trade unions. Fabians were among the founders of the Independent Labour Party in 1893 and the British Labour Party in 1900. They did not, however, concentrate on the Labour Party alone but tried to propagandize the ranks of the other parties as well. They were particularly successful with the left wing of the Liberal party which gradually veered under Lloyd George's leadership toward social legislation and Socialist ideas. A young ambitious apostate from the Tories with very radical ideas delighted Lloyd George and enchanted Beatrice Webb. His name was Winston S. Churchill.[76] Indeed many of the great social reforms before World War I were enacted by the Liberals but promoted, suggested, and sponsored by the Fabians. The program adopted by the Labour Party in 1918 was drawn up by Sidney Webb and in the years to come the Fabians were not only extremely active in the field of social legislation but also in foreign politics where they later strongly supported the League of Nations and methodically promoted leftist causes all over the globe.

The influence of the Fabians on the American scene was and remains considerable. They have always maintained intimate connections with a number of American universities and with the Foreign Policy Association which they often provided with speakers lecturing all over the United States. Typical of them was Professor Harold Laski, famous for his correspondence with Oliver Wendell Holmes, Jr., for his clever formulations, and for his sometimes unbridled imagination.[77] In the moral

142

disarmament of the English-speaking countries vis-à-vis the Soviet Union, the Fabians played an eminent role. They loved disarmament —an affection influencing labor policies during the 1930s and leading, in combination with Tory provincialism, to the state of dangerous unpreparedness that prevailed when the Nazi menace appeared on the horizon. One really could not disarm, ridicule "Colonel Blimp," sneer at "militarism," and make a stand against the brown bullies. It was dangerous to rely on the Red Army alone.

Fabians, on the other hand, supplied socialism in Eastern Europe with ample intellectual ammunition. One of the Fabians, J. A. Hobson, together with G. D. H. Cole, an initiator of "Guild Socialism," was the author of *Imperialism,* published in 1902.[78] This book inspired Lenin to write his pamphlet *Imperialism as the Last Stage of Capitalism* which came out in 1915. In this work the Russian Social Democrat living in his Swiss exile claimed that capitalism, as a last means of expansion, has to engage in aggressive wars not only to conquer new markets, but also to divert the masses from the class struggle.

Fabianism is more than just the organized and publicized outlook of a group of intellectuals. It represents a version of leftism most congenial to Britishers and Americans. Fabianism has been instrumental not only in undermining the belief in free enterprise, individuality, and personal responsibility in favor of the *Versorgungsstaat,* the "Provider State" rather than "Welfare State," but also in spreading an atmosphere of illusion and confusion as regards the dangers from the East. Psychologically and intellectually American pseudoliberalism, the entire left-of-center mentality not only west of the Atlantic but even west of the Channel is deeply indebted to Fabianism which in that area, to be true, often met halfway with popular notions and concepts. The ideology of the "moderate left" in the English-speaking countries, however, is by no means harmless or only of academic interest. As we are going to see in another chapter, this mixture of prejudices and ignorance has already led twice in our century to major catastrophes whose effects are still with us all. It might even lead to further evil developments.

Chapter 10

From Socialism to Communism

It was not in the industrial West, as Marx had predicted, but in Eastern Europe that socialism reaped its first concrete, tangible victories. When Marx and Engels wrote the *Communist Manifesto* they also provided for a Danish edition but not for a Russian edition. Yet the Socialist victory in Russia is one of the most important facts in modern history and is worth being a subject of special study. However, there are only three aspects of the Russian Revolution we would like to put under the magnifying glass.

Problem One concerns the question of whether there is something inherently "communist" or collective in the Russian soul.

Problem Two poses the question of whether the Russian Revolution was in any way the "natural reaction" to the "horrors of Czarism," a swinging of the pendulum to the other side, if not a continuation of the old regime in a new form.

Problem Three leads us to the examination of the factual strength of "Maximalist Socialism," i.e., of communism at the time of the Revolution.

As to the first question, we must state emphatically not only that there is nothing inherently collective or conformist about the Russian mind and outlook, but that the Russians are extreme individualists with an anarchical bent of mind. Those who defend the theory of the "inborn trend toward collectivism" usually cite the institutions of the *mir* (land communities) and of the *artel'* (common workshops) as well as the principle of *sobornost'* (commonalty) in the theology of the Eastern Church. Yet the *mir* was such an abysmal failure that Stolypin had to liquidate it in the early twentieth century, and *sobornost'* has its (admittedly not too close) analogy in the Catholic concept of the Mystical Body. Still the Catholic world no less than the world of the Eastern church has always been the cradle of anarchist parties. It is the world of the Reformation Churches which cultivated strict order, discipline, frugality, conformity, sticking to rules, cooperation, and consensus through massive persuasion and compromise. (In Europe *black* has always been the symbolic color for Catholics *and* anarchists!) Russia stood for extremes at all times, but conformity is only possible where the accepted norm is the "happy medium," the spirit of "fifty-fifty" remote from all absolutes, the *juste milieu* which Alexander Herzen despised so much.

Edward Crankshaw was perhaps the first author in the English-speaking world who used the anarchical mentality of the Russians as a key to their character and thus to their political behavior. "The Russian," he wrote, "is a man who regards compromises not as a sign of strength, but as a sign of the dilution of the personality, or self-betrayal, who is, moreover, susceptible in the extreme to outside influence of every kind, who is, in a word, completely experimental and mentally *free*, in the way that, in the West, only artists are experimental and free (and by no means all of those)." He then went on to explain how such a profoundly anarchical people, despairing of finding an inner cohesion, are willing to accept as a necessary evil "control from above." He added, finally, "All this, I suggest, is the rigidity of a naturally fluid people who have to forge hoops of iron around themselves or disintegrate utterly. And it all comes from a natural individualism which makes our vaunted, rugged individualism look like an abandonment of personality."[1]

Russia, Spain, Italy, and France had, by no means accidentally, the largest anarchist parties at the turn of the century. In Russia the Anarchists (S.R., "Social Revolutionaries") were the ones who committed practically all the acts of violence. The Communists were too shrewd, too clever to engage in mere terrorism. Conspiracy, organization and mass risings were their means.

The anarchical bent of the South and East Europeans (and of the Catholic or Orthodox nations living in other parts of the world) also makes for a proliferation of parties which, together with an uncompromising extremism, render parliamentary life difficult if not impossible. Hence the almost inevitable failure of the "democratic experiment" in that area.

Point Two is concerned with the swinging of the pendulum. "Where there's smoke, there's fire" is an often quoted proverb in America and Britain, presupposing a certain "rationality of emotions." Yet history (like nature) shows that a big fire can produce very little smoke, and a small fire a lot. And before answering the "pendulum" argument, let us remember that the bolsheviks did not replace an absolute or even a constitutional monarchy, but a democratic republic—the republic of Alexander Kerensky, a moderate Social Revolutionary. And if we apply the smoke-fire theory to Germany, then the Weimar Republic must have been unmitigated hell—which was not the case either. Let us therefore burn many of our history textbooks and give up the idea that history makes "sense" in a mathematical or mechanical way. Neither does great drama.

When we talk about Imperial Russia we ought to bear in mind that after 1905 it was in many ways very different from what it had been in, let us say, 1890. One might easily imagine a bearded man with a newspaper under his arm walking across a street in St. Petersburg in 1912. Who is he? A deputy of the bolshevik wing of the Russian Social Democratic Party—in other words, a bolshevik sitting in the Duma. What sort of paper does he carry under his arm? *Pravda*. Where did he buy it? There, at the street corner. Of course, before 1905 people were less free, but Vyera Zassulitch, who tried to assassinate the police prefect Tryepov, was acquitted by a jury. Trotsky described how delightful Russian jails were, with what respect political "criminals" were treated by their wardens. Lenin suffered *ssylka,* exile in Siberia, but simple exile merely meant that one was forced to live in or near a certain village, received a meager pension but was still able to read, write, hunt, and fish. Life in Siberia around 1900 was no worse than life in North Dakota or Saskatchewan at that time. A friend of mine has even seen the copy of the letter Lenin's wife wrote from Shushenskoye to the Governor in Irkutsk protesting against the insufficient staff she had been alloted.

Nor should one have wrong conceptions about the agrarian situation. At the time of the outbreak of the Revolution in 1917 the peasantry owned nearly 80 percent of the arable land,[2] whereas in Britain more than half of the fertile soil belonged to large estates. (Yet Britain had no violent agrarian movement and Russia had.) Illiteracy was down to about 56 percent, and the schools were multiplying by leaps and bounds. It is also important to note that from a sociological viewpoint the lower classes were much better represented in the Russian high school-colleges than in those of Western Europe.[3] The misconceptions about the Russian class structure prevailing in the Western world are so manifold and so deeply rooted that they seem ineradicable. Reading the brilliant three volumes by Anatole Leroy-Beaulieu on late nineteenth-century Russia, *L'Empire des tsars et les Russes,* one gets a glimpse of a totally mixed society not based on birth or money. Needless to say, the same impression is conveyed by the great Russian novelists of that period.[4] As a matter of fact, Russia before the Red October was Europe's "Eastern America," a country where social mobility was greater than anywhere else, where titles had by no means the nimbus they had in the West, where fortunes could be made overnight by intelligent and thrifty people regardless of their social background. And if one knew *how* to speak and to write one indeed had total liberty even before 1905.

Naturally, the lot of the worker was as difficult in Imperial Russia *as everywhere else in a nascent industrial society.* This was as true of England in the first third of the nineteenth century as it is of contemporary Socialist India. Yet the Imperial government had never any intention of favoring manufacturers unilaterally, nor did it ever side unilaterally with the large landowners. (The emancipation of the serfs—who had never been slaves—was the work of "autocracy" against the wish of the landowning class.) Manya Gordon could say without exaggeration that "records have proved conclusively that Russia was a pioneer in labor legislation."[5] The *Okhrana,* the secret police, actually started to aid the workers in the establishment of trade unions so that they could defend themselves against exploitation. Actually, a quarter of a century after the Red October the living standards of the workers were lower than they had been in 1914, a fact we find well documented in Manya Gordon's book, *Workers Before and After Lenin.* Ilya Ehrenburg, in his recently published memoirs, tells us that in the early 1950s there were fewer domestic animals in the USSR than on the same territory in 1916.[6] This situation has not changed much since.[7]

No doubt certain aspects of the Imperial regime had not improved much even after 1905. There was discrimination against Catholics (but not against Lutherans) in the higher ranks of the administration, but this was also the case in Scandinavia. The Jesuits were outlawed, but they still are in Switzerland. Jews could not reside in the northern and eastern provinces unless they held university degrees or were "merchants first class." (These restrictions were lifted for those who became Christians: The discrimination was purely religious, not ethnic nor racial.) Only a certain percentage of the university students could be of the Jewish faith, but a *numerus clausus* of this sort was not unknown in American universities, especially in medical schools priding themselves on their "liberalism."

In higher female education old Russia was also a pioneer. It was the literary leader of Europe before World War I and had some of the best textbooks on the Continent. Its universities were as good as any in the Western world. Its *intelligentsiya* (a Russian word!) was perhaps confused but in richness and diversity of ideas it was unexcelled.[8]

However, this brings us to Problem Three: How did it happen that communism could overpower that great nation? Obviously the turmoil following the lost war provided the setting for the Revolution which was not made by the industrial proletariat. There were practically no workers among the leaders of the Russian Social Democratic party. And when in 1903, at the London congress of this then illegal party, the majority voted for a radical program while the minority stuck to more moderate demands, a real schism took place. The *bol'sheviki* (majoritarians, maximalists) opposed the *men' sheviki* (minoritarians, minimalists), though both still called themselves Social Democrats: Only the bolsheviks favored the Communist label which they have used officially since 1918.[9] By 1921 the schism had become permanent: The Social Democrats remained loyal to the Second International, while the Communists established the Third International.

The Bolsheviks, no less than the Mensheviks, were led by men who either belonged to the lower nobility (*dvoryane*),[10] or had a middle-class intellectual background (there were Jews and gentiles among them), or were ex-seminarians. When Joseph de Maistre prophesied that the coming Russian revolution would be led by a "Pugatshov with a university background,"[11] he was not far wrong. This description fits Lenin[12] only too well, but it could be applied to most other leaders who combined more or less the three great revolutionary gifts: intellectuality, the talent for organizing, and oratorical magnetism.

Yet all these talkers and doers rolled into one could never have won without the aid of rebellious soldiers and sailors consisting mostly of peasants and sons of peasants. The working class of Russia was then only a very small percentage of the population. (We have no exact statistics.) After fighting a rough foreign enemy under oppressive discipline, the soldiers and sailors were now looking for an easy victory. They also wanted to get rid of their officers. Strongly represented in the "Councils (*sovyeti*) of Workers, Peasants and Soldiers," they helped the intellectual rabble-rousers to win the day. The middle classes were not only a relatively small layer, they were also unorganized and lacked all cohesion. The Kerensky government fought the rebellious soldiers in the last stage with a female regiment that was decimated, defeated, and taken prisoner by the half-drunken Red heroes. The scenes which followed would have delighted the Divine Marquis, as would the bestial slaughter of the Imperial family in Yekaterinburg.[13] Kerensky wanted to have them shipped to Britain, but Lloyd George refused because to the "liberal" Prime Minister, eager to achieve victory at all costs, Nicholas II, desperately wanting peace, was a traitor. The British public would not stand for it, he declared.[14] It was manifest in World War I that we have to see in the "moderate left" the force most opposed to peace and prone to the worst excesses of nationalism. In England the main culprit was the leftist David Lloyd George, in America the Democratic Party led by Woodrow Wilson, in France the old *Communard* Clemenceau and in Russia the "progressive republican" regime of Alexander Kerensky. Those who were eager for peace were the crowned heads, the Pope, and, it must be candidly admitted, the representatives of the working class who tried to gather in Stockholm.

It was evident, however, that in Russia the fall of the monarchy in March 1917 had destroyed the center and object of all loyalty. It was impossible to stabilize the country on a *juste milieu*, in a middle of the road position. Effective opposition against the victorious Communists came only from the right and from the Anarchists. A series of civil wars (1918-1920) followed, fought on a military rather than a revolutionary basis. From these wars the Communists emerged as victors not only because they held the center of the Russian railroad net but also because they had the support of the peasantry which was thoroughly intoxicated by dreams of further land gains.

The first big agrarian partition had taken place after the emancipation of the serfs, when land was allotted in the form of the *mir* to entire communities. The *mir* was a complete failure, so Stolypin,[15] Minister of the Interior and then Prime Minister, decided to carve up the *mir*-lands and to give them in permanence to individual holders, which set an end to the periodic famines. He planned additional partitions of latifundia so that by 1930 the large landowners would have held no more than 11 percent of the arable land. (They had only slightly more than 22 percent in 1916).[16] While thrifty peasants now got ahead, the lazy ones sold their plots to the more ambitious, the so-called *kulaks*. Since ambition is not considered a great virtue in Russia,[17] the *kulaks* became generally disliked.

The Communists promised to divide *all* estates not owned by peasants. The result was a fairly general adherence of the peasantry to the Communists. (This was less true in the Ukraine or in the Cossack—Don and Kuban—areas.) The "Whites" fought a losing battle because the soldiers (practically all of them peasants and peasants' sons) ran over to the Red Army which promised them land. After the collapse of the White Armies (which had some battalions consisting of officers and noncoms only), the peasants failed to till the land they had, and new famines were the result, whereupon the Red authorities started to confiscate food. The reaction to this was a further lessening of production: Money, after all, was worthless. Then collectivization had to be enforced. First the *kulaks* were denounced, attacked, expropriated, and frequently deported. Next the lesser peasants were enslaved. The Russian countryside, far more so than the cities, went through incredible agonies. In a sense this was poetic justice. To this day the agrarian sector of the USSR is the poorhouse of the nation—and its unhappiest part too.

As one can see, each part of Russia has its share of guilt in the Revolution. So too, of course, have other "Christian" nations and, last but not least, those Germans such as General Ludendorff who reimported Lenin to Russia in 1917. (Which only proves that it is criminal to commit immoralities for the benefit of one's nation. Right causes *are* universal causes—such as the Christian tradition in government. The thinly disguised contempt with which the bolsheviks treated the Germans during the peace negotiations in Brest-Litovsk was well deserved.) The Russian working class was perhaps the least guilty. Eminently guilty were the avaricious peasants and, above all, the brilliant, scintillating, amiable *intelligentsiya*. For generations it had undermined the fabric of Holy Mother Russia, either by siding with the Social Revolutionaries, the *Narodnaya Volya,* the Social Democrats, or by being "open minded,"[18] by deriding the national heritage, by spreading polite doubt, by stupidly imitating Western patterns, ideas, and institutions which never would do for Russia. Dostoyevski in *The Possessed* (*Byessy*) has shown very vividly how liberal relativism and skepticism spawned the monstrosities which came to the surface in the last decades before the Revolution.[19] And Dostoyevski knew. In his youth he had been a leftist himself and, as a member of the Pyetrashevski conspiracy, he had been condemned to death and had lived in a Siberian prison, in "The House of the Dead."[20]

In one of the most brilliant books on the Communist Revolution, *Tsarstvo Antikhrista*,[21] Dmitri Myerezhkovski wrote: "Not on account of their own strength are the Bolsheviks powerful but only thanks to your weakness. They know what they want, but you do not know what you want. They all want the same thing: among you everybody wants something else.''

And he also quotes Rozanov: ''The deeper reason for all that has happened now has to be found in the fact that in the civilized world vanishing Christianity has created enormous cavities and now everything tumbles down into them.''[22]

In Russia, however, (and some time later in Germany) these cavities were not only of a religious but of a political nature. It is important to remember that there always will be a more or less obvious, a more or less subtle, a more or less invisible connection between the two. In the case of Russia it was the small, evil glow of communism that lit up the entire dark void until, at last, in our days the residue of Christianity along with the natural protest of man against an inhuman ideology generated a spirit of resistance.

The picture offered to us by dogmatic socialism[23] in action is strikingly similar to that of the French Revolution. No wonder, since the leadership had a very similar sociological structure: bitter and confused members of the nobility,[24] murderously idealistic intellectual bourgeois, alienated wicked priests, friars, and seminarians. There were almost the same high-flown speeches, the destruction of ancient buildings, the desecration of tombs and cemeteries, the furious attacks against religion, the declamatory pathos of writers, the complete one-track-mindedness in political thought, mob violence, and turmoil in the countryside accompanied by arson and robbery. Gracchus Babeuf, after all, was worshiped and exalted by the *bolsheviki* as their forerunner. And instead of the virtuous *citoyen* the virtuous proletarian was now arrayed against the ''rotten old order'' as a new ideal.

This was an image to gladden the heart of ''progressives'' the world over. However, what they overlooked was the price for introducing what was really a retrogressive system: the thousands of people killed in the Revolution, male and female soldiers;[25] the two million killed in the two years of civil war; the six million who died in the famines of 1920-1922; the eight million who perished under the same circumstances; the hundreds of thousands executed by the Tshe-Ka,[26] the GPU, the NKVD, the MVD, the KGB; the millions who died in Stalin's concentration camps, including Estonians, Latvians, Lithuanians, Tartars, Jews, and Volga-Germans, all deported under inhuman conditions. But even this gigantic massacre is dwarfed by the record of Red China. Mao Tse-tung murdered in a shorter period millions more than Lenin,

Stalin and his successors combined. And today we see how a heroic Chinese communism in Indochina fights to the last Vietnamese while the Americans at least risk their own skins in preventing the massacre of at least four million innocents. To these staggering numbers must be added those killed in "foreign wars" fought over ideological issues.

Indeed the calamities caused by Soviet communism are not confined to Russia. (Nor did Chinese communism remain a "local" affair.) World War II would never have taken place had not Stalin given the "green light" to Hitler by promising a simultaneous attack against Poland.[27] One of its consequences was (with Western acquiescence, to be sure) the tyranny established in Europe between the Soviet border and the Iron Curtain. Going further back, there was the Russian intervention in Spain and, at the root of all this, the reaction to the Soviet challenge in the form of Fascism and, even worse, of German National Socialism. In character and basic doctrine these reactions very much resembled "communistic socialism" (which is genuine socialism) and differed from it only in financial techniques. While the Western totalitarians accepted statism and the total subordination of the individual to the whole, while they clearly represented another form of materialism, they nevertheless revolted against the Russian edition of Communist danger, against the new imperialism emanating from Moscow.[28] They were not the "enemies" of communism but its "competitors," which is a very different matter, even if there can be greater bitterness in rivalry than in opposition. And, as a matter of fact, the tensions and hatreds mounted literally to a cutthroat competition, a term which under the circumstances very well illustrates this tragic and terrifying issue, expressed geographically in one of the worst wars history has ever seen, the "Third War of Austrian Succession," commonly called World War II. In this struggle the economic left overpowered the biological left, while the "moderate left" shared in none of the spoils and was in spite of all their efforts and merits the loser.

152

Chapter 11

From Marxism to Fascist Nationalism

The first systematic leftist and nationalistic opposition against Moscow-centered communism came from Italy. It was *fascism*; it had clearly socialistic origins. The *fasces* were the Roman symbols of authority and they reappeared in the symbols of the French Republic and on the American dime at a later period. In the earlier 1890s *fasci* ("bundles," leagues) of workers so-called *fasci dei lavoratori* created grave disturbances primarily in Sicily, but also in parts of Tuscany. They were imbued with romantic socialist ideas and could only be subdued by force.

The founder of this century's fascism was Benito Mussolini, the son of an Italian Socialist blacksmith who had two sons; the older he called Benito (and not, in the Italian way, Benedetto) after Benito Juárez, the Mexican Indian who, supported by the United States, had defeated and then executed Emperor Maximilian Ferdinand Joseph, a Hapsburg and brother of Franz Joseph. The younger Mussolini was baptized Arnaldo after the medieval revolutionary Arnaldo di Brescia, a cleric who protested against the wealth and power of the Popes. Young Benito Mussolini was also a fanatical Socialist and started out to become, like his mother, a teacher. Later he went to Switzerland to take literature courses at the Universities of Lausanne and Geneva while earning his livelihood as a mason. He had difficulties with the police, was temporarily jailed, and later went to Trent, then in Austria, where he worked as a journalist for two newspapers, printed in Italian, which had nationalistic and

Socialist tendencies. He became convinced that the local population, though ethnically Italian in its vast majority, preferred Austrian rule and, due to clerical influences, hated the idea of joining Italy. Mussolini also considered the Austrian administration superior to that of his own country.[1]

The future *duce del fascismo* also used his stay to study German quite thoroughly, but was finally expelled by the Austrian authorities who were suspicious of his nationalistic and irredentistic propaganda. Back in Italy Mussolini became an agitator against the Italian War with Turkey over Tripolitania (Libya). As a good Socialist young Mussolini considered this an imperialistic war of aggression. In 1913 he published a book in Rome, the fruit of certain contacts he had made in Trent with Czech nationalists. The book was called *Giovanni Hus, il verïdico*, "John Hus, the Truthful." It was badly written, showed a marked anti-Catholic bias (as did his one and only novel *The Cardinal's Mistress*), but was far more political than religious. Actually Mussolini was also attracted in earlier years by unorthodox Socialists such as Sorel and by anarchists such as Prince Kropotkin.[2]

What interested Mussolini more than anything else was the popular movement which had sprung up after the burning of Hus at the stake in 1415—one of the great blunders the history of the Catholic Church abounds in. The more moderate followers of Hus, the Utraquists, soon made their peace with the Church and were given concessions in their rite while the Taborites, the radical wing, embraced extreme religious, social, and political propositions. In the Taborite movement (so-called after the newly founded fortified city of Tábor in Bohemia) nationalism ("ethnicism"), democracy, and various socialistic trends were united in a new synthesis for the first time in Europe. It was obvious that such a violently *collectivistic and identitarian* current immediately encountered the strongest opposition from the Catholic Church, which is supranational, has always recognized the principle of idoneity against all egalitarian manias, and has a long tradition of patriarchalism, of respect for the father image.[3]

The Taborites waged violent racial-ideological wars not only in the Lands of the Crown of St. Wenceslas (Bohemia, Moravia, Silesia), but also in the surrounding areas—Austria, Saxony, Upper Hungary. They were feared for their utter inhumanity; for their tendency to kill all men, women, and children in the cities they conquered; for their limitless hatred for everything German. In Komotau, for instance, all males were slaughtered—except thirty who had to bury the others.[4] The Hussite women were completely "emancipated" and worse than the men in committing atrocities—against other women. In one case they undressed their victims completely and burned them in groups, reserving special cruelties for those who were pregnant.[5] When the Taborites stormed Prachatitz (Prachatice) in 1420 they spared the lives of the Utraquists but burned all the other men alive.[6] Their hostility for everything Catholic and German was matched only by their loathing for the nobility—and this in spite of the fact that, as in the later leftist revolution, members of the nobility frequently acted as leaders for the bestialized masses. Žižka of Trocnov was one of them. Here again one has to remember that sadistic tortures are the expression of hatreds and that hatreds always originate from some sense of inferiority, or some sort of weakness. When we feel or really are superior, we have the choice to treat others with contempt and pettiness or, much better, with love and magnanimity. It is the truly inferior person in a superior position who yields to his sadistic drives. Moreover, there is also a statistical aspect to this state of affairs. It is almost always the inferior majorities who try to *exterminate* the superior minorities, who surely would agree with Ovid's *Bene vixit qui bene latuit.* Privileged minorities might have a strong *libido dominandi,* but the drive toward physical extermination always has a root in the inferiority complex of the suspicious and envious masses, who in a deeper sense always are and feel helpless, hence their cruelty.

The importance of these events, centering in fifteenth-century Bohemia, cannot be exaggerated. They constitute a phase in the development of the entire Western world which produced currents of a decisive and irrevocable character. (Of course, all history is, in a sense, irrevocable.) True, we should not forget that John Hus is unthinkable without the intellectual fatherhood of John Wyclif, an early nationalist (in the British-American sense of the term[8]). Hus *himself* was a theologian rather than a political theorist, and we have investigated elsewhere the connections between Hus and Luther.[9] Hus's ideas remained alive in the German-speaking regions adjoining Bohemia until Luther's days. What then was precisely the political character of the Taborite, the radical Hussite, movement? In the second half of the nineteenth century, while it was considered not only as fiercely nationalistic as radically leftist, we have to tone down this extreme judgment somewhat. But what is important to us is not so much the *reality* of a movement's character but rather the historic evolution of its *image.* (Something similar can be said of the American War of Independence in which the American folklore has become an "American Revolution" and as such frequently affects the mind of the average American.) However exaggerated the picture of Taborism, it had a great effect primarily on the Czechs, but in the long run also on their German neighbors (the so-called "Sudeten Germans") and they were often prepared to forget the anti-German character of Taboritism while cherishing its anti-Catholic and sometimes also its anti-Austrian bias.

Professor Josef Pekař was probably right in his hotly contested thesis that the Taborites were neither quite as democratic nor as socialistic as had been maintained earlier, and that the presentation of other scholars (Masaryk, Palacký, Krofta, Hajn, Czerwenka) was at least in part erroneous.[10] Until the middle of the nineteenth century the Taborite movement was morally rejected by the vast majority of Czechs and Germans as an outbreak of primeval savagery. Palacký's mythological presentation changed all this. With the simultaneous rise of nationalism, democracy, and socialism, the Czechs came to cherish the idea that they were the forerunners of modernity, and Taboritism received a reinterpretation which went hand in hand with a reevaluation of Hus among the Germans. The end of the nineteenth century saw the organization of the "Away from Rome" movement (*Los-von-Rom-Bewegung*)[11] especially strong among the Germans from Bohemia and Moravia, and now the memory of Hus, hitherto a despised Czech nationalist hero, suddenly became sacred. An entire German nationalistic literature sprang up in praise of Hus (whose name, written with a "double s," suddenly sounded quite German). Here it is interesting to note that to the Czech nationalists (then as now) the Catholic Church appeared as the German-Austrian Church of the Hapsburgs, and when Thomas G. Masaryk joined the Bohemian Brethren (*bratři*), his break with Rome had simultaneously a religious and national significance. (Needless to say, to German nationalists and Nazis the "Church of Rome" appeared to be "Latin-Slav" and "alien"—*artfremd*—almost like the allegedly pro-Slav Jews who were excoriated by Masaryk as pro-German Hapsburg protégés.) As a form of neurosis, race-conscious nationalism almost always ignores logic and knowledge: In the East European civil wars between 1918 and 1920 Jews were slaughtered for a variety of contradictory reasons, as capitalists and as communists, as friends of the Ukrainians, as Polonophiles, as pro-German—just as it suited the circumstances. However, it can be argued that during World War I the Jews in Eastern Europe sympathized with the Central Powers who gave them civil equality (as, for instance, in the Treaty of Bucharest, 1918).

What other momentous effects the "National Socialist" presentation of Taboritism had in central Europe we shall discuss later. At this stage we are primarily interested in its influence on Mussolini who was an Italian Socialist with a nationalist outlook and, at the outbreak of World War I, was immediately in favor of intervention. He berated the Catholic Church, the House of Savoy, and the conservative circles for not immediately bringing Italy into the war on the side of the Allies, and it is likely that he received monetary aid from France for his newly founded dissident Socialist newspaper, *Il Popolo d'Italia*. We cannot doubt, however, that even in his heart he really stood for intervention on the side of the Western Powers, although Italy, together with Germany and Austria-Hungary, formed the Triple Alliance and her national interests would have been served much better had she remained in it.[12] Italy could—and did—gain rather little from the defeated Austria-Hungary except territories inhabited predominantly by non-Italians. Italy's belligerence on the side of the Central Powers would have resulted in their speedy victory, since this would have forced the French to fight in the north as well as on a second front in the south, thus enabling the Germans to outnumber them more effectively and the Austrians to devote themselves wholeheartedly to the war in the East. Mussolini, however, had *ideological* reasons for his switch from pacifism to belligerence on the "wrong" side, and when Italy joined England and France, he immediately volunteered and was severely wounded near the front by an exploding mortar.[13] By that time he had also given up his purely Marxist views and according to his own avowal became increasingly interested in Proudhon, Sorel, and the French Syndicalist movement.[14] Péguy, Nietzsche, and Lagardelle also had made a deep impression on him.[15]

Mussolini returned from the war as a non-Socialist and in order to stem the tide of chaos and anarchy this still staunch republican and leftist founded the *fasci di combattimento* whose real fighting force were the *squadristi*. They wanted to save Italy from total anarchy toward which the country indeed was headed. They also wanted to Italianize the newly-acquired regions wrested from Austria in total defiance of the principles of self-determination. They considered the preservation of the Austro-German character of the Central Tyrol a "national scandal" and brutally attacked the local population. The formal founding of the Fascist party, however, took place only late in 1921, the March on Rome in October 1922. (Mussolini went most of the way by train.) By that time the *Fascisti* already had wise support not only from ex-Socialists but also from the middle and upper classes.

Who was to blame for this development? Primarily the Communists and Socialists who had plunged the country into an indescribable confusion leading to near collapse. One strike followed the other. The present state of Italy (which is bad enough and shows ominous historical parallels) does not offer a complete analogy. At that time Communist bands occupied factories, paralyzed communications, established local soviets, and defied the central authority. There is no doubt that the constitutional monarchy, far too loyally adhering to the then existing constitutional laws, could no longer cope with the situation. It would have been the duty of the Crown to establish a temporary royal dictatorship with the help of the Army. Yet Victor Emmanuel III probably considered it more "democratic" for an existing party to shoulder the responsibility and thus he refused to proclaim the state of emergency desired by the weak Facta government whose resignation was accepted. Mussolini, appointed Prime Minister, had a hard time putting the brakes on the more radical (and more emphatically leftist) Fascists. Full dictatorship did not develop until 1925-1926. The transitional period lasted several years and the diarchy (King and *Duce*) until 1943, when the monarchy saved the country by having Mussolini arrested. Such a finale was not possible in Germany where Hitler fought to the bitter end and left the country divided and in ruins. Mussolini, "saved" by Otto Skorzeny and brought to Hitler's headquarters, proclaimed (in all likelihood upon Hitler's advice) the Italian Social Republic which collapsed in 1945.[16] A year later the Republic was revived with decisive Communist support.

Today it is possible to review Italian fascism more dispassionately and to see it in its right context: as an ideology *and* as a historic phenomenon within the Italian scene. We subscribe to the view of Hannah Arendt who pointed out that, compared with Nazi Germany or the Soviet Union, the Italian scene under fascism was hardly totalitarian. There can be no doubt that Fascist Italy was far more humane than the two tyrannies in the North.[17] The temperament of nations is a highly important factor in the character of any government, and Italian *umanesimo* and *umanità* have had their effects.

There was another aspect to fascism, although less apparent than in Russian communism and not at all present in German National Socialism. The countries of southern Europe, having played such an eminent part in history until enlightenment, liberalism, and technology speeded up the evolution of the North, were fatally eclipsed and "left behind." Italy was no exception. While Britain, the Netherlands, Germany, and Scandinavia were forging ahead, acquiring military and naval fame, and rapidly increasing their living standards, the Mediterranean nations, engaged in *dolce vita* and in *dolce far niente,* enjoyed blue skies, soft melodies, and delightful conversations—with a great deal of poverty. However, the presence of tourists from the affluent north created an inferiority complex which in turn fostered the desire to compete successfully with these progressive and powerful nations. The remedy seemed to be hard work, discipline, punctuality, cleanliness, the fight against corruption, control of morality, military prowess, artificial industrialization, obligatory sports, and propaganda for "national greatness." Fascism tried to promote all these efforts and drives. Foreign tourists were gratified to see the beggars disappear from the streets and the trains running on time. George Bernard Shaw, the great Fabian, had nothing but praise for Mussolini and thereby elicited cries of protest from Socialists. He was called a traitor, but he stuck to his guns: the Fascists were "progressive." Similarly, many a Russian nationalist was delighted by the industrialization of the USSR. Russian refugees gloated: "They are going to show the decadent West!" One has to know the USSR, as I do, to realize how desperate the Soviet desire is to outdo the United States above all.[18] Even Lenin's surrealist slogan: "Communism means all power to the Soviets plus electrification of the country," which one still sees everywhere, is a morbid piece of pseudo-Americanism.

Yet apart from this competitive urge conditioned by an inferiority complex there is still a purely ideological aspect to fascism, a solid piece of Socialist heritage and also of *Religionsersatz,* of synthetic religion, which made coexistence between fascism and the Catholic Church so difficult.[19] Fascism also had a Maurassian side insofar as it said "yes" to the Catholic Faith as a "national religion" and this attitude had a Machiavellian, a pragmatic basis.[20] In this and other respects fascism differed strongly from Spanish falangism and the Rumanian rather spiritual even if savage Iron Guard ideology.[21]

One need only read the pertinent passages about Italian fascism in the very interesting diaries of Victor Serge, a dissident Russian Communist, to understand the deep and lasting connection between the national and international leftist ideologies, socialism-communism and fascism. Serge writes about Nicola Bombacci, a Socialist who later returned to Italy and "collaborated." When Serge met him in his exile in Berlin (1923-1924), Bombacci told him that Mussolini owed much to the ideas of the Communists. "Why," Serge asked, "didn't you get rid of Mussolini at the time of the destruction of the cooperatives?" "Because our most militant and energetic men had gone over to him." Serge confesses that he then realized how much he was tortured by the attraction fascism exercised on the extreme left.

Equally interesting are the confessions of Henri Guilbeaux, another founder of the Komintern, made to Serge. Guilbeaux saw in Mussolini the real heir of Lenin. Serge concluded that fascism attracted so many of the revolutionaries by its "plebeian force and violence" and by its constructive program: to build schools, to drain swamps, to promote industrialization, to found an empire. Moreover, there was the vision of a New Order which, to the leftist mind, would come about when the groundwork done by the Fascists was crowned with socialism. "It is impossible to review the Fascist phenomenon without discovering the importance of its interrelations with revolutionary socialism,'' Serge confessed.[22]

In Massimo Rocca's well documented *How Fascism Became a Dictatorship* we find even more material about the leftist ties of fascism. Rocca insists that Mussolini in his last days thought of surrendering to the Socialist party, expecting to be spared by his old comrades. (Twice he had saved the life of Pietro Nenni.) Toward the end of 1922 (which means at the very beginning of Fascist rule) Mussolini was still trying in the Chamber to win over the extreme left through fiery appeals.[23] "For Mussolini," Rocca writes, "fascism was nothing but an interlude between his exit from the Socialist party and his future triumphal readmission, a hope nourished for twenty years."[24] In 1919 Mussolini still had praised the Communist seizure of the factories in Dalmine and in 1921 he had offered the Socialist party (P.S.I) cooperation in an antimonarchical and anticapitalist revolution. Mussolini's "conversion" to the monarchy came a few weeks before the *Marcia su Roma*, but his last truly trusted friend was a Socialist, Carlo Silvestri. And during his rule of the "Social Republic" (with the capital in Salò) Mussolini's loathing for the "bourgeoisie" and the "capitalists" again came out into the open. His hatred and contempt for the aristocracy had been strong at all times, as Vittorio, his son, confirmed. This also explains in part his hostile attitude toward his daughter Edda's marriage.[25] In this respect he felt very much like Hitler, to whose spell he succumbed tragically toward the end of his life, even accepting the *Führer's* racist ideas, though racial prejudices have no place in the Italian mentality. After his rise to power Mussolini had a Jewish mistress who wrote his first biography. Hitler, his pupil who became his teacher, had been influenced by the Taborite image in a more devious way. In practice Hitler certainly subscribed to Mussolini's *"Tutto nello Stato, niente al fuori dello Stato, nulla contro lo stato* (Everything within the State, nothing outside the State, nothing against the State)."[26] Theoretically, however, both could have repeated another monistic formula referring to their own rule as intended to be a "government of the people, by the people, and for the people."

"Hitler and Mussolini," Jules Romains wrote in *Les hommes de bonne volonté*, "are despots belonging to the age of democracy. They fully profit from the doubtful service which democracy has rendered to man in our society by initiating him into politics, by getting him used to that intoxicant, by making him believe that the domain of catastrophes is his concern, that history calls for him, consults him, needs him every moment. Dictatorship of the Nazi type is a late cancer which has blossomed on the soil of the French Revolution."[27]

Chapter 12

National Socialism and Socialist Racism

At heart Mussolini was always a Socialist. Hitler, on the other hand, had never formally belonged to the Socialist party, although he had drunk from almost the same ideological sources. His *Weltanschauung* too had been largely fathered by the image of the national socialist Taborites.

Let us go back to the revived interest for the Taborites in Bohemia during the second half of the Nineteenth century. Bohemia then had a Social Democratic Czech party fully cooperating with the Austrian Social Democrats. Both belonged to the Second International. Yet the nationalistic fervor of that period was such that it strongly affected the Czech party and led to a split in 1896. A faction under the leadership of Klofáč, Stříbrný, and Franke seceded and formed the *Národně Socialistická Strana Ceská*, the "Czech National Socialist party" thus introducing for the first time in European history a party sporting the national socialist label. The popular notion of the Taborite movement became immediately the guiding image of this party.[1] We can look up practically any Czech handbook or encyclopedia[2] and find that the main characteristic of this important party was its emphasis on the Hussite-Taborite tradition which, in fact, became the "official myth" of Czechoslovakia after its formation in 1918. After 1919 the N.S.S.C. adopted Dr. Edvard Beneš as its leader and changed its name to Czechoslovak National Socialist party. Karel Hoch in his essay *The Political Parties of Czechoslovakia* gives us the following characteristic of the N.S.S.C.: "Collectivizing by means of development, surmounting of class struggle by national discipline, moral rebirth and democracy as the conditions of socialism, a powerful popular army, etc."[3]

A study of its programs reveals other important points: anticlericalism, an intimate synthesis between nationalism and socialism, trust in the working class, the peasantry, and the lower middle class, opposition to the nobility—all reminiscent of German National Socialism except that no anti-Jewish stand was mentioned. But, contrary to a widespread notion, anti-Jewish feelings had been quite strong among the Czechs and had led to outbreaks of popular violence against the Jews in Prague and other places. As a matter of fact, anti-German riots had led to demonstrations against Jewish shopkeepers (they spoke German too!) and to the killing of three persons on December 1, 1897. Thomas G. Masaryk's criticism of the Hapsburgs for their support of the Jews was seconded by Wickham Steed, the great British apostle of the Czech case.[3] Still, Czech National Socialism was strongly identitarian, far more so than Italian fascism which, after all, put the accent on the State rather than the people. As a political party the N.S.S.C. disappeared under German occupation and reemerged in 1945, when it eagerly collaborated with the Communists.

We should not consider it accidental that the big "Masaryk Encyclopedia" (*Masarykův Ottův Naučný*) features under the heading "National Socialism" both the Czech and the German National Socialist parties. The first foundations of the latter were laid among the Germans of Bohemia in 1897 when a small periodical, *Der Hammer* was transferred from Vienna to Eger. Its editor was Franko Stein, a member of an organization that called itself "German National Workers' League." Backed by his paper this man was able to organize a German National Workers' Congress in Eger (northwest Bohemia) in 1898, where a program of twenty-five points was adopted, a program rather similar to the Linz program of Georg von Schönerer, Austria's most prominent nationalist leader. (This nationalist program had been partly drawn up by Victor Adler, who later left the nationalist camp and became Austria's leading Social Democrat.) These nationalist workers, however, soon headed by a bookbinder called Ferdinand Burschofsky, distrusted Schönerer and considered him too "bourgeois" to lead or to rally class-conscious workers. They wanted socialism, they wanted a nationalism of a distinctly leftist pattern.

They were not unsuccessful. In April 1902 a meeting of the Organization of Nationalistic Labor took place in Saaz, and in December of the same year a mass demonstration was held in Reichenberg. The group was then renamed "German Political Labor League for Austria" and boasted 26,000 members. Schönerer's national-liberal attitude was flatly rejected. On November 15, 1903, a further step was taken in Aussig: A *political party* was formed which called itself the "German Worker's Party in Austria" (D.A.P.). Its program was formulated a year later in Trautenau, where the following declaration was made: "We are a liberty-loving nationalistic party which fights energetically against reactionary tendencies as well as feudal, clerical, or capitalistic privileges and all alien influences."[5]

There were other demands: for instance, separation of Church and State, adherence to democratic principles in army appointments, nationalization of mines and railroads—the usual postulates of "progressive" leftist parties in Europe. In the same year (1904) however, we hear about a plan to change the name of the rising new party. Hans Knirsch, who hailed from Moravia, proposed to call it the "German Social Workers' party" or the "National Socialist German Workers' party." After a long debate this proposition was rejected by the Bohemian delegates for a very obvious reason: They were afraid of the charge that they were copying the Czech National Socialists. And yet their programs were almost identical and not at variance from that of the Social Democrats, members of the Second International. Karel Engliš, professor at the Masaryk University in Brünn (Brno), speaking about the program of the successors of the German Workers' party said that "German Socialism does not differ from Marxism in its critique of capitalism and in its concept of the class struggle."[6]

At a local election in Reichenberg the German Workers' party was able to marshal 14,000 votes in 1905. In 1906 it sent three deputies to the *Reichsrat*, the Parliament in Vienna, thus appearing for the first time in the center of Austrian life. An "All-Austrian" congress of the German Workers' party took place in Prague in 1909 and again the Moravian effort to change its name was defeated. Now new men were coming up. There was a Rudolf Jung, a man with an engineering degree who had been transferred from Vienna to Bohemia by the state railway since he engaged too much in nationalistic propaganda. There was also a lawyer, Dr. Walter Riehl. There were "bourgeois" elements, to be sure, but we find them in all Socialist parties.

In the beginning World War I had a paralyzing effect on all political activities, but in 1916 *Die Freien Stimmen*, the paper of the D.A.P., started to propagate anew the adoption of the term "National Socialist." In April 1918 a motion to rename the party along these lines was again defeated by a vote of 29-14 in Aussig, but a month later the change was effected at a large congress in Vienna. Thus a "German National Socialist Workers' party" (D.N.S.A.P., not yet N.S.D.A.P) was born months before the end of the war, while Hitler was still a *Gefreiter*, a private first class, on the Western Front.

The program formulated in Vienna had a purely Leftist character. It said: "The German National Socialist Workers' party is not a workers' party in the narrow sense of the term: It represents the interests of all honestly creative labor. It is a liberty-loving and strictly nationalist party and therefore fights against all reactionary trends, against ecclesiastical, aristocratic, and capitalist privileges and every alien influence, but above all against the overpowering influence of the Jewish-commercial mentality in all domains of public life. . . .

" . . . it demands the amalgamation of all regions of Europe inhabited by Germans into a democratic, social-minded German Reich. . . .

" . . . it demands plebiscites for all key laws in the Reich, the states and provinces. . . .

" . . . it demands the elimination of the rule of Jewish banks over business life and the creation of national people's banks with a democratic administration. . . ."[7]

This program, as the perceptive reader can see, oozes the spirit of identitarian leftism: It was democratic, it was anti-Hapsburg (since it demanded the destruction of the Danube monarchy in favor of the Pan-German program); it was against all unpopular minorities, an attitude which constitutes the magnetism of all leftist ideologies. The Jews of Austria, we have to bear in mind, were slowly evolving (as they had done further west) into a new upper crust.[8] A Jewish proletariat, such as in Poland, Russia, or the Ukraine, no longer existed. Jews were nobilitated. Hence the mobilization of envy against them. Hence also the declaration of war against all nonnational, cosmopolitan elements like the Jews, the clergy, the bankers, the aristocracy and royalty.

Six months later the Austro-Hungarian monarchy was no more. But Germany survived. Lloyd George, Wilson, and Clemenceau actually helped to realize the noble program of the D.N.S.A.P. by eliminating the biggest stumbling block in the path of Pan-Germanism, the Hapsburg monarchy. Though the birth of Czechoslovakia did not quite fit into the plans of the National Socialists, Hans Knirsch congratulated Masaryk and Tusar, the Czech leaders, for having helped to destroy the old monarchy,[9] but he wept for the unfulfilled "old nostalgic dream of all German democrats," the Pan-German state.[10] Still, in the first elections held in Czechoslovakia, the D.N.S.A.P. received 42,000 votes. It suffered some losses too: Men who lacked the legal grounds for Czechoslovak citizenship were expelled. Rudolf Jung went to Munich and Dr. Walter Riehl to Vienna. The party now had three branches: one in newly-founded Czechoslovakia, a smaller one in what remained of Austria (headed by Dr. Riehl), and a tiny one in Poland whose members were German-speaking. It was Rudolf Jung who contacted a small nationalist group in Munich and instilled in them the spirit of early National Socialism. Referring to this, Josef Pfitzner, a Sudeten German Nazi author, could write with pride that "the synthesis of the two great dynamic powers of the century, of the Socialist and national idea, had been perfected in the German borderlands which thus were far ahead of their motherland."[11]

What happened in the meantime inside Germany? Konrad Heiden, Hitler's earliest biographer, mentions the creation of a Free Committee for a German Workers' Peace early in 1918. Anton Drexler organized a branch of this league on March 7, 1918 in Munich.[12] In January 1919 this local group was renamed "German Workers' party" with Drexler the proud possessor of membership card number 1. A certain Adolf Hitler became the seventh member, but he did not like the name of this budding organization and proposed to call it "Social Revolutionary party." Rudolf Jung, who joined these men and brought much material and literature[13] from the D.N.S.A.P., persuaded them to adopt the slightly reshuffled name "National Socialist German Workers' party" (N.S.D.A.P.). Hitler's contribution to the party program consisted of several ideas on foreign policy: A teacher and organizer of the Democratic party from Franconia by the name of Julius Streicher provided some additional, anti-Jewish arguments.[14]

Who was this amazing person, Adolf Hitler? As with every human being, one has to study his development in the light of environment, personal experiences, and the ideas to which he was exposed. He was a tragic and not attractive figure. To understand him fully one has to know the Austrian and especially the Viennese atmosphere.

There cannot be much doubt that Adolf Hitler's father was of part Jewish origin which explains the son's twin hatred for his father and the Jews. His father's mother, a Fräulein Schicklgruber, had been a servant in the home of the Jewish family Frankenberger in Graz. She had a child, Hitler's father, and it is an established fact that she received alimony from her employers—and alimony in such circumstances is rarely paid without good reason.[15] She later married a man called Hiedler or Hitler. This marriage automatically legitimatized the child. Hitler's father married twice and was a custom official in the city of Braunau on the Austro-German (Austro-Bavarian) border.

One really should see Braunau and the house where Hitler was born.[16] The city's main square is completely open toward the Inn River separating Braunau from (Bavarian) Simbach. The town, a county seat, seems to be cut in half as with a knife. Hitler's father spent much of his time on the bridge, stopping the passersby to inspect their suitcases, bundles, and sacks, thus symbolizing to his son the separation of Austria from Germany. There were, of course, several reasons why Hitler, who knew of his father's origin, did not get along with him. Given the importance attached by the Nazis to "racial purity," Hitler's ancestry was a state secret. It was known, however, to a number of people.[17]

Since his father, wearing a uniform with the imperial insignia, personified to young Hitler the Hapsburg monarchy, it is not so surprising that he soon developed a real loathing for the country of his birth. His teachers in the secondary school were mostly Pan-Germans and thus also anticlericals. There is no evidence that he ever harbored religious feelings. As an adolescent and as a young man he seemed to have been possessed by endless animosities. Before concentrating on the Jews his morbid hatred had turned against the higher social layers: the officers and the aristocracy.[18] He entered a high school-college of the scientific type[19] but was intellectually not able to make the grade. He painted and became interested in architecture. He wanted to study at the Art Academy (*Akademie der bildenden Künste*) of Vienna but was not admitted because he had neither a B.A. nor a B.S., nor did he show extraordinary talent which would have served in lieu of a degree. The examining professor advised him to study architecture, but this too proved impossible because he lacked a degree which the Polytechnic required.

His hatred for the imperial regime was so strong that he did everything within his power to avoid military service in Austria. (For those without a degree it was three years while the others served one year and almost automatically received a commission.) So he emigrated to Bavaria and at the outbreak of World War I joined the Bavarian army.[20] After the war when Hitler, already the recognized leader of the National Socialist movement, wanted to extend his oratory to Austria, the Austrian Federal Chancellor, Monsignor Seipel, warned him that he would have him arrested and tried for desertion. This gave further nourishment to Hitler's hatred for the Catholic Church.

Hitler was never a paperhanger. He sold hand-colored postcards in coffee houses, a far more humiliating way to earn a livelihood than any honest craft. (Theoretically it is quite possible that he offered his art to Lenin, Stalin, Trotsky, or de Gasperi who used to frequent the

Café Central in Vienna's Herengasse.) Easily hurt, quickly offended, tortured by inferiority complexes, he was also highly superstitious. The fact that he was born in Braunau created in him a fixation for the color brown. The Nazi storm troopers wore brown shirts, the headquarters of the National Socialists in Munich was the Brown House: Hitler became a German by acquiring the citizenship of Braunschweig (Brunswick) where the local Nazi government gave him an administrative post.[21] Finally he married his mistress called Eva Braun.[22]

His social inferiority complex weighed heavily on him. Carl Burckhardt, grand nephew of the famous Jacob Burckhardt and last League of Nations Commissioner in Danzig, explained to what extent this factor contributed to the outbreak of World War II. In *Meine Danziger Mission 1937-1939* Burckhardt reports his conversation with Hitler in August 1939 about the prospects of war and peace. Hitler shouted, "I have read idiotic reports in the French press to the effect that I have lost my nerve, whereas the Poles have kept theirs." (Hitler was so furious that for a few moments he was unable to continue.)

Burckhardt: "You do these journalists too much honor if you take their views so seriously. A Chancellor of the Reich ought not to get upset about such trifles. . . ."

Hitler: "This I cannot do. As a proletarian and due to my origin, my rise, and my character, I am incapable of seeing things in this light. This the statesmen have to understand if they want to avoid a catastrophe."[23]

Here was definitely a man with a genuinely leftist turn of mind, an identitarian, a *leader,* not a ruler, a personifier of the masses.[24] Big Brother, but not a father, a loveless man who wanted to see Germany in complete monotony, with local traditions eliminated, regional self-government destroyed, the flags of the *Länder* strictly outlawed, the differences between the Christian faiths eradicated, the Churches desiccated and forcibly amalgamated. He wanted to make the Germans more uniform, even physically, by planned breeding[25] and the extermination, sterilization, or deportation of those who deviated from the norm. The tribes (*Stämme*) should cease to exist. Still, Hitler's lack of education and preparation for the enormous power he held endeared him to the masses (who usually adore the successful amateur), and so did the amazing mediocrity of his tastes (especially in art), and of his views on almost all subjects. There was a "regular guy," a "fellow like you and me"!

His *Table Talks,* noted down by a physician, Dr. Henry Picker, are a most frightening human document because they show the banality and, at the same time, the diabolism of the final logical consequences in the thinking of the man in the street.[26] And, as so often happens with basically mediocre neurotics, certain romantic notions established a firm hold on Hitler. Before his emigration to Bavaria he read the curious pamphlets of a defrocked Cistercian monk from Heiligenkreuz Abbey, Georg Lanz, who called himself Lanz von Liebenfels.[27] This somewhat mentally disturbed man even published a periodical propagating a Nordic racism. These ideas, combined with his increasing hatred for the Jews and his violent rejection of the multinational Austrian Empire, impressed Hitler deeply. A close community can only be established among near-identical people, and all this ties in well with the haunting vision of a perverted, secularized monastery.

Connections between the newly emerging N.S.D.A.P. and the D.N.S.A.P. of Czechoslovakia, Austria, and Poland were quickly established. In 1920 and 1922 so-called Interstate Meetings of Deputies of the three (or four) Nazi parties were held in Salzburg (Austria).[28] In 1920 a violent clash occurred there between Hitler and two Austrian representatives, Dr. Riehl and Herr Schulz, during which Hitler, in the best proletarian fashion, declared that he would "prefer to be hanged in a bolshevik Germany rather than be happy in a Gallicized *Reich*."[29] At the 1920 meeting the Vienna program of 1918 was repeated almost verbatim, which just shows how strongly even German National Socialism was determined by the Bohemian pattern. The new declarations were signed collectively by the National Socialist party of the German people. Even at the meeting in 1922 the German Nazi group seems to have been the smallest—if we discount the tiny German-Polish splinter.

In November 1923 Hitler tried a *Putsch* in Munich which ended fatally. The revolutionary demonstrators were met by the *Reichswehr* under General von Lossow and were mowed down by bullets. Hitler and General Ludendorff[30] got away with their lives by throwing themselves on the ground. The conservative Prime Minister of Bavaria, August von Kahr, also helped to quell the rebellion and for this "betrayal of the national revolution" the German conservatives not only earned Hitler's undying hatred, but Kahr had to pay with his life in the *Reichsmordwoche* (the mass executions on and after June 30, 1934). After the Munich *Putsch* Hitler was apprehended and jailed in Landsberg fortress, where he had a splendid opportunity and the leisure to write *Mein Kampf*.[31]

Released from jail, he was accepted by all three National Socialist parties as the undisputed leader, though Schulz established a dissident group in Austria. In Czechoslovakia the National Socialists were dissolved in October 1933 and replaced by the *Sudetendeutsche Partei* which was certainly National Socialist in character. It was led by Konrad Henlein, a gymnastics teacher. The most militant element in the Czech national movement was always the *Sokol,* a calisthenics association founded by Miroslav Tyrš, a fervent admirer of Jahn and Darwin. The majority of the German and Austrian calisthenic leagues, the *Turnvereine,* were also nationalistic—the identitarian nostalgia of identically dressed men and women making identical movements in mass performances!

In 1923 Hitler failed to take over Germany by force. The Weimar Republic, however, with its democratic constitution offered an ideal frame for a peaceful and legal takeover by just winning elections. Any party could either achieve supreme power by attaining a majority and thus provide the government or, as a strategically placed minority in the parliament, make a mockery of democratic principles. Of course the Weimar Constitution was extremely democratic in its intentions: It prescribed proportional representation and provided one deputy for every 60,000 voters. The number of deputies was thus flexible and depended upon the size of the electorate.

A study of the numerical development of the different parties in the four elections preceding Hitler's advent to power is most interesting. We can learn a great deal from their geographic-regional distribution as well as from changes in the support they got. Maps which I have published elsewhere show distinctly that religion was a main factor in the territorial growth of National Socialism.[32] In Germany the denominations used to live in specific circumscribed areas—the result of the historic *cujus regio ejus religio* principle—and even today, after the tragic migrations following the collapse of the Third Reich, the old pattern survives with surprisingly few differences. There is no doubt that the Nazi victories were gained primarily with the aid of the Protestant or, to be more precise, the "progressive" post-Protestant areas: A mere glance at the statistical maps proves it. On the other hand, one of these maps also proves that the Communist votes show *no* denominational implications.[33] In a way, we should expect this when we remember that Luther was a firm political authoritarian, that he thought *utter* severity in government essential in view of the totally corrupt nature of man, and that he had become (after vainly striving for the conversion of the Jews to his faith) one of the world's most rabid Jew-haters and racists.[34] The idea of a concentration camp for Jews was his,[35] and at the Nuremberg trial Julius Streicher invoked Luther, insisting that, if the Reformer were still alive, he would be sitting among the defendants.[36] Streicher (but not only Streicher) had carefully studied Luther's anti-Jewish pamphlets. It shows the ignorance and confusion in which we live that America's late leading professional anti-racist carried the Reformer's name, and so did a well-known Jewish movie actor who vied with Charlie Chaplin in impersonating Hitler.

These facts unfortunately must be mentioned because they are essential to an understanding of the German tragedy which has aspects of a global calamity. I refer to them with a heavy heart not only because the ecumenical spirit always had a strong hold on me, but also because, having engaged for years in studies of Luther,[37] I have developed a sincere affection for this true "wrestler with Christ," a compassion for this irascible and melancholy theological genius who is, moreover, the creator of the German language.[38]. Hitler, to be sure, never showed any specific enthusiasm for Luther and despised the Evangelicals even more than the Catholics. However, he had left the Catholic Church to all practical purposes and declared National Socialism to be not a "cultic religion" but a "popular movement based on the exact sciences."[39]

Perhaps even more interesting than the denominational aspects of the spread of National Socialism were its ideological conquests. Looking at the three or four elections before the brown wave finally buried everything, we get a curious picture. Let us put the many parties into three separate categories: the National Socialists; the parties with fixed ideologies (Communists, Social Democrats, Catholic Centrists, German Nationalists, Bavarian People's party); and the parties belonging to the liberal-democratic dispensation (German People's party, Democratic party, Economic party). The German People's party was the successor of the National Liberals of Bismarck's day and was led by Dr. Gustav Stresemann until his death. The Democratic party had been renamed the State party. The Bavarian People's party was monarchist and conservative. In our tabulation we include the March 1933 elections, though their genuineness is most questionable. They were held under Nazi control and we know of specific cases where the results were falsified.

First of all, we also have to bear in mind that only 481 deputies had been elected in 1928 as against 647 in 1933, an increase explained by the fact that more and more habitual nonvoters came to the polls: the wishy-washy and the withdrawn, indifferent and skeptical people. Their imagination, obviously, had been caught by the Nazis and thus they strongly contributed to their victory. (Of course, this cannot be

ELECTION DATE	DEPUTIES		
	National Socialists	Non-Nazi Ideologists	Demo-Liberals
May 20, 1928	12	363	116
September 14, 1930	107	351	119
July 31, 1932	230	358	20
November 6, 1932	196	364	24
March 5, 1933	288	346	13

proved "scientifically"; *theoretically* it is possible that they now voted for the Socialists, Centrists, or Nationalists, while former voters became Nazis, but nobody knowing the German scene would dare to argue like this.) Yet just as important as the mobilization of the old nonvoters was the switch of the "Demo-Liberals," the uncommitted left, the "progressivists" and the middle-roaders to the Nazis. The Democratic party, which in 1919 still had 80 deputies, had only two in November 1933. The Economic party of the middle class went down from 23 in 1928 to zero, the German People's party, the former National Liberals, decreased from 45 in 1928 to a mere 2 in March 1933, but the Catholic Centrists increased during the same time from 61 to 73, the Bavarian royalists from 17 to 19, even the questionably conservative German Nationalists rose in the years 1930 to 1933 from 44 to 53 seats. This shows quite clearly *what* resisted and tried to stem the Nazi tide: certainly not the forces of agnosticism, polite doubt, left-of-centrism, progressivism, and enlightenment.

The Social Democrats decreased, but only slightly. From May 1928 to November 1932 their seats in the *Reichstag* numbered 153, 143, 133, and 121. To whom did they lose?

We find a hint in the totals of their fellow Marxists, the Communists: 44, 77, 89, and 100. This shows that by July 1932 the two big totalitarian parties, the Nazis and Communists, held 319 seats out of 608—an absolute majority which proves that *more than half of all Germans emphatically rejected parliamentary democracy* and that another large sector regarded it with the greatest skepticism. This again means, in other words, that the democratic republic uncompromisingly demanded by Wilson, was the basis of future slavery in Germany, the door through which tyranny entered. Plato's and Aristotle's dictum that tyranny always arises out of democracy was well confirmed.

German democratic parliamentarism had reached a complete impasse by 1932. Chancellor Brüning knew that there was only one way to preserve basic liberties, the restoration of the monarchy through a referendum. But the President, Paul von Hindenburg, rejected this solution because he considered a plebiscite for a monarchy incompatible with the principle of legitimacy and also because he had actually given an oath of allegiance to the Republic (in which he basically did not believe).[40] A cabinet enjoying the confidence of the majority could not be formed. Franz von Papen, a dissenter from the Centrist party and one of the stupidest men ever to emerge in German political life,[41] tried to rule without the Parliament, merely with the aid of the old War Emergency laws. He was supplanted by General Kurt von Schleicher, an intellectual military man who desperately tried to find a formula resembling that of Primo de Rivera's regime, a combined dictatorship of the army and trade unions. Yet the conservative forces, already too deeply imbued with democratic notions and not believing that in the long run a government could subsist without popular support, had a genuine failure of nerve. On January 30, 1933 a government was formed with the National Socialists who, unfortunately, had the relative plurality in the *Reichstag*. Hindenburg, too old and too tired to resist and ill-advised by his nephew, also gave in to what was actually a victory *of the democratic though not the liberal principle.*[42]

It had been Papen's idea to form a coalition government in which for every Nazi in an important ministerial post, a non-Nazi would be appointed to counterbalance him. Hitler was to be Chancellor of the *Reich*, Papen Vice-Chancellor, and so on along the whole line. Papen and his friends expected—as did the outside world—that Hitler would never be able to master either the gigantic economic difficulties or those in the domain of foreign policy. Internally, however, Hitler solved the unemployment problem by armament and public works, and the West was so frightened of him that they made every concession they had denied to Dr. Brüning. Still, an earlier offer by Papen to enter such a coalition government had been rejected by Hitler in a haughty letter whose salient passages highlight the leftist character of the Nazi movement. In his analysis of Papen's predicament Hitler puts the following words into his mouth:

"In this emergency only one thing could help. We wanted to invite them, i.e., the Nazis, into our cabinet which enjoys not only the support of all Jews, but also of many aristocrats, conservatives, and members of the *Stahlhelm*. We were certain that they would accept our invitation without guile, freely and gladly. Then we would slowly have started to draw their poison fangs. Once they had shared our company, they could hardly withdraw. Caught together, hanged together!''

172

The "open letter," printed by the thousands and distributed, was terminated in the best leftist "common-man" tradition:

"As to the rest, Herr von Papen, stay in the world in which you are, I will go on fighting in mine. I am happy to know that my world is the community of millions of German workers of the forehead and the fist, and of German peasants who, although mostly of humble origin and living in dire poverty, want to be the most faithful sons of our people—for they fight not only with their lips, but also with a suffering borne thousandfold and with innumerable sacrifices for a new and better German *Reich*."[43]

But in January 1933 Papen gave in on far less advantageous terms, and was duly cheated and outsmarted. The tragedy ran its full course. The outcome is only too well known.

In the meantime, misinterpretations of the real character of National Socialism continued almost unchallenged. Against these it must be emphasized that, not only in the judgment of the historian and the political scientist, but of its own leaders and ideologues, National Socialism had a distinctly leftist pattern which generally can clearly be traced back to the French Revolution.

The Danzinger Hermann Rauschning was the first man to analyze from a conservative viewpoint Hitler's utterances made to him in private. In his highly revealing *Gespräche mit Hitler* he tells of Hitler's utter contempt for Italian fascism,[44] his special hatred for the Hapsburgs,[45] his complete legal nihilism[46] so reminiscent of the legal positivism in the United States. Hitler naturally knew very well that the Nazi Revolution was "the exact counterpart of the French Revolution" and he imagined himself not only as "the conqueror but also the executor of Marxism—of that part that is essential and justified, stripped of its Jewish-Talmudic dogma."[47] He was particularly proud of having learned so much from the political methods of the Social Democrats. He went on record to say that, "Workers calisthenic associations, cells from the factory workers, mass demonstrations, propaganda pamphlets written especially for the multitudes, all these new means of the political struggle used by us, are Marxist in origin."[48] No wonder, since Socialism brought the principle of totalitarian organization to Germany, a fact duly noted by the late Wilhelm Röpke.[49] "National Socialism is socialism in evolution," Hitler insisted, "a socialism in everlasting change."[50] And he also admitted, "There is more that unites us with than divides us from bolshevism . . . above all the genuine revolutionary mentality. I was always aware of this and I have given the order that one should admit former Communists to the party immediately."[51]

Talking about the coming war, Hitler said, "I am not afraid of destruction. We will have to part with much that seems to us dear and irreplaceable. Cities are going to be transformed into ruins, noble edifices will disappear forever. This time our sacred soil will not be spared, but I am not afraid of it. We are going to set our teeth and fight to the bitter end. From these ruins Germany will rise bigger and more beautiful than any country of the world."[52] This idea the mobmaster repeated ecstatically in the last weeks of his rule. Demolition delights all leftists, fills them with diabolic glee. Mr. Herbert Read (quite some time before he was knighted, to be true) praised destruction in a book appropriately called *To Hell with Culture* (No. 4. of the series, "The Democratic Order") in which he spoke about the necessity to destroy all "nondemocratic, aristocratic or capitalist" culture: "To hell with such culture! To the rubbish-heap and furnace with it all! Let us celebrate the democratic revolution with the biggest holocaust in the history of the world. When Hitler has finished bombing our cities, let the demolition squads complete the good work. Then let us go out into the wide open spaces and build anew."[53] This was written in 1941 when the barbarians dominated *everywhere*. Still, Sir Herbert had the courage to write in 1943, "Communism is an extreme form of democracy, and it is totalitarian: but equally the totalitarian state in the form of fascism is an extreme form of democracy. All forms of socialism, whether state socialism of the Russian kind, or national socialism of the German kind, or democratic socialism of the British kind, are professedly democratic, that is to say, they all obtain popular assent by the manipulation of mass psychology." And then he went on to explain why Nazi Germany was much more thoroughly democratic than either Britain or the United States.[54]

Official utterances to the effect that Nazism stood firmly on the left, that it represented a democratic and republican, socialistic and antiaristocratic ideology, always abounded. Just like a fanatical Laborite Hitler attacked Eton and Harrow.[55] He called himself an "arch-democrat,"[56] National Socialism the "most genuine democracy,"[57] the Nazi constitution "truly democratic."[58] In *Mein Kampf* he wrote about the "Germanic democracy of the free election of a leader."[59]

Goebbels called National Socialism an "authoritarian democracy" or a "Germanic democracy," if not the "noblest form of European democracy":[60] He maintained that National Socialists did not talk about much democracy, but nevertheless were the executors of the "general will."[61] Rudolf Hess termed National Socialism "the most modern democracy in the world" which rested on the "confidence of the majority."[62]

Michael Oakeshott of the London School of Economics said, very much to the point, in confirming Goebbels' stand, "An authoritarian regime, no doubt, can 'liquidate' the liberal supporters which, for one reason or another, helped to bring it into being, but no modern authoritarian doctrine can liquidate its debt to the doctrine of Democracy. . . . It is impossible to understand either communism, fascism or National Socialism without first understanding the doctrine of representative democracy. . . . It is the parent of these ungracious children."[63]

No wonder, therefore, Goebbels had stated unequivocally that he "paid homage to the French Revolution for all the possibilities of life and development which it had brought to the people. In this sense, if you like, I am a democrat."[64] There was, to be true, a more radically Socialist wing among the Nazis, led by the brothers Strasser and by Röhm, a group which had suffered as much in the *Reichsmordwoche* as the conservative opposition, but men like Goebbels were even more frank about their hatred for the traditional forces of Germany. Dr. Goebbels asked in 1932: "Where would we take the moral right from to fight the idea of the proletarian struggle between the classes, if the bourgeois class-state were not first destroyed and replaced by a new Socialist structure of the German community?"[65] And when Mussolini was arrested by the King of Italy, Goebbels' indignation knew no limits. He declared on October 31, 1943 in the Sports Palace in Berlin, that something of this sort would never happen in the Third Reich because: ". . . first of all, the Reich is headed by the *Führer* and not by a traitor like Badoglio. And secondly, because we have kings only in fairy tales and musical comedies. Germany is a republic *Führer*-state." Hitler, as a matter of fact, always loathed the King of Italy, and after his last official visit to Rome before the war he said openly, "Now I would have become most certainly an antimonarchist, if I had not always been one."[66]

The leftist character of Nazism was also apparent in its attitude towards Christianity. For a variety of reasons National Socialism was bound to take an anti-Christian attitude. Not only did it reject the Jewish background of Christianity and of the Old Testament, but Christian ethics—compassion, charity, mercy—militated against the Nazi creed no less than against Marxism. Nazism was moreover a materialism deeply pledged to Darwinistic and Spencerian ideas.[67] It preached biological determination but entered a (not truly realized) conflict between the belief in an automatic survival of the fittest and the urge to intervene with legislation, to eradicate, to sterilize, eliminate, castrate, exile, and exterminate "undesirables." The bellicose attitude of the Nazis made them blind to the fact that in a war the best, not the cowards, are killed off. *Ares ouk agathôn feidetai allá kakôn*, "Mars does not spare the good but the bad."[68] And one of the most criminal aspects of Nazi racism was the handling of the Russian and Ukrainian people by its party minions. The German troops were first greeted as liberators and Russia could be had on a platter. But then the party moved in and the Russians were treated as slaves, the Ukrainians never were given self-government,[69] and the disappointed and disgusted masses started to resist. Evil prejudices and a false doctrine destroyed a unique opportunity.

Yet the Nazis were slow in showing their cards, which explains why, at the beginning of their rule, many wellmeaning, naive people willingly collaborated with them. Even the plans to amalgamate the Churches forcibly emerged only slowly and foundered when it became evident that a sizable majority of upright Lutherans and Calvinists resisted "Nazification." "Mercy killings" of the incurably insane got under way only at the beginning of the war, and immediately aroused protests from the Catholic bishops. As time went on and the population was occupied more and more by the war in its critical stage, by the food problem, by the losses at the front and the increasing air attacks, the Nazis became bolder. A circular letter, violently anti-Christian like the one issued by Martin Bormann, the deputy leader, early in 1942, would have been unthinkable a few years earlier—and this in spite of a rather frank forerunner, Alfred Rosenberg's *Mythus des Zwanzigsten Jahrhunderts*.[70] Bormann's massive attack was entirely in keeping with scientism and materialism and could have emanated from a Soviet propagandist or from certain American professors. Plans were made for a total crushing of Christianity to be carried out after a victory which, fortunately, never came—the crushing was left to the Communist competitors in the Eastern two-thirds of Europe.

The fundamentally leftist and identitarian character of National Socialism can certainly not be questioned. The Marxists tried to prove that Nazism was "financed by the rich" merely to browbeat organized labor, an interesting theory which implies that political persuasions (and therefore elections) are a mere matter of cash: the bigger the propaganda, the more posters and newspaper ads, the more certain the victory at the polls. This, however, would be the most powerful argument against parliamentary democracy because in the light of this theory the man in the street is either a venal little swine or a mere echo. Yet, as Gustav Stolper has demonstrated,[71] the Nazis were quite capable of financing themselves with the millions coming from their membership dues. The contributions of industrialists and bankers (some of them "non-Aryan") had the same character as the sums shamefacedly paid to gangsters by shopkeepers who want to play safe because they cannot trust the police.

The economic order under the Nazis, indeed, was Socialistic, also from an economic point of view, because in a totalitarian state the factory owner or banker no longer automatically holds genuine property. He is merely a steward, the tolerated representative of an almighty government which can expropriate him at the drop of a hat. Not by accident was the Nazi flag the *red* banner. In early 1933 many Nazi flags were only adapted Communist and Socialist flags, the center having been cut out and replaced by white cloth or a so-called "mirror" sewn on. (When it rained the red naturally shone through.) In the concentration camps the Communists, who were very well organized, murdered their rightist opponents under the very noses of their jailers, who did not much care.[72] As a matter of fact, Nazi-Soviet collaboration was planned at an early date. The Reventlow-Radek negotiations are well documented, and this joint Red-Brown hatred was directed mainly against Poland, the *bête noire* of leftists all over the world.[73] In this respect Stalin, Hitler, Lloyd George, and the American left formed an unholy alliance.

Who were the real Nazis? Professor Theodor Abel found among the leading Nazis (i.e., those known to the broad public, the historians, etc.) 7 percent who belonged to the upper layer, 7 percent peasants, 35 percent workers and 51 percent who could be described as middle class. In the party the largest single occupational group were the elementary school teachers, a group well known in Europe for its inclination toward authoritarianism and its intellectual curiosity sadly combined with a lack of scholarly preparation. (European elementary schools usually last only four or five years and in the past the teachers almost never had the equivalent of a college education.) Yet what about the army? Since army officers (or even soldiers) were *not* permitted to belong to the National Socialist party, the Nazi fanatics with military ambitions were almost all in the *Waffen-SS* which paralleled the *Wehrmacht,* the regular army, where there were very few high-ranking officers with Nazi convictions. (Men such as Keitel—"*la* Keitel"—and Jodl were exceptions.) This situation changed radically following the last attempted assassination of Hitler (there had been several), and after the end of July 1944 members of the Nazi Party and *Gottgläubige* (non-Christian theists) could be members of the officers' corps; the "German Greeting" (Heil Hitler!) was also made obligatory. Thus the army was Nazified at that late date. Before these events even the draftees had to return their membership cards to the party and show a deposit slip that they had done so. Membership could be resumed only after military service. Until July 1944 the higher officer's corps, including the General Staff, consisted about half noblemen and half commoners, and most of the latter were also anti-Nazi. (Names such as Beck, Halder, Rommel, Speidel immediately come to mind.) Yet besides the Jews, the groups most hated by the Nazi leaders were royalty and the nobility, and it was primarily the nobility within the armed forces which, as a group, really struck—in July 1944. The retribution was terrible. Hitler had the hanging of the conspirators *filmed*—including the suspension of their naked corpses on butchers' hooks. Here again we encounter the sadistic drives of a genuine, Sade-inspired leftism.

Still we must bear in mind that the horrors perpetrated by the Nazis during the war in occupied areas and inside their country were perfectly "logical." Leftists all over the world have tried to portray these horrors as typical deeds of reactionaries, of "right extremists," of "counter-revolutionaries," if not of "conservatives." Another school tried to nail these chilling crimes to the German character. But here must be borne in mind that nobody in Europe tried to explain the delirious crimes perpetrated by the French Revolutionaries with the darker and seamier sides of the French character. Few people ascribed the atrocities of the Spanish Civil War to the "Spanish soul," or the frightfulness of the Russian Revolution to "Eternal Russia." The shock which the Nazi horrors produced was so great, because they came after two hundred years of Roussellian propaganda about the goodness of human nature and also because the Germans were literate, clean, technologically progressive, hard working, "modern," sober, "orderly," and so forth. Yet about human nature we get more concrete and more pertinent information from the Bible than from statistics dealing with secondary education, the frequency of bathtubs or the mileage of superhighways. Nevertheless, it is true that there is something in the German mind which prompts it to make final logical deductions from specific premises. Baron Hügel has written about this German propensity in a memorable article[74] and Ernst Jünger said rightly that Germany, due to its central location (central in a metaphysical rather than geographical sense) is the place where one expects the appearance of a symptomatic figure such as Hitler,[75]—the man, as another author said, who put the Prussian sword in the service of Austrian folly. Ernst Jünger described this situation in other words when he wrote in his diary (*Strahlungen II*, October 6, 1941): "After that long period of fasting the German was led by Kniébolo [Hitler] up a mountain and the might of the world was shown to him. Not much prompting was needed that he worshiped his tempter."

We have dealt with the horrors of Nazism or communism in Russia because these are, as we perhaps rashly assume, sufficiently well known. The world, however, is indebted to Germany in a terrifying way, because she demonstrated to everyone what the ultimate conclusions of negative and destructive ideas really are. Ideas which in London or New York are repeated as seemingly harmless abstractions have been shown up by the Germans in all their blood-chilling finality. In this sense Nazi Germany has become the Gorgonian Mirror in which a decadent West could study its own features. This is a characteristic shared by the whole spine of Europe which stretches from the Straits of Gibraltar via Spain, France, Germany, and Poland into Russia, where people tend to be *pèlerins de l'absolu*, "pilgrims of the absolute," to use the phrase of Léon Bloy. While the rest of the world has only too often been engaged in small talk, the "absolutists" have transformed abstraction and theories into concrete realities. Have not American and British so-called Liberals repeatedly voiced ideas and notions leading directly in ice-cold logic to the gas chambers and cremation stoves of Auschwitz, Treblinka, and Majdanek, to the icy graves of Siberia, the gloomy forest of Katyn, the orgiastic cemeteries of Red Spain? The case of Germany, however, should be a *memento* to the English-speaking world because there was a nation to be admired in so many ways, the heart of the Holy Roman Empire, the cradle of the Reformation, a land of *Dichter und Denker,* (poets and thinkers), degenerating into a land of *Richter und Henker,* (judges and hangmen).

By divorcing themselves from religion and wilfully turning their backs on great traditions, the Germans made of their katabasis an inferno which, historically speaking, they will never be able to forget . . . a fall worse than that of France, the "Oldest Daughter of the Church," and equaling that of "Holy Russia." All the visions of Sade, all the nightmarish dreams of the French *Révolution Surréalists*[76] had become true, all the consequences of American pragmatism and universal positivism were drawn, all the "eugenic" blueprints of biological visionaries were carried out and illimited materialism found its fulfillment. Man was conceived as a mere beast that could be crushed like an ant or a bedbug, and all the laws on the Tables of Sinai, all the words of Christ were eradicated.

Just before the outbreak of World War II in Europe a leftist author under the pen name Nicolas Calas wrote a book of essays entitled *Foyers d'incendie,*[77] making a passionate appeal for "more sadism among leftists." He claimed that, like the early Christians, they succumb too often to a masochist urge for suffering. "Fascism, therefore, must be fought with Freudian as well as Marxist weapons. And, like fascism, communism will have to call on sadistic and masochistic love. Masochist tendencies must be excited in the Fascist masses, and sadistic tendencies among the Communists. . . . But we must never forget that the dominant of the revolutionary complex is to be the sadistic. This means that hatred of the father should always be stronger than love of the brother.''[78]

"A real reeducation of the younger generation should take place for this purpose. Let the child learn to do more than admire the beauty of flowers and the intelligence of bees: let us show him the pleasure of killing animals. Let him go hunting, let him visit the butcher's, let him enjoy suffering.''[79]

But that is not enough. "The bourgeoisie know what they're about when they give their children soldiers and cannons for toys. Let us do the same, let us give our own children armies of leaden workers, barricades, buses, factories, and an enemy army as horrible as the heart desires, made up of capitalists, preachers, and cops. For the child, play should be a game of massacres. Our holidays need no longer be those of the bourgeois calendar, for the chocolate Easter eggs let us substitute chocolate guillotines.

"Excite desires! Monogamy does not exist yet. After the butcher, the prostitute! It is up to her to give the child a taste, and not a disgust for love. . . .''

And here a final word about the ideally educated child. "When he wants to read, put in his hands the works best calculated to excite his desire. Show him succulent dreams, the syrups of passions, the wines of blood, the burning kisses, the moist looks, all that bread of life, that whole body of love.''[80]

Only a poor French degenerate hiding under an obvious pseudonym? Who is the man who said, "I do not think that man at present is a predatory animal. It seems to me that every society rests on the death of men''? It was a Justice of the United States.[81]

Nicolas Calas exhorted leftists with the words, "Comrades, be cruel!'' Hitler followed this call. Not in vain have we been told by Charles Fourier, grandfather of socialism, in his *Théorie de l'unité universelle*:

"The office of the butcher is held in high esteem in Harmony.''

Part III

Liberalism

Chapter 13

Real Liberalism

Another grave, this time semantic misunderstanding between America and Europe lies in the concept of *liberalism*. In Europe the significance of this term has also undergone several changes, but its essential meaning always has been kept. In the United States today the word "liberalism" has a content diametrically opposed to its etymology, and to its original sense as understood not only in Europe but also in Latin America, Australia, New Zealand, the Soviet Union, Southern Asia, and Japan. In its process of deformation the idea of liberalism has suffered nowhere more than in the United States, although a certain degenerative process of this term also has taken place in Britain. The liberalism preached by the Whigs at the beginning of the last century, the liberalism of Palmerston, of Asquith, of Lloyd George, and the younger Churchill, and obviously that of Mr. Acland-Hood—each have somewhat different meanings.

Let us look at the verbal meaning. The root is *liber* ("free"). The term *liberalis* (and *liberalitas*) implies generosity in intellectual and material matters. The sentence "he gave liberally" means that the person in question gave with both hands. In this sense *liberality* is an "aristocratic" virtue. An illiberal person is avaricious, petty-minded, tight-fisted, self-centered. Up to the beginning of the Nineteenth century the word "liberal" figured neither in politics nor really in economics.

We explained the political content of the term in Chapter V. While democracy answers the question as to *who* should rule, liberalism deals with the problem *how* government should be exercised. The answer liberalism gives is that regardless of who rules, government must be exercised in such a way that each individual, each citizen enjoys the widest personal liberty still compatible with the common good. Yet in spite of the fact that the "common good" can be wilfully interpreted in the narrowest way, it is clear that liberalism rightly understood stands essentially for *freedom*.

As far as our research goes, the first time this term was used in a political sense was in the year 1812, and the "place of action"—not unnaturally—was Spain, a nation famous for its individualism, its inordinate sense of liberty, its strong anarchical drives. The supporters of the Constitution of Cádiz were called los *liberales* and their opponents (among them the *Apostólicos*) were nicknamed *los serviles*. Yet even at this very early stage of the game a certain amount of misunderstanding had crept into the use of this term inasmuch as the Constitution of Cádiz also had democratic features while the majority of the *Apostólicos* had federalistic (local rights) leanings which became even more marked when the Carlist Wars broke out and the Liberals rallied around Queen Isabel II who also enjoyed the aid of enthusiastic British volunteers.

It took several years for this nomenclature to make its appearance in England. Southey used it for the first time in 1816 and, significantly enough, employed the Spanish form, speaking of "our liberale*s*." Sir Walter Scott, soon afterward, copied it from the French, referring to the liberals as *libéraux*. In the early 1830s, when after the reforms of Sir Robert Peel the new parties emerged, the Whigs became the Liberals and the Tories the Conservatives. This evolution was not surprising. Whigs and Tories were both "aristocratic" parties (as we have pointed out in Chapter VII), but the Whigs were more genuinely aristocratic in that they saw in the king a mere *primus inter pares,* whereas the Tories were the party of the aulic nobility fawning in a rather unaristocratic way upon the monarch. (At least this is the way the Whigs saw it.)

In other words, there is in all genuine aristocracies a certain republican undercurrent: The typical aristocratic state is always an open or a disguised oligarchic republic. This is borne out by Venice and Genoa on one side, and the Polish Commonwealth and Britain after 1688 on the other. The *classic* ally of the monarch is not the nobility or the clergy, but the burgher class. Only with the French Revolution do we see a radical and tragic change.

184

Thus the *idea* of liberalism existed well before 1812. During the eighteenth century an economic school was in the ascendancy (particularly in Britain and in the Netherlands) which, without straining our semantics, can be styled *preliberal* because it still did not use the liberal label. We are referring here to the Manchester School whose philosophical (or theological) roots were deep in the soil of deism. God, the Great Architect, had created the world nearly perfect. All evils were due to human intervention which upset the Divine plan. This could easily happen because this deist God had withdrawn from His creation: Neither priestcraft nor white magic, neither prayers nor other incantations moved Him any longer. It was up to man to work out his own salvation, i.e., his terrestrial happiness by interfering as little as possible (or, preferably, not at all) with a universe existing in a preestablished harmony which rested on divine laws. If state and society never intervened in commerce and industry, these would automatically flourish, while all artificial limitations, rules or regulations—for instance, guilds, labor laws, tariffs, currency reforms, etc.—would bring about the downfall of prosperity.

As Alexander Rüstow[1] has pointed out, there is a true theological background to the thought of Adam Smith and the entire Manchester School, a "theology" which has to be understood partly as a logical continuation of Calvinism, partly as its dialectical contradiction. In other words, there is in the ideology of Manchesterism and its *laissez-faire* a synthesis of John Calvin and the Renaissance. Of course there is also a good deal of practical truth and common sense to this outlook. With its appeal to human egotism and ambition, the different schools of economic liberalism have delivered the goods much better than the various economic orders based on a pseudomonastic collectivism and/or statism.

At the same time one ought to recognize that Manchesterism was a truly "grand bourgeois" ideology related to but not identical with Whiggery. The second phase of liberalism (which, indeed, bears the liberal label) we will call *early liberalism*. Though perhaps not entirely unaffected by deism, it had to a large extent the leadership of thinkers with decided religious affiliations or at least strong sympathies for the Christian tenets. This early liberalism reached its apogee in the 1850s, but its forerunners were active already in the 1820s and 1830s while some of its exponents died around 1900. Let us name only a few of them in chronological order: Royer-Collard, Alexis de Tocqueville, Montalembert, Gladstone, Jacob Burckhardt, Lord Acton. Half of them, significantly enough, were aristocrats; the others belonged to what is sometimes called the patriciate. Not a systematic thinker but a statesman of the same school is Count Camillo Cavour. Nor should one omit the name of Achille Léonce Victor Duc de Broglie.[2] In other words, from a sociological viewpoint we are here faced with upper-class men, none of whom had an antireligious bent. (Jacob Burckhardt has to be styled an agnostic, but in his declining years he developed warm feelings for the Catholic Church.) Did early liberalism have a forerunner? A man who inspired most of them? Inevitably one thinks here of Edmund Burke, not a preliberal, but certainly an early conservative who influenced de Tocqueville as well as Metternich.

Many of these early liberals were not lovers of freedom *besides* being Christians but took their political inspiration either directly from Scripture or from theology. As we can see, it was their "religious anthropology," their picture of man which invited or forced them to walk the road of liberalism. Man has an immortal soul, man has a personality, man is not an accident of blind forces of nature, man needs freedom because God wants him not only to develop his personality in the right direction but also to live a moral life, freely (but rightly!) choosing between good and evil.

From the aforementioned it is obvious that the religious aspect of early liberalism was more strongly developed among Catholics, Eastern Orthodox, and those supporters of the Reformation faiths who had broken with the strict views of the Reformers, who were "Erasmian" and Zwinglian rather than Calvinistic or Lutheran. Among the names we have mentioned we do not find a single supporter of what is loosely called "Protestant orthodoxy." Calvin and Luther certainly were not liberals in the decadent American sense, but they were not "libertarians" either. "Libertarianism," that is to say true liberalism, in the Reformation faiths makes itself felt only in the Eighteenth century as a result of the impact of the Enlightenment and of rationalism, both late descendants of the Renaissance and therefore alien in themselves to the spirit of the Reformation. The man in the street, to be sure, more often than not associates the Enlightenment, rationalism, and individualism with the "Protestant" outlook, if not with the Reformed religions. He knows nothing about the 180-degree turn the bulk of the Reformed faiths took 200 years ago, nor has he taken much notice of the return of a number of Reformed theologians to the orthodoxy of the Sixteenth century, a relatively recent development which, so far, has not had the time (or the chance) to affect the faith of the masses.

But whereas liberalism in the beginning received support from certain Catholic *thinkers*, its supporters were probably more numerous among the Reformed *people*. In the Catholic world the early liberal parties were small and largely composed of elites. There economic thinking and economic considerations played a rather minor role and early liberalism placed its emphasis on other sectors of human endeavor. It was different in the Evangelical areas of Europe, where commerce and industry always occupied a more honored position than in the *orbis catholicus* and where the ideas and notions of a very economic-minded preliberalism were still very much alive. Here we must bear in mind that the lacking prestige of the businessman in the Catholic world is due partly to the realization that the merchant is the representative of the only profession ever to have been physically chastised by Our Lord. (What a wonderful subject for our great painters in the past!) St. Thomas Aquinas' views on the trader were frankly hostile,[3] and modern capitalism rising in Northern Italy in the Fifteenth century had many technical and psychological hurdles to overcome. (Double entry bookkeeping was invented in the Fifteenth century by Fra Luca Pacioli di Borgo, a Franciscan, but with the rise of Calvinism the center of business quickly shifted to the North.) No wonder the Catholic renewal in the Nineteenth and Twentieth centuries had certain bitterly anticapitalist aspects.

Nevertheless, it is interesting to see how rarely the early liberal thinkers were preoccupied with economics, whereas the next wave of liberalism, the *old liberals* (paleoliberals, to use the phrase coined by Frau Heddy Neumeister)[4] became as intensively interested in economic problems as the preliberals. Early liberalism was characterized by a rather limited pragmatism. It was intuitive rather than scientific. Montalembert's thinking rested squarely on Christian premises. De Tocqueville, profoundly influenced by Madame Swetchine who was also the great soulmate of Lacordaire,[5] coordinated at a more advanced age his political and social vistas increasingly with his reviving Christian faith. Jacob Burckhardt was deeply imbued with Christian ethics: It is indeed moving to see an agnostic solemnly choosing celibacy in his young years to be able to devote himself entirely to knowledge, research, wisdom, and truth. In the early liberals there is very little of that equation of freedom and usefulness prevailing among the preliberals and the old liberals of a slightly later period. The early liberals considered freedom as something to be treasured and defended because man needed it, because it was a postulate of a moral, not of a practical order, because—as many of them acknowledged—"Christ had liberated us to liberty" (Galatians, V:1). An early liberal would hardly have shaken in his belief if somebody had proved to him that freedom is impractical, or expensive, or less apt to produce higher living standards than some effective form of slavery.

Precisely because the early liberals were "idealists" in the narrow sense of the term, because their background was aristocratic or patrician, because they were intellectuals of a high order, without exception educated in the classics, because they founded their demand for freedom on religious and philosophical principles, they were not friendly toward democracy. As a matter of fact, most of them could frankly be styled antidemocrats. This, however, is often not fully realized by those interested in the history of ideas. Acton's remark to Bishop Creighton in a letter addressed to him in 1887, "Power tends to corrupt, and absolute power corrupts absolutely," is frequently cited by well-meaning democrats who forget (or do not know) that Acton, quite an antidemocrat himself, would have applied this formula to parliaments or popular majorities without batting an eye. The mere fact that de Tocqueville wrote a standard work called *Democracy in America*, foretelling a further extension of democracy on a worldwide scale, has made him an apologist in the eyes of so many an American. But de Tocqueville was much too clever to believe that, with the coming upsurge of democracy, political history and its every-changing forms would come to an end. He realized, we can be sure, that the world would outlive the democratic age, which he did not like at all. Yet he wrote in such a detached way that one has to read carefully between the lines. The man who, disgusted by the July Revolution of 1830, had left France for a United States, then under its first Democratic administration, was not a democrat. But, let us admit that even a few of his more intelligent readers were not quite sure where he actually stood. When once asked peremptorily about his convictions, he replied:

> I have an intellectual inclination for democratic institutions, but I am instinctively an aristocrat, which means that I despise and fear the masses. I passionately love liberty, legality, the respect for rights, but not democracy . . . liberty is my foremost passion. That is the truth.[6]

This is not the Alexis de Tocqueville known to the average American.[7] Nor, to be sure, does the ordinary Swiss burgher, looking at a stamp featuring Jacob Burckhardt, realize how much this great man loathed democracy—as did Burckhardt's liberal friend, J. J. Bachofen, similarly honored by the Swiss post office.

Outstanding men who have a certain pride in their experience or their knowledge are not likely to be admirers of democracy which refuses to distinguish between the various degrees of knowledge, is indifferent toward truth (as Berdyaev pointed out)[8] and takes its stand on the basis of quantity and biological age rather than quality. In this system of government the votes are counted and not weighed, an observation Aristotle made well over 2,000 years ago. Indeed it would be difficult to find in Europe more than a handful of truly outstanding thinkers who believed or believe in democracy. As a matter of fact, only Bergson and Maritain come to my mind, and Maritain joined the democratic group only in his early forties. Before that time he was fairly close to the *Action Francaise*.[9] We mention Bergson only because in one of his philosophical works we find a passage hinting at his democratic convictions. However, he was strictly a philosopher and not in any way a political scientist. Naturally, one could produce a long list of *literary* men of the greatest talent adhering to democracy. Thomas Mann who also had such friendly words for the Soviet Union, is a case in point.[11] But literary people address themselves to a broad public; they are primarily artists and not systematic thinkers.

The aversion of the early liberals for the two democratic postulates of equality and majority rule also had other important roots. They knew about the incompatibility between the liberal and the egalitarian principle, they saw very clearly that the enfranchisement of the masses would inevitably lead to the rise of political movements exploiting the envy of the many, they realized that the concept of the "politicized" nation was in itself *totalitarian*—a term then not known or used but clearly sensed and understood as in de Tocqueville's vision of the new tyranny to come.[12] It was also evident to the early liberals that democracy would replace the search for truth in the light of reason with the mere whim, the emotions, the naked desires of the many expressed in numbers. Burckhardt spoke about dangers coming from political decisions based merely on the *Gärungen der Völker,* on the "peoples in ferment." Royer-Collard no less than Montalembert emphasized the lights, *les lumières*, the quest for truth which obviously is a task of the few but not of the many. They have neither the training, the time nor the money to get and to digest the information necessary for the judgments they have to make. (Needless to say, moral qualifications are also necessary for one to arrive at decisions which demand immediate sacrifices ensuring a better future. "Blood, sweat and tears" can usually be promised only to a people with its back against the wall.)

Not all the early liberals were safe at all times in the face of the temptations of democracy which, as we have pointed out, has a paradisiacal character and all the lure of a "clear but false idea." One has only to bear in mind that even Acton leaned temporarily toward democracy and that Constant de Rebecque also had a great moment of weakness when this brilliant essayist and politician suddenly decided to collaborate with Napoleon during his Hundred Days. And yet nobody had written a better and more scathing analysis of the democratic French Revolution and the Bonapartist dictatorship than the early liberal Benjamin Constant during his exile. These things, unfortunately, do happen. Still, the early liberals are certainly nondemocrats or antidemocrats whereas their successors, the old liberals, had usually a philosophical and ideological outlook which predisposed them to view democracy in more positive terms. The main reason for this state of affairs *is the strongly "agnostic" bent of the old liberals.*

Genuine liberals always wanted freedom. It is, however, precisely this quest for freedom which in certain minds started the idea that every firm conviction, every strong affirmation *automatically* results in intolerance. As we have pointed out in Chapter IV, the *possibility* of a truly convinced man's intolerance (and "illiberality") *exists*: It is a hurdle, a temptation he has to overcome. Those, however, who do not believe in absolute truth or in the human ability to attain truth, are naturally not tolerant but merely *indifferent*. Still the confusion between tolerance and indifference hardly bothered many old liberals who thought they could "play safe" by preaching a basically agnostic attitude (to use the word in a much wider than merely theological sense) and by waging a real intellectual and political crusade against all who believed in absolutes. These were decried as "dogmatists." Such an attitude, as could be expected, put the old liberals all too frequently in opposition to Christianity and especially to Christian orthodoxy of any denomination.

It is precisely this leaning towards "agnosticism" which facilitated the old liberals' armistice or even alliance with democracy. Democracy—as democratism—is an ideology, though in its simpler form it can also be seen purely as a system, as a mere procedure for "producing," i.e., for selecting, a government. A democratic constitution offers a frame into which a picture can be fitted through the voting process. It is the majority vote which usually determines the character of the picture. Now, according to *standard* democratic doctrine—there are a few others—every full citizen has the right not only to vote, but also to organize a party or to propose local candidates. The guardians of the democratic constitution have to adopt a neutral position toward all candidates, all parties, all ideas represented. One man is as good as any other man, one opinion as good as any other, all men and all opinions are invited to participate in the race, and he who wins numerically gets the prize. Democracy as an abstract principle has to insist on fair play, must express no preferences, and thus also has to give a "break" to parties which would put an end to the democratic order.

If 51 percent or, better still, two-thirds of a people vote one or several antidemocratic parties into power, the end of democracy is at hand. In other words, *democracy can commit suicide democratically.*

This quandary, this dilemma of democracy appears in many parts of the world. Italian law gives democratic rights to Communists but not to Fascists. (The M.S.I. is not exactly the successor of the old Fascist party.) In Argentina the real Peronists could not run for office either. (They might actually have won as much as a good one-third of the votes in free elections.) In short, democracy often distinguishes undemocratically between supporters of its own ideology and its adversaries—whereby the totalitarian aspects of democracy, perhaps tragically and unavoidably, become manifest.

An ideal democracy does not discriminate. Fearful of violent dissent which rends asunder the fabric of state and society, it not only tries to be neutral but knowingly-unknowingly considers an "agnostic" attitude to be the natural lubricant for the democratic process. Precisely here we find the golden bridge between old liberalism and democracy. People in a democracy should have tenuous party affiliations: Their convictions should not be too well grounded and their loyalties ought to be superficial. Otherwise they might always vote in the same way. A happy democracy of a liberal character where freedom survives, rests on *change*, however, not permanance. The citizens should be in the mood to switch their votes and individuals, parties, and party leaders should always be ready to engage in compromise, in fifty-fifty arrangements which are the lifeblood of parliamentarianism. (Here one should not overlook the coalition cabinets on the Continent which—in contrast to the Anglo-American world—are the rule and not the exception.)

Democracy and old liberalism have something else in common. They share the optimistic Roussellian view of man. Man is basically good and wise; let him act according to his whims, his desires, his intuitions, and everything will be all right. The good people will prevail—almost automatically. In this attitude democracy is far from Calvin and the argument that it really has its historic roots in Calvinist synods (the Synod of Dordrecht has been named as a conspicuous example) becomes somewhat questionable. Of course the term "good" implies a value judgment. The true agnostic would be rather inclined to say, "Man is as he is; you prefer him to act this way and I that way, and that is where we are." Such would be the position of the grandfather of democracy, the Marquis de Sade. Still, whatever the formulation, democracy and old liberalism give a basically unqualified "yes" to man, though not to each individual man. In this respect, needless to say, old liberalism shows that it has its roots in preliberalism rather than in early liberalism. The fear of "interference" is very highly developed in the first and third stage of genuine liberalism. Here again the deist and subtly pantheistic attitude of the Manchester School and Adam Smith comes to the fore. Democracy as an ideology maintains that if one voted after mature reflection and in an "unfettered" way, the relatively best decision could be made and progress thereby assured. "A million eyes see better than a single pair!"

This, however, as we all know, is certainly not borne out by the facts. Such belief is a fetish of the democratist, a magic formula which, as history teaches, sometimes works and sometimes doesn't. For reasons we shall give elsewhere, it will work less and less as time goes on last but not least because the "Information Explosion" has brought us confusion and bewilderment rather than enlightenment and balance. To know facts still does not mean to know how to weigh evidence.

The democratic optimism as to man, his nature, and the entire universe also animated the old liberals who, to be sure, unlike certain democrats, always insisted that man needs first to be educated. (We guardedly said "certain democrats" because there are many people who seem enchanted if elections are held in African jungles where the illiterates are gently guided by the choice of animal symbols. Knowledge and maturity are undemocratic principles! The vast majority of democrats, however, still believe that literacy is a prerequisite for the vote—the new American "voting rights" bill notwithstanding!—and that a free press and witty radio commentators can do the trick.)

This emphasis on education in an intellectual and a moral sense has definitely an elitarian character. Just like the preliberals, the old liberals thought that the sum total of all enlightened self-interests would, in a mysterious harmony, automatically make for happiness and a life of plenty, that especially in the field of economics this would lead to abundance and the survival of the fittest. These in turn, by their pull and their shining example would raise general levels. Half truths, one can say, are optimistic exaggerations. Still, the old liberal stand caused infinitely fewer tragedies than the opposite errors of the leftist gnostics (in the sense Eric Voegelin uses this term) and of the red "Monasticists" whom we have mentioned earlier.

As one can easily see, there is a certain psychological connection between the social Darwinism adopted by the old liberals (strongly rejected by most of the early liberals)[13] and democratic optimism believing not exactly in the survival of the fittest, but in the identity of wisdom and majority opinion. (There is a precursor to this in the Christian adage *securus iudicat orbis terrarum*: The judgment of the big wide world is infallible.) It should not be surprising that this old liberal social Darwinism not only had a Manchesterian root but also played into the hands of the Nazis at a later period.[14] In the whole Manchesterian calculation, however, there always lurked the danger of mammothism and colossalism, of cartels, trust, and monopolies which are an evil not *so* much because they are big and dwarf the individual, but because they are menacing the most important aspect of a free economy, i.e., *competition*. Without a free choice for the customer to buy this or that product and without the competition between enterprises trying to produce the best and the cheapest, there is no free economy. True, the evils engendered by a private monopoly are sometimes as great as those due to the state monopoly of socialism. We say "sometimes" because the monolithic aspect of state-controlled economic production, as well as the repetitious rewards for party loyalty which are crucial in the managerial appointments inevitably lead to corruption and inefficiency—and these indeed are the far greater evils. Thus the private enterprise monopolies, though lacking the proper incentives of competition, will still give better service, will be better administered, will make greater efforts than their state-owned counterparts. There is an example of this in the United States where the Bell Telephone System is a virtual monopoly but still vastly superior to the United States Post Office with its strongly political character, the job of postmaster being one of the typical plums in the spoils system.

Old liberalism in Europe also had the tendency to enter into various alliances and combinations. On the one hand it preached an extreme liberalism in the economic field, but on the other it merged with nationalism which, in Europe, has an ethnic connotation. Bismarck derived his main support from the National Liberals and not from the Prussian conservatives who were Prussian patriots and not nationalists with Pan-German leanings. Ethnic nationalism was always anti-Catholic, anti-Papal—with the exception of Irish and Polish nationalism—and above all this animosity played into the hands of the old liberals. Since they hated anything they called "dogmatism," they were, as we have hinted before, opposed to religious orthodoxy and above all to Rome. Bismarck's *Kulturkampf* pleased nationalists, old liberals, and national liberals almost equally. (It won *no* applause from the Prussian conservatives although they were staunch Lutherans.)[15] Obviously the aristocratic character of early liberalism was not inherited by the old liberals who got their main support from the upper and middle bourgeoisie, precisely the layers of society which had anticlerical and nationalistic leanings. In some countries—we think here above all of the Latin nations—old liberalism allied itself strongly with Freemasonry, which in these countries has a character quite at variance with its counterpart in the English-speaking world. There was and there remains a real antagonism between the Grand Orient of Paris with all its affiliates and the two main British rites.

Given all these alliances and connections it is not surprising that old liberalism became illiberal. If one is solemnly convinced that all strong stands, all firm affirmations, all orthodoxy, all absolutes in thought are evil, then indeed one becomes inclined to show hostility to all representatives of "absolutism" (religious, political, philosophical, or otherwise) and, if one had the chance, to persecute them methodically and mercilessly. Since the old liberals in the second half of the Nineteenth century and also frequently in the early Twentieth century had, thanks to the property qualifications for voting, great parliamentary power, they could also abuse it. Owing to their intellectual appeal they had a near monopoly in the universities and acquired an iron grip on the press, the theater, and the entire intellectual life. Thus they could painfully discriminate against their conservative and Christian opponents. The Holy American Illiberal Inquisition, as we see, had a forerunner.

The old liberals, moreover, had some supporters in the working class, even in the aristocracy and quite frequently in the royal families. They were, in fact, only rarely antimonarchists. They were favorable to democracy, as we have pointed out before, but they did not underwrite it without reservations and usually considered it as just one useful element in a mixed government. The Spanish aristocracy was largely liberal.[16] So was a sizable part of the Italian, the Portuguese, the Bavarian,[17] the Hungarian, and the Scottish nobility. Franz Josef's sympathies lay with the liberals and so, notoriously, did his son's, the ill-fated Crown Prince Rudolf. His brother the tragic Maximilian of Mexico, contrary to what the average American or European tends to believe, was even an ardent liberal. The royal houses of Italy, Spain, and Portugal were largely liberal.[18] "Privileges" were not decried by the old liberals provided these were held by the "right people." Whatever might be said against the old liberals—and a great deal can be—they were never really a party of the left.

Actually the old liberals were responsible for their own decline around the end of the century. In Austria the introduction of the one-man-one-vote principle in 1907 was a great blow to them. Their anticlericalism led to a rather well-organized Catholic opposition which astounded and dismayed the old liberal leadership. It is obvious that the Church did not at all like the idea of descending into the political arena and competing with other secular ideologies. It was the (inofficially Catholic) Center party which defeated Bismarck and made him eat humble pie. These Catholic parties, after all, had the allegiance of a good cross-section of the people—peasants, craftsmen, shopkeepers, professional men, intellectuals, and the nobility. (The evangelicals could not found a similar party because they were already doctrinally too much allied with old liberalism and/or nationalism.) All the troubles the old liberals had caused in marriage and school legislation, all the laws they had enacted which were alien to the spirit of the Church (*compulsory* civil marriage, as an example) now boomeranged against them.

A boomerang, however, also came from the other side: the rise of the Socialist parties which had partly benefited from the "anticlerical" attitude spread rather unwisely by the old liberals. Neither the new Catholic nor the Socialist opposition against old liberalism was characterized by an appeal to liberty. As a matter of fact, old liberalism had contributed by its ambiguous attitudes to rendering even the word liberty suspect.[19] In France liberty meant expelling religious orders. In Hungary it was used to justify compulsory civil marriage. In Spain it worked as a screen for the confiscation of almost all Church property. In Switzerland and in Germany it was invoked to exile the Jesuits.

By the outbreak of World War I old liberalism found itself in a very grave crisis. It remained entrenched in certain intellectual strongholds, but it was totally beaten in the field of power politics. The liberal parties on the Continent had been decimated: What remained were specific positions in the universities and the still sizable liberal press, which had become a middle-of-the-road institution promising (not always truthfully) "objectivity" to its readers. In the practical political sphere, however, it no longer could "deliver the goods." This startling phenomenon could be observed all over Europe. Papers such as the *Frankfurter Zeitung,* the *Corriere della Sera, Le Temps, Die Neue Freie Presse,* or *De Algemeene Handelsblad* still held their leading position, but they ceased to affect elections. Deeply allied with nationalism, the old liberals could not take an independent line in World War I either. Among the Allies they were tied to the war interest, felt that they had a real stake in it and naively hoped that the murderous struggle would foster their cause. Among the Central Powers old liberalism was haunted by the thought that its followers were better entrenched in the Allied camp. And when it came to the Paris Peace Conference, Western old liberals were among the most fanatic supporters of a "hard peace," thus contributing to the rise of National Socialism in Germany, while in Central Europe they tended to blame their old governments for the beginning and the end of the war and thereby invited the wrath of the totalitarian nationalists, who denounced them as traitorous collaborators with the West. Whatever they did, they did wrong, which is not so surprising in the light of the fact that they had completely parted with absolutes and played politics "by ear." History does not honor mere goodwill or good intentions.

When the totalitarian wave started, the old liberals were persecuted, in a sense, more bitterly than the people on the left. Those on the left —Socialists, Communists, and Jacobin democrats—were totalitarian competitors, not mutual enemies. The Social Democratic worker in Essen and the Socialist worker in Sesto San Giovanni or in Turin could very easily switch sides: The worker in Essen gave up international socialism and embraced National Socialism. The directors of his factory were now mere stewards of the state. The worker in Turin knew that Benito Mussolini had been a Socialist and that the Fascist movement had grown out of Italian socialism, shedding first of all its international outlook.[20] (This is just what the Czech National Socialists had done when they seceded from the Czech Social Democratic Party in 1897.) The old liberals had nothing but declared enemies and no competitors. They could not easily "switch." The new, big totalitarian parties stemming from the French Revolution boasted of being "democratic." They called themselves "Socialist": They too were engaged in that perennial trick of successful leftist parties ever since 1789, the "mobilization of envy." The old liberals, whatever their faults (and they had many), abstained from this tempting strategy which proved so rewarding at the polls.

Professor Eduard Heimann, a German "Religious Socialist," wrote very correctly during World War II:

> Hitlerism proclaims itself as both true democracy and true socialism, and the terrible truth is that there is a grain of truth to such claims—an infinitesimal grain, to be sure, but at any rate enough to serve as a basis for such fantastic distortions. Hitlerism even goes so far as to claim the role of protector of Christianity, and the terrible truth is that even this gross misinterpretation is able to make some impression. But one fact stands out with perfect clarity in all the fog: Hitler has never claimed to represent true liberalism. Liberalism then has the distinction of being the doctrine most hated by Hitler![21]

We, however, would go a great deal further than this author who

196

by conviction was a democrat and a Socialist. Still, his thesis is correct—even in the light of the curious fact that "National Liberalism," this particular central European compound, had and even today still has subtle links with Nazism. Since the death of the so oratorically gifted German Social Democrat leader Kurt Schumacher, a real nationalist, the Nazi old guard rather sympathizes with the Free Democratic party (F.D.P.), aptly called by the foreign press the "liberal party." Exactly the same situation exists in Austria where the *Freiheitliche Partei Oster-reichs* (F.P.O, Liberal party of Austria) is the joint party of surviving old liberals and of ex-Nazis. And it is not so much the "National Liberal" past, but rather "anticlericalism" which brought both camps together. It was also, needless to say, not the enthusiasm for liberty but the hostility towards organized religion in general and Christian orthodoxy in particular that caused the old liberalism to be energetically attacked by the Catholic Church. Pope Pius IX in Proposition 80 of his *Syllabus errorum* (December 8, 1864) condemned the following statement: "The Roman Pontiff can and should reconcile himself and cooperate with progress, liberalism and modern civil society."[22]

This antiliberal trauma remained for a long time a very potent force in orthodox Christianity (not only in the Catholic Church!) and when neoliberalism developed in the 1930s and 1940s it was often difficult to persuade freedom-loving Christian thinkers that this new phase of liberalism differed in many important and even decisive ways from its immediate predecessor, because the word "liberal" created a mental block among many devout Christians.

The term neoliberalism, denoting the fourth phase of liberalism, hardly appears before the end of World War II. When in 1946 a remnant of liberal scholars met at the Mont-Pèlerin Hotel near the northern shores of Lake Geneva to coordinate their forces and form an organization, it soon became apparent that a certain fission had taken place in and outside the domain of economics. There were now, mostly in central Europe, thinkers who viewed the problem of liberty in a different light than the men who belonged to a somewhat older generation and in many ways could have been called their teachers. (Almost all of them, to be sure, as far as economics go, had been inspired by Ludwig von Mises.) But in matters of economics these newer lights were less radical in their outlook and they admitted curbs on mammothism and colossalism to preserve competition. They thought that the state had a right and even a duty to correct possible abuses of economic freedom—just as we give to a mature person a driving license and the right to travel wherever he wants but still make him submit to traffic laws. Yet probably more important than this change was the reappraisal of religion, especially of Christianity. Many of the neoliberals declared that it is not sufficient to prove that "liberty delivers the goods," that freedom is more agreeable or more productive than slavery. There must be philosophical and even theological reasons why liberty must be achieved, fostered, preserved. One of the neoliberals, perhaps the one best known in the United States, the late Professor Wilhelm Röpke, maintained that even if it could be proved to him that a planned and collective economy is materially superior to a free one, he would still, in an "ascetic" spirit, prefer the latter. Under these circumstances sacrifices of a material order would have to be made to preserve the dignity of man. From such views we can deduct that the neoliberals had, in a certain way, a greater affinity with the early liberals than with their immediate predecessors. Interested in economic problems, they refused, however, to make a fetish of economics and they tried to integrate their economic views into a metaphysical humanism. The great early liberal thinkers, from de Tocqueville to Burckhardt, were seriously studied by new liberals who in many cases were professing Christians.

The new liberalism started in the German-speaking countries. This is not an accident because in this area the old liberalism had suffered its major bankruptcy and had helped to undermine the older Christian civilization, a process from which the totalitarians derived the greatest profit.[23] Who are the leading neoliberals? Three of the founders of the new liberalism have died: Walter Eucken, professor of economics at Freiburg University in Breisgau,[24] Alexander Rüstow, professor emeritus of Heidelberg University, and Wilhelm Röpke, professor at the Ecole des Hautes Etudes in Geneva. Alexander Rüstow was the son of a Prussian general who, out of juvenile enthusiasm, joined the Spartacist movement in 1919.[25] Penniless and near despair, he was aided by that famous Catholic priest and charity organizer, Dr. Carl Sonnenschein who provided him with a desk and a typewriter. Rüstow, never adhering formally to a church, and always cultivating a somewhat anarchical outlook, became first deeply interested in Greek philosophy (especially in the pre-Socratics) and only later in his life concentrated on economic problems within their historical, sociological, and theological context. When Nazism made research impossible and academic liberties illusory, Rüstow emigrated to Turkey in order to remain near to his country. He taught for many years at the University of Istanbul.

Alexander Rüstow is famous not only for his essay on Manchesterism but mainly for his stupendous three-volume *Ortsbestimmung der Gegenwart*. Like all other neoliberals, Rüstow (who died in 1964) always

198

refused to deal with economics in an isolated way, detached from all the other disciplines. His book, whose title in English, literally translated, means "Location of the Present" offers us a sweeping historical view of one of our last polyhistors, a work in some ways more impressive than Toynbee's *A Study of History*. Today, however, the use of any language other than English is a grave handicap to worldwide fame. Jacob Burckhardt (*orbiit* 1897), for instance, was unknown in the English-speaking world until the middle of World War II, and even Max Weber gained only posthumous recognition in America. Very little, indeed, is known in the United States or even in Britain about the conservative authors of the Continent.

The late Walter Eucken, professor of economics, and Franz Böhm, professor of law at Jena University, were both active in the German resistance. (Eucken was jailed for some time.) After the war they founded *Ordo*, a liberal (predominantly neoliberal) yearbook containing essays of a very high quality. Professor Wilhelm Röpke also fled first to Turkey but finally went to Switzerland, where he taught until his untimely death in Geneva in 1966. During the last years of the war he published his first stirring books. These dealt either with basic economic problems or with political, social, and cultural questions in which he equally espoused the cause of liberty. At the end of the war he wrote a memorandum for the Allies recommending a monarchic restoration in Germany, a step advocated by Chancellor Brüning as early as 1932. In Brüning's case it was the aging Hindenburg, in Röpke's case it was the Allies who ignored these suggestions. As a matter of fact, the Soviets vied with the United States in imposing, fostering, and promoting the republican form of government. Moved by her self-interest, they were seeking a parliamentary frame for Communist parties to cooperate with legally in a constitutional form—eventually to kill the constitution.[26]

Professor Goetz Briefs, another eminent star in the galaxy of neoliberal thinkers, has been living in the United States ever since the earliest days of Nazism and was for a long time professor at Georgetown University. Originally he came from the school loosely identified as "Catholic Social Thought," the tradition emanating from Ketteler and Vogelsang. He started as professor at the *Technische Hochschule* in Berlin-Charlottenburg and is a prolific writer. In recent years he has occupied himself with the problem of trade unions acting as a state within a state and developing here and there into a real menace to a free society—and even to democracy.

The neoliberals are hardly organized and it is significant that in the

A CHART OF THE LIBERALISTS

	PERIOD	TIME	MAIN LEADERS	MAIN INTEREST	POLITICS	RELIGION
I.	Pre-liberal	1750-1810	Adam Smith Manchester School	Economics	Libert-arian	Deist
2.	Early Liberal	1812-1900	(Burke) de Tocque-ville Mont-alembert Guizot Burckhardt Acton	Political Social	Mixed Govern-ment non- or anti-democratic	Christ-ian Pro-Christ-ian
3.	Old Liberal (palaeo-liberal)	1840-1939	Mazzini Gladstone Cavour Cobden Bismarck Clemenceau Croce Asquith L. v. Mises Herriot	Political Economical National	Parlia-mentary Monarchy pro-democratic	Liberal Protest-ant agnostic
3a.	Late British Liberal-ism	1900-1960	Lloyd George Young Churchill	Economical Social Political	Parliam-entary (symbolic) Monarchy Democratic	Indiff-erent
4.	New Liberal (Neo-liberal)	1945-cont.	Rüstow Röpke Eucken Rougier A. Müller-Armack L- Einaudi L. Erhard Franz Böhm Goetz Briefs Daniel Villey	Political Economical Social	Mixed Govern-ment Skeptical towards demo-racy	Christ-ian or pro-Christ-ian

NB. Obviously, a man such as Cobden might also figure as a late preliberal, Edmund Burke as an early conservative. We have omitted American names deliberately.

Germanies they have no special love for those parties which do not quite wear the liberal label but are usually referred to as "liberal." Many of the neoliberals are contributors to *Ordo,* published annually in Düsseldorf. Naturally they collaborate with the *Institut für freie Marktwirtschaft* in Heidelberg-Bonn, an organization engaged in economic research and in propaganda for the "free market economy," i.e., free enterprise. In 1962 they held a memorable private roundtable conference in Augsburg with Catholic sociologists, but the demarcation lines were blurred inasmuch as some of the attending neoliberals were professing Catholics. It became evident that the viewpoints expressed on this occasion were indeed not far from each other.[27]

In a few cases it is not easy to draw the dividing line between neoliberals and certain later old liberals. Professor Friedrich August von Hayek, for instance, is a thinker on the borderline (but rather "old" than "new"). While Wilhelm Röpke could be called a conservative, F.A. v. Hayek declines this label.[28] Alexander Rüstow was in many ways a conservative.

Recapitulating the four phases of genuine liberalism, it might be helpful to make a tabulation which (permitting for certain simplifications) would roughly look like the table on page 200.

Realizing, however, that European new liberals and modern conservatives often have become practically indistinguishable from each other, we cannot help remembering how different the situation is in the United States—not in fact but purely from the point of view of current labels. Indeed, we have before us two problems to be solved: first, to find out how it happened that liberalism in the United States evolved into the very opposite of what it set out to be—if it did "evolve"!—(thereby morally forfeiting the right to call itself "liberal"), and second, later on, to analyze what conservatism, old and new, really stands for or, at least, ought to stand for.

Chapter 14

False Liberalism

Toward the end of World War II the *American Mercury,* then under the editorship of Eugene Lyons, featured a series of articles in which a variety of authors defended their political-social stand. This writer's interest focused on an essay by Oswald Garrison Villard, entitled "Credo of an Old Fashioned Liberal." The article made it evident that Villard's stand showed strong analogies with the gentlemanly and "Erasmian" version of Continental old liberalism—a liberalism, one might add, not so different from the liberalism once prevailing in England and in the United States during most of the nineteenth century. We do not thereby imply that there were no differences on that score on both sides of the Channel.[1] In England, too, where, in a way, the Whigs had been "replaced" by the Liberals, the latter were increasingly exposed to leftist influences. In the Nineteenth century it seemed for a time that the Conservatives (Tories) had a chance to become the party of social reform—especially so under Disraeli and under the influence of Lord Randolph Churchill. This is by no means surprising if we recall that Continental conservatism and certain forms of paternalism went well together as illustrated by the patriarchal character of large land ownership. (In Sweden, in the past, Socialists and Conservatives, often have voted together against the Liberals, the party of big business and industry.) Yet by the end of the nineteenth century in Britain the competition of the Labor Party made itself felt and some of the Liberals drifted toward the left. Fabian influence was by no means innocent in this evolution. A Gladstone, a Rosebery, an Asquith, needless to say, were anything but leftists; but another factor also played a certain role, the split over Irish Home Rule, which was instrumental in facilitating the switching of sides of those Liberals who had nationalist leanings. Under the leadership of David Lloyd George the Liberal party moved to "left of center." Their social program was strongly radicalized and this change had been promoted, fostered, and abetted by an ambitious young man who had deserted the Conservative party to become an ardent Liberal—the son of Lord Randolph Churchill, Mr. Winston Spencer Churchill, whose elevation to the rank of a "Great Conservative" is one of the most amusing misunderstandings in our time. (As a not-so-young Radical he campaigned for Lloyd George's "war budget" against poverty, which was designed to make indigence as rare as the "wolves who once infected England's forests." The "Great Society," Act One!)

As could be suspected, the Labor party finally reduced the Liberals to such a size that they became impotent in British politics and retained only some local influence in Wales. All they can do now is tip the scales in Parliament, provided a near equality in the number of Conservative and Labor MPs makes this possible. Nor does British party Liberalism have any longer a real program—neither politically nor economically.

The evolution of the term "liberal" in the United States, an evolution which took place only in the last thirty years, shows certain minor analogies with the change in Britain but has few equivalents on the Continent. This is so because there the "sectarian liberal," as Carlton J. H. Hayes defined him, might have been prejudiced, inflexible, and petty, especially in his "anticlericalism," but he had no leftist bent and, apart from his nationalistic proclivities,[2] no identitarian mentality. How then did this change really take place? How was it possible that in the United States the word that means freedom-loving, generous, tolerant, open-minded, hostile to state omnipotence and antitotalitarian, came to stand for the very contrary of all these notions and virtues?

This process is easily explained. The "old-fashioned liberal" was often the man who refused to resist what might be called the Wave of the Future. The conservative (and even more so the "reactionary")[3] usually decided to make a stand against change, and change was largely a leftward movement. The leftist ideologies had all assumed (inevitably so, one might say) a "futuristic" character, a term we also find in the history of art, and it is not accidental that its major spokesman,

Marinetti, became an ardent Fascist. The leftist ideologies all claimed the future, they claimed utopia, they claimed the millennium in a chiliastic spirit. They believed in the concept of a near-automatic progress (which needed just a little "push"). The road in this fictional direction had in their eyes the character of an "advance," whereas conservatives merely adhered to the *status quo* and the reactionaries to a "backward trend." The situation in this respect was not radically different on the Continent. It is certainly with a sense of irony that the *Guide Bleu* (Paris: Hachette) edited by Professor Marcel N. Schveitzer of the Sorbonne, said in its 1935 edition, "Málaga is a city of very advanced ideas. On May 12 and 13, 1931, no less than forty-three churches and convents were burnt down" (p. 562). The monarchy had fallen and the short-lived, infamous republic was moving "ahead." It is obvious that an unimaginative martinet such as General Franco wanted to stop this kind of "advance."

There were old-fashioned, i.e., genuine liberals who clung to their convictions; Albert Jay Nock, even H. L. Mencken were among them. But many others dreaded being called conservatives or reactionaries. As long as there existed a utopia at the end of the road, painted in the colors of absolute personal freedom, the genuine liberal was sure to be a "progressive." Before the 1930s the "ultraradical," the extremist (especially in America) was not the Socialist, not the Communist, but the *anarchist*. As a matter of fact, it took Americans quite some time to distinguish between the Communist and the anarchist, and to the average American for a long time the *bolshevik* was an unshaven, rowdyish creature who wanted no law, no order, but the eternal overthrow of everything—in other words, an anarchist. The more spectacular acts of violence were all carried out by anarchists, whereas Communists, believing in mass action at the right time, in military conquest and in civil wars, abhor individual action. Even in Russia the Communists (or, to be even more exact, the radical wing of the Russian Social Democratic Workers' party) had never carried out assassinations or acts of terror, and the very first Communists (*Bolsheviki*) who had suffered death for cause were those executed in the Civil War. *Russian communism up to 1918 had no martyrs.*

When I arrived in the United States for the first time in 1937 I had to give written assurance that I was neither a bigamist nor an anarchist. Violent, rampaging lawless freedom still seemed to be *the* menace. It was also the direction in which the world—to the less initiated at least —gradually seemed to be moving. Respect and authority were declining, divorce was becoming easier and more common, crowned heads were toppling, censorship was disappearing right and left, travel was becoming simpler, liberal parties were still scoring in elections in parts of the Western World. Thus the genuine American liberal could be fully convinced that with his political convictions the future belonged to him. It was only because of the leniency and the tolerance of Americans and British liberals of an age gone by toward the real leftists, that liberals became suspect.

The Great Change, however, came only in the 1930s when certain Americans, who saw in their country primarily not their fatherland but the "American Experiment," suddenly thought that the "Soviet Experiment" offered even more to mankind. This was the "Red Decade," to quote the title of a book by Eugene Lyons.[4] In other words, the vision of tomorrow now took another form. Liberty no longer was the ideal. Security and equality, the promises of international Socialism, rather than individual freedom now were the new goals. Mrs. Anne Morrow Lindbergh, in her book *The Wave of the Future,* pleaded for a more realistic understanding of National Socialism. Yet the disease of democratic utopianism and a certain materialism had already too deeply affected the American liberals for them to overcome the fear of clinging to a "lost cause." They were too afraid to "miss the bus," and the horror of "getting stuck with the ideas of yesterday" troubled them profoundly.[5] They had no consistent system of ideas, no principles, no real leadership. They were drifting, and drifts are determined by winds and currents. These now carried them toward determinism and collectivism, toward a "secular monasticism," and thus toward what can be called the opposite direction from their initial stand, into rank illiberality. At the same time they preserved a few hardly essential notions from their past and, as could be expected, flatly refused to give up their label. In the end we got the Great American Semantic Confusion, and it lives on to this very day.

The old liberal ideas on matters such as sexual morals, prison administration, capital punishment, and the emancipation of women largely survive, but it is in their *basic* outlook on the state and society that the old liberals in the United States (far more so than in Britain) have made an about-face of 180 degrees. Liberals in all ages have looked at the state, always prone to annexations, with a great deal of suspicion. This tendency of the state is especially marked in the democratic order, not only because democracy is inherently totalitarian but also because it works (to use John Adams' term) with *largesses,* large-scale bribes, promises rashly and shrewdly made by the *demagogoi.* It matters little that the encroachments of the state tend in a subtle way to undermine democracy. Bureaucracy quickly assumes oligarchic and autocratic traits. Yet expansion, encroachment on personal rights, remains inseparable from democracy.[6]

The old liberal did not necessarily like the democratic notion of the "politicized citizenry." As a matter of fact, he often suspected it of being fundamentally illiberal. However, his resistance against the new winds and currents was not only weak because he cherished so deeply the idea of belonging to the camp of the innovators, progressivists, and "dawnists" (an expression of Michael de la Bédoyère) hailing the new and damning the obsolete, but because *he had previously been robbed of his sense of values*. He had lost his philosophical props at a much earlier date. These had been eliminated half a generation before by philosophies such as instrumentalism and behaviorism, as well as by "polite doubt," actually a refined form of positivism. This view has been represented so well in the American scene by Oliver Wendell Holmes, Jr., grandson of a Calvinist clergyman, son of a theologically liberal physician and essayist, himself a Justice of the Supreme Court of the United States—and a complete nihilist. Whereas pragmatism came on the American educational scene through that notorious institution of pedagogical training of which it has been said that there false pearls were thrown to real swine, the Justice influenced legal thinking, which in the United States is equally important to education.

As a real positivist Holmes could write that, "Sovereignty is a form of power, and the will of the sovereign is law because he has power to compel obedience or punish disobedience and for no other reason. The limits within which his will is law, then, are those within which he has, or is believed to have power to compel or to punish."[7]

If these were his true convictions there was certainly no reason why he should have condemned the horrors of the French Revolution, of Sachsenhausen, or of the *kontslageri* of Stalin. Or was this only a *lapsus linguae*? Holmes could hardly have been more explicit when he wrote: "I think that the sacredness of human life is a purely municipal idea of no validity outside the jurisdiction; I believe that force, mitigated so far as may be by good manners, is the *ultima ratio*, and between two groups that want to make inconsistent kinds of a world I see no remedy except force. . . ."[8]

What a pity, a Nazi might say, that Holmes was not one of the judges at Nuremberg. (He died in 1935.) The Nazis also could have made monkeys out of the Allies simply by quoting him. And if the reader is not convinced by these passages, let us add another: "I see no reason for attributing to man a significance different in kind from that which belongs to a baboon or a grain of sand. I believe that our personality is a cosmic ganglion, just as when certain rays meet and cross there is a white light at the meeting point, but the rays go on after the meeting as they did before, so, when certain other streams of energy cross at the meeting point, the cosmic ganglion can frame a syllogism or wag its tail."[9] There we have it: a grain of sand, baboon, Jew, "bourgeoisie"—let's rub them out!

Does it make us much happier to learn that the late Justice Holmes had a most humble opinion about himself? His pessimistic nihilism surely extended to his own person as we feel when we read, "I may work a year or two but I cannot hope to add much to what I have done. I am too skeptical to think that it matters much, but too conscious of the mystery of the universe to say that it or anything else does not. I bow my head, I think serenely and say, as I told to someone the other day, O Cosmos—Now lettest thou thy ganglion dissolve in peace."[10]

This admission is not less dangerous because it is melancholic in spirit. It has, however, helped to establish a pattern which still is going strong, witness the opinion given by Justice Vinson in 1951 in connection with a trial of Communists: "Nothing is more certain in modern society than the principle that there are no absolutes, that a name, a phrase, a standard has meaning only when associated with the considerations which give birth to nomenclature. To those who would paralyze our Government in the face of impending threat by encasing it in a semantic strait-jacket, we must reply that all concepts are relative."[11]

Oliver Wendell Holmes, Jr. would have subscribed to this formulation half a century earlier. He once said that Emperor Franz Josef was a gentleman, but that the monarch was a "perfect illustration of my old saying that no gentleman can be a philosopher and no philosopher a gentleman: To the philosopher everything is fluid—even himself."[12] This means, in other words, that there is a real antithesis between philosophy and permanence, that there can be no immutable truths. The consequences of such an attitude, clearly catastrophic, have shocked a number of European philosophers,[13] though others expressed analogous ideas. An Austrian legal thinker of considerable influence on both sides of the Atlantic, Hans Kelsen, drafter of the still valid republican constitution of Austria, has said that, "Justice is an irrational ideal. However indispensable it might be for man's will and action, it cannot be reached by knowledge."[14] The real danger of this nihilism lies in the fact that its disciples find no reason to resist evil and are intellectually defenseless in the face of such diabolical menaces as

National or International Socialism. Kelsen was once asked by Wilhelm Röpke what cogent argument he had against the Nazi extermination camps, whereupon he just smiled and shrugged his shoulders—even though, had he stayed on in Austria, he would have been one of their victims.[15]

The lack of well-grounded convictions, the absence of a belief in truth create a dangerous hunger. And since nature abhors a vacuum, the absolutes of the totalitarian systems suddenly find customers. The isms then appear on the scene and, as Fëdor Stepun said, "Give to the hungry demo-liberal-nihilistic world the 'truth,' but this 'truth' in reality is a lie and a travesty of religion."[16] Of course, as Keyserling has observed, there also exists, a real absolutism of the relativists (who remind one of Hayes's "sectarian liberals"), but they fail in the emergency. They can be petty, stupid, and stubborn, but they cannot make a stand for the true good, even if such stand is in favor of the positive values inherent in the great religions of the West.[18]

This nihilism goes very well with the naturalism represented by Edward Lee Thorndike, who had a great influence at Teachers College, Columbia University. Dr. S. J. Holmes has well summed up the philosophy of Professor Thorndike in the following words: "Man's traits, insofar as they are a part of his inheritance, owe their origin and biological meaning to their survival value. All natural traits and impulses of human beings must therefore be fundamentally good, if we consider the good as the biologically useful. Cruelty, selfishness, lust, cowardice, and deceit are normal ingredients of human nature which have their useful role in the struggle for existence. Intrinsically they are all virtues. It is only their excess or their exercise under the wrong conditions that justly incur our moral disapproval."[19] Was Professor Thorndike an isolated case of the lonely thinker or a real former of minds on a large scale? Dean Seashore of the University of Iowa said of him: "No school is uninfluenced and no humanistic science is unaffected by his labor." Dean James E. Russell insisted that, "In developing the subject of educational psychology and in making it fit study for students in all departments, Professor Thorndike has shaped the character of the college in its youth as no one else has done and as no one will ever have the opportunity of doing."[20]

There are interesting parallels between the nihilistic and materialistic undermining of the old-fashioned American liberal faith with relativist ideas and the erosion of the faith of the French upper layers prior to the Revolution through Voltairean skepticism, followed by the fanatical, yet in a way consistent philosophy of Rousseau. The nihilism inherent in the instrumentalism and pragmatism of John Dewey's philosophy also provided Marxism with an opening wedge. If all spiritual values, if Revelation, if the concept of the natural law, if the Aristotelian tradition were "illusory" and Christian existentialism from St. Augustine to Kierkegaard were "unscientific," then a naked materialism within and outside existentialism might well be the answer. As we have seen, de Sade had established this bridge between a subjectivist relativism and rank materialism.

In other words, not only the "drifting" of lost old liberals, but also a corrosive agnosticism helped to transfigure this set of ideas into the very opposite of what they first were. This is not the first time history has seen such a metamorphosis. One has only to remember the ideas and ideals the Reformers stood for, then look at the form and content of religious thought offered to students in the *average* "Protestant" theological seminary in the United States. (Here we are obviously not talking about the admirable fundamentalist or orthodox institutes of theological learning, which are in a minority and often sadly lack prestige.) The "outstanding" theological seminaries of the Reformation faiths are normally victims of the grandchild of Catholic Scholasticism, that is to say Rationalism, and of the grandchild of Catholic Renaissance, the Enlightenment. To make matters worse, there is the lamentable tendency to project modern, popular notions about "Protestantism" back to the Reformers.[21] Not only would it have been interesting to see Luther's reaction if anybody had called him a "Protestant," a term of contempt coined by the budding Counterreformation,[22] he would also have been amazed at being accused of advocating "private interpretation,"[23] an early liberalism, the abolition of auricular confession, or of the Latin language in the ritual,[24] humanitarianism, individualism, racial equality, democracy, etc. The Reformation was a rigoristic, conservative movement, a reaction *against* humanism, against the Renaissance, which eventually became totally transformed by highly secular tendencies emanating, to be true, from cultural trends in the *orbis Catholicus*. In other words, if we exclude fundamentalism and orthodoxy (or neoorthodoxy), "Protestantism" became its very opposite. And we cite this religious analogy because the same can be said of American liberalism, though even here we have glaring exceptions. Professor Milton Friedman, for instance, who teaches at the University of Chicago and acted as advisor to Senator Goldwater during the latter's presidential campaign, still calls himself proudly a liberal.[25] And so do others.

Since American freelancing leftism, parading under the stolen liberal label, is the result of an inversion of its former self, it does not present us with a truly systematic and coherent logical picture. It suffers from inconsistencies and contradictions. No wonder, since it is a halfway house, after all. Thus the American leftist or left-of-centrist,[26] while talking basically the identitarian jargon of leftism, will suddenly inject into his talk ideas belonging to the liberal past. Not being a systematic thinker, but a person subconsciously torn between parts of American folklore, nineteenth-century reactions to Calvinism and radical leftism, he is not really aware of his dilemma.

And not being aware of his dilemma, he is prone to the worst miscalculations in dealing with truly systematic thought abroad. Hence his naive belief that (to quote only one instance) Russian Marxism could be liberalized to the extent that Western "capitalism," treated with Socialist hormones, could finally meet it halfway. The meeting, naturally, can be effected, but only in such a way that the flexible is bent like a blade against a concrete wall until it touches the rigid. We can be gradually socialized, communized and sovietized: Industries can be "nationalized"; but it is difficult to see how Russian industry or agriculture could ever be transformed into private property without (a) the collapse of the secular religion of communism, and (b) a transitional period of total chaos and anarchy. Revolution always remains a possibility (though in a totalitarian state a fairly remote one) but from an evolutionary viewpoint socialism is always a dead-end street. Yugoslavia now experiences this difficulty. If you have the two long legs of free enterprise you can run; with the short legs of socialism you barely walk; but with one long and one short leg you fall on your nose.

We must also beware of believing that ideologies can be dealt with in the abstract, i.e., without any reference to national psychological situations. British and American thought looks with disfavor upon "systems," airtight explanations of history, religion, psychology, economics, etc.[27] It does not like extremes. It has a horror of going down to roots ("radicalism") or of embracing the Absolute.[28] Thus it is not merely the transitional aspect of American left-of-centrism that gives it its confused character, but also the "Anglo-Saxon" isolation made worse by a dislike for system, method, and logical rigidity. Witness Oliver Wendell Holmes's insistence that no gentleman can be a philosopher.[29]

If one peruses the Thirty-Nine Articles of the "Liberal Creed" as presented in James Burnham's brilliant *Suicide of the West*,[30] one is immediately aware of the frequency of contradictions and of the highly eclectic character of the "tenets." Point 9, for instance, saying that

210

governments have the right to expropriate (though not without reasonable compensation) its own nationals or foreigners, is clearly a leftist proposition. But to say, as Point 17 insists, that Communists have a right to express their opinion, is a liberal, not necessarily a leftist view. Yet when it is deprived of its corollary, i.e., that Fascists and Nazis ought to have the same right, it is a *parti pris* for a specific type of leftism against another one and thus becomes illiberal. Point 38, declaring that everyone has the right to form and join trade unions, is liberal rather than leftist, but if the formulation were to the effect that everybody gainfully employed should be *forced* to join a union or a specific union, then we would be face to face with a genuinely leftist, antipersonal and coercive demand stemming from a social totalitarianism that might even be endorsed by the state. (Of course the closed shop and the union shop are rather "democratic": no escape from conformity and horizontal pressures.) Point 19, stating that corporal punishment, except possibly for small children, is wrong, is also liberal and not leftist. The pros and cons of such an issue have a great deal to do with ethnic-cultural patterns. (Corporal punishment has a stronger tradition in Northern and Eastern than in Central or Southern Europe.) Point 8 is interesting because it states that progressive income and inheritance taxes are the fairest form of taxation. Is this liberal or leftist? Here the answer is not easy. It is not only part of American, but also of Western folklore that the rich ought to be "soaked." As long as the majorities endorse this practice (and they do), it must be considered democratic—even though it is contrary to the democratic principle of equality, because if the rich man pays 50 cents and his less affluent fellow-citizen only 25 cents of his dollar in taxes, equality before the law becomes a sham.[31]

Yet, whatever our exegesis of Mr. Burnham's test, it is obvious that American leftism, which no longer deserves the name of liberalism, has a transitory character, but the transition takes place progressively from rightist to leftist positions. This evolution, moreover, is not only in harmony with the likings and leanings of the semiintellectuals who provide American moderate leftism with leadership but is also largely consonant with the instincts and aspirations of the masses—of the American masses as well as of the masses anywhere else.

There exists, primarily in America, a myth to the effect that the masses are noble, good, decent, honest, and that they are merely misled by diabolical eggheads of the leftist persuasion, by a tiny minority with key positions in education, publishing, the press, the theatrical world, and the movie industry. This, however, is a gross and dangerous oversimplification. There might be certain "sound instincts" in the multitudes, but since they consist of human beings and not angels, they are also subject to animal instincts and to specifically human frailties: envy, jealousy, egotism, greed, avarice, pettiness. Their sense of justice is not always strong, their sadistic drives can be well developed, their sense of fairness impaired, their knowledge limited, their historic memory bad, and so forth. Thus the question remains whether the American moderate leftists have injected new and evil ideas into the American scene or whether they have not rather exploited negative drives, have appealed to the seamier side of human nature and, above all, have achieved whatever popularity they have by merely formulating cleverly and coherently the ideas and notions which could be found inchoately before their rise to eminence, before they took over the intellectual leadership of the nation. In spite of the fact that American leftists were quite adroit in importing ideas from Europe and have acted consistently as agents of European ideologies, propagating them either in *toto* or in selected fragments in a new synthesis, they were never insensitive to local American notions. Take merely the curious expression "Americanism": Communist propaganda in the late 1930s and early 1940s operated with the slogan "Communism is twentieth-century Americanism."

In other words, American leftism derives its strength from an interplay between imported ideas, cherished popular American traditions, and appeals to the higher or, if need be, to the lower human appetites. Communism, socialism, "welfarism,"[32] ideas from the French Revolution, or "democracy" are clearly importations. The anticolonialist crusade, which has done such tremendous harm to all concerned, rests on American folklore (as far as it does not also derive some impetus from the democratic dogma), whereas Woodrow Wilson's program to "make the world safe for democracy" has idealistic undertones, and the "sexual revolution," so dear to the non-Marxist left anywhere, appeals to baser instincts.

It is in the domain of sex, "below the belt," and probably in this region only, that the liberal principle has been preserved. (To which one might add another "biological" stand, antiracism.) American leftism not only is antipuritanical, it stands for libertinism. (To what extent the defense of homosexual practices, a cause popular with the uncommitted left the world over, is due to the strong identitarian strain in leftism, will always remain an element of speculation.) The American non-Marxist leftist is naturally feminist, and the leftist bent of the female feminist—the ex-suffragette type—is very marked in America.

212

But the American leftist is not really a lover of women, and one also has to keep in mind that the American matriarchy is a myth.[33] Women in America have a very wide ghetto in which they rule supreme, but they have neither the influence women have in France nor (of a different type) in Italy, nor in the upper layers of central and Eastern Europe. In Spain, nay, even in misogynist England, one can imagine a ruling Queen, but America could not conceivably elect a female President. (A female Vice President succeeding a male President? Perhaps. But a lady "stumping" the country?)

Libertinism, however, is frowned upon by the stricter leftist ideologies. Although homosexuality was not infrequent in certain Nazi circles and even had its advocates in proto-Nazi groups,[34] it was savagely punished by the Nazi authorities. In the concentration camps the homosexuals were assembled into punitive units with distinctive marks on their uniforms. In the Soviet Union, too, homosexuality is considered a crime—which indeed makes no sense taking into consideration the deterministic character of the official Soviet philosophy.[35] (As a matter of fact, since materialism rejects the notion of free will, why should there be any punishment for anything? De Sade asked this question earlier.)

The American uncommitted left retains, apart from its sexual antipuritanism, a few humanitarian residues from its genuinely liberal ancestors. It usually has a dislike for capital punishment, though this sort of retribution was first abolished in Western civilization by the Hapsburgs in Tuscany[36] and Austria and by Catherine II in Russia. It was later temporarily reintroduced in Austria and Russia, but after 1898 Emperor Franz Josef pardoned every culprit condemned to death— with one exception. (In 1898 the Empress Elizabeth was murdered in Geneva by an Italian anarchist: Franz Joseph's *practical* abolition of the death penalty was a Christian reply to his own loss in a great dialogue with God. Nor was Gavrilo Prinćip, murderer of his nephew and heir to the throne and virtual initiator of World War I, executed.)[37] In Russia the death penalty was practically reabolished by Alexander II (after having been once abolished by Catherine II) and remained almost in abeyance until the Communists became the masters of the country: It was reserved mainly for assassinations or attempted assassinations of members of the Imperial family. As a matter of fact, it is psychologically very difficult for a monarch to sign the death warrant for one of his subjects with whom he is connected in a father-son relationship. (Here also lies the reason for the ready abdication of dynasties, since they cannot easily fire at their "children" in times of stress and revolts.)[38] In republics the situation is radically different, because the person of the magistrate is less important, the democratic republic works with abstractions (the constitution, the law, the general will) whereas monarchy is personal government.[39] According to democratic doctrine the citizen revolting against a "duly elected government" is revolting against himself. He is not a parricide; he is a suicidal maniac. He deserves no pity.

Yet apart from these humanitarian leftovers, the not strictly Marxian (but usually Marx-tainted) uncommitted American leftist, the man arrogating for himself the label of "Liberal" is by no means a friend of liberty, of personal freedom. Even when he seemingly espouses the cause of liberation and emancipation, as in the case of the American of part-African ancestry, he immediately invokes the strong arm of the law, the intervention of secular government in the social domain. The net result of such ubiquitous and total legislating and intervening might then be another "noble experiment" such as we had in Prohibition.[40] Here precisely lies the false "liberal's" radical deviation from the ideals of those liberals whom he brazenly but wrongly claims as his ancestors: in his adulation of the omnipotent state and his genuine contempt for the independent person. His real or pretended "humanism" in the "biological" domain[41] (sex, race, death penalty) is matched by a totalitarian outlook in nearly all the others. The Roussellian strain is here even more evident than the earlier and milder American leftist tradition as represented by Jefferson, Paine, Rush, and Jackson.

We shall have more to say about the American pseudoliberal later on. Here we merely want to cite a few passages from a book which was published in a moment of great fear and tension among uncommitted leftists living in the United States, i.e., after the fall of Paris in June 1940. At that time the German armies had reached the Channel and the brown heirs of the French Revolution, together with their Fascist allies, were ruling all over Europe from central Poland to the Spanish border and from the North Cape to Libya. Only Sweden, Finland, Switzerland, Spain, Portugal, the Balkans, and, of course, Britain were not in their grip. The Third Reich, moreover, was intimately allied with the Soviet Union, which provided Germany with much needed raw materials and above all with high octane gasoline enabling the Nazi war machine to retaliate savagely against the British air attacks.[42] Poland was divided between two totalitarian empires, Rumania had been shorn of Bessarabia with German permission, and the rape of the three Baltic republics happened with Hitler's connivance.[43] The Soviet press sided completely with the Third Reich and Soviet foreign policy gave full support to the National Socialists.[44]

214

The disappointment in the left-of-center camp was great because National Socialism, especially in America, had been regarded as a "rightist" movement. Red Russia and Brown Germany now were in the same camp and nontotalitarian democracy was fighting with its back against the wall. Some of the American leftists hoped that their country would come to the aid of "European democracy." (There were also American conservative interventionists because their heart was on the side of the liberty-loving British monarchy and of the valiant Finns during the "Winter War" of 1939-1940.) Yet in the immediate future there was no indication that Congress would declare war against Nazi Germany and a very large number of American leftists, in their boundless sympathy for the Soviet Union, were radically isolationist. The "American Youth Congress," a Red front organization, convening in late 1939, booed President Roosevelt because he had seemed sympathetic to the fighting Finns, but applauded Mrs. Roosevelt who (thanks to the kind ear she lent to Joseph Lash) spoke words very much to their liking. Up to the invasion of Russia there were practically no American leftist volunteers who came to the aid of Britain, although they had flocked in very great numbers to the International Brigades in Spain in order to participate lustily in the greatest sadistic orgy the Western World had experienced before 1939. There were volunteers for Britain, there were people raising funds for the Finns, but those were not leftists.

At this juncture the non-Marxist left in the United States went into a huddle and produced a "Declaration on World Democracy" also signed by a few people who (so one would think) did not really belong to their camp. There is something exceedingly hurried about American life. There is a certain affection for publicity and little time to read full texts to which people affix their signature. Thus it happened that the book called *The City of Man—A Declaration on World Democracy*[45] was published over the names of Herbert Agar, Frank Aydelotte, G. A. Borgese (Thomas Mann's son-in-law), Hermann Broch, Ada L. Comstock, Dorothy Canfield Fisher, Christian Gauss, Oscar Jászi, Alvin Johnson, Thomas Mann, Lewis Mumford, William Allan Neilson, and Gaetano Salvemini. But it also bore the signature of William Yandell Elliott, Hans Kohn, and Reinhold Niebuhr. Especially in the case of Niebuhr I had great doubts that he saw the complete text.[46]

The small book has a Declaration, a Proposal and, finally, a Note as to the origin of the document—and a real *document humain* it is. The Note informs us that a group of friends began meeting in October 1938 and that they drew up a memorandum in May 1939. A "Letter of Invitation" for a "Committee on Europe" was drafted and mailed on March 28, 1940. This letter was signed by G. A. Borgese, Robert M. Hutchins, Thomas Mann, Lewis Mumford, William A. Neilson, and Reinhold Niebuhr. The first conference of the committee was held May 24-26 in Atlantic City. Further meetings took place in Sharon, Connecticut, on August 24 and 25, 1940. There the final drafts of the book were made. It is significant that though new members lined up, Mr. Robert M. Hutchins dropped out. He was too shrewd to put his name to a text about which the late Father Walter Farrell, O.P., then a leading Thomist in the United States, commented quite rightly: "This book represents one of the earliest and most concrete conquests of Hitlerism in America."[47]

The "Declaration" and the "Proposal" are also interesting because they still use the term "liberal" in its classic context, yet they defend a clearly illiberal (or antiliberal) totalitarian democracy quite in the Jacobin tradition. The language in which this document is written is distinctly of an extreme leftist character and, whereas socialism is mentioned as something here to stay, and as organically pertaining to the "Janus head of democracy," communism gets only a few snide side remarks. ("Monopoly capitalism" and the "ruling classes," however, get it really in the neck.) The book merits special attention because it expresses its message in ringing terms and openly identifies democracy with religion, presenting it *as* a religion. According to the signers it is "the plenitude of heart-service to a highest religion embodying the essence of all higher religions. Democracy is nothing more and nothing less than humanism in theocracy and rational theocracy in universal humanism."[48] Involuntarily the remarks of R. H. Gabriel and Crane Brinton come to one's mind: that owing to its irrational-unscientific character the only chance of survival for democracy is its metamorphosis into a religion.[49]

The signers are kind enough to find some virtues in the "higher religions" and indeed very exalted ones in the faith founded by "Jesus, highest of the Jewish prophets," but democracy is the highest all-embracing religion which as a "universal religion of the Spirit acknowledges with reverence the incorruptible substance of truth which lies under the surface and errors of the separate confessions risen from the common ground of ancient and medieval civilization—democracy, in the catholicity of its language, interprets and justifies the separate creeds as its own vernaculars."[50] In other words, as long as the Catholic, Lutheran, Eastern or Anglican theologies talk the jargon of Democratese, they will be tolerated.[51] Democracy in the meantime will practice a severe and eclectic benevolence towards these slightly obsolete denominations: democracy "explains and annexes all dogmas as symbols."[52]

How this is done we discover in a passage which reads, "The fundamental principle is that the democratic concept of freedom can never include the freedom to destroy democracy and freedom. If no liberty is granted to the murderer and arsonist, no liberty can be granted to whosoever and whatsoever threaten the divine spirit in man and above man.

"This is—in an interpretation suited to modern man—the spirit which Christ called the Holy Ghost."

This seems to take care of the whole theology concerning the Holy Trinity by infallible deduction—not from the Vatican but from the White House, because we also read, "The religion of the Holy Ghost, and nothing else, is the 'spirit of the New Testament' of which the President of the United States spoke.

"This universal religion, harbored in the best minds of our age, this common prayer of democracy militant, was anticipated by sages and saints of all ages. Its substance matured out of whatever rose highest in man's speculations and hopes."[53]

One wonders who these sages and saints were—certainly not Dante, St. Thomas Aquinas, Shakespeare, Milton, Calvin, Luther, Nicholas of Cusa, Goethe, St. Ignatius, or Kierkegaard. The Enlightenment, naturally, fares quite well. Hence, after enumeration of the virtues and foibles of the Christian and Jewish faiths,[54] we get the statement that " . . . finally, the optimistic philosophies of enlightenment which provided a background for America's Declaration of Independence, postulated the primal goodness and nobility of man as a myth conducive to his final nobility and goodness."[55] This sentence is heartening in at least one respect: It declares a myth the Roussellian concept of good and noble man.

The Catholic Church, as one might expect, comes in for a great deal of criticism, and one is amused to hear that the allegiance of Catholic Christians to the City of God (not, for a change, to the City of Man) must be disentangled from "bondage to Vatican City as a foreign potentate in feud or trade with other potentates."[56] And with the "foreign potentate" we come clearly to the language of the Know-Nothing movement.

The future is reserved almost exclusively to the super-religion of democracy. There is no return to the spiritual fleshpots of the past. "We shall not imitate the backward course of Julian the Apostate . . . or of the Roman populace running for asylum and atonement to the old gods after the capture of their city by the Goths. We shall not return, under the counsel of despair, from a higher and vaster religion to lesser ones.''[57] The "higher and vaster" religion is not symbolized by the Cross and the Lamb that bears the sins of the world; not by Baptism of water, not by Mount Sinai and Mount Tabor and Mount Carmel, not by the Torah and the Gospels, the Lord's Prayer and the Nicene Creed, but by the click of the voting machines behind the green curtains, by the swish of the guillotine, by the ghastly tragicomedy of the Storming of the Bastille, and even more so by the nauseating massacres in the Vendée.

It is obvious that under these circumstances the Religion of Democracy takes precedence over all the other creeds of lesser breeds, and that therefore they ought to be placed under surveillance. The Proposal tells us bluntly that too much separation between Church and State is not good and that certain controls of religion are quite in order.[58] "The hour has struck when we must know what limits are set by the religion of freedom, which is democracy, to the freedom of worship." (As symbols of the "religion of freedom" one might mention Socrates and the cup, Le Mans and the *noyades*, the hunger blockade of 1918, Dresden, and Hiroshima.) For this purpose an inquisitorial investigation is necessary in order "to determine what religious and ethical traditions are of greater or lesser value for the preservation and growth of the democratic principle. . . . An inquiry into the religious heritage of the Western World should try to discover which of its elements are more apt to cooperate with the democratic community and consequently more deserving of protection and help by it, and whether other elements, conversely, are by their nature and content committed to the support of fascism and other autocratic philosophies and intrinsically so inimical to democracy, or at least so ambiguous, as to become a source of additional danger in the hour of peril." A careful reading of the book shows that neither the Four Square Gospel Church nor the Mennonites nor the Assembly of God is meant by these oblique references. It is primarily the same "international" Church, run by a "foreign potentate," which the National Socialists also had singled out for their most violent attacks, and in the second place the Church founded by Martin Luther, without whom the Reformation as we know it, would never have taken place.[59] It is comforting to know that Rome and Wittenberg (though Geneva less so) draw the common ire of American and German identitarian leftists—not to mention the masters of the Kremlin.

As we can clearly see, there is no burning love for real freedom among the signers of this noble declaration. This is proved partly by

218

their repeated attacks against liberalism and against the freedom of religion, as well as by their desire to amalgamate all "higher religions" into "vernaculars" of Democracy, the new State Religion. This new religion was also to have a ritual, an "unsectarian liturgy" for which "university and college chapel services and exercises" provide a "provisional model."[60] Here we are very near to the worship of Robespierre's "Supreme Being" in colorful ceremonies and perhaps equally near to the efforts of the Nazis to establish a national Church by forcefully amalgamating Lutherans, Calvinists, and Catholics into a "folkic" and "dejudaized" Christianity, which would supplant pity and charity with heroism and other ancient Germanic virtues. Hitler tried to start the process of unification by appointing bishops in Germany's Lutheran Church—there were none since the Reformation[61]—and while many a pastor donned a brown shirt, the best minds in the Evangelical Church started to protest and to band together in the *Bekennende Kirche* ("Professing Church").[62] These men, who met for the first time at Barmen, refused to see in their Church a "vernacular of National Socialism."

One might take in one's stride the book's constant socialistic propaganda and the remarks to the effect that a "planned economy is implicit in the spirit of democracy."[63] More total and totalitarian are the visions of a world state with a rather amusing nationalistic undertone. "Of all fading fatherlands, one brotherland will be made, the City of Man; and that the United States must be made the Uniting States. No number is prescribed to the stars on its flag."[64] It is nice to think that the signers had a vision of the coming world state with the United States as its Piedmont, its stepping stone, that they craved a global state representing a Greater America. This would not be so terribly bad if this Greater United States were loosely federated and not strictly centralized. Yet the language we hear provides us with a rather different impression. "The day comes when the heresy of nationalism is conquered. . . . Then above the teeming manifold life of free communities . . . there will be a Universal Parliament representing peoples, not states—a fundamental body of law prevailing throughout the planet in all those matters that involve interregional interests . . . an elected President, the President of Mankind—no crowned emperor, no hereditary king . . . embodying for a limited term the common authority and the common law; and a federal force ready to strike at anarchy and felony."[65] This sounds grim. "The President of Mankind"—maybe Julian Felsenburg out of Robert Hugh Benson's *Lord of the World*. On top of it we have the federal forces ready to strike everywhere. Thus if anybody were to challenge the "dictatorship of humanity" (p. 34) in the name of God, or perhaps only in the name of personal freedom, the federal forces would collar him.

One has to read a bit between the lines in order to guess the total and totalitarian character of the "religion of democracy." I will help the reader by emphasizing certain words in the following passages with italics: "In the decline of Western civilization the *collective* purpose of democracy, with its commandments of *discipline* and *loyalty*, had given way to a *corrupted liberalism with its claim of unrestricted liberty for each one to act as he pleased* . . . the concept of a vital democracy must be dissociated from the notion of a *disintegrated liberalism*. . . . There is, indeed, *no liberty but one*: the right, which is a *duty*, of making oneself and others free through *absolute allegiance* to the final goal of man. All other liberties are the rewards of battle. There is *no comfort but one*: pride in the *duty performed.*"[66]

Democracy must be dogmatized, it must be "redefined." It should be "no longer the conflicting concourse of uncontrolled individual impulses, but a harmony subordinated to a plan, no longer a dispersive atomism, but a purposeful organism."[67] Here we have clearly another case of "African democracy" for the white man, of Mr. Sukarno's "directed democracy." Democracy, according to the signers, teaches that "everything must be within humanity, nothing outside humanity."[68] This viewpoint results automatically in either atheism or in a modified pantheism. Here we have Rousseau, Robespierre, Marx, Lenin, and Hitler rolled into one.

In the *City of Man* we see quite clearly the Thirteen Point Program of American pseudoliberalism behind whose mask hides the not strictly Marxian left. And here are the points:

1. *Utopianism.* Some sort of salvation for all lies in the *future.* The great promise refers not to the theistic Heaven but to a coming "Age of Man"—or Mr. Henry Wallace's "Century of the Common Man."[69]

2. *Planning* which is "implicit in the spirit of democracy."[70] It begins with economic planning, continues with "social engineering" and finally produces "planned elections." Man no longer has the primacy; he is made subordinate to *The Plan.* In the end we have the total victory of geometry and arithmetic on the human level. Man as a cipher is the end of man.

3. *Centralization* as opposed to local rights and "privileges." (The Rule is supreme; there are no exceptions, no "privileges," no deviations.) No planning is possible without centralization, and there is no utopia without planning. (Utopia will come automatically, yet we have

220

to plan for it: an inner contradiction without solution and present in *all* leftist creeds.) Free Will is rejected as a dangerous fiction (if it existed it would have to be respected) and there is little freedom—"individualism" would become a term of abuse!—because it interferes with the blue prints guaranteeing the "foreseeable."

4. *Identity, Sameness.* The "masses" (Humanity) consist of identical units of mere "individuals" (exchangeable grains of sands) not "persons." To be different, to think or act differently, becomes a crime. Where differences exist, they are declared to be meaningless. Where they cannot be "explained away" and when they cause trouble to The Plan, they call for enforced standardization, expropriation, demotion, exile, and, in the more extreme cases, execution—measures, to be sure, which could *not yet* be taken. But they are encouraged abroad where all leveling movements and actions get the full sympathy and encouragement of the "local left."

5. *Majoritism.* There are minorities (*never* majorities) who are obnoxious and are declared to be the real cause of all or at least most iniquities. These conspiratorial and domineering minorities are not content to be "like everybody else"; they crave privileges, thus depriving the "underprivileged" of their rights; they destroy equality, identity and "social harmony."[71] The main criminals are the "ruling classes" composed in the United States of the "white Anglo-Saxon Protestant minority," of the "Catholic hierarchy," "anti-Zionist Jews," "big industrialists," "brass hats," bankers, and "ultraconservative rightists," a rather motley crowd. (In other countries the minorities forming objects of leftist hatreds are noblemen, Jewish newspaper owners, Armenians, modern artists, lawyers, "clerical" politicians, stockbrokers, etc. Leftist ideologies rest on the existence of "badmen" who can be made objects of general hatred.)

6. *The hostility against organized religion.* The standard leftist reaction to religion—as long as it does not bow to the leftist establishment in humble subservience and permit itself to be infected with leftist ideas—is the effort to eliminate it from the market place, from all public life. (Leftist forces in other climes act differently: There extreme separationism is supplanted by complete state control.)[72]

7. *The Socialist hatred for free enterprise* ("anticapitalism") because a free economy puts a premium on hard work, thrift, and ambition—the natural enemies of "equality." A free economy gives man the chance to build up a little fortress of his own, to escape state omnipotence. (State welfarism is just one more means of firmly establishing state control over the citizenry.)

8. Closely connected with this attitude is *antifamilism*. The family as a closed and emotionally marked-off unit is an obstacle to total sameness and contains a hierarchic element (authority, domination) which the leftist with his hatred of the "father image" thoroughly dislikes. "Dynasties" of all sorts are a special target for leftist attacks.[73] The inheritance of fortunes and all other forms of the accumulation of wealth[74]—regardless of how it is used—must be prevented by the jealous and envious state with a system of progressive taxation.

All attitudes, all laws and regulations designed to protect the family (and sex, its root) morally are ridiculed and rejected. The only element inherited from a liberal past is the American leftists' indifference to man's biological views and behavior patterns. While prone to deny it, he is in all other domains a subtle or even shameless authoritarian.

9. *Intolerance.* "Inflexible principles must be stated in a renovated law, beyond which freedom is felony" (*City of Man,* p. 77). Genuine liberalism stands for freedom and tolerance. American leftism wants freedom only for the different shades of the "Liberal" Establishment and thus carried out on a social basis a kind of "Internal Inquisition"[75]—especially so in the intellectual field (universities, colleges, stage, film industry, radio, television, publishing, press, administration).

10. Allied with this attitude is *statism* which characterizes leftism perhaps more than anything else. When the designers of *The City of Man* accuse the teachers of totalitarian philosophy of proclaiming, "Everything within the state, nothing against the state, nothing outside the state," they merely want to divert our attention. And it is the state at the highest level, in its most centralized aspect that the American Leftists worship, i.e., the federal government.

11. Linked with utopianism is *Messianism* which more often than not has not a personal but rather a racial or national character. The vision of the signers who see the world state as global-scale United States shows what a provincial role they assign to the American people—or rather, to the American government. Their collective Messianism is twofold. Not only is the American Republic pressed into the role of a Messiah but also democracy, the "ancient hope of man" (p. 28). Democracy rests, according to this text, on the "common prayer of democracy militant which must be the hymn of democracy triumphant" (p. 36). We have here, no doubt, an analogy to Comte's Positivism which was a secularized version of the institutionalized Catholic faith.[76]

12. *Anticolonialism.* This Messianism has the task of eventually sav-

ing all mankind, but in the meantime it must be the savior of the colonialized nations and tribes. Thus anticolonialism forms part and parcel of the American leftist's creed.

13. *Interventionism.* Finally, there exists, last but not least due to Utopianism and Messianism, a highly aggressive interventionist and bellicose element in American leftism which, however, is not serving *genuine* American interests but those of the great leftist ideologies—provided they bear the *official* leftist stamp. The American leftist indeed is not pledged to pacifism. "Peace at any price is peace at the price of submission," the signers of the *City of Man* (p. 22) explain to us bluntly. Such statements, to be sure, become invalid if America is menaced by distinctly leftist powers of the international brand. Then the "better Red than dead" formula is only too frequently appealed to. Yet holy wars against "reactionaries" (be they real ones or merely competitors of other leftist groups) are quite within the American (and frequently the British) leftist program. As a matter of fact, leftists usually love armed conflicts because during modern wars the state necessarily has to take illiberal emergency measures.[77] Leftists always hope that wartime policies will be made permanent. Their ideal is the secular monastery or the civilian barracks.

All these thirteen points, needless to say, are as characteristic of the leftist outlook in English-speaking countries as they are of the ideologies animating the French Revolution and its evil offsprings: socialism, National Socialism and communism. They have nothing to do with the convictions of men and women called "liberals" in the rest of the civilized world. And it must also be added that the leftist outlook in America and Britain has hardly changed since 1940 when this rather unique manifesto was published. In America, we must admit, there is today a highly increased emphasis on "racial equality"; yet leftist antiracism, it must be borne in mind, is of a very different character than that of the genuine right. And the same is true of the leftist stand towards (ethnic) nationality. Leftism with its strongly identitarian bent and a nonspiritual, materialistic enthusiasm either declares race and nationality to be supreme values to which everybody has to *conform* (as the Nazis did) or they want to "explain them away" and ignore them with iron determination. . . because they are an obstacle to identitarian *uniformity.* The Nazis wanted to eliminate by brute force those who did not *racially* conform, those *nationally* (ethnically) not conforming by cultural high-pressure methods. The "international leftists" wants us to close our eyes and ignore facts. This is just another process of "elimination." The rightist, who is a liberal in the genuine sense of the term, keeps his eyes open and gladly and charitably accepts the diversity of mankind. Rejecting egalitarianism (no less than identitarianism), he knows that God's gifts are distributed in mysterious ways—not only among persons but also among nations and races. Though they cannot be expressed in a simple scientific formula and never work out mathematically in time or space, they do not invalidate the rightist principle of *suum cuique*.

Part IV

The Left and

U.S. Foreign Policy

Chapter 15

The American Left

and World War I

Dealing not only with American foreign policy but also with British foreign policy in our century, I am obviously addressing readers from English-speaking countries as an alien—as an Austrian who, during all his lifetime has been at the "receiving end" of political decisions which were largely identified with the national interest of the United States and Britain. Certainly not every American, not every Britisher subscribed to every movement his government made during the crucial World War I years and if the party he voted for was in opposition, he had good reason to disassociate himself from his government's official policy. And yet he could not possibly avoid identifying himself—at least up to a point—with the actions of his country. Writing as an Austrian, nevertheless I have to tell my readers in all candor that I am also writing as a man who still has a "home," a *Heimat*, but since my childhood, since November 1918, no longer a fatherland. The Alpine Republic of Austria has made every imaginable effort to deny its historic roots going back to the Austro-Hungarian monarchy. It shed all the symbols recalling the Hapsburg monarchy either in the form of the Danubian monarchy or its real matrix, the Holy Roman Empire. Thus politically I am representing a *void*. This, however, gives me the courage to criticize the policies of the English-speaking nations vigorously though endeavoring to remain objective. I think that as a citizen of Christendom, as a product of the Western World it is my duty to point to a chain of errors committed by Britain and America in the past, because these countries still have an armed might, a freedom of decision, a responsibility which Austria no longer possesses. This is the reason I am not dwelling on the faults and mistakes of my own people, now a small pawn on a big chessboard. I am not even putting much stress on the sins of omission and commission of the German people or of its masters prior to 1933, a people to whom as an Austrian I feel attached in many ways. Great nations have fallen very low—the Jews when they rejected *their* Messiah; France, the "Oldest Daughter of the Church," when it engaged in the Revolution, Pandora's Box of centuries to come; "Holy Mother Russia," when she fell for the abstruse ideas of German intellectuals; the "Germanies," heart of the Holy Roman Empire, when they submitted to Hitler and his evil creed. Of course these peoples have no *common* guilt. There is no such thing as collective guilt. However, as Theodor Heuss has pointed out, there is collective shame.

Nor, obviously, are the Americans (or the British) collectively guilty of the fateful errors and misdeeds committed by some of them. The words of Count Benckendorff, last Imperial Russian Ambassador in London, about the Germans—*"Il n'y a pas 'les Allemands,' il n'y a que des Allemands"*—are equally valid for the English-speaking nations. The vast majority of my friends in Britain and America never belonged to the left, they rarely subscribed to its errors, they have little, sometimes no responsibility for the tragic situation the modern world is in at present. If I am accusing, I am hardly accusing them and the accusations themselves are made in order to show *errors of the past*. The only thing we can do now is to learn from them.

Certainly in no domain has the influence of American (and the British) left been more nefarious than in matters of foreign policy. The effects of their interventions were tragic not only in the United States and in Britain but for the world at large. Yet let us also admit that, while the left has actively participated in political and military activities that powerfully contributed to the decline of the West, the more conservative forces in the English-speaking world cannot be entirely absolved from the guilt of omission rather than commission, of inaction rather than intervention.

Here, however, we must bear in mind that, viewed from the angle of American native mythology—this has little to do with factual history!—the United States were born on the flight from Europe. A certain tradition likes to speak about the "American Experiment" (What is it? Can it be "called off" if found "inconvenient"?) and tends to see in America an island of the blessed totally removed from the rest of the world. There can be no doubt that the nascent American Republic needed a rest, needed a period of internal reconstruction and crystallization and that, thanks to two oceans, a policy of isolation was feasible and desirable. In spite of the fact that the foundations of the American Republic are whiggish and aristocratic, we nevertheless soon witness the buildup of another myth on *both* sides of the Atlantic: the United States as the "big democracy," as the haven of all persecuted and the downtrodden, as the supranational, global fatherland of equality, and so forth. Nineteenth-century America had many outstanding conservative thinkers and writers—Melville, Brownson, Sumner[1]—but a countercurrent also existed. Walt Whitman, to quote just one instance, is a typical democratist, invoked *qua* homosexual as a representative of democratic *camaraderie* by Thomas Mann in his confession of faith in the Weimar Republic.[2] In *Leaves of Grass* Whitman chanted:

One's self I sing, a simple separate person

Yet after the word democratic, the word *en masse*.

This looks like a solidly identitarian program, yet there are passages with a more pompous and less liberal wording. Thus when Whitman says in his *Democratic Vistas:* "I demand races of orbic bards, with unconditional and uncompromising sway. Come forth, sweet democratic despots of the West!"[3] The despots came rather from the East and they were not sweet either. The very foundation of this democratic order was largely in the hands of "literary men" (as in today's leftism), and indeed, "The priests depart, the divine literatus comes." (Should this be a prophecy related to Mr. James Baldwin?) Literature, according to Whitman, should be as revolutionary, as traditionless as all other cultural manifestations. "I say that democracy can never prove itself beyond cavil, until it founds and luxuriantly grows its own forms of art, poems, schools, theology, displacing all that exists, or that has been produced anywhere in the past, under opposite influences," says another passage in the same book. Here we have a totalitarian, anti-traditionalist program like that of the spokesmen of *Proletkult* in the Soviet Union. A new race should grow up in America, the "ideal race of the future—divine average!" Almost a Nazi vision.

Reinhold Niebuhr has rightly pointed out in one of his best books that the United States were "God's American Israel" called upon to save the world.[4] It is important to recall, however, that American national Messianism had a decidedly leftist tinge which, for instance, the *earliest* Russian Messianism did not have. The grandfather of American Messianism is Jefferson and its character was and still is republican (i.e., antimonarchical) and democratic (i.e., antiaristocratic). American nationalist feelings seem very strong to a foreigner and, as all nationalist sentiments, they have a certain "intellectual" character. Unlike patriotism, nationalism is argumentative: The nationalist tries to prove the superiority of his nation by pointing out its unique characteristics, achievements, virtues, qualities, institutions, traditions. The patriot sees in his attachment merely a manifestation of loyalty, just as an intelligent man would never try to argue that his parents were the "best in the world"; he would consider it an accident to have been born as a citizen of a specific country—which he did not choose. He did not choose his parents either, but he will naturally love them, and if he does not love them he will be loyal to them in obedience to the Commandment—even if they are very ordinary, even if they are manifestly inferior people. American nationalism, however, has been conditioned to a large extent by the "indoctrination" of the children of immigrants.[5] Naturally a German, an Italian, an American gentleman will defend his country against patently unjust accusations (loyalty demands this), but he will not try to convince us that his nation has the highest qualities in the world, has the most gifted inventors, the best writers, the finest painters, the profoundest philosophers, the fastest trains, the most beautiful women. These boasts are reserved for the drummer after a third highball in a commercial hotel, to the Nazi, the Russian Communist, etc.[6]

Yet in America moderate leftism and national nativist nationalism have gone well together. Witness Whitman, witness a certain aspect of Carl Sandburg's writings, witness the poem of Emma Lazarus on the Statue of Liberty in New York harbor. This gigantic symbol of freedom greets the immigrants thus:

"Keep, ancient lands, your storied pomp!" cries she
With silent lips, "Give me your tired, your poor,
Your huddled masses yearning to breathe free,
The wretched refuse from your teeming shore,
Send these, the homeless, tempest-tossed to me,
I lift my lamp beside the golden door."[7]

It is interesting to investigate the ideological background of the Spanish-American War of 1898, a war in which purely nationalistic motives most certainly were mixed with leftist prejudices. The enemy was one of the rotten, ramshackle, "backward," "priest-ridden" monarchies of the Old World. Obviously there existed at that time in the United States a highly cultivated upper crust which neither participated in folkloric notions about European governments nor was affected by leftist ideas. Yet in the intellectually less ambitious minds a number of dangerous simplifications had already taken root. The United States with its institutions, habits, traditions, and customs was assumed by the masses to be at the top of a ladder of evolution. The more a foreign country was similar to the United States, the more it was considered "progressive"—and friendly. The more dissimilar it was, the more it was seen as "backward" and worthy of contempt. Simple or (sometimes quite consciously) rather odd classifications were used; such items as forms of government, freedom of the press, formality of class differences, emancipation of women, literacy percentages, the number of bathtubs and telephones, religion, church-state relationship, the legal status of denominational minorities, cleanliness of hotels, punctuality of trains, and others functioned as measuring rods. Historical elements also came into play: Britain was remembered for 1776 and Nathan Hale, France's role in the War of Independence improved its score, Germany's excellent record in almost all points was offset by its monarchical form of government. And so forth. In the case of Spain in 1898 the balance sheet looked perfectly hopeless. The *leyenda negra*, the "Black Legend"[8] of English fabrication made it even worse. The yellow press of the United States represented the Spanish people as bigoted, fanatical, cruel, treacherous—and the Cubans as their high-minded, heroic, innocent victims.[9]

Antimonarchism became the driving element in America's European policy during World War I and its aftermath which helped to crystallize American leftism to an even greater degree. At the so-called extreme left in the United States were the anarchists, but there was also a Socialist party (with a splinter) and a fair amount of "radicalism" without definite political ties. World War I had actually started in Europe as a war between nations but rapidly lost the character of an old-fashioned cabinet war. All participants, with the exception of Great Britain, had conscription and the press was instrumental in engendering broad waves of collective national hatreds. In St. Petersburg a "patriotic" mob even stormed the German Embassy. The lights—in the words of Sir Edward Grey—were really going out all over Europe. Especially in the West collective loathing had reached dangerous levels that marked the decay of the Old World. Dachshunds were killed in Britain, Germans greeted each other with *Gott strafe England!*,[10] "enemy aliens" were brought behind barbed wire in Germany, England, France, and Italy (but not in Austria-Hungary or Russia).[11] The Germans tried to starve out Britain, and the Western Allies tried to starve out the Central Powers. Allied propaganda represented the German armies as composed of assassins and sadists: Atrocity stories were faked in droves and were widely believed.[12] A fanaticism was roused that had not been known in past ages.[13] Still, by the end of 1916, when the senseless butchering almost reached its zenith, there was only one European republic in the Allied camp—France; and with Russia (and Japan) fighting in the Great Coalition, it was difficult to give to that war an ideological character. A small group of Czech nationalists wanting to break away from Austria spoke in their manifesto about a Romanov prince on a Bohemian throne. Who bore the main guilt for this senseless holocaust? Each nation was honestly convinced that the responsibility lay with the other side, but it can be said without danger of refutation that the guilt was divided—not evenly, to be sure, but in a different degree among men and groups and cliques in the various countries.[14]

By the end of 1916 and early 1917 a compromise peace was still possible and great efforts were made in that direction. In a diminished form hopes still existed until early 1918, when the last Austro-Hungarian peace offensive took place. Of course, Emperor Charles I was not the only person trying desperately to end the frightful butchery. The Vatican, certain German parties, the Socialists, Conservatives, English groups, and Spain were also engaged in major efforts to put an end to the almost universal suffering. By the summer of 1917 the Russian emperor had abdicated, the Kerensky government was tottering, the Italians awaited a major blow, Rumania had been defeated, a stalemate existed on the Western Front, and a partial mutiny had weakened the French army. Lord Lansdowne's famous letter (rejected by the London *Times*) had been published by the *Daily Telegraph*. But the non-Marxist left in Britain and France, represented by Lloyd George, Clemenceau, and Ribot, was relentless. It counted on American aid. And the decision over peace or war really lay with America. As a matter of fact, never was there a greater chance for a genuine *Pax Americana*. If the United States had then been blessed with an outstanding President, with a great leader endowed with real vision, he could have called a peace conference and treated all those refusing to attend as *prima facie* partisans of the war.

Now, one might argue that the great errors committed by the German Government—Franz von Papen's stupidities, the Zimmermann telegram, the sinkings of the *Lusitania* and the *Sussex*, and many other provocative acts so severely castigated by Count Bernstorff, last Imperial

Ambassador to Washington[15]—had created a most difficult situation. This is quite true but one need not believe in the inevitability of America's entry into the war. It is not too rash to assume that the election of the Republican candidate, Charles Evans Hughes, so narrowly defeated by Wilson in 1916 would probably have changed the course of events and with it the fate of the globe.[16] (Obviously, one could also argue that Teddy Roosevelt's stubbornness in 1912, when he split the Republican vote and made Wilson's first election possible, was the beginning of the end. A reelected Taft in 1917 would have made America's entry into World War I highly unlikely.)

Certainly 1917 is the fateful year of our century. Woodrow Wilson decided to throw the American sword on the scales without realizing that he lacked the knowledge to win the peace and the power to make it lasting. This started a catastrophic development which is by no means terminated. Actually World War I with its seemingly permanent aftermath is still with us. And the "aftermath" is due to the fact that the monumental ignorance of the left, their absolute nonunderstanding (rather than misunderstanding) of human nature, of the simplest facts of history, geography, psychology, economics, strategy, and politics, have led to one wrong decision after the other. Let us remember only two things: Twice it was a Democratic administration (comprising the greater part of the leftist forces)[17] which engaged the United States in a global war, and twice it happened that two hierarchical organizations —the industry and the military—won the wars. But democratically elected or appointed politicians lost the fruits of these costly victories— costly in blood and money—at the conference tables.[18] In the long run genuine achievements do not come from mere intuitions, but only through knowledge. The engineers and the captains of industry, the generals and the admirals, had *learned* their trade. The politicians had their jobs solely because they were popular.[19]

The collapse of the monarchical government in Russia, the switch to the Republic and the presidency of the relatively temperate social revolutionary Alexander Kerensky sharply changed the ideological picture of Europe. France still continued the revolutionary tradition, though in a moderate and "bourgeois" form. Britain not only had strong sentimental and cultural ties with America but also ranked as a "parliamentary democracy" in which the monarch was a mere figurehead. Japan was considered to be the torchbearer of "progress" in Asia. Italy was a monarchy more or less in name only. Though the Germans were considered industrious, clean, and musical, there existed in America the myth that "after 1848 all decent Germans went to America," leaving the country open to arrogant, heel-clicking, monocled Junkers and that sinister autocrat, William II.[20] The Austro-Hungarian monarchy hardly figured in the popular American mind, but all the more so among leftist intellectuals. They had heard the name of Metternich and agreed with Gladstone that "there is not an instance, there is not a spot upon the whole map, where you can lay your finger and say, 'There Austria did good.' "[21] They remembered the tirades of Margaret Fuller against Vienna. No wonder, then, that the upshot of it all, the most tangible result of World War I, was the dismemberment of Austria-Hungary. This really changed the map of Europe and incidentally provided Germany with a geopolitical position of mastery which gave Hitler an ideal start for his nonmilitary and military conquests. For Germany was bordered in the East by a power vacuum. The fall of the monarchy in Russia made Wilson extremely happy. "Here is a fit partner for a League of Honor," was his reaction to the abdication of Nicholas II.[22] Wilson was a genuine ideologue in the narrow sense of the term; his plan, unfortunately, was not to make democracy safe for the world, but rather to make the world safe for democracy. He was working towards a *Djihad*, a holy war to extend what he considered the American form of government. This was already evident in his dealings with Mexico before America's entry into World War I. About America's neighbor south of the Rio Grande he said, "Our friendship is a disinterested friendship, so far as our aggrandizement goes . . . leaving them to work out their own destiny, but watching them narrowly and insisting that they shall take help when help is needed."[23] What sort of help he thought about we can gather from a conversation between Walter Hines Page, his ambassador, and Sir Edward Grey, Britain's Foreign Secretary. Page recorded it himself:

GREY: Suppose you have to intervene, what then?

PAGE: Make 'em vote and live by their decisions.

GREY: But suppose they will not so live?

PAGE: We'll go in again and make 'em vote again.

GREY: And keep this up for 200 years?

PAGE: Yes. The United States will be here for 200 years and it can continue to shoot men for that little space till they learn to vote and rule themselves.[24]

This is, in a way, what happened also between the United States and Central Europe. Wilson's prejudice against monarchy, however, was not only intellectual, it was also "folkloric" and based on the conviction that monarchs loved wars whereas nations were always peaceful. Now, *revanchisme* was the great *popular* passion of the Third French

Republic until 1914, but evidence is easily ignored. (One need only remember Hegel who, upon being told that the facts contradicted his theories, severely replied: *"Umso schlimmer für die Tatsachen"*—all the worse for the facts.) The identification of democracy with peace was mirrored in a letter of Wilson's Secretary of State, Robert Lansing, who wrote to Colonel House: "No people can desire a war, particularly an aggressive war. If the people can exercise their will, they will remain at peace. If a nation possesses democratic institutions, the popular will will be exercised. Consequently, if the principle of democracy prevails in a nation, it can be counted upon to preserve peace and oppose wars. . . . If this view is correct, then the effort should be made to make democracy universal."[25]

Wilson's famous message to Benedict XV, (conveyed to the Pope by Lansing), at a time when America was not yet a belligerent, breathed more or less the same spirit.[26] The German people might be fine, the letter said, but its government had to go. As a result Germany and Austria were saddled after the war with regimes whose character had been dictated by the Allies—the alternative being the hunger blockade. Any historian could have told the victors that political forms imposed by the triumphant enemy *never* last.[27] The mistake committed by the Holy Alliance in 1814-1815 was repeated by the Allies in 1918-1919 and by the Unholy Alliance in 1945.

Needless to say, Wilson suffered from the Great American Malady, the belief that people all over the world are "more alike than unlike," in other words, that they are just inhibited, underdeveloped could-be Americans saddled with the misfortune that they spoke another language. Once in the past Wilson had been tortured by the suspicion that in other parts of the world a very alien mentality could be found. In an article written for the *Atlantic Monthly* in 1889 he mentioned the "restless forces of European democratic thought and anarchic turbulence" which were brought to the United States by "alarming masses" of immigrants who were "apt to tell disastrously upon our Saxon habit of government."[28] When it came to the showdown at the conference table in Paris, Lloyd George, himself a Methodist Machiavelli, said that he was wedged in between a man who thought he was Napoleon (Clemenceau) and another one who thought that he was Jesus Christ (Wilson). By that time the Southern racist had developed into a savior of mankind.

The ignorance of the former president of Princeton in matters of history and geography was simply prodigious. The Italians showed him a spurious map on which a mountain in the very heart of Austria appeared fittingly named "Vetta d'Italia"; it served as a proof that "historic Italy" (there never was such a country) extended right to that spot. As a result the Italians received the South[29] and the Central Tyrol with the Brenner Pass for the first time (and for the second time in 1946, with the result that the shooting and dynamiting in this restless, tortured area is still going on to this very day). Harold Nicolson, who was at the Peace Conference, wrote about the current feeling that "if Wilson would swallow the Brenner, he would swallow everything."[30] Terrified by his own mistake, Wilson then wanted to prevent the annexation of Fiume (predominantly inhabited by Italians) by Italy, and tried somewhat undiplomatically to appeal to the Italians over the head of their government.

As in the arrangements and treaties after 1945, almost everybody was deprived of something that was legitimately his and got something else to which he really had no right. Nations were thus prevented from living again peacefully with neighbors whom they had wronged or who had wronged them.[31] The era of Pan-Democracy and Peace, in fact, started an endless series of wars—cold, lukewarm, and hot. Wilson, however, was in a way as "lost" at the Peace Conference as he had been lost before in the thick fog of factual ignorance and mythological concepts. John Maynard Keynes, who as a young man had been present at the Paris Conference, gave a shattering picture of his qualities: "He not only had no proposals in detail, but he was in many respects, perhaps inevitably, ill-informed as to European conditions. And not only was he ill-informed—that was true of Mr. Lloyd George also—but his mind was slow and unadaptable. . . . There can seldom have been a statesman of the first rank more incompetent than the President in the agilities of the council chamber."[32] Of course, thanks to the "democratization" of the Western World ever since the Congress of Vienna (1814-1815) and the Congress of Berlin (1878), a tragic lowering of general standards had taken place. The representatives of the nations no longer spoke a common vernacular and the era of interpreters had started. In Paris Clemenceau "alone among the Four could speak and understand both languages, Orlando knowing only French and the Prime Minister and President only English, and it is of historic importance that Orlando and the President had no direct means of communication."[33]

Woodrow Wilson's greater guilt, nevertheless, lay in his attitude *during* the war, in his flat refusal to cooperate in any peace efforts and in his determination to carry the war to the bitter end, thus laying the foundations for the next one. (Human lives? The number of mercenaries is limited by cash and their natural willingness to join, but draft boards can squeeze out an almost endless number of unwilling death candidates.) World War I, surely, is a far more crucial historic event than most Americans think. Modern man is overoccupied with stems and leaves, he wilfully disregards the roots. George F. Kennan is perfectly right when he says, "All the lines of inquiry lead back to World War I."[34] Had World War I been terminated earlier, the old Germany with certain modifications would have survived. About this by now impossibility Kennan wrote in 1951, "Yet, today, if one were offered the chance of having back again the Germany of 1913, a Germany run by conservative but relatively moderate people, no Nazis and no Communists, a vigorous Germany, united and unoccupied, full of energy and confidence, able to play a part again in the balancing-off of Russian power in Europe—well, there would be objections to it from many quarters, and it wouldn't make everybody happy; but in many ways it wouldn't be so bad, in comparison with our problem of today. Now, think what this means. When you tally up the total score of the two wars, in terms of their ostensible objectives, you find if there has been any gain at all, it is pretty hard to discern."[35]

This sort of reflection is not necessarily the outcome of *two* major disappointments. *One* ought to have been sufficient for an unprejudiced mind. Lord Newton, indeed, could write in 1929 in connection with the failure of Lansdowne's letter in the *Daily Telegraph*: "If peace had been made at the end of 1917, it is clear that the Germans would have escaped their legitimate punishment. On the other hand, the failure of their criminal aggression would have been inconcealable, the Kaiser and the military caste would have been discredited and disposition to embark upon another similar enterprise would have vanished. A negotiated peace, although it might have disappointed many aspirations, would certainly have effected a more permanent European settlement than exists at the present day. Millions of lives would have been saved and the load of human misery substantially reduced. We ourselves at a moderate computation would have been spared hundreds of thousands of casualties, and more than 1,500 millions of expenditure."[36]

"Objections from many quarters," "disappointed aspirations"— these would have been exclusively on the left eager to slaughter in order to achieve its aims, the nationalistic left, the radically democratic left, the Socialist-Communist left looking for an opportunity to enact a major revolution. President Wilson's thinking, however, was somewhat determined by his religious tradition (he was the son of a Presbyterian minister in Virginia)[37] which earned him Calvinist sympathies in Europe, and predominantly, by his antimonarchical bias. Nevertheless, it is questionable whether his religious position was one of affirmation or merely of negation. His Calvinism (*if* it genuinely existed in a theological sense) hardly shows in his speeches or in his writings, whereas his anti-Catholic attitude was quite obvious. In this one respect he fully concurred with Lloyd George and Clemenceau. His hatred for Rome was strong enough to make him sacrifice his other shibboleths, such as self-determination. He said that "German Austria should go to Germany, as all were of one language and one race, but this would mean the establishment of a great central Roman Catholic nation which would be under the control of the Papacy."[38]

In his antimonarchism, in other words, in his endeavors to foster in Europe a form of government bound to fail (as a semihierocratic, semiaristocratic Catholic monarchy would in Alabama), he was perhaps not really a scholarly professor of government, but just a "plain American." He was convinced that the key to his success in the United States lay in the repetition of American popular notions, relating them to the rest of the world. He once said that "the best leaders are those with ordinary opinions and extraordinary abilities, those who hold the opinion of the generation in which they live, outhold it with such vitality, perceive it with such excessive insight, that they can walk at the front and show the paths by which the things generally purposed can be accomplished."[39] This is nothing but the despicable principle of that great demagogue, Ledru-Rollin: "I am their leader, so I have to follow them!"[40]

All this is not surprising since so few Americans were indifferent to the accusation of lacking patriotism—and unfortunately the blind belief in "democracy" (which in an altruistic nation fosters the urge for its exportation) is only too often identified (even if falsely) with patriotism. Hugo Münsterberg could rightly say about America two generations ago, "I believe sincerely that no European country knows a patriotism of such fervor and explosiveness."[41] Actually we are in this respect faced with nationalism rather than with patriotism. Patriotism is never aggressive in relation to other nations, but nationalism, which was reborn in the French Revolution, curiously enough "knows no borders." It incites nations to force other nations to adopt their pattern of political "happiness."

Münsterberg also pointed out the deep-seated antimonarchism of Americans. It is extremely difficult to make them see a monarchy's advantages and virtues in specific situations since they consider it a "rotten" institution.[42] (In the youth-worshipping American mind there is a far-reaching identification between "old" and "rotten.") Another

German, Ernst Bruncken, remarked that in America "every teacher of comparative government will discover what an enormous effort is required to impart a clear notion of European monarchical institutions to even quite mature students. A Napoleonic tyranny, a dictatorship—that is easily within the realm of their comprehension. But a legitimate monarchy seems to the Americans a simple absurdity, and he cannot understand how otherwise quite intelligent people can have faith in such a thing.[43] For too many Americans there is a mysterious-mystical connection between the monarchical and the religious concept, bolstered by the misunderstood slogan of the 'divine right of kings.' "[44] Still, there are exceptions to the rule. Reinhold Niebuhr, who does not belong to the conservative camps, has written with great awareness of the intrinsic merits of constitutional monarchy, the traditional form of European monarchical government:[45] "The institution of monarchy, shorn of its absolute power, was found to possess virtues which neither the proponents nor the opponents of the original form anticipated. It became the symbol of the continuing will and unity of a nation as distinguished from the momentary will, embodied in specific governments."[46]

During World War I American leftism in action was probably embodied not so much by Wilson himself as by his left hand (in every sense *left* hand!) in foreign relations—by George Davis Herron. (His right hand was, naturally, Colonel House, though this friendship finally foundered and failed.) Herron is hardly mentioned in the *Encyclopaedia Brittanica,* but he is featured in one-third of a column in the *Encyclopedia Americana.* To assess correctly Herron's *actual* importance is extremely difficult. It is quite probable that "he took himself more seriously than he was taken by Wilson."[47] And yet Herron's part in preventing an early peace in 1917, and much more so in February-March 1918, should not be underestimated. Our interest in Herron is almost equally divided between his historic role and his significance as a person, as a typical representative of "progressive" and leftist thinking which caused such enormous harm in our century. His ideological affinity with Wilson was complete. Both belonged to the post-Protestant age[48] and it was easy for Herron to persuade Wilson to establish the proposed League of Nations in Geneva,[49] the city near which Herron finally made his headquarters.[50] Wilson was delighted and enthusiastic about this proposition.[51] Geneva was, after all, the city of Calvin and Rousseau, whom Herron in his confusion adored simultaneously. Though Calvin can hardly be imagined without Luther, Herron completely rejected the German Reformer. Herron was a "national Messianist'' (of which he was fully aware) and therefore these two Genevans with their great, even if mutually contradictory influence on America attracted his mind. After the war he wrote from Geneva to William Allen White, ''I labored unceasingly to make America a really messianic nation in this world crisis and to help the President in his divinely appointed stature.''[52]

Both Wilson and Herron were naturally more susceptible to a dislike, if not a real hatred for Austria-Hungary rather than for Germany. William James in the 1860s also sided with Prussia against Austria and in his case too there were religious motives: His was the typical attitude of the son of a Swedenborgian minister.[53] Now, with America engaged in a war which Sir Denis Brogan rightly called the Second War of Austrian Succession (a third was to follow in 1939), Herron no less than Wilson was exceedingly prone to anti-Austrian feelings and to anti-Austrian propaganda. Hence we should not be surprised about Masaryk's swift victory in his encounters with Wilson. He quickly won over the President to the idea of a radical breakup of the evil, ''backward'' Danubian monarchy[54] and convinced him that Austria, by declaring the war against Serbia, had acted on her own and not under German pressure.[55] The enthusiasm of the Czechs for their self-appointed leaders in exile was by no means great.[56] Yet there can be no doubt that the American left leaped into action. ''American democracy,'' as Masaryk wrote, ''buried the Hapsburg Monarchy and the Hapsburgs with it.''[57] (But thus also helped bury hundreds of thousands of young Americans in World War II.) Masaryk worked hand in glove with Herron: They shared common quasireligious ideological prejudices and thus we had a truly ''triangular'' situation. We also owe it to Herron's pressure and persuasion that Woodrow Wilson brought Congress to declare war against Austria-Hungary,[58] an action not at all in the interests of the United States.[59] To the American leftists, we must strongly bear in mind, Austria was far more wicked than Germany: It existed in contradiction to the Mazzinian principle of the national state, it had inherited many traditions as well as symbols from the Holy Roman Empire (doubleheaded eagle, black-gold colors, etc.), its dynasty had once ruled over Spain (another *bête noire*), had been leading in the Counterreformation, had headed the Holy Alliance, had fought against the *Risorgimento,* had suppressed the Magyar rebellion under Kossuth (who has a monument in New York), had morally supported the monarchical experiment in Mexico.[60] Hapsburg—this evoked memories of ''Roman Catholicism,'' of the Armada, the Inquisition,[61] of Metternich, of Lafayette jailed in Olmütz, and Silvio Pellico in

Brünn's Spielberg fortress. Such a state had to be broken up, such a dynasty had to disappear. So finally the House of Austria went into exile and was replaced by a simple common man from Austria, allegedly a "house painter," who drowned the world in a flood of blood and tears.

Now, who was George Davis Herron, one of the gravediggers of old Europe? Who was this curious bearded, bespectacled poet, mentioned in some documents as "Reverend," in others as "Professor" or more rarely as plain Mr. Herron? Romain Rolland, the great pacifist, once referred to him. The reason? Herron had written an article against Rolland in Geneva's *La Revue Mensuelle* (April 1917) entitled "Pacifist Immorality." At that time Herron was tortured by the fear of a compromise peace and spoke out in ringing words: "Darkness is rising rapidly over the skies of the nations. It is as if the soul of the human race were gripped by the crushing fear of a prehistoric night. Yes, it is Thor and Wotan who are now about to establish a reign of spiritual death. . . ." Romain Rolland replied by calling him a "virtuous hypocrite" and a "gigantic idiot." Herron was the latter rather than the former, an eternally confused youthful enthusiast, rather than a scoundrel, steeped in deepest ignorance and drunk with words. Part of the key to his behavior and his thinking was his idealistic-romantic leftism.

He was born on January 21, 1862 in Montezuma, Indiana, the son of a humble couple of Scottish descent, William Herron and Isabella Davis. In 1879-1882 he went to Ripon College (Ripon, Wisconsin), a rather "progressive," coeducational, nondenominational school. In 1883, only 21 years old, he married Mary Everhard.[62] Herron already had decided to become a minister: It was practical humanitarianism rather than a mystical or a spiritual urge that determined his choice.

Herron became a minister when he was still a student of theology. He was made doctor of theology by Tabor College, then was ordained minister of the First Congregational Church in Lake City, Minnesota, and finally was appointed minister in Burlington, Iowa. Apparently he found no fulfillment in his pastoral work and turned to an academic career. He also embraced socialism as a secular creed. He received a professorship at Iowa (later Grinnell)[63] College, where the very wealthy Mrs. Rand[64] founded a chair for "Applied Christianity" which Herron kept until 1899. Theoretically he belonged to the ministry but was unfrocked when his wife (who bore him five children) sued for divorce which was granted to her on the grounds of "cruelty, culminating in desertion." The reasons for this separation, however, seem to have been more romantic, because very soon afterward he married Carrie Rand, a girl of rather delicate health, the daughter of his kind patron. (The first Mrs. Herron received $60,000 from her former husband's new mother-in-law, a considerable sum in those days and an interesting financial transaction.) Herron was not happy about the attitude of his Church and he tried to counter the decision of the disciplinary committee with an "Open Letter," dated May 24, 1901, but his protest was to no avail.

The day after his suspension a secular celebration of his new marriage took place in New York's Gotham Hotel; America's leading Socialists (Norman Thomas among them) were invited. Poems were recited and dramatic speeches delivered. In order to get an idea of the atmosphere of this wedding a sentence from one of the addresses might suffice: "Our Comrade George D. Herron arose, careworn and sorrowful as one who had passed through the Valley of the Shadows of Death, yet stronghearted and gladsome withal, and beside him stood Carrie Rand, clad in pure vestal white and bearing lilies-of-the-valley in her hand."[65] This marriage lasted until 1914 in which year the second Mrs. Herron died, whereupon he left the more orthodox forms of socialism and pacifism, and he also married Miss Frieda B. Schoeberle.

Until World War I Herron was active in the ranks of America's Socialist party to which many men of German descent belonged. Herron, financially independent, was a public orator and pamphleteer. One of his speeches, "From Revolution to Revolution: Lessons Drawn From the Paris Commune," delivered at the Boston Socialist Club on March 21, 1903, was republished in St. Petersburg.[66] His pacifism was coupled with socialism, and in those years Herron also developed the exceedingly florid style which stamped him as ex-preacher, a seer, a demagogue, and a hysteric. His writings abounded in hyperbolic enunciations. For example: "Capitalism is but the survival of animal in man."[67]

World War I surprised Herron in Italy. In the beginning Washington tried vainly to ascertain the character of this struggle and even Wilson was still hesitant to commit himself,[68] but Herron's mind was made up quickly. The Italian Socialists were just as blind as the American Socialists. This was a Holy War of all the forces of progress, enlightenment, and tolerance against the most unholy alliance of the Vatican, "Mother of Harlots," the Prussian Junkers, the wicked Hapsburgs and the Lutheran gun manufacturers of the Ruhr Valley!

The precise nature of Herron's status in American *and* British Service, (he also "informed" the Foreign Office) especially before 1916, seems rather ambiguous. In the voluminous *Herron Papers* we find only two meager documents concerning his financial dealings with London and Washington and his official position. One contains an admission that he was recognized by Washington as representative of the *American Socialist Mission*—which certainly had no ties with the American Socialist party, whose leader Eugene V. Debs, a great idealist, was sent to penitentiary in September 1918 for his pacifist views.

The *Herron Papers*, kept in the Hoover Institute in Stanford, California, are a unique collection. They were given as a present to the "Hoover Library" by Herron during his lifetime in 1924, yet these papers cover only the years from 1917 to 1924, not the previous period. A few letters, papers, and pamphlets are in possession of the U.S. Department of State and of the Public Library in New York City. I have read not only the *Herron Papers* but nearly forty books and pamphlets either written by Herron or dealing with him.[69]

Wading through this mass of material one is simply terrified by the mixture of misinformation, naiveté, hubris, and goodwill which characterize the activity of this fantastic person. Wilson seems to have taken serious notice of him only as late as 1917 and their contacts remained epistolary until the Paris Peace Conference, when they finally met. There is little doubt that Wilson was deeply impressed by the information imparted to him by Herron—and perhaps also by the fulsome praise which Herron bestowed upon him.[70]

The books which pleased Wilson so much were *Germanism and the American Crusade, Woodrow Wilson and the World's Peace,* and *The Menace of the Peace*[71] in which Herron cried out his desperate fear that the senseless slaughter might be shortened. Some of his words —memorable for their style and content—merit recording:

> As one who hopes passionately for the victory of the Allies, I would say that a complete Prussian triumph would be preferable to a compromise between the contending peoples and principles. For even under the baleful bondage of a German dominion mankind might still through high rebellion, through hard suffering awaken to its mission in the universe—to cosmic intimacy and infinite choice. But if the war end in universal evasion, if the race refuse its great hour of decision, then downward into long and impenetrable darkness we shall surely go. One can imagine such an issue as the very despair of the heart of God, vainly broken for a dastard and derelict humanity. (*The Menace of the Peace*, pp. 9-10.)

The President wrote to Mr. Kennerley, publisher of *Woodrow Wilson and the World's Peace*, a highly congratulatory letter in which he said that he read the book with "the deepest appreciation of Mr. Herron's singular insight into all the elements of the complicated situation and into my own motives and purposes."[72]

By late 1917 Herron sat like a spider in the center of an information network with admittedly ill-defined powers of negotiating. It is certain, however, that he met a very large number of people, emissaries from Central Europe as well as from other nations. In a way this poor, ambitious man was lost in a maze: He had the greatest trouble in sizing up the character or the importance of his visitors, yet he continued to write his reports in the usual high-flown prose, issuing relentlessly one oracle and one judgment after the other.[73] His great moment, however, came when he was empowered to receive Professor Heinrich Lammasch on a confidential peace mission from Vienna. Lammasch was a personal friend of the Emperor Charles, a first-rate scholar and three times president of the International Court of Arbitration in the Hague. It is easy to imagine what exaggerated prestige Herron enjoyed in Germany and Austria-Hungary where professors are demigods, and what importance one attached to getting the ear of a man whose opinion weighed so heavily in the White House. (Herron, according to his mood, claimed or disclaimed this importance.)

The meeting between Herron and Lammasch took place on February 3-4, 1918, on an estate near Berne, belonging to Dr. Muehlon, a self-exiled and embittered German industrialist. During a whole afternoon and evening Lammasch explained to Herron the plans of Emperor Charles, plans which were identical with those of his uncle, the murdered Archduke Francis Ferdinand. Lammasch described the envisaged transformation of the Austro-Hungarian monarchy into a federated political body in which, entirely in keeping with one of Wilson's Fourteen Points, the individual nations (ethnic groups) should be "accorded the freest opportunity of autonomous development."[74] Actually, the picture painted by Lammasch was such that Herron at first saw no reason to reject the proposal and, without giving an answer, reflected over it during the night. Then he began to wrestle with this "temptation" as "Jacob wrestled with God near Yabbok."[75] In the morning he knew that he had gained a complete victory over himself: Lammasch had been only an evil tempter. No, the Hapsburg monarchy had to go because the Hapsburgs as such were an obstacle to progress, democracy, and liberty. Lammasch returned to Austria a broken man. Herron wrote a negative report for the President which he immediately transmitted to Hugh Wilson, American *chargé d'affaires* in Berne, and on February

11 the President made a speech which implicitly rejected the Austrian peace overtures.[76]

Had Austria-Hungary been taken out of the war, Germany could not possibly have fought on (as in 1943, after Italy's defection) and hundreds of thousands of lives could have been saved. But Herron was a leftist bellicist: Human lives meant nothing to him. His reaction to Lansdowne's one-man peace offensive had also been strong in the extreme. To Mr. Bland of the Foreign Office he wrote, "It had an almost shattering effect upon me. I have been sick at heart for a week—sick unto death almost. . . . I have never been as fearful of an ultimate peace and a lost world as I am now. And behind my fears are portentous forces—not merely echoes like Lansdowne, but the occultism of the international financiers in alliance with the Vatican."[77] Curiously enough, Herron liked Lammasch personally and gave him (to Lammasch's immense surprise) two of his own books against peace.[78] Herron's schizophrenia knew no limits. Later, at the Peace Conference at St. German-en-Laye, when Lammasch was treated as a criminal, Herron's indignation was overpowering.[79] After all, he was the man who had "really believed that we would come out of this war into something like an approach to the kingdom of Heaven."[80] Nothing came of it (as after World War II, when similar hopes were voiced) and Herron's ire now turned mainly against the French in wild invectives[81] paralleling Wilson's outcry: "I should like to see Germany clean up France, and I should like to see Jusserand [the French Ambassador] and tell him so to his face."[82]

Herron's remark about the "occultism of the international financiers" had, as the sensitive reader might perhaps surmise, an anti-Jewish bias. Socialism and the Jewish mind in its more sophisticated form do not easily get together. The Jewish outlook is rather individualistic and only in specific sociological situations and under great exogenous pressures will Jews join wholeheartedly the Socialist (or Communist) camp.[83] It was therefore quite natural for Herron with his Socialist background to have anti-Semitic leanings and in his *Papers* the anti-Jewish references (usually in an anticapitalist spirit) abound.[84] Frequently these assume the character of the vague and wild accusations we heard from National Socialists.[85] Typical for his mind are baseless remarks such as these: "Béla Khun [*sic*] was the most flagrant agent of French Jew financiers and was put there by them."[86]

Herron's revulsion and disgust for the actual peace treaties, however, were certainly sincere and not a result of his split personality. The disappointment may not have come immediately but evolved within a year or so. Mr. Wilson's failure to rally the country in favor of the League of Nations undoubtedly had much to do with it. Herron's *Umsturz und Aufbau* was published in German in 1920,[87] since such a violent diatribe against the Paris Treaties could not have been brought out in the United States or in England. His book, *The Greater War* (New York, 1919), still shows him worried about the danger of a "Prussian Germanization of Europe from Calais to the Gates of India,"[88] but his German pamphlet, dedicated to the youth of Europe, proves that at times he was not devoid of prophetic gifts. He foretold an "age of murder and slaughter, if not a century of Tartar tortures," of the "worst wars the world has ever seen." Hitler could not have been more extreme in the denunciation of the Versailles Treaty whose "paragraphs abounding in ferocity, lust of conquest, contempt for the law, and lack of honor are as cruel, as shameless, as senseless, as vulgar. . . ."[89] And sorrowfully he admitted that it was "Wilson's word [the Fourteen Points] which had undermined the German Reich and prepared the victory which Foch, finally, reaped with the sword."[90] In this analysis he pronounced the same judgment as a certain Captain Charles de Gaulle who spent several years as a prisoner of war in Germany and described in his first book, *La discorde chez l'ennemi*,[91] in ringing words Germany's demoralization through enemy propaganda. There can be no doubt that the Germans and Austrians firmly believed in the sincerity and official character of the Fourteen Points. If the Germans had not accepted the Fourteen Points at their face value, they probably would have fought on;[92] Max Weber had faith in Wilson but advised continuation of the war in the fall of 1918 because he thought that otherwise the wild chauvinists among the Allies would sidetrack the President.[93] And this is precisely what happened.

Herron returned to Italy after the war but visited Germany a few times. He died in Munich on October 7, 1925, on the way back to Florence. He had become disgusted with the European Socialists, not only because they had tried to make an "early peace," but also because they—men such as Ramsey MacDonald and Henderson—were spending up to $25 a day in exclusive hotels. About events in Russia Herron was less sure. He wrote to Norman Thomas in 1920 that the "bolsheviks" were bad, but that the "future civilization of Europe is coming out of Russia and it will be at least an approach to the Kingdom of Heaven when it comes."[94] The old leftist Utopia of the Kingdom of Heaven just around the corner! To another Socialist he wrote late in 1919, "I am inclined to think that the Soviet system will ultimately prevail. But you are making a very great confusion between bolshevism and the Soviet system. . . . The Soviet system does not differ economically from the Old England town meeting, or politically from the early Christian communities."[95] We have here a foretaste to the "translation" of Mao's murderous minions into peaceful "agrarian reformers."

Slowly Herron began to see that the Italian Communists were ruining Italy economically and politically. His hopes now turned to the use of force against force. His Socialist friend, Roberto Michels,[96] had embraced fascism which, after all, had started as a deviation in the Socialist camp. In a book about Italy, published in 1922, Herron already expressed highest praise for the Fascists,[97] and, after Mussolini had taken over, his enthusiasm, as his correspondence shows, became almost limitless.[98] After all, there was nothing extraordinary about his evolution. It had been duplicated in many other cases—from socialism and communism to fascism and National Socialism—and back again.

Chapter 16

Leftism Goes from War to War

By the end of 1925 Wilson and Herron no longer were among the living, but the seed they had sown (or helped to sow) was slowly maturing. The day was not too far—as Herron had foreseen—when the Germans and the Japanese at least thought they could join hands on the Volga River. The Nazi monster was already born at that time. Instrumental in its rise was Germany's humiliation. This humiliation, however, did not derive from military defeat. The theory, so popular in the West before 1939, that the brown evil was due only to the fact that the Allies held no victory parade in Berlin in 1918 is blatant nonsense. (Such a parade, if anything, might have accelerated the rise of the Nazis.) The root of the trouble lay in the moralizing attitude of the West, especially of America, culminating in Article 231 of the Versailles Treaty which put all the guilt squarely on the shoulders of Germany.[1] (The Treaty was signed on June 28, 1919, exactly five years after the double murder of Sarajevo, proving that crime *does* pay.) There is no better way to generate greater hatred than by forcing a person to sign a confession of guilt when he is sacredly convinced that the confession is untrue. This wanton humiliation, unprecedented up to that time in the annals of Christendom, created the thirst for revenge which the Nazis so cleverly exploited.

It has been argued that such an article had to be inserted in order to provide a moral basis for Germany's reparation payments.[2] It would have been not only simpler, but more honest and manly, to insist on reparations based upon the argument that in a complex war, whose origins historians were going to dispute during several decades, the loser obviously had to foot the bill—not the winner. If one compares the Congress of Vienna, which terminated twenty years of aggression, with the Paris Treaties, one sees all the difference. (France, as a matter of fact, emerged slightly enlarged in 1815 and thanks to Talleyrand's diplomatic genius immediately joined the Holy Alliance.) True, the moral indignation game was played not only by official America but also by Britain—witness the "Hang the Kaiser" campaign of Mr. Lloyd George.[3] After the defeat of a nation the situation is the same as after the physical defeat of a person. The victor has only one *logical* alternative: to cut his enemy's throat or help him to his feet by offering him a peaceful hand. Democracies during a war, however, cultivate collective hatreds, work up a feeling of moral indignation against entire nations (not just against their governments, which sometimes might be perfectly warranted) and thus an equitable settlement becomes extremely difficult, if not impossible.

In the case of the outcome of World War I the most amazing decisions were made. Germany, not Austria-Hungary, was presented to the masses in the West as the real evildoer. (This was not always the conviction of responsible statesmen and we know of Clemenceau that his hatred was greater for Austria than for Germany.)[4] Lloyd George is said to have declared a few times that for denominational reasons Austria-Hungary, not Germany, had to be carved up.[5] Whatever the case may be, the fact remains that after 1919 Germany bordered only on one great power (France) whereas before 1914 her expansion had been hemmed in by three great powers—France, Russia, and Austria-Hungary, powers with a grand total of 230 million inhabitants against Germany's 62 million. Geopolitically Germany's situation had now vastly *improved* and bright Germans were quite aware of this. Professor Ernst Kornemann, Rector of Breslau University, declared in his inaugural address on October 15, 1926, that in spite of all her losses, Germany must be glad that she survived the war as by far the strongest and ethnically most homogeneous political unit of Central Europe: "Let us take fully advantage of this situation, which our opponents have created by Balkanizing and atomizing Europe," he exhorted his audience."[6]

Poland, the only stronger state with a historic background bordering on Germany, had been handicapped from the beginning by the enmity of Lloyd George (and, later, of Winston Churchill). In the rest of the area to the south and east of Germany a political order which made an eventual catastrophe absolutely inevitable was established *jointly* by American leftist idealism, inane British cynicism, blind French chauvinism, and Italian neoimperialism, all intensively collaborating with the local forces of an antihistoric nationalism. The elements of criminality and insanity had achieved a perfect synthesis *so that it was only a question of time until this area would fall under the sway of Berlin or Moscow or both.* H. A. Macartney, one of the very few first-rate experts on Central Europe, said rightly, "For a very considerable proportion of the peoples of the [Danubian] Monarchy, then, the Monarchy, with all its faults, represented a degree of protection and of national security which was not lightly to be hazarded."[7] Yet as in the case of the decolonialization of our days, the leftists of the West combined with the nationalists of other countries in order to break up larger units, thus giving adjoining truly oppressive imperialist powers an unexpected chance to enslave these unviable fragments thoroughly and completely. And when Macartney says, "Of all the Danubian peoples only the Czechs have succeeded in creating anything like democracy. The rest either stuck to their old hierarchies or relapsed into despotism,"[8] he is still somewhat charitable.

The Czechs only numbered 47 percent of the population of Czechoslovakia, but by "annexing" the Slovaks, very much against their expressed will, into a hyphenated "nation" which never had existed in the historic past,[9] they suddenly formed a "majority." As a matter of fact, there were more Germans (24.5 percent) in Czechoslovakia than Slovaks. By clever gerrymandering devices the Czechs could maintain a parliamentary majority and exercised an oppressive rule which drove the German minority (inexactly called "Sudeten Germans") into the arms of a rebellious and disloyal nationalism evolving into National Socialism. Czechoslovakia foundered on the fact that while it actually represented a multinational state, it offered no place under the sun, it gave no chance for a "national fulfillment" to its ethnic minorities which together actually formed a majority. Like Yugoslavia it was a caricature of the defunct Austro-Hungarian monarchy. And with the dithyrambic praise bestowed by the Czech government upon Czechs behaving treasonably against the old monarchy, a real cult of disloyalty was created. The Czechs who had fought against Austria in the Czech Legion on the side of Russia from 1914 to 1917 were praised as national heroes. Why then should the "Sudeten Germans" not side "treasonably" with the neighboring Germans?

The trick of combining several nationalities into one was repeated by the Serbs who, copying the Czechs, promulgated the existence not of a "Serbocroatoslovene," but of a "Yugoslav" nation, a historical, psychological, religious, and ethnic "non-sense." Whether we peruse the official "Czechoslovak" or "Southslav" atlases,[10] we encounter in either case a flat refusal to distinguish between the different "ruling" nationalities (of which one ruled while the others had to obey)[11] and the same was true of the official statistics. (The Serbs also "annexed" the Bulgars of Macedonia and forbade the term "Macedonia" which had to be supplanted by "Southern Serbia.") The West accepted all this without protest, but the reaction probably would have been different if the Germans had claimed the Dutch as "Germans" just because they spoke a language based on Low German. Up to the sixteenth century at least, the Dutch considered themselves to be Germans (inhabiting the lowlands—the *Netherlands*—of Germany), but subsequently they developed a national conscience entirely of their own which only certain Dutch Nazis dared to question. Yet the Slovaks never had been Czechs, the Croats and the Macedonians never were Serbs, the Slovenes had never been ruled by Belgrade.[12]

Before taking paper and pencil to make an inventory of what had become politically of the former Danubian monarchy, let us recall Disraeli's words: "The maintenance of the Austrian Empire is necessary to the independence and, if necessary to the independence, necessary to the civilization and even to the liberties of Europe." He feared the deep-seated antagonism of Britain's moderate left toward Austria, of the Liberals already then influenced by radicalism, of men who measured foreign countries by their affinity to British institutions. "You looked on the English Constitution as a model form," he said to the Liberals in the House of Commons. "You forced this constitution in every country. You laid it down as the great principle that you were not to consider the interests of England, or the interests of the country you were in connection with, but that you were to consider the great system of Liberalism, which has nothing to do with the interests of England, and was generally antagonistic with the interests of the country with which you were in connection."[13] How easily one could substitute "democracy" for "liberalism" and address these sentences to American no less than to British leftists who had served neither the real interest of their country nor of the countries whom they saddled with representative governments of a democratic character.

Winston Churchill, who during his life repeatedly crossed party lines and was by no means a "true conservative" (but, rather, a pragmatic Deist), held views similar to those of Disraeli. He had seen what not only the republican form of government in Germany, but also the destruction of Austria[14] had brought to the world. "For centuries this surviving embodiment of the Holy Roman Empire had afforded a common life, with advantages in trade and security, to a large number of peoples," he wrote, "none of whom in our time had the strength or vitality to stand by themselves in the face of pressure from a revivified Germany or Russia. All these races wished to break away from the federal or imperial structure, and to encourage their desires was deemed a liberal policy. The Balkanization of Southeastern Europe proceeded apace with the consequent relative aggrandizement of Prussia and the German Reich, which, though tired and war-scarred, was intact and locally overwhelming. There is not one of the peoples or provinces that constituted the empire of the Hapsburgs to whom gaining their independence had not brought the tortures which ancient poets and theologians had reserved for the damned."[15] Churchill repeated these views in a note to the Foreign Office on April 8, 1945: "This war should never have come unless, under American and modernizing pressure, we had driven the Hapsburgs out of Austria and Hungary and the Hohenzollerns out of Germany. By making these vacuums we gave the opening for the Hitlerite monster to crawl out of its sewer onto the vacant thrones. No doubt these views are very unfashionable."[16] No doubt they were in April 1945, because world leftism was already busy laying the foundations of World War III so that more young people, nay, people of all ages could again be plowed under for the sacred cause of progress, democracy, enlightenment, social justice, security, and so forth.

Taking the inventory of what has happened to Central Europe half a generation after the Treaties of Versailles, St. Germain-en-Laye, Neuilly, and Trianon, we will find that Germany in 1934 was ruled by a totalitarian dictatorship of the Nazis, that the Czechs of "Czechoslovakia" uneasily bossed the non-Czechs who were waiting for a day of revenge, that Poland and Austria were authoritarian states under Pilsudski and Dollfuss, that Hungary was ruled oligarchically with a very limited democracy, that the Iron Guard in Rumania was preparing for the conquest of the country, that in Yugoslavia ever since the murder of Radić the terror-regime of Belgrade ruled through assassination and execution, that parliamentarism prevailed neither in Bulgaria nor in Albania or Portugal. Lithuania and Estonia had become dictatorships. Latvia and Greece had two more years to wait for this transition. In Spain we saw the buildup for the civil war. In Japan parliamentary life had become as farcical as in Turkey, in Russia the Duma had disappeared a long time ago. In other words, the Holy Crusade to make

Europe safe for democracy, with its billions spent and its millions killed, had ended in a total defeat of democracy and also, which was far worse, of the liberal principle of personal freedom. Where did personal freedom still exist? Where was it constitutionally protected? Certainly not in Czechoslovakia where Professor Tuka was jailed because on the tenth anniversary of the very spurious Pittsburgh Agreement he published an article entitled *Vacuum Iuris* in which he merely showed that the terms of the agreement had come to an end. *Freedom outside of Switzerland and France existed only in the historic monarchies of Europe,* of Northern Europe to be more precise. In this connection the text of the decision of the Conference of Ambassadors (of the Allies), issued in April 1921 when a similar resolution on a Hapsburg restoration had been passed in February 1920, makes interesting reading: "The Principal Allied Powers consider that the restoration of a dynasty which represented in the eyes of its subjects a system of oppression and domination over other races, in alliance with Germany, would be incompatible with the achievements of the war in liberating peoples hitherto enslaved, as well as with the principle for which the war was waged."[17]

In view of the fact that now twenty-two million people in the area formerly ruled by the Hapsburgs were under the control of nations of other tongues, whereas before 1918 just about the same number were "controlled" by German-Austrians, Magyars, and Croats,[18] one is truly amazed. Now the Hapsburgs figured as the villains in the eyes of the great worldwide left from Washington to Moscow (and, later, in the eyes of Brown Berlin!), while the Karagjorgjevićs of Serbia, who had come to rule by murder, governed through murder and had erected a monument in Sarajevo for the murdered Gravrilo Prinćip, [19] were probably viewed as representatives of progressive, tolerant liberalism. To a Central European blessed with a modicum of education and common sense this declaration by the Conference of Ambassadors of the Principal Allied Powers must have appeared as the height of suicidal folly and hypocrisy. *Quem Deus vult perdidi, prius dementat.*

An equal amount of stark madness also characterized French strategy in Central Europe. The American idea to destroy utterly the Western brake against Russian aggression and the Far Eastern obstacle to Chinese expansion, practiced in 1945, had its precedent in the French policies on the Danube.[20] Austria-Hungary had been supported by Germany, therefore Austria-Hungary had to go. The successor states, however, now had to assume the role of effective dams against Germany *and* Russia. Austria had to be reduced to an area she roughly held in the thirteenth century; Hungary was deprived of 70 percent of her area

253

and of two-thirds of her population. Austria was allowed to keep an army of 30,000, Hungary one of 35,000 men. (The Austrian army was not even permitted to use gasmasks.) Austria could not feed herself; one out of three Austrians was a Viennese, and she lost all major coal deposits.[21] As a result the vast majority of Austrians thought of reunion with Germany and Nazidom flourished in Austria because the Nazis offered a speedy *Anschluss*.[22] The Hungarians were automatically driven into the arms of those powers which promised a radical revision of the peace treaties—Italy and, later, Germany. The same was true of Bulgaria: One-third of the Bulgarians were living under a foreign flag.

Czechoslovakia, Rumania, and Yugoslavia—countries whose names before 1850 could never have been found on a map, a dictionary or an encyclopedia[23]—formed the "Little Entente" and received an enormous amount of French military and financial aid. Billions of francs, extorted from unwilling French taxpayers, were poured into these countries designed to stem Germany's *Drang nach Osten*. Two of them, Rumania and Yugoslavia, together with Greece and Turkey, also belonged to the Balkan League. The avowed purpose of this league was to oppose all territorial demands of Bulgaria (and Albania). The Little Entente and the Balkan League thus formed a huge "Z" stretching from the gates of Dresden to the borders of Iran. Yet, as any child could foresee, the French investments were hopelessly squandered. Greece and Turkey were not so much anti-German as merely anti-Bulgar, and the other three states were primarily interested in (a) preventing a Hapsburg restoration, and (b) thwarting Hungarian (or Austrian) revisionism. Their common interest was their common loot, their common fear, and their common bad conscience.

When the Nazis appeared on the scene as staunch enemies of the Hapsburg restoration, Prague, Belgrade, and Bucharest immediately collaborated with them and, in a way, betrayed their French protector. On top of all this it must have been evident to any intelligent person (and it *was* evident to any intelligent Frenchman not belonging to the leftist establishment) that the members of the Little Entente never would nor really could fight the Germans even if they wanted to. Their armies were the most heterogeneous units, their nucleus had been formed by small groups of traitors who had deserted from the old Imperial-Royal army and now were serving the new masters of Central Europe, many coming from the Balkans.[24] We shall see later how these armies stood up to the grim realities of the years 1938-1941. Let us remember that Yugoslavia between 1918 and 1919 was officially called "Kingdom of

Serbs, Croats and Slovenes," *Kraljevina Srba, Hrvata i Slovenaca,* abbreviated "S.H.S." which was interpreted by those speaking German to mean *Sie hassen sich,* "they hate each other." It is significant that to this day U.S. foreign language newspapers with a Central European background almost never call themselves "Czechoslovak" or "Yugoslav," but Slovene, Croat, Serb, Czech, Slovak, Ukrainian, Macedonian, etc. Not even under the tremendous pressure exercised by Communist dictatorships have these nationalities jelled into synthetic "nations."

However important that seismic area, however tragic American intervention in that region, the fact remains that the American public at large was not really interested in that part of the globe—at least until the "Sudeten Crisis" in September 1938. This is less true of the American left, and here we come to the great sin of omission of the American right—or perhaps *of the right of conservative circles almost anywhere in the West.* When Hitler actively intervened on behalf of the Sudeten Germans in Czechoslovakia in 1938 and effectively blackmailed England, Neville Chamberlain referred to Czechoslovakia as a country "of which we know so little." This, at least, was an honest and candid confession.

But let us not lose the thread of our investigation. To begin with, it is true that the study of foreign history and geography is a weak spot not only in American, but also in British schools. It has rightly been said that European history is often taught in American schools as "French history with frills."[25] (The usual frills are Philip II, the Reformation, Peter the Great, Bismarck, and Cavour.) Geography is the very stepchild of higher American education.[26]

To this calamity must be added another. Leftism in the United States was always international-minded whereas American conservatives tended to be nationalistic, introspective, and isolationist. There is, as we all know, a strong and durable connection between leftism (radical democracy, socialism, communism) and nationalism—a genuine ethnic nationalism or merely its clever exploitation. Yet, while leftism is trying to keep one eye on national realities and national susceptibilities, the other eye tries to encompass the globe. There can be little doubt that nationalism as well as anti-intellectualism in America grew at first on leftist soil. Jefferson in his remarks on foreign countries[27] showed himself a fanatical nationalist and, as Professor Hofstadter has shown us so convincingly, anti-intellectualism in the United States went hand-in-hand with democracy. Intellectuality in America originally was considered to be an aristocratic vice.[28] What could be more obvious than the antiegalitarian character of higher knowledge, training, or education? The American upper crust, the American aristocracy used to be great travellers; they enjoyed the value of foreign countries, whereas the *early* democratic element of the United States, the frontiersmen, had neither the disposition nor the time to scan foreign horizons. The China clippers, the rise of big banks with worldwide connections, the international relations of the leading universities interested the top layers of New England and the Middle Atlantic States. Thus the anti-intellectual and "localist" (isolationist) lower classes with subtly leftist views faced an international-minded and "brainy" upper class. F. J. Grund's picture of the United States in the 1830s confirms this.[29]

It would be interesting to make a thorough study about the reasons why a change of attitudes actually has taken place. This evolution in America, however, has *certain* analogies and relations with shifts of emphasis in Europe. There, we should never forget, conservative thought (as opposed to mere traditionalist sentiments) developed more in those countries where the Reformation had triumphed than in the Catholic or even in the Greek-Orient ones. Maurras is not a conservative, de Maistre is more of a reactionary. What we get in Southern and Eastern Europe are rather emancipated thinkers who in the sovereignty of their outlook *overcome the leftist myths*—this, however, is not necessarily "conservatism." The Reformers, Luther above all, as it cannot be stressed sufficiently often, were anti-intellectual and anti-rational. And since conservatism in Northern Europe leaned heavily on religion, this antirational and antirationalist attitude crept into conservative thinking. Professor Hofstadter is most emphatic about the influence of "Protestantism" on anti-intellectualism in America—especially so of the purely emotional sects with ecstatic undertones. Another factor was the international character of America's socialism and the protectionist character of the American manufacturer. To make matters worse, it soon became evident that new ideologies were constantly imported into America by Continental immigrants and these new *Weltanschauungen* of a strongly political character, of an extremist and "radical" bias, were opposed to many facets of "Americanism" and a large part of the American folklore.[30] Similar feelings prevailed in England. As a child I remember a comic strip in the London *Daily Mirror* which featured a black-haired, bearded anarchist who added the ending "ski" to every word he said, thus indicating his Slavic origin. And indeed it cannot be doubted that the Mediterranean and East European element played a very large role in the anarchist and Socialist movements in America until the 1930s. To be true, they also had an Irish admixture. It is obvious that Anglo-Saxons do not like to throw bombs or mount the barricades. Their civil wars, nowadays at least, if any, are waged in an orderly military fashion—and not in the Viet Cong way.

By the early twentieth century the internationally minded forces in America were the Marxist left, the anarchist left,[31] the moderate, unorganized left composed of radical democrats, suffragettes, Single Taxers, the Catholic Church (with all sorts of mental reservations), and a great part of American Jewry. And the more these international-minded groups cast interested glances to Europe, Latin America, and Asia, the more the average solid "conservative" American stiffened in his retrospective parochialism. Obviously, there is a sane and even God-ordained patriotism (remember Our Lord crying over the fate of Jerusalem), as there is also a patriotism which in the words of the conservative Dr. Johnson is a refuge of scoundrels. Equally there exists a reasonable, rational, and honorable Christian internationalism as well as a perverted and irrational form. Yet, whatever the case, the fact remains that internationalism no less than the crucially important field of international relations was "left to the left." And so were intellectual and cultural affairs which, by default, became the monopoly of long-haired professors and short-haired ladies—a truly perverse situation, considering that intellectual and artistic creativeness is the only undisputed realm of male supremacy.[32] (There always have been amazons, *pétroleuses*, and women of Herculean strength in the better circuses.)

Thus we should not be surprised to see American foreign policy following an ever-increasing leftist pattern. Originally the leftist pressures were exogen, came through the mass media, emanated from well-organized groups, from radio commentators and columnists. By 1938 the State Department was not yet the happy hunting ground of the leftists, but the leftist critique of it was increasing by leaps and bounds. As a result a leftist administration started its successive purges until the State Department assumed an increasingly leftist character. This was equally true of the diplomatic service which is largely under the control of the U.S. Department of State. (Ambassadors, however, need confirmation by the Senate, and fortunately, for one reason or the other, the right man might get into the right place, as in the case of Robert Murphy.) Under the crucial Democratic administrations from 1933 to 1953 many appointees were leftist professors a la William E. Dodd[33] and leftist millionaires of the Joseph E. Davies type.[34] Driven by their missionary zeal and their fatal vanity they often luckily left us their impressions, actions, and reactions in print, which gives us a marvelous opportunity to study the simple monumental leftist ignorance in its historic international relation.

This leftist monopoly on foreign affairs, however, is not only due to a conservative default, to a sour suspicious retreat in disappointment and offense. At the back of it lies something even more tragic: the imminent fear in the American noncommitted right that the left, so nicely rooted in American folklore, after all, is riding the Wave of the Future. How, otherwise, could one understand that temperamentally very conservative boards of trustees of colleges and universities have repeatedly hired professors notorious for their leftist ideas? How could one understand that archconservative American businessmen have sent their sons and especially their daughters to institutions of learning equally well known for their exorbitant rates and their extreme leftism, a leftism pertaining to politics, history, philosophy, economics—and morals? How often do well-paid Marxists in such places indirectly and even directly tell intellectually innocent maidens—at their hard-toiling fathers' expense—that their procreators are real scoundrels and blood-suckers? Yet the hard-toiling fathers know all this and both parents accept this state of affairs with a sigh: it is, after all, the "proper thing to do" to provide the dear little thing with a highbrow education in a college with high social rating and to acquaint her with all "advanced ideas." They might hope that, once safely married to an equally hard-working stockbroker, the good girl would wake up from sweet leftist dreams and end up as secretary of the local Women's Republican Club.

One apparently has to leave "brains," "ideas," and "new vistas" to those budding leftist eggheads (even if they stand badly in need of a haircut). How, otherwise, can one explain the fact that newspaper owners, editors-in-chief, or radio station proprietors, who have safely overcome their adolescent flirtations with leftism, again and again employ wildly leftist reporters, columnists, and commentators? I have especially in mind a leading midwestern daily and its correspondent covering the Spanish Civil War. The paper was well-known for its strictly conservative attitude and the correspondent for his boundless sympathies for the *mixtum compositum* known as "Republican Loyalist Spain." (Of course the Communists also were republicans and they were exceedingly loyal but not exactly to Spain.) That correspondent also was blessed with absolute and total ignorance of Spanish history, but leftists are always "forward-" and not "backward-" looking persons: They do not heed the maxim that those who ignore history are condemned to repeat it.[35] Still, the attitude of that paper can be understood only in view of the repressed and well-hidden inferiority complex of the frequent American adherence to conservative principles without being intellectually able to defend them. Just because he also had a notion of "progress" practically in the leftist sense, he feels strongly

258

that he is only fighting a rearguard delaying action. All he can usually look forward to is a certain *Schadenfreude*, a spiteful pleasure at the inevitable setbacks and failures of leftism. This attitude gives to a certain type of American conservative (far more so than to the Continental one) a petty, morose, and melancholy character. He stands in need of a rather lighthearted, humorous, and magnanimous aggressiveness, a will to win, coupled with the liberality of those who believe in diversity.

The American left in the 1920s was nevertheless building up its positions. They were strengthening their various camps intellectually, achieved an increasing control of education and the arts, and slowly gained a monopoly in fashioning public opinion on foreign issues. The rise of fascism in Italy was not overly noticed, however, and certain representatives even of the Democratic party were friendly toward Mussolini.[36] Yet the Soviet Union was far more successful than Italy in winning the sympathies of the writers known to be "open-minded"—though only in one direction. And just as France had its Dreyfus case—a Jewish captain of the French Army was unjustly accused and convicted of having betrayed military secrets to the German military attaché[37]—the United States had its Sacco and Vanzetti case which drove a great many people into the leftist camp, some of them even right into the arms of communism or procommunism. (Among them was Eugene Lyons, a great idealist, who went as foreign correspondent to Moscow where he was cured of his leftism. But how many Americans had the advantages and the opportunity of such a splendid reeducation?)

There were many aspects to the Sacco and Vanzetti case, but to the outside world the *least* important of all was the question of the two men's guilt or innocence. Whatever the answer might be, they themselves never admitted any guilt except their belief in political anarchism. Nontotalitarian Europe, however, was in modern times very lenient to political criminals and thus almost nobody cared whether these two men (and a third, a Portuguese, Celestino Madeiros) were assassins or not.[38] By 1927 very few Continental countries had the death penalty. Sacco and Vanzetti had waited for death no less than seven years and this idea seemed intolerable to Europeans. Americans argue that justice in the United States is so meticulous that every appeal of a condemned man will be so carefully investigated that between the original trial and the actual execution years might elapse. Europeans would maintain that an agony lasting for several years is worse than a quick death. Therefore practically all of Europe protested. Rightists and leftists alike, monarchists and republicans, Fascists and Communists, Catholics and atheists. The Pope tried to intercede. Mussolini demanded pardon, the President of Portugal (then already a "Fascist dictatorship" under Salazar) also asked for grace. I mention all this in detail not only because the Sacco and Vanzetti case is of importance to American "ideological history," but because it shows how little the Continental outlook is understood by Americans.[39] The reaction among pious European Christians of the right is very simple: "Either these men are innocent, then their execution is a crime, or they are guilty, then they will hardly commit another murder. And as to a punishment, they will surely get it in after-life."

In Fascist Italy the execution of these two anarchists was taken as a national insult. In 1928 Luigi Rusticucci published a book in Naples, *Tragedia e supplizip di Sacco e Vanzetti*, whose preface was written by Arnaldo Mussolini, brother of the Duce. Vanzetti's earthly remains were brought back to Italy and buried. Around his grave (with the connivance of Fascist authorities) a local cult developed. The fact that these men were anarchists (and not Communists) was an aggravating circumstance in European feelings. "That's what we all are," was a not infrequent reaction, "but unfortunately, it is an irrealistic attitude and conviction." This is also one of the reasons why the Rosenberg trial and the execution of the ill-fated couple did not create the same stir in Europe as the Sacco-Vanzetti case had. Against the background of millions dying in Red concentration camps and hundreds executed for "speculation," the protest movement in Europe did not materially transcend the Communist camp.

The next stage in the unfolding drama of American-European relations came in 1929 through the Black Friday on the New York Stock Exchange and the powerful crescendo of the world economic crisis. This mighty blow, striking free enterprise without preparation, almost immediately engendered in America a wave of "anticapitalist" feelings, an increased interest and enthusiasm for Socialist ideas and notions, a new, benevolent attitude toward Russian communism. When I visited the Soviet Union for the first time in the summer of 1930 I was struck by the fact that 80 or 90 percent of the tourists came from the United States—and also that a very large sector of the *Innospyetsy*, the "Foreign Specialists" were Americans. America's *Red Decade* (to use the title of one of Eugene Lyons' books) was then already in full swing. Certain Americans were lapping up the books of Maurice Hindus and a great many salient features of the USSR recommended themselves to the American mind—the fostering of community feelings, the methodical warfare against "outworn traditions," the emphasis on "progress," industrialization, the demophile atmosphere of Russia (which had *always* existed), the welfare institutions, from kindergartens to hospitals, the experiments in the penal system,[40] the efforts to create "something new."[41] Among the American tourists (the majority of them female), one frequently could discover an almost hysterical enthusiasm.[42] For most of them communism filled a void caused by the loss of religious faith or faith in Wall Street. However, these tourists, visitors, and "students" had no means of measuring the achievements or failures of communisn. They had not known Imperial Russia, they did not speak Russian, they were completely in the hands of their guides, they had no contacts with the run-of-the-mill Russian population (contacts at that time were very difficult to establish), they knew nothing about Russian history, they were frequently so helpless that without "outside aid" they could not distinguish the door of a men's room from that of a powder room. (Comment, "I find this sort of alphabet rather confusing!") Had they ever been to an *obshtshezhitye,* "a common apartment," seen a kitchen, or eaten in a *stolovaya,* a communal restaurant, they might have started thinking. But they had nothing to go on except their subconscious determination to be enthusiastic, and enthusiastic they usually became. He who knows human nature realizes to what extent a previous disposition can warp the human mind and destroy objectivity thoroughly and completely.

The economic crisis profoundly affected the patriotism of all these Americans who saw in their country not the mother who loves even when she is old, ugly, fragile, and "difficult," but merely the provider, the "land of plenty"—quite in keeping with the immortal poetry of Edgar Guest.[43] Mr. Hoover's presidency was drawing to a close and Mr. Franklin Delano Roosevelt, one of the most dynamic gravediggers of the Western World, succeeded on a platform not dissimilar to that of his predecessor. Though Mr. Roosevelt belonged to the Democratic party, his social background made him not originally disposed to leftist policies at home and abroad. His wife (from another branch of the Roosevelt family) was more deeply inured with leftist ideas, the natural result of higher feminine education in the United States,[44] be it public or private. Whereas Mr. Roosevelt in his politics was "playing by ear," his wife, wielding a considerable influence, was (as we shall show) ideologically far more consistent. Mr. Roosevelt, moreover, had the scantiest of education for his task; he hardly knew Europe, his knowledge of foreign languages[45] was as modest as his acquaintance with the mentality of other nations. Being largely ignorant himself, he really had no way of judging and evaluating expert opinion, or of coordinating conflicting expert views. He was profoundly anti-intellectual[46] and his sense of objective truth was gravely impaired. His handicap was by no means predominantly of a physical nature. He certainly would have needed treatment from a competent psychiatrist.[47]

Hitler's takeover in Germany and Mr. Roosevelt's first inauguration speech were only a few weeks apart, and in the beginning there was a certain amount of Nazi admiration for President Roosevelt, his administration, and the New Deal which slowly crystallized, trying to solve the economic crisis with statist and planning measures. (The end of the economic crisis in the United States came, however, as it did in Germany, with *rearmament*.) The German traveler, writer, and lecturer, Colin Ross, who had decidedly Nazi views, was also an admirer of the "New United States." Most Nazi authors writing about American history showed themselves favorably to the Jeffersonian-Jacksonian (populist and anti-Federalist) tradition,[48] and Herr Johst, President of the *Reichsschrifttumkammer*, the Nazi Chamber of Literature, wrote a play about Tom Paine. The Roosevelt administration was hostile to big business and this was entirely in keeping with Nazi notions. (While the Nazis tolerated the manufacturers, they were especially hard on finance which they called "grasping but not creative capital," *raffendes aber nicht schaffendes Kapital*.) The Nazis, moreover, were convinced that capital in the United States was largely in Jewish hands. They respected Henry Ford (the "history-is-bunk" man who had once written a book against the Jews) but they were dead certain that names like Mellon or Morgan were Jewish. Mr. Roosevelt's highhanded dealings with the business world, with Congress, and the Supreme Court were greatly admired by the Nazis.

Nor was Mr. Roosevelt in the beginning too hostile toward Hitler or his henchmen. As a matter of fact, even the *Anschluss* was right away recognized by the United States, and the American Legation in Vienna swiftly transformed into a Consulate General. The *Reichsmordwoche* ("Reich Murder Week"), starting on June 30, 1934, during which the Nazis assassinated hundreds of opponents, "traitors," and rivals within a few days, did not trouble American-German relations. American public opinion had neither been particularly upset by Japan's grabbing Manchuria (aggression should have been stopped right there), nor by Mussolini's conquest of Ethiopia—which even Mr. Herbert L. Matthews of the *New York Times* "underwrote." (Only a black pilot in Harlem volunteered for the Abyssinian air force—a mulatto in sympathy with Semitic Amharas under the flag of "Negro solidarity.") Americans, however, were duly aroused by the Spanish Civil War which broke out in July 1936. To the American left this was the Crusade of Crusades, a far more sacred cause than either World War I or World War II.

What were the reasons for this enthusiasm which, in a certain way, still has not abated? It is obvious, as we have hinted before, that the (British manufactured) *leyenda negra*, the "Black Legend" about Spain, was still very much alive. Spain had been the pillar of the Counter Reformation and it was the last country to have been at war with the United States before World War I. Other reasons were Spain's Catholic and allegedly aristocratic character.[49] And Spain, on top of it all, received aid from Germany and Italy. Therefore, the reasoning went, the Nazis and the Fascists, envious of the wonderful democratic progress of Republican Spain, were scheming to destroy it. Franco was a "stooge" of Hitler and Mussolini; Franco "conspired" with Nazis and Fascists. ("Conspirationism" as a key to the understanding of history is by no means a privilege of unimaginative reactionaries, but also of the left.) It was Franco's task to make Spain into a bastion of "racist fascism" and thus help to encircle democratic progressive France, which was run by a popular front government. It was therefore America's duty to come to the aid of Loyalist Spain.

The truth is different and, as always, complex. The Second Spanish Republic was just as much a failure as the first. Born in April 1931 as a result of *communal* elections which showed the left in strong ascendancy in certain key places, it went through a never-ending series of crises. As a constitutional monarchy nineteenth-century style, Spain clearly had not been viable. The dictatorship of General Miguel Primo de Rivera in the 1920s brought stability as long as it lasted: It drew support from the army and the trade unions, but the latter finally went into opposition, whereupon Primo resigned, shortly to be replaced by General Berenguer. It would certainly have been the duty of King Alfonso XIII to establish a provisional royal dictatorship and to use force if necessary. Given the fanatically opposed, ideologically so thoroughly divided parties, from anarchists to Trotskyites to Carlist Traditionalists, a parliamentary regime along classic lines was and always will be bound to fail in Spain. Such a failure is all the more certain if the parties in question are grimly determined not to abide by the rules of the game and to revolt if circumstances permit. Modifying Clausewitz' aphorism—war is the continuation of diplomacy by other means—one could say that *in ideologically divided countries civil war is but the continuation of parliamentarism with other means.* Miguel de Unamuno, a very independent-minded and original liberal who lived in exile during Primo's dictatorship, had advocated civil war for years[50]—as a necessary means to purify the air and to rejuvenate the country. The politically inflammable material was getting larger and larger every year. At the last free elections in February 1936, no less than twenty-eight political parties competed and got a sufficient number of votes to send representatives to the Cortes. When I mentioned this to a Spanish friend he pounded the table and shouted, "This is a dirty lie! We have not twenty-eight but twenty-eight million different parties." He clearly referred to the number of inhabitants of Spain.

The birth of the Republic was marred by endless acts of mob violence, by the burning of churches and monasteries (see p. 269), by endless strikes, by outbreaks of brigandage and a rapid decline of general security. To every unbiased observer it was evident that a democratic Spanish republic is a grotesque proposition. The democratic republic might work in the United States and in Switzerland, but since Spaniards are radically different from Genevans or Philadelphians, it was obvious that the experiment would fail—and fail only slightly less than it did in Russia.

The inner division of Spain was shattering. The elections of 1934 produced a right-of-center government. The result was a rising of the miners in the Austrias, most of them Anarcho-Syndicalists of the *Federación de Anarquistas Ibéricos* (F.A.I.). Delirious atrocities were committed already then, horrors worse than those depicted by Goya in his *Desastres de la guerra.*[51] This savage outbreak could only be quelled with the aid of the *Tercio,* the Spanish Foreign Legion, a body of professional soldiers known for their courage and their brutality.[52] Part of them stood under the command of a young general who had distinguished himself in the Riff War and who came from a notoriously Republican family. His younger brother Ramón, the first man to cross the South Atlantic by plane, had thrown leaflets from the air in 1931 asking the King to abdicate. The Prime Minister of the Spanish Republic in 1934, however, was Don José Maria Gil Robles, son of a well-known professor of political science and himself an outstanding Catholic lay leader. He tried to persuade the general in question to establish a military dictatorship because Spain had proved ungovernable by constitutional means. The general energetically rejected the proposal. His name is worth remembering: Don Francisco Franco y Bahamonde.

He certainly was not the most likely man in the Spanish Army to do what had been repeatedly done in Spanish America—establish military rule. General Sanjurjo was the man to do this. Sanjurjo failed, unfortunately, in a premature uprising and went to Portugal. After the elections in 1936, when matters went from bad to worse, Sanjurjo planned another uprising. Franco at that time had been sent to the Canary Islands by the leftist government; he had become suspect. At the same time the left also planned a takeover which was scheduled for late July.

Things came to a head when, in the Cortes, Rosa Ibarruri, La Pasionara, told the monarchist deputy José Maria Calvo Sotelo that he would speedily meet his end. On the same night he was arrested and murdered by the Assault Guards—a new police force created by the regime which did not trust the old Guardia Civil. It was now evident to everyone that Republican Spain had totally ceased to be an *estado de derecho*, a land of constitutionality, of law and order. Sanjurjo therefore proclaimed a military dictatorship and took a private plane to Spain to organize the takeover. Unfortunately the plane crashed. Sanjurjo was killed while the pilot barely survived the accident.[53] Franco's flight from the Canaries to Morocco, where he joined the Tercio, was better managed by Luis Bolín,[54] and the transfer of the Tercio and of the Moorish regiments was partly financed by the Jewish quarter, the Mellah of Tetuan.[55] The army rebellions in Barcelona, Valencia, and Madrid quickly collapsed, but the commander of Seville, the quixotic Queipo de Llano, who was not "in" the conspiracy, rose to everybody's surprise. The initial stage of the revolution went so badly that General Mola was about to give up, when the *Requestés*, the military formations of Carlists, reorganized literally overnight and virtually forced him to fight. The fathers and grandfathers of these men had been defeated in the war against the liberal monarchy in 1872.[56] Now they were again, miraculously, in on the plan. No doubt theirs was the lion's share in the victory.[57] Franco was just one of the generals in the junta that took over. The chairman of this committee was General Cabanellas, also a well-known republican. General Franco emerged as the undisputed leader only by the end of 1936.[58]

The situation at that time was this: The larger part of the army and a minor part of the navy had joined the military rising. The air force was almost wholly Loyalist. The richest parts of Spain were under the control of the Republicans, the poorest and most "backward" on the Franco side. Almost all the industrial areas were Loyalist, but the most historical provinces (Old Castile, Léon, Galicia, part of Aragón, and Navarre) were Nationalist. The term "Nationalist" is not entirely wrong in view of the fact that the Franco side stressed national values, and that the cry "Viva España!" was used among the nationalists, but was strictly taboo on the Loyalist side.

There can be no doubt that all the great lights, the great thinkers, the genius of Spain were traditionally rightist: Leftist Spain's intellectual or artistic contribution was almost zero. True, there is Picasso, an artist of real genius and a Communist, but he leads an exceedingly "bourgeois" life and is repudiated by the Communists *as an artist*.[59] Men such as Unamuno, José Ortega y Gasset, Federico García Lorca, Machado, Américo Castro, Salvador de Madariaga, Gregorio Marañón, and Menéndez Pidal were or are individualistic old liberals, but not Leftists.[60] On the Loyalist side none of the great Spanish traditions was represented—except the anarchist bent embodied in the F.A.I. But in 1937 open warfare broke out between the Anarchists and the Communists, and the former were defeated in street battles, jailed, massacred en masse and murdered individually.[61] The G.P.U. also brutally persecuted the P.O.U.M. (*Partido Obrero de Unificación Marxista*), the Trotskyite group.[62] Their leader, Andrés Nin, perished in one of the purges.[63]

As for population, the Loyalist area had about three times as many inhabitants as the Nationalist side, and, as we said before, its wealth was far more substantial. Republican Spain had almost all the industries, by far the best agricultural lands, and on top of it all the treasury, a big gold hoard which went largely to the Soviet Union and a smaller part to Mexico. The outlook was dim for the Nationalists, but they had the greater faith and by far the better leaders. Besides the Carlists, the toughest of the tough, they had the *señorito* on their side and most of the officers' corps. This also prevented the fiendish massacres so prevalent in the Loyalist camp. It is true that in the confusion of the first weeks many people were shot, many innocents died. Georges Bernanos in *Les grandes cimetières sous la lune*[64] has given a terrible account of the frivolous executions in Majorca, but I know of no case of slow tortures preceding death and of sheer bestiality which abounded in the leftist sector. Here the balance is entirely in favor of the Nationalists.[65] The Loyalists have shown themselves faithful disciples of de Sade and the Bluecoats in the Vendée. The horrors of the Congo were anticipated in this war, and the great leftist delight, i.e., the defiling of cemeteries, was practiced as an exquisite art.

I had the chance to see the cemetery of Huesca, a city under siege, between September 1936 and April 1938. Only one road connected the city with Nationalist Spain and trucks could enter it only very early in the morning or late at night with the lights switched off and traveling at great speed. Life within the city went on normally, but the cemetery, to the east, was in Red hands all the time. And since the forces of progress, democracy, and enlightenment could not take Huesca, they vented their hatred on the dead.[66] The vulgarities, the obscenities, the corpses torn out of their graves and assembled in obscene positions gave one a never to be forgotten impression of the fine spirit which received such enthusiastic support from the American and British left. I saw these horrors just a few days after the liberation of that cemetery and on the way back to Huesca, riding on an army jeep, we passed a stalled ambulance which bore the inscription, "Gift of the Friends of Spanish Democracy, Tampa, Florida Chapter." My Spanish companion could not eschew the remark that we now had seen a splendid example of Western democracy. I protested—still, the "Revolution of the Eighteenth of July" as the Red counterrising was officially called,[67] had indeed been an orgy of rape, sadism, torture, and unspeakable obscenities perpetrated by our dear friend, the Common Man, and which has its analogies wherever leftism lifted its ugly head. A detailed account of some of the horrors would hardly be fit to print. That they showed the need for a spiritual reeducation of vast sectors of the Spanish people is also not to be denied.[68]

As usual in ideological conflicts there was foreign intervention in the Spanish Civil War. The parties in question took help from whoever offered it. The Americans fighting against British rule accepted French aid and it is virtually certain that without the efforts of France, Spain, and the Netherlands (but, above all, those of France) independence would not have been achieved or only after a long time and at a terrible price. Yet the mere fact that the Founding Fathers were allies of Louis XVI and Charles III does not prove for a moment that they were imbued with Bourbon traditions or that the United States showed everlasting gratitude to the Bourbons of France and Spain.[69] However, one radical difference exists between the two interventions. There *was* a Communist party in Spain which worked hand in glove with the Soviet interventionists, whereas there was no big Bourbonist organization in the nascent United States.[70] To call the Falangists *Fascists* is far more erroneous than to call the Nazis Fascists (as the Soviets do, for very obvious reasons). The old Falangist doctrine, which is admittedly *rather* left than right, has certain totalitarian aspects and so had the J.O.N.S. (*Juntas ofensivas nacional-sindicalistas*), but the political theories of José Antonio Primo de Rivera and of Alfonso García Valdecasas, cofounder of the Falange, put the person first, not the state or society, a theory absolutely in keeping with the Spanish tradition.[71]

Whereas the Spanish Communists, the heroes of the "Revolution of July 18th," collaborated with Moscow from the very beginning,[72] the

267

military men worked independently from the Nazis and the Germans, and German as well as Italian help was only forthcoming after the heavy aerial attacks by the Red air force.[73] There were comparatively many civilian victims. Only German and Italian aid assured to the Nationalists superiority in the air which was probably not achieved before the summer of 1937. In the spring of 1938 I still witnessed Red air attacks.

German aid, outside of aviation, was merely technical (pioneers, materiel, signal corps) and after the conquest of the north Spanish industrial area (Basque provinces, Asturias) Nationalist Spain was financially quite independent. Italian military aid, for some time, had been substantial and the conquest of Málaga was carried out largely by Italian troops. But after the defeat of the Fascist units at Guadalajara the number of Fascist "volunteers" decreased and they were hardly visible during the spring offensive in 1938. As to mere manpower, the Loyalists had the edge over the Nationalists all the time and they were well provided with materiel, especially with tanks, by the Russians. The number of volunteers in the International Brigades—more genuinely convinced and certainly more fanatical than the Italian Fascist units—were considerable: Guesses vary from 40,000 to 60,000. A few volunteers, other than Germans or Italians, also fought on the Nationalist side. There were 600 to 700 Irish who withdrew relatively soon because they could not stand the Spanish food. There were some individual Portuguese and French volunteers (active Catholic monarchists). Actually, the only way to join was to enter the Spanish Foreign Legion—and to sign up for five years was a rather unattractive proposition.

There was not too much unity among the Nationalists, except that they were determined to have Spain's fate settled by Spaniards and that Spanish traditions and a Spanish way of life should be maintained. Unlike the Republicans, they not only wanted bullfights to continue, but they insisted that a man should be able to go to church without being clubbed to death or a woman join a religious order without being undressed publicly, raped, slaughtered, and exhibited on a butcher's hook.[74] Franco, however, had the greatest difficulties in bringing the various supporters of his side under one hat: He forced the Falange, the J.O.N.S. and the Carlists to join in a common organization (which, by American standards, would be like amalgamating the Birchers with A.D.A.) and this led to many a local explosion.[75] The Falangist leader Hedilla had been three times *en capilla*, "in chapel" prior to execution for insubordination and revolt, but he was pardoned again and again.[76] On the Aragon front I met with a Carlist captain who loudly regretted that they fought only Communists, Socialists, and Anarchists, but not the Nazis, *enemigos de Nuestro Señor Jesús Cristo*. Liberal monarchists, (*Alfonsinos*) and many moderate Republicans (Lerroux, etc.) were on Franco's side. The vast majority of moderate Republicans and Liberals, who had fled Spain altogether because they opposed *both* warring sides, either returned during the Civil War, during World War II, or soon thereafter.[77] Naturally, the devout Catholic element had no choice; Loyalist Spain persecuted the Church with far greater savagery than even the Russian Communists did, so it had to side with Franco.[78] The situation was different only in the Basque Provinces.[79]

The Loyalist or Republican side, without hesitation, could be called "Red" because the Communists and, to a lesser extent, the Socialists were the only well coordinated international bodies within Spain. As to worldwide connections, the precision of their ideology, their fanaticism, and energy, the forces of "liberal democracy" could not compare with the Second (Socialist) and Third International. The Communists fully cooperated with the Socialists—after all it was the time of the Popular Front flirtation and Largo Caballero, the Socialist leader, was called the "Spanish Lenin" by Stalin himself—but gunned after the F.A.I. and the Fourth International, the Trotskyites. Even Freemasonry, officially persecuted in Nationalist Spain, was fairly divided because it was, after all, a "bourgeois" movement and would have faced an even worse fate in Red than in Nationalist Spain. (There was the example of the USSR.)[80] The non-Socialist democratic element in Red Spain merely served as an alibi: It was powerless. A man such as President Azaña probably did not like the murders and the executions,[81] but he did not have the power to stave them off. Over 6,000 priests, friars, and nuns were massacred under his eyes, but what could he have done? He was not master in his own house. And in this connection it is interesting to note that the Communist party was not at all numerically strong in the last elections (something equally true of the Falange). This fact is usually adduced by naive minds to prove that a Communist danger did not exist in Spain, and that the Communist plans for a takeover were merely a phantom evoked by the right.[82] Yet a small determined minority can always conquer a disorganized state and a deeply divided society: The Russian Revolution of November 1917 proved it. And the takeover of the Spanish Communist party in the Loyalist section of the country proved it again.

The pro-Loyalist hysteria, however, existed mainly in Britain and in the United States. (It was, for me, an interesting sociological experience to talk to the prisoners from the Abraham Lincoln Brigade in their provisional encampment near Zaragoza. As one could expect, a very large segment came from the West Coast between San Diego and Vancouver.) Still, the majority of Americans sympathized with the "Republic" and merely Catholics had largely another orientation. A small sector of Catholics, however, changed sides under the influence of Jacques Maritain[83] and tried to assume a "neutralist" position. It is not easy to see how they could do this, knowing all the facts (or most of the facts), but, of course, they could not grasp the happenings as they did not know the Spanish character—and the day-to-day reporting did not offer a coherent picture. They were horrified by the excesses of the Nationalists in the first weeks and these cannot be denied. They were shocked by the Nazi and Fascist aid. Yet if—to quote an example—a man discovers that his country, fighting a war for a just cause, has immoral allies and that his own army has committed atrocities, he certainly has the moral duty to protest loudly against this state of affairs. But should he therefore "call it quits" and consider himself a "neutral," refusing to take sides? There is nothing more dangerous than perfectionism. Inevitably the words of Gonzague de Reynold come to one's mind, "Often behind a false moderation quite simply a real cowardice is hiding."

American Catholics did not know all the facts; neither did the non-Catholics. In a country as wealthy as the United States there is usually no dearth of information. Information costs money and it can be bought—correct information as well as wrong information. To get all the right information and to *reject* the false, the deceitful, the fabricated one, a special gift is necessary, the *ability to weigh evidence*. Living in the United States during World War II, I found it always possible to find the truth and to get excellent information, but I had to go out of my way and I had to read everything with a critical eye. Believe it or not, *it could be done,* partly because I knew Europe well and had been brought up in Central Europe where the printed word is looked upon with greatest suspicion. *"Er lügt wie gedruckt—*he lies like print," is a standard phrase. (It might legitimately be questioned whether bibliolatry is not a specific gift of the Reformation.) Especially the "editing"[84] done by newspapers, slants, distorts, and colors the news. While in Spain I met the correspondent of the *New York Times* on the Nationalist side. He told me grimly that only a small fraction of his reports ever got printed whereas the cables of Mr. Herbert L. Matthews, stationed on the Loyalist side, received a far better treatment. Finally the *New York Times* sent one more correspondent to the Red side, Mr. Lawrence Fernsworth, featured as a "liberal Catholic," a man who later wrote for the pro-Communist publication *The Protestant.*[85]

From him we could hear the glad news that religious tolerance was on the increase in Republican Spain: Why, only a few days before he had been able to attend Mass in a private home.[86]

Neither the Nazis nor the Italians were able to cash in on their "investments" in Spain. Franco saw Hitler only once and, as an old specialist on criminals from his days in the *Tercio,* he immediately sized up his partner. There never has been an Axis Madrid-Berlin; The Rome-Berlin Axis, on the other hand, had been largely the work of Western leftist ineptitude. Fascism and Nazism, as we have pointed out, were never sufficiently close to agree on a common foreign policy. Masters are often furious if their disciples go their own ways or achieve greater fame. The crucial point in Hitler's expansionist plans was Austria—not because it was his (despised) land of birth, but because the geopolitical edifice of Central Europe as constructed by the Paris Treaties was such that the elimination of only one brick was enough to bring it down; with the *Anschluss* perfected, the most important part of Czechoslovakia (Bohemia, Moravia, Silesia) was totally encircled and could be strangled by merely closing the borders. When Czechoslovakia was incorporated into the *Reich,* Poland was similarly encircled, and so forth.

It was in Italy's self-interest to preserve Austria's independence and in the crisis of the summer 1934, after the murder of Dollfuss and the pitched battles fought in Central and Southern Austria between the *Heimwehr* and the illegal Nazi formations, Mussolini mobilized against Germany. Several divisions stood at the border of the North Tyrol and of Carinthia. The Italian army, for better or for worse, was then the guarantor of Austria's survival.

In the eyes of the left, Austria was hardly worth saving because it was a "Fascist" state. It had started as a democratic republic in 1918, but ideological differences tore the country asunder. Already in 1927 a demonstration in Vienna had degenerated into a revolt, the Palace of Justice was burned down by a mixed Socialist-Communist mob, and there were over a hundred casualties. The non-Socialist element started to counterorganize and thus the *Heimwehr,* the "Home Defense League," was born. But the Socialists too put up a private army, the "Republican Defense League" (*Republikanischer Schutzbund*), and although either formation hardly ever appeared with arms in public, it was obvious that they possessed weapons illegally. The Socialist bailiwick, naturally, was the city of Vienna which, for years, had engaged in big housing programs: Enormous fortresslike buildings were erected in a belt around Vienna and created the impression that, in a civil war, the Red city was ready to defend itself against the rest of the country whose predominantly non-Socialist convictions were only too well known.

In the meantime the Nazi peril arose. The Nazis also organized along military lines, also established para-military formations and prepared for the "Day X." All through 1933 and in early 1934 the Nazis engaged in a terror campaign, similar to that of the Viet Cong. They threw bombs, committed arson, destroyed bridges, etc.

The government in the meantime consisted only of members of the Christian Social Party and the *Heimwehr*. The parliament had ceased to function due to a technicality, i.e., the absolute equality of mandates of government and opposition. The constitution stated that the largest party was to provide the Speaker, but since the government had eighty-one mandates, the opposition eighty (Socialists, Communists, and pro-Nazi Pan-Germans), and the Speaker was not permitted to participate in the voting, a complete stalemate had ensued. With the aid of a war-time emergency law the cabinet continued to be in power without consulting the parliament. No elections were decreed since a number of Nazis would have been voted into parliament, creating a situation *not quite as bad but similar to that of Germany in 1932*. There was no possibility for democratic government—and the government, relatively unmolested by the Socialists, desperately fought the terroristic Nazis.

The situation unexpectedly came to a head when the police received information about a large deposit of arms in Linz, which probably belonged to the Republican Defense League. Policemen who came to search the premises were fired at and they counterattacked. The trade unions replied with a general strike which was tantamount to stabbing the government in the back, a government engaged in a life and death struggle with the Nazis. In other words, the trade unions and the Socialist (Social Democratic)[87] party had virtually become allies of the Nazis. The communal apartment houses in Vienna were now transformed into fortresses and the army, combined with the police and the *Heimwehr*, attacked this fortified belt successfully. The Socialist rebellion also spread to other parts of Austria but was suppressed in a few days. Significantly enough, the railroadmen and the postal employees, knowing more about the outside world and the general state of affairs, refused to sabotage the means of communication. At times the fighting was bitter, many of the Marxist leaders fled to Czechoslovakia (among them Otto Bauer) and some of them transferred to Russia. One local Socialist leader (Koloman Wallisch) and eight more organizers, unfortunately, were executed. Jail sentences were imposed upon others. The moderate Socialists had been opposed to the rising against the government, some members of the Christian Social party were against the quelling of the rebellion and would have preferred negotiations.[88] The result was an increased isolation of the government.

Among leftist circles between San Francisco and Moscow the indignation against "Austro-Fascism" and "Clerico-Fascism" was boundless. The crackdown on the Social Democrats (often represented as kind democrats with social leanings) was construed as an action of the Dollfuss regime in obedience to Mussolini's orders, which was by no means the case. Mussolini was interested only in having a buffer between Italy and Germany. A right-of-center government suited him well. Yet the fact remained that in this outbreak the Socialists had in fact acted as Nazi collaborators—as certain Buddhists in South Vietnam acted in fact as Viet Cong collaborators—and that the Nazis had received orders from Berlin to stay put. The Socialists were ideologically nearer to the Nazis than the *Heimwehr,* the Monarchists, the Catholic Church, or all true right-wingers. True, there was an *entente* between Dollfuss and Mussolini (the only effective protector of Austrian independence!), but the Nazis loathed Austria's cooperation with the Latin-Catholic world. Therefore they planned to murder Dollfuss before his forthcoming meeting with Mussolini, which was scheduled for the last days of July 1934.

The larger part of the British and American press was anti-Nazi, but also anti-Dollfuss. Mr. Stephen Spender wrote his ringing poetry about the Vienna troubles, and Mr. W. H. Auden, then firmly in the leftist camp, put his pen at the service of the same cause. United Press published the news about 10,000 dead in the streets of Austria's capital (there were less than 300 in Austria all told, more than 100 of them on the government side) and this piece of information came from their correspondent, Mr. Robert Best. His case is psychologically interesting. He hailed from Georgia, had the usual scanty education of American foreign correspondents who start their careers reporting about fires and suicides in love-nests, but one nice day are jerked out of their cosy surroundings and land in far-away countries—such as Austria. Usually not familiar with the language spoken there, these (in their majority) political middle-of-the-roaders almost regularly associate with the left. They do not come from "radical" families but, up to the gills in the myths of their local folklore, they are neither overly friendly toward the "Catholic hierarchy," nor toward "titled aristocrats," and they lack the proficiency to talk with peasant leaders—nor would they ever really understand their minds. The only ideological language they *possibly* can understand is that of the Marxist and non-Marxist left which uses the vocabulary of the French Revolution mixed with expressions one remembers from the economics courses in college.[89] Mr. Best, obviously, could not understand the talk about the *Reichsidee,* the *Ständestaat, organischer Staat, Ganzheitsphilosophie, Volkstumswerdung, Heimatverbundenheit,* or *Ordnungsbild*—concepts that cannot be translated with precision into English. He could understand the Socialists, though. So he sided with the International Socialists and when they disappeared from the political surface and went underground, he quite naturally transferred his enthusiasm to the National Socialists. This transition must have come to him quite easily: Racial prejudices, after all, were something he had always been familiar with; as a matter of fact, he had them himself. So he stayed on even after the *Anschluss,* made no move to quit Vienna after Germany's Declaration of War, became a radio speaker for the Nazis, and agitated against his land of birth. Why be surprised? The Nazis were progressive, built superhighways, provided the people with cheap cars and cheap radio sets, and were riding the wave of the future. They were in his mind the fulfillment of the American dream. His kind of evolution was frequent, has numerous analogies, and is perfectly natural.[90]

The murder of Dollfuss was organized in Germany and "Millimetternich's" successor, Kurt von Schuschnigg, could not possibly stave off the final disaster. The amity between Vienna and Rome was heavily mortgaged by the South Tyrol which the Fascists brutally tried to Italianize by all conceivable means. Nazi propaganda in Austria (which in sentiment was strongly anti-Italian) portrayed the Austrian government as a handful of traitors because they kept silent about Mussolini's policies in the South Tyrol. (Not even the Austrian Nazis could foresee that Hitler in 1939 would agree with Mussolini to resettle the South Tyroleans in "Greater Germany.") Yet Italy remained the only power to protect Austrian independence.[91]

This also was fully understood in London and Paris and led to the Stresa Conference which resulted in a London-Paris-Rome Axis for the preservation of Austrian freedom. A public declaration of a guarantee by these three powers followed. Schuschnigg himself tried to strengthen anti-Nazism in Austria and to achieve a greater understanding between the Successor States of the Old Monarchy. He knew that the *Ständestaat* ("Corporate State") designed to overcome class antagonisms and party strife, was not enough. Man does not live by bread alone. He therefore wanted to restore the monarchy in Austria in the long run and this idea had many supporters: practically all members of the Christian Social party, of the *Heimwehr*, and even a few moderate Socialists. Only the Nazis, the radical Socialists and the Communists opposed such a solution with violence and fury. The greatest difficulty, however, was made by Prague and Belgrade. These two governments collaborated closely with Hitler in the "Austrian Question." Beneš declared in conversations that he would rather see the Nazis in Prague than the Hapsburgs in Vienna.[92] Czechoslovakia and Yugoslavia were deadly afraid that their countries would melt away the moment the Hapsburgs appeared on the horizon. They melted away a few years later, and Beneš, in his exile, acknowledged freely that the countries of Central Europe had not had the opportunity to solidify and to acquire an inner cohesion.[93] In fact, as faithful minions of Hitler, they declared restoration to be a *casus belli,* which in itself shows the brittleness of the house of cards built by leftist endeavor at the Paris Peace Conference.[94] The hatred of the "United Left" for the Hapsburgs lasts to this very day[95] and is typified by the Austrian Socialists who in so many ways continue the Nazi traditions, especially in the field of legislation.

Ideological reasons in the West, however, were responsible for Mussolini's withdrawal of his support for Austrian independence and with the ensuing inevitable fall of Austria,[96] with the *Anschluss,* the stage was set for World War II, the Third War of Austrian Succession. And with the outcome of World War II the chance for new, bigger, and more terrible calamities was given. The ideological reasons for this entire development—from 1917 over 1935 and 1938 to our days—are of a distinctly leftist character.

At the Stresa Conference Mussolini informed Sir Samuel Hoare, the British Foreign Minister, and Monsieur Laval, that he intended to attack Abyssinia, a country with whom the Italians (as now the Somalis) had border difficulties. He made it clear that he would use the opportunity to take revenge for the defeat of Adowa in 1896 and would conquer all of Abyssinia. In the beginning his declaration made little impression and since he met with no protest he proceeded to prepare this war—no doubt a war of aggression against the spirit and the letter of the League of Nations Charter. To make matters worse, it was Italy who had introduced Abyssinia into the League of Nations, an entry opposed by Britain because Abyssinia was suspected of tolerating slavery and practicing barbaric punishments (mutilations, etc.).

With the buildup of Mussolini's overseas forces British public opinion became increasingly restive and leftist circles, which also had a hold on a certain sector of the Conservative party, demanded that Britain adhere strictly to the League of Nations Charter and that military-economic sanctions should be imposed on Italy for breaking the rules. Of the great powers only the Soviet Union, Germany, the United States, and Japan did not belong to the League.

From a higher moral point of view the situation was singularly complex. There can be no doubt about Italy's infringing upon the stipulations of the Charter. It was also certain that Italy could and would introduce a more civilized, a more humane life in a colonized Abyssinia[97] and that from the point of view of the Common Good of the Abyssinians, Italy's rule would have been preferable to that of the local autocracy. People with such diverging political views as Mr. Evelyn Waugh and Herbert L. Matthews have been with the Italian army in this struggle and have seen the Italian administration afterwards.[98] They both (for rather different and yet so similar reasons) favored the Italian side. There was, moreover, the case of the tribes and "nationalities" subjected by the real Abyssinians, the Amharas, after their victory in 1896. The arms they collected from the defeated Italians enabled them to subject vast tracts of land, especially to the east, southeast, and south of the provinces of Amhara, Tigre, and Shoa, i.e., the regions inhabited by the Dankalis, Gallas, and Somalis. Conquered by the Italians, they were merely to pass from one alien rule to another, and probably from a harsher to a more lenient one.

British public opinion was worked up to a high degree while Sir Samuel Hoare and Pierre Laval racked their brains about what to do in order to save the "Stresa Front" (Austria!), to let the League of Nations keep its face, and to reach a compromise preserving order in Europe. The war had already started, Italian troops advanced in the North, when Hoare and Laval secretly drew up their famous plan to avert the worst. The idea was that the harassed Abyssinians cede their conquests to Italy which thus would have obtained a direct connection between Erythrea and Somalia: The Italian colonial empire in Africa would have been consolidated in this way. Mussolini showed himself not too difficult[99] but the Hoare-Laval Plan was actually torpedoed by the indiscretion of two leftist journalists and, above all, by the well-organized "Peace Ballot." (Who does not want peace?) Due to this wave of moral indignation Britain adopted a rigid policy in the best tradition of League of Nations orthodoxy and Sir Samuel Hoare was made to resign, to be replaced by Mr. Anthony Eden, until then Minister without portfolio for League of Nations affairs.[100] The sanctions were ineffective, Soviet oil reached Italy, and Abyssinia was defeated in 1936. Haile Selassie, the hapless Emperor, took up residence in London, but the "Committee for the Defense of Abyssinian Democracy" refused to terminate its propaganda actions. Whether Abyssinia was then or is now (or even has the capacity to be) a "democracy" is quite another question.

The tragic results of the sanctions soon made themselves felt. The Nazis in Austria greeted each other with a knowing smile saying "Haile Selassieh!" instead of "Heil Hitler!" They knew that the West's stand in the Abyssinian case was the beginning of the end of Austria's independence. And so it was. England could not possibly assume moral leadership in a general action to prevent Italy from acquiring colonies: Being the archcolonialist herself she could not really turn to Italy saying, "Colonial conquests were possible until 1919, but now that we have the League, now that we all believe in peace, democracy, equality, progress, universal brotherhood and other niceties, you have to stay where you are." In Italian (and not only in Fascist) eyes England behaved like a millionaire organizing other rich men to prevent a shiftless proletarian from becoming a skilled worker. (Of course, Italy would not have greatly benefited from Abyssinia, but that's not the point. Colonies meant *prestige*, and only in exceptional cases *eventual* riches!)

Mr. Anthony Eden (today the Earl of Avon) thus is the creator of the Axis. He embodied the policy that drove Italy into the arms of Germany. Mussolini, being not a gentleman but a common man personally hurt by all and any criticism, burst into obscene rantings against England. American public opinion under leftist leadership sided with Britain and the League. Germany, however, derived a great profit—material and political—from this development. Isolated Italy was her prey.

Without effective Italian protection Austria's enslavement was only a question of time. Britain had lost all interest in Austria, and no longer Hitler but Mussolini now appeared to be the main villain to British public opinion. It can be said without danger of refutation that London wanted to avert Hitler from the West and therefore gave him practically a free hand in the East. In 1940 the advancing Germans found in La Charité a deposit of documents from the Quai d'Orsay among them a note of Lord Halifax to the French Foreign Office exhorting the latter not to make the slightest gesture which Kurt von Schuschnigg, the Austrian Chancellor, might interpret as an encouragement to resistance.[101] An enormous amount of ink has been spilled about Schuschnigg's tactics and his "missed opportunities," but the fact remains that as soon as Italy was Germany's partner, not even the greatest political genius could have saved Austria. It had been written off by the West, by the pro-Nazis as well as by the anti-Nazis—even if for very different reasons. And, indeed, not too much could be expected from the resistance of the Austrian people because it had lost the center around which its loyalty could rally: the Hapsburgs. Besides, the Austrians in their majority felt German[102]—though not necessarily Nazi. As a matter of fact, a great deal of Austrian resistance against the *Anschluss* had the character of the struggle between the "other Germany," "Christian Germany," and "Brown Greater Prussia."[103] It is too easily (and often too conveniently) forgotten that the first Austrian Constitution, promulgated under Social Democratic leadership in 1918, declared *Deutschösterreich*, "German Austria," to be part of the *Reich*.[104] The driving motor against the *Anschluss* were the Monarchists and after the calamity happened, they really got it in the neck. (This went so far that the members of the Austrian nobility, being a race of traitors against Germandom, were forbidden by Hitler to use their titles.)[105]

Americans and Britishers knew very little about these subtleties of a tragic struggle. Only in Jewish circles in the English-speaking world could a greater restlessness be observed. Ambassador Dieckhoff, who spoke to the American Secretary of State Cordell Hull[106] on March 12, 1938, the day after the *Anschluss,* informed the Reich's Foreign Office that Mr. Hull had no words of disapproval of Austria's annexation and even two days later he was still courteous. (Only Mr. Sumner Welles seemed bitter.)[107] Knowing Mr. Hull's mental horizon one can hardly be surprised.

The disturbing lack of quality in the Foreign Service under the Roosevelt administration made the American government as uninformed as the American public was through leftist reporters and news commentators. The American Ambassador in Germany prior to the *Anschluss* was Professor William E. Dodd[108] whose *Diary* was published by his son William E., Jr. and his daughter Martha.[109] According to an unconfirmed rumor President Roosevelt wanted to appoint another Professor Dodd to head the American Embassy in Berlin (probably Walter F. Dodd), but thanks to a clerical error (or to some leftist intrigue?) it was the Chicago history professor who got the plum.

The reading of *Ambassador Dodd's Diary* is almost as rewarding as the study of the far more voluminous *Herron Papers*, because in sheer backwood, parochial leftism these two men vied with each other. There are, of course, passages of historical value such as Dieckhoff's admission that he would have liked to see Hitler overthrown,[110] or the Polish Ambassador's belief (as early as 1934!) that Hitler was secretly negotiating with Russia. Bullitt's avowal that Lord Lothian and Lloyd George wanted to give a free hand to the Germans is as interesting as the Czech

Minister's claim that neither Czechoslovakia nor Yugoslavia would permit a return of the Hapsburgs to Vienna[111]—the old collaboration of Beneš and Belgrade with the Nazis! The funnier part of this *Diary* concerns Ambassador Dodd's aristophobia and democratism. He is scandalized that his German butler packs his suitcase, is shocked by Sumner Welles who has fifteen servants, is critical of American diplomats with a Harvard accent, and his description of a requiem for Pilsudski (which poor Dodd had to attend) is priceless. ("Candles were burning and priests were chanting in Latin which no one understood, and occasionally falling upon their knees and scattering incense, which I think Jesus never used. It was the medieval ceremony from the beginning to end . . . to me it was all half-absurd.") A hillbilly from the Shenandoah Valley lost in the neon jungle of Broadway could not have felt more bewildered. However, the most terrifying aspect of his diary was Dodd's total ignorance of history, a proof of the tragic specialization to which learning in America so frequently is subjected. He had published (in German!) books on Thomas Jefferson and Woodrow Wilson, but the not inconsiderable rest of history remained to him a book with seven seals.

We want to present our readers with only a few specimens of the Ambassador's reactions to impressions and events. It is interesting to note that everything he thought odd or obsolete was immediately styled "medieval," a habit he shared with Franklin Delano Roosevelt. It also was perhaps a hangover from reading Mark Twain's *A Connecticut Yankee at King Arthur's Court*. Göring, naturally, had a "medieval hunter's uniform." Savagery and barbarism, Dodd thought, were a "curious quality of the Nazi mass mind which passed away in England with the Stuart kings in 1688."[112] Himmler, in Professor Dodd's eyes, was probably another James II. University professors who confessed to him their despair drew the following comment: "They do not know the real cause of Germany's reign of terror: the failure of the 1848 movement to resolve itself into a democratic parliamentary system." As if a democratic parliamentary system had not been installed by the victorious Allies in 1918—but with what results! The following reflection, jotted down on March 11, 1935, is delightful: "The Pope is in a tight place. He must help Lutherans and Lutheran universities to save Catholicism in Germany. At the same time he must support Nazi philosophy in the hope of defeating communism in Russia and checking the advance of socialism in France and Spain." One wonders where these "Lutheran universities" are and what effect Nazi philosophy might have had on the *Front Populaire* in France or on the C.G.T.

in Spain. Professor Dodd informed Franz von Papen that "Father Coughlin is always breaking loose" and then found out to his surprise that "Von Papen is a Catholic, but he showed no sympathy with Coughlin." Should every Catholic be enchanted by every priest? One is totally perplexed by sentences like these: "It is an unprecedented move to abolish such historic states as Bavaria or Saxony dating back to the time of the Caesars. Hitler, as much as he hates France, is imitating Napoleon I who abolished all French States."[113] Was Dodd raving mad? And such a man not only represented the United States in the worst trouble spot of the world, but taught history—history!!—at the University of Chicago.[114] After such pronouncements one should not be surprised to hear that it was Germany's "thousand-year aim to annex or at least subordinate all the Balkan countries."[115] Of course it is difficult to know whether such ignorance is of a historic or rather geographic nature. Sir Robert Vansittart, GCB, GCMG, MVO, Chief Diplomatic Advisor of the Foreign Office, published a book in 1940 replete with such historic nonsense that he would have flunked out of every secondary school on the Continent,[116] but he played a significant role before and during World War II. The *New York Times,* priding itself on its high standards, not only put Hungary on the Balkan Peninsula, but even Czechoslovakia.[117] Mr. Raymond Moley, another professor and former "braintruster" to President Roosevelt, wrote in his column in *Newsweek* in 1943 a piece of pro-Soviet propaganda about the Baltic States which contained a record number of historic, geographic, and political errors. Facts are sacred? After a storm of protest had broken loose, Dr. Moley sent a stenciled reply "To my critics" which ended in the sentence, "My critics are entitled to their opinions and I to mine." If there are no absolutes, there are no facts—there are only opinions. All this is partly the psychological-practical result of our age which demands that everybody should have an opinion on almost anything and that everybody should be able to "think on his feet." But it can't be done.

The end of Austria created very little commotion in the West.[118] Kurt von Schuschnigg was the *only* head of government who did not flee abroad but stayed on and "faced the music," making the rounds of jails and concentration camps. This did not much impress the American left, because he was a "Fascist" and when he came to the United States in 1947 demonstrations were organized against him by native leftists and by what the French called *la résistance de la Cinquième Avenue.* But now that Austria had been crushed, Hitler turned against his willing collaborators, the men and the governments that had been "kept" by the French, had taken their money but, as Jacques Bainville had clearly foreseen,[119] failed their employer. Paris now started to see the light, recognized the folly of having destroyed Austria-Hungary (as they had seen in the eighteenth century the folly of having built up Prussia), but now it is too late.[120] Beneš, to prevent a restoration of the Hapsburgs in Vienna, had secretly negotiated with the Nazis[121] and had encouraged Mussolini in his anti-Hapsburg stand. He had even been opposed to any type, any kind of Danubian Federation to stem the Nazi tide, though he openly admitted that his antagonism rested on sentimental and psychological, rather than on political or economic reasons. He intimated that the Little Entente would "always be opposed with intransigence and under all circumstances" even to a union between Austria and Hungary—after all, two sovereign states.[122] He also served notice on France that all these or similar solutions of the Central European problem were "inacceptable to Paris because, above all, they were condemned by the Little Entente." Naturally, it was difficult for this little man with the narrowest of political horizons to forget the ideological stand of his party, the National Socialist party, or his wartime activities, his ceaseless endeavors to prevent an early peace that would have ended the senseless slaughter. "Any compromise with Vienna in the summer of 1917 would have been unmitigated disaster for us," he shamelessly confessed later on.[123]

Why did this spiteful, drab, and puritanical man, who had helped to build an impossibly synthetic country and had waged such a suicidal policy based on resentment that led to sovietization of Czechoslovakia, gain such prestige in certain Western circles? For this there are a variety of reasons: One was his anti-Catholic attitude, and "anti-Catholicism," as Peter Viereck has pointed out, is the "anti-Semitism" of the moderate left. Another reason for his posing as liberator of "Czechoslovakia" from the yoke of the Hapsburgs, the "Viennese bureaucracy," an "alien aristocracy,"[124] "big landowners," and "Pan-Germanism," all arguments one can beautifully present to those prejudiced in ignorance. Sometimes one wonders to what extent he was ready to "modify" them. Discussing the possibility that the Western Allies might not energetically support Czechoslovakia against German pressure, he told Count Sforza, "If we should remain without support against the German menace, we will surprise the world with a limitless subservience to Berlin."[125] At the bottom of his heart this man always despised the West and longed for Russian cooperation. His contempt was greater for Britain than for France. In England he saw a future colony of the United

States and "there is no greater impertinence than the American one."[126] A perusal of the articles he wrote for the antireligious periodical *Volná myšlenka* ("Free Thought") and *Beseda* before World War I is most revealing in this respect.

The most fatal aspect of his role, however, lay in his absolute determination to prevent a Hapsburg restoration even if the alternative was the *Anschluss*—and with the *Anschluss* the encirclement and the end of Czechoslovakia.[127] Better the Nazi flag over the Hradčany in Prague than Otto in Vienna's Hofburg! Yet is it conceivable that the man was so stupid[128] that he thought Hitler might reward him for his anti-Hapsburg stand? An American journalist of renown who saw Beneš immediately after the *Anschluss* found that he "pooh-poohs the idea that Hitler might succeed in any way in interfering with the affairs of the Czechoslovakian Republic." It is obvious, on the other hand, that Beneš never regretted the course he took[130]—except perhaps in 1948 when it was too late. He always had a sneaking and at times a very open admiration not only for perennial Russia, but also for the Soviet Union. In 1938 he must have expected aid from Moscow, and this all the more so as the Third Soviet Army Air Corps was inofficially stationed in Czechoslovakia. He was sure that "communism in its philosophy and morality has certain similarities with democracy. It is also humanitarian, universalist, intellectualist, and rationalist. It is also pacifist, internationalist, and for the League of Nations policy."[131] This, after all, was typical for the way "moderate leftists" in the United States liked to look at communism. Beneš was dead certain that the Soviet Union would evolve to a freer form, but, as soon as he returned to Czechoslovakia under Russian auspices, this leader of the Czech National Socialist party proved to be one of the most docile pupils Hitler and Stalin ever had. Personal freedom no longer seemed to interest him. True, while still in exile he had claimed that Hitler should serve as an example in many ways. In January 1942 *Foreign Affairs* (New York) published an article by Beneš in which he said openly that Hitler was to be imitated as a "forerunner of minority settlements."[132] He repeated this thesis again in March 1944 when he spoke about the "grim necessity" of the transfer of populations,[133] which meant in practical terms the total expropriation and deportation of fully one-third of the population of the historic countries belonging to the Crown of St. Wenceslas (Bohemia, Moravia, Silesia). Dr. Beneš, being a "good democrat," believed in majority rule. But since all the German inhabitants of this area would vote, he could hardly expect a solid majority for radically leftist experiments. The logical conclusion was quite simple: the German-speaking population had to be expelled. The Soviets agreed

282

with him because they knew that in the old elections the Sudeten Germans produced only a tiny Communist vote. Beneš might have argued that these German-speaking Bohemians and Moravians would not only vote the "wrong ticket," but also had been "disloyal."

Yet since Mr. Wilson, Mr. Lloyd George, and M. Clemenceau had handed over these areas inhabited by a people of German extraction against their wishes to the artificial state of Czechoslovakia, why *should* they have been loyal to the nationalist government of the Czechs? The Slovaks, the Hungarians, the Poles, the Ruthenians who had to join this curious state without being asked, had not been loyal either.[134] In 1918-1919 the "Sudeten Germans" proclaimed their loyalty to Austria, but a self-determination was denied to them by the Great Western Democracies.[135] Their efforts to unite with Austria were put down by force of arms.[136] By the fall of 1938 Austria no longer existed and the Germans of the Third Reich figured as the only conationals of the Sudeten Germans. Now, if these Germans of Bohemia-Moravia, appealing to the principle of determination to deny them the fulfillment of this then it was highly undemocratic to deny them the fulfillment of this wish. Or, if after 1945 they wanted to remain under the rule of Prague, then why deport them? Of course, Dr. Edvard Beneš was a democrat and not a liberal. This comes out clearly in his tirade against the freedom of the press in July 1945. "Unbridled freedom to publish newspapers must not be reestablished," he declared. "We all say that liberalism has been discarded. This is a fact, and we must realize that one of the factors in public life that is, above all, subject to today's socializing trends, is journalism. How to harmonize this fact with freedom of speech is another matter. But here, too, the principle that the freedom of the individual has to be subordinated to the freedom of the whole, holds good."[137] Liberalism goes out, socialism comes in. Why not? Dr. Beneš headed a National Socialist, not a National Liberal party! And when Jan Masaryk was thrown out of the window this was probably one of the finest acts of subordination of the individual to the "whole," i.e., the interests of the Czech Communist party.

So much about Dr. Beneš, one of the gravediggers of Europe, a man so highly esteemed by the leftist press, a man who was destined to die in ignominy, isolation, and despair.[138] When Hitler shrewdly whipped up the passions of the Sudeten Germans, who had very genuine grievances against the Czechs and asked more energetically than ever for self-determination, the Western powers were put into a far more awkward position than the average leftist journalist surmised. *Could Great Britain*—just to quote one instance—*fight in good conscience against the realization of the principle of self-determination?* Czechoslovakia had not only the three-and-a-half-million Sudeten Germans (as many people as there were Americans in 1776) but also a million Hungarians and Poles who wanted to break away—not to mention the Slovaks who, at the very least, demanded autonomy. The whole edifice of contradictions, built in 1918-1919, was coming down with a crash. And what should a democrat say if people, invoking the democratic principle, demanded for themselves an undemocratic order? As a matter of fact, Hitler, without even threatening invasion and war, could have coldly strangled Czechoslovakia. Even without treason or terror, simply by being compelled to arm excessively, the Czech Republic (already suffering badly from a grave economic crisis) could have been driven into total bankruptcy. Actually, the foolish experiment of the Treaty of St. Germain-en-Laye was drawing to a close. And when "Czechoslovakia" rose again in 1945, it had changed from a German protectorate to a Soviet satellite. This to all practical purposes entailed one not inconsiderable difference: The Czechs had never been forced to accept the Nazi philosophy or to deny their religion. Now they were required to embrace Marxist-Leninism, i.e., the ideology of a Prussian Jew and of a half-German Kalmyk.

The abuse heaped upon the head of Mr. Neville Chamberlain for his surrender in Munich was almost entirely unjustified. First of all it must be realized that Mr. Chamberlain inherited a totally unarmed country from his predecessor, Mr. Stanley Baldwin, one of the most insular political leaders England ever produced. Baldwin not only knew little about the outside world, he actually hated it.[139] The pacifist Labour Government preceding Mr. Baldwin's premiership had been working very hard to disarm Britain, and when the Nazi danger loomed around the corner, the Labourites engaged in the highly amusing pastime of calling for disarmament while insulting the Tories for not standing up to the Nazi menace. The Liberals did even worse: Lloyd George admired Hitler and declared after his visit to the Obersalzberg, "I have never seen a happier people than the Germans. Hitler is one of the greatest of the many great men I have ever met."[140] Democracy means rule by public opinion numerically arrived at. British public opinion was as little prepared to fight over Czechoslovakia as over Austria, and though certain leftist circles were highly enthusiastic about Czechoslovakia, they were not sufficiently organized to sway the masses. Czechoslovakia was indeed a country about which the British (in the words of Mr. Neville Chamberlain) "knew so little," and whoever wanted to look it up in the 1911 edition of the *Encyclopaedia Britannica* could not find it—nor its people.[141]

To declare war against Germany in September 1938 would have been a suicidal gesture for Britain. Even if it is untrue that there were less than a dozen modern antiaircraft guns in Britain at that time, the armament was exceedingly poor and there was no conscription.[142] The French left was torn between pacifism and interventionism. The Soviet Union had a military pact with Czechoslovakia dating back to 1935, but no common border. The argument that a war at that moment would have given the edge to the Allies is so silly that it hardly needs refutation. The army of Czechoslovakia would not have resisted for forty-eight hours. The Czech officers would have been killed by their own soldiers and the Czech population after defeat would have been treated like the Poles. As it happened, the Czechs were not called to military service, there was full employment all through the war, the people received the same rations as the Germans, the birthrate rose, and in spite of isolated cases of atrocities (Lidice), civil casualties were very small, the losses through aerial warfare almost zero.

In other words, Chamberlain, abused and ridiculed as the "umbrella man" (which Englishman does not sport an umbrella?) had *almost* no choice—in fact, none at all, *unless* he accepted the word of the conspirators in the German General Staff. The conspirators of the Halder-Beck combine were powerless against Hitler who was well supported by the masses.[143] There, after all, was the man who had licked unemployment, the man who had wiped out peacefully the results of a truly iniquitous treaty, the man who showed himself able to enlarge the Reich without firing a single shot. Intellectual liberty was down to almost nothing, but the masses have few ideas they want to express: Bread and games are more important to them than the freedom of the press or academic freedom. The generals, however, not only despised Hitler as an upstart (Hindenburg called him the "Bohemian private first class");[144] they fully understood the lowness of his character which had become evident in the Fritsch case[145] and, above all, they were afraid that he might bring about the ruin of Germany in a fatal two-front war. Generals, on the average, are far less bellicose than journalists or patriotic housewives: They know the horrors of a war and they dislike any break in the routine.

The conspirators were determined to arrest Hitler in case a war broke out. Only then a very large sector of all males would be mobilized and under military orders, thus no longer able to follow party directives.[146] The masses would also be impressed by the fact that Hitler, who promised their country territorial aggrandizement without spilling a drop of blood, had brought them the agonies of a war after all—in other words, that he had broken his pact with the German nation. The conspirators even stationed a division in Thuringia between Munich and

Berlin in order to paralyze Nazi party formations in case of an emergency—especially Hitler's bodyguard (*Leibstandarte*) stationed in Munich. (Hitler's arrest was planned to take place in Berlin.)

Theodor Kordt, a German diplomat in London and brother of one of the conspirators, went to 10 Downing Street where he informed the Foreign Minister, Lord Halifax on the evening of September 5, 1938, about the conspiracy, insisting that Britain should not deal with Hitler, that the Prime Minister should not negotiate with him but should allow war to break out—the conspirators' only chance to strike against the idol of the common man. By that time, however, Chamberlain had already consented to meet Hitler, but the conspirators were not told this. The German officers risked their lives, but they were not considered worthy of confidence.[147]

The Beck-Halder group was desperate when Chamberlain went to Godesberg,[148] though they became more hopeful when the crisis approached a new climax. The date for Hitler's arrest was set for September 29, but then, prompted by Chamberlain, Mussolini intervened and the conspirators gave up. Hitler had gained another "moral" victory.

Why did Neville Chamberlain not collaborate with the conspirators? No ideological reasons were involved, only the curious inability of the Britishers and Americans to project themselves into the minds and temperaments of other nations. I can almost visualize the faces of the men in Downing Street after Theodor Kordt's departure. They must have looked at each other with a mixture of embarrassment, suspicion, surprise, disdain, uneasiness, and discomfort—until one of them exclaimed, "Damn it, this is a preposterous E. Phillips Oppenheim story! Can any one of you chaps imagine a bloody general arresting His Majesty's Prime Minister?" Indeed, no one could visualize a British general handcuffing Mr. Churchill or Mr. Attlee. Here, however, we are up against an old Anglo-Saxon limitation and an insoluble dilemma. The dilemma arises in the minds of the British or the Americans when their belief in radical human differences, if not in racial superiority, suddenly and mysteriously collapses giving way to the very opposite conviction, i.e., that human beings everywhere are "basically the same," that they are "more alike than unlike." Here is a source of endless miscalculations, misinterpretations, and catastrophic errors.

Thus only God knows whether one can make Mr. Chamberlain's Englishness a major point of accusation. This limitation certainly is not of a moral but only of a psychological order. No doubt the man was an English gentleman in the best sense of the word, honorable, without guile, perhaps somewhat simple-minded, but future historians will surely judge him with infinitely greater fairness than the hysterical newspapers of his days. Was the United States perhaps ready to fight for Czechoslovakia or merely egging on England to go out on a limb? True, the United States had no military alliance with that brand-new country, but it was its brainchild, the joint creation of Woodrow Wilson, Thomas Masaryk, and American citizens of Czech[149] and in some cases of Slovak origin.[150] Still, President Roosevelt himself admitted that he was "not a bit upset" about the results of the Munich Agreement.[151]

The vilification of Neville Chamberlain is usually accompanied by the statement that Winston Churchill always had seen the light, that he had always known exactly what a scoundrel Hitler really was and that Chamberlain's naive exclamation upon his arrival from Munich about "peace in our time" would never have been made by the Old Bulldog. Certain Conservatives would fully subscribe to this myth, firmly believing that Churchill, a "typical Conservative of the old school" is, in this respect at least, beyond reproach. Churchill, however, never was a genuine conservative, but rather an old-fashioned eighteenth-century Liberal and Deist. His father, Lord Randolph Churchill, belonged to the "left-most" wing of the Tories and, after a short flirtation with the Conservative party, young Winston became an ardent British Liberal *of the leftish, of the Lloyd George dispensation*. He was considered a "Radical," supported Lloyd George after the war when the Welsh politician disliked the strong stand Churchill adopted towards bolshevism. Lloyd George's pro-Russian and anti-Polish attitude was partly due to his loathing for Poles (which Churchill inherited), partly to his desire not to lose the indirect support of the Trade Unions who wanted to cripple Poland's resistance in her life-and-death struggle against the Red army.[152]

After the break with Lloyd George Mr. Churchill worked his way back into the Conservative party where the old diehards (who always valued character more than brains) never quite forgave him his switches.[153] But when, upon his return from Yalta, he told the House of Commons (February 27, 1945) that he did not know any government that kept its obligations, even to its disadvantage, as faithfully as the Soviets did and that he was thoroughly opposed to debating Russia's loyalty to pacts and treaties—what did he really think? If he believed his own words he was a great deal more naive than Chamberlain with his "peace in our time."[154] And his famous perspicacity about Hitler? In November 1935—well over a year after the June 1934 massacre—Churchill called the *Führer* a "highly competent, cool, well-informed functionary with an agreeable manner" and added that "the world lives on hopes that the worst is over and that we may yet live to see Hitler a gentler figure in a happier age."[155] As late as 1937 our great Epimetheus wrote about Hitler, "If our country were defeated I hope we should find a champion as indomitable to restore our courage and lead us back to our place among the nations."[156] Churchill's conversion did not take place until sometime in 1938.

Chapter 17

Another Leftist War

Whereas the fall of Czechoslovakia (consummated in March 1939)[1] was a bitter blow to the left the developments later in 1939, disturbing to all people of good will, did not bother them too much. Mr. Churchill, always uninformed about the geography and history of countries away from seashores, berated in his memoirs Hungary and Poland as "beasts of prey" devouring parts of prostrate Czechoslovakia.[2] The leftist press viewed Poland with even greater hostility: To them it was a country of "Fascist aristocratic landowners" inhabited by miserable serfs, a country where Jews had to live in ghettos[3] and heel-clicking army officers administrated the country together with fat Roman Catholic bishops. Polish realities, however, were almost as complex as those of Imperial Russia and at the outbreak of World War II this was especially true of the social conditions and structures.[4]

British enthusiasm for Poland was never excessive, but Mr. Chamberlain was certain that another of Hitler's "peaceful grabs" could not be permitted. In France pacifist feelings were strong (*Nous ne voulons pas mourir pour Dantzic!*), but British public opinion was outraged by Hitler's march on Prague and regarded this, quite rightly, as a breach of promise. Negotiations were started between the Western Allies and the Soviet Union to build up a solid front against Hitler. *There is very little doubt that peace would have been preserved if Germany had been faced by the specter of a two-front war.* The German-Russian military pact, concluded between Ribbentrop and Molotov, gave to Hitler the necessary guarantee for a free hand in the West. Even after the *joint Nazi-Communist conquest of Poland* Soviet economic aid to Nazi Germany was increasing: In the fall of 1940 Nazi planes engaged in the battle of Britain were using Soviet gasoline. The prospect of a two-front war, on the other hand, would have resulted in a reorganization of the conspiratorial forces within the German army. Surprised by the political developments and the successful negotiations in Moscow, the German generals started only in November 1939 to close their ranks again.

In September 1939 there were no valid reasons or excuses whatsoever for Hitler's attack against Poland. Contrary to a certain German propaganda, the eastern boundary of Germany, as set down in the Versailles Treaty, was not particularly unjust. As a matter of fact, certain areas which Prussia acquired in the First and Second Partitions of Poland had not been returned to Poland. The so-called "Polish Corridor" was not an iniquity: These districts were ancient Polish lands mainly inhabited by Poles. The separation of East Prussia[5] from the rest of Germany involved a few minor hardships, but anybody traveling from the Continental United States to Alaska on the Alcan Highway also has to cross Canada. Hitler, however, had his eyes set on another triumph, another bloodless conquest, and there is good reason to believe that he did not expect Britain to live up to her new treaty with Poland. This speculation was unfortunately not baseless; there had been much vituperation of Poland by a considerable part of the English and the French press; and a British radio commentator, Commander Stephen King-Hall, had announced that he would shout "Sieg-Heil!" if Hitler were to invade Poland. Hitler told Ciano that he was convinced that Britain and France would never start a general conflagration by supporting Poland. Thus the surprise among the Nazi leadership when Britain's declaration of war came on September 3rd was almost boundless. Hitler suffered from the typical Continental Anglomania[6] and not even Britain's entry into the war cured him from his complex which resulted in his passivity at the time of the evacuation at Dunkirk. Ribbentrop too, was dead certain that Britain would not move.[7]

All this came as a terrible surprise to the American left, the most naive people under God's sun. Only on August 23, one week before the outbreak of the war, the "Committee on Cultural Freedom" under the signature of a huge crowd of "leading intellectuals" had published a full page advertisement in America's most important papers. Signatories were among others Jay Allen, Henry Pratt Fairchild, Waldo Frank, Leo Hubermann, George Kaufmann, Paul de Kruif, Max Lerner, Clifford Odets, Frederick L. Schumann, George Seldes, James Thurber, Richard Wright, Dashiell Hammett, Vincent Sheean, Maxwell Stuart. Here are a few excerpts:

290

"The fascists . . . are intent on destroying such unity [i.e., of all "progressive forces"] at all costs . . . realizing that here in America they cannot get far with a definitely pro-Fascist appeal, they strive to pervert American anti-Fascist sentiment to their own ends . . . they have encouraged the fantastic falsehood that the USSR and the totalitarian states are basically alike. . . .

"The Soviet Union considers political dictatorship a transitional form and has shown a steadily expanding democracy in every sphere. Its epoch-making new constitution guarantees Soviet citizens universal suffrage, civil liberties, the right to employment, to leisure, to free medical care, to material security in sickness and in old age, to equality of the sexes in all fields of activity and to equality of all races and nationalities."

Convinced "evolutionists" should remember that these brilliant facts, figures, and forecasts were stated nearly one-third of a century ago and had ample time to become reality.

World War II started with an unparalleled depression and despair among all peoples involved. Germany and Austria were countries in tears, the spontaneous demonstrations of 1914 were not repeated.[8] Far from being terminated,[9] the resistance of many German generals and rightist leaders was to increase as time went on until it reached its culmination in July 1944. Nor is it true that they turned against Hitler only when his star was sinking. A perusal of the diaries of Ulrich von Hassell[10] shows the despair created by the successive victories in the earlier period of the war. Indeed rare is the country whose leading men are driven to think, to pray, and to act for the defeat of their fatherland. Do Germans merely love to obey orders blindly, unconditionally, and loyally? But where else could one find the chief and not just a treacherous employee of the Counterintelligence—a magnificent man such as Admiral Canaris—working full blast for the downfall of the Third Reich?[11] There were men galore in Germany eager to put an end to their country's criminal leadership and the self-destruction of Europe, but they had to fight alone and to go down in this fight because the combined, well-scheming forces of the left wanted it just that way—and the feeble and confused forces of the right among the Allies were not prepared to make a stand.

At first the Stalin-Hitler Pact, which made the war possible, and the subsequent outbreak of the fighting stunned the leftist camp all over the world. The leftists, needless to say, forgot that the Nazis were archleftists and that the alliance with the Soviet Union, concluded to destroy Poland, was by no means an act of political perversion. Hitler had

291

always preferred communism to the free way of life and Goebbels, especially as a younger man, had a genuine admiration for a socialist Russia, the natural ally of Germany.[12]

Though used to acting like sheep, many leftists in the Western World discovered that they were still human beings; others stuck blindly to their Red loyalties and found that the Nazis weren't so bad after all. Needless to say, the Brown press in Germany had made a complete *volte face* and all anti-Communist propaganda ceased overnight.[13] Ribbentrop[14] shocked not only Ciano but also certain old Nazis when he recounted how happy he had felt in Moscow among Stalin's buddies, "men with strong faces."[15] In the Soviet Union the papers had to feature the German war news before the Allied. Soviet economy worked full blast for Nazi Germany and after the annihilation of Poland Mr. Vyatcheslav Molotov declared grandiloquently: "One blow from Germany, one from the Soviet Union, and this ugly duckling of the Versailles Treaty[16] was no more." He then accused the "ruling classes" of Britain and France of "diverting attention from their colonial problems," adding that there was "absolutely no justification for a war of this kind. One may accept or reject the ideology of Hitlerism as well as any other: That is a matter of political views. But everybody would understand that an ideology cannot be eliminated by war. It is therefore not only senseless but criminal to wage such a war for the destruction of 'Hitlerism' camouflaged as a fight for 'democracy.' " The Soviet Union, having just gobbled up Eastern Poland and occupied strategic places in the three Baltic republics (all with Nazi connivance), was suspected of having further designs on the latter. Mr. Molotov indignantly declared: "We stand for a scrupulous and punctilious observance of pacts on a basis of complete reciprocity and we declare that all nonsense about sovietizing the Baltic countries is only to the interest of our common enemies and of all anti-Soviet provocateurs."[17]

Not much later the Soviet Union (without Nazi protest) attacked Finland and decent people all over the world were outraged.[18] Of course the mere existence of Finland only sixteen miles from Leningrad was in itself an "anti-Soviet provocation." Though Leningraders could not possibly visit the seaside resorts between Terijoki and Viipuri (Viborg), the news had leaked through to the Soviet Union's second largest city that in Finland, a country which apart from timber had hardly any natural resources, living standards were infinitely higher than in the Workers' Paradise. Thus the borders had to be pushed back to where they had been temporarily in the eighteenth century which also had the effect that the USSR (as once Imperial Russia) could launch a swift attack on the heart of Finland at any time. The Finnish Communist party, percentagewise one of the largest in Europe,[19] was expected to rise, but nothing of the sort happened, and the "Finnish People's Democratic Republic" under Otto Kuusinnen, established in Terijoki[20] soon after the first attack, remained without visible support. Clearly the Finnish Communists wanted to have their own brand of communism and no defections occurred. After the surrender of Western Karelia in 1940 only *one* family remained in that area.

The leftist forces in the West slowly recovered from the blow. The switch in the German-Soviet alignment happened just as described by Orwell in his novel *1984* where in the permanent world war the change of alliances occurs during a public demonstration: The orator is given a slip of paper informing him of the startling fact and he quickly revises his message. Of course weasel words had to be used by the left; the Nazis were somehow lost from sight; the fact that Germans stranded in America now regained their *Vaterland* via Vladivostok was overlooked.[21] Only a few days before the announcement of the Nazi-Soviet Pact a flaming manifesto of protest against the very insinuation that such a thing were possible, signed by the whole shining phalanx of the leftist American intelligentsia appeared as a full-page advertisement in leading newspapers. Now the left quickly concentrated on the "forces of reaction" at home and denounced those who wanted to wage a "capitalist war" for bigger and better profits. Nazism? A bugbear! The American Youth Congress—as we mentioned above—hooted at President Roosevelt when he mentioned valiant Finland. In England "People's Congresses" sprung up overnight, drew up resolutions, demanded reforms and "peace," and protested against armaments. The Communists in the United States were entirely on the side of isolationism (so were, naturally, the members of the German-American *Bund!*), and Georgi Dimitrov could write in 1940: "The brave fight of American Communists against the United States being drawn into the war finds an ever-increasing sympathy among the Labor unions and even from the ranks of the A.F. of L. run by reactionaries."[22] A song was composed and distributed: *The Yanks Are Not Coming*.

Yet they were coming after all to repeat the old tragic performance: to win a war and to lose a peace. I do not share the frequently found opinion that a full Nazi victory in World War II would have been preferable to the present state of affairs. A victory of the German armies would have enhanced Hitler's prestige to a point where any revolt by the army would have become unthinkable—and no other revolt there was possible. A revolt of officers, moreover, is feasible only if the soldiers obey their orders—even if they are most "unusual." With a progressive diefication of Hitler in the eyes of the success-centered Common Man this would no longer have been the case. The rank and file of the soldiers would not have followed their officers in a rebellion against the *Führer* and "Supreme War Lord."[23] With Britain on her knees and the Russian war materiels under the control of Berlin, the Nazis would have become well-nigh invincible. Naturally our argument falls flat with the completion of the A-bomb in August 1945. But would it have existed without America's entry into the war? The German scientists certainly had boycotted its manufacture in the Third Reich. And, we will admit, in the long run, it would have been most difficult to dominate the Old World with the help of a *racist* ideology. This particular weakness of Nazism made itself felt even during the war.

Still, whereas we can insist that America's entry in 1917 was a truly fateful decision which paved the way to World War II, a Nazi victory in Europe—for one or two generations—would have been an almost unmitigated disaster. Nearly as disastrous, however, was the political-psychological warfare waged by the Allies as well as the "order" which actually emerged from World War II. Taking into consideration the ignorance, the prejudices, and the ideological trends prevailing in the West and in the Soviet Union, not much else could be expected. This was also the reasoning of a few intelligent American isolationists.

Mr. Churchill, as we have pointed out, was not a genuine conservative, but a pragmatist and Deist of a certain aristocratic cast, of a terrifying cynicism and an astounding ignorance concerning most countries. Nevertheless, he was very gifted by nature in many ways but had a comparatively poor schooling: He never was a *student* of anything. His biographer, Mr. Robert Sencourt, said that to him "Christ was a socialist" and "men who had principles were 'goody-goodies.' With one grandfather a duke and the other an American impresario, he had grandeur in his zest for adventures and huge gambles. This enabled him to seize one of the greatest occasions in history and gradually to turn it into a calamity for Europe and a triumph for America."[24] The triumph, however, was only momentary.

His colleague, Mr. Franklin D. Roosevelt, was less gifted and even less informed, was totally ignorant of the big wide world, perhaps had less oratorical proficiency than Mr. Churchill, but played on a far larger instrument. Let us here remember Kierkegaard's remark that the preparation of a minister nowadays does not teach him how to be one, but how to become one.[25] The manifold efforts, talks, intrigues, chats, and rubbing of shoulders in order to finally jockey oneself into a leading position in a democracy consume so much time and energy that the factual knowledge absolutely necessary for *statesmanship* (as opposed to the qualifications of a mere *politician*) is almost never acquired. Though more cautious in his public utterances, Mr. Roosevelt knew even less than Professor Wilson. There is little doubt that he could have read *Mein Kampf*—if ever!—only in 1941.[26] (The Nazis to him, of course, were "medieval.") His wife stood very far to the left: A study of her writings is most rewarding and we shall return to her later in this chapter. His Secretary of State, Mr. Cordell Hull, had received the intellectual preparation for his exalted role in the most amazing way.[27] He owed his later career largely to his specialization in trade and tariff agreements which in the good old days used to be the crux of American foreign policy. His contribution to the profound, almost fatal crisis in which our world actually finds itself is a not inconsiderable one. His successor, Mr. Stettinius, an industrialist, was not much more qualified, and we owe thanks to Pan Jan Ciechanowski, the former Polish Ambassador to Washington, for a candid glimpse of Mr. Stettinius catapulted into the important position of an Undersecretary of State two years prior to his taking over the entire State Department. "I congratulated him on his appointment," Ciechanowski wrote, "and asked him how he felt in his new surroundings. He replied that he felt 'very bewildered.' "[28]

Barely a few days after taking over his duties he had become Acting Secretary of State in the absence of Mr. Hull. With boyish frankness he admitted that he not only felt ignorant of the affairs he had to deal with but, what made it even more difficult, he did not know most of the officials of the department who had suddenly become his subordinates and collaborators. Sheer amateurism characterized not only the Americans but also the British war effort, whereas the Russians and Germans were held in thralldom by ideologies untrue to life—a different handicap. Yet a very bad plan is sometimes superior to none at all. A human being will plan ahead and might err in his calculations. A beast does not really plan: *Unerring instincts* will induce it to build a nest or to collect food for the winter. But apart from such isolated activities conditioned by *inherited* instincts, the animal merely acts and reacts pragmatically, as the momentary circumstances demand. There exists in "Anglo-Saxonry," as Keyserling stated, a strong anti-intellectual current[29] which, by the way, harmonizes well with the democratic tradition.

Our "conservatives" have a tendency to compare the President with the Prime Minister, and the Prime Minister comes out far better. To the historian and moralist this is by no means evident. Apart from the fact that Churchill was not a "conservative" (and, for this particular reason, there should be no *parti pris*!), we must remember the "mythomanic" tendency of the President, the promises he broke without the slightest reason or provocation, the statements he made without any backing of facts, the directions he gave on the spur of the moment and which had no realistic substance—all of these add up to the fact that he could not be held morally responsible for many of his utterances and actions. (Thus he sent the Polish Premier Mikolajczyk on a wild goose chase to Moscow and exhorted him to stand up to Stalin, to make no territorial concessions, insisting that the President and the people of the United States stood solidly behind him. Molotov told the surprised Premier in the presence of Eden and Harriman that at Teheran Roosevelt had solemnly promised Eastern Poland to the Soviet Union.[30] Mikolajczyk was thunderstruck.) The President's sense of responsibility was startling, his frivolity was of an extraordinary character.[31] Mr. Henry Morgenthau, Jr. relates in his *Diaries* how every morning the price of gold was set by the President at breakfast. One day Mr. Roosevelt proposed a rise of 21 cents because "it is a lucky number, three times seven." Finally, Montagu Norman, Governor of the Bank of England, protested. This outcry of indignation amused "Henry, the Morgue": "I began to chuckle and the President roared with laughter."[32] Roosevelt had only hazy ideas on a future order for our planet, but they clearly bordered on the abnormal and were characterized by a strong leftist bias. (There was to be a plebiscite in Norway to see what sort of constitution the people really wanted to have, also in the Netherlands, in Belgium, in Italy and in Greece—but, of course, none in Czechoslovakia, a model democracy; and Russia, according to FDR had the noble calling to dominate Europe.)[33] Yet apart from vague notions, there was no coherent vision. All a man like Roosevelt could do was to wage war, declare "Unconditional Surrender" a policy, thereby prolong the war beyond his own life span and play politics "by ear." The Russians had a plan. The Americans had none.

Nor, indeed, had Mr. Churchill and the British. It is pure myth that Mr. Churchill insisted on his brilliant idea to invade Europe through the Balkans and to occupy Budapest, Vienna, and Prague before the Russians did. He yielded quickly and without much resistance to the "American" plan to attack Italy instead, and called Italy no less than the Balkans the "soft underbelly of Europe." (How many Allied soldiers, especially Poles bound to lose their homeland, found their graves in this allegedly so soft highly mountainous underbelly?) And it is a mere saga that Churchill opposed the Unconditional Surrender formula. His reaction to this piece of psychological strategy was that "that poor Goebbels is going to howl."[34]

General Albert C. Wedemeyer wrote quite adroitly about the war aims and the two key men in the Western camp of the Allies: "Without a clearly defined political objective, war is but aimless or senseless slaughter. This fact is understood by every military man with any pretensions to professional knowledge. Winston Churchill, correctly described by his own Chief of Staff as no strategist, but as acting on intuition and impulse without regard to the implications and consequences of the courses he favored, waged war more like an Indian chieftain from the Arizona Territory intent upon obtaining the largest possible number of enemy scalps. . . . In order to kill a maximum number of Germans, Winston Churchill dismissed politics or policy as a 'secondary consideration,' and on this and many other occasions said that there were 'no lengths of violence to which we would not go' in order to achieve his objective."[35]

The Russian alliance was of great psychological importance for the entire left in Britain and in the United States. It cannot be denied that the German attack on the Soviet Union was a break for Britain engaged in bitter aerial warfare with the *Reich*. Contrary to a widespread opinion, though air warfare was not begun by the Nazis, in 1935 they had offered an air pact to the National Laborite Government, which would have limited the role of the air force to the support of operating ground forces. This was turned down by Air Secretary Thomson as a clever, but immoral ruse to humanize warfare: Frightfulness should terminate war, this blot on humanity! Yet Hitler originally acted *as if* it had been accepted and signed, and the first big German raids on England had the character of mere reprisals. (The attack on Rotterdam, with 945 people killed, had been erroneously unleashed after the armistice when the German troops were within nine miles of the city.)[36]

There exists a *very large and conclusive documentation* on this whole issue. Mr. Churchill speculated, quite rightly, that Britain eventually would win the air war because she could build up an air force in safely distant lands while Germany would always remain under her nose. This much we can gather partly from his notes written on July 8 and 11, 1940.[37] The documentary proof that the RAF started a methodical bombing of Germany before the Germans opened their so-called *Blitz*[38] on Britain can be gleaned from such authoritative books and articles as J. M. Spaight (Assistant Secretary, Air Ministry), *The Battle of Britain*[39] and *Bombing Vindicated*,[40] and Basil Liddell-Hart, "War

Limited," in *Harper's Magazine*.[41] General J. C. F. Fuller in *The Second World War, 1939-1945* says frankly, that "it was Mr. Churchill who lit the fuse which detonated a war of devastation and terrorization unrivaled since the invasion of the Seljuks."[42] Yet the suffering inflicted from the air took not only a huge toll among the Germans (without too seriously incapacitating their industry) but also among foreign laborers, concentration camp inmates, and Allied nationals.[43]

Even before Pearl Harbor American public opinion had to be prepared for an alliance in which not only Britain but also the Soviet Union had a leading part. The German attack on the USSR played a role similar to the abdication of Nicholas II in 1917. Now American public opinion could more easily be made to change its stand. In this connection Cannon Bernard Iddings Bell recorded a rather significant wartime experience: "At a dinner in New York at that time, I sat next to a high-up officer of one of the great news-collecting agencies. 'I suppose,' I ventured, 'now that the Muscovites are on our side, the American people will have to be indoctrinated so as to stop thinking of them as devils and begin to regard them as noble fellows.' 'Of course,' he replied, 'we know what our job is in respect to that. We of the press will bring about a complete and most unanimous *volte face* in the belief of the Common Man about the Russians. We shall do it in three weeks.' "[44]

The major trouble about deceit and untruth is not that misinformation is imparted to certain persons but that the originators of the lies tend to consider them to be truths. Finally they are unable to distinguish between fact and fiction and *act* in accordance with their fabrications. In Britain the news of the first Soviet victories came as such a relief that even people of considerable integrity lost their balance.[45] A feminine hysteria broke loose in the British Isles: Visions of sturdy Cossacks, nagaikas, vodka, the sweat of galloping horses, bearded muzhiks, progressive commissars, and heroic girls in boots and coy fur caps fired the imaginations. Many Britishers were ready to throw themselves into the arms of Unholy Mother Russia, absolutely forgetting that it was Stalin who, with the Molotov-Ribbentrop Pact, had wilfully started World War II, later discarding all British warnings about an impending attack from the Germans as idle capitalist talk. A policeman who finds that the two gangs he is fighting have fallen out among themselves does not proclaim that the weaker of the two consists of cherubs and seraphs; he merely takes practical advantage of the "break." And when the USSR demanded a much larger chunk of Poland than Hitler ever had—52 percent of Polish territory, to be precise—the British by and large failed to remember that it actually had been the Polish issue that had made them declare war on Hitler. What did Lord Halifax say in December 1939? "We have tried to improve relations with Russia, but in doing so we had always maintained the position that rights of third parties must remain intact and unaffected by our negotiations. . . . I have little doubt that the people of this country would prefer to face difficulties and embarrassments rather than feel that we had compromised the honor of this country and Commonwealth."[46] Yet the most curious part of the bill to be paid for that almost limitless *libido serviendi* as regards the Soviet Union was presented only in late spring 1945. Then the majority of the British People, expecting the left millennium, sided with Labor and voted the Conservatives out of power who, after all, had brought them military victory. If the Communist USSR was so marvelous the British people was drawn to the next-best thing: Socialism.[47]

In the United States the great enthusiasm for the Soviet Union came only after Pearl Harbor, the cleverly organized back door to get the United States into the war. We have no reliable demographic statistics, but it is my impression that the pro-Soviet fervor was less strong in the United States than in Britain if for no other reason (and there were others) than that America had too many citizens of East European and East Central European descent who could not so easily be hoodwinked. But they were rarely to be found in the higher and highest social layers, with the result that the Red Hysteria was much stronger in Boston or Philadelphia than in Pittsburgh or Johnstown, not to mention Sauk Center. I still remember a cocktail party in Manhattan in 1943 where a lady in mink, balancing her highball, screamed that it was America's most urgent task to show herself "worthy of her gallant Soviet Allies." "To think," she sobbed later, after some more libations, "that I called them 'Bolsheviks'!" I had to reassure the good woman that there was nothing pejorative in this appellation.

Joseph E. Davies' *Mission to Moscow* contained propaganda sufficiently deceitful to make it a best-seller (which was even filmed.)[48] It helped a great deal to give to the American public a revised picture of the "New Russia."[49] Miss Dorothy Thompson, during the war years perhaps America's most outstanding columnist, wrote that one thing was certain about the Soviet Union: They never broke their word or reneged a treaty. Yet she was by no means the worst of the whole lot.

When one looked at the material which was published, read, and favorably commented, one had to despair about the sanity of a large sector of the American public. Take for instance the book of Mr. Quentin Reynolds, *Only The Stars are Neutral*,[50] published in 1942. The best anecdote in the whole book can be found at the end when the author, on his way home from the USSR, describes himself talking to Sir Miles Lampson, British Ambassador in Egypt, in Cairo. Sir Miles plies him with questions about the USSR but repeatedly Mr. Reynolds has to reply that he does not know. " 'Sure,' I said, 'after I had been in Russia three weeks I knew everything about the place. I could have written a book about it. But I made the mistake of staying there three months. After three months I realized I didn't know a damn thing about the country.' "51 The reader is probably moved by so much modesty. But what does he hold in his hands if not?

Well, for instance, Mr. Reynolds makes a few admissions about the 800 women (political prisoners) working hard near Kuybishev, the wash basin costing 15 dollars, the great risk which Soviet citizens run by associating with foreigners, and even the lack of freedom of speech "in spite of so much smartness," but he expects that the youngsters will learn "soon from the older democracies."52 Notice the little legerdemain: "from the older democracies." In other words: the Soviet Union is a "younger democracy," as of course it would be *if* it had the support of the majority of the people. The subtle lie is placed quite unobtrusively. Other lies are far less subtle and presuppose an immensely unintelligent, i.e., average reader. Here we want to go into a few details because the technique is typical for the propaganda poured out by the left during the war in America. Mr. Reynolds (who had the best preparation imaginable for his task because he had started as a sports reporter) wrote: "In the Czarist days the priests had a wonderful racket in Russia. They were paid by the State and collections taken up in churches went to the State. All Stalin did was to separate the church from the State. In short he did the same thing we did in our country back in 1776. . . . Their priests are no longer government officials who have almost the power of life and death over them. . . . Had any of us ever troubled to read the Soviet Constitution (as vigorously upheld as our own) we might have got the true picture of religion in the Soviet Union. I looked it up the day after the Kremlin dinner. I talked with Father Braun. I mentally apologized as a Catholic for the things I've thought about Russia's attitude toward religion."53

Now let us look into this interesting revelation. The priests, indeed, were paid by the State, as were *all* priests and ministers everywhere on the Continent, except in France, after 1905. Yet if the collections went back to the State, why then call it a racket? (Of course they did not "go back.") Stalin did not separate the Church from the State, Lenin did it. Now Mr. Reynolds is entitled to his opinion that the

Church should be separated from the State, but this just is not the European tradition, least of all in Switzerland, a freedom-loving, highly democratic state. Most *free* European countries cooperate with *several* churches. Nor did the separation in the United States take place in 1776; and the First Amendment, enacted in the years 1789 to 1791, merely *prohibited an established church on a federal basis.* Cooperation of state and church is not necessarily establishment. And establishment on a *state* basis in the United States continued well into the nineteenth century.[54] It is of course totally untrue that Russian priests had "almost the power over life and death": They had neither the power nor the prestige that either Catholic priests or Evangelical ministers traditionally enjoy in the West. In Russian folklore the priest (and his wife) always played the role of the fool.

The high praise given to the Soviet Constitution seems to be a real hoax. We have only estimates about the number of persons in concentration camps at the time of Stalin, but these estimates all run between eight and twenty million.[55] Furthermore, separation between Church and State is one thing, persecution is something else. When Mr. Reynolds visited the Soviet Union, the second big wave of religious persecution (1934-1941) had just come to a close. (A third wave was to follow after 1958; it still lasts.) From 1917 until the outbreak of World War II more than 110 bishops of the Eastern Church alone were executed and more than a dozen had "disappeared."[56] Yet these data give only a weak idea of the real extent of the persecution and the savageries it involved. When Mr. Reynolds "mentally apologizes as a Catholic" one is even more puzzled. And before his mental apology he had talked with Father Braun, an American Assumptionist, who was then Chaplain to the foreign diplomatic service. He does not say what the priest told him, whether he confirmed or denied his views and experiences, but just mentions the fact. One has to assume that his mental apology was not only the result of his perusal of the Soviet Constitution but also of his talk with Father Braun. There is another choice bit: A captain of the Red army talks to our author referring to a British officer. "My friend Colonel Hill was here in Russia in Czarist days. He will tell you that only 10 percent of our citizens owned shoes then. He will tell you that only 1 percent of our people was literate. Now education—classical, scientific or industrial, is open to all. . . . Remember our world has only lasted twenty-four years. Yours in America has lasted since 1776. . . ."

And then comes the climax: " 'We haven't had to chuck religion overboard,' I suggested. 'We have not chucked religion overboard,' he smiled. 'We've chucked overboard the religious abuses we suffered from. . . .' ''[57]

This is really worth going into. Reynolds does not tell us anything. He makes no statements. He is merely a reporter. He was told all that by a Red army captain who refers him to a British colonel who in turn is not consulted and reaffirms nothing. Fine. But according to this conversation, only 10 percent of the people had shoes and only 1 percent was literate. As we know about 44 percent were literate in 1917, and if only 1 percent had been literate at the outbreak of the Revolution, how many were there let us say in 1882, the year Dostoyevski died: one in two hundred? One in five hundred or in a thousand? Just think, out of 110 million people perhaps only half a million people could read and write, and at the end of the nineteenth century such a country produced Europe's then leading literature! Of course, this is utter nonsense, but the dear reader will gobble it up. He will also swallow the 10 percent shoes. Amusing to visualize Imperial Russia in the winter of 1910 with 90 percent of the people staying home between early October and late April—and then going barefoot. Yet the greater the nonsense, the greater also the idiotic public's delight. The dear reader also will believe that American life before and after 1776 ran along different lines, that a big social and economic Revolution with a capital "R" had taken place. But in Russia nothing radical had happened as far as religion was concerned; only "abuses" were corrected. A civil servant who is fired because he is seen regularly in Church on Sunday has shown that he is a reactionary; a university professor getting married in church proves that he cannot be a real scientist; a wedding in the registry office is scientific and everything connected with religion is unscientific; and to teach children or adolescents religion is "intolerable" because it alienates them from Marxism-Leninism. The "abuse" of religion in old times consisted in the anarchic freedom that everybody could stay home or go to church without danger of reprisal—just as he wanted. Or does anyone believe that two gendarmes fetched Dr. Antoni Tshekhov every Sunday to drag him to "Holy Liturgy?" "In Russia, anyone who criticizes the government is an enemy of the State," Quentin Reynolds admits. "Harsh as Stalin's methods are, he has a complete answer, a complete justification for the ruthless quelling of opposition. Today there is not one Fifth Columnist, not one Quisling at liberty in Soviet Russia. . . . Stalin knew what he was doing back in 1938. Russia's magnificent unity today and her completely unbroken spirit after the tragedy of that German advance, is proof of the fact that Russia accepted the purge and approved of Stalin's policy."[58]

This "magnificent unity" while almost half a million Russian *Vlas-sovtsy* fought under the German flag, needs no comment.

But then, what do we make of Mr. Reynolds' message to the reader on the wrapper? He says that this "is a war to decide whether or not men can sit around the crackerbox in the general store and lift their voices in praise or criticism. It is a war to decide whether or not we can worship Christ or Mohammed or Buddha or a clay pigeon, or anything else which we, as individuals, decide to worship." Yet, if some of us worship navel-gazing Buddhas and the others clay pigeons, while sitting around a crackerbox, where do we get that so necessary "magnificent unity" for which Stalin has a "complete justification"? Here we are certainly faced with complete schizophrenia.

In my novel *Black Banners* I have described this orgy of lies which took place in World War II and which engulfed the entire globe. The hero listened to the various short-wave broadcasts:

And all he heard were lies, small lies so small that they needed a magnifying glass, and lies so monumental that they literally darkened the mental horizon, slippery lies hiding in a mountain of truth designed to be swallowed with the most innocent-looking commonplaces, lies so cleverly camouflaged that it needed endless efforts to reach their poison after removing one protective layer after the other, and lies so gross, so stupid, so blunt that they could make a pasture of horses laugh and neigh themselves to death. There were bitter lies and sweet lies, lies which tried to gain the battle of persuasion by a straight assault, by surprise and a direct hit, and lies so circuitous and oblique that they needed gentle allusions to other lies, to other distortions, other misrepresentations. There were lies so new that they looked like silver coins just fresh from the mint, and lies so old that they had acquired friendly, familiar faces: they gloried in the patina of respectability and nobody even suspected that behind age-worn surface there lay enshrined untruth petrified and undisturbed already for centuries. And there were lies brazenly shouted over the ether and others muttered humbly, lies floating lonely and almost boredly carried by electric waves and others coming in packs like hungry wolves ready to attack, to bite, to kill: there were lies coming in erect and proud, pronounced in naive honesty, and lies whispered in all malevolence, bad conscience and malicious cunning, lies in drops, in whole oceans, in thin rivulets, lies in the form of powerful, foaming rivers, lies as a thin mist obscuring all views, lies, lies, lies. . . .[59]

There were, of course, notable exceptions in the chorus of ignorants, fakers, and liars receiving the favors of the government for their aid in "moral warfare"—under the circumstances quite a misnomer. In a "people's war," however, the frenzy of the masses has to be whipped up to a high degree of indignation, hatred, and fanaticism. Under such circumstances liberal democracies distinguish themselves very little from leftist dictatorships.[60] Men and women such as Thomas F. Woodlock of the *Wall Street Journal*, Henry J. Taylor, W. H. Chamberlin, Joseph Harsch, Anne O'Hare McCormick of the *New York Times*, the Packards and others refused to play the evil game. In quite a different role were commentators such as Gabriel Heatter, Frederick L. Schumann, Raymond Gram Swing, Lisa Sergio.[61] A hotbed of leftist, pro-Communist and Communist propaganda was the Office of War Information (OWI) which had its fill of leftist refugees from all over Continental Europe. Its German Department was one of the worst.[62] Since so many of these refugees in the United States had been Marxists they started to indoctrinate the American public with a Marxist version of global events, and the Americans, unfortunately, were able to digest this fare because it was offered to them in terms they understood.

Man is emphatically not a *homo oeconomicus* pure and simple, but the explanation of political events in terms of material interest, cash, financial ambition, production, etc., is the simplest and even a dim-witted person can understand it. To make matters worse, the United States (just like Britain) has an emphatically commercial civilization and thus the Marxist argumentation could be followed. In terms of Marxist doctrine "fascism" could not be anything but a last-ditch stand of "dying capitalism." Nazism, therefore, had to be explained as the desperate defense of German industry ("monopoly capitalism") and high finance, and Hitler, naturally, was a mere "stooge," a "puppet" of money-crazed monsters who had hired the "Bohemian Private First Class" to club the trade unions into submission. Under the circumstances one could not expect a nobler ally in such a final battle for progress, liberty, and equality than the Soviet Union which knew how to deal with the evils of capitalism. Gustav Stolper, also an exile, had well seen this danger in America.[63]

This exegesis of Nazism, playing into the hands of a blind and irresponsible pro-Soviet attitude, could be linked with a piece of American folklore, with the notion that "rotten backwardness" was reigning supreme in Europe,[64] that misery and poverty there were caused by big landowners who miraculously transformed themselves into monocled, saber-rattling, heel-clicking officers allied with slick bankers and fat bishops. The clichés of World War I, when the United States had been at war with the Hohenzollerns, were revived, and the demoniacal shadows of aristocratic arrogance magically projected onto the Nazis, of all people. During my wartime years in the United States I could never find a single "morale-building" story about Central Europe in which a Nazi nobleman was not involved. Unfortunately they did exist —just as there were Jews who paid conscience money to the Nazis, as there were Catholic priests with "Brown" sympathies. Exceptions confirm the rule. Nazism, however, was a plebeian movement, and it is significant that at the big Nuremberg Trial there was not a single nobleman among those condemned to death.[65] In the abovementioned type of literature (some of it transformed into movies) the "carryover" of World War I clichés is remarkable. As a result, slowly but surely, a fairly general feeling arose in the United States that this war, like its lamentable predecessor, was fought to aid the *Common Man*. He was the victim of noble and arrogant Nazi-Fascists; organized as well as spontaneous leftism in the United States was to turn the emancipation of the Common Man into some sort of war aim. A century of the Common Man had to be ushered in. This idealism worked in synchromesh with "anticolonialism" and while America and Britain fought shoulder to shoulder, the President of the United States dreamed not only of a Red overlordship over Continental Western Europe,[66] but also of a total destruction of the "British Empire," the "Commonwealth of Nations." This is a fact not sufficiently realized by many Americans and much of the resentment of certain European circles against America (de Gaulle!) has to be explained by this still unforgotten phase of American foreign policy.

The Common Man hysteria was amazing because actually the real source of evil in Europe *was* the precipitated and unwarranted rise of the Common Man into positions where he could not possibly use his own training, his knowledge, his experience but was asked to carry out tasks way beyond his capacity. Stalin's preparation consisted of a little theology, some highway robbery, and an artificial, very limited study of political science; Hitler had sold hand-colored postcards in Viennese cafés; Mussolini had been a mason in Switzerland; Daladier was the son of a baker. Still we do not want to insist on a purely sociological concept of the Common Man: *The truly Uncommon, the Superior Man obviously can be born in a log cabin.* In Austrian history, for instance, we find men such as Joseph von Sonnenfels, son of a little rabbinical scholar, and Baron Thugut, son of a little army paymaster, pillars of Maria Theresa's reign, Dr. Karl Lueger, son of a school janitor, founder of the Christian Social Party, and famous Mayor of Vienna, Monsignor Ignaz Seipel, University professor and Chancellor of Austria, son of a cabby, and Dr. Engelbert Dollfuss, illegitimate son of a peasant girl. Yet these *Uncommon Men* were men who had studied, *were trained*. The leftist-inspired and leftist-directed American wartime hysteria wanted to impress the broad public with the existence of a situation which was completely imaginary and the coming of a New Age which was totally unreal. "Dawnism" is always the great psychological approach of the left which is eager to paint a possible paradisiacal future.[67] The wartime utopia contained not only social and political promises, but also plastic cars, new gadgets of all sorts, nylon hose for all pretty girls, education through tape recorders under the pillow during sleep, twenty-five-dollar trips by air across the United States, and boundless liberty and equality amidst plenty all over the globe. This promising future had a few melancholy aspects because Mr. Sumner Welles in a memorable book[68] advocated a total partition of Germany, Mr. Henry J. Morgenthau, Jr. had the plan to transform Germany into a goat pasture,[69] and Mr. Theodore N. Kaufman in his essay *Germany Must Perish!*[70] showed even greater imagination. He proposed to sterilize all Germans and to distribute Germany and Austria among their neighbors. A map in his work showed the interesting changes: Holland and Poland had a common boundary; France, Czechoslovakia, and Holland met in Thuringia. Yet it ought to be mentioned for the sake of the record that the genuinely Socialist camp did not participate in this orgy of Soviet adulation mixed with outbreaks of sadistic hatred for the partly guilty and partly innocent German people. A Socialist weekly such as *The New Leader* was absolutely honest and fair:[71] Some of its editors had been born in East Europe, most of them were Jewish, but they knew precisely who was who and what was what, which was not the case with the semiliterate and far more affluent mob which gladly danced the new Carmagnole.

This euphoria was hardly troubled by the Soviet Union's announcement that demanded permanent possession of the three Baltic Republics as well as of the largest part of Poland. This did not even come as a shock. Americans of nearly all political persuasions supported the shameless demands of the USSR which quickly also claimed further pieces of Finland (which they had wantonly attacked for the second time in less than two years),[72] Germany, and Czechoslovakia. The area "requested" by the Soviet Union was precisely thirty-four times that of Alsace-Lorraine; it comprised 482,000 square kilometers—more than Germany in 1937—and over twenty-two-million inhabitants, as many as the United States had in 1850. The Soviets knew that they could get what they wanted because Mr. Churchill and Mr. Roosevelt were opportunists without a real sense of honor or obligation. As long as they won the war, who cared what the peace would be like? The *New Republic*, one of the mouthpieces of the uncommitted left, declared on February 20, 1943 in an editorial about the Russian demands that "however forceful or dubious Russian legal claims, the crux of the problem must not be sought in legal genealogies but in the need of an enduring friendship between Russia and America." These words remind one of the famous discussions between Fitzroy MacLean and Winston Churchill recorded in *Eastern Approaches*: Brigadier MacLean, who had been staying with Tito's partisans, informed the Prime Minister that unlike Draža Mihajlović, the wily Croat was a true Communist, Churchill asked him bluntly: "Do you intend to make Yugoslavia your home after the war?" "No, sir!" "Neither do I," Churchill replied, "and that being so, the less you and I worry about the form of government they set up, the better. . . . What interests us is, which of them is doing most harm to the Germans."[73]

Cynicism, however, is luckily not a main characteristic of the American people and thus reasons had to be found for supporting the Soviet demands. The Soviets' insistence on the Molotov-Ribbentrop Line in Poland was suddenly bolstered with the silliest, flimsiest, and most infamous arguments. The left immediately stamped prewar Poland as a den of iniquity and the men who valiantly fought the Germans as "Fascists."[74] The Molotov-Ribbentrop Line was identified with the Curzon Line, but the public was not told that this line was never even by the congenitally anti-Polish British considered as a border but merely as a demarcation line of Poland's minimum demands.[75] It extended from Central Lithuania to the Galician border only and never to the Carpathians. In *Time for Decision*, a manual for "peace planning," Mr. Sumner Welles, former Undersecretary of State, berated Catherine the Great of Russia for having been "primarily responsible for one of the greatest international crimes in history," the first three partitions of Poland. Yet then Mr. Welles goes on defending Stalin's demands not only for the Russian share of all the first three partitions, but even for half of the Austrian share of the first partition.[76] I am sure that Mr. Welles (or his ghost writer) could not read maps.

The Soviets founded their claim against Poland neither on an ideological nor on an historical but on a national, i.e., ethnological basis. Although the Soviet Union is basically a Great Russian State shrewdly and methodically Russianizing the rest of the USSR[77] with the help of schools or planned migrations, it has given a minor ethnical autonomy to "member states" such as Byelo-Russia ("White Ruthenia") and the Ukraine. White Ruthenians and Ukrainians thus are minorities in the USSR. The same ethnic bodies are represented in Eastern Poland. There the Poles mostly formed the middle and upper class, as well as the *largest ethnical group*,[78] followed by the Ukrainians, the White Ruthenians, the Jews, the Lithuanians, and the Germans. Only a nationalist, however, will insist on ethnic borders; and one of the main accusations against Hitler was always that he wanted all those who were ethnically German to live in the Third Reich, a tendency which goes rightly under the name of Pan-Germanism. His demand for the *Anschluss*, his peremptory request for the border districts of Bohemia-Moravia-Silesia (inhabited by the so-called Sudeten Germans), his insistence on the return of certain areas of Poland (which brought about World War II), his incorporation of Alsace-Lorraine in 1940, all this was based on a racialist-nationalist attitude, condemned, decried, execrated, and vilified by the more international-minded left.[79] Now Stalin did the same, and in the United States (or in England) hardly anybody asked whether the people living in Eastern Poland *really wanted to join* the Soviet Union. (Just imagine the indignation if Hitler had declared that all of German-speaking Switzerland had to join the *Reich*!) I had an exchange of letters with a leading American journalist who defended the Soviet stand on ethnic grounds. The idea never came to his mind that a Ukrainian of Volhynia, in spite of his dislike for the Poles, might prefer to live as member of a minority in "bourgeois" Poland rather than as a member of another minority in the Great Russian USSR.[80] It probably never occurred to him because he could not imagine that free Poland and Red Russia were worlds apart. In the United States one frequently heard that the wily Poles, with French aid, had defeated the Red army in a moment of weakness and thus brutally wrested lands from a helpless Soviet Russia.[81] This also is nonsense. In 1920 Lenin offered to the Poles peace and a boundary *a great deal farther east* than the one violated by Stalin in 1939.[82] The Poles did not accept because Pilsudski felt that he was morally bound to come to the aid of Petlyura,[83] the Ukrainian Nationalist leader, then engaged in a life and death struggle with the Russian Reds. Yet Petlyura was defeated, the Red army advanced deep into Poland and arrived at the very gates of Warsaw (which filled Lloyd George with glee,[84] enthused the British Labour Party, and made Thomas G. Masaryk very happy.)[85] But at the very gates of Warsaw Pilsudski (*without* French aid)[86] defeated the Red army—the "Miracle of the Vistula." The Red army retired and in the compromise peace of Riga the Poles achieved a boundary which returned to them the Russian share of the Third Partition and a few tiny fragments of the Second Partition —none from the First Partition, and this in spite of the fact that the partitions of Poland had been solemnly abrogated as a piece of Russian imperialism at the beginning of the Soviet régime, (August 29, 1919). In the previous offer of the Soviets, cities such as Polock, Minsk and Kamieniec-Podolski had been promised to the Poles. Now they received less and, as a result, the *Great Soviet Encyclopedia* considers that that war had been *won* by the USSR.[87] And indeed in the following years a stream of refugees came at great danger from the Soviet Union over to Poland—Ukrainians, White Ruthenians, Jews, and naturally Poles.[88]

Little it mattered that on July 30, 1941, the Soviets had even solemnly abrogated all treaties they had made with the Nazis on the subject of Poland's territory.[89] The pro-Soviet hysteria,[90] coupled with a mounting defamation of Poland, swept the press. Czechoslovakia was strongly played up with the horror of Lidice, but the fact that the Poles had an endless number of Lidices hardly mattered.[91] Their perhaps ungenerous treatment of the Ukrainians and Jews was constantly held against them, although there was no doubt which side[92] these minorities would have taken if given the choice. A Ukrainian (or Jewish) lawyer, doctor, priest, monk or nun, peasant, teacher in the humanities, labor leader, artist, banker, or shopkeeper could not possibly prefer the Soviet regime which was sure to annihilate his way of life and deprive him of his property if he had any.[93]

Then came the news of the Katyn Massacre, swiftly followed by two Soviet blows: Moscow's rupture with the Polish government in exile because it had dared to demand an impartial investigation of the Nazi charges, and the Soviet allegation that the crime had been committed by the Germans after their advance into West Russia in the fall of 1941—whereas the horror had been perpetrated in spring 1940, almost a year-and-a-half earlier. The American and British governments assumed a "neutral" position, but this was an occasion for the vast majority of American newspapers to feel ill at ease.[94] Today hardly anybody left of center would dare to maintain that this crime belongs to the Nazi register of sins, but the Soviets still tried to ascribe it to the Germans as late as 1946 at the Nuremberg Trial. This, however, embarrassed their noble Western Allies so much that they quietly dropped the accusation.[95] They probably felt that before such a mixed body of judges the Russians could not repeat their delightful techniques used at the stage trials under Andrzey Wyszyński[96] in the late 1930s.

Katyn should have been a signal, as should the establishment of the Communist Polish Committee in the Soviet Union, which was later transferred to Lublin, or the fatal halting of the Red army before Warsaw while the heroic *Armya Krojowa*, under the leadership of Count Komorowski ("General Bor"), bled to death; or the murder of the two Jewish labor leaders Alter and Ehrlich;[97] or the deportation of thousands upon thousands of Poles to the Arctic and to Siberia;[98] or the distrust and contempt displayed toward Allied missions. Yet all these signs which, one would have thought, could not be overlooked, did not shake leftist admiration for the Soviets—neither their admiration nor their inferiority complex. Their earlier American Messianism was now transferred to the USSR.[99] Did Mr. Roosevelt wake up to the danger? According to legend, the last months of his life were darkened by the increasing realization that another totalitarian power was menacing the world's freedom, but we find no documentary evidence to prove that this was the case. It seems rather as if his conviction that he could "charm" the sinister Georgian never left him. (How can a man "charm" another if he cannot even converse with him?) Churchill never really liked bolsheviks and his attitude towards Stalin will remain forever a riddle.[100] On the other hand he disliked Poles and entertained no hope that he could ever understand anything about Russia. Before he came to Yalta he arranged for the ghastliest single massacre in modern history, the annihilation of Dresden, in order to impress Stalin with the might of the Western Allies. But the weather permitted the holocaust to take place only on the day Churchill *left* Yalta, having committed the "Crime of the Crimea" by arranging for the West's suicide before sealing its fate at Potsdam. So the ghastly mass murder was completely in vain: The number of victims in this unfortified and nonindustrial city, crammed with refugees, is estimated to have been between 135,000 and 170,000—all noncombatants, mostly women, children, and old men, but including foreign slave laborers (a few thousand "only"). Hiroshima or Nagasaki were child's play compared with this and at least two-thirds of the victims were *burned alive*.[101] The Inquisitors at least were after people they thought to be individually guilty. The number of those killed in the name of progress, democracy, freedom, enlightenment, and brotherhood, on one nice *afternoon* is a multiple of the Inquisitors' victims during *centuries*. (And how it boomeranged: Every year three minutes of silence are observed on the Day of Infamy in Communist-dominated Dresden for the victims of "Western Monopoly Capitalism"—as if the shareholders of DuPont or Courtauld's had instigated the crime.) When the American Mustangs appeared over the smoking ruins, all they could do was to machine-gun fire-scarred refugees running for their lives. This war, as senseless as its predecessor, could have been considerably shortened.

In 1943 German army leaders desperately tried to obtain the collaboration of the Western Allies but failed completely. They made efforts to establish contacts through the German Embassy in Ankara and through George H. Earle, former Governor of Pennsylvania and U.S. Naval Attaché in Turkey during the war. Earle flew to Washington in May 1944 and vainly tried to make the President see the light,[102] i.e., the Russian menace. Other truly unceasing efforts were made by the German opposition in Sweden, Switzerland, and Spain.[103] The Western Allies, however, were adamant in *not* giving any hint as to the meaning or content of the Unconditional Surrender Formula.[104] Thus they paralyzed not only the activities of the opposition groups but also gave to Goebbels and to the Russians an undreamed-of propaganda advantage. The Soviets wanted to fight to the bitter end (while getting assurances from the West that it would *leave* them half of defeated Germany) and so did the Nazis because it was the only way to prolong their lives (or, at least, their liberty). *Never in history has there been a more suicidal collaboration between a power at war, its political opponents in the enemy nation, and its allies preparing to be its enemies of tomorrow.*[105] We should not fool ourselves into believing that the British, even ignoring the wishes of Washington, would have pursued a very different policy. Mr. Churchill in the House of Commons vilified and ridiculed the conspirators[106] and Mr. Anthony Eden was as adamant in rejecting the advances of the conspirators (high officers, labor leaders, professors, administrators, writers) as were his American counterparts deeply influenced by real traitors who had a leftist victory far more at heart than peace or their country's welfare. Thousands of Americans were sacrificed to a mixture of vanity, treason and stupidity, to a buildup for World War III. These Americans were expendable; they were plowed under.

When, finally, on July 20, 1944, assassination of Hitler was attempted by the desperate German Resistance, American public opinion was fed more nonsense of the lowest moral order. What editorial do we find in the *New York Times*? On August 9, 1944, when much information was available, they wrote: "The underworld mentality and methods which the Nazis brought from their gutters and enthroned on the highest levels of German life, have begun to pervade the officers' corps as well." The *New York Herald Tribune* on August 9 of the same year wrote: "Americans as a whole will not feel sorry that the bomb spared Hitler for the liquidation of his generals. They hold no briefs for aristocrats as such, especially those given to the goosestep. . . . Let the generals kill the corporal, or vice versa, preferably both." The ensuing massacre in which not only "generals" and "goose-stepping aristocrats" were killed—Moltke! Goerdeler! Leber! Bonhoeffer! Dalp! Stauffenberg!—deprived Germany of such an important segment of its moral and intellectual elite that it has not recovered from this loss to this very day.[107]

The possibility of an earlier peace was not realized by America's or Britain's man in the street because he was never given the necessary information. The information, we must admit, *could not* have been given to him. The men he had directly or indirectly elected to office failed, nay, refused to act on their information—out of stupidity, vanity, ideological prejudice, and their subservience to the USSR (which by the way had taken up secret contacts with the Nazis in Stockholm). In this connection one has to ask oneself whether the Western "statesmen" did not know about the *extermination* camps since they disposed, after all, of an elaborate system of espionage all over Nazi-occupied Europe. The Germans in their overwhelming majority, though fairly well acquainted with the horrors of the concentration camps, knew nothing about the swift mass murders. I conducted private investigations in 1947, interviewed Church leaders, etc.[108] Léon Blum, who was in Buchenwald for a long time, ignored the tortures and murders committed there until the bombing of the camp by the Allies and accidental contacts with men from other sectors made him realize the terrible truth.[109] For many years we had nothing but the Gerstein Report[110] as the only coherent eyewitness testimony of the horrors of the extermination camps in the East. The Vatican, famous for its lack of reliable information, had no concrete information either—just hearsay.[111] Yet what about the Allied sources of information? By early 1943, American Jewry had reports about the extermination camps.[112] Did Washington and London not know anything about this?[113] There are, as we said, indications that they did after all. The Western Allies had air superiority by late 1942; they could have menaced Hitler with specific retaliatory measures; they could have enlightened the German people (which listened to Allied broadcasts)—but nothing of the sort was done. Stubbornly, doggedly they continued the war under the motto of Unconditional Surrender. Perhaps certain people wanted to put all trump cards into Soviet hands.

The confusion in America was enormous and the circulating legends numerous. People desperately clung to the belief that in the Allied camp "at least Churchill knew better," which was not the case. The responsibility for the switch from Draža Mihajlović to Tito was also due to Churchill, not to Roosevelt, but few people realized that Mihajlović's *Cetnici* was purely Serb and that an anti-Nazi Croat (who opposed the *Ustaša*) therefore had no other choice but to join the *Partizani*, which he did without qualms last but not least because the BBC told him that Tito's outfit was "really democratic." (Mihajlović had murdered Croats on a large scale, and the *Ustaši* had murdered Serbs *en masse*—the dragon seed of 1918-1919 produced its evil harvest[114]—and the *Partizani* murdered in every direction.)

To be quite frank, a government consisting of rank amateurs could hardly cope with an immensely complex situation that required at the helm of the state men with moral[115] and intellectual qualities such as any form of government rarely, but democracies almost never supply. (The man in the street, no doubt, has neither the time nor the preparation nor perhaps even any interest to grapple with monumental issues.) The answer to the alternatives—Mihajlović or Tito—was naturally that Mihajlović represented by far the lesser evil. The real key to the whole problem is the fact that Yugoslavia should never have been created. It had been largely created by refugees in 1917-1919, and other refugees were active in the United States during World War II. As we have pointed out, the majority belonged to the leftist camp, they cooperated intimately with the American left and, more often than not, they were the men who had helped in the past to undermine the fabric of traditional Christian Europe, thus creating that frightful void which communism, socialism, and later on National Socialism were to fill. "Deserted altars are inhabited by demons." (Ernst Jünger). Of course Jews and persons married to Jews often had no other choice but to emigrate. Had they stayed on, they would have faced certain death. The same was more or less true of those who had been in important positions and who were on the list of the brown headhunters. But it can be said without much danger of refutation that the Marxists and the representatives of the "left center" were the more "mobile" people, the rootless element which made its way to the American fleshpots and then wrote "courageous" anti-Nazi pamphlets or novels, safely sheltered beyond an ocean.[116] The most courageous people stayed on and "faced the music."[117] Hermann Borchardt, a conservative Christian writer of Jewish extraction, beaten to pulp in a Nazi concentration camp, was invited for a lecture by a group of moderate leftists, Marxists, and Progressives in New York. Eyeing his audience he started his speech with the remark: "Seeing you, gentlemen, sitting here, you the gravediggers of

Germany, I regret that Hitler permitted you to escape. . . ." He did not hear the indignant outcries because the beatings in Oranienbaum had almost completely deprived him of his acoustical faculties. Indeed, truth alone offends.

America's leftists had been strongly reinforced by those newcomers, the *émigraille*, and the more extreme among them fostered the cause of the Soviet Union. Such an attitude, even more so for those born in the country and those who had solemnly sworn allegiance, was criminal. It was downright treason, whatever the government's own attitude, and when it became apparent that treason actually had been committed and that the culprits had to be found out, great excitement broke loose among the leftists, native or foreign born. These supporters of an alien totalitarian government suddenly invoked for their treatment all the sacred principles of classic liberal tolerance.

The betrayal itself cannot be doubted: its documentary evidence is unimpeachable. I personally am viewing these activities with the eyes of a non-American, of a person dead-set against the whole development of identitarian and egalitarian frenzy to which Jefferson was not alien and which has affected American popular concepts and American political folklore. (Which does not mean that the evil seed is not also sprouting in other parts of the globe—and more powerfully so than in the United States.) The question I want to raise is this: *Where are we going to draw the line?* The line between objective treason and loyalty is very clear. A man who puts the interest of a foreign country above that of his own is not acting patriotically—*provided no moral issues are involved*. (Obviously "My Country Right or Wrong" is an immoral, an un-Christian device. It is Churchillism pure and simple.) A man who secretly, illegally hands over vital information to a country which is a potential or an actual enemy of his country is legally a traitor.

Now, a man might commit treason from a legal point of view while he actually follows his conscience. "Legally" Admiral Canaris was a traitor because he collaborated with Franco in keeping Spain out of the war on Germany's side. For this and many other actions he was executed in Flossenbürg concentration camp. Yet while legally a traitor, he fought courageously for all the values our Western World stands for. Count Klaus Schenk von Stauffenberg, a Catholic, tried to assassinate Hitler. *Iustum est necare reges impios*[118] is a concept in the best medieval Catholic tradition. In an ideological war mere nationality becomes a secondary consideration. "Citizenship," from the point of view of the higher loyalties, is only a relatively valid concept. The *Vlassovtsy*, i.e., the Russians and Cossacks who fought under General Vlassov against the Red army, were patriots in a deeper sense. The American with Communist convictions whose first loyalty is to the Communist idea and thus to the men in the Kremlin, is in *similar* position. We said "similar," not identical. Admiral Canaris did not want to make an American (or a British) crown colony out of Germany. An American Communist to whom Sovietism is the highest ideal works quite naturally for the transformation of the United States into a member-state of the USSR (such as the Ukraine) or into a "satellite" such as Rumania or Bulgaria. On the other hand, the American Communist (or fellow traveler) working in the interest of the USSR is acting like Canaris inasmuch as he puts his political faith, his convictions higher than a loyalty due to the accident of birth. In the conflict of loyalties, those to one's convictions always should take precedence. This, however, is the reason why a political community, a state, has to eliminate persons from positions of importance if they hold convictions which sooner or later will conflict with the real interests of the polity. And there can be cases when an individual, without adhering to a systematized ideology, simply finds himself unable to carry out an order given by the state. I do not think that a hangman can put to death a person of whose innocence he is absolutely convinced. Yet these are "unforeseen cases." It is certainly not an act of unjust discrimination if a restaurant refuses to employ a convinced vegetarian as a meat cook or a devout Moslem as a wine taster or if a board of education does not appoint a declared misogynist as principal of a girls' school.

The trouble about the so-called witch-hunt in the United States was the question where to draw the line. To me it is evident that the revival of ancient democracy in the French Revolution spawned a whole interconnected and coherent series of leftist ideologies visibly filiated, and that it is not easy to separate them neatly from each other. They are all identitarian, they are all statist, they are all egalitarian and more or less materialistic, they have *affinities* with atheism and, even more so, with agnosticism. Mr. Robert Green Ingersoll[119] was not a Communist, but he was an ardent and devoted propagandist of atheism. Lenin's views about God were roughly the same; Stalin (and later Khrushchev) shared Hitler's views about modern art, Jewish influence, the Catholic Church, and the "practical solution" for ethnic minorities. The Second, Third, Fourth and even the Fifth French Republic worship the memories of the French Revolution and celebrate an event as nauseating as the Storming of the Bastille. (Remember the young cook *qui savait faire les viandes.*) Pathological butchers such as Danton and Robespierre were again honored on French stamps fifteen years ago:

Mr. Harry S. Truman, who with Mr. Attlee and Stalin had voted the starvation program for the Spanish people (perhaps not really destined to starve the Spaniards but to achieve the victory of bolshevism in Spain so that the Soviets could have the base in Rota), is still considered a respected elder statesman. In the United States it is not always easy to draw the line between a "liberal" and a "conservative" republican, between a "liberal" Republican and a middle-of-the-road Democrat, between such a Democrat and a highly liberal Democrat of the ADA type. Let us imagine a typical pragmatist, product of Teachers College of Columbia University, formerly an avid reader of *P.M.*, devotee of *The Progressive*, financial supporter of a Committee for Decolonization which supports the sacred cause of the Liberation of the Peoples of Angola. No doubt, one can subscribe to *Soviet Russia Today*, clamor for the admission of Red China to the United Nations, regard the late Mrs. Roosevelt as the brightest woman that ever trod the earth—and still not be a Communist. But under such circumstances one gets nearer and nearer to the Communist position.[120] Mrs. Roosevelt's contribution to the cause of world communism has been sufficiently substantial for the "New Hungary" to commemorate her with a stamp. Whether "New Czechoslovakia" or "New Rumania" did the same, I do not know.

I think that the case of Mrs. Roosevelt is typical. I am sure, however, that she was never singled out by Senator McCarthy as an object of his methodical investigations since, apart from her status as the wife and, later, widow of a President, she was probably never in the civil service of the United States.[121] It is well known that she was connected with many organizations which, to put it mildly, were left of center. She had a considerable prestige among common people and her column *My Day* as well as her articles and her question-and-answer column in a ladies' monthly were read by millions. It is fairly common knowledge that she stood further to the left than her husband and her public remarks on the actions and institutions of the Soviet Union were always on the whole favorable or only mildly critical.

In order not to rely on mere hearsay I once studied her column *My Day* in the years 1948-1949—a time when the vast majority of Americans were waking up from the stupor into which they had been cast by their own government's pro-Communist propaganda. That the waking-up process had taken such a long time is amazing, because there was every indication that Sovietism represented unmitigated horror: displaced persons fleeing Communism were moving all over Europe,[122] the promises given by the USSR were broken right and left, a regular war had been fought in Greece, but only now the euphoria came to an end.

Of Mrs. Roosevelt's dicta I would like to take only a few samples which I consider characteristic. Let us look at *My Day* in the *Chicago Sun-Times* of July 7, 1948. There she says:

> One wishes very much that the USSR could be brought to see the light and to give those countries on her borders which have genuine Communist governments sufficient latitude to let them feel they are acting as free and independent people. There is no question [!] but that the Yugoslavs have a great admiration for Soviet communism.[123] They feel that, from the economic standpoint, the Russians have the only solution, both industrially and agriculturally. They are not opposed to Soviet political theories, and are even willing to follow along. They have an efficient [!] secret police and all [!] they ask is that the secret police be their own and that they be allowed to enjoy their own brand of nationalism. I happen to think that their desires could be achieved quite as well [!] under democracy as under communism, but they will have to find this out as time goes on.

There is more in this column than immediately meets the eye. One has to read it two or three times and then draw one's own conclusions. Here is another piece. (January 19, 1949):

> I am in receipt of two interesting communications relative to a column I wrote about the imprisonment of Cardinal Mindszenty. What I was trying to say, of course [!], was not that the cardinal was an altogether admirable character, but that it is stupid [!] of the Communists to imprison people where it can be said that they have been imprisoned because of their religion. Our correspondent—a man who edits a publication which claims to be completely factual—writes that the arrest is not a matter of religious persecution, but of opposition to progress. He claims that the cardinal is a reactionary, if not a fascist and a notorious anti-Semite.
>
> He also says that every fairminded correspondent in Hungary would bear him out in this assertion that the cardinal was the main opponent to the general welfare of the Hungarian people. Cardinal Mindszenty controlled a million acres of land, says my correspondent, for the Roman Catholic Church was the largest landowner of Hungary, therefore the cardinal opposed all agrarian reform and opposed the separation of state and church.[124]

So far, so good. Mrs. Roosevelt obviously said nothing. She merely related what one of her correspondents *told* her. She is perfectly innocent of all pro-Communist propaganda.

Naturally, in her column, she sided with Alger Hiss against Whittaker Chambers on whose word "nobody could rely." She opposed Cardinal Preysing's visit to the United States. She thought that Franco's Secret Police were just as bad as the Gestapo and that the only persons who should teach German youths are those who "have proved *their democracy*," a phrase which undoubtedly would surprise a student of the English language. Was Mrs. Roosevelt deeply imbued with pro-Communist ideas or merely naive? Probably both. Witness an article she published in *McCall's* (February 1952) about the President's unease with Stalin at the Teheran Conference. "My husband was determined to bend every effort to breaking those suspicions down, and decided the way to do it was to live up to every promise made by both the United States and Great Britain, which both of us were able to do before the Yalta meeting. At Yalta my husband felt the atmosphere had somewhat cleared, and he did say he was able to get a smile from Stalin." Indeed, how many people would not sell millions into slavery to get a smile from that dear old man!

Mrs. Roosevelt obviously was not alone in kowtowing before the Soviets. Mr. Wendell Willkie, presidential candidate for the Republican Party in 1940, went on a goodwill tour around the globe during the war. His impressions were published in a book priced at one dollar and entitled *One World*, a cliché which either he or his ghost writer invented and which became exceedingly popular in leftist circles.[125] Here we can read that "there is hardly a resident of Russia today whose lot is not as good or better than his parents' lot was prior to the revolution."[126]

Thus we come back to our original question: Where would one draw the line? We have no reason to assume that Mr. Alger Hiss (or even Mr. Harry Dexter White) took money from the Soviets, not even the men involved in the Amerasia Case, or the Rosenbergs, but their loyalty belonged to the Communist Utopia and not to the American reality. It is even possible that Mr. Alger Hiss was not a convinced "Sovietist," but that he saw in the Muscovite faith the shape of things to come, while he considered the order prevailing in his own country as "obsolete." He was not even condemned as a traitor (which in a legal sense he fully was) but as a perjuror, and no doubt he had committed perjury.[127] However, the attitude an impartial committee of investigation should *theoretically* have taken was simply this: "Ever since the days of the Founding of our Nation we have gradually drifted away from the original spirit of the Constitution and have let ourselves be influenced by trends and ideas which found in communism a perhaps not unavoidable but logical conclusion. Such a development we might deplore; we might even decide to alter or reverse it; but it has been a reality in the past. To make matters worse, we have found ourselves in a military alliance with the leading Communist power and to cement it, our own government, by distorting facts and offering to our population a false picture of that state, has strongly contributed to Communist propaganda. Let us review the damage done; let those who have been deluded make a clean breast of their deeds; let us measure the whole extent of that criminal folly which found its consummation in the last decade but which has been going on for some time." Such a stand, I readily admit, could not be expected because it implies a denial of too much of what had happened in the past. And yet, if in our peregrinations we have taken a wrong turn, we have to go back to the point where we took the wrong turn—or at least reconstruct, recalculate this point.

If I have not made myself sufficiently clear, I would like to point out that, just to quote one instance, a typical burgher of the city of Pamplona in Navarra in the seventeenth century confronted with the Marxist-Leninist message would have shrugged it off as a piece of egregious nonsense. Accepting none of its premises, he would have listened to none of its conclusions. The average American with a degree from his progressive college is much nearer to the Red message; the devoted uncommitted leftist even more so. There comes the moment when the non-Marxist leftist inadvertently steps into the magnetic field of the Red Doctrine and then his guardian angel or his last residues of rationality will prevent the worst. Just a few more *symbolic* reminders mentioned occasionally much earlier: Columbia on the old half-dollar with the Jacobin cap; the *fasces* on the dime piece which reappear on the French Republican and in the Fascist coat of arms; the first battleships of the Soviet Union named Danton and Marat; the studied utopianism in terms such as "the American experiment"; *the replacement of the Calvinist outlook (which, after all, is still a Christian one!) with Roussellianism* which lies at the bottom of all utopian leftist heresies. (Herein lies the root of the entire internal moral and political crisis of the United States.) In other words, an American conservatism, any movement on the true right (which of course could *not* in any way be totalitarian) has to return to far distant historical sources—not to *stay* there but to get the right start. Back to the imaginary burgher of Pamplona in the seventeenth century? Though he hails from another part of this world (and therefore is not a fitting reference), he certainly had a grasp of basic truths. It is the Great Western, the Great Christian tradition which has to be reconstituted, and this is a gigantic task requiring *radical* thinkers and far-going measures.

Toward the end of the war the leftist follies increased. Mr. Hull, who went to Moscow to proclaim a resolution in favor of Austrian independence, was neatly tricked into signing also a declaration of Austrian war guilt. One is aghast at the stupidity of the formula which said that "Austria was reminded, however, that she had a responsibility which she could not evade for participation in the war on the side of Hitlerite Germany, and that in the final settlement account would inevitably be taken of her own contribution to liberation."[128] Anthony Eden apparently first sponsored the declaration and there can be no doubt that Molotov added the above quoted paragraph, because with this injunction the Soviets had a "legal title" to stay in Austria and confiscate property right and left.[129] Yet neither the forger of the Axis nor the former student of the National Normal University of Lebanon, Ohio, seemed to have been aware of this clever snare which had an adverse effect on the Austrian Resistance. No doubt there were many Nazis in Austria, but there also were not so few in Norway, in the Netherlands, in Belgium, and quite some eager collaborators in France.[130] To say, however, that these occupied and incorporated countries helped the German war effort willingly and spontaneously is a gross and unjust exaggeration. The Soviets knew only too well what to do in this situation and the two fall-guys from the West walked straight into the trap.[131] So did an American delegate in Potsdam when the Soviets demanded the "German assets" in their occupation zone of Austria.[132] This had been rejected by the American delegation, last but not least because the Soviets demanded German real estate—oil-fields, barracks, training fields. The debate over the German assets in the satellite world lasted until the small hours of the morning when, finally, the agreement was put down in writing. Mr. Pauley, head of the delegation, could hardly keep his eyes open. Then, in enumerating the countries to which this treaty would apply, the Russians quickly inserted Austria. When he signed, Mr. Pauley was too exhausted to be aware of the change. This thirty-eighth parallel in Korea was similarly accepted as a demarcation line in a state of ignorance, torpor, and confusion.

The Potsdam meeting was a worthy culmination of its predecessors, the Teheran and the Yalta conferences. The only "survivor" of the previous encounters was the Georgian highwayman who had committed his crimes in the service of the Social Democratic Party of Russia. Mr. Roosevelt was dead and had been replaced by a man who got his education at no college and his political training from Tom Pendergast[133] and his associates in Kansas City, Missouri. Mr. Churchill was present at the first sessions, but the grateful British had voted him out of power and in his stead a man attended who had greeted Spanish loyalists with the clenched fist: Mr., later Lord Attlee, the new Prime Minister. The outcome of the meeting was not at all surprising. Most of the great evils had already been settled in previous conferences, so for instance, the Oder-Neisse Line. This demarcation line, which artificially attaches Poland to the Soviet Union (because the Poles must be permanently afraid of the inevitable German revindications) continues to represent the worst and largest wound in the fabric of Europe. The brilliant idea to move the entire Polish nation westward had been originated by Churchill and he even boasts of it in his memoirs.[134] Warsaw (under whatever government) was placed only 115 miles from the Soviet border, but that did not bother him. Non-Britishers did not matter to Mr. Churchill, who sacrificed human beings, their lives, their welfare, their liberty with the same elegant disdain as his colleague in the White House. Lwów? What did Lwów mean to him? A city whose name was difficult to pronounce, inhabited by unknown East Europeans whom he had never met: Poles, Jews, Ukrainians who hardly belonged to the Nordic race. Let's give it to Stalin, the "great father of his country." Mr. Churchill in his own words was "not prepared to make a great squawk about Lwów."[135] And as the Polish Premier Mikolajczyk refused to sign away half his country, Churchill menaced him with its total annihilation.[136] The man who had said "there are no lengths of violence to which we will not go"[137] had become a terror to his allies. The Anglo-Polish Treaty of Mutual Assistance, concluded on August 25, 1939, which made the Poles decide to fight and not to "play dead" like the clever Czechs, contained eight articles: Six of these were openly broken by Britain.

When the three men sat down in Potsdam and when, later, Mr. Truman played the piano with Lauren Bacall lolling on it, the fate of Poland was already completely sealed. Other fresh acts of folly were still to come. One of them consisted in soliciting Stalin's aid in the war against Japan. This gave "Uncle Joe" a splendid opportunity to capture the entire Japanese industry in Manchuria, to acquire territories (Sakhalin, Kurile Islands), to occupy North Korea and, later, indirectly, help to communize China. This invitation to our own disaster will always be a great puzzle to historians. Just prior to the meeting the first atomic bomb had been brought to a successful explosion at White Sands, New Mexico, and while Stalin was implored to aid the Western Allies, the American general staff already knew that this hellish invention worked. Of course, men like General Henry Arnold of the AAF saw no difference between Stalin's and Roosevelt's ideologies—a delightful reflection on the New Deal—and thought that it was a mistake to think that Stalin was a Communist.[138] Yet in spite of this enormous advantage, this certainty of a speedy and easy victory, the grizzly tyrant was asked to come in on the deal—with tragic results for America. (Just close your eyes and think how many Americans have paid with their lives for this folly!)

Excuses are frequently offered for this piece of maddening stupidity, one of them being that one did not realize whether the atomic bomb could actually be "delivered"—dropped and exploded upon contact. This excuse is patently nonsensical and even *if* the argument had substance, it does not really hold water because the Japanese had already made two peace efforts: one via Moscow and the other one through the Vatican. However, we have to ask ourselves whether leftist circles in Washington had not worked feverishly for the continuation of the murderous and costly war. Men such as Mr. Owen Lattimore protested in 1941 against any *modus vivendi* with Japan.[139] Apparently they wanted Japan's total defeat and we probably owe it primarily to Mr. Joseph C. Grew, former American Ambassador to Tokyo, that Japan was not transformed into a "democratic republic" (like Bulgaria or Hungary). The dropping of "the Bomb" on a *populated* center was another totally superfluous crime. Even if one is callous enough to make an argument for the annihilation of Hiroshima, one fails to understand the necessity for the slaughter in Nagasaki, cradle of Japanese Christianity. Within a split second the bomb wiped out one-eighth of Japan's Catholic Christians. Here again we hear the argument that Mr. Truman wanted to impress the Russians, just as Mr. Churchill had wanted to impress them with the Dresden massacre.[140] Yet what butcher could really impress the arch-butcher from the Caucasus? Not even the late Adolf Hitler could!

And here we come to another point. I am dead certain that at the turn of the century, historians will try to find out the answer to two crucial historic questions:

1. What caused the United States to withdraw its armies immediately after the armistice from all parts of the world? Was the clamor "Let's Send the Boys Home" somewhat "organized?"

2. What prevented the United States—as *sole* atomic power between the years 1945 and 1948—from using its deadly monopoly to "ease" the Soviets out of their ill-gotten gains? A war never would have been necessary. The mere threat would have been sufficient. Panic on an unprecedented scale would have been the immediate result. Of course the answer is tragically simple: A "democracy" rests on the "fermentation" of the people. It merely hits back if attacked and is more perplexed by victory than by the task of defending itself (which belongs to the military hierarchy and not to amateurish politicians).

The Armistice[141] was not only conditioned by the preliminary arrangements and agreements concluded at Teheran and Yalta but also by military moves determined by these talks. It is perhaps true that Vienna could not have been occupied by the Western Allies in the last stages of the war, but why, then, had it been savagely bombed on the anniversary of the *Anschluss*—an act of revenge facilitating the Russian conquest?[142] Neither Prague nor Berlin, two European key cities, need have been left to the Red army. They were given to the Soviets, staunch Nazi collaborators between 1939 and 1941, on a platter. The Americans and the British stopped at the Elbe[143] and later even surrendered all of Thuringia to the Soviets while Berlin could easily have fallen into American hands.[144] The same is true of Prague: The Americans under General Patton had advanced as far as Pilsen when they were ordered back.[145] Clearly, all important places in Eastern and Central Europe according to leftist ideas were to be handed over to the Soviets leaving to the Western World a mere toehold on the Continent. The craziest arrangements were those concerning Berlin and Vienna. In these two cities the Western Powers were to control mere sectors and no stipulations were made as to the accesses leading to them.[146] Mr. Roosevelt is said to have been opposed to discussing these details because he thought that only a complete show of confidence and trust would soften the Soviet regime and would create an atmosphere of "fellowship" and "goodwill." Soon the Americans were "undeceived" and the airlift had to be organized at great cost in money and even in human lives.

The worst result of the Potsdam meeting were the stipulations concerning the mass transfer of the German population from east of the Oder-Neisse Line,[147] from Czechoslovakia, Rumania, Hungary, and Yugoslavia. No less than 13 to 14 million people had to be removed under enormous hardships and this created tensions, hatreds, demands, and counterdemands from which even a de-Sovietized Europe could hardly recover. These brutal transfers, accompanied by atrocities and spoliations continued all through the winter of 1945-1946 and ended only in 1947. Poles from Eastern Poland were dumped into East Germany, a process by which people from underpopulated areas were "massaged" into overpopulated ones—the height of perversity. Yet no legal title over Eastern Germany was given to the Poles.[148] Vast tracts of land remained uncultivated (as in Bohemia-Moravia) and on the trek from East to West millions of people perished.[149] What were the Western Allies to do with the part of Germany they were given for occupation? It is interesting to note that the Western army leaders went into a huddle to discuss what they should do if there should be any resistance or sabotage. They decided that they would take hostages and shoot them—perhaps the only thing they could "reasonably" do, but the Germans had been vilified for having acted the same way in the same predicament.[150] As to the political order and cultural institution, the American left (thanks to its preoccupation with foreign affairs) had a field day in West Germany. Professor Wilhelm Röpke, an outstanding German neoliberal, exiled in Constantinople and later in Geneva, had written a memorandum about the necessity of a monarchical restoration which, by the way, we find in the program of practically all the heroes of the Twentieth of July. Nobody in his right mind and with any sense of history planned to revise parliamentary democracy, already obsolete by 1919 and tragically terminated by 1933. Yet the American left naturally thought about a Constitutional development which would give the forces of the left a frame for a free development. Had not Engels demanded the democratic republic as the ideal form of government, conducive to the victory of Marxism?[151] Above all, the Soviet Union had a true "vested interest" in the establishment of democracy in preference to forms of government in which parties could not develop freely, gain victories, and take over the government.[152]

What the leftist establishment did in Germany is most notable. In many parts of the country, in Bavaria, for instance, it put into power Social Democrat (i.e., Socialist) governments which had by no means the backing of the majority of the population. The prevailing idea in the civilian sector of the occupation authorities was that "Clericals" were reactionary, backward, and "Fascist," but that Marxians were "progressive." Dorothy Thompson had already told us that what Germany needed was not less, but "more socialism" (though not exactly "national socialism").[153] Now the Germans got it at the expense of the American capitalist system duly milked to provide for socialism and socialization all over Europe from Land's End to the Iron Curtain. There was a special bias against the German nobility, many of whose members had courageously opposed Hitler, but here folklore and leftism again

324

combined against genuine American interests.[154] The famous *Fragebogen*, the questionnaire prescribed by the American authorities, that had to be filled out by all those Germans who wanted to do anything more than just work in a factory or in the fields, contained questions which in their content or their wording revealed the whole leftist bias and betrayed the sure little hand of Marx. (One of the questions aped the Nuremberg Racial Purity Laws: "Did any of your or your wife's four grandparents have a title of nobility?")[155] For a time the American leftists in the military administration could work hand in glove with the British occupation, directed by the Labour government in London which was also determined to create a leftist Germany—a "national socialist" Germany under the rather demagogical Social Democrat Schumacher, but minus racism. One of the early victims of this combine was Dr. Konrad Adenauer, who immediately after liberation had become Lord Mayor (*Oberbürgermeister*) of Cologne. One nice day he was ejected by the British from his office under the (written) pretext "that he lacked the qualifications to run a city as large as Cologne." This egregious piece of nonsense *der Alte* kept as his most cherished souvenir.[156]

"Reeducation" also ran into a few snares. Luckily the leftist plans never came to fruition but what they would have been like one can guess from the "Zook Report," published in parts by the *New York Times* (October 16, 1946). Dr. George F. Zook, head of a mission of nine men and women (among them a Catholic priest!) sent to Germany by the State and War Departments, declared that the goal of democracy is "democratic man." This commission found the main ills of Germany to be "discipline in the family" and the high school-college, which begins at the age of ten. "The survival of democracy would warrant an invasion of the German home," the report suggested. It referred to the "stern German parental authority" that produced Freudian ambivalence, or a clash of tenderness and hostility in children, undermining individual self-reliance, if not also self-respect, while women were confined to cooking, children, and churchgoing, thus converting "worthy enough functions into antidemocratic sterilities." The report went on to say that to "shun the majority rule principle was to play into the hands of a Hitlerian 'superman.' " Ninety percent of the Germans went to vocational schools and "this separation of children at an early age was an important factor in developing the superiority complex of the privileged class and the subservience of the trade class which had led Germany to totalitarianism and war."

A most amusing light is thrown on this report by the fact that the

Nazi movement had been basically a youth movement against the older generation, that the Nazis wanted to radically revamp the educational system to eliminate the classically educated elites, that they had tried with all means at their disposal to undermine parental authority. In other words, most of the propositions of the Zook Report were entirely in keeping with Nazi ideas, and Nazism was represented in retrospect as a conservative and patriarchal movement: Hitler appeared to the signatories as some sort of *Patriarcha* and not at all as Big Brother whom he actually represented.[157]

The Zook Report and the various efforts to "democratize" German education in an intellectual sense were partly of a temporary nature.[158] As soon as West Germany recovered some sovereignty, most of the various leftist experiments were given up. As we all know, a "reinfection" took place in the mid-1960s when the New Left, the student revolt and hippieism invaded Germany via the Free University of West Berlin and the University of Frankfurt where the various aspects of this particular disease were abetted by part of the German press and a number of intellectuals with distinctly American background.[159] No wonder, because there was a field in which the American occupation authorities were able to achieve a permanent victory for leftism: in the "Fifth Estate." After 1945 the license for the publication of a newspaper and books had to be obtained from the occupying powers and here was an opening wedge for the leftist returnees and for their friends. Later it became extremely costly to start a new paper. The conservative forces, viewed with great suspicion by the leftist establishment, thus were the Johnnies-come-lately and to this day from a journalistic point of view, they have not overcome this handicap. It is important, however, to remember that the left in Europe was soon to turn anti-American and that the anti-American propaganda profited from the support it had been given earlier by the very country it was later to attack.

It is difficult to enumerate the calamities enacted in the years immediately following the Armistice. There were serious diplomatic mistakes such as the pressure exercised upon Switzerland to surrender the German assets to the Allies (whereas the Swiss had not even been approached by the Nazis to surrender emigrant savings and investments.) There were the Nuremberg Trials which definitely ought to have been handled by the Germans themselves[160] and which was totally mismanaged. The notion of "legal precedent" is Anglo-Saxon:[161] Even American generals were horrified by the trial (thinking of their possible difficulties in World War III): and the very idea that the assassins of Katyn sat in judgment over the assassins of Auschwitz is tragicomic.

Points of accusation like the wanton attack on Norway, an accusation *per se* justified, make no sense if one remembers that Mr. Churchill admittedly prepared an attack on Norway himself.[162] The thing to do would have been to have the Nazis tried by German courts simply for *common crimes* according to the Code of Penal Law. The principle *Nullum crimen sine lege* was as much ignored as that of the impartiality of the judges—for instance, when the Russians condemned the German attack against Poland in which they themselves had participated. Even worse were the following minor Nuremberg Trials, almost completely based on Marxist principles: An effort was made to implicate German industry and high finance.[163] No less infamous was the Krupp Trial in which Alfried Krupp von Bohlen and Halbach[164] was placed on the bench of the accused *instead* of his gravely ill father.[165] Here again Marxism, financed by American taxpayers' money, was celebrating orgies. In the writ of accusation against Alfried Krupp von Bohlen and his ten codefendants of the same firm we find the words: "The origin, the development, and the background of the crimes committed by the defendants, and the criminal plans, in which they participated, can be traced back to 100 years of German militarism and 133 years—four generations—of the manufacturing of arms."[166] Apart from the fact that the Krupp works normally produced arms on the average of only one-fifth of their total output, one recognizes in this sentence and, even more clearly in other passages of the accusation, the Marxian verbiage. The accusation was presented by General Taylor, U.S.A., formerly of the Federal Communications Commission, then 40 years old. His aides were Mr. Joseph Kaufmann from New York and later Mr. Raggland from Texas. The director of the Chief Trial Team was Mr. H. Russell Thayer who had been Assistant Secretary of the North American Committee to Aid Spanish Democracy during the Spanish Civil War. The basic notion of the trial was to prove in the best Leninist fashion that "big business" (especially in the form of "monopoly capitalism") creates and fosters wars.[167] All of the accused were condemned and later released and the confiscations annulled. In retrospect the trial appears too preposterous. On the other side of the ocean we had the Yamashita Trial, a travesty of justice.[168] When Yamashita's lawyer, Frank A. Reel[169] published a book about his tragically innocent defendant, the rather conservative director of the publishing company, the Chicago University Press, lost his position.

Leftist forces mismanaged the world situation practically everywhere. Working through the occupation authorities, where the much saner military were unable to interfere with the civilians, they set up a witchhunt against monarchists in Austria (thus continuing Nazi policies!) and they also prevented the return of the South Tyrol to Austria: For this the British Labour government was mainly responsible. Self-determination was obviously only desirable if it benefited leftist issues, but the South Tyrolians, being mostly conservative agrarians would, once returned to Austria, have prevented a full Socialist victory.[170] The damage done by the *dinamitardi*, the tortures committed by the *carabinieri*, the wall of hatred between Austrians and Italians —this only "bleeding border" left in Free Europe we owe first to Mr. Wilson, then to Mr. Bevin[171]—and to the Soviets who supported Mr. Bevin, and thus incidentally ratified the Hitler-Mussolini Agreement of 1939 pertaining to the iniquitous Brenner Border. It seems that Nazi decisions, Nazi thought, Nazi mentality, and Nazi institutions in many ways are here to stay.[172]

True, other people, other groups, fared much worse than the Austrians. The 150,000 cases of rape perpetrated by the Red army in Eastern Austria was perhaps only a practical demonstration of "sexual democracy."[173] (Let us remember Mr. Henry Wallace's charming formula: "We have political democracy, they have economic democracy.") Many Austrians were deported, some returned, others disappeared forever. Still, it was on Austrian soil, in the East Tyrol, that large numbers of Russians and Cossacks who had fought against Communism were clubbed half dead, packed into box cars and sent back as "unpatriotic traitors." A British major (Davis) had given his word of honor that England did not think to surrender the Cossacks and Russians to the Soviets. When the truth leaked through, the disarmed anti-Communists resisted His Majesty's soldiers in the services of bolshevism: Many Russians were killed on the spot,[174] fifteen more were killed during the transport while trying to escape, six committed suicide, seventeen succeeded in disappearing during the transport to the Russian occupation zone. There were twelve generals in the group handed over to the USSR by that great conservative, Mr. Winston Churchill to placate, to mollify, to befriend his Communist comrade-in-arms. But even this act of prostitution did not buy their friendship and less than a year later this Epimetheus of European politics uttered the Great Warning in his famous Fulton speech.

An Austrian eyewitness has described the scenes in Lienz, worthy of Breughel's brush. (He estimates at about three hundred the number of Cossacks who hanged themselves in the Lienz woods after being surrounded by the 8th Brigade.) With bayonets and clubs these men and many women were subdued. A Russian who had escaped to tell the tale, S. G. Korolkov, now living in the United States, has painted the memorable scene of the "Hell of Lienz."[175] And while Mr. Churchill perpetrated such wonderful deeds, the Americans, apparently, could not stay behind. The *New York Times* reported the ghastly scenes that took place in Dachau when the Russians who had fought against Communism were made "ready" to be "shipped" eastward. The long somber report ended with the description of the evacuation of the second Russian barrack. "The inmates . . . barricaded themselves inside and set the building afire. Then all tore off their clothing, apparently in a vain effort to frustrate the guards and, linking arms, resisted the pushing and shoving of the Americans and Poles trying to empty the place. The soldiers then tossed in tear bombs and rushed the building. Some prisoners, they discovered, were already dead, having cut their own throats, while others had used pieces of cloth to hang themselves."[176] One can easily imagine what confidence in the United States and Britain these actions engendered inside the USSR, but hatred and suspicion against the West were precisely the feelings which not only the Soviets but also their faithful collaborators in the American leftist establishment wanted to create. And it ought to be remembered that the American heirs of the Nazis in Dachau (of all places!) perpetrated these horrors three-quarters of a year *after* the end of the war—and this in accordance with the agreements made at Yalta, at least half of which Soviets had already broken. Remembering the American tradition in regard to political refugees through the ages, one cannot but be aghast at the betrayal of such trust, such a noble tradition.

The so frequently followed British example, too, was at times exceptionally evil. The Austrians have seen not only the "Hell of Lienz" but also the bestial surrender of the *Domobranci*, the Catholic Slovene Home Guard, which had protected Slovenes against the depredations of Tito's *partizani*. Thousands of them were rounded up, shipped over the Karavanken Mountains, to be mowed down in masses and their corpses used as natural fertilizer for the fields. One should never forget: Sadism is the outstanding characteristic of the entire left.

Errors were ubiquitous.[177] Italy in 1946 was helped back to the republican form of government it had under Mussolini as *Repúbblica Sociale Italiana*. A plebiscite in which the vast majority of the non-Communist vote was cast for the monarchy, gave Italy the ideal form of government to be captured some day by communism *the legal way*, a danger still with us. Obviously the Communist vote was totally in favor of the Republic, remindful of Engels' aforementioned formulation (confirmed by Dallin) that the democratic republic is the ideal frame for a Red conquest of the State. In Greece, luckily, a referendum—itself an impossible procedure—produced a sound majority for the monarchy. The principle of monarchy cannot be subordinated to the principle of majority decisions. Its very essence is independence from the vagaries of the voting process.

Yugoslavia, another miscreation of World War I, was restored and even territorially enlarged. (Yugoslavia and Bulgaria were the only countries, apart from the Soviet Union, emerging from the war with a bigger territory.)[178] Yugoslavia, however, can only exist and survive as a harsh dictatorship, if not as a tyranny. Since its constituent nations do not want to form a whole, they can be held together by coercive measures: either the sway of one nationality over the rest, or the rule of an oppressive ideology through a party over all.

It would be an error, however, to believe that the horrors of leftist oppression and revenge were merely confined to Eastern, Central, and Southern Europe. In France a large sector of the collaborators were recruited from the left, embracing ideologies which were "national-leftist" in character. Neither Laval nor Darnand, Déat or Doriot belonged to the "right." The Germans suspended *Le Figaro*, the conservative daily, and supported the leftist paper *L'Oeuvre*. The French Communists fully collaborated with the Nazis between 1939 and 1941. De Gaulle, who went into opposition, had belonged to the *Action Française*. Other French rightists and conservatives fled France (Henri de Kérillis was one of them), but there were also men of the French right who stayed without collaborating and others again who (rightly or mistakenly) considered it their duty to protect whatever remained of France as well as they could. Among them was Marshal Pétain whose patriotism should no more be questioned than General Weygand's. Pétain had negotiated with Churchill an agreement which (in order not to irritate de Gaulle) Downing Street tried to deny, but we have documentary evidence of its existence.[179]

After the German attack on the Soviet Union, the French Communists, whose real *patrie* had always been the USSR, went into opposition and, having more practice in clandestine political and military activities than the other parties, they soon assumed some sort of leadership in the resistance.[180] After the collapse of the German occupation in 1944 the Communists started to wage a terror warfare of their own against all the people they disliked politically, socially, or just personally. An American observer who arrived in Southern France with the army of General Patch estimated the number of people assassinated by the *Résistance* in that region was around 50,000.[181] French estimates speak of about 120,000 all told. To this number must be added all those who were "legally" condemned, more often than not by courts staffed with Communist jurors. Now, it is quite true that many of the *bona fide* collaborators literally sacrificed French citizens in order to get a breathing spell for France. It can well be argued that the ends do not justify the means. But then what about the *Résistance* men who, with *false* information, were played by Allied authorities into the hands of the Nazis who finished them off?[182] Were they expendable? And were the Allied air massacres, butchering not only Germans,[183] but Frenchmen, Dutch, Belgian, Serbs, and foreign laborers,[184] morally justified?[185] Much of de Gaulle's *ressentiment*[186] has to be explained by the gratuitous massacre of Frenchmen and women who,[187] it seems, were at times even wantonly killed by Allied ground forces.[188]

Leftist control of foreign relations was equally apparent in all imaginable domains. UNRRA, an American organization designed to aid "displaced" persons in distress, repeatedly assumed a pro-Communist character. The Mayor of New York, Fiorello La Guardia, who directed its activities and who had once been U.S. Consul in Fiume, had a strongly leftist bent. In a Yugoslav camp in Egypt he insulted the inmates, berating them for not returning to their homeland.[189] The problem of the "displaced persons" (read: desperate refugees)[190] was one of the most baffling to all moderate leftists: the "Fascists" had been defeated. Now whom did they flee? Why did they not return to the places they had left?[191]

The left, from the more moderate groups to the Communists, now turned their eyes toward Spain. There still was a "Fascist dictatorship" to be liquidated: It created a welcome "problem" which diverted public interest from the annexationist activities of the Soviets. At the time of the landing of the Allied troops in North Africa in November 1942, President Roosevelt had written a letter to Franco addressing him as "My dear friend." A "distinguished Roman Catholic layman," Professor Carlton J. H. Hayes acted as American Ambassador in Madrid and tried (successfully) to keep Spain out of the war. This was not too difficult because Franco had met Hitler and, as we said before, immediately a cordial antipathy sprang up between the two.[192] Spain, we have to bear in mind, made extraordinary efforts to protect the Jews, although predominantly those of Sephardic origin.[193]

More than 200 years after the Jews had been collectively expelled from Britain[194] in 1290 the Spaniards placed before their Jews and Moslems the alternative either to embrace Christianity or to leave the country. Most of them left (1492), a certain number became sincerely Christians, others again only seemingly changed their faith. The Jewish refugees went partly to Morocco and Algiers, partly to Turkey, a few of them to Italy and to South America. This harsh measure was a great loss to Spain: It had a purely religious and not a racist character. In the nineteenth century a trickle of Jews returned. King Alfonso XIII was known for his friendly feelings toward the Jews. When the Republic was established in 1931 the Jews in Spain already numbered more than 2,000.[195] In 1924, under the rule of King Alfonso (and the military dictatorship of General Miguel Primo de Rivera, father of José-Antonio, the founder of the Falange), a law had been issued which invited the descendants of the expelled Sephardic (i.e., Spanish) Jews[196] to return to Spain and offered them immediate citizenship. A few followed the call. When the civil war broke out the Spanish Jews, above all those living in Northern Morocco, a Spanish Protectorate, sided with the right. And when in World War II many Jews fled to the West, passing through Spain, *not one of them* was surrendered to the Germans.[197]

As a matter of fact, the Spanish consulates and embassies all over Europe started to issue passports for Jews of Spanish descent on the basis of the law of 1924. An estimated 30,000 to 40,000 passports were granted, which makes "Franco Spain" *the* greatest protector of Jews at the time of the last war. The Spanish government, through economic pressure, succeeded in having the French Jews of Sephardic origin exempted from wearing the Star of David. The Spanish consular agents sealed the apartments and houses of Sephardic French Jews. And more: The Spanish government forced the Nazis to disgorge Jewish inmates from concentration camps who actually came by whole trainloads to Spain. Mr. Maurice L. Perlzweig in a resolution adopted at the Jewish Congress in Atlantic City (November 1944) thanked the Spanish Ambassador in Washington for his government's efforts to aid and protect Jews. "The Jews are a race of long memory; they will not easily forget the chance given to thousands of their brothers to save their lives."[198] (Similar messages were sent to the Swiss Government, the King of Sweden and Pope Pius XII—all not exactly representatives of leftism.)[199]

Now that the Allies were safely entrenched all over Western Europe and still had not waked up to the danger from the East, Franco no longer was "My dear friend." Stalin, who butchered more Jews than Franco could ever have saved, suggested to the Right Honourable Clement Attlee of clenched fist memory and to Mr. Truman to blockade Spain, so that the Spaniards might rise and overthrow their "Fascist" government. The result was not a reduced breakfast table for Generalissimo Franco, but years of misery and starvation for the Spaniards who, whatever their opinion about Franco, now really rallied to him in a feeling of national indignation and collective pride. The Potsdam plan luckily miscarried and here one can say with a sigh of relief that God at least sometimes takes care of children, drunkards, fools, and the foreign policy of the United States of America.[200] Today Spain, undergoing a gradual process of liberalization, is a military pillar of the Free World.

Luckily Japan preserved the office of Emperor,[201] yet one wonders what would happen to its Parliament at a time of grave economic adversity and its "demilitarization" is a tremendous burden on the shoulders of the victorious United States. Japan and Germany, for better or worse, played important parts in keeping the equilibrium of Eurasia. America now has to fill this military void. "Moderate leftist" foresight was even less successful on the Asian mainland. The "agrarian reformers" of China transformed themselves into a roaring tiger, "anticolonialist" American hostility toward France in Indochina resulted in another American liability and responsibility: the joint British-American intervention in favor of Sukarno, a collaborator of the Japanese, and against the Dutch, their wartime ally, was another case in point. What characterizes the leftist mind, however, is a would-be pragmatism combining two things which normally tend to be opposites: an impractical utopian idealism coupled with the lack of a sense of honor. Usually idealism goes together with a sense of honor and loyalty. Don Quixote is not practical but he is a man of honor: Sancho Panza ignores honor, but he is a realist. The typical leftist is a dreamer without honor and that is a pretty bad combination.

Inevitably one remembers the letters of Franklin Delano Roosevelt to Pius XII in which the President tried to convince the Pope that he ought to come down to earth and realize that his picture of the Soviet Union was obsolete and no longer conforming to truth—an interesting change after Woodrow Wilson's reply to Benedict XV's peace effort, reminding the Pope that the war was a moral issue which practical considerations could never eliminate. Granted that the Vatican is neither a powerhouse[202] nor even a prime center of information, but there is perennial value to sound Christian reasoning and to a profound knowledge of man in all his glory and misery, which leftist emotionalism and ratiocination cannot replace.

More blunders were made in the years after 1945: the failure of nerves in the Hungarian Revolution; the failure at Suez; the failure in the Bay of Pigs; the horrible blunder in Vietnam in 1963, when a deceitful leftist propaganda portrayed the rule of Ngo Dinh Diem as a "Roman Catholic dictatorship" oppressing kind Buddhist monks,[203] with the resulting speculation on a possible All-Buddhist Crusade against communism with American support, some sort of Buddhification of the war in Vietnam. (One could as well imagine an American Army led by Quakers, devout Mennonites, and conscientious objectors.)[204]

Needless to say that the blunders of American leftists have their analogies in other parts of the world. French, Spanish, Italian, German, Austrian, and British "moderate leftists" are no less silly and supercilious; however, their influence, their weight, their historic importance is now a great deal less than that of their American *confrères* who have an establishment with which the others cannot vie, because it is in a key nation deciding the fate of the world. One can listen to certain Spanish (or Peruvian) students—who are filled to the gills with most incredible nineteenth-century nonsense—be informed by sophisticated Frenchmen how the Texan oil millionaires murdered President Kennedy, or be instructed by Italian *Repubblicani* about Italy's economic exploitation by the Vatican. The stupidities uttered by Greek intellectuals, soft-headed German *literati* or sixth-rate English university professors are just as bad, except that they matter less. From the masses no intelligent man expects a superior knowledge anyhow: they can only throw back what has been fed to them by the information manufacturers or by the opinion makers. Common sense is valuable, no doubt, but not without knowledge, just as knowledge is worthless without common sense. The masses cannot really be blamed.

Naturally the picture of what happened since 1945 is not completely black. There has been resistance in the case of Korea, though a resistance which was never fully developed. Nationalist China has not been thrown to the dogs, as so many leftists wanted. In Formosa as *intelligent* agrarian reform has taken place and that island is a real showcase in Asia—now economically on its own feet.[205] The Marshall Plan in free Europe was a success, and the more private initiative was given a scope, the greater the success.[206] Support for the sadists in Angola and Mozambique has abated.

The negative, the blinding effects of leftism even in its moderate form, derive mostly from envy and jealousy, the main dynamic forces of the left. It is this driving element which links up the whole sequence of revolutions from 1789 to 1917 and 1933. Envy and jealousy are capable of dominating not only internal politics but, even more so, foreign policy where they support the sadistic drives which so strongly color international relations in our progressive, democratic century. No wonder, since today the ultimate means of foreign policy is not only total war but also the fomenting of revolutions and rebellions in foreign countries, which was taboo in an earlier age. When Sir Roger Casement, in World War I, tried to get the aid of the German Ministry of Foreign Affairs, the *Aussenamt*, his plea for active support against British rule in Ireland was rejected for the reason that this meant meddling in inner British affairs. It was the German *army* which cooperated first with Casement and later with the Communist exiles in Switzerland who were shipped to Russia: it was a non-Junker, Erich Ludendorff, who utilized revolutionary disloyalty, imitating the Allies who partly won the war through these tactics (as young Captain de Gaulle insisted).[207]

The Soviets needed the democratic restoration of 1945 very much indeed. We know about a leading American general who, after World War II, met a Soviet leader. We quote: "Circumstances had brought the two together on a number of occasions and the American had noticed an attitude of considerable friendliness on the part of the Russian. One day he commented on his attitude.

"The Soviet leader made no reply for the moment, then he drew his chair closer to the table and from a matchbox he took four matches which he placed methodically on the table, each match about an inch from the next and parallel to it. Then he said, 'Now this first match is what you call "Capitalism"; the second is what you call "Democracy"; the third is what you call "Socialism"; and the fourth is what you call "Communism".'

"He paused a moment, and then, looking up at the American, said, 'Now, I like your country because it is moving straight down the line from capitalism through the others to communism.' "[208] The distinguished American, according to our information, was nobody else but General MacArthur.

Today, world conflicts move on several levels. The time of the old-fashioned cabinet wars is over, war has become total, partly because technology gave us staggering means of destruction, partly because, due to the withering away of religion, totalitarian ideologies capable of mobilizing the masses and fanaticizing pragmatists, have filled this void. Hot wars destroy bodies, cold wars are waged for immortal souls. Still, what strikes one today, more than ever, are the words of Rivarol,[209] one of the most brilliant spirits of old France: "Politics is like the Sphinx: It devours all those who cannot solve its riddles."

Part V

Leftism Today

Chapter 18

Anticolonialism

Anticolonialism has been one of the worst traps into which American foreign policy fell during this century. Naturally its stalwarts were and are the leftists. Yet the anticolonial sentiment is quite generally represented in the American people and, in the United States, one has to be something of an *esprit fort*, an emancipated spirit, to be able to resist its temptation. The fact that anticolonialism has two distinct roots, and not just one, contributes powerfully to its strength. To make matters even worse, it has become a tactical weapon in the Cold War where Washington uses it with the greatest sincerity. Now, since anti-imperialism seems to sound better than anticolonialism it has partly but not entirely replaced the latter term in Soviet harangues. When I was asked in Irkutsk a few years ago what I thought about Eastern Siberia, I replied that it is a wonderful example of the dynamics of Russian colonialism. With this remark I horrified most of my interlocutors (by no means all convinced Communists) and one of them told me that the term colonialism was out of place here: I should have called it *osvoyeniye*, which means "incorporation" (or the German *Landnahme*), whereupon I opened my notebook and took down this valuable piece of information and education with the straightest of faces—whereupon a few in my audience started to laugh. I am sure, however, that some of the young among those present became aware for the first time in their lives that their country truly was a colonial power.

I witnessed something similar in America, when I once started a lecture with the remark that I, belonging to a nation which never had colonies, was addressing myself to the citizens of a colonial power. It was immediately pointed out to me that the United States never possessed colonies in the past and none at the present. When I mentioned the Philippine Islands, Guam, and Western Samoa, I created a minor sensation. The fact had been known all along, but its realization had been blocked. When I defined a colony in the modern sense as a distant area administrated by a motherland granting either only limited or even no autonomous power, we had to include some other areas as well.

There is, of course, nothing evil and nothing extraordinary about colonialism. It is the inevitable result of a historical law according to which not only nature, but also political geography, does not tolerate a vacuum. Where no effective resistance can be expected, other powers, other nations, other tribes will occupy, dominate, and administer an area. Our history could not be imagined without the forces of colonialism constantly at work. Without Greek colonialism Magna Graecia would not have existed, Stagira would not have existed (in a way Aristotle would not have existed), Paestum or Pergamum, Ephesus, or Agrigent would not delight us with their ruins. Without Phoenician colonialism, there would have been no Carthage—and eventually no St. Augustine. Roman colonialism (or "imperialism") is responsible for the French language, for Racine and Molière—and also for Cervantes, Lope de Vega, and Calderón. Without Bavarian colonialism there would be no Austrian people. And so forth. As we should all realize, there is good colonialism and bad colonialism, just as we have good rule, which is government conscious of the common good and the welfare of the citizen or subjects, and bad rule which is selfish and exercised solely for the profit of the rulers.

The twin roots of American anticolonialism are (a) insistence on self-rule (democracy), and (b) a misinterpretation and an illegitimate application of the reasons for American independence. We have dealt elsewhere with the mirage of self-rule, which admits at best to a collective, but never to a personal-existential interpretation. The only individuals who enjoy self-rule are citizens in a direct democracy, deciding all issues with unanimity (a purely theoretical case) and absolute monarchs, dictators, or tyrants. The dream of everybody becoming his own monarch could especially be fulfilled by the anarchists (provided such fulfillment is possible and desirable), but the democrats can explain their system as a pantocracy only with the help of amazing abstractions, psychological arguments, and axiomatic suppositions which hardly fool the independent thinker.

Yet more often than not it is the memory of history classes and the uncritical listening to Fourth of July speeches rather than the democratic argument which emotionally dominates American anticolonialism. As a result a genuine fusion of leftist and "patriotic" arguments against colonialism is possible, and this is usually fostered assiduously by the more clever leaders of the American left. Here we have an ideal opportunity to quote again Dr. Johnson's "Patriotism is the last refuge of the scoundrel."

What is usually forgotten in the "patriotic" (i.e., historic) appeal to anticolonialism is, first of all, the fact that here we are not facing any "ism" whatever. The term "colonialism" will hardly be found in authoritative dictionaries before 1914 or even 1924. Colonizing is not the result of a systematic ideology, of a *Weltanschauung*, of a philosophy, political or other. A second fact has to do with the great variety of situations actually covered by the term "colony." There have been and there still exist a few colonies which before the arrival of the white man were totally void of the human element. This is true, for instance, of a number of islands in the Indian Ocean. Is it an iniquitous situation if such settlements are governed by the motherland? When does their God-given right of secession and independence begin? Certainly not with the landing of the first settler. When are they "ripe" for autonomy? All answers of necessity will be arbitrary.

We have to place into the same category areas which were practically deserted and where the indigenous population at best had tribal but not political organizations. It would not be too easy to prove that the Britishers were infringing on the natural law (or on God-given rights) when they started to colonize Australia. Whatever may be the case, the colony *in the classic sense of the term* was a city or a whole area settled by people from a "motherland" (*metropolis*) speaking the same language, adhering to the same laws, praying to the same gods as the people in the motherland. In the remote past their independence usually resulted from the impossibility of long-distance administration. Political decisions had to be made on the spot without much delay. In antiquity independence always evolved in an organic process. The moral and emotional ties between motherland and colony were rarely broken. As a result, military alliance was the rule rather than the exception.

In spite of the American *War* of Independence, (often referred to as the "American Revolution" starting the "American Experiment"), the relationship between America and Britain falls entirely into the category of *classic colony* where people of the same culture, language, and civilization, with equal intellectual and moral levels, are separated by a considerable geographic distance. Any equation of the secession of the Thirteen Colonies with, let us say, the "War of Liberation of the Peoples of Angola" is based on complete ignorance of the facts.

A *second* type of colony is the one found in isolated spots. Here the purpose of colonization is merely one of civil or military communications.

The *third* type of colony very frequent until recently, had a relatively numerous local population of a manifestly lower culture and civilization than the motherland. The former Belgian Congo would be a case in point.

Now, there exists a school of thought which hesitates to talk about higher and lower cultures. We, of course, use the term culture in the German sense, now generally adopted by the English-speaking nations: the intellectual, moral, and artistic status of nations as opposed to their civilization, which includes the civic (political) institutions and the servile arts. Obviously there are domains which do not fit neatly into one category or the other: Sanitation and industry obviously belong to civilization; religion, painting, and poetry to culture; jurisprudence and table manners to both. High levels of culture and civilization are related, but do not operate in synchromesh. Often history shows us great discrepancies between both, among persons as well as entire nations.

In talking about levels we need measuring rods. We need standards. The assumption that Western *culture*, in its present stage, is inherently superior to others is not easily proved. I am convinced of it, but I have to omit a lengthy argument here. Still, I want to go on record as affirming that the overwhelming part of mankind wants to adopt Western culture and, even more so, Western civilization—if not in all, at least in many or most of its aspects. (I will return to that theme). In occupying and administering areas inhabited by primitives and semiprimitives (central Africa, to quote an instance), the Western powers were driven to their colonization by psychological motives ("national pride", expansive patriotism, etc.) as well as by practical considerations, i.e., advantages of a military or economic nature. Nor were altruistic motives entirely absent. Missionary zeal as well as a desire to help these populations from a medical, educational, and civic point of view—they all played their part.

Fourth and finally, we had colonies whose populations had a culture and civilization as old as ours, if not older. These nations either had stagnant cultures or civilizations, or both. The technological side of their civilizations ceased to develop and this particular inferiority resulted in the conquest of their ancient states by Europeans.

There exists, however, a curious interconnection between culture and civilization. There can be hostility and conflict between them (as is evident if we put the masses of our big cities under the magnifying glass), but they cannot exist too far apart either. Jointly they form (to use an expression of Arthur Koestler) a "package deal" which precludes the possibility of taking individual items arbitrarily and successfully out of their compounds. The European masters of these old and proud nations (our fourth type of colony) usually tried to provide them with the blessings of Western civilization rather than culture, but soon the desire for cultural assimilation (within arbitrary limits) followed. There is a real inner conflict between the study of mechanical engineering and the natural sciences and Buddhism or Hinduism, whereas in the case of Christianity, such an antithesis does not exist, except, perhaps, in the minds of leftist semi-intellectuals who have never taken the trouble to study systematic theology.

The American anticolonialist is usually unaware of the fact that his protest against the survival of colonies practically never can be based on arguments valid for the independence of his own country. The United States in 1776 were as cultured and civilized as Britain at the same time. Americans then were honestly convinced that they were "just as good as the British" and the same argument, on the other side of the Atlantic, was used by and large by the agent of the Province of New York, Edmund Burke. One has only to visit New England towns which have not materially grown since 1800 in order to evaluate the levels attained by Americans more than a century-and-a-half ago. The controls by London (humiliating rather than vexatious) were resented as insulting and superfluous. To compare Holden Roberto with George Washington or Patrice Lumumba, the embezzler of the Stanleyville post office, with Nathan Hale is ludicrous: to liken the *évenements regrettables* of January 6, 1959, which grew out of a senseless riot of football fans in Leopoldville, to the Boston Tea Party or to Bunker Hill is an insult to the American people. American Independence, after a few difficulties, led to the progress of the United States in almost all domains, whereas the precipitated decolonializations of the mid-twentieth century have resulted in an endless series of calamities.

The average American has also partly been driven to his anticolonial stand by his switch from Calvinistic ideals to the very opposite of Calvinism, to Rousseau's "philosophy" of the noble savage. There might be an added guilt complex because in the past so many noble savages had been brought as slaves to the American Colonies and then to the United States, though it is frequently not realized that they were sold by *Africans* to Yankee slave traders. (In many cases the blacks could

343

have been grateful to have ended as house slaves in Virginia rather than as human sacrifices in bloodcurdling ceremonies such as the *Zenanyana*, the "Evil Night" in Dahomey.) This conscious or subconscious guilt complex of Americans mingles with the suspicion that Europeans merely "exploited" their colonies (which, up to a certain point, they indeed *wanted* to do). The *dolce vita* of Europe was considered to be largely the result of huge profits from the colonies. Such gains had been normal in the more remote past though only in certain areas, as, for instance, in the West Indies. In the second half of the nineteenth century and in our age, however, the vast majority of European colonies ran in the red. Local budgets showed deficits, the balance of trade was largely adverse. Among the German colonies prior to 1914 only little Togo was profitable.[1] All the other colonies needed huge investments in road and railway construction, in machinery, in medical care, in education. A modern economy can hardly be managed by savages or slaves: It needs well-trained and even ambitious men. Eventually the efforts of the European colonialists would have borne fruit, but decolonialization came too early to let the plans mature and thus the colonies left their European tutelage before they became economically independent.[2] The problem of balancing their payments is now for the ex-colonies a major issue in the Cold War which is primarily but not solely responsible for the premature severance of their ties with the motherland.

The American protest against *all* forms of colonizing activity actually presents us with an interesting medico-psychological problem. Let us imagine a man forty or fifty years old, a man in his "best years," who is generally respected, is proud of his achievements and his standing in the community, is happy with his wife and his possessions. This man has one great grudge: He is opposed to *parenthood*. He is proud of his ancestry in general but emphasizes that he has been conceived in shame and that a similar calamity should not happen to others. Obviously such a man would need expert psychiatric treatment. The American anticolonialist is in exactly the same boat. Without British colonialism his own country would exist as little as mine without Bavarian colonialism, or Indonesia (which bears a European name) without Dutch colonialism. It would be interesting to find out to what extent we are here faced with a modified Oedipus complex, with the desire to "murder the father."[3]

American anticolonialism also supplies a hidden motive to the foreign policy of the United States. Too many Americans hoped for the eternal gratitude of the peoples liberated and released owing to American pressure. *Nothing of that sort, however, has ever happened.* Even the material aid given to the "emerging nations" has not modified the attitude of these peoples or their governments in favor of the United States. Recall the speech of Senator John F. Kennedy in 1957 against France in favor of a "free Algeria"; the concerted efforts of America and Britain's Labour government to "stop the Dutch" in Indonesia; the American activities on behalf of "Indian freedom"; the highly positive and encouraging attitude of the United States toward "decolonization" in tropical Africa. Then look at the UN record of the "emerging nations," supported at great material sacrifice by the United States. More often than not we have seen them voting against the stands of the United States.[4]

Yet while not receiving any recognition for its moral and financial aid to these nations,[5] the United States has by this aid effectively antagonized small influential (not necessarily wealthy) groups of Europeans, turning them into fanatical anti-Americans and thus severely weakening the fabric of the Free World. These Europeans are not necessarily expellees from Africa and Asia—former landowners, civil servants, factory managers, teachers, doctors, and merchants. They might be their relatives; they might be people, even little people, who had lost their investments in overseas areas; they might just be patriots who hate the thought that their country's flag had to be taken down somewhere in the big, wide world. The expellees very often had been *born* in the colonies, the mother country to them is a strange country and they felt bitter pain when they were torn away from their native soil. Many of them believed they had a mission among the natives. (Some of them actually were missionaries.) They naturally deplored the demagoguery of a small semi-intellectual minority. Others were victims of mob violence, of rape, mutilation, and other indignities as a result of the "decolonizing process." And since decolonization is being preached simultaneously by Moscow and Washington (by Moscow hypocritically and by Washington sincerely), these victims of the Cold War talk about a decolonizing Moscow-Washington Axis engaged in a permanent auction, an incessant bidding during which the battle cry, "I can be more anticolonialist than you are," can be heard all the time. In this noble-ignoble competition Moscow (with much smaller bribes) is almost always the winner, while the bill for this senseless struggle is being paid by Europeans and "natives" alike. It is on issues like these that it becomes eminently clear that the American left, spearheading this anticolonialist drive, is the *competitor* of communism, *not* its *enemy*. Competitors do not contradict each other; they try to outdo each other.

The negative results of "decolonization" could have been foreseen easily. However, two legitimate views are possible on the subject of decolonization: (1) It was inevitable but should not have taken place at so early a period; and (2) it was not at all inevitable but happened in a historical impasse—just as did the destruction of the Austro-Hungarian Empire. Indeed very few historical events should be called inevitable. We should be content to speak of greater or lesser probabilities, in extreme cases of "virtual impossibilities" and "greatest likelihoods." True, it belongs to the leftist mentality to visualize a fixed point of historic evolution, a utopia behind which there is no genuine historical development but, at best, improvement. All roads lead to utopia which will be reached automatically, but intelligent people help to increase the speed of this evolution. "Progressive people" thus promote the coming of paradise on earth; reactionaries in vain try to delay the arrival of the millennium. (They are merely "turning the clock back.") Actually the machinations of the left are often in the nature of a real fraud because they try to create the impression that the events favoring their cause were *bound* to come. But *if* they are so truly convinced of "historic automation" along their lines, why are they not waiting patiently and passively for the inevitable fulfillment of their Great Dream? This is a question legitimately addressed to the left progressivist no less than to the orthodox Marxist. Certainly, if you stand on the right, then rightly you have no reason to adopt such complacency.

I lean toward the view that decolonization was neither inevitable nor even desirable. I am convinced, however, that *eventually*, in the long, very long run, the globe might be federated politically and that such a process could have positive aspects as I shall explain in the last chapter.

The continued existence of the colonial empires would have greatly facilitated the federation of the globe because it would have aided the Westernization of the colonized tribes and nations, a process not completely terminated today but greatly handicapped and considerably slowed down. We must bear in mind that we saw in the European colonies by 1945 not only a steady advance of Western culture and civilization, but also the growth of education and an increase in local self-government. As a matter of fact, in the years immediately following World War II Europeans emigrated in increasing numbers to the colonies, and when we ask where the most dynamic Europeans could then be found, where the great modern and thriving European cities were located, we would have had to point to Léopoldville and Dakar, Singapore and Hongkong, Casablanca and Lourenço Marques, Luanda and

Algiers, Elizabethville and Nairobi, Hanoi and Bombay. Here the energies and the adventurous spirit of the Old World found their concrete expression; here we had the counterpart to the American drive toward the West and the Russian drive toward the East.

There is every reason to believe that if this process had gone on uninterruptedly the Europeanization, linguistic and cultural, of the original primitive nations and tribes and also of the peoples with an ancient culture would have progressed in a far more organic way than at present. The process, to be sure, is still going on because the common denominator of the globe continues to be Western. Even China, with all its frantic Red nationalism, is only succumbing to one of the most primitive by-products of the Western mind, to Marxism. And in spite of the official program to replace English eventually with Hindi as the official language, English is steadily winning and is actually the uniting bond of India. India, in fact, is as unimaginable as a unified country without the preceding British *Raj* as the *Republik Indonesia* without Dutch rule. The "emerging nations" of Africa owe whatever cohesion they have not at all to tribal customs, traditions, or boundaries, but to European administrations and European languages. A *Nigerien* (a citizen of the *République du Niger*—provided he is Europeanized, *évolué*), differs from an educated North Nigerian (a citizen of formerly British Nigeria) by the fact that he uses French for intellectual purposes while the latter has adopted English as a vehicle of "advanced thought." Both might belong to the same tribe, the same "race," and one might speak in the same idiom to their less literate or even illiterate friends or members of the family. In other words, the "emerging nations" in most cases (Ethiopia and Cambodia, for instance, would naturally be exceptions) are European creations. They were obviously not designed as such, but they still are the product of treaties of European powers. They received their very shape as a result of boundary arrangements between European nations. In other words, they were, in a way, extensions of European states and thus, in a way, could be considered as constituting preparatory steps for the unification of the world. And while free (and "Colonial") Europe after World War II groped desperately for its unity, the colonies not only seceded (prompted by the USA and USSR) but went through the process of fragmentation and "balkanization" that we had already witnessed after the "liberation" of Iberic America. In 1920 all of Africa was under eight flags. It is now subject to no less than forty governments. French Indochina broke up into four states, British India into three or four.[6] In this respect decolonization was a *recessive movement*, in contradiction to a great many ideas and ideals professed by the American left.

A great many other features of decolonization were also antiprogressive and recessive. Before we deal with the desirability of the Westernization inaugurated by the European powers, we have to ask the preliminary question whether the Afro-Asians *wanted* to be Westernized: a legitimate question because nations should decide whether they really like to be subjected to a specific evolutionary process. Talking in Africa to *évolués*, highly critical of "colonialism," I very often asked point-blank whether they would have considered it preferable if, 200 years ago, we Europeans had put a *cordon sanitaire* around Africa, leaving it to its own evolution unaided by the immense knowledge and experience we had acquired and accumulated—at great cost, at great pains, in the last three thousand years. A few extreme nationalists explained to me with profound conviction that, left to their own devices, they would have achieved the same inventions, the same improvements, the same advances, but the vast majority, less possessed by brazen optimism, were usually put on the spot. A few even admitted that in all likelihood they would not even exist, since the substantial decrease in mortality and the phenomenal increase in population were gifts of the medical services introduced by the Europeans. The unqualified "yes" to European civilization was, to be true, not always followed by the same enthusiastic assent for European culture. In most of the "emerging nations" the belief exists that one might opt for one and not the other, but this is true only to a very limited extent. One can, for instance, ride a bicycle half or three-quarters naked, one can read Plato (though not in Linguala!) and eat couscous, one can use the most modern automatic rifle and, at the same time, practice cannibalism which might be defined as "nutritional democracy." There are, however, certain limits to these arbitrary selections from what, as Arthur Koestler pointed out, in reality are *package deals*.

In the Congo one was well aware of this in the good old days of Belgian rule when one made a trip from Usumbura to Bukavu and saw the large number of cars stranded and deserted on the wayside. Such sights were rare in the environs of Elizabethville for the simple reason that the population of Katanga had close contacts with technology and had been industrialized for two to three generations. The people from Upper Katanga had gone through the school of applied Aristotelianism without knowing it. They had genuine knowledge of the connection between cause and effect. They realized, for instance, that if one of the foremen in the foundry made a grave error in timing or calculation, this might result in grave material loss or in the death of several people.

The Upper Katangese industrial worker whose car stalled did not call for a medicine man to dance around and imprecate the evil spirits to depart. He lifted the hood, investigated the wires and spark plugs, tested the carburetor and water pump. In short he looked for the *reason* for the trouble. This of course, leads us to the statement that Europe and North America owe their phenomenal technological rise—which gave them the edge over much older, more cultured and more numerous nations—to their acute sense of objective reality (resting on the triad of Aristotelianism, scholasticism, and rationalism), as well as to their assent to the Biblical command to dominate the Earth, to make it subservient. However, I have written of this elsewhere.[7]

All this does not mean that Afro-Asians have always and everywhere accepted most forms of Westernization with open arms and immediate joy. This happened only after a longer acquaintance with these values, inventions, and institutions: They came to desire them. As a matter of fact, the remark is very often heard in Africa and Asia that the colonizing powers did *too little* in imparting these values: Their educational effort was too haphazard, their medical services not sufficiently comprehensive, their road-building program too sketchy, their slum clearance not effective enough, their granting of self-government (autonomy) too slow. The American left has always been extremely vocal in denouncing the colonial powers for their egotism, their selfishness, their neglect, their "exploitation," their "undemocratic" ways of dealing with "natives." And, unfortunately, since these leftists control so much of the press and the other mass media, they were frequently seconded by well-meaning good Americans who otherwise are not leftists by conviction.

This colossal misunderstanding (sometimes amounting to a truly wilful falsification of facts) was evident in the case of the independence of the Belgian Congo and the subsequent catastrophic developments. First of all, it must be borne in mind that the Belgian Congo is located in "darkest Africa"—in other words, in an area which was among the last to be explored. It contains the least civilized and the most primitive tribes if we exclude the Bakongos, who had a political organization in the late Middle Ages around the mouth of the Congo and northernmost Angola.

The earliest efforts at colonialization of the Belgian Congo go back to the last years of the 1880s and the subsequent establishment of the Congo Free State under Leopold II, when the Congo was exploited (and, we must admit, quite brutally exploited) by private companies. It became a colony only in 1908 and the reports of Mr. (later Sir) Roger

Casement decided the Belgians to make of their only possession a model colony. (European nations at that time had a free press and parliaments in which the opposition was only too happy to expose mismanagement or an inhumane administration. Whether they realized it or not, the "victims of colonialism" were morally represented in the European parliaments. The countries without parliaments were those with no colonies.)

The Belgians in the more remote past may never have contemplated total independence for the Congo. The avowed plan of most of the colonizing nations of Europe was not complete secession, but autonomy, and autonomy with equality. Race-minded nations had their doubts whether the natives would ever become peoples like those of the motherland, but others were more optimistic. The French wanted to make Frenchmen, the Portuguese Portuguese, the Spaniard Spaniards and the Italians Italians of the Afro-Asians. The Belgians were handicapped because they had an ethnic struggle at home which deeply divided the nation and also an ideological rift between active Catholics and anticlericals, antagonisms which had their distinct echo in the Congo. There were natives (although in a minority) who studied Flemish rather than French because a majority of the administrators were Flemish and not Walloon. Schools were either religious or areligious, and when the university age dawned over the Congo the Belgian bicephalism in higher education also made its appearance in the heart of Africa. The Catholic University of Louvain founded the Lovanium, the "free-thinking" University of Brussels, the "liberal" University of Elizabethville. Still, the Belgians did not spare time nor money to fashion the Congolese after their own image. Almost everything in the colony was run by Catholics *or* by *les frères*, i.e., the Masons, and people knew and in a way respected this curious duality. I doubt, however, that Tories and Whigs or Conservatives and Labourites tried to penetrate the Gold Coast or India ideologically, even if the British succeeded in getting hold of African and Asian students, westernizing them abroad in Britain.[8]

Official Belgium had a real plan—a wise and constructive plan about the Congo. Unfortunately "time" (which largely means Washington and Moscow) did not permit it to mature. The basic idea was to avoid the French pattern, i.e., the hasty establishment of a few elementary and secondary schools from which the best scholars were shipped to French universities where more often than not they became uprooted. The Belgians wanted rather to cover the entire country with a net of primary schools to provide the vast majority of the Congolese with a basic education. After having developed the elementary schools, the Belgians started secondary schools and seminaries. Unlike the French colonial system, university education (which to Continentals is a graduate and not a "college" education), was also to be given in the Congo itself. The idea of the Belgians was to avoid tearing the young men and women away from their own land, for a life of isolation and miserable cold in Belgium (which lacks the warm sites of southern France). Their plan was to build universities around the Equator. We have mentioned two of these; a third was scheduled to be set up in Usumbura for the Ruanda-Urundi area which did not form an integral part of the Congo but was actually a United Nations mandate.

The Lovanium preceded the University of Elizabethville and both of these places of learning were provided with the best guest professors from Europe. In the very first years the percentage of whites among the students was high (a minority in the Lovanium, a majority in Elizabethville). There were, needless to say, no racial barriers and the universities were coeducational; yet no African girl attended before 1961 because *none* qualified! The administrators and professors of the Lovanium stayed with their families in Livulu, a village for racially integrated living.[9] In 1960 (when I gave a few lectures to the students) the buildings of the Lovanium together were almost four miles long and the university was designed to house and eventually teach more than 10,000 students. The University of Elizabethville was more decentralized. The equipment of the universities was first-rate. The Lovanium had an atomic reactor years before the University of Vienna.

The Belgians, indeed, thought that the main burden of the administration should be transferred to the Congolese, but at first no specific date was set for a more systematic takeover. The Lovanium was opened in 1957 and the University of Elizabethville a year later. When the fatal riots started on January 6, 1959, the Belgians were no less startled than the Africans themselves. It all came like lightning out of a blue sky. The "ignition" came from a brawl between two factions at a football game. This developed into an attack against the Portuguese traders in the former native section of Léopoldville. (All racial discriminations and the zonings were abolished in 1954 and the new laws were applied from one day to another without any protest.) The traders defended themselves with the usual Portuguese stubbornness, courage, and skill, but the army failed to receive orders to shoot from the Governor General who completely lost his head. General Janssen of the *Force Publique* thereupon delivered an ultimatum to him: "I will wait for three hours to get your orders to shoot, sir. If I don't get them by that time I will act on my own." The Governor General consented and Janssen restored order with the *Force Publique* which, together with the *Union Minière du Haut-Katanga*, was considered one of the two great success stories of the Congo.

The *événements regrettables* of January 6 were not at all directed against the Belgians but they created a mood of unrest and were fully exploited by the forces of "anticolonialism" in the United States and in the Soviet Union. Suddenly people began to remember the brutalities of the rubber companies (which no longer existed).[10] Washington or rather the State Department put great pressure on the Belgian Government to "free" the Congo. The Belgian extreme left raised the same clamor and the government, in which the Socialists participated, declined to cling fanatically to this overseas possession; after 1957 (as before 1940) the colony had been in the red again. As a matter of fact only the Upper Katanga, that small appendix in the southeast corner of the colony, had a real economic value and provided almost three-quarters of the revenue. There also, work ethics had reached a somewhat satisfactory level.[11] The *Union Minière* (belonging to the *Société Générale*) paid with its taxes for about 55 percent of the expenses of the colony. The rest of the country (apart from the diamond fields of the Kassai Province) is practically worthless and could, from an inhumanly economic point of view, be dumped right into the Atlantic Ocean. As one can very easily imagine, a movement to separate the Katanga from the rest of the Congo had existed for some time because black and white in that province were sick and tired of paying for the glories and luxuries of Léopoldville, the very remote capital, as well as for the other provinces.

While the American State Department pressured the Belgians to give up their wicked colonialism, the Pentagon had rather different sentiments. The military men thought about the big base of Kamina and they had no squeamish anticolonialist complexes. They knew, moreover, a bit more about the realities of the big wide world than the leftist theorists. Yet, even in spite of the Republican administration at that time still holding office in Washington, the bureaucracy in the State Department prevailed and the Belgians, who had finally made plans to give full autonomy to the Congo in 1975, changed their timetable and promised freedom by July 1, 1960. They relied on the *Force Publique* which was to be officered by the Belgians as in the past. The vast majority of Belgian civilians were also expected to stay in the country. The leader of the Bakongo party, Joseph Kasavubu, was to be the President, Monsieur Patrice Lumumba, leader of the Lumumbist wing of the *Mouvement National Congolais* (strongly centered in Stanleyville), became Prime Minister. This man had been indicted as an embezzler while employed by the post office. He had received another conviction for revolutionary activities but benefited from an amnesty. At the ceremony in Léopoldville, when King Baudouin solemnly handed over the power to the new local government, this petty thief insulted the *Bwana Kitoko* (The Young Master). Yet a few days later the red carpet was literally rolled out for him in Washington. (Maybe his theft was just a piece of "economic democracy"!)

Soon the mutiny of Thysville broke out. All order collapsed in the Congo; the Katanga region seceded. The Golgotha in the heart of Africa had begun thanks to the follies of Western leftist anticolonialists and the shrewd calculations of their brothers under the skin in the East.

Africa (and other underdeveloped overseas areas) are in a sense magnifying mirrors of the West or Gorgonic mirrors,[12] if one prefers. This is partly the reason why we go into such detail in describing the grim "evolution" of the Congo. The events in Thysville and in the neighboring districts and the mutiny of the highly trusted *Force Publique* simply were due to the change of authority and the psychological breakdown it caused. Traditionalists can make a most valid point here. When the pictures of the *Bwana Kitoko* were taken down in the barracks on the last day of June, 1960, and replaced by those of Joseph Kasavubu (who once upon a time had dreamed of becoming King of Lower Congolia) all authority had gone. The soldiers asked their (largely white) officers whether they now considered Monsieur Kasavubu their sovereign. When they got a positive reply, all respect for them disappeared. Joseph Kasavubu looked like everybody else. He was an "ordinary man," a "Negro like you and me," and this just did not impress the Congolese. To make matters worse, Kasavubu, unlike a King, was exchangeable and replaceable. He could be—with the aid of votes—hired and fired like a domestic. Of course, exactly the same reaction had taken place in Europe when monarchies were overthrown: Disrespect and disorder or fear and fanaticism took over. Hell now broke loose in the Congo. When the Belgian paratroopers arrived to save the lives, the health, and the honor of Belgian men and women, the Soviets protested against this "violation of the sovereignty of a nation," whose existence could be measured in days and hours. Africa certainly cannot be ruled by abstractions—nor can most of the more civilized nations in the long run either.[13]

The reaction of the free Western press to the atrocities was worse than could be expected. Let us bear in mind that in order to be a "good journalist" it is apparently not sufficient to be a good reporter or to have access to a certain amount of "inside information" (which, more often than not, cannot be checked easily). Above all, it takes a thorough study of history, geography, economics, sociology, political science, religion, anthropology, languages, etc. In Europe at least, a very large sector of the newspaper correspondents and responsible editors have been to graduate schools.

But even so there is the danger that a half-baked element with scanty education, little experience of the world, and badly grounded knowledge may get access to key jobs in journalism. (The handicap of the European press consists in the lack of funds; this results in *theoretically* qualified people judging world affairs *from afar*, which is just as disastrous as the ignoramus writing on the spot.[14]) And since the press has to work with speed, it is tempted to write and to inform in a way that pleases the public. The average reader puts a premium on writing skill rather than on a valid commentary. Thus the press has become in many countries a haven for the *terrible simplificateur* in the form of the leftist semi-intellectual who, more than anybody else, indulges in *fausses idées claires*, clear but false ideas.[15] For reasons which we have given elsewhere the leftist element is much more strongly represented among the "foreign correspondents" than among local reporters, and the reporters are usually more "liberal" than their bosses. Worse, the editors and newspaper owners in the United States and Great Britain suffer from an amazing inferiority complex. They often feel themselves not sufficiently "progressive" and with a sigh leave "advanced views" to the younger men who (so they think) understand better the shape of things to come. Thus, more often than not, they yield—with resignation—to their informants abroad and to their leftist commentators. Nobody in his right mind would call the *Chicago Tribune* a leftist paper, yet Jay Allen, correspondent in Loyalist Spain, provided this paper with the Red version of events. Britain's conservative *Evening Standard* featured cartoonist David Low, whose work was of a distinctly leftist inspiration.

In the case of the Congo horrors a large part of the press (and not only the notoriously leftist press) turned against the Belgians. They were accused of not having sufficiently civilized and educated the inhabitants of the Congo Basin "for independence." First of all, it has not been considered a primary task in the past to educate any conquered or incorporated area "for independence." No doubt the United States is doing its level best to foster and promote welfare in Puerto Rico: It can even be said that it is aiding education in Puerto Rico in every imaginable way. But it simply is not true that the United States is training the Puerto Ricans for "independence"—nor is the United States doing anything along these lines in Guam, in Samoa, or on the Indian reservations.

On the other hand it is a fact that the Belgians tried to build up education in the Congo: They had to start from rock bottom. Yet it is impossible to provide one of the world's most primitive regions with an intelligentsia within fifty years and with men sufficiently trained to take over the administration of 20,000,000 people in an area three times the size of Texas. The Indians in the Southwest have been wards of the United States ever since the middle of the nineteenth century. I have lived among them and studied several tribes, and there can be little doubt that many of them originally had a level of culture a great deal higher than that of many Congolese. Yet, we may ask, "What is the level of education on the reservation today?" How many of these Indians have been trained to work at white collar jobs? How many of them are professional men? The United States, with enormous monetary resources and relatively few Indians to deal with, could *theoretically* have done a magnificent job. We say theoretically because we know the tremendous obstacles, the immense human difficulties of Western acculturation. I am ready to exonerate the United States government, but why attack the hapless Belgians?[16]

It is interesting to see in this case precisely how the democratic dogma and all the other deeply ingrained prejudices (some of them not ideological in the concrete sense of the term but pertaining to American folklore) contributed after "liberation" to the criminally stupid and uncharitable judgments on Belgian colonial policy. The horrors of July-August 1960 (and many of the horrors committed later by revolutionary groups right through 1965)[17] were reported but considered merely as outbursts of rightful indignation after years of "colonialism." All people are equal, all identical, people are "more alike than unlike"—and thus the noble savages of the Congo were "driven" to their misdeeds.

The fact that the I.Q.s of Africans *on the average* are a great deal lower than ours could not be accepted: It was contrary to the democratic notion of equality. And yet it exists, it has been established statistically, and it has nothing to do with race. *But it is there*. It is due to the fact that the child between the ages of two and seven—any child anywhere—needs a maximum of contacts with adults when the cortex of the brain is being developed. In the first two years maternal love is the most important factor and this the African child gets—regardless of whether it is black, as in the Congo, or white as in Algeria. Then, about two years after the child's birth, a new child is likely to appear. The older child will be relegated from the back of the mother and left to play in the village, in the slum, in the forest. At the age of two the African child is superior to its Euramerican counterpart; at the age of seven it has the mind of a Euramerican child of five. This difference, this *décalage*, is scientifically established and it continues as the years go on. Needless to say, we have the same problem in our orphanages where a few adults have to deal with hundreds of children. Their I.Q.s are shamefully low. The African mother, to make matters worse, is miserably educated or even uneducated. The girl longs for motherhood and does not finish school—if she goes to school at all.[18] In most cases her parents are opposed to the education of females, and men are not particularly eager to get well-educated wives.

In other words, to begin with, Africa is intellectually handicapped.[19] Yet the American leftist not only overlooks the basic difficulties in educating decolonized people, he also suffers from a curious schizophrenia. On the one hand formal education is his great shibboleth and he "measures" nations by their percentages of illiteracy. (If literacy is taken as a measuring rod, Latvia should be superior to France.) He is a fanatical educationist. Yet, on the other hand, education from a political point of view seems to have no specific value for him. Sometimes he insists on literacy as a necessary qualification for voting.[20] The voter ought to be able to read a newspaper. Of course this no longer is really necessary, because radio and above all television can "instruct" him acoustically and pictorially. Sitting in front of his magic box he can decide whether he "really likes" a given candidate or not. And for this as well as for a number of other reasons the "emerging nations" have often dispensed with literacy tests for their voters. They deem it sufficient if, according to a purely vegetative principle, the voter is more than eighteen, twenty, or twenty-one years old and still "on the hoof." A UNESCO study has demonstrated that *today more than half the world's voters* (admittedly many of them participating only in the mock elections of totalitarian tyrannies) are illiterate. They vote guided by mere animal symbols, for or against the rhinoceros or the parrot. American leftists are not in the least shocked about these performances. As a matter of fact, they often feel indignant if a government refuses the franchise to illiterates, as does Perú or, much nearer home, any state government.

Thus, neither the American left nor the various demagogues in the Congo were upset about the fact that a still largely illiterate nation should go to the polls. Switzerland does not have female suffrage though educational levels for Swiss women are very high; yet the Congolese women were naturally permitted to vote. Actually, there should be no reason for a real democrat to get upset about it. Literacy alone does not guarantee knowledge. The mere fact that somebody can read and write does not mean that he has any grasp of the political problems his vote (however infinitesimally small in relation to the grand total) might contribute to decide. As we have said before, the twenty-one-year-old prostitute and the sixty-five-year-old professor of political science have one vote each. Equality and not knowledge, quantity and not quality are the keynotes of democracy; the Hitlers defeat the Brünnings.

In this respect I received a wonderful object lesson when I discussed with a group of Congolese their forthcoming independence and the demo-republican constitution. This happened in Bukavu (Kivu Province) in February 1960. We sat in a restaurant and my newly acquired friends were MNC, men of the Lumumbist faction. "Your womenfolk, too, will vote," I declared. "But tell me now, honestly, what do they know about the Congo and the world? Have they here in Bukavu any idea what the Katanga is like or what the economic problems of the Katanga are, or what reasons the Luluas have to hate the Balubas? Do they understand the arguments for and against federalism in the Congo? What do they know about the Cold War, the United Nations, free trade, nationalization, educational problems, the issue of highways versus railroads, the world market in copper, uranium, and diamonds? Can they judge any of the issues with which the free Congo will be confronted—judge them seriously, not merely following hunches, whims, and emotions?"

One of the men looked straight at me and asked, "What about your country, Austria? Do women vote in Austria?" "They do." "And are the Austrian women capable of judging domestic politics seriously? And world affairs? What do they know about free trade, the United Nations, railroads, nationalized industries, the Cold War?" "I'll be frank—they know nothing at all. They repeat what they read in the newspapers, if they remember at all what they read. And so do the men."

"All right, then," my interlocutor replied grimly, "So why should you have all the fun of voting—and not us!"

This reaction was not at all stupid. He almost had me. Yet the answer is that it is not popular representation that makes a country tick, but the executive and the administration. Without its administration France would have gone the way of all flesh a long time ago. The intellectual

357

level of the voters and the politicians with the general franchise and a political Gresham's Law affecting the quality of modern political life has shifted many of the responsibilities to the civil service which still insists on qualifications, whereas elections and parliamentary life require neither knowledge, nor practical experience, nor wisdom, nor higher moral standards. A lieutenant in an army, a locomotive engineer, a bank cashier behind a grill—nay, a plumber, an electrician, or a traveling salesman needs infinitely more knowledge, more experience than politicians (especially in countries where party slates and not individual candidates compete).

But it is clearly the civil service which in the underdeveloped countries cannot be established overnight. A good civil service needs not only an intellectual infrastructure of relatively high quality, but also a sound moral fiber. A civil service which is competent but corrupt is as valueless as one which is honest but untrained. And inevitably when we speak of moral qualities we mean those emanating from the Judaeo-Christian tradition, and these standards are not universally accepted or at least not uniformly evaluated. The taking of bribes (to quote just one example) was not equally condemned in eighteenth- and in late nineteenth-century England: it was treated differently in early twentieth-century Germany and Rumania. It is not viewed in the same way in contemporary Burma and in Switzerland.

We have talked about the Congo at length because in dealing with such an area and its problems, the American leftist (independent of the degree of his anticolonialist fervor) is uniquely unqualified to pass judgment, to design a policy, to make forecasts. His handicaps in this matter are so manifold that it is difficult to enumerate them all. Let us, therefore, merely recall his basic alienation from the existing world, from *human nature*. About human nature he makes *two* mistakes: One is dictated by his Roussellian heritage and by his blind reaction to Calvinism: He overrates the character of the average man (i.e., his moral qualities). The other mistake stems from his utopian visions which have a global and symmetric character: He underrates human variety. Anthropology, egalitarianism, and identitarianism mar his outlook even more so than those of the European leftist.

His utopianism has other drawbacks. Utopia comes through *progress* and progress for him has an automatic character: It is one of the hidden laws of this world. Progress in his view and in the long run will always reassert itself even if, here and there, minor setbacks occur, engineered by evil reactionaries. Man is good, but reactionaries do not deserve to be treated as human beings. Thus the evils of decolonization are of short duration (as in the United States). After a slight detour the emerging nations will be safely back on the swift uphill road of progress.

All comparisons are imperfect, but in certain cases the beginnings of a "national" existence can be likened to bad starts in individual human lives, to premature births with complications creating permanent debilities and physical handicaps, infirmities that can never be straightened out. I am convinced that Hispanic America suffers from such a bad start and that it will take much time, courage, and great effort to overcome its flawed beginning. Haiti is a second case of decolonization in the Western hemisphere, but under auspices so radically different from those in the United States that it is idle to make comparisons. Boston was, in a way, another English city in 1776, but Port-au-Prince *minus the French* was not another Bordeaux or Nantes. As a matter of fact, Haiti might be a prefiguration of what tropical Africa will be like tomorrow: A dictator demanding divine honors and exploiting witchcraft à la Nkrumah, the exhibition of the decaying corpses of murdered political adversaries to a frightened populace, the establishment of concentration camps (such as Fort Dimanche), a brutal police force such as the Tonton-Macoutes, spectacular if uneconomic new cities such as Duvalierville. All this would be possible in the Africa of tomorrow—though perhaps not in the same degree, because important sectors of Africa had a longer training and education by the evil colonialists than Haiti ever had. As a matter of fact, large parts of Colonial Africa never had *serfdom* (neither did considerable parts of Europe),[21] and it always must be kept in mind that Europeans were in many ways kinder to Africans and Asians *than to each other*. The victorious Americans were harsher to the Loyalists than the French to the Tonkinese. In many ways the British were more liberal toward the Hindus after 1854 than the Union to the former Confederacy. The atrocities committed by the Belgian adventurers before the Congo became a colony are nothing compared with the delirious horrors of the Spanish Loyalists or of the Jacobins in the Vendée. And we don't even go into the savageries of the Nazis and the Stalinists, both of them boasting of being the heirs of the French Revolution.

All this shows that, contrary to the American leftist dream, progress is by no means automatic and that relapse into barbarism is always around the corner. It is true that there is a certain cumulative quality to material progress. After having made certain discoveries and inventions, man can make further advances in the same direction. Without Hertz and Clerk Maxwell there is no Marconi. Yet progress is not essentially material—unless we consider an ultramodern concentration camp with a technologically refined human slaughterhouse more "progressive" than building such as the Cathedral of Chartres or Nkrumah, who watched television, more "progressive" than King Albert of the Belgians. Progress is the assertion and the ascendancy of virtues and of wellbeing (which in turn is much more than mere comfort). Progress, however, rests on spiritual and moral foundations which are not separate but interconnected. It is obvious that if you see in man merely a biological link in an evolutionary chain (as, among others, the National Socialists did), a soulless economically conditional animal (as the orthodox Marxists do), a state subjected mammal (as the Jacobins and the Fascists did),[22] then the accumulation of material knowledge might go on, but hell can break loose any moment. Every bestiality becomes possible and compatible with either general opinion or the opinion of the responsible leaders. If the horrors perpetrated by these groups were not greater, we owe this only to the still effective "whiff from the empty bottle" of a vanishing Christian tradition. Yet the typical American leftist is in the same boat without really knowing it. He is less of a logician than his brothers under the skin in the Old World and therefore is more subject to Christian residues. But how long will this last?

Haiti was decolonized before Christianity had struck deep roots and the same process has taken place in most of Africa and in parts of Asia. Hence we have to expect among the "emerging nations" nightmares similar to those perpetrated by National Socialists, by international Socialists and by the minions of Duvalier, who are Voodooists and spiritual grandchildren of the Jacobins. When the "long-suffering" East Indians were "liberated from the British yoke" in 1948, few people in the Western world knew history sufficiently well to have real apprehensions about a negative development. The horrors of the Indian Mutiny—the Black Hole of Cawnpore 91 years earlier, were forgotten a long time ago. Here again it must be borne in mind that not only had the unification of India been the work of the British, but that India had also been liberated from the rule of a Muslim minority. India did not pass from freedom to "colonialism," but from Moghul to European sovereignty. There can be no doubt that the rule by London brought greater individual and national freedom to India than the rule from Delhi by the descendants of Mongol-Tartar invaders who were racially less akin to the Hindu than the British who, after all, are Indo-Europeans. When the British Labour Party decided to give up British rule in India the Moslems, who formed about one-fourth of the Indian population, demanded a state of their own. Since India was scheduled to become

360

a democracy where the majority rules over the minority, the pre-British masters of India did not want to fall under Hindu sway and the Hindus did not want to revert to their old rulers. The tragic answer was partition.

There was never complete agreement as to where the new border should be drawn (especially not in Kashmir). There existed, however, a considerable reluctance to leave large minorities on either side of the new demarcation line. The *Pax Britannica* had gone. Mass expulsions took place and they degenerated into the worst, the most fiendish, the most nauseating spontaneous massacres the world had ever seen. Diabolical tortures, the most nightmarish sex crimes, the most delirious blood orgies resulted in the death of *four-and-a-half million people*, perpetrated by pious Moslems and the believers in *Ahimsa*, "nonviolence." Even Gandhi's *Satyagraha* (fasting) could not stop the butchery. This incident alone—unthinkable under the British Raj—annuls the morality of such a form of independence. And actually, if one talks with the plain people in India, one finds very little enthusiasm for the present order. On the contrary, the old times appear to many as a Golden Age. Only a very small and very thin upper layer of politicians profits from this new situation, and this is true not only in India but elsewhere in the decolonized world. Again and again one meets people who inquire whether there is really no chance that the British sahib might come back. (A friend of mine was asked by a native in the Cameroons: "When is this *terrible indépendance* going to end?")

There exists a myth—and not only among American leftists—according to which the wicked Europeans with their missionaries brutally invaded overseas areas (which they often did) in order to destroy the idyllic life of the innocent natives, a life without a sense of guilt, without disease, without fear and unhappiness—all blatant nonsense. They defeated and enslaved vastly superior civilizations which merely lacked the machine gun, civilizations of a much greater spirituality, intellectuality, profundity, with a greater artistic sense and a more balanced life than ours. That is nonsense too. Anybody who knows the world and has not been seduced into building up elegiac dreams about faraway tribes and nations realizes only too well that the Dayaks, nay even the Japanese or the Aztecs, if they had been technologically able to colonize Europe, would have established an iron rule resulting in lasting tyranny.

It is quite true that European civilization exported hitherto unkown diseases and vices to a few islands. Yet European know-how finally triumphed not only over the exported diseases but also over the far more terrible local ones. The accusation that only narrow-minded missionaries gave to these "children of nature" a sense of sin and therefore caused them mental anguish is so silly that it hardly needs refutation. Most of these natural religions are based on choking fears—fear of spirits, fear of witchcraft,[23] fear of sorcerers, fear of gods. Take only one case, common in the highlands of New Guineas (Papua). There every mother must give birth to her first child in the jungle—which is also an unwritten law in large parts of Central Africa. She must then take the child firmly by its feet and bash out its brain against a stone. Then several sows who have litters are driven to that rock, and the first sow starting to munch up the little corpse becomes her comother. From the litter the poor woman has to choose a piglet which she adopts and feeds with her milk. Her attitude toward the piglet will also determine her moral standing in the community. This is her chance to demonstrate what a "good mother" she is. And this is by no means the most unappetizing performance in that area of the world: The sucking of decomposed corpses is far worse.[24]

Now, one might object that this is a "low" religion, a mere superstition of savages, and that nothing like it can be found in the higher religions of the East. Yet I remember a talk I had with a highly educated Hindu in Agra, outside the Imperial Hotel. He was a civil engineer and he had received part of his training in England. We discussed the British Raj and he admitted that it had benefited India in many ways. He added, however, that the provincialism and the narrowness of the British had been silly and harmful in many other ways. The prohibition of *suttee*, the burning of widows, is only one example. "If a woman really loves her husband she obviously wants to immolate herself. If she throws herself on the funeral pyre, she will be knocked unconscious in five to ten minutes, suffocated by the fumes if not actually killed. And then she has a chance of being reunited with her husband in another incarnation."

"You mean to say that you approve of this? Personally? Now and for every woman?" I inquired.

"Naturally. Take the case of my married sister. Her husband had a quarrel with his father and committed suicide by taking poison, cutting his wrists and hanging himself. Two days later my sister did the same. After all, what is the alternative? There is nothing worse than to live as a widow, especially in the higher castes."

"Were there any children?"

"There were three, but what are families for? They were taken care of."

In cases like these one might raise the argument that such behavior

362

is sanctioned by religion, that woman by nature is made to suffer, that the Papuan mother practicing infanticide and the Indian mother engaged in self-cremation are committing acts which really are in conformity with their beliefs, that they knew from childhood what was expected of them. In reality, however, the Papuan mother is endowed with the same maternal instincts as Mrs. Grey or Mrs. Green of the Anti-Colonial League in Kankakee, Illinois. She *does* go through agony bashing out the brains of her firstborn baby, and, as I got my Indian friend to admit, his sister acted from a sense of duty and propriety, and probably suffered enormous anguish carrying out her suicidal act. Still the man relished his sister's heroism. Societies and religious systems, however, which make such self-inflicted cruelties a norm, have to be judged negatively. "Colonialism," which tends to eliminate these precepts, is doing a good work.[25]

Here, however, we have to put in a word of warning. These horrors are not "racially conditioned." *Ideas*, primarily specific religious ideas, were or are working against them. *Ideas Have Consequences*, to use the title of the late Richard Weaver's book. We have to ask ourselves whether we too would not still be indulging in such practices without Christianity intervening (whether, without the British Raj, *suttee* would be as rare as it is now).

The "destruction" of widows is probably an ancient Aryan rite; witness the account of Ibn Fadlan, an Arab diplomat who was in a Viking town in Russia around 920, only a thousand years ago. He watched the funeral of a Nordic chieftain whose corpse was put on a riverboat. The Chief's friend raped his bride in a tent on land and then had sexual intercourse with her on the boat. After this she was held in an iron grip so that an old woman called the Angel of Death could strangle her. Finally the boat was set on fire and the two bodies were burned together—a performance surely not much more humane than *suttee* or our own legal procedures in the Middle Ages.

What efforts it took even Christianity to overcome this pagan inheritance *internally*![26] It was a slow process and a mark of *real progress* (the only kind worth mentioning). Every lapse from Christian standards brought its own retribution, an immediate relapse into barbarism. Jacob Burckhardt foresaw this when he spoke about the catastrophes to come if the level of our culture were to sink only "a hand's width. Then the pale horror of death would be over us and naked power would rule supreme."[27]

Here we also have to consider the "speed" at which the various nations progressed in different periods of history. It cannot be denied that in judging such matters we have to use rather subjective measuring rods. If we view the first 1,500 years of Western history in our terms, we might arrive at a rather interesting answer to the question how long it took our forebears, after the collapse of the Roman Empire, to reach a level of culture and civilization roughly commensurable with that of, let us say, 250 or 330 A.D. Seven hundred, eight hundred or a thousand years? A similar question might be raised in connection with the termination of European colonialism in various parts of the globe. Of course modern times are telescoped but still it is evident that the old levels cannot be reached overnight. Taking this into consideration, a phenomenon such as *Apartheid*—we mean Big *Apartheid*—must be judged somewhat more leniently than it is usually done.[28]

The fact remains that we continue to move ahead along the road of Christian development—both as a faith and as a civilization—while the newly Christianized or un-Christianized nations are trailing. This is true morally, it is true intellectually, and it is also true economically. We already mentioned the fact that, from an economic viewpoint, the colonizing powers have rarely seen their plans mature and their expectations fulfilled. The reasons why the European powers clung to their colonies, as we said before, were psychological and military rather than economic—even when nations nourished great hopes for economic gain. Their loss of colonies, needless to say, was for most colonial powers a blessing only thinly disguised, since the colonies were more often than not a constant drain on their finances. It is significant that Europe's present prosperity coincides with the loss of her colonies. Now, at long last, the former colonial powers have a chance to reach the material standards of the noncolonial powers—Scandinavia and Switzerland.

Looking at decolonization in the last twenty years, we ought to liken the colonies to adopted children of European powers, children going through the process of puberty. Adolescence is always a difficult time for children as well as parents. It is usually a period when children start to become critical of the persons exercising authority over them. Not rarely their dissatisfaction is so great that they think it would be better for them to run away—from school, from the paternal home. They are convinced that they are quite as bright, experienced, and educated as their parents. Usually, of course, they do not carry out their plans because they dimly realize that their formal training is not finished, that a start on their own would be difficult, that it would be wiser to swallow one's silly pride and stay on.

But what would happen if just outside their parental home were two powerful men with fat wallets encouraging a promising child to make the break? "The way you are being treated by your parents is a disgrace. We would never have put up with that at your age." Matters would be worse, of course, if the children were merely adopted.

This is a good analogy if we think of the elites, the *évolués*, of the colonies as adopted children, while Uncle Sam and Uncle Ivan represent the powerful men who can fleece their taxpayers at leisure. Uncle Ivan's subjects have no say in the matter and Uncle Sam's citizens have been indoctrinated by the left. If, to make the situation more troublesome, Uncle Sam and Uncle Ivan were to engage in a real competition for affection, shouting at each other, "I can be more anticolonialist than you!" while assuring the child that it would be taken care of materially, the rebellious brat could hardly be held back. He would leave home, repair to a hotel, and write blackmailing letters, playing off one big man against the other.

The foster parents, for their part, are rid of an ungrateful child, have less responsibilities and expenses, but are naturally hurt in their pride and develop a real hatred for the seducers of their adopted child with whose plight they nevertheless do not sympathize. Let them now pay through the nose! And when the two seducers—one of whom has acted in good faith prompted by idealism while the other was bent on real mischief—find that their financial resources are now being unduly strained and appeal to the former parents to contribute to the support of their ungrateful child, the latter are not receptive. They well remember the insults and invective of well-meaning Americans (as, for instance, President Roosevelt and the then Senator John F. Kennedy)[29] and are reluctant to help the "underdeveloped countries." Even the Italians were approached by the United States to participate in the aid to the "emerging nations," whereupon the Italians quite rightly replied that much of their own country, the *mezzogiorno* (Italy's Deep South) is in many ways worse off than some of the new nations beyond the seas.[30]

The aid now given can be viewed from several angles. If it were true that these hapless *quondam* colonialized peoples and tribes had been brutally exploited in the past and had also been artificially stunted in their development (as, for instance, the Poles were under the Nazi occupation), the argument might be raised that aid given to them is a compensation for the mistreatment they had suffered. This, however, is not the case. The usual outcry of the ex-colonials is that they had been insufficiently Westernized. They do complain about exploitation (as many Latin Americans do in relation to their post-liberation period), but here the dual question must be posed: What was the exploitation

365

of natural resources and manpower before the arrival of the Europeans, and what were the living standards before and at the end of the colonial period?

The Europeans and Americans have achieved their high standards after an immensely bitter uphill fight lasting 2,500 years. They have gone through agonies to arrive at their present levels. The Industrial Revolution is only one of the many periods of large-scale sacrifice. All this knowledge, all this thinking and planning and endless experimenting, all the fruits of savings, of studies, of scheming, of wars (*Polemos pater chrematon!*) have been put at the disposal of overseas peoples and nations, and in a sense, this has been done without charge. To learn, as we all know, is not always pleasant. Remember the Greek proverb: *Ho me dereis anthropos ou paideuetai*. There is no education without tears.

However, realities in politics are very often less important than myths. We have a widespread feeling between Valparaiso and Hanoi, between Jamaica and Zanzibar, that the wealth of Europe and the United States is due not only to exploitation in the past but to an economic servitude which is far from terminated and which sails under the name of "economic imperialism" or "neocolonialism." Rare is a man such as King Hassan II of Morocco who told his subjects early in 1965 that wealth does not come automatically with political independence, but only as the fruit of hard work. Early in 1961 a poster of the *Unión Republicana* could be seen in the streets of Buenos Aires which, speaking about the great natural wealth of Argentina and the misery of the masses, said: "We are poor because a treasonable government hands over the possessions of the Argentine people as a colonial tribute to her British Majesty."[31] It is obvious that this truly general feeling (which I had the opportunity to encounter in such different places as Egypt, Peru, Senegal, Cambodia, Ceylon, and Santo Domingo) is based on a variety of superficial impressions and on propaganda, not however on concrete data.[32]

Here we must bear in mind that humanity has existed probably for one-third to one-half million years and that living standards which we now call "compatible with human dignity" could be found in a few isolated areas of this globe only during the last 1,000 years and in a more general way in Europe and North America only in the last 200 years. The living standard of a skilled Swiss worker today is infinitely higher than that of professional people a century ago.

But this very recent and sporadic material progress is generally not seen as exceptional. Socialists violently protest that within a nation some people live a great deal better than others, and we encounter in the last twenty years a mounting tide of protest against differences in economic levels between nations. Just as today the poor man is prone to blame the rich man for his own indigence and considers income differences as highly "undemocratic,"[33] such differences between nations are also developing into a challenge, a piece of collective impudence. The wealth of other nations is becoming psychologically an "act of provocation," and the uncommitted left in many a Western country (and this includes America) is talking about *a real duty, a moral obligation* on the part of the richer nations toward those less well off (just as richer individuals ought to aid poorer ones). As long as this is merely a call for Christian charity, we have no quarrel at all with aid to the indigent. There are people who labor harder and are more inclined to a frugal life than others, and the same comparison can be made between nations. Thus the Italians took it for granted that the Germans who visited them were richer since they worked harder, saved more money, concentrated more on industry and banking—but on the other hand had less time for relaxed conviviality, for the *dolce far niente* and the *dolce vita*. The Italians envied the North Europeans for their money, but envied them in a civilized, moderate manner, knowing pretty well that the Northerners paid a price for it that the South Europeans were not willing to pay—in time, effort, and an ascetic way of life. There was no talk about exploitation. If anybody was exploited, it was the Northern tourist in the South who did not mind too much, until or unless he felt himself to have been excessively swindled, "taken in."

This, however, is not the mood of many overseas nations who are in the shoes of a runaway brat. This lovable child is now blackmailing Uncle Sam and Uncle Ivan at the same time. We saw the case of a Latin American republic sending trade missions simultaneously to Washington and Moscow. Obviously a crucial reason—for the "generosity" of the West is the fear that in case of nonpayment the Soviets might "muscle in"—and vice versa.[34]

But this is not the only reason. The uncommitted left in America (far more so than in Europe) is promoting this yielding to blackmail on "moral grounds" and as a move designed to foster egalitarianism. Why should economic egalitarianism be fostered merely *within* the nation? Let us carry it to the international scene! There is very little fear or realization that all this penalizing of the hardworking element (on the individual or national level) will finally act as a brake to progress, as a positive discouragement to all extraordinary effort which alone assures progress.

There is another reason why the American left favors aid to the "emerging nations." More often than not the self-appointed leaders of these nations belong to the leftist camp. Various types of socialism —"Indian socialism," "African socialism," as well as "African democracy"—are duly fostered. The handouts, as a rule, are given to *governments* and not to individual enterprises—often, to tell the truth, because the latter hardly exist. Thus the taxes of "capitalist" countries are used to finance leftist governments which, more often than not, are using them in order to (a) bolster up their oppressive regimes and (b) build up a war machine which one day might easily be used against their benefactors. Needless to say, it is a very different proposition to aid Nationalist China where not only an army is being equipped for the Western camp, but (as I know through repeated visits) the living standards of the population have been improved to the extent that we now have on Taiwan the third highest per capita incomes in Asia,[35] and this although *economic* aid has been discontinued since 1962.

Yet in many another country profiting from development grants the masses see and get very little. Certain sums disappear into the pockets of the oligarchy (which might be deep Red), others are used to equip the secret police or paramilitary formations to keep the dear subjects in check, huge sums are squandered on sumptuous buildings and other objects of no economic value, designed merely to raise the prestige of the ruling group within the country and the prestige of the "emerging nation" in the international community. It would be most interesting to learn the real expenses of the emerging nations incurred not only in the fields of policing and armaments but also in foreign representation. Today a newly appointed minister or ambassador in a capital such as Washington, London, Paris, Bonn, or Tokyo has to make at least *one hundred* "first visits" to the various foreign representatives[36]—which shows precisely to what extent the modern world with its alleged "progress" has become balkanized, atomized, fractured.

Still, although this misuse of funds from hardworking citizens (who never have been asked whether they want their monies employed in such a frequently very wasteful fashion) is regrettable, it might be argued that the erection of a sumptuous presidential palace somewhere in the tropics—infinitely more luxurious and costly than, let us say, the residence of the King of Norway—contributes in a minor way to the income of the natives hired for its construction. But obviously a sugar refinery would be a greater asset to an emerging nation's economy than a presidential palace or a mammoth "Monument to Democracy." (I have seen one in Southeast Asia, in a not at all democratically governed country.) In other words, these foreign aid funds are either "conscience money" paid because truly progressive nations are ashamed of their wellbeing or have been made to feel guilty for having carried the white man's burden in the past—or they are bribes. But are they effective as bribes? In the last few years the divine Mr. Nkrumah has received from the United States alone $160 million, Ethiopia over $200 million, Burma $120 million, Cambodia—which threw the American diplomatic representatives out—$367 million, but if we look at the voting record of these nations in the UN we will see that with few exceptions they are engaged in that popular overseas sport of biting the hand that feeds them. Americans should derive only a meager consolation from the fact that the Soviets also have "miscalculated" a few times and that the citizenry of the USSR is boiling mad about foreign aid—an indignation for which perfectly innocent overseas students, especially the Africans, are made to suffer. Talking to Russians and Ukrainians in 1963, I was informed that the economic situation in the USSR was so miserable because, due to the selfishness of the United States, it fell upon the Soviet Union to feed the starving two-thirds of the world. "And now 'they'[37] even import these black students who receive scholarships which are 50 percent higher than those given to our own boys." These African and Asian students have a real Jim Crow place for their studies in the Patrice Lumumba Friendship University located in an old barracks. I do not remember ever having seen them in the company of their Soviet colleagues of either sex.

To make matters worse there are cases when American dollars handed out as a bribe aid have been used as grants or loans to third nations. Yugoslavia, which tries to play a leading role among the "uncommitted" nations (the "Third World"), has tried to bribe its way into this illustrious society. While taking U.S. dollars with one hand she hands them out with the other. Thus the American taxpayer helps to finance Yugoslavia's foreign policy.[38] Yet even Yugoslavia had to experience what the United States and, to a lesser extent, the Soviet Union and Red China had learned: that the majority of "emerging nations" have an extraordinary firmness of character. They are for hire but not for sale. They have the character of prostitutes rather than domestic animals.

(Why are the Soviets and the Chinese more successful with smaller handouts than the United States? America is more *envied* than the two Communist powers. China, moreover, is "colored" and the Soviet emissaries, as Russians, are less "insular." The heroes of Dostoyevski are more "universally human" than the moralizing do-gooder types who so often represent America abroad.)

Apart from Taiwan, where the United States has tried with admirable

tenacity to correct her enormous errors committed on the Chinese mainland in the years 1944-1948, one sees little wisdom employed. In her
anticolonialist policy the United States, under leftist guidance, has made
mistakes very similar to those in her European policy. Here we
encounter again the assumption (dealt with in the preceding chapter)
that human beings all over the world are "more alike than unlike,"
a piece of miscalculation always connected with the silly, "Well, how
would *I* act in his place?" Yet the typical American (or Britisher or
Canadian) is radically different from the typical or average Dayak or
Khmer or Chinese or Tamil (or even Italian or Austrian): People in
given situations in given countries *do* act differently. Although I have
spent a total of fifteen years all over the United States, have read more
Americana than the average American, know more about American history and geography, and have perhaps a greater affection for the real
United States than many an American citizen, I am still in my thinking,
acting, and reacting quite different from the average American, and I
do not fool myself that it could be otherwise. As a matter of fact, when
I wrote a novel with an American background a few years ago,[39] I
did not dare to use as my leading hero a real American; I chose an
immigrant. Soviet writers, who often have to concoct novels about the
capitalist world, willy-nilly have to be propagandists, and they have
provided us with works of fiction which are unintentionally hilarious
in the extreme.[40] American writers, without undue pressure, have
depicted the European scene and European heroes and heroines—and
the result is usually disastrous. There was a whole crop of such books,
plays, and movies published during World War II.

"Tragically typical" is the history of American intervention in Vietnam. The French can point out with bitterness that, as long as they
were engaged in the struggle to hold North Vietnam against Communist
aggression, the United States did not lift a finger to help. The French,
like the Dutch in Indonesia, were convinced that Southeast Asia was
not ready to resist the assault of the forces of decomposition and
tyranny. They were obviously not afraid of *local* decadent ideas but
rather of ideologies which either had failed in Europe or had established
unspeakable tyrannies: communism, socialism, Jacobinism, nationalism, National Socialism, one-party tyranny of an authoritarian character, or nationalistic communism. And after the "Colonialists" had left
there never was a question in Southeast Asia *or anywhere else overseas*
of restoring forms of government or social systems which had prevailed
prior to the arrival of the European powers. As a matter of fact, if
such local, such "native" forms continued to exist (or coexist) under

colonial rule or protection, they now were crushed, persecuted, snuffed out. *So great is the hatred* of the new "nationalistic" masters for their own native traditions, so abject their admiration for the worst ideologies, for the fecal matter of the West.

The elimination of Dutch power in Indonesia under the threats of Washington, just as the fall of French power in Indochina, was applauded by the American left as an evolution in the direction of "progress." Yet in whatever direction we look, we see that decolonization has never meant *material or practical progress*, nor even *political advance*. If we eliminate entirely the religious (missionary) viewpoint from our speculations, we have put at least these two aspects under the magnifying glass. The material decay is obvious and intimately connected with the lessened internal security through brigandage and revolutionary movement. Yet it might be argued that, had the Portuguese handed Java over to the native princes instead of to the Dutch, this return to local ("native") government then and there (in the seventeenth century) would have been quite sensible. In the meantime, however, the globe entered a period of Westernization, and political independence in the twentieth century means joining a more or less Westernized society of nations. For this task the new ruling groups, classes, and cliques are not really prepared, the masses, obviously, even far less so. Whatever our view about the United Nations—and it is indeed a rather dim one we have to take—it is based on a Western concept: International trade, stock exchanges, currency regulations, the world of diplomacy, international traffic, cooperation between police forces, disease control and sanitary laws, international scientific bureaus and educational systems—all these are Western, Western, Western. The Sultan of Jokjakarta on Java in the seventeenth century could easily have taken over after a Portuguese evacuation of his domain, reassuming local rule with few outside contacts. Today the birth of a new nation means facing the entire gradually Westernized globe with its institutions and currents and cooperating with it. And for this dangerous existence in a strange world the new nations were and are totally unprepared.

The damage done by present-day anticolonialism, American or other, is enormous. It will take a long, long time until the ill effects of this premature birth will disappear. Countries such as Haiti, Bolivia, or Guatemala to this day are suffering from their acquisition of "freedom"—which took place a century-and-a-half ago.[41] Will they or the new batch of "emerging nations" ever recover? Or will they, like a baby, crippled in the process of birth, suffer from it all through their existence?

Chapter 19

The New Left

To begin with, the New Left is not so very new and it is not genuinely left either. Its existence, however, cannot be understood without a knowledge of the leftish soil in which the new plant started to grow. Furthermore, this newcomer on our ideological scene must be viewed as a reaction against our present profoundly left-influenced culture and civilization. Here we also have to face the fact that much of the New Left's critique of our way of life is—unknowingly rather than knowingly—copied from conservative sources. Finally, one can only fully comprehend the New Left if one realizes that it happens to be tied in with the student movement, the "academic unrest,"[1] as well as with the worldwide disillusionment with the Classic Left, which by now is morally bankrupt. (Moral bankruptcy, unfortunately, causes physical decline only in the very long run.) In its refusal to yield to the right, the New Left, moreover, shows us its profile against the background of all the many gruesome failures of the leftist movements, the leftist establishments which have accumulated in the last 200 years. Yet it is equally certain that the New Left cannot take over the receivership, the inheritance of the Great Leftist Drive because it offers no real alternatives: Unlike genuine leftism it has produced neither a coherent ideology nor a concrete utopia. It offers criticisms but no real answers.

Let us first look at the geographic origins of the New Left. In 1918 we have grave political disorders at the University of Córdoba in Argentina. The year 1918 was bad and Córdoba has bad memories. The Córdoba massacres in the 1820s mark a low point in Argentine history, a low point not so easily overcome.[2] After 1918 the disease spread in a northwestern direction, reaching the oldest university of the Americas, San Marcos in Peru eight years afterward. Under the leadership of young Victor Raúl Haya de la Torre (later to become the leader of the leftist APRA) the students succeeded in forcing the authorities to grant them comanagement (*cogobernación*).[3] This thoroughly ruined the university which to this day has not overcome either ideologically or academically, this particular shock. After World War II the anarchical student unrest gripped Japan, where authority, *all* authority had been gravely shaken by utter defeat. The virus then crossed the Pacific again and affected the third seismic area, California. From there it was carried to the Eastern United States and then made its appearance in West Berlin, the European point of infection. This is not surprising because West Berlin has no conscription laws and thus became the haven for draft-dodgers from the Federal German Republic. The student rebellion then quickly spread to Frankfurt and from there to Paris, Rome, and Madrid.

There are good reasons for this development which, so far, has spared the Nordic countries from England to Finland. In Latin America we have not only the Catholic faith with all its anarchical implications[4] but also the specific irrationalism of that part of the world which had been so cleverly described by Count Keyserling—the emphatically emotional way of life determined by *gana*, by "disposition" and "indisposition," by "likes" and "dislikes" rather than by logic, reason, and planning.[5] If we recall the terrible words of the deeply disappointed Simón Bolívar about his countrymen, we can well understand how the New Left came to have South American origins.[6] The Japanese student troubles (started by the *Zengakuren*) followed upon a total breakdown while the American disorders had a rather different character. Certainly the steady decay of authority is a natural phenomenon in a gradually democratized society when parental authority[7] (as the last stronghold) slowly vanishes, but there are also other and probably stronger factors which will be dealt with presently. The German "infection" is not at all surprising in view of the fact that Western Germany is the most "Americanized" country in Europe, the country where the experiment of (leftish) reeducation and indoctrination had been carried out with the greatest intensity. As a result the American imported New Left could quickly strike roots, and this all the more so as the three most important New Left ideologues had lived as German refugees in America: Theodor W. Adorno, Max Horkheimer, and Herbert Marcuse who alone stayed on in the New World, whereas Adorno and Horkheimer returned to their native country.

Viewed from a biological angle, the New Left movement is carried largely by the young, but its original minds belong to men of an advanced age, to a European generation which has become successively disillusioned by Wilhelminian *grand-bourgeois* Germany, the Weimar Republic, Nazi totalitarianism, Stalinist communism, and the materialistic society of consumers. Having been formally on the left (and often still publicly professing to be so), they have seen all their gods fail, all their illusions destroyed.

None of the three could or would deny their original leftist outlook. Yet it was far more young Marx, the frustrated artist, the "libertarian," the Herostratic visionary, than old Marx, the inverted commercialist, who inspired them in their thinking. At the same time their vision remained riveted on *freedom* and this, without their ever openly and directly admitting it, put them into the neighborhood of the *anarchists* rather than of the Communists. Their criticism of "bourgeois" society is perhaps even more savage than that of the deep Red Marxists—and it is more sincere, more to the point, because Sovietism is essentially petty bourgeois and bureaucratic, it has no affinity with the bohemian, the artist, the intellectual hungry for originality, the free peasant, the aristocrat.[8]

Marx's lasting enthusiasm for the working class was due to his belief that within the framework of bourgeois society the factory hand would be condemned forever to a life of misery in eternal bondage. He never realized (as Marcuse, Adorno, and Horkheimer did very clearly) that modern technological society, with or without exploitation, could even provide the working man with a middle-class existence, with a great deal of security, a modicum of luxury, a minimum of work. Though revolutionary at heart, the New Left had to abandon its innermost hopes for a revolutionary rising of a no longer existing proletariat now integrated with all its material interests into the process of production.[9] In addition, no modern industrialist wants merely to exploit his workers —they should be happy, well-paid consumers. The utter inanity of Marxian economics[10] is now evident and thus the person who is first and foremost a revolutionary and merely seeks for a rational excuse—an intellectual overstructure—to preach the overturn of the existing order, has to look in other directions, toward other social layers to whom to preach the revolutionary gospel. In this case the ideologies of the New Left appeal to the outcasts of modern society, the eternal *Lumpenproletariat*, the term to be understood not only in the sociological

374

sense.[11] The call for destruction without any constructive or even utopian blueprint is also somehow in keeping with the spirit of our fast-living time which quickly forgets the past and shrinks from looking to the future—described no longer by the Bellamys, but by the Huxleys and Orwells (hence *also* the reluctance to have any or many children).[12]

The present order, no doubt, is iniquitous in many ways. However, life according to Christian precepts, is a vale of tears and the "pursuit of happiness" on this earth is more or less bound to fail. Christianity does not eliminate suffering, but gives sense to it. It does not make people "happy"; it offers joy and by giving a sense to suffering, *prevents despair*. We have to admit that the present state of our Western civilization (and of the rest of the world as well) is worse than has been in almost any period of history. In spite of good dentists, anesthetics, better health conditions, moon flights, television, birth control, and a greatly decreased mortality, it would be easy to prove that human *un*happiness has reached a very high level. Fear, loneliness, alienation, aimlessness, anguish, and melancholia are more prevalent than ever. There is not the slightest reason to believe that "progress" has made people happier. It has (above all in its technological form) an inflationary character. Technology moreover means more regulation, the need for more controls; it increases responsibilities, makes us more dependent, more vulnerable.

All this is evident to the New Left which therefore assumes the antitechnological stand of young Marx. Not only in this respect, but in many other ways, the New Left repeats knowingly-unknowingly the nineteenth-century conservatives' critique of modern society. When the latter felt that they were defeated, that the immediate future belonged to "progressive" industrial society, their prophecy as to the shape of things to come was roughly this: "You think that you can establish a social, political, economic order based merely on the profit motive, that you can achieve happiness for yourselves or for the masses with the aid of technology, medicine and the provider state. You think that your 'system,' your establishment, will guarantee liberty for everybody, that you will be able to eliminate a feeling of inner independence by destroying the old historic estates. You are wrong! You will actually lay the foundations of a society in which servitude will assume a more subtle, more ubiquitous, a more oppressive character than ever before. Life will cease to have color, to be spiced with adventure, and people will revolt against the inhuman boredom and the drabness you offer them. In the long run man will not be satisfied with a social system giving him nothing but security and a near anonymous government of laws and regulations—rotating, impersonal, lacking all glamor. Emperors, kings, princes, cardinals, bishops, and noblemen will be replaced by general directors, bureaucrats, manufacturers, bankers, trade union leaders, party bosses, and dictators: This will make rule not less burdensome, only duller and, in many ways, more oppressive. Young people especially will rebel against an order based on the counting of noses, an order giving them nothing to live or to die for. Once all great dreams are gone, this society of identical and equal people in their purposeless solitude will start to scream!''

Indeed, if we read Marcuse carefully, we shall discover just these accusations, just this lament. Theodor Adorno has actually intimated that ''reactionary'' arguments should be used for the Second Enlightenment, the New Left. [13]

Yet, as was to be expected, the masses, especially the working class, could not be won over to the New Left because—as its ideologues fully realize—the wage earners have at long last achieved middle-class living standards, and are not (and never will be) prepared to sacrifice them to some rather sophisticated doctrine without ''practical'' aims and material rewards. Marxism could be popularized, the New Left with its sophisticated intellectual somersaults cannot. The worker, as we said, has been totally assimilated by the industrial machine which might offer him extremely monotonous work but at least feeds him well. The financial interests of workers, management, and investors are, in fact, identical—a maximum of production, an optimum of sales.

The more moderate New Left had unforeseen experiences with the young generation. It was only a question of time until, thanks to the innate radicalism of the young, old sorcerer's apprentices would find themselves first isolated and then ridiculed as timid innovators lacking the courage to draw the final deductions from their daring premises. No wonder Professor Marcuse was lambasted and shouted down at an international student congress in Rome by Daniel Cohn-Bendit, the French-German student leader, and that Theodor Adorno was indirectly murdered by his followers. In one of his last lectures at Frankfurt University a number of female students stripped to the waist and tried to kiss the dazed scholar who fled with tears in his eyes. To the press he declared that this, indeed, was not the evolution he had hoped for, that his aims and ideas had been completely misunderstood. A few weeks later he succumbed to a heart attack in Switzerland. The third founder of the New Left, Professor Max Horkheimer, a particularly close friend of Theodor Adorno, has since been moving in another direction. In an interview [14] he declared that man can be properly understood only by taking his *transcendent* character into account, and that we have to return to theology, a declaration which caused shrieks of indignation from pious agnostics and atheists.

Yet, regardless of whether we look at the founders or at their undisciplined and even more confused disciples, the fact remains that the New Left no longer is basically left: It rather represents an *inverted* mental product of the Old Left plus a number of Rightist *vistas*, though not enough to make it a rightist movement. It is anticonservative inasmuch as it rejects and fights the existing order, the establishment. Yet rightism is not conservative either in a strict etymological sense, since, after all, the present is largely leftist inspired. In fact, as we shall see later, conservatives are not always bent on preserving whatever exists; they are, in a basic sense, far more evolutionary, far more nonconformist than either the Old or the New Left.[15] What the New Left has in common with the rightist outlook is only a critique—the critique of the materialist, technological "identitarian" consumer society dominated by anonymous forces. Nevertheless, mere analogies do not determine the essence of a movement or a political-social philosophy. The Nazi Third Reich was a provider state: Sweden and New Zealand, too, are typical provider states. This obviously does not mean that the Third Reich with its biological identitarianism was basically similar to and animated by the same moral and political outlook as either Sweden or New Zealand.

If we now ask why the New Left has not developed a constructive program, a blueprint, a utopia all its own, we find several reasons. We already alluded to the fact that mankind today is not "futuristic" and that the typical New Lefter lacks all family sense, all generational vistas. Also, curiously enough, a certain rather anti-ideological substratum can be observed in the New Left and, consequently, a real aversion to produce a precise program. Any program already smacks of "prescription" in the Kirkian sense. Whenever I asked young New Lefters about their New Order the answer was that this problem is to be settled by discussion after "victory." Debate and discussion—they are the delight of the ill-prepared, inexperienced, unread theoretician. Talking to a group of Catholic Bolivian students of the New Left persuasion about their vision of a "New Bolivia," I found that their only immediate aim was the *destruction* of the entire old order. Unpleasantly winking, they told me that it would not be difficult to occupy the waterworks of the city of La Paz, as well as the electric plants, and thus force the surrender of the capital. And what if the government was not going to yield? What about the 400,000 inhabitants? Would they not have to leave the city? What would happen to the hospitals? The insane asylums? The homes for the aged? They could not have cared less. Liberation always has a high price. And the new order? That would be debated, discussed.

The whole student movement from Tierra del Fuego to Tokyo and Berlin is characterized by the shortsightedness and the cruelty of youth.[16] To be sure, certain external reasons made this large-scale rebellion altogether possible. In many parts of the world a degree of prosperity reigns which most of us have not become used to. Before World War II students had to study very hard and frequently also to work. Today they have parents willing to shell it out for them. And this all the more so, as these have abdicated morally and intellectually. Whatever their conviction, they frequently see in the Left the "Wave of the Future" and thus are afraid, unprepared, and unwilling to criticize the views of their enthusiastic progeny. Not only have they, without any true religious convictions, parroted the precepts of Christian ethics, often paying mere lip service without living up to them, they have also failed politically. In America the generation of the parents and grandparents died on battlefields all over the world only to usher in an age of deadly fear of an atomic World War III. In Germany one grandfather has betrayed the Kaiser, the other the Weimar Republic, the father Adolf Hitler. The young men in Germany have become, in the words of Armin Mohler, *die Richterknaben*, the "boy-judges" who sit in judgment over their fathers.[17] An analogous situation exists in Italy, Spain, France, Japan, and Austria. And now these rather despised but prosperous fathers tend to buy the affection of their offspring with permissiveness and hard cash. Thus the young generation of the middle and upper classes is given "freedom" when they are most in need of guidance and authority, and the means enabling them to loaf, demonstrate, and smoke pot rather than study and work. *Without strong ideals* (religious or other) young men and women of considerable vitality will almost automatically become "rebels without cause" and, if imbued with purely negative and critical ideas lacking a concrete aim, they will surrender to purely destructive instincts.[18] Vandalism and nihilism of a physical or intellectual order will be the result. This goes hand in hand with a process of depersonalization. Eros is replaced by mere sex, and the debasement of sex assumes a cardinal role in the New Left "philosophy"; by destroying "taboos" it strikes at the very roots of life.[19] The negation of all ties ends in promiscuity, in a flight from life through drugs, and in a consuming hatred for every form of organic existence.[20] Nihilism *is* diabolism since everything created by God or man has a positive value. Satan thrives on nothingness, on not-being.[21]

Old classic leftism likes to destroy, but only in order to replace memories of the past with a vision of the future. It aims at the establishment of a cast-iron order, at symmetry, at monolithic sameness: The young New Left, on the contrary, delights in disorder and chaos. An "authoritarian person" might be neatly dressed and scrupulously clean,[22] whereas the typical representative of the New Left loves sloppiness, informality, and the reflection of his mental disorderliness in his appearance, in his entire way of life. His parents worshiped the Golden Calf. He venerates the Golden Swine.[23] The New Left represents the left's suicidal conquest of the children of the so-called exploiters. It is suicidal because the young *bourgeois* who turns to the New Left is no more a genuine leftist than an albino in the Central Congo is a "white man." The authentic left might *occasionally* use the destructivism of the New Left as an aid in the struggle against the forces of "reaction," but it will always be highly suspicious of its "progeny" because it retains a live memory of anarchism, its old competitor from the days of Bakunin, Kropotkin, Ravachol, and Dieudonné.

The New Left has shown that it can successfully disrupt, that it can gravely upset, if not all but paralyze the public order. In May 1968 the revolutionary efforts of the New Left made a strong bid for the cooperation of the French working class, but failed—except in a few isolated cases. However, the fact remains that France, as in May 1958, was again within inches of a military dictatorship, the army having been ready to act if the near-revolutionary riots had not stopped.[24] The Communist party was put on the spot. Neither daring to disavow "the young" completely nor to side with them openly since they subscribe to a law and order program *of their own*, the Communists found themselves between the devil and the deep sea. And, at the same time, there arose among the masses a feeling of silent but furious opposition against this new menace, and it was not long before the right triumphed at the elections.

The same reaction could be observed in other countries. During the grave Frankfurt riots wives of workers were seen hitting the demonstrating students with heavy umbrellas and shouting, "Go back to your university and study. After all, we're paying for it!"[25] They knew that almost none of these students were the sons and daughters of working men who, if they make the grade, study very hard, and do not want to endanger their scholastic progress. Alfred von Thadden, leader of Germany's national-authoritarian NDP,[26] declared that he knows how to deal with rioting students: he would send two brigades of hardworking, tax-paying factory hands to the respective universities to clean them up.[27] A significant thing happened in Italy: Pier Paolo Pasolini, a leading Communist poet and movie director wrote a piece of poetry which might almost be called an "Ode to the Police" in which the author sides with the Forces of Order (sons of workers and peasants, after all) against the sons of the fat bourgeoisie who attacked and vilified them.[28] In other words, the "Student Revolt" of dirty, bearded, well-heeled quarter-intellectuals[29] might evoke—and is in the process of evoking—something very close to a Fascist reaction in the lower classes. Over in Vietnam, among the young men in the armed forces, one can already observe the steady rise of such sentiments. They feel literally betrayed by those young men and women whose parents can afford to send them to colleges, to graduate and postgraduate schools to escape conscription; but, instead of keeping mum and lying low, these draft-dodgers impudently try to play the role of real saviors of humaneness and humanity. Once they have seen the ghastly horrors of Vietcong atrocities,[30] the American soldiers in Southeast Asia, certainly a rough sometimes even brutal crowd, know the political scores on this globe infinitely better than the screaming and shouting bearded spooks back home, who display their heroic virtues only in face of defenseless college administrators or nearly defenseless policemen. They may yet achieve their immediate aim, i.e., to bring down American (or European) universities to the level of the Latin American ones which started so much of the trouble.[31] But, oddly enough, our "saviors" forget that man is a dialectic creature and that their actions provoke reactions. These reactions might be made much worse than whatever caused them. Many countries today are dangerously near to the same spot Germany was in 1932; in spite of a lack of well-organized nationalistic mass movements, the similarities are ominous, to say the least.[32]

It is touching to see how the New Left, a romantic movement not so unlike the one that "carried" young Marx, is engaged in a cult of heroes. These may only be lugubrious assassins or hairbrained intellectuals such as Castro, Guevara, Debray, Torres, Dutschke, Teufel, Cohn-Bendit, Mao, Ho Chi Minh or Thich Tri Quan,[33] but they are literally worshiped. The New Leftists want leaders. Still, in summing up the situation, we must not forget that the New Left expresses certain truths and truisms and provides us with not a few straws in the wind. However immature, destructive, sterile, and confused, it is a cry of anguish and protest against a mechanized, profoundly leftish age. It is, in a sense, leftism to end all leftism.

Chapter 20

Conservatives and Liberals

It might come as a surprise to American and British readers that today Conservative *parties* in Europe exist exclusively in countries which are predominantly "Protestant." This is certainly true as far as the conservative label goes. One might, naturally, argue that the CSU (Christian Social Union) of Bavaria is more or less a conservative party and the same can be said of the Austrian *Volkspartei*. Before the Soviet expansion there was no "Conservative party" in either Poland, Hungary or Czechoslovakia. This is not only due to the "unpopularity" of the conservative cause—"conservative" to the popular mind means "no progress"—but also to the revolutionary and anarchical temper of the Catholic nations. The situation overseas is not very different either.[1] And it is equally significant that, North or South, due to a similar lack of mass appeal the Liberal parties are small. The only sizeable liberal party exists in Switzerland which has escaped the impact of two World Wars.[2] Today these liberal parties could as well be called denominationally neutral (if not slightly "anticlerical"), parties of an upper-middle-class pattern. They are in many ways conservative. In the past, however, in the days of pre-, early, and old liberalism, the parties and factions under the liberal banner had often not only a *grand bourgeois* but even an aristocratic character. Liberal monarchs were not rare, not even in the House of Hapsburg—witness Joseph II,[3] Leopold II, Franz Josef. Frederick II of Prussia and Catherine II of Russia were liberals in a sense, and personal friends of Voltaire[4] that arch-preliberal. The prototype of the autocratic, nay, tyrannic "liberalizer" was, of course, Peter the Great.[5] Like Atatürk, he hanged people because they did not want to become "free," "modern," "progressive." The desire to compel change can lead to far greater oppression than the reluctance toward change. This is not surprising because the ordinary man is not at all eager to change existing conditions, until or unless he is in desperate straits. For this reason alone revolutions of the "Progressivists" have resulted in worse bloodshed than traditional ones. The pressure they had to apply was always much greater. The new shoe always pinches more than the old one.

At the same time it is obvious that the conservative aim cannot be a totally static world, because that is undesirable and impossible. It would be *inhuman*. The "state" and "society" of the ants, the termites, or the bees are completely immutable. Man is always faced with change—be it revolutionary (involving destruction) or evolutionary. If evolution is not revolution in slow motion (this also exists) it will be characterized by accretion and synthesis; and if it does move in the right direction, it can indeed be called "progress." In the Church, for instance, this would be the *profectus ecclesiae* of which more than fifteen hundred years ago St. Vincent of Lérins spoke in his *Commonitorium*. An evolution of this sort is necessary and salutary. There must be action among men and there must be thought, and with these two elements in the Western World change is unavoidable. The problem is to achieve organic progress, which means the preservation of real values, the resuscitation of past, forgotten or abandoned values, and the addition of new values harmonizing with the patrimony we have received. Of course not everything that is old or taken over from the preceding generation is good; not everything seemingly brand new is bad. (There is very little that is brand new!) Man is created in the image of God, he is the measure,[6] he has to evaluate the concrete things and the abstract thoughts he encounters. The Christian is "priest and king." He participates in the Royal Priesthood of all believers.[7] He is emphatically not a parrot or an automaton, not a slave or an IBM machine.

Nor is the Christian a reactionary. Those who use the conservative label are, at times, unfortunately mere *reactionaries*, which means that they react with hostility against new trends, often against *all* new trends. There are many aspects to Luther, but *as* an enemy of the Renaissance and of Humanism he was a reactionary. There is one aspect to Metternich which is also reactionary. (Other aspects make him a product of Enlightenment,[8] others a prophet and seer of extraordinary perception.) In other words, there are "conservatives" who in reality react only negatively to existing trends. Usually such an attitude is sentimental rather than rational, or it is merely based on rationalizations of sentiments and emphatically not on cold reason. The case of the reactionary is very similar if not identical to that of the "uncommitted leftist" who is uncritical (and in this word lies the key) toward the order of the day, who says uncritically "yes" to currents or events which he believes to be leading to *his* utopia. (Sometimes he cheats and adjusts his utopias to the "straws in the wind.") In other words, the reactionary is a no-man and the non-Marxist leftist is a yes-man. This is the reason why I personally prefer the reactionary as a representative of the human race to the leftist, the "liberal" in the debased and perverted American usage. I respect more the man who wants to swim against the stream than the one who is determined to ride "the wave of the future." After all, he who wants to reach the sources has to swim against the current: There is always something honorable in swimming against the current—even if it is quixotic. I also find somewhat more reasonable the man who looks backward (into the known) than the one who pretends to know all about the future, which is unknown and, except for the seer, unknowable. I consider more rational the person who clings to existing foundations or to a cellar than the man who tries to climb roofs over nonexistent buildings.

Still, the reactionary position should be rejected as antirational. Reason rather than sentiment is the distinguishing mark separating man from beast. Naturally reason, wrongly employed, perverted and under the yoke of emotions, is worse than mere sentimentalism[9]—and this, precisely, was the "rationalism" of the Enlightenment. God created man, after all, in such a way that his head is *above* his heart.

It is, however, this false rationalism of the dying eighteenth century[10] which created a reaction against reason, and this particular reaction again affected not only the nascent conservative camp of the early nineteenth century but even the Catholic Church. (One cannot blame the faiths of the Reformation for their attitude, since antirationalism belongs *organically* to their theology.)[11] Instances of anti-intellectualism (which is closely related to antirationalism) in Catholic theology are the more surprising since scholasticism is the grandfather of modern rationalism.[12] The revival of scholasticism in Catholic theology was delayed until the last quarter of the nineteenth century. The Encyclical *Aeterni Patris* was promulgated in 1879. Then, as we know, there appeared in Catholic theology a scholastic ubiquity and exclusiveness which were particularly noticeable in America.[13]

When we speak of conservatism on the European Continent we are talking not only about a movement (though not a mass movement) but also about a *coherent set of ideas*. Whereas the term movement might be criticized because it imparts the notion of a large number of people with identical sentiments developing a dynamism based on numbers, there can be no doubt that Continental conservatism represents a *doctrine* or, much better, a variety of related doctrines. It would not be completely illegitimate to talk, *horribile dictu* about an "ideology," a *Weltanschauung*, *mirovozzreniye*,[14] or *világnézet*. Continental conservatism also represents an effort to establish a synthesis of irrational and rational values in which the irrational values are never antirational but belong to the category of suprarationality, to a realm which has not been conquered intellectually and perhaps might never fall entirely under the sway of human reason. Continental conservatism represents a philosophy of life, a *practical* philosophy, yet one to be exercised by a philosopher as Unamuno ideally conceived him: "Man ought to be a philosopher not only with his reason, but also with his will, his sentiments, his flesh and his senses, with his whole soul and his whole body."[15] In other words, Continental conservatism is intellectual though not cerebralist. Joseph de Maistre, one of the first systematic conservatives, wrote in his "Letter to a Royalist from Savoy": "You must know how to be royalists: In the past this conviction was based on an instinct; today it is scientific."[16]

The term *conservatif*, *conservateur* in the political sense, like the term liberal, originated on the Continent. The French were the inventors, and when it was introduced in Britain for party purposes in the 1830s, it was not accepted without a struggle. Sir Robert Peel protested against this label for the reformed Tory Party as "un-English," but he yielded later and used the un-English term. An endeavor was made to rename the Tories "Constitutionalists" and this effort was repeated in the 1880s but without success. Lord Randolph Churchill, who belonged to the leftmost wing of the Conservative party, called himself a "democratic Tory." Today parties calling themselves conservative exist in Great Britain, Denmark, Sweden, Switzerland, and Canada. Then there are conservative parties which use other labels. The Anti-Revolutionary party of the Netherlands is Calvinist in inspiration and most decidedly conservative in outlook. The Monarchist parties of Italy are conservative and so are, up to a point, the Liberal parties of Australia, Italy, and India (i.e., "Swatantra"). Italy's *Democristiani* and the Christian-Social party of Belgium have conservative wings. Conservative thought, however, exists in many other countries, layers, and groups, especially in "study circles," *Kreise*, especially in Germany. Quite a number of periodicals are conservative in policy and appeal.

Yet, as the reader probably senses, conservatism on the Continent and in Britain are not the same. Systemization and absolutism in thought are alien to the relativistic post-Protestant mind and just as the Labour party by and large was the first to drop orthodox Marxism, British conservatives, representing a party with its roots deep in British soil, eschewed at the very beginning the notion that a conservative could espouse a whole coherent body of doctrine. The Conservative, then, is a gentleman, and a gentleman (British version) is not in need of elaborate ratiocinations. Life to him is a series of attitudes, a way of behavior, an instinctive knowledge of the right thing to do, a positive reaction to everything "natural" (in a deeper sense), and a healthy suspicion of "constructions," of length and involved argumentation, of intellectual formulations of what to him is obvious. Needless to say, there is much that is aristocratic about the British Conservative, much that Britain consciously-subconsciously inherits from Greek *kalokagathia*.[17] This is not so on the Continent where the predominant religion is Catholic, where the rational scholastic background is stronger, where the "cleric" had an influence at least equal to if not greater than the nobleman's. Yet the "cleric" was originally not only a priest but also professor. The nobility, moreover, in some countries (Italy, for instance) was always strongly urbanized and not agrarian. There exists a certain tendency in various aristocracies to be leery of intellectuality, a tendency which, more often than not, has a military or agrarian background. But it is strongly developed only in the British upper crust[18] (and, for good reasons, is absent in the Boston Brahmin set which is neither military nor markedly agrarian, but urban).

Commercialism and industry, which want to "get things done," are also frequently "anti-intellectual." Here we get the clash between the "doers" and the "talkers." This combination of an industrial-commercial with an agrarian-military-naval upper crust created a general anti-intellectual atmosphere in Britain, and this inevitably had a greater impact on the conservatives than on the leftist (Laborite) attitude. The Laborites as a Socialist party are a Continental if not an international party—and this in spite of their amazing parochialism. There is such a thing as the parochially minded internationalist, and he is indeed also to be found in America, which a German author once called a *Grossinsel*, a gigantic island wedged in between three oceans and the Caribbean.

What we have said of Britain is true *mutatis mutandis* of the United

States. The intellectualized aristocracy of the United States consists even today only of thin layers on the East Coast, and here and there in the rest of the country. The captains of industry and the big traders are not excessively given to thought and art. Therefore the intellectual life of America gets little human, little moral, though often a substantial material aid from them, and, unfortunately, they do not often reflect whom and what they are supporting. The result is that intellectual and artistic life in the United States is not tied to conservative thought, and conservatives until very recently were not overly interested in intellectual and artistic affairs. All this had nothing to do with the totally fallacious concept of the "young nation" which allegedly has to "mature" in order to develop a dynamic intellectual and artistic life. (Luxor, Karnak, Mohenjo-Daro are "young," the Acropolis is older, present-day American culture and civilization—as an integral part of the West—are *very old* because they have such a long prehistory!) An Oxford don (just like a "long-haired" American professor) is always in danger of appearing as a funny figure to his countrymen. A professor of the Sorbonne, on the other hand, until recently was a demigod, a member of the French Academy a god. And the son of a Ruhr industrialist who is a self-made man will consider it natural that he study to become a *doctor utriusque iuris* (doctor of civil and canonic law). The obsession with *la pensée, les lettres et les arts* in France is just as great as the preoccupation with *Kultur* in Germany or with *Kul'tura* in Russia.

Since the intellectual will always have a natural inner leaning towards systemized thought, the Continental conservative will tend in the same direction. In other words, he will be an ideologist. (This term, by the way, has been coined by Napoleon, the devoted empiricist.) Thus it would not be surprising to see a German book called *Die Welt-anschauung eines Konservatives* whereas it would be rather odd to find one entitled *The Conservative Ideology* written or published in America or Britain. Here let us return to our question: "Is there really a basic difference between Anglo-Saxon and Continental conservatism?" And *if* the difference is not so marked: "Are we faced with two ideologies, one systematic and the other loosely constructed?" Geography in these matters is of importance. The word Tory, after all, originally had an Irish and Catholic (Jacobite) implication. The term Whig is Scottish and Presbyterian. The word conservative in its political implications was born in France, the word *liberal* in Spain, the word socialist in England.[19] All this, perhaps, is not so accidental.

This introduction is necessary to remind the American and the British reader that the formulations, "Conservatism is opposed to all ideology" and "Conservativism is alien to intellectuality" have only local significance. From these formulations to John Stuart Mill's high-handed declaration that the Conservative party is the "stupid party," the distance is not so very great.

Conservativism on the Continent was based on disciplined thought from the start. Chronologically it falls into the period of late Romanticism and opposes ideas and ideologies emanating from the sentimental disorders of early Romanticism. Its opponent is the French Revolution (including the Napoleonic aftermath) with its egalitarianism, nationalism, and laicism. But, as it so often happens in the battle of ideas, the good old principle *fas est ab hoste doceri* is applied a great deal too liberally, with the result that early nineteenth-century conservativism has a rigidity and harshness reminding us of the hard school through which these early conservatives had to go: the school of the French Revolution and the interminable sanguinary wars caused by the Napoleonic aftermath.[20] Their school, as we said, was tough and therefore an element of severity and repression characterizes early conservativism, a certain belief in force if not in brutality, an unwillingness to enter any sort of dialogue or to conduct a gentle and shrewd reeducation of its opponents. One does not discuss with assassins from whom one never expected humaneness, leniency, or tolerance.[21] They must be mastered, fought, jailed and, if worst comes to worst, locked up or exiled. In view of the horrors of the French Revolution and Napoleon's trail of blood all over Europe from the gates of Lisbon to the heart of Moscow, this attitude is not surprising.

Continental conservatism was liberal only inasfar as it was a continuation of the *Ancien Régime*—which it was only in parts. Yet "popular movements," movements of the masses, are automatically more sanguinary than reactions coming from small elitarian minorities. The collectivist left always wanted and, if in power, has tried to exterminate minorities—royalty, aristocrats, priests, "bourgeoisie," intellectuals, Jews, "capitalists," bankers. *It never happened the other way round*. There never has been an attempt from the most fanatical reactionaries to exterminate workers or farmers. And something similar is true of verbal warfare. There exists a whole polemical literature charging minorities with every imaginable or unimaginable vice and describing in detail their evil character. Yet who would dare to denounce the character of one's own country's entire working class? Or its peasantry? In his memoirs a former butler might denigrate a duke (or, even better, a duchess) who once employed him: a lovely piece of scandal titillating the prurient. But what duke would write an abusive book about his former butler? This, indeed, would be considered a total denial of the principle of *noblesse oblige*.

Let us admit that the older conservativism on the Continent had a strongly authoritarian bent and that it operated with affirmations which brooked no discussion. Much of conservative thought had been stimulated by Edmund Burke whose speeches and letters had been translated into several languages, but this Whig infusion did not generate much flexibility. The idea that one could rule *fruitfully*, effectively and efficiently through an executive of policemen, *gendarmes*, informers, and jail wardens was (let us admit it) pretty widespread. This is the way Metternich was running Central Europe. Foreign armies intervening to crush local revolts did the rest. Yet early conservatism, we must bear in mind, was only authoritarian: It was never totalitarian. Its weakness was that the pendulum had turned: The image of man was no longer Roussellian. Europe had practically gone back to Calvin without having stopped at St. Thomas Aquinas.

Unfortunately, as we see, the worm of reaction was at work in early conservatism. It was unfriendly to popular representation in many forms[22] and had a bias against republican forms of government under almost any circumstances. Thus the Congress of Vienna (which strongly reflected conservative feelings and views) transformed the Dutch Republic with its hereditary stadholder into a kingdom reuniting the two constituent parts of the Netherlands which had been separated since 1579. The old Italian aristocratic republics of Venice and Genoa were incorporated into neighboring countries and the only remaining *independent* republic in Europe was Switzerland. (There were, of course, the small German city republics, and Cracow, San Marino, and Andorra—places of no importance.)[23] Yet the total identification of monarchy with the conservative principle was not really conservative. The establishment of the Kingdom of the Netherlands was a "reactionary" deed (the resuscitation of an order of the remote past)[24] and the incorporations of Venice and Genoa into Austria and Sardinia-Piedmont were contrary to tradition. As Constantin Frantz, that great Prussian "anti-Prussia" conservative, pointed out, the reconfirmation of the partition of Poland was the great crime of the Congress of Vienna, partly because it destroyed one of the largest realms in Europe, partly because the redrawn demarcation lines of the partition—the fourth—pushed the Russian borders right into the heart of the continent and thus made Russia the arbiter of the larger part of Europe for a long time. In the reconfirmation of Poland's partition an antirepublicanism of the leaders at the

Vienna Congress played an important role. Aristocratic Poland was an elective monarchy, a *rzeczpospolita* (republic, commonwealth). The reaction of the Poles to this state of affairs was, as one could expect, leftist and republican. A very large sector of the Polish lower nobility, the *szlachta*, became socialistic. Józef Pilsudski, the great general, "militarist," and dictator, was formally almost all of his life a leading member of the Polish Socialist party, which was filled with noblemen who were sentimentally conservative and intellectually leftist.[25]

Popular representation, the Diets of old in most parts of Europe, was a *traditional* institution, whereas the modern parliaments made up of parties were decidedly not. Yet the French Revolution had dishonored, in the eyes of many an early conservative, the very idea of representation, so that only local representations composed of the various estates did survive. The French *parlements* never reappeared. As a result we see that the early conservatives had cast their lot with the *absolute* monarchy, and this Gerlach, a great conservative, called quite rightly "the Revolution from above." In other words, the early conservatives conveniently forgot that *mixed government* and not absolute government is the great Western political tradition. The conservative concept of monarchy envisages the king in a dialogue with the people whom he patriarchally (but not paternalistically) treats as his children—but as adult children and not as minors. The trauma caused by the howling mob of Paris had gone too deep.

Yet the early conservatives were antinationalistic and in this respect they had reacted in a very healthy way against the nationalism of the French Revolution, this mass outbreak of ethnic identitarianism. French (ethnic) nationalism had provoked German nationalism and nationalisms fostered also by German Romanticism (Herder!) sprang up in every nook and corner. People speaking the same language now wanted to live in one country under one government, as *nation une et indivisible*. Against this "herdist" outbreak Metternich reacted as violently as the Hohenzollerns, Frederick William III, and Frederick William IV. This new nationalism of a leftist character was rampant among the German students who were also enthralled by democratic and republican ideas: These young men, who had in many cases fought against France, now proved that they were taken with identitarian, with leftist ideas—though not quite as much as their former enemies. And the way conservative governments repressed their movements showed that even these leaders had been affected by the tyrannical spirit of the French Revolution. Force called for Force.

In purely *human* terms the young German republican-minded

nationalists merit our sympathies. They sensed, as the supporters of leftist movements always do, the "dawn of a new Age." They had that juvenile enthusiasm for turning a new page in the book of history. The fate of a man such as Karl Ludwig Sand, the student whc murdered A. von Kotzebue,[26] seeing in that German playwright the worst enemy of nationalist-minded Germandom, is very moving.[27] There can be little doubt about the idealism animating these young Germans at that time. Yet we should not forget that these currents, which Metternich and his collaborators tried to suppress and eradicate, led to a very evil evolution at whose end we can clearly see the big leftist movements of our age, socialism, communism, and above all National Socialism which, naturally, saw in the nationalist movement of the post-Napoleonic period one of its spiritual ancestors.

A typical representative of this new nationalism, of this leftist ethnic collectivism copied from the French Revolution was Friedrich Ludwig Jahn, who developed mass calisthenics in Germany, which he called *Turnen*. He also inspired a fanatical notion of Germanism. Jahn invented an "old Germanic" costume and during the Prussian-Austrian-Russian occupation of Paris he walked, lonely, furiously, aggressively through the streets of Paris with crossed arms and his long hair falling over his shoulders. He tried to climb the *Arc de Triomphe* to knock the tuba out of the hands of the symbol of Victory. Inside Germany this very popular man waged a one-man war against the French language, and declared that for a young girl to learn French was just as wicked as to become a prostitute.[28]

This very popular demagogue was later arrested by the Prussian authorities, jailed for several years, but acquitted in a public trial.

Jarcke, the great Prussian Austrophile, comments very rightly on German nationalism, especially the type fostered by Jahn and Arndt, as an imitation of French patterns. He also hinted at the possibility that the Slavs, in turn, would copy the Germans—as indeed they did.[29] The German calisthenic associations (*Turnvereine*) with their rhythmic mass performances and their nationalistic choral singing, found enthusiastic imitators among the Western Slavs whose "Falcon Leagues" (*Sokol*) were nationalistic, democratic, and socialistic in their ideology. The *sokol-slets* ("Falcon Flights"), gigantic mass performances in Prague, Zagreb, Laibach, and Belgrade, were later taken over under new names by the Communist masters of these countries. Their identitarian character is most evident:[30] The individual appears merely as a cog, as a constituent part of a whole, pronouncing identical words, making identical movements in performances which aim to overwhelm by their *size*.

390

Ethnic nationalism, as the early conservatives saw very clearly, would destroy the whole fabric of Europe and would even act as social dynamite because in many areas the ethnic units though mixed, still represent specific classes. In a place such as Brünn, capital of Moravia—a typical example—the burgher class was solidly German and only the lower social layers were Czech. Now, with the rise of nationalism, replacing the geographic and dynastic patriotism of an earlier period, they viewed each other with a twofold hostility. In East Central Europe we encounter situations where class, language, and religion form a triple pattern filled with explosive possibilities.

In their antinationalism the early conservatives were certainly right. They were less right, however, in their gradual acceptance of another evil gift of the French Revolution: conscription. This institution rests on the democratic notion that everybody has the same rights. And people who have the same rights have the same duties. Taine spoke about the French *citoyen* who held in his hand the ballot and therefore was burdened with the knapsack. Militarism, as an ism, was really born with the French Revolution, and it is evident that, if a major power introduces conscription, its neighbors, in self-defense, have to do the same. (Luckily, Britain, protected by her fleet and profoundly liberal, had to introduce conscription for the first time only in 1916.) With this new order ended the era of the old-fashioned cabinet war, a war between mere governments employing armies of volunteers who fought for money. These "mercenaries"[31] were professionals who liked soldiering as a career and usually picked a good general.

These limited wars came to an end with the French Revolution. And since all able-bodied men had to serve, whether they had a natural talent and enthusiasm for war or not, they and their families had to be *propagandized* and *indoctrinated*. Now nation was pitted against nation, not merely government against government. This new concept of total war was the natural result of the two totalitarian trends toward democracy and toward identitarian nationalism.[32] Another "democratization" and escalation of warfare took place in World War II when not only civilians were massacred from the air, but also noncombatants were encouraged to attack occupation armies. Thus the *partizani* of the Russian Civil War became the new pattern: The murder of the occupants resulted in the shooting of hostages and other atrocities. Amid the applause of the American and the British public and the enthusiasm of their press a new level in savagery had been reached.

The early conservatives were not fully aware of this basic deterioration. No real efforts were made in Europe to return to the old system of professional armies. The leaders liked the idea of oversized military establishments. Later even the old antinationalist attitude was given up. This evolution was largely due to the rise of Marxism with its accent on "internationalism." With the decline of early liberalism and its replacement with old liberalism even the word liberty became more and more suspect. Had not liberty been one of the slogans of the French Revolution with its triple program of Liberty, Equality, and Fraternity? The fact that liberty was almost immediately betrayed by the Revolution was slowly forgotten. Economic freedom, a free market economy, world trade—all these became increasingly unpopular with European conservatives who, without realizing it, assumed increasingly reactionary traits by just saying "no" to the prevailing currents.

These changes in the old European conservatism cannot be entirely understood without bearing in mind that its leadership consisted less and less of intellectuals,[33] more and more of men with agrarian roots: landed gentry (with second sons in the army) and farmers. Thus by the end of the nineteenth century anti-intellectual trends were clearly noticeable and *with them* a fair amount of anti-Jewish feeling.[34] Many Jews, for social, religious, and historical reasons, preferred old liberalism or even socialism to a political outlook with a strongly Christian background. While the Jewish elites remained attached to monarchy, the rank and file of the European Jewry, very much to their undoing, were receptive to democratic and republican ideas.[35] With the aftermath of World War I we find in Germany, for instance, a party such as the *Deutschnationale Volkspartei* which figures in the public mind as *the* conservative party of the Weimar Republic. Upon closer examination we find, however, that very few of its tenets could have been called conservative. The party was militaristic and nationalistic. Its feeling for the great traditions did not extend beyond the nineteenth century. Again this has to be understood historically. The Second German Reich, founded in 1871 in the Hall of Mirrors of Versailles, was very definitely what real conservatives called a "child of the Revolution," referring to the spirit of destruction which started with 1789. A restoration of Old Germany in a conservative spirit could only have been carried out by Vienna and not by Berlin, by the Hapsburgs and not by the Hohenzollerns, by the Old South and the Old West (Vienna, Frankfurt, Aix-la-Chapelle) and not by the colonial Northeast. (Historic Prussia[36] lay *outside* the borders of the Holy Roman Empire, which is Germany's "First Empire.") The mere idea of a "national monarchy" is nonconservative.[37] For this very reason Bismarck, himself a Prussian *Junker*, was opposed by the Prussian conservative diehards. Earlier, Friedrich

Wilhelm IV had flatly rejected the idea of becoming German emperor as long as the Hapsburgs were around. And for all these reasons genuine conservatism in North Germany had no real parliamentary representation—no more than Italian conservatism, because Italy's unity also had a revolutionary, anticonservative background. In Italy it was even impossible to concoct that curious brew of conservatism and nationalism which we have seen in Germany. Italian nationalism rests more obviously than any other on leftist foundations: Mazzini, Garibaldi, Gioberti, and the House of Savoy (formally excommunicated from the Catholic Church between 1870 and 1929).

In France, however, Charles Maurras succeeded in establishing a synthesis of some sort of conservativism, monarchism, nationalism, and agnosticism. It was only a matter of time until this weird concoction was condemned by Rome and it happened in the pontificate of Pius XI.[38] Maurras, who, in spite of his hatred of the Germans, collaborated with the Nazi occupants and spent several years in the jails of the Fourth Republic, was reconciled with the Church before he died. The newspaper *Action Française* was taken off the *Index* in summer 1939 by Pius XII.

Maurras was a brilliant man with deep insights, but he had basically an un-Christian mind. People of all age groups supported him fanatically and faithfully. Yet it is a painful question whether we can call him a conservative. A certain German school of thought, interestingly enough, insists that Christianity and conservatism are mutually exclusive, because Christianity has a "linear" and conservativism a "circular" concept of existence.[39] Now, it is true that Christianity thinks in terms of Creation, Incarnation, Salvation, a Day of Judgment: Christianity believes in time, in an unfolding of truth, in a historical mutation. Yet, is conservatism a *Weltanschauung* according to which past, present and future are blotted out, and there is no "fulfillment"?

We are back to the problem posed at the beginning of this chapter. In the earlier parts of the book we have defined democracy, totalitarianism, and liberalism. The definition of conservatism is all the more difficult because this term bears a relation to time and space. Can it perhaps be understood only in a framework of Historicism? What about a Japanese conservative? Would he have to oppose Christianity in the name of Buddhism? Or Buddhism in favor of Shintoism?[40] If this is the case, then conservatism becomes a completely relative term, unlike democracy which always and everywhere means equality and majority rule, or liberalism which stands for a maximum of personal liberty. I am afraid that conservatism in a purely etymological sense can only be understood in the context of a given culture and civilization. If we, on the other hand, speak here about conservatism, we can only do so in referring to a set of values which are *perennial* in our Christian civilization,[41] values which we want to conserve, which we want to defend not only because we like them, because they are congenial to us, but also we carry the deep conviction that they are true. And if they are true, they are true independently of time and space.

Naturally the true and beautiful (they are *not* necessarily identical) can appear in different "outward" forms. The cathedral of Trondhjem in Norway and the Cathedral of Mexico City are very different in form and expression. They were built in different ages. They have to be loved and respected across national boundaries. There are, on the other hand, limits to our worldwide acceptance of other values. A highly conservative Portuguese administrator in central Angola might advocate the building of a courthouse in an African style but he will not "respect" the age-old tradition of sacrificing small children.

Talking about conservatism in practical, programmatic terms, we must insist that we are talking about *our notion* of conservatism. As we have seen, the term itself is not a very lucky one. In *Neues Abendland*,[42] a defunct German conservative review, the proposition was once made to use instead of the word conservative the complicated triple adjective "Christian, liberty-loving, tradition-connecting" (*christlich-freiheitlich-traditionsanknüpfend*). One might argue that the middle term (liberty-loving) is superfluous because this postulate is implicit in the Christian concept of the person. Somebody might insist that for the sake of a more universal appeal "Christian" should be supplemented with "Judaeo-Hellenic," but the Synagogue is implicit in the Church: There is no New Testament without the Old and no Christian theology; no Christianity as we know it, without the Hellenic, Platonic, Aristotelian, and Patristic background. It also might be argued that there were and are Jews who are conservatives without being Christians.[43] It is surely significant that they were and are widely read in Christian writings. I am thinking here of men like Franz Werfel, Uriel Birnbaum, Martin Buber, Thomas Chajmowicz, Hans Joachim Schoeps, Raymond Aron, Robert Aron.[44] (I am not thinking of the Jews who have become Christian *and* conservative thinkers. Among them we would have to name Friedrich Julius Stahl, founder of Prussian conservatism, Benjamin Disraeli who became Lord Beaconsfield, René Schwob, Hermann Borchardt, Daniel Halévy, and many others.) Still, "historically" (i.e., in its development), ever since the beginning of the nineteenth century, conservatism existed in the affirmation of Christian values. Even

Charles Maurras, personally through most of his life an agnostic and a nationalist, was a "fellow traveler" of Christianity.[45] Even the conservative Jews, as intelligent persons, know that, as a small minority they themselves have to refer to Christian semantics. Historically speaking it was, after all, an attack against the Christian order not by noble, but by ignoble savages that made conservatism necessary—primarily as a *restatement* of values under attack.[46] In this sense—important to remember—conservatism is not an "ism" but *the systematization and reaffirmation of the permanent values of Western culture and civilization.*[47]

In the domain of "social thought," early conservatism was strongly determined by two factors: the opposition against preliberalism and old liberalism (paleoliberalism), the opposition against deism and *laissez-faire* (as well as against Guizot's *Enrichissez vous!*)[48] which resulted in a very receptive mood for social reforms and a negative attitude against a far-reaching economic freedom. It is in matters like these that we can sense the American errors and misconceptions about earlier conservatism in Europe. (There are others about the New Conservatism.) The old agrarian-aristocratic leadership in conservatism demanded from the manufacturers that they should treat the workers in the same patriarchal way as they treated their house servants and frequently their agricultural laborers. In Sweden Socialists and Conservatives often voted together against the Liberals *in these matters*. The founders of modern "Christian Social Thought" are almost without exception members of the first two estates.[49] Baron Wilhelm Emmanuel von Ketteler, Bishop of Mayence, Count Georg Hertling, Baron Vogelsang, Prince Alois Liechtenstein, Count János Zichy, Vicomte A. de Villeneuve-Bargemont, Count Albert de Mun, Father Heinrich Pesch, S. J. Naturally there are exceptions: Frédéric Le Play and the highly sentimental Frédéric Ozanam.

Social reforms in the sense of "social security"—the insurance of the workers first against accidents and sickness, then against old age and unemployment—started more or less in Central Europe under the direction of the Hapsburgs and the Hohenzollerns. Conservative forces of a paternalistic character were behind these innovations. As a matter of fact, the violent dissent between William II and Bismarck (a national liberal) on the whole labor question led directly to the break between the two.[50] (There were, needless to say, also subtle personal reasons for "Dropping the Pilot.") Joseph A. Schumpeter in his *Capitalism, Socialism and Democracy* describes how William II, aided by "conservative civil servants" (von Berlepsch, Count Posadowsky), inaugurated these changes: "The monarchy, after having for a time given in to economic liberalism [Manchesterism, as its critics called it], simply returned to its old traditions by doing—*mutatis mutandis*—for the work-men what it had previously done for the peasants.[51] The civil service, much more developed and much more powerful than in England, pro-vided excellent administration machinery as well as the ideas and the drafting skill for legislation. And this civil service was at least as amen-able to proposals of social reform as was the English one. Largely con-sisting of impecunious Junkers, entirely devoted to their duty, well educated and informed, highly critical of the capitalist bourgeoisie, it took to the task as the fish takes to water."[52]

In retrospect we might say that these reforms were an error because the worker was treated as a child and his welfare was placed in the hands of the State rather than his own. But taking the conservative out-look of the *fin-de-siècle* and the early twentieth century into considera-tion, the reforms could be expected as some sort of Continental version of "democratic Toryism." The American reader, in this connection must remember that royalty is distinguished from nobility, and that agrarian reforms might have the full backing of the crown. He also has to bear in mind that royalty and nobility are not by nature friendly to the plutocracy, that the nobleman on the Continent dislikes the man-ufacturer and the banker, and, one should add, that "the university" has a position apart while the clergy was usually torn between populism and royalism. Today royalism is no longer a temptation. A large part of the clergy (including their theological inspirators) are hell-bent on ingratiating themselves with their "customers."

Nor should one think for a moment that the Russian autocracy was hostile to the working class. In the absolute monarchy until 1905 there was no special love lost between the emperors and the manufacturers. Here the German case was repeated. Subjects, according to monarchist theory, are "equidistant"[53] from the sovereign, who might *socially* attract aristocrats (or even plutocrats)[54] to his court but might have a better political understanding with other layers. The termination of serf-dom, which had prevailed over a large part of European (Central West-ern) Russia, was the work of Alexander II. The first efforts to establish trade unions under Nicholas II were made by the secret police, the *Okhrana*, to prevent the exploitation of the workers. Very comprehen-sive laws to protect the laborers were issued in Russia as early as the reign of Anna Leopoldovna in 1741.[55]

Still, if we try to visualize conservatism on the Continent before 1914 or even before 1933, the general picture we get is not too reassuring.

The conservatives of that age are largely negativists. In opposing a naive and utopian pacifism, they show themselves in favor of conscription and militarism. In opposing an inane humanitarianism they become spokesmen of an excessively disciplinarian outlook and defenders of physical and capital punishment.[56] In rejecting the internationalism of Socialists and Communists they accept the identitarian nationalism of the left. Despising an inefficient and demagogical democracy, they tolerate tyranny and dictatorship. Faced with the Jewish old liberalism alliance they often adopt anti-Semitism. Seeing the rapid growth of big business, of industry and finance, they develop an agrarian hatred for a free economy. Revolted by a sterile leftist intellectualism they become pure sentimentalists. It is almost always a negation that determines their stand and gives them a "reactionary" character. While often, though not always, sympathizing with their "no," one misses a constructive, positive stand.

The people calling themselves conservatives surely were not negativists in *all* matters. In this or that domain they had preserved their sense of what we have called the perennial values of the West. They did make a stand for local institutions and traditions against the centralizing tendencies. They defended religion, knowing that without religious foundations our civilization[57] would neither exist nor last. They had no illusions about the dangers of popular representation and were on the Continent fully aware that it was not the task of the monarch to be merely a sacred cow: It was his duty to refuse his signature to a law he could not accept in good conscience. (This, after all, is the reason he receives a civil list.) Conservatives knew that the very poor had to be helped and to be protected against exploitation—just as those envied by the mobs needed safety and security. Yet they saw the liberals as just as much their enemies as the Socialists and were convinced that Marx was merely the answer to the egotism and the avarice of the liberal capitalist—a gross oversimplification yet solemnly believed by the conservative Christian world (Another *fausse idée claire*, de Tocqueville would have exclaimed, but it was *not totally* lacking in substance.)[58]

It is true that in the 1920s and 1930s state and society, torn within the framework of parliamentarism by bitter strife, were heading for disaster and that some conservatives were looking desperately for ideas which might "sway the masses." Elections could be won only by majorities, and parliamentary majorities served as the basis for cabinet choices, yet it was evident on the Continent that conservatism could hardly act as a dynamic idea and grip the multitudes. Wherever conservative parties existed, they were too small to be decisive. In short, conservatism could not really engage in demagoguery. It could not promise to nationalize the factories, to expropriate the land, to abolish military service, to lower the standards of school examinations, to decrease the tax on liquor or cigarettes or entertainment, to facilitate abortion and divorce, to improve social security or to lower the income tax.[59] The leaders of the conservative parties (wherever they existed) more often than not had gentlemanly notions about keeping their word. Usually they were not even good stump orators.

Their country came first in the thoughts of these conservatives, and they found themselves in a most difficult situation when the parties of the nationalistic left became engaged in a bitter warfare against the parties of the international left. Should they just call down a plague on both houses? Or did they have a moral obligation to join what they considered the lesser evil? The average conservative, looking over the situation, saw on one side the Marxist parties—Socialists (Social Democrats), independent Socialists, Communists—all pledged more or less to the dictatorship of the proletariat. The Socialists, after all, were Marxists who had poured some water into their wine, while the Communists were Marxists who preferred to drink their whisky straight. But both had the same origin, both used the Red Flag, both frequently joined in alliances ("Popular Fronts") against the "bourgoisie."

Looking in the other direction, the conservatives saw the nationalistic leftists, Fascists, Nazis, and so forth. The example of the Fascists was rather confusing. Their totalitarianism was not overly developed. Italian fascism became gradually totalitarian, and it is a matter of speculation whether, without the evil influence of Nazi Germany, this development would ever have reached a climax. The general situation in Italy had worsened in 1921-1922 to such an extent that almost any change would have been welcome. And since only the nationalist left had the drive, the energy, the brutality to lead the country out of its parliamentary chaos and trade union terrorism, even such an errant son of socialism as Mussolini had to be welcomed. Only those who recall Italy's situation in the early 1920s will be able to understand today the embarrassingly often quoted reference of Pius XI to "this man of Providence." Did an alternative to fascism exist? In theory, yes. The King, with the support of the army, should have established a "provisional absolute monarchy." An authoritarian rule from above would have created a stability without inviting totalitarianism and the hubris of a dictator whose head is turned by power.[60]

Still, in a way, the Italian example paralyzed the resistance of conservatives against nationalist leftism and cast a spell of evil fascination upon them. Not that conservatives could have prevented its rise. Their small if not tiny parties were incapable of stemming the tide or changing the course of history, but stronger opposition or louder protestations could have kept their record cleaner. In Germany the *Deutschnationale Volkspartei* played along with Hitler willy-nilly. Herr Hugenberg,[61] owner of the *Berliner Lokalanzeiger*, joined the Nazis in a parliamentary arrangement, the "Harzburg Front." The paramilitary organization, *Stahlhelm*, imbued with a stronger spirit of opposition, was later forcibly dissolved.[62] Herr Treviranus tried vainly five minutes before twelve to found a popular Conservative party, but as could be expected, popular success was denied it. Only in Austria did the conservative forces battle to the last moment against nationalistic and international leftism, against Brown and Red—and therefore went through a real Golgotha in the dark period of Nazi oppression. However, when we say that conservatives on the Continent chose nationalistic leftism in preference to its international brand as the lesser evil, we do not want to imply that they were really in favor of it. Conservatives on the Continent, with the exception of Switzerland, were and are monarchists, and the nationalistic totalitarianisms were either openly or implicitly antimonarchical. (This is also true of Italian fascism.) Conservatives had to choose between their legitimate *ruler* and a *leader*. A nationalistic monarchy does not exist, because Christian monarchy, as we said before, is an international and interracial institution. Conservatives are federalists ("States' righters") and totalitarians are centralists. Conservatives also stand for the privileges of the Church; leftists of all dispensations want to reduce her influence, drive her from the marketplace, or eliminate her altogether. Conservatives are "diversitarian," totalitarians are egalitarian and identitarian. Conservatives are patriots; leftists *at best* are nationalists. Conservatives are traditionalists; leftists always want to make a "clean break with the past."

Yet though this is often not realized sufficiently, cooperation of conservative forces with nationalistic leftism was at least suicidal as frank opposition would have been.[63] In all countries where cooperation was attempted, a visible or invisible break came at a given time and the forces of tradition, the *enemies* of nationalistic leftism, as much as its *competitors*, the deep-Red leftists, had to face the concentration camps and the axe of the executioner. Again and again we have seen how conservative leaders, thinkers and writers who had just escaped the Brown hangman fell victim to his Red colleague. A conservative Prussian, Hungarian, Rumanian, or Croat is just as badly off today as he was under the Nazis. The Italian monarchist is just as much in opposition today as he was in the First Italian Republic, Mussolini's *Repub-blichetta*. A Czech monarchist, faithful to the Hapsburgs, is just as swiftly jailed today as under the Nazis or under Dr. Beneš, the former darling of American "liberals."

Still, the black period of dictatorship in large parts of Europe served as a beneficent if terrible and tragic school for European conservatives. In so many ways they were cleansed of the leftist poisons which had affected them in the first and, even more so, in the second half of the nineteenth century. First of all, they again learned to appreciate the great value of liberty fully. In jails and concentration camps, in fear and trembling due to the silencing, the boycotts they were subjected to, the suspicion cast upon them, their bereavements through assassination and execution—out of all this they learned the bitter lesson that liberty is necessary to the dignity of man, necessary for the preservation of tradition, necessary for educating their children in their own image. In the past they had often sneered at the liberty the democratic interlude had accorded them because they had been free even before 1918, and because they saw in the liberty of the time between the wars the reason for paralysis and chaos—an error, no doubt, because it had not been liberty that created the disorders but the entire political-social framework. Now they realize that truth has the chance to be attractive in liberty only, because all suppression provides the halo of martyrdom, and truth aided by force loses its luster. An error shouted from a flaming stake has more power than the truth proclaimed by a public loudspeaker protected by a dozen *gendarmes*.

They found out that though pacifism as an ism is a utopian error, peace is nevertheless a great good and war really only an *ultima ratio* (more "ultima" than "ratio," we would be tempted to say), that thorough "militarization" of a nation has paralyzing and debilitating effects, and that, ideally speaking, those should be soldiers who have a real calling—which is true of all professions, sacred and worldly.

They found out that there is such a thing as Christian humanism and even humanitarianism; that there is nothing uglier than severity for severity's sake, brutality for brutality's sake; that the basic attitude of the Christian is one of love.

They made the amazing discovery that a free economy really delivers the goods, that manufacturers are not all devils incarnate and that "social justice" can be based only on economic realities and not on generous hearts alone. They also gave up much of their leaning toward the conspiratorial explanation of history, which sees history mainly as the work of secret societies and religious sects. They found out that

400

the average man has a fair amount of goodwill but is weak and often overpowered by evil emotions and that his political acumen is exceedingly modest (to say the least)—all of which suffices to explain the vicissitudes of modern history without constant resorting to involved theories.

They also parted with that childhood disease of so many conservative movements, anti-Judaism. They now saw that anti-Jewish feelings inevitably must turn against Christianity. After all, the Synagogue is the Mother of the Church, a fact symbolized in stone inside and outside so many medieval cathedrals.[64] Anti-Jewish sentiments never characterized conservative thinking in Portugal,[65] Spain, or Italy. Nor are they really at home in the conservative movements of the Americas—unless we make the gratuitous mistake of calling Nazi movements "conservative"—which, unfortunately, is done again and again.[66]

This "chastising" of the conservatives which invited them to return to their roots, has an analogy in the reforming (and re-forming) of the liberals. The neoliberals, as we have pointed out before, have waked up from their Roussellian dreams and have cooled in their affection for democracy which, however, is now such a shibboleth that not many of them are too emphatic in their critiques. In jails, in camps, in hiding, the liberals found out that the average man is not abounding in either goodness or shrewdness, and the Common Man[67] can be just as monstrous as the despot corrupted absolutely by absolute power. They also discovered, just as the conservatives did, that parliamentary democracy does not at all favor the spreading of their ideas, and that they have to work for the common good through entirely different channels—deviously, laboriously, often in a clandestine way, communicating their ideas from brain to brain and less from heart to heart. The latter would be so much simpler, but neoliberalism could no more engender a dynamic mass movement than conservatism, new or old, can.

In view of these facts it is not surprising that the New Conservative and the New Liberal in Europe are nearly the same. There is only a slight shift in emphasis. It can be said that all existing European monarchs (and all pretenders of vacant thrones) are neoliberals and that most neoliberals write for conservative publications and often work through conservative parties. Many an American will consider certain European thinkers to be conservatives while they call themselves liberals, humorously accepting or nonchalantly rejecting the conservative label.[68]

There is the question of what attitude a European conservative of the old or new dispensation should take vis-à-vis the existing order.

A conservative, as we said earlier, is a conserver. Yet does the average European conservative loyally and unreservedly underwrite the present state of affairs—or should he oppose it? I am afraid the latter is the case, and it is precisely this circumstance which renders the term "conservative" in its etymological sense so precarious. The term "revolutionary conservative" is frequently used[69] and although it sounds like a contradiction, it is not unjustified. As a matter of fact, a real conservative, European or American, cannot possibly accept the world he lives in, nor the direction in which this world moves. If we analyze his mind, his views, his ideals, he is *far more of a revolutionary than either the Communist or the uncommitted leftist*. It is immaterial whether he wants to change the political and social order of his country through "peaceful means" and using the Constitution, or whether he wants to effect the revolution through a violent overturn. (There are various methods: conspiracy, large-scale organization or the patient-impatient waiting for the collapse of the old order.) If the change can be evolutionary, by reform rather than by revolution, organically and constitutionally rather than by sheer force, the conservative, will *obviously* prefer it because he respects the past, his entire historic heritage. A conservative east of the Iron Curtain is, most naturally, a revolutionary because he wants to make mincemeat of the existing order. Yet what about an Austrian conservative? An Italian conservative? Can a Continental conservative believe in the supremacy of parliaments, in the principle of majority and equality? Or should he take his stand against "ex-quality" and for *quality, truth, justice, reason, loyalty, and charity*? The voting systems of all existing democracies wilfully and programmatically disregard quality. The notion of majority rule (as Berdyaev and so many others have pointed out) disregards truth (parties representing contradicting philosophies get equal chances and equal treatment). Justice has nothing to do with equality, but with the principle of the "everybody his due," as Royer-Collard said. Not the sovereignty of the "people" (a mere abstraction) should be dominant, but the sovereignty of reason; not just volition, but thoughtful, methodical reflection. Loyalty is incompatible with democracy, which rests on switches of allegiance and change. (Without change totalitarianism is the immediate danger.) Love, which in its ideal form is not only deep but also permanent, has no place in a democracy—except in the form of abstractions. Christian love is for persons, for God, for men, for women, for children, for families. It is incompatible with the notion of a supreme public servant who can be hired and fired like a domestic.[70]

The conservative in the free West has to reject not only much of the political order, but also social conditions, artistic trends, cultural institutions, human relations. It is evident that these are all interconnected. One need only remember one item: the affirmation of state omnipotence which characterizes all of leftist thinking, as in the present system of social security which makes the individual hopelessly dependent upon the state. The conservative does not for a moment deny the importance of security for old, ill, or unemployed persons. But to achieve protection for them there are other and better avenues besides the omnipotent state which (terrible European experience) can be wiped out the day after tomorrow. And what then? To the Christian conservative who is deeply conscious that *stat crux dum volvitur orbis*, the idea of the total collapse or bankruptcy of his country is a tragic one, but it remains for him a distinct possibility. Where will the old, the sick turn if money *completely* loses its value, if the paper becomes mere paper,[71] or if the government, the state which signed the banknote, disappears? Certainly the best security is a large and faithful family ready to help when help is needed, but there are other values of greater permanence: real estate, fields, pastures, small houses, domestic animals, gold, other valuables, even stocks or private insurance. The whole underlying notion of our social security system is that the average man is improvident, that he does not think about tomorrow, that he is incapable of taking care of himself and his savings, that he has to be treated like a child. *This is largely true*, but the answer is not to treat the person as a child forever, but to educate that overgrown child, to teach him to stand on his own feet.

And here lies one central point of a conservative program, i.e., to educate people according to their ability though not to saddle them with responsibilities out of proportion to their capacities, their knowledge, their experience, by giving those on top the illusion that each individual's vote is decisive.[72] Imagine if one should drag an innocent passer-by from the street to the operating room of a nearby hospital and force him at gunpoint to perform a delicate operation. The man would burst into tears. However, if one were to ask him to sound off on problems such as nuclear experiments, Vietnam, the borders of Israel, support for Indonesia, aid to Latin America, or recognition of Red China, in most cases he would start spouting opinions. Demographic inquiries have been made in both the Old and the New World, and the results of both are shattering beyond belief.[73] The reply of the convinced democrat is that the man in the street merely votes for a representative, but is the representative better equipped? In order to practice medicine (i.e., perform the delicate operation mentioned above) one has to study from six to eight years. In order to become a representative in a diet (or a member of a Cabinet), one need fulfill no other requirements than to have been on the hoof for several years, a purely vegetative principle.[74]

The attitude of the Western occupiers of Germany toward the Nazis, and their notion of "denazification" shows a curious inner contradiction in the light of these facts: The Allies, professing democratic convictions, based their attitude on the conviction that one man is *not* as clever and well informed as any other man. An industrialist with a substantial education or a professor of a university who joined the Nazi party and made a few silly speeches was amply punished—and perhaps rightly so. *"They should have known much better."* A postman who distributed the mail and also joined the Nazi party was merely a *"kleiner Mitläufer"* and got off very lightly. This is entirely in keeping with the principle of the *suum cuique*, to everybody his due. *But then, why on earth restore democracy and give each one an equal vote*? Why punish "the German people" if, as a result of the Djihad to "make the world safe for democracy," they (i.e., not "they" but the majority of them) had been made in 1918 "masters of their own destiny" with the "privilege" of "deciding at the polls"? As a matter of fact, the greater the percentage of voters, the worse the outcome of German elections. In America usually less than 70 percent of the voters actually take advantage of their "privilege." (If everybody can do it, is it still a privilege?) In the German elections of 1932, free and unfettered elections in a most unbecoming atmosphere of hysteria[75]—more than 98 percent cast their vote. Poor fish, they really did not know what they were doing! They were really *überfragt* und *überfordert*; they were given questions and asked for judgments way above their capacity.[76]

Continental conservatives have also learned or unlearned other things. They found out that man is not totally wicked (which they tended to believe). They never fell for Roussellianism, of course, but they came to see that Pascal was right in describing man as neither beast nor angel, *weak*—very weak!—rather than wicked. (And naturally they remembered Pascal's afterthought: ". . . and, unfortunately, he who wants to act like an angel becomes a beast.")[77] They also found out that one has to face not only new political ideas but also scientific discoveries and artistic trends without prejudice, coolly, reflectively, not automatically rejecting the new or fostering the old. In other words, they have learned not to cling furiously and childishly to untenable positions if reason told them that they were really wrong. Not everything Marx,

Darwin, Freud, Picasso, or even Voltaire produced is wholly bad. There existed and in part there still exists such a thing as a "conservative demonology"[78] but it has been largely overcome in Europe—far more so, I am sure, than in the United States. Of course the position of American conservatives is psychologically a very different one from that of their European political coreligionists. America is more basically conservative than the European Continent, but precisely because American conservatives derive a greater strength from the subsoil (the "grass roots") of their country than Continental conservatives do, they are more hated, more intellectually combated, more vilified and vituperated by the leftist establishment. The position of European conservatives is much weaker, but more generally respected, if not secretly admired. Such bodies as the *Académie Française* with its enormous prestige are not dominated by leftists. Nor are our universities, if we disregard Italy and Sweden (intellectually the most backward countries in Europe). The European conservatives, however, are not given a chance to rule. They are sometimes considered brilliant, witty, profound, learned, or gifted, but nobody expects them to sway the masses or form a body of men who will decide the future. (A man such as Adenauer was "venerated," but he was never "popular.") Their basic chance is the total collapse of modern Western civilization, in which case they might take over by *default* from the Big Left. The general attitude toward them (as, only too often, toward monarchy) is a melancholy-apathetic one: "They're basically right, they probably have the answers . . . but, unfortunately, they have no chance."

American conservatives probably have a better chance. But what is the Continental conservative's attitude toward conservatism in America? Economically-socially speaking he is at first surprised to find it deeply imbued with preliberal ideas. Adam Smith never had the slightest place in European conservative thought, but upon some reflection the European will understand why "Manchesterism" does indeed belong to the traditional American scene. What the Continental conservative misses most in the American conservative outlook is, as we hinted, something like a coherent system of thought. Naturally, he will encounter feelings and emotions, but not a cogent philosophy. Professor Eliseo Vivas, a conservative Venezuelan thinker who teaches in an American university, has said quite succinctly that it should not be

> necessary to show in detail that the problem of conservativism is a difficult problem that touches on all domains of human interest, scholarly no less than practical, philosophical no less than legal,

moral and theological no less than economic and social. I take it as agreed that if the conservative movement is going to make more than a trivial and fugitive impact on the life of the nation, it will have to develop a philosophy that is systematic, that is comprehensive, that takes full and honest account of current positive knowledge, and that is, therefore, no mere repetition of dried-up old chestnuts that appealed to men a generation or two ago but have lost their flavor and freshness.

Professor Vivas then went on to say that this involves "one major negative job," i.e., to show the falseness of the current liberal (leftist) ideology. But besides this task there is also the necessity to have "some working notions as to which of our values are basic and which are not."[79] Our author puts *truth* in the first place. But this can serve merely as a *basis* for a blueprint. *As far as we can see, the blueprint to this day has not been worked out.*

It might be objected in the best Anglo-Saxon[80] fashion that true conservatism cannot be bothered with utopias and that the cry for a "philosophy that is systematic" comes dangerously near to a demand for a coherent ideology, which is also "unconservative" and of the left.[81] But what is the alternative? An empiricism, so dear to the American or British heart? ("This works; that doesn't work.") A discussion based on noble feelings is impossible. Any program to which a large number of people is pledged needs a rational profile. Conservative movements (anywhere and at any time) must have a clear demarcation line which separates them from those merely disappointed by the evil trends of the present age and therefore prone to be moved primarily by hatred. Charity as the foremost Christian virtue (charity properly understood, not mushiness) must head up every genuine conservative program. Leftism is always motivated by hatred. Let us beware of taking in the haters of the haters. The spiral of hatred should be left to the mutually *competing* (not "opposing") leftist camps, forming a dialectically organic whole. But to draw a clear demarcation line we must have a concise philosophy. It does not yet exist and thus there is a real danger that American conservatism may remain a mere "reaction" to the soft, hysterical loathsomeness of American leftism (a reaction condemning the nascent conservatism to sterility), or that it will be nothing but a literary movement—something the French simply call *de la littérature*—very smoothly even beautifully written but nothing concrete, magnetic, or dynamic.

The roots of this state of affairs are manifold. There is the aforementioned dislike for systematization. There is also the fear of looking into the future, of envisaging something radically different from the present order, in other words, not only of breaking with the present leftward trend, but of advocating something revolutionary: something too old, too new, or too farfetched.

Let us ask this painful and crucial question: Can American conservatives hope for a better world on the basis of the *present American Constitution*, as it is now interpreted, i.e., within the framework of a political order which is more or less (though not fully) democratic? I personally do not believe that such hope is realistic. Yet, to say so openly, an American conservative needs a great deal of courage. In the last 150 years the American left, through repeated Constitutional changes and latitudinarian interpretation, has democratized the originally far less democratic Constitution as designed by the Founding Fathers. We must now ask whether the *majorities* within the American people are ready to reverse this trend, whether this process can be terminated democratically, whether the system can evolve into other directions. I am rather pessimistic about this possibility, though we should not discard it from our calculations altogether.

There is, admittedly, a lack of *pietas* in planning about what will happen to us once our parents are no more. At the same time we can be certain that such a moment will come and that we have to face it emotionally and even financially. The American conservative (or any American, with the exception of the radical of the New Left) has no program as to what order to establish in place of democracy in America should it once cease to exist. The historian knows that nothing is permanent on this earth and a popular Viennese witticism says that "everything has an end, only the sausage has two." Let us only think for a moment what effects a total atomic war might have on the American Republic. Before, in, and after such a war the present system of legislation might prove too slow, too cumbersome.[82] Elections might be out of the question. The devastations and the mutual recriminations would render Congressional legislation impossible. A system of many parties after the European pattern might paralyze Congress to the extent that America would have become an absolute monarchy with a time limit.[83] Under these circumstances a military dictatorship represents a great likelihood, and since such a rule is usually pragmatic rather than ideologically very tinted, it is the least oppressive among the authoritarian forms.

Even if we rule out catastrophes, there are other forces working quite automatically against the present strongly democratized order. Among these the most important is the rise of the experts and of expertise. Most American conservatives have a strong dislike for this trend. They put their main hope in the "people" and in Congress. Yet the increase in weight of expertise and (as a concomitant of the administrative-executive branch of the government) is *well-nigh unavoidable*. This is an undemocratic if not antidemocratic evolution, observable all over the world, because, as we have demonstrated elsewhere, the gap between the *scita* (what is known) and the *scienda* (what ought to be known to arrive at rational judgments) is ever-widening. It is widening because our civilization and culture become more and more complex, because our globe is shrinking, and because (unlike in the very ideal direct democracy of the Swiss canton Glarus with 45,000 inhabitants) the man in the street is completely bewildered by the issues of the day and the problems he is called upon to decide directly or indirectly at the polls. This bewilderment, as we have said before, is shared by the vast majority of the Congressmen or parliamentarians. And, to repeat another argument, only a budding expert can judge between several expert views and coordinate them. Conservatives such as the late President Hoover and Ralph Adams Cram have insisted on the importance of a first-class administration.[84] Morally and intellectually the democratic age was terminated a very long time ago, but so few people are contemporaries of their own time. At the end of the last century Eduard von Hartmann, the German philosopher, wrote: "The belief that the liberty of the people can be guaranteed by parliamentary government has ceased to exist for some time. . . . The world is fed up with parliamentarism, but nobody has a better solution, and the knowledge that this despised institution has to be carried over as a necessary evil into the twentieth century fills the minds of the best of our contemporaries with anxiety."[85] Of course, the problems of preserving liberty under majority rule or of governing rationally with amateurs are not the same. Since the masses increasingly prefer that what they *think* is security to what is real liberty and since the complexity of the world has grown by leaps and bounds, this statement is today even more true than seventy years ago.[86]

Institutions more than men have the tendency to survive themselves. Thus we face the curious situation in which totalitarian dictatorships with an ideologically limited expertise and[87] ideologically paralyzed economies are facing democracies politically weakened by rank amateurism but provided with a strong economic system based on liberty. This looks like a semi-plus and a minus versus a minus and a plus. In the United States, however, expertise is increasing, especially

408

so in administration, *and in this domain, unfortunately, the leftists occupy important positions.* There are several reasons for this state of affairs. One of them is the aforementioned American "conservative" anti-intellectualism. As a result, American conservatism tends to be proamateur and antiadministrational, a position European conservatives would rarely take.[88] In this respect American conservatism follows American folklore, which loves to sneer at the expert-intellectual-egghead and adores the (successful) amateur.[89] Yet American conservatives in continuing such an attitude are fighting historically a losing battle. Instead of adopting a sour, standoffish, offended attitude they should try to get *good* men into permanent positions in the executive (civil service, diplomacy, etc.) and not leave the field to the forces of destruction. Unfortunately, they have not done this in the past.[90]

Naturally, it is difficult to enter institutions and organizations which already are under the control of the opponent (not to say "the enemy"). American conservatives have a valid excuse inasmuch as they started to become conscious of their position and of their need to organize only in the last decade or so. The same is true not only of much of the administration but also of the universities, the colleges, the publishing houses, the press, cinema, theater, and all the other means of mass communications. The leftists, as the Children of Darkness, in this respect have been much more clever than the Children of Light. In the positions where the leftists now are safely entrenched they can use against their opponents every imaginable tactic. They can give them the "silent treatment."[91] They can boycott them, use defamation and discrimination of every sort. And this, indeed, they are doing.

Yet American conservatives have to be careful not to become reactionaries by just blindly negating everything America's leftist establishment stands for. They have to use the scholastic *distinguo.*[92] Thus, to quote an instance, a conservative coming to the conclusion that a man is innocently indicted, has to protest the verdict, even if he finds himself suddenly in the company of other most loathsome protestors. Thus during World War II it was quite a scandal that the cause of the Americans of Japanese descent on the West Coast was almost entirely "left to the left." The laws and regulations which sent them to "relocation centers" (humane concentration camps) were, in a way, harsher than the Nuremberg Laws, since even a *drop* of Japanese blood put these American citizens into the category of enemy aliens. (The whole procedure was declared superfluous by the FBI and no such measures were taken in Hawaii, where 37 percent of the population is of Japanese descent and which was far more exposed to Japanese invasion than, let us say,

Nevada.)[93] The record of American conservatives on racial tolerance in the United States is rather poor. Here is another field "left to the leftists" who sometimes act as idealists, but sometimes just love to exploit an iniquitous situation. Of course the cause of the mulatto—there are hardly any Negroes in the United States—will not be helped by laws emanating from federal legislation.[94] Leftists, deeply unconscious of the complexities of the human soul and almost always apt to refer all problems and troubles to the central government, think that all that is needed is "the right law." America has always been a country of lawyers. The cry, "There should be a law against it!" conforms to the popular temper. Yet the "Noble Experiment" of Prohibition shows that laws which go against the grain of vast majorities are not really enforceable: At best they will be obeyed according to the letter but not the spirit. The full emancipation of the BASP, the "Brown Anglo-Saxon Protestant," will be a painfully long process since racial differences clash with the prevailing trend of identitarianism. (We therefore have to expect racial tensions in "modern" rather than in "backward" countries.)[95] Delight in diversity will help solve the racial problem, and this precisely ought to be a point in the psychological program of conservatism, which is opposed to equality and identity.[96]

"Internationalism"—conservatives must remember—is leftish only if it wants to establish an identitarian global brew, an odious uniformity encompassing the whole world. In this sense internationalism is only a global nationalism. The nationalist wants the powerful centralized "national state" which assimilates (or exiles) minorities and establishes perfect uniformity within the state. Revolutionary France, Italy after the *Risorgimento*, the Republic of Indonesia, the Soviet Union *in fact* (but not in theory)[97] represent such patterns. The internationalist of the leftist dispensation dreams of a unitary world state with a globally elected President which then would administer our planet from one capital, imposing laws voted for in one quarter of the globe over the rest. Under the circumstances this would spell the end of our civilization. This, however, should not mean that some time in the remote future a federation (but never a centralized) government with limited powers might not come into existence. Here as in so many other domains, *timetables* play a crucial role. It can well be argued that even today many governments are far too centralistic and curtail the free and sane development of the constituent parts of the State. This is even true of the United States whose federalist principles are part and parcel of the Constitution. It is also true of Spain where the centralism of Madrid often suffocates provincial life.[98] "Federalizations" or "unifications" represent exceedingly delicate and complex tasks. Just as broken bones can grow together the wrong way, so too with countries. The Italian *Risorgimento*, which led to a centralized state, has had the most deteriorating effect on the once so rich Italian culture. Something similar can be said about the establishment of the Second German *Reich* in 1871. Even though it was far less centralist than the Italy of Cavour, Mazzini, and Garibaldi, its federal structure was vitiated by the fact that it represented really only a Prussian conquest. It resulted in a Prussia with frills. Prussia with all its annexed areas comprised almost two-thirds of Germany. A cultural slump without parallel was the result, which took time to be overcome.[99]

Wise people in Europe realize that it would be a terrible mistake to have an omnipotent central government in a unified Europe or even a common parliament.[100] Though de Gaulle's stand on many a question was open to grave criticism, his concept of *une Europe des patries*, a "Europe of Fatherlands" was basically sound. And when we speak about the federalization of the world in the not so near future, we readily admit that the term "world government" is debatable. There might be a "global Chairman;" a global President or a global Emperor is conceivable, but not desirable; a global Parliament would be madness. It would be an idiomatic and philosophical madhouse. As a matter of fact, without at least some vague common religious denominator, such a federalization would have no inner cohesion. Theists and atheists do not speak the same language. This alone should make us ponder over the timetable. The notion that "We must get together in order not to hurt each other" is not a sufficient foundation. World citizenship in the full sense of the term would not be desirable either—nor European citizenship for a "United Europe." Just imagine five million Spaniards or Italians planning to settle in Norway. When we talk about other "United States" we refer to an orchestra with many well-tuned instruments. There is no happy family in which the members do not respect each other's personality. Still, the world is tending toward unification, and as an ultimate goal this can and should be envisaged on a federal basis. On the other hand, the time has not yet come. In this respect, the leftists of the United States are like people who see a small boy and a small girl. They *might* one day get married; it would be gruesome, however, to marry them off at the ages of seven and five. Without exaggeration we might call such an idea a perversity. The Greeks had a word for the right time: *kairós* (as opposed to *khrónos* which is any time). The *kairós* for the world state has not yet come—unless it were the conquest of the world by a morally and practically superior state, as the Roman Empire used to be in its best days, when it was imposing the *Pax Romana* on the Western world.

American conservatism must be revolutionary in the sense that it must have the will to *renew radically* the face of the country. And for this purpose it needs a systematized idea, a philosophy animating a *concrete vision* of America *and* the rest of the world as they ideally ought to be. I am convinced that such a philosophy must be universally valid and that the vision cannot remain a local affair. We are living in a world where, it is true, small things must be protected and the sense for what is locally and organically grown should be reawakened.

Colossalism is an evil. Nevertheless, the time of parochialism is over. One of the greatest conservative writers, Hermann Borchardt, said in his *The Conspiracy of the Carpenters*:

> For we too, my friends, are partisans—let us be honest. We too, my friends, we Christian conservatives, are, *let us hope*, an international party: and if we are not as yet, we mean to become one. The difference between the Urbanites and us is not, then, that they are international and we are national. I hope not: A national party in our day is about as important as a bridge club or an association of canary breeders. No, the difference is that we are the party of God, while they are the party of Satan, the Lord of the World. Because we are the party of God, not a single soul and not a single government need fear us, for we hate intermeddling unless it is forced upon us. We are glad to live in isolation if people will let us live in isolation. We do not believe that we have a mission, or that salvation will originate with us. We do not believe that God has created individual men and nations as equals: therefore they cannot be ruled in the same way. We believe that equality is of the devil, and that the Lord our God delights in multiplicity.[101]

Chapter 21

The Outlook

The great hope of leftists and, to be sure, not only of leftists is the United Nations. Here again conservatives err when they reject in principle an organization of this order. In a radically different form (and, perhaps, in another age) it might have been quite useful. Born in 1945 at the Conference of San Francisco (nicknamed "San Fiasco") this almost stillborn organization suffered right from the beginning from the Russian veto which paralyzed it in its most important functions. Its effectiveness has been impaired by the same debility which besets all parliaments composed of parties belonging to diametrically opposed philosophies and ideologies. As long as the various member nations do not speak the same "language," as long as they do not have *a bloc d'idées incontestables*, a common intellectual and spiritual denominator, they cannot have a real dialogue. They cannot really "talk" to each other.[1] The Soviet delegate who utters the word "democracy," the Indian, the American, the Thailandic,[2] the Yugoslav, the Mexican, the Swedish delegate each mean something else, something radically different.

One does not even have to use this many-faceted political term as a measuring rod. What about *man*? The Soviet, the Portuguese, the Cambodian, the Tanzanian representatives cannot possibly mean the same thing when they mention man. To one he is a biological accident in an inexplicable universe, to another a creature created in the image of God, to a third an odd animal tending into nothingness, and so forth.

To make matters worse, we have all over the world a fantastic proliferation of states and "nations" of the most varied importance (which is a lesser problem) but also of the most varied cultural levels which, indeed, should not be overlooked. The democratic dogma, of course, wilfully tried to overlook the difference in quality, in educational levels, in experience and moral values, and relies completely on the volitional element. It can be argued that the Polish representative at the UN represents a government which in no way has a mandate from its people, but it also seems obvious that the Danish delegation to the United Nations can make a more reasoned, sounder contribution than that of the Sudan which massacres its black Christians, or that of Papa Doc in Haiti,[3] or of some "emerging nations" where not such a long time ago "long pig," i.e., human meat was happily digested.

At the present moment the United Nations in no way reflect the lasting values of this globe. Numerically they do only in a very remote way, qualitatively not at all. Their entire record ever since their inception is very poor. They had some successes in very minor issues, but they have failed in all crucial ones (the Korean War, the Hungarian Revolution, the Congo troubles, the many critical phases of the Southeast Asian or the Near East imbroglio, disarmament, etc.). In other words, we have another case of a typical leftist timetable error combined with an idealistic failure in the face of harsh realities. In (a) another time, (b) another form, and (c) another composition, the United Nations might be viable. Of course the argument might be raised that politics is the art of the possible and that, under the present circumstances, the United Nations is better than nothing. He who cannot buy a big, shiny, expensive new car has to content himself with a secondhand one. This argument sounds sensible but becomes questionable when we reflect that a ramshackle vehicle might be a death trap. Under such circumstances it is wiser to walk or go by bus.

Viewing this globe in our times, one often wonders about the cocksureness of so many representatives of "moderate" leftism. As far as we can let our eyes roam, we see nothing but misery and ruin, created by the moderate leftists, the self-styled "progressives" unattached to any party discipline or ideology with a clear profile; or we see the same ruin caused by radically totalitarian philosophies which have thought out their premises to the bitter end, which disdain compromise and prefer to work without a mask. It is difficult to find a single large area where we do not have to say: "Here leftism has caused suffering, mischief, and destruction." And by leftism we mean that attitude, usually

414

rationalized and systematized into an ideology, which stands on identitarianism, egalitarianism, collectivism, statism, centralization, majoritism, materialism, coercion, and slavery. We mean movements which are antipersonal, antidiversity, antiprivilege, antispiritual, antifederalist and, indeed, antiliberal even if they misuse the liberal label—because the only liberty they are interested in is sensual liberty, which ordinarily means slavery.[4] It is true that crimes of commission as well as omission must be attributed to the forces of the great Western tradition: the loquacious bombast of a William II, the bureaucratic lack of imagination of Franz Josef, the melancholic inertia of Nicholas II, the callous sloth of certain Latin American big landowners, the indifference to human values of early capitalism, the stubborness of the old clergy, and the arrogance of the aristocracy, the cynicism of a Ludendorff[5] who sent Lenin in a boxcar to Russia, the misplaced liberality of a Louis XVI, the avarice of certain colonial administrators, and so forth, but all these are mere peccadillos in comparison with the disastrous, murderous, and suicidal actions of the left.

Let us take a map of the world, a brush and a pot of red ink. Then let us paint in the areas where people live in slavery and desperation, where they are less free, less well off materially, more controlled, more curtailed in their expressions and actions, more terrified about their future than 40 to 60 years ago. I do not think that we could even leave out the United States from this blood-colored manifest of unhappiness. Take the average American parent looking over the breakfast table, counting the heads of his children. If he has any degree of intelligence he must realize what frightening menaces are hanging over them—menaces by no means unavoidable at one time. The history of the world since 1917—since America's entry into the war and the Red October—only *seemingly* resembles a Greek tragedy that starts with certain words and actions and mounts to its inexorable tragic climax: the situation we are all in now. The historian, the philosopher, the theologian know better. Along the path of this catabasis decisions were taken—or not taken. And these decisions, far more often than not, lay in the hands of the left: the quarter-left, the half-left, the full, thoroughly committed left. And in spite of all their minor or major quarrels, in practice they all banded together, mutually aiding, pushing, and confusing each other. In one of my novels, whose background is the United States during World War II, a Hungarian government emissary confesses: "If you had an inkling of what I know you would have to despair of the logical faculties of those governing us—not only here, but everywhere. These chaps can be compared to drunk criminals who have

415

been hit over the head with a club and now are reeling in darkest night across wooded swamps. Or one might even liken them to madmen who have put the noose around their neck and wait impatiently for an opportunity to jump from the chair."[6]

The mischief was done for a variety of reasons. There is a blindness, a danger in any system of thought, a danger which those on the right (and in the right!) also have to face, mindful of the Spanish proverb: "All science is madness if it is not balanced by common sense."[7] Ideological closed-mindedness, however, was always a greater weakness among the left. We remind the reader again of Hegel's reply to the admonition that the facts contradicted his theories: "All the worse for the facts." The second factor is the intellectual arrogance of the moderate left which forms everywhere (and in American far more so than anywhere else) a well-organized mutual admiration society enjoying a number of monopolies and therefore is rarely seriously challenged. To be sure, they suffer defeats in the practical order but the Common Man's memory is no longer than his nose and thus the old follies are rarely reviewed. Cut off from the great traditions of the West, rootless and parochial, ignorant of the big wide world and its cultures, languages, institutions and religions, the American leftist (more than his overseas *confrère*) has been a babe in the woods, stubborn in his error and unfortunately sustained by a large sector of "public opinion" representing specific trends in, or rather strains from, the American tradition. We should never lose sight of the fact that the American leftist does not hang in midair. The American conservative will one day have to come to grips with certain cherished American notions. (This, by the way, is not only true of America, but of everywhere. The conservative, as we have said before, cannot just underwrite the past[8] or the entire tradition of his nation.)[9]

The *moderate* leftist is not always aprioristically opposed to liberty. Often he sacrifices it with a sigh. Yet he has no higher reason to cling to it, and his weakness in opposing the radical forms of leftism partly comes from his Roussellian stand and partly from his inferiority complex. He sees in the unabashed totalitarians the wave of the future. They have "done things." They are carrying out programs he himself has not the courage to advocate openly or, given the opportunity, to execute. He therefore falls into the category of Lenin's "useful idiots."

It is his Roussellian heritage which tells the quasiliberal that Socialists, anarchists, and Communists are "human beings after all," that they will one nice day see the "light of reason," that, faced by harsh reality, they will have to "come to terms" with it, that totalitarian

416

leaders will sooner or later have to "fulfill the aspirations of the masses" which can be expressed in washing machines and in the right to pull levers[10] on election day and to read *Lady Chatterley's Lover* in the unexpurgated pocketbook edition for 75 cents. The religion of the moderate leftist is "progressivism" and since its final victory is assured, all roads lead directly or indirectly to it. Lenin, Stalin, Mao, Ulbricht, Ho Chi Minh, and Castro might be only detours, disagreeable but unavoidable intermediary figures useful for getting obsolete survivals out of the way to establish a better tomorrow.

The situation, however, is not quite so simple, especially in America where the moderate leftist has evolved from the old-fashioned liberal and has not entirely shed certain liberal notions. He would not like to see a Lenin in the United States but has a sneaking suspicion that the contemptuously grinning corpse in Moscow's Red Square was "good for the Russians," that these "medievally backward priest-ridden serfs" (who, by the way, had produced Turgenev, Dostoyevski, Tolstoy, Rimsky-Korsakov, Mussorgsky, Tschaikovsky, Metchnikov, Mendeleyev)[11] "needed just that sort of reformer." Our liberal is hardly aware of the fact that he is a fervent nationalist.

Finally we have that most dangerous of all types, the "halfway" man who sees in the Communist utopia the terminal station. He has no real argument against it except the trembling hope that it will come about in an evolutionary rather than revolutionary way: All that America can do is start to subordinate its temporary existence to the eventual coming of the Red Paradise. This is precisely the position of Alger Hiss and all the others like him (whether they actually acted on their convictions or not). It was a mere historic accident (explicable by the preceding evolution of general political thinking) that they did not in any appreciable number fall for the National Socialists.

The havoc wrought by leftism is simply colossal. If humanity had any common sense, had been permanently endowed with reason, knowledge, a sense of history, it would have renounced the leftist gods a long time ago. The left, however, has by far the better catchwords, and man's brainpower has to be viewed in terms of potentiality, not of actuality. It needs enormous moral and spiritual qualities to mobilize one's intelligence fully; it just does not work automatically.[12] However, an unbiased glance backward and around us reveals an ocean of misery, unmitigated horror, and colossal stupidity: the fiendish massacres perpetrated by the French Revolution, the *noyades*, the *batteries nationales*, the blood orgies in the Vendée, the forests of guillotines, the silly and vain risings of 1848, the bestialities of the Paris *Commune*,

417

with its mass slayings of innocent hostages, the senseless overthrow of the Mexican and Brazilian monarchies[13] which alone could have insured an orderly development to these two big Latin American nations. There is the suicidal order of 1919 in Central Europe which provoked World War II, the idiotic transformation of Germany into a republic,[14] the ignominious treatment of Hungary and Bulgaria that forced them into the Axis camp; the horrors of the Russian Revolution and the hell of Stalinism culminating in Katyn and the icy inferno of the *kontslageri* on two Continents; the Nazi Revolution with its countless bestialities, the *"Kazetts"* and the extermination camps; the "democratic" aerial warfare that burned alive myriads of noncombatants of all ages, the infamous cruelties of the Spanish Loyalists and the Chinese "agrarian reformers"; the sadistic doings of totalitarian police forces in Poland, Hungary, Czechoslovakia, Rumania, Bulgaria, Yugoslavia, and Albania; the fiendish tortures applied in North Vietnam and North Korea; the unspeaking depredations of the Mexican, Cuban, Colombian, and Venezuelan "Revolutions"; the nightmares of decolonization in India and the Congo, in Angola and Mozambique, in the Cameroons and the Sudan; the brutalities of *Genosse* Ulbricht's repression of the Berlin Rising, of dear old Khrushchev's quelling of the Hungarian Revolution—not to forget the millions of Kulaks deported, starving and dying; the famines in the Ukraine and in the Kuban Region; the deportation of untold East Germans, Sudeten Germans, East Poles, Latvians, Lithuanians, Esthonians, Krim-Tartars, Volga-Germans, and even the Communist victims of Stalin caught in their own net. Remember the French massacred by the Communists working within the Résistance, the Italians assassinated by their own Reds, the Yugoslavs victimized by the *Partizani*. Remember the slaughter of the *Domobranci* by Tito (surrendered to him by the British), the fate of the *Vlassovtsy* (surrendered jointly by the Americans and the British), the scenes of terror at Dachau, when the Nazi cremation stoves were hardly cold and the Western Allies packed good Russians into railroad cars to have them shipped as traitors to the Soviet Union—desperate men then tried to commit suicide by biting their arteries. Think of the innocent victims of Red Chinese bands in the jungles of Malaya, of Catholics executed in Mexico, of the Lutheran pastors slain in Riga, of the 256 human roasts in the Montagnard Village of Dak-Son, the 4,000-odd Christians slain in Hue, the buried Benedictines of Thien-An. If one were to take paper and pencil to make an estimate of how many people were murdered or killed in battle because of the ideas of the French Revolution in their various stages, guises, and evolutionary

418

forms, because of the ideas of equality, ethnic or racist identity, a "classless society," a "world safe for democracy," a "racially pure people," "true social justice achieved by social engineering"—one would arrive at simply staggering sums. Even the Jewish holocaust offered by the National Socialists with five or six million dead would seem almost a drop in the bucket. There must have been at least 120 or 150 million victims, perhaps even 300 million. The victims of the French Revolution were relatively few, but sadistic bestiality had entered Western Civilization through that door and we have had increasingly "bigger and better" slaughters ever since—as the Western World moves nearer and nearer to the abyss.

However, we have already reached the brink of the abyss—hence the so much talked about "brinkmanship" which is indeed a grim reality. As Spengler said, "Optimism is cowardice." We are now passing through a phase in history when the forces of the left in conjunction with the technological development have created a situation (the "world we live in") in which hope based purely on rational grounds can hardly subsist and only Hope as a theological virtue is justified. It is significant that such outstanding Christian thinkers as Romano Guardini and Josef Pieper[15] emphasized the legitimacy of a religious pessimism or, let us say, realism in relation to this world.

But let us view the future, given our physical survival, in the light of a continued evolution and revolution in our midst. We are now living in a time when in the realm of art and thought the essentially new no longer appears,[16] when basic patterns tend to repeat themselves or merely show new combinations. Science, technology, and techniques create additional factors, but man remains man. Ever since Pandora's Box of the French Revolution had been opened, ever since Prometheus was replaced by Procrustes, leftism had its sway. Nor should we harbor any illusions: Even in spite of its suicidal tendency leftism is going to stay with us, not *necessarily* as a dominant power, but certainly as a permanent factor, as a trend, as a constant temptation. It is there to stay, even in the best of systems, up to the very threshold of eternity. This is so because the leftist element, due to its animal-material character, is part and parcel of the human person. And *persona* means soul *and* body, personality *and* numerality, uniqueness *and* repetitiveness.

Today democracy is still with us, but all observers with a modicum of insight see it drawing to a close. It has been popular (and by no means only among the most primitive) because it did, almost miraculously, enter a synthesis with the liberal principle, but this union, as was clearly foreseen by de Tocqueville, is heading for a divorce. This is perhaps least felt in the United States where political theory in recent decades has become curiously one-sided, moving in one direction, provoking no *substantial* contradiction.[17] Yet Madison was already aware of the liberal essence of democracy[18] and he would have been surprised to see that today it is brought into intimate connection with pluralism, a dangerous catchword so generally used and misused.[19] As we have always pointed out, democracy needs a maximum of conformity, not variety, in order to work properly and efficiently.[20]

Nevertheless, we have to look upon the end of democracy with fear and trembling. The evergrowing gap between *Scita* and *Scienda*, as well as the swiftness and secrecy so necessary in the domains of foreign policy and military affairs make a change in the long run unavoidable. However, rule from above might herald an Augustean age as well as its very opposite. An authoritarian regime by leftists without any controls would be at least as oppressive as was its initial phase—the French Revolution. In other words, in the coming authoritarian regimes in which diets will be no more than advisory bodies or at best, mere organized pressure lobbies, the real problem will concern the moral and intellectual qualities of the administrators, the experts and those in supreme control. Even if (as it is to be hoped) checks and balances will function in relatively good governments, the quality of the top is of crucial importance.[21] *It is obvious that the left will try to capture and monopolize the top*, and the outcome of these efforts will decide the fate of nations, perhaps even of the globe. The danger is this: that the "conservatives," that the right, might lose this new opportunity again by default because they will hesitate—if necessary—to use revolutionary means and rather do what they so often have done, i.e., optimistically watch developments, hoping that they will go their way automatically. They constantly forget how perverse history can be, because they have lost the Biblical skepticism as to the nature of man. They must remember what Horkheimer said in his famous interview: that conservatives today are nearer to true revolutionaries than to fascists and that true revolutionaries are nearer to conservatives than to communists. Yet the possibility unfortunately exists that the right people of the right at the right time, the *kairós*, will just produce another "great book" although—we will borrow this from Marx—the moment approaches when we should not merely philosophize but actually change the world.

Yet whatever the authoritarian character of the *top*, according to a rightist conception of state and society, in order to save the dignity of man and the freedom of peoples, it will be necessary to create "areas," "domains," "little kingdoms" in which man can move freely and decide freely; where not only can he be master but where his judgments are valid because they are based on knowledge and experience. In a Tyrolean village, for instance, where the community council (*Gemeinderat*) is elected on the basis of universal suffrage, where the mayor as well as every councilor is personally known to everybody, where the problems to be dealt with are within the intellectual grasp of almost everybody (including the councilors and the mayor!), democratic institutions still do make sense. The problem is to secure (and to insure) the autonomy of such a village. Now, a village is a "geographic" unit but there are other well-marked-off domains where a person can find his freedom and face it with a sense of responsibility because right proportions still exist between his knowledge and the affairs of this area. (Codetermination in a factory—as it exists in Federal Germany—also makes sense and should by no means be viewed as a socialistic venture.)[22] Yet to confront the average man with issues he is not able to judge, or to force even exceptional men to handle affairs for which they are not competent, is either mocking madness, a crime, or both.

It is quite possible that now constitutions are evolving which may prove to be more promising than our systems. We might look in this respect to despised Latin America[23] or to contemptuously treated Spain whose constitutional development in the last twenty years (hardly realized even by the average Spaniard) deserves serious study.[24] Peter F. Drucker, certainly not a rightist radical, is very much to the point when he says:

> Ultimately we will need new political theory and probably very new constitutional law. We shall need new concepts and new social theory. Whether we shall get these and what they will look like, we cannot know today. But we can know that we are disenchanted with government, primarily because it does not perform. We can say that we need in pluralist society a government that can and does govern. This is not a government that "does"; it is not a government that "administers"; it is a government that governs.[25]

Such a government might even be a hereditary monarchy and to him who knows world history in its depth and width, this should not be surprising. Marcuse himself admits that the Father always returns and overthrows the association of Brothers in a Thermidorian style.[26] Mitscherlich's views are not dissimilar.[27] As a matter of fact, in the broad masses the (largely subconscious) thirst for monarchy and monarchs is amazing—sometimes even a bit nauseating. Bored with and tired of all forms of "modernity," fed up with technology and its uniformity, disinterested in an abstraction like "government by law," the masses long for persons and personalities they can look up to, whom they can love, for whom they can have "sympathy" in the original sense of the word. A perusal of lowbrow weeklies in Europe reveals an inordinate fascination with royalty, with their loves, marital troubles, weddings, pregnancies, courtships, friendships, affairs. Obviously, as long as the family as an institution exists, as long as patriarchalism in some (however diluted) form survives, the familistic principle in politics will exercise its magnetic attraction.[28] This might be exploited "in parts" by a single person rather than by an entire family. A very recent poll among Italians—who not such a very long time ago have emerged from a one-man dictatorship—has shown that two-thirds of them would be willing to submit to a new dictator with a time limit.[29] The dangers possibly (but not inevitably) inherent in such a development also have to be seen in the light of the fact that our present society, devoid of a sense of authority, has not been prepared to cope with *power* in any sense—neither those subjected to it nor those exercising it.[30] This crisis of our time is also a crisis of manliness and true masculinity which the left always suspected as "reactionary." There is no room today for male aggressiveness except in underdeveloped countries and within the framework of New Left destructivism. The "Father State,"[31] the "Provider State" is but a faceless father substitute. The failure of man as a warrior and as a father is now being followed by his resignation as a lover, after the sinister looking shock worker we are getting the long-haired dope addict.[32]

There is, however, a certain interrelationship between the totalitarian Provider State, Leftism, and atheism. Leftism, obviously, tends in its identitarian, unitarian enthusiasm towards *monism* and not toward dualism or pluralism. Clemenceau declared in the National Assembly: "The clergy has to learn to give to Caesar that which belongs to Caesar—and *everything* belongs to Caesar." Jules Ferry, another leftist Prime Minister of the French Republic said that "we want to organize a humanity which can do without God or kings" and that by "feeling part of humanity" one "will be free from the fear of death." Fifteen years later Viviani, Premier and Minister of Foreign Affairs stated in lyrical terms: "We have extinguished the lights of Heaven and they are not to be lit up again." Jaurès, in his socialist and democratic fervor, even did one better: "If the idea of God, if God Himself in some visible form were to appear before the multitudes, the first duty of man would be to refuse Him obedience and to consider him as an equal with whom one enters in discussion, not as a master to whom one is subject."[33] Bourgeois leftist laicism and atheism, needless to say, was soon outdone by its socialist-proletarian version.

As one can see, it would be the eminent task of Christianity to fight the leftist temptation in the world and in ourselves, but the untimely crisis of Christianity, not only but above all in the Catholic Church, is the most glaring of all present defaults. Triggered off by a wrong interpretation of Vatican II on the part of the Catholic and secular press, the crisis has a predominantly *theological* nature, not among the still conservative flock, but among priests, monks, nuns, hierarchs, "intellectuals." It produced a theology of the beaten dog,[34] with resentment-loaded argumentations characterized by purely negative "antipositions."[35] We are here faced with an evil spirit flattering and courting the world;[36] the peremptorily demanded concessions to the world are mostly incompatible with the character of a great religion.[37] Leftist poisons, the nearly total immersion in "social thought" and in "social action"[38] have created an impasse in Christianity depriving it of its magnetism precisely for those who most thirst for the supranatural and the eternal. A leading French Dominican who declared during a lecture in São Paulo that he suspects God to be rather on the side of the Communists than of the capitalists, and that he is not at all unhappy about this state of affairs,[39] expresses very much the spineless spirit of a "changing faith in a changing world," with an unfettered libido for corporate survival which disgusts the faithful and causes contempt among the enemies of Christ.[40] Here indeed lies a real responsibility of Christianity, of all Christian faiths toward the rest of the world. By giving up basic positions, by relinquishing their role of defenders of freedom, by becoming prototalitarians, relativists, and drifters, they jeopardize the very center of our culture and civilization, its heart and soul—the Christian minority. Polite doubt or relativism, on the other hand, will neither lead to "progress" nor protect us against the assaults of the organized or unorganized left, old or new.[41] Man is willing to die only in the service of genuine convictions, for an exclamation mark, not for a question mark. And since we are touching here upon the "rather dead than Red" formula, we must remember that in history man's readiness to die for ideas and ideals has always been the most decisive factor.[42] There is victory, there is noble failure, and there is also defeat in ignominy. One thing, however, is absolutely certain and this precisely from a Christian point of view: We have no right to offer our throat meekly to the assassin—because we are permitted to tempt neither friend *nor foe*.[43]

While the Old Left proposes a false order, the New Left proposes chaos which,[44] oddly enough, is nothing but the other side of the same medal. External "reforms," naturally, will not establish a lasting and right order: All such plans can only be transformed into reality if our hearts and minds are prepared for it, if a *metanoia*, a change of mind and mentality has taken place. Only then can we be ready and summon the courage to do the right things right and leave the wrongdoing to the eternal left.

ABBREVIATIONS: D = "Democracy" (National Democracy, Radical Democracy, Jacobinsim)
NS = National Socialism (Fascism)
SC = Socialism, Communism

Left

MAN

The individual is subject to the will of the majority (*volonté générale*). He is a mere number in the "democratic process" (D), who can be added or subtracted. He is embodied and personified by a "leader" (*Führer, Duce, Vozhd*) (NS) or by a delegate (D). The individual is nothing—the "People" everything (D,NS,SC). The individual is a mere fragment of the "collective masses" (SC). "Nobody is indispensable" (D). Man is a creature of the stomach and wallet (SC), the reproductive organs (NS) or of the larynx (D).

LIFE

a) *Slavery and Coercion*

Equality is achieved by slavery and coercion (SC). Equality is only possible if we remove the mountain tops and fill the valleys. Full mobilization of envy to foster equality by taxation (D) or confiscation (SC) or "naturalization" (SC,NS).

b) *Identity (Sameness)*

Political equality of the uneducated and unexperienced (D), sameness of language, custom, way of life (D,NS), sameness of race (NS), sameness of class (SC—Theory).

c) *Quantitativism*

Moral conclusions are drawn from the moral or intellectual propensities of the many (D) at elections, plebiscites, polls, sex-investigations.

STATE

The State as ultima ratio and end in itself:
Monolithic structure (centralized, unitary state), *absolutism* of monarchs, leaders, dictators but also of parliamentary majorities (D,NS,SC). "Politics." The citizen is the subject (serf, slave) of the State (NS,SC).
The "interest of the State" takes the place of the common weal.
Centralization, statism, geometrism and identitarianism in the administration (D,NS,SC). Opposition to all private spheres, to all "privileges."
To be different as such becomes a crime (D,NS,SC).

SOCIETY

Structure: No estates, but *"classes."* Tendency towards the amorphous, towards the static, the egalitarian or identitarian mania, or towards a new caste system. Mass movements: Dominion of the instincts and the passions. Bureaucratic reactions against tendencies leading to chaos and anarchy.

NATION

Nationalism of an ethnic order (D,NS) or *racism* (NS): Complete unity within the framework of the State. Antinomian reactions: *Internationalism*, grey worldwide uniformity (D,SC).

CHURCH & FAITH

Either complete hostile annexation of the Church ("Josephinistic" establishments under State control) or persecution of the Church by separation. Religion then is first removed from the marketplace and the school, later from other domains of public life. The State will not tolerate any gods besides itself (D,NS,SC).

POLITICAL STRUCTURE

All problems, all matters of individuals and of groups are always left to the discretion of the *central government*, which cannot tolerate any autonomous developments. The end of all private and local enterprise, or at least of the spirit sustaining them. Repression of all "minorities," of all dissenting groups (D,NS,SC).

IDEALS

Utopianism. The nihilistic tendency to recreate and refashion all forms of human existence after a *tabula rasa* of total revolution (D,NS,SC). Total planning and "social engineering," methodical uprooting. Geometrism and symetrism instead of organic growth. Life as a "mathematical formula." The expectation of a social and technological paradise on earth either after a series of revolutionary hells (NS,SC), with appeals to accept sacrifices for coming generations, or along the lines of an endless, evolutionary, humanitarian "progress" (D).

WELFARE

The material security of the individual is entirely in the hands of a *provider state*, which controls the material weal of the citizenry through a centralized agency. "Welfare" as opium of the people and as tool of the cold or hot totalitarianism. The controls are directed at the "weak points" of the defenseless individual: old age, unemployment, illness. Practical affinity between the provider state and socialism (D,NS,SC).

LAWS

Legal Positivism. The "law" in the service of a triumphant ideology. Laws are "made." Justice is prescribed and fabricated, not "looked for" and found (D,NS,SC).

INTERNATIONAL RELATIONS

Efforts to refashion all other nations after one's own image. Eternal crusades motivated by the spirit of a (usually only subconscious) *imperialism of structural forms* (D,SC). Local crusades for the liberation of "underdogs" and other "enslaved minorities," "democracy" (Wilson, Lloyd George, Roosevelt), national socialism and communism as modern "Islamic movements" engaged in *Djihads*, "holy wars."

INSTRUCTION & EDUCATION

Uniform education according to a uniform scheme "for all," thus coddling the worst and stultifying the most talented. State monopoly in education which tries to be education and not mere instruction, thus increasingly arrogating the rights of parents. Cutting or totally eliminating religious instruction (D,NS,SC).

ECONOMICS

Either paleo-liberalism, which leads to the concentration of wealth in very few, if not "one," hand (monopolies), which then can be expropriated or controlled by totalitarian states and only theoretically continue to figure as "private property" (D,NS) or State capitalism (socialism), where the State owns everything. Currency completely controlled by (SC) the State (occasionally laws against private ownership of precious metals and coins). Robbing of the money-saving citizen by inflation and sly expropriation through excessive taxes (D,NS,C).

THE SEXES

a) *Sexes:* equal.
b) *Family:* relative and horizontal (therefore "generation gaps").
Relativism due to the "sand heap" concept of society as simultaneously individualistic and collectivist: many grains, one heap.

HUMAN COHESION

Power. (Naked power, terror).
Fear and resentment.

Right

MAN

A person with an intransferable destiny, unique, created in the image of God, responsible to God, endowed with an immortal soul. A creature with "heart" and "reason" (ratio directed towards wisdom *and* knowledge). Enfeebled by original sin, but not just a "product of environment."

LIFE

a) *Freedom*

"Equality" is merely accepted as an "administrative simplification" and as a fraternal attitude towards others, because we do not know *exactly* who is superior to whom, who stands nearer to God who alone knows the full truth.

b) *Diversity*

Joy in the diversity and in the richness of all forms of creation.

c) *Efforts towards perfection and excellence*

Realization of the "royal priesthood of all believers."

Timocracy.

STATE

Guardian of the freedom and dignity of man:

"Mixed government" with an interior balance. Tendency towards a "patriarchal" (even hereditary) monarchical head. "Statesmanship." The people always asked for their desires and these are seriously taken into consideration without being accepted as *ultima ratio*. They are not placed above knowledge, reason and experience. Primacy of quality over quantity. Administration of an elitarian, nonpolitical character. Church and State, State and society as separate entities—although cooperating. The State is the servant of the common weal, the servant of the people's true interests. The federal principle and personal freedom are the guiding stars of its structure and function.

SOCIETY

Estates, not "classes." An "open society." The estates are functional. They are not hierarchic units, not castes. Demophily. Leadership of changing, but tradition-connected (not tradition-determined) elites.

NATION

Patriotism and Supranationalism. Unity in diversity.

CHURCH & FAITH

Church and State are *separate, but cooperate* as equals within society in all domains where their collaboration and mutual understanding are indispensable (school, legislation, spiritual care of the army, the prisoners, hospital inmates, care of certain art treasures). Such cooperation with several churches (or non-Christian denominations) is (by experience) as feasible as with a single one.

POLITICAL STRUCTURE

Principle of Subsidiarity. In state and society the larger (higher) unit only then becomes active and effective when the smaller (lower, more immediate) is incapable of coping with the problems: Where the person fails, the family takes action; where the family fails, society steps in; where society is powerless, small and then progressively larger political units come into play. The necessity of creating small "kingdoms" in which the person can be sovereign.

IDEALS

Development in the light of tradition. (Without tradition there is no progress, but endless fresh starts from zero.) Respect for the achievements of the past and institutions organically grown. Progress through additions, corrections, adaptations. Full comprehensions for the glories, but also for the limitations of man. "Sovereign," which means objective and thoughtful, attitude towards the world "organic concept" of life.

WELFARE

"Social security" through general prosperity and respect for the independence of the person. Ideal climate for acquiring and retaining property which, except for the "saint," is indispensable for his liberty. In the financial-material crisis of the person his primary sources of aid are the family, cooperatives, professional associations, charities. The State intervenes only where all other agents fail. Fostering of the natural virtues: saving, providence, planning.

LAWS

Legislation, the law, jurisdiction are based on the natural law, on revelation, on tradition, on intelligent differentiation. Motto: *suum cuique*.

INTERNATIONAL RELATIONS

Acceptance of the fact that the nations are different, ofter radically different from each other; that they have, therefore, different traditions, institutions and dreams. Nevertheless: distinction between the political genius of the various nations and political-ideological aberrations which might menace the well-being of the world.

INSTRUCTION & EDUCATION

The principle of the natural *aristoi*. Intellectual-moral selectiveness coupled with the effort to ensure the social rise of the more gifted and more laborious. Instruction and education for a full and noble life. Respect for the rights of the parents. Importance of religious instruction. Public, private and/or corporate education.

ECONOMICS

Free market economy with free competition but also protection for the free choice of the consumer. A sensible (not petty) intervention of the State to keep competition alive. Emotional attachment of the workers to their enterprises—affection for and pride in them. Facilities for acquiring capital. Absolute stability of the currencies.

THE SEXES

a) *Sexes:* Here too the principle, "to everybody his due."
b) *Family:* Vertical, hence dynastic feelings tying together the generations. Absolute. The family as cell of society and State. It is also the frame for the development of the personality. Families are as different as personalities are.

HUMAN COHESION

Authority. (Direction through inner ties, not outside pressure.)
Love and respect.

Appendix

The Tragic Life of

Charles-Armand Tuffin,

Marquis de la Rouërie

Some people will never tire of repeating that the American War of Independence was essentially a prelude to the French Revolution, and that the latter was a mere continuation of the former. They will cite Lafayette and Tom Paine, but they will pass over in silence Jefferson's and Gouverneur Morris's critical remarks and they probably will not even have heard of the crown witness for the gulf separating America's noble struggle for freedom from the infamous horrors of the French Revolution—Charles-Armand Tuffin, Marquis de la Rouërie, born on April 13, 1750 in Brittany, a man lamentably overlooked by most historians on both sides of the Atlantic.

Charles-Armand, unfortunately, lost his father early in life and his mother found it difficult to deal with the temperamental but generous and high-minded young man. Sooner than was good for him he was sent to Paris where he joined the guards. There he fell temporarily in love with an actress, the famous Mademoiselle Beaumesnil, naively tried to join the Trappists to forget the grief of his unsuccessful suit, was retrieved by his uncle, became infatuated with another actress, Mademoiselle Fleury, and ended up by having a duel with a remote relative of the King, Count Bourbon-Busset. He almost killed the man and fled to Geneva. From there he handed in his resignation and, accompanied by three servants, started for America which he finally reached at the end of April 1777.

Did the young Marquis take leave of Marie Antoinette before he sailed for America? This was standard procedure for all volunteers because the Queen had a special enthusiasm for the cause of American liberty.[1] On account of the scandal which had forced his resignation we doubt very much that he did. However, his arrival on the shores of the nascent United States was as dramatic as the circumstances of his departure. The crossing had taken almost two months, and the ship was in sight of land when it was attacked by a British cruiser which sank it on the spot. Charles-Armand with his three companions swam to shore and climbed onto the beach without a stitch on them but luckily still in possession of a full purse. Thus our hero arrived before Lafayette, and he also left after his noble rival had returned to France.

His difficulties in the beginning were considerable. After spending $480 for the command of a volunteer corps previously organized by a Swiss major (one had to pay in those days—when nobody owned draft cards—for the privilege of a commission, for the privilege to die on the battlefields), he finally received permission from George Washington to raise a legion. Under the name of "Colonel Armand" he enjoyed great popularity with the Americans.

The Marquis de Chastellux, another of the many volunteer aristocrats from Europe, met him in 1780, and from him we know that Charles-Armand had lost the gaiety of his earlier years and become a rather serious young man. He was then operating under General Gates and fighting with Baron de Kalb. In the Battle of Camden he suffered grievous losses in men and material and, finding it difficult to obtain a new supply of arms or even uniforms, he took the next available boat to France, slipped through the British blockade and, back in his own country, borrowed 50,000 livres at the handsome interest of 50 percent in order to buy new equipment. The Congress finally owed him $12,000, a quite respectable sum in those days.

After his return to the United States he distinguished himself at the siege of Yorktown where he started a lifelong friendship with a Frenchman of German extraction—Gustave de Fontevieux de Deux-Ponts, a nephew of the Duke of Zweibrücken. George Washington was so impressed by his bravery that he permitted him to select fifty of the best men available for his brigade.[2]

"Colonel Armand" was one of the very last French officers to go home. He had stayed in America until the end of 1783, he was in possession of a special letter of commendation from George Washington, he also owned the Grand Medal of the Order of the Cincinnati.[3] Yet hardly had he returned to France accompanied by Major Shaffner, his American friend, than he realized that he had arrived too late to receive a commission. By his delay he had actually "missed the boat" of promotion. So, while Lafayette became a big public figure, doing a great deal of harm, blissfully ignoring the warnings of Gouverneur Morris, the American minister, "Colonel Armand" perforce retired to his castle, Saint Ouen de la Rouërie. There he brooded over the dry rot into which France had fallen.

In this mood of disgust and resignation he suddenly decided (though up to his neck in debts) to found a family. Through a quirk of circumstances this proved his undoing. The young woman who followed him to the altar was the daughter of the Marquis de Saint-Brice. Major Shaffner was one of the two witnesses at the ceremony and George Washington wrote him a warm letter of congratulation. Only six months later, however, his bride, always of precarious health, was dead of pulmonary tuberculosis. All the care lavished upon her by her devoted husband, who never forgot her, and by his personal friend Dr. Chévetel, had been in vain.

Charles-Armand, ardent hunter and crack shot that he was, tried to bury his grief in the wilderness of Brittany. In the meantime clouds were gathering on the political horizon. The American War had emptied the French treasury and the government tried desperately to repair the damage. Now we are in the year 1788. France is in the throes of a deep restlessness. Charles-Armand, who tried to forget his loss in hunting and shooting, was upset about the King's refusal to restore the old constitutional order and to respect the *parlements*. The Estates General were not convoked, only the local *parlements* met and were constantly in danger of being dissolved by Louis XVI's Minister, Beau de Loménie. Charles-Armand attended the Breton *parlement* in Rennes which sent a delegation of twelve noblemen to demand Loménie de Brienne's "head" from the King. Just arrived in Paris, they were told that the King would not receive the rebellious Breton nobles. On July 14 they gave a huge dinner to certain members of the Breton colony in Paris and in fierce speeches told the King to watch out. When they returned to their respective abodes each of them was met by police officers who arrested them with *lettres de cachet*. Thus they ended in the Bastille.[4]

There they spent forty-two days, each accompanied by a servant.

They hired a billiard table, drank innumerable bottles of champagne, and had a marvelous time. As soon as Loménie de Brienne fell, they were released and returned triumphantly to Brittany. Still, Charles-Armand was not too happy about this temporary victory. He went back to his castle but his anxiety increased. In a letter dated June 18, 1789 (less than a month prior to the storming of the Bastille) he had already written to his friend George Washington: "I fear two great evils for my country—anarchy on the one hand, despotism on the other." He intimated to the President that he contemplated leaving France "to take the oath of allegiance and fidelity to the laws, government, and people of North America."

Charles-Armand's apprehensions grew with the increasing tensions between State and Church. Then his correspondence ceased.[5] He had become aware that it was his duty to face the evil, to fight against democracy and for liberty where liberty was threatened. His voyage to America, under the circumstances, would have been nothing but an escape.

Always hostile to absolutism, Charles-Armand was in the beginning rather in favor of a return to a constitutional form of government which had been interrupted by Louis XIV. However, the Estates General, now merged into a single body, the National Assembly, as well as the privileges of the nobility were soon abolished. This meant little to our hero because in the west of France—Normandy, Brittany, and Vendée—the relationship between nobility and peasantry had always been a very friendly one. This area was and still is famous for its profound religious convictions[6] and thus a real class consciousness hardly arose: Nobody could possibly know who was superior to whom in the eyes of God. The peasants took part in the festivities in the castles, and the nobility appeared at peasant weddings and baptisms, conversing, dancing, and drinking with them.

Not far from La Rouërie was Count Ranconnet de Noyan's castle which served as hospital and dispensary for the entire region. The Count, a widower, ate at the same table with his servants. He acted as amateur physician and his daughters as nurses. Like Charles-Armand he had opposed royal absolutism and fulminated against the frivolous life at Versailles. Now, however, he was worried about the turn events had taken. Not only the Crown was under attack, but religion as well. The priests who had given the oath to the Constitution and were automatically suspended by the Vatican (because the oath had an anti-Papal character) were not accepted by the peasantry. These "intruders," as they were called, soon had to flee the countryside. The spirit of resistance was growing everywhere.[7]

Old Ranconnet de Noyan sat down with Charles-Armand and drew up plans for a counterrevolution. It seemed imperative to establish contact with the insurgents and the emigrants who had gathered in Germany around the Comte d'Artois, the King's younger brother. Charles-Armand decided to carry out this mission himself and journeyed to Coblentz and Ulm via London. There financial help and military cooperation were promised him. His hopes somewhat buoyed up, he returned to France. In Paris, where he stayed a couple of days, he met not only his old comrade-in-arms, Gustave de Fontevieux, but also Dr. Chévetel, whom he trusted as a sincere friend. Little did he dream that, in the meantime, the physician had become a rabid Jacobin and kept close touch with Danton and the infamous Marat. After telling Chévetel about his plans Charles-Armand returned to his ancestral home.

The moves preparatory to the insurrection were soon underway. There were minor clashes between the bluecoats and the peasantry in which Charles-Armand appeared as a leader directing the hand-to-hand fighting. The authorities tried to arrest him, but he slipped easily through their hands. On his side there appeared his trusted friend, Major Shaffner, and his youthful cousin, the mysterious Thérèse de Moëlien who acted as a messenger. Dressed as a huntress, the Medal of the Order of the Cincinnati around her neck, this beautiful amazon dashed across the country on a black stallion to forward letters, money, instructions. As far as we can make out, it seems that Charles-Armand, never forgetting his wife, was unable to respond to her affection for him, and that George Shaffner was deeply infatuated with her. The tragic element was the dominant note in Charles-Armand's life.

And then the authorities, warned by Chévetel, invaded his castle from which he was forced to flee. It was ransacked from top to bottom. Now calling himself "Monsieur Millet," Charles-Armand appeared one day here, another day there—a "Lone Ranger" in the service of God and Country. And just as the insurrection in the neighboring Vendée had been organized by one peasant and one nobleman—Jacques Cathelineau and the Count de Larochejaquelin—the rising in Brittany was also headed by such a pair: our Charles-Armand and Jean Cotterau, nicknamed "Jean Chouan."[8]

In the meantime the treacherous Chévetel continued his activities. The true motives for his activities will probably never be known, but after receiving definite instructions from Danton, he went to Brittany. Charles-Armand, warned about him by his Parisian friends, told the doctor bluntly that he knew about his connections. Anybody else would have been disturbed by these revelations, but Chévetel readily admitted everything, telling the conspirators, however, that Danton and his charmed circle were fed up with the Revolution and were willing to make common cause with the insurgents.

He lied so brazenly and convincingly that not only credence was given to his words, but he was even entrusted with an important mission to London and to Liège, where he conferred with the Comte d'Artois. After all, it was expedient to make use of a man who could travel abroad freely as Chévetel could.

It had been agreed upon at Liège that the rebellion should break out the moment the liberating armies of the Coalition (Austrians, Prussians, and the French Volunteers) entered the city of Châlons-sur-Marnes. Hence the Paris government, duly warned by Chévetel, concentrated all their efforts on defending the town. The peasants under Cotterau were becoming impatient. At Saint-Ouen-des-Toits they had fought the bluecoats and were slowly gaining control of the countryside. Advancing at night, using the sinister shout of the screech owl, ''Eyoo-eyoo,'' to keep in touch with one another, they had become the terror of soldiers and policemen.

Charles-Armand, disappointed by the successful defense of Châlons, now set a new date for the general uprising—March 10, 1793. He made the castle of La Fosse-Hingant his headquarters and, accompanied by two servants, traveled by night from castle to castle, from village to village, organizing the rebellion. His dream was to enter Paris at the head of a peasant army.

But God, who alone fully comprehends the mystery of suffering, decreed otherwise. Not far from Saint-Malo there is the castle of La Guyomarais, then inhabited by the family of the same name. Count Guyomarais was a freedom-loving, God-fearing man, father of a large family, and loyal to his king. On January 12th at 1 o'clock in the morning Charles-Armand arrived—nearly dead from exhaustion—before the gate of the castle. Night after night he and his companions had slept under trees and in ditches, to cover better the vast expanse of France's far west. Charles-Armand had had a bad fall from his horse, but the first of the group to be struck by illness was his servant Saint-Pierre whom he nursed back to health.

Hardly had Saint-Pierre recovered when Charles-Armand was afflicted with an enigmatic disease, probably meningitis. Tortured by high temperature he had to stay in bed. A searching party of bluecoats raided the castle, but the owner, previously warned, transferred Charles-Armand to a peasant hut where the half-delirious man escaped detection. Once the danger had passed he was brought back to the castle.

In the meantime both Fontevieux and Shaffner, back from London after a dangerous crossing, arrived at La Guyomarais. The most important piece of information they had picked up in St. Malo was the fact of the King's execution, but they hid it from Charles-Armand. A day later the papers carried the sad news. Fontevieux who read the gazette aloud to his sick friend carefully left out all references to the dramatic end of the trial, but while he was answering a sudden call, Charles-Armand got hold of the paper and with a heart-rending cry fell back on his bed. His temperature again mounted, the doctor spoke of brain fever, and a serious crisis set in. Soon, after frightful agony, Charles-Armand rendered up his soul to God. He died without receiving the Sacraments as no nonjuring priest was available in the neighborhood.

La Rouërie dead was no less a liability than La Rouërie alive. The Count decided to bury him in a nearby wood, and with the help of a few servants and the Countess, the mournful ceremony took place in the middle of the night. No coffin was obtainable and amidst the tears of those present the earthly remains of Charles-Armand were lowered into a dark hole. A howling, icy wind made the prayers almost inaudible.

Saint-Pierre, inconsolable after his master's death, volunteered to bring all the money, papers, and documents to La Fosse-Hingant. But whom did he meet there but Chévetel who eagerly listened to his story and suggested a hiding place for the documents Saint-Pierre had brought from La Guyomarais.

From this moment events assumed the inexorable character of a Greek tragedy. Lalligand, a collaborator of Chévetel, arrived with a large band of soldiers at La Guyomarais, and it did not take long before definite proofs were found of La Rouërie's sojourn there. One of the servants admitted it after being soaked with liquor. The grave of Charles-Armand was discovered, the badly decomposed corpse was exhumed and a *gendarme* severed the head from the body.

The Guyomarais family, meanwhile, were brutally grilled by their inquisitors and, in order to force the Countess to talk, they threw the head of Charles-Armand in her face. She fainted but her husband now ceased to stall. "Yes," he admitted, "this is the head of the man before whom you quailed. He is dead and now, of course, you are greatly relieved." The whole family with the exception of the two youngest daughters, mere children, were arrested and dragged away. These little girls were left alone, crazed with grief, in the empty halls of the plundered castle.

And then a second blow struck La Foss-Hingant. Lalligand and Chévetel pursued the investigations and the Desilles and de la Fonchais families, Gustave de Fontevieux and the glamorous Thérèse de Moëlien were arrested. The mammoth trial of this group and of the Guyomarais family ended with twelve death sentences.

Young Madame de la Fonchais was given a chance to escape the "Nation's Razor" if she would divulge the name of the person who had given her the money she had forwarded to Charles-Armand. This she refused to do. "But you are a mother and you have children!" the prosecutor shouted at her. "The person who gave me the money is in precisely the same position," she replied with tears in her eyes. It was actually her sister-in-law whom she was shielding by her courageous silence.

The jailers offered the conspirators the solace of religion provided they would accept suspended priests, the "intruders." These, of course, they flatly rejected. Thérèse de Moëlien also refused the aid of the barber to cut off her beautiful hair and she handled the scissors herself. The painful preparation for the execution took two hours: Prayers were said and they exhorted each other to fortitude. The usual howl of the mob was not heard: The dignity and noble bearing of the "Breton Conspirators" impressed everyone. And in Gustave de Fontevieux one of the many volunteer fighters for America's freedom had gone to his reward as a martyr for his Christian convictions.

We do not know what happened to Major Shaffner. The great rebellion broke out on March 10 as planned. The major then joined the ranks of the "Chouans" and we know that he was taken prisoner near Nantes, but then suddenly all trace is lost. In all likelihood, together with other prisoners and nonjuring priests, he was placed on one of the many rafts which were sunk in the middle of the Loire. These *noyades* (mass-drownings) were the precursors of the indiscriminate extermination of prisoners which disgraced World War II. They were the first Katyns in modern history.

Lalligand ended on the guillotine, but Chévetel became the fat and prosperous mayor of Orly. He had switched from the Jacobins to Napoleon and from Napoleon to the Bourbons. It is not here on earth, but in the beyond that man is finally judged. The wars of the Chouans continued unabated until 1795. Only with the help of the "Infernal Hordes," the "Black and Tans" of the Revolution, could the rebellious peasantry be subdued.

The bravery of these sturdy farmers, the determined efforts of "Colonel Armand," of Thérèse, of George Shaffner and Gustave de Fontevieux had been in vain. The French Revolution was victorious and its evil aftermath is still with us. Our heroes themselves are almost

442

forgotten. This in itself is strange because virtually every nook and corner of American history has been explored. Oceans of ink have been spilled over Lafayette, a vain man who had never properly understood the real spirit of the American War of Independence and who had done such great harm at the beginning of the Revolution in France.

"Colonel Armand," whose letters to George Washington until 1791 mirrored such admiration for America and melancholic despair for France, the gallant and enigmatic Thérèse, Fontevieux, the hero of Yorktown, and—last but not least—Major Shaffner are figures worthy of consideration by budding historians of the New World.[9] Let us hope that young Americans will get to know and love them, so that, one day, they will live again in the pages of novels, on the stage, and on the screen.

Notes

INTRODUCTION

¹ There is, of course no program without an ideology. This is the reason Whittaker Chambers could write, "The Right has no program. A distaste for communism and socialism is no program." *Cf. Odyssey of a Friend. Whittaker Chambers, Letters to William F. Buckley Jr.* Privately printed (1969) p.69. This is certainly the situation in the English-speaking world today. Chambers also insisted that capitalism and conservatism are mutually exclusive. (*Ibid.*, p. 229). He did not profess to be a conservative: "I am a man of the Right. I am a man of the Right because I mean to uphold capitalism in its American version." (p. 228) Klemens von Klemperer in his *Konservative Bewegungen. Zwischen Kaiserreich und Nationalsozialismus* (Munich and Vienna: Oldenbourg, 1961), p. 23, insists that conservatism has different forms of expression, but no doctrine, no tenets. (The American original of this interesting book was published in 1957 by the Princeton University Press under the title *Germany's New Conservatism. Its History and Dilemma in the Twentieth Century.*)
² *Cf.* Alexis de Tocqueville, "De la démocratie en Amérique," *Oeuvres d'Alexis de Tocqueville* (Paris: Michel Lévy Frères, 1864), vol. 3, p. 526.
³ *Cf.* Foster Rhea Dulles, *The Road to Teheran* (Princeton: Princeton University Press, 1944) p. 6.

Chapter I

¹ *Cf.* p. 169.
² Dr. Marcel Eck says in his essay "Propos de la sexualité" (in *Qu'est-*

ce-que l'homme. Paris: Pierre Horay, 1955, p. 110) that the "hell of homosexuality" lies precisely in the fact that it avoids genuine dialogue and that homosexual love is not in quest of the other but is merely seeking the self.

[3] José Ortega y Gasset says in *Invertebrate Spain*, trs. Mildred Adams (New York: Norton, 1937), pp. 170-171: "Probably the origin of this anti-individual fury lies in the fact that in their innermost hearts the masses feel themselves weak and defenceless in the face of their destiny. On a bitter and terrible page Nietzsche notes how, in primitive societies which were weak when confronted with the difficulties of existence, every individual and original act was a crime, and the man who tried to lead a solitary life was a malefactor. He must in everything comport himself according to the fashion of the tribe." (Not to be found in the Spanish edition of *España invertebrada*. Madrid: Calpe, 1922). On the antagonism between liberty and equality, liberalism and democracy, see also Roger G. Williams, *Free and Unequal: The Biological Basis of Individual Liberty* (Austin: University of Texas Press, 1953): A. D. Lindsay, *The Modern Democratic State* (London: Oxford University Press, 1945), vol. 1, pp. 46, 79: Franz Schnabel, *Deutsche Geschichte in Neunzehnten Jahrhundert* (Freiburg i.Br.: Herder, 1933), vol. 2, pp. 97-98: Heinz O. Ziegler, *Autoritärer oder totaler Staat* (Tübingen: J. C. B. Mohr, 1932), p. 10: Wilhelm Stählin, "Freiheit und Ordnung," in *Der Mensch und die Freiheit* (München: Neues Abendland, 1954), p. 17. Werner Jaeger in his *Paideia* (Berlin: Walter de Gruyter, 1954, vol. 2., p. 104) emphasises the fact that Athens was democratic, that it laid stress on *to íson* (equality), but not on personal freedom. Professor Goetz Briefs in his *Zwischen Kapitalismus und Syndikalismus* (Bern: A. Francke, 1952, p. 75) reminds us that all democratism (which he distinguishes from democracy) must end in despotism since it is opposed to the realities of man and society. Herbert Marcuse, referring to Hegel, came to a very similar conclusion. *Cf.* his *Reason and Revolution*, (Boston Press, 1960), pp. 242-243.

[4] *Cf.* Jacob Burckhardt in his letter to Friedrich von Preen dated January 1, 1879: "You are perfectly right: One wants to train people for meetings. Finally, people will start to scream if they don't form crowds of at least a hundred." (Jacob Burckhardt, *Briefe an seinen Freud Friedrich von Preen 1864-1893* (Stuttgart: Deutsche Verlaganstalt, 1922), p. 130.

[5] *Cf.* Friedrich Nietzsche, *Werke* (Leipzig: Kröner, 1917), vol. 12, p. 140.

[6] Witness President Wilson's declaration shortly before America's entry into World War I: "Conformity will be the only virtue. And every man who refuses to conform will have to pay the penalty." (*Cf.* Harold U. Faulkner, *From Versailles to the New Deal* (New Haven: Yale University Press, 1950) p. 141.

On the dangers of standardisation see Josiah Royce in *Race Questions*, p. 74 cited by Ralph Henry Gabriel, *The Course of American Democratic Thought: An Intellectual History since 1815* (New York: The Ronald Press, 1940), pp. 275-276.

446

[7] *Cf.* "Monita quibus Stephanus filium Emericum instruxit, ut regnum recte pieque administraret," Chap. VI, in J. P. Migne, *Patrologiae Cursus Completus, Series Latina*, vol. 151, pp. 1240ff.

Chapter II

[1] See the excellent contribution of W. H. Hutt, "The Complexities of South Africa" in *The African Nettle*, Frank S. Meyer, ed. (New York: John Day, 1965), pp. 157ff. *Cf.* W. H. Hutt, *The Economics of the Color Bar* (London, André Deutsch, 1964), p. 58ff., and Ray Marshall, *The Negro and Organized Labor* (Sydney: John Wiley, 1968).

[2] The address of Pius XII to the World Federalists condemning virtually the one-man-one-vote system and the worship of numbers received little publicity in the Catholic press—anywhere. For a full text of *The New York Times*, No. 34,041, April 7, 1951, p. 3 or *Acta Apostolicae Sedis*, annus et vol. XLIII, 1951, pp. 278ff.

[3] As, for instance, John Stuart Mill, so frequently and enthusiastically quoted by our leftists. Equality of vote Mill considered "in principle wrong, because recognising a wrong standard and exercising a bad influence on the voter's mind. It is not useful but hurtful, that the constitution of a country should declare ignorance to be entitled to as much political power as knowledge." *Cf.* his "Considerations on Representative Government" included in *Utilitarianism, Liberty and Representative Government*, no. 482 of "Everyman's Library" (London: Dent, 1910), p. 288.

The criticism of the one-man-one-vote principle is naturally almost universal. See also Rosalind Murray (Mrs. Arnold Toynbee), *The Good Pagan's Failure* (New York: Longmans, Green, 1939), pp. 137-139: Sir Henry Maine in R. Sellars, *The Next Step in Democracy* (New York: Macmillan, 1916), p. 216: John Adams, Letter to James Madison, June 17, 1817, in *The Selected Writings of John and Quincy Adams*, A. Koch and W. Peden, eds. (New York: Knopf, 1946), p. 202: Jacob Burckhardt, *op.cit.* p. 200: Charles Péguy, *Pensées* (Paris: Gallimard, 1934), pp. 21-22: Gabriel Marcel, "Considérations sur l'égalité," *Etudes Carmélitaines*, vol. 24-2, pp. 164-165: *Letters from Albert Jay Nock* (Caldwell: Caxton Printers, 1949), p. 176: D. H. Lawrence as quoted by Witter Bynner, *Journey with Genius* (New York: John Day, 1951), p. 226: Antonio Rosmini-Serbati, *La società e il suo fine*, Carlo Brocca, ed. (Milan: Edizioni di Uomo, 1945), pp. 45-46. Recently the attacks of Professor Max Horkheimer against the principle of majority rule (coming from a former supporter of the New Left) created in Europe a minor sensation. *Cf.* his *Zur Kritik der instrumentellen Vernunft* (Frankfurt am Main: S. Fischer, 1967), p. 38.

At present Laborite Great Britain in the humble service of democratism (and a number of African States) is boycotting and blockading Rhodesia because that country, rejecting the democratic one-man-one-vote system, adopted a timocratic (and by no means "racist") electoral law. It is true that the Rhodesian parliament is elected by a minority but so is the Swiss Diet. Of the entire Swiss population (residing in the country) about 29 percent (before female suffrage on the federal level was introduced two years ago) had the right to vote and between 19 and 20 percent actually vote. Yet nobody so far has thought of organizing an economic warfare against Switzerland, with the possible exception of Stalin in 1945.

[4] How low the Soviet birthrate is actually, is open to conjecture since reliable statistics about the USSR do not exist. We know only about the catastrophic decline of the birthrate in the satellite states. In the "German Democratic Republic" it is the French rate. *Cf.* "Die Ausbeutung der Frau in kommunistischen Osteuropa," in *Neue Züricher Zeitung*, February 15, 1970, p. 19.

[5] *Cf.* Friedrich August (von) Hayek, *Individualism and Economic Order* (Chicago: University of Chicago Press, 1947), p. 15.

[6] Castes are inherited by birth and are immovable and unchangeable: estate status is usually inherited but is not unchangeable. A nobleman could become a priest or friar, a burgher could be nobilitated, a peasant could receive the "freedom" of a city and thus become a burgher. Contrary to the general notion there were no "higher" or "lower" estates. They just had different functions. (There are higher and lower classes, though).

Chapter III

[1] Marchese Vilfredo Pareto's *Trattato de sociologia universale* (Florence: G. Barbèra, 1923) also exists in an English translation by Arthur Livingston under the title of *Mind and Society* (New York: Harcourt, Brace, 1935). Livingston also translated a part of Gaetano Mosca's *Elemmenti di Scienza Politica* (Turin, 1923) and published it as *The Ruling Class* (New York: McGraw-Hill, 1939). Robert(o) Michels' *Zur Soziologie des Parteienwesens in der modernen Demokratie* (Leipzig: Duncker und Humblot, 1911) saw many editions.

The thesis that all democracy is in practice always oligarchy has also been defended by Enrique Gil y Robles in his *Tratado de Derecho Político según les principios de la filosofia y el derecho cristianos* (Salamanca: Imprenta Salmaticense, 1902), vol. 2, pp. 882ff. This professor of Salamanca University was the father of Don José Maria Gil Robles, founder of the CEDA and Prime Minister of Spain in 1934.

[2] Article 21 of the Weimar Constitution insisted that the deputies are only subject to their conscience and not to the desires of their voters. We find the same stipulation in Article 91 of the Swiss constitution. *Cf.* William F. Rappard, *The Government of Switzerland* (New York: Van Nostrand, 1936), pp. 59, 64. The contrary (democratic) position had been taken by Hans Kelsen,

author of the present Austrian constitution, in his *General Theory of Law and State*, trsl. A. Wedberg (Cambridge, Mass., Harvard University Press, 1946).

[3] Rappard reasoned that Switzerland rejected female suffrage because she is essentially middle class. Only the aristocracy and the proletariat truly accept female equality.

[4] The critique of proportional representation (P.R.) was the life work of Professor Ferdinand A. Hermens, formerly of Notre Dame, now of Cologne University.

[5] Naturally, in old times, *unanimity* was the rule and *had* to be achieved (as today among the jurors in Britain and in the United States). Unanimity was also required for the election of the king in the Polish *Rzeczpospolita*, only the nobility (the *szlachta*) voted and a nobleman could not possibly be subject to a man who was not his own choice but somebody else's. The Golden Bull abolished unanimity in 1356 and in the Imperial Diet (of the Holy Roman Empire) in 1496 decisions were taken by majority vote. *Cf.* J. Stawski, *Le principe de la majorité* (Geneva: Officina Boeniningiana, 1920), pp. 29-38, also Carl Ernst Jarcke, "Prinzipienfragen" in *Vermischte Schriften* (Paderborn: Schöningh, 1854), pp. 175-176.

[6] *Cf.* Herman Melville, *Mardi—And a Voyage Tither* (Boston: Small, Maynard, n.d.), p. 183. Majoritism seems to have been strongly backed by Marsiglio of Padua, *Cf.* Felice Battaglia, *Marsiglio da Padova e il pensiero politico medievale* (Firenze: Sansoni, 1928): Sigmund Riezler, *Die literarischen Widersacher der Päpste zur Zeit Ludwigs des Baiers* (Leipzig: Duncker und Humblot, 1874), p. 203. Yet Alan Gewirth insists that the purely majoritarian character of the passage in the *Defensor Pacis* (XII, 3) is the result of mangled manuscripts. *Cf. Marsilius of Padua, The Defender of Peace*, trsl. and edit. Alan Gewirth (New York: Columbia University Press, 1956), vol. 2, p. 45, n 6, Orestes Brownson, the brilliant and original American Catholic thinker rejected majorities in strong terms. *Cf.* the *Collected Works* (Detroit: T. Nourse, 1882-1887), vol. 15, pp. 5, 40, quoted by Lawrence Roemer, *Brownson on Democracy and the Trend Toward Socialism* (New York: Philosophical Library, 1953), pp. 36-37, 45: Carl Ernst Jarcke, *op.cit.* pp. 172-173. Most revealing is Herman Finer, a leftist professor who, replying to a F. A. v. Hayek's question whether the Nazi Reich should be credited with exercising rule of law if Hitler had had a clear majority in the elections said, "The answer is 'Yes,' the majority would be right, the Rule of Law would be in operation, *if* the majority voted him into power. The majority might be unwise, and it might be wicked, but the Rule of Law would prevail. For in a democracy right is what the majority belives it to be." *Cf. The Road to Reaction* (Boston: Little, Brown, 1945), p. 60. An injunction against the moral dangers of majoritism we already find in II. Moses, XXIII, 11, which can be summed up in the words, "Thou shalt not follow a majority to do evil."

[7] This author is convinced that (contrary to the teaching of St. Thomas) the State (as we basically conceive it) is the result of original sin, i.e., of

man's imperfections, *Cf.* also Erik von Keuhnelt-Leddihn, *Liberty or Equality* (Caldwell, Caxton Printers, 1952), pp. 92-93 or Isdem, *Freiheit oder Gleichheit?* (Salzburg: Otto Meüller, 1953), pp. 235-237. It is a commonly held view that St. Augustine and Luther saw in the state a result of the Fall. Yet Otto Schilling in his magistral work *Die Staats und Soziallehren des hl. Augustinus* (Freiburg i Br.: Herder, 1910), pp. 45-63 has proved the contrary and from Luther we have no exact formulation: we can only deduce such a stand. St. Bonaventure, Hugo of St. Victor and Aegydius Romanus, however, blamed the state on original sin. (Exact sources and materials can be found in *Freiheit oder Gleichheit?*, notes 680-685 on pp. 507-508. Nevertheless, I am convinced that *society* would have existed under all circumstances, and with society —leadership and arbitration.)

[8] The connection between love and service has been well brought out by Franz von Baader, "Vierzig Sätze aus einer religiösen Erotik," in *Gesammelte Schriften*, F. Hoffman, ed. (Leipzig: Bethman, 1853), vol. 4, p. 186: Gustave Thibon, "Christianisme et liberté," in *Recherches et Débats* (Paris 1952), new series 1, p. 16: Georges Bernanos, *La France contre les robots* (Paris: Laffont, 1947), p. 87. The relationship between loyalty, law and love was the guiding idea in the defense speech of Sir Roger Casement. *Cf.* Geoffrey de C. Parmiter. *Roger Casement* (London, Barker, 1936), pp. 303ff.

[9] Is polygamy (unlike polyandry) against the natural law? We doubt it.

[10] Cited by Richard Hertz in *Chance and Symbol* (Chicago: The University of Chicago Press, 1948), p. 107.

[11] *Cf.* Elliott Roosevelt, *As Father Saw It* (New York: Duell, Sloane and Pearce, 1946) and Winston S. Churchill, *The Second World War* (London: Cassell, 1952), vol. 5, p. 330.

[12] *Cf.* Peter Wust, *Ungewissheit und Wagnis* (Salzburg: Anton Pustet, 1937), *passim*.

[13] This distinction between liberalism and democracy we can find among nearly all outstanding political scientists and essayists. Here are just a few authors and works containing references to this piece of semantics: Irving Babbitt, *Democracy and Leadership*; W. H. Chamberlin, *The World's Iron Age*; Christopher Dawson, *The Judgment of the Nations*; Luis Legaz y Lacambra, *Introducción a la teoria del Estado Nacionalsindicalista;* José Ortega y Gasset, *Castilla y sus castillos*; Gustav Radbruch, *Rechtsphilosophie*; Wilhelm Röpke, *Die Gesellschaftskrise der Gegenwart*; Frank Thiess, *Das Reich der Dämonen*; Georg Freiherr von Hertling, *Recht, Staat und Gesellschaft*; Max Weber, *Grundriss der Sozialökonomik* 111, Abteilung; Franz Schnabel, *op.cit.*; Heinz O. Ziegler, *op.cit.*; Winfried Martini, *Das Ende aller Sicherheit*; Carl Schmitt, "Die geistesgeschichtliche Lage des heutigen Parlamentarismus" in *Bonner Festausgabe für E. Zittelmann*; Hermann Hefele, *"Demokratie und Liberalismus,"* *Hochland* XXII; Georges Vedel, *Manuel élémentaire de droit constitutionnel*; Guido de Ruggiero, *Storia del liberalismo*

europeo; Denis de Rougemont and Charlotte Muret, *The Heart of Europe*; Bernard Wall, *European Notebook*; Everett Dean Martin, *Liberty*; Georges Bernanos, *La liberté pour quoi faire?*; Nicholas Berdyaev, *Novoye srednovyekovye*; Petko Staynov, *Kompetentnost i narodovlastie*. Probably the best *semantic* analysis of the terms "liberalism" and "democracy" can be found in Giovanni Sartori, *Democrazia e definizioni* (Bologna: Il Mulino, 1969). The authors dealing with the incompatibility of democracy and freedom, democracy and liberalism are legion. An identification of democracy and freedom can be found, however, in the work of a strictly positivist scholar denying a hierarchy of ethical values—Hans Kelsen in his *Vom Wesen und Wert der Demokratie* (Tübingen: J. C. Mohr, 1929), pp. 3-4.

[14] *Cf.* J. L. Talmon, *The Origins of Totalitarianism* (London: Secker and Warburg, 1952). In this book Talmon puts the main emphasis on Gracchus Babeuf. There have been plans during the Terror to put all Frenchmen into a uniform, a "national costume" (p. 245). Similar plans were entertained by Morelly. (See p. 107 of this book.) About the educational theories of the *Babouvistes cf.* pp. 245-247.

[15] *Cf.* Alexis de Tocqueville, *op.cit.* vol. 3, pp. 517-523.

Chapter IV

[1] J. J. Bachofen maintained that matriarchal civilizations generally consider the left side to be superior to the right. *Vide* his *Das Mutterrecht*, Basel, 1948, p. 54ff. The Gnostics identified "left" with the lower and "right" with the higher elements of creation. *Cf.* Francois M. Saguard, *La Gnose Valentinienne et le témoignage de St. Irénée* (Paris, 1947), pp. 544-545. A very witty analysis of the leftist mind can be found in the small book of Leon Plumyène and Raymond Lasierra, *Le complexe de gauche* (Paris: Flammarion, 1967). As *leitmotif* of the leftist mentality the authors see "the murder of the father."

[2] In German the sentence, "The just, saved and judged, were on the right" would sound like this: "Die *gerichteten* und *geretteten Gerechten* waren auf der *Rechten*." In Spanish and Portuguese the word for "left" is taken from another language, from Basque, (*Izquierdo*).

[3] In the non-Latin Continental languages we distinguish between citizenship, nationality, and race. The first, a legal concept, can easily be changed; the second, of a cultural-linguistic nature, will be difficult to transform; while the third, a biological-material notion, is immutable *for the individual*. "Nationalism" in the Germanic and Slavic countries, therefore, implies an exaggerated emphasis on language and culture ("way of life"). In the Roman languages the same confusion prevails as in English. The Nazis, naturally, were nationalists as well as racists (and socialists) which shows their identitarian character. A Swiss, for instance, can be a patriot and he might even become

a racist but he cannot become a nationalist without seriously questioning the idea of the Swiss state. *For the sake of a workable semantics* (and respecting etymology) *we employ the term nationalism in its original nonlegal connotation throughout the book.*

[4] Nowhere is this more evident than in the natural sciences, where most visibly one generation learns from the preceding and *adds* its own discoveries and inventions. Mortimer Adler said quite rightly, "The substitution of one thing for another would leave us going around in a circle, neither advancing nor declining. . . . Progress is conservative, because it is cumulative, not substitutional." *Cf.* his essay "God and Modern Man" in *The Critic* (Oct.-Nov., 1966) p. 19.

[5] *Cf.* Etienne Gilson, *L'esprit de la philosophie médiévale* (Paris: Vrin, 1944), p. 402.

[6] *Cf.* I. Peter, 11:9, and St. Thomas Aquinas, *De Regimine Principum*, 1,14. We find the origin of this concept in Exodus XIX:6. The uniqueness of each one of us entails our inequality in the eyes of God. *Cf.* also E. I. Watkin, *A Philosophy of Form* (London and New York: Sheed and Ward, 1951), pp. 229-230.

[7] Yet what about Russia, Prussia, Italy, and Portugal, the reader might ask. The Romanovs died out in the eighteenth century and were actually replaced by the German House of Holstein-Gottorp. Prussia was ruled by South German Suabians, the Hohenzollern, whose main line remained Catholic. Italy's crown belonged to the Savoys, who were French. Portugal's legitimate dynasty was in exile, the "Braganças" ruling there until 1910 in reality were Saxe-Coburg-Gothas.

[8] *Cf.* Chapter 20, Note 45.

Chapter V

[1] On Socrates see the excellent article in the *Encyclopaedia Britannica* by Professor Henry Jackson (in various editions), as well as Werner Jaeger, *op.cit.* pp. 76ff., 124; A. E. Taylor, *Socrates*, (Garden City, N.Y.: Doubleday-Anchor Books, 1953), p. 111: Heinrich Maier, *Sokrates* (Tübingen: Mohr, 1913), pp. 133, 417ff. 419, 470: Tuttu Tarkiainen, *Die Athenische Demokratie* (Zürich; Artemis, 1966), p. 340.

[2] Isocrates had even larger visions of unification transcending the Hellenic-Macedonian frame. *Cf.* Arnaldo Momigliano, "L'Europa come concetto politico presso Isocrate e gli Isocratei," *in Rivista di filologia d'istruzione classica* (Turin, 1933), pp. 477ff. Isocrates, besides, was a confirmed monarchist. *Cf.* his "Nicocles" in *Isocrates*, trsl. George Norlin, The Loeb Classical Library (London: Heinemann, 1928), vol. 1. pp. 17-18, 21, 26.

[3] *Cf.* Polybius, *Works*, trsl. W. R. Paton, The Loeb Classical Library (London: Heinemann 1923), vol. 3, p. 288 (Book VI, 2-10).

[4] *Cf. Aus Metternichs nachgelassenen Papieren*, Fürst Richard Metternich-Winneburg, ed. (Vienna: Braumüuller, 1881), vol. 3, pp. 236-237. Compare also with Henrich von Treitschke, *Politik*, Max Cornicelius, ed. (Leipzig: Hirzel, 1900), vol. 2, p. 196.

[5] On this subject also *Cf.* Otto Seeck, *Geschichte des Underganges der antiken Welt* (Berlin: Siemenroth und Troschel, 1879), vol. 1, pp. 11-14.

[6] This concept is almost the tenor of the brilliant work of Fritz Kern, *Gottesgnadentum und Widerstandsrecht in früheren Mittelalter. Zur Entwicklungsgeschichte der Monarchie* (Leipzig: Koehler, 1914). There are translations into English and Spanish both, very much to their detriment, radically out.

Similar if not identical concepts also prevailed in Hispanic South America. *Cf.* F. Javier de Ayala, *Ideas políticas de Juan de Solórzano* (Seville: Escuela de Estudios Hispano-Americanos, 1946), pp. 194-195, 203.

[7] An "absolutistic" government will not consult its subjects. A totalitarian government, however, will intervene in all domains of life. A government can be absolutistic and totalitarian at the same time—but it is not necessarily so. Monarchies in their internal expansion tend to be absolutistic, democracies totalitarian. The notion of the "politicized" nation is in itself totalitarian. All forms of "populism" lead naturally towards totalitarian extension.

Therefore, a free market economy and free trade might fare better in monarchies—hence the political conservatism of the Physiocrats. *Cf.* Roberto Michels, *Introduzione alla storia delle dottrine economiche e politiche* (Bologna: Zanichelli, 1932), pp. 15ff.

[8] *Cf.* Josef Leo Seifert, *Die Weltrevolutionäre. Von Bogumil über Hus zu Lenin* (Vienna: Amalthea, 1930).

[9] A German translation of this query was popular on the Continent and a burgher of Innsbruck nailed it to the door of the Imperial Palace where Maximilian I resided. He was famous for his genealogical mania. The Emperor replied the next day in a German rhyme, "I am not better than any other man but for the honor that God did me." Maximilian knew perfectly well that, had he been born a hundred yards from the palace, he would be in another position altogether. Yet the great mobmasters of our day, all self-made men, believe that they owe everything to their own genius. Hence their megalomania.

[10] *Cf.* Marsilius of Padua, *Defensor Pacis*, Richard Scholz, ed. (Berlin: B. G. Teubner, 1914), pp. 16-29 (Chapters VIII-XIII).

[11] Typical is the gradual disappearance in the arts of Christ the King, of the royal crown in favor of the Crown of Thorns. Frequent in Romanesque art, the triumphant crowned Christ is replaced by the *Schmerzensmann*, the "Man of Pain," in the Gothic period.

[12] Bishop Tunstall in a letter to Erasmus in 1523 lamented the continuation of Lollard ideas and sentiments in Britain. *Cf.* also James Gairdner, *Lollardy and the Reformation of England* (London: Macmillan, 1908), vol. 1,

pp. 314-366-367, and J. C. Garrick, *Wycliffe and the Lollards* (New York: Scribner's, 1908).

[13] In the exegetic works of Josef Schmid, *Regensburger Neues Testament* (Regensburg: Friedrich Pustet, 1954), Vol. 2. p. 196, we find an outline of Christ's attitude toward the rich.

Did Christ speak about a camel or a rope being unable to pass through the eye of a needle? Not only in Greek but also in Hebrew the words for camel and rope are very similar. The *kamilos* (rope) interpretation is found for the first time in Origen's scholion of Wettstein. *Cf.* also Georg Aicher, "Kamel und Nadelöhr," *Neutestamentliche Abhandlungen* (Münster: Aschendorf, 1908), vol. 1, No. 5.

[14] Abel Bonnard said very correctly about the ancient monarchy, "The king was father of the people only because every father was king in his family." *Cf.* his *Le drame du présent*, vol. 1. *"Les modérés"* (Paris: Grasset, 1936), p. 35. All these concepts are ancient. The "pious king" figures in almost all political writings of the Middle Ages, such as, for instance, in *De institutione regis ad Pippinum regem* of Jonas d'Orléans. See particular chapters II, IV, and VII in Migne, *Patres Latini*, vol. 106, col. 287, 291, 295-296. Here lies, of course, an innate connection with Christianity. Ida Görres (Coudenhove) has seen very clearly the analogies between physical and transcendental fatherhood ("in a sense more miraculous than motherhood") pointing to the God who is essentially *the* Father. *Cf.* Ida Friederike Görres, *Nocturnen* (Frankfurt: Knecht, 1949), p. 115. And the rather left French Catholic philosopher Jean Lacroix sees in democracy first the revolt against God, resulting in the revolt against all fatherhood, *"One could say that to a large extent the present democratic movement is the murder of the father."* (His emphasis.) *Cf.* "Paternité et démocratie," *Esprit*, vol. 15, no. 133, May 1947, p. 749. He would probably have support from Jerome Frank who said that "modern civilisation demands a mind free of father-governance." (*Cf.* his *Law and the Modern Mind*, Boston: Peter Smith, 1930, p. 252.) Hence also the great American inability to understand monarchy. Mom, or even "Big Brother," can be more easily understood by the American mind. *Uncle* Sam is not a father, but essentially a New England bachelor. It is also the thesis of Friedrich Heer, another Catholic with leftist inclinations, that democracy demands brotherhood, not fatherhood. (But do brothers exist without a common parent?) The problem of fatherhood in politics, society, and family is well treated in Alexander Mitscherlich *Auf dem Wege zur vaterlosen Gesellschaft* (Munich: R. Pieper, 1963).

[15] *Cf.* note 7, this chapter.

[16] *Cf.* Chapter VI, Note 16.

[17] Soren Kierkegaard was convinced that the "real royalists" with a homogeneous outlook all lean towards the Catholic faith. See the remark in his diary, dated October 13, 1835, in *The Journals of Soren Kierkegaard, A Selection*, trsl. and edit. Alexander Dru (London: Oxford University Press, 1938), p. 21.

[18] *Cf.* Josef Pekař, Žižka a jého doba (Prague: Vesmir, 1927), vols. 1 and 4, *passim*.

[19] It is precisely in order to set the record straight that Cardinal Roncalli when elected Pope chose the rather odious name of this counter-Pope. Historians now have to cope with two Johns XXIII, a fake one (who was a pirate in his younger years) and a real one.

[20] *Cf.* Chapter IX, Note 3.

[21] The term "propaganda" stems from the Papal *Congregatio de Propaganda Fide*, the supreme authority for all the missions.

[22] *Cf.* E. v Kuehnelt-Leddihn, *Liberty or Equality*, pp. 209-217 (*Freiheit oder Gleichheit*? pp. 325-333).

[23] Typical of this total misrepresentation of the Reformer and of the absolute ignorance of modern scholarship is de Rochemont's American film *Martin Luther* which Germany's leading daily, the *Frankfurter Allgemeine Zeitung* (March 3, 1954) lambasted bitterly as *der amerikanische Luther*. The Catholic monthly *Herderkorrespondenz* (April 1954), under the title "Martin Luther Made in USA," called the film "an intervention of alien money and an alien spirit," a film "against whom Adolf von Harnack and Martin Rade would have violently protested," a "repetition of nineteenth-century platitudes," a "misdeed prompted by American naiveté" and "after all the Catholic and Evangelical efforts to come to a real understanding of Luther's personality and the spirit of the Reformation, a truly evil surprise." (col. 319). Since the Reformation is the terrible wound that divides the German people to this day, it was very much resented that Americans exported a film to Germany which rubbed salt into this wound. "The next time," a German told me grimly, "we'll make a film about the American race problem." The German Evangelicals produced a Luther film, *The Obedient Rebel*, which was sound in scholarship and thoroughly acceptable to enlightened Catholics.

[24] Walter Nigg, himself of the Reformed Church, warned, "Too often we overlook the fact that the Reformation was born in the quiet cell of a monastery." (*Rheinischer Merkur*, vol. 11, no. 21, May 25, 1956, p. 3.) On "Monasticism" *cf.* pp. 104-105 of this book.

[25] The real reason for Luther's break with Zwingli was not so much a different view of the Eucharist as on the salvation of non-Christians. Luther was furious over Zwingli's *Christianae Fidei Expositio ad Christianum Regem* in which Zwingli forcefully defended his stand. *Cf.* Luther's "Kurz Bekenntnis vom heiligen Sacrament" in *Werke*, Erlangen Edition (1842), vol. 32, pp. 399-400. We must always bear in mind that Luther was a *Gothic man*. *Cf.* Alexander Rüstow, *Ortbestimmung der Gegenwart* (Erlenbach-Zürich: Eugen Rentsch, 1952), vol. 2, pp. 235, 269-270, 299-300, and Vicente Rodriguez Casado, *De la monarquía española del barroco* (Seville: Estudios Hispano-Americanos, 1955), p. 52. On the traumatic importance of Luther's journey to Rome, *cf.* Karl August Meissinger, *Der katholische Luther* (Munich: Leo Lehnen, 1952), pp. 55-57, 272.

Nietzsche saw all this very clearly when he wrote about "that German monk

Luther" who went to Rome and hated the Renaissance. *Cf.* his *Der Antichrist* no. 61.

Friedrich Heiler saw in Luther's antipaganism one of the main roots for the reformer's stand against the Catholic faith. *Cf.* F. Heiler, "Luthers Bedeutung für die christliche Kirche," in *Luther in ökumenischer Sicht*, A. v. Martin, ed. (Stuttgart: Fromann, 1929), pp. 167-168. Compare also with J. A. Möhler, *Symbolik* (Mainz: Kupferberg, 1832), pp. 49ff. and Konrad Algermissen, *Konfessionskunde* (Celle: Giesel, 1959), p. 514.

[26] We do not like the expression "Protestant," a term of ridicule and opprobrium invented by the Catholic Counter-Reformation. None of the so-called "Protestant" Churches on the Continent officially uses it. (Needless to say, it had not been derived from the Latin *protestave*, to bear witness, as it has claimed since the nineteenth century only.) We use the term Evangelical which *is* official, although it might confuse American readers since Evangelical in the United States has a "low church" implication. In Prussia an order of the King forbade in 1821 the use of the terms "Protestant" and "Protestantism"; only the word *Evangelisch* was admitted, an adjective which has *no noun*. *Cf.* Franz Schnabel, *p. cit.* vol. 2., p. 263. Nor do we use the frightful term "Catholicism" which never figures in Roman documents. (Encyclicals do not even mention "Catholics," but only "Christifideles," "faithful in Christ.")

[27] The highest virtue in the Scholastic traditions are the "theological virtues" (faith, hope, charity), followed by the "intellectual virtues," while the "moral virtues" are of the lowest order. The lowest of all was *temperantia* which included chastity. Even *fortitude* (courage) ranked higher. Unchastity, however, is considered a "cardinal sin" because it is the *source* of so many other failings.

[28] *Cf.* pp. 104-105.

[29] On the Anabaptists in Münster *cf.* Dr. Heinrich Detmer, *Bilder aus den religiösen und sozialen Unruhen in Münster während des 16. Jahrhunderts* (Münster: Coppenrathsche Buchhandlung, 1903, 1904), 2 vols.

[30] *Cf.* C. A. Cornelius, *Geschichte des Münsterischen Aufruhrs* (Leipzig: Weigel, 1855 and 1860), vol. 2, pp. 279ff.

[31] *Ibid.*, p. 73.

[32] *Cf.* Ludwig Keller, "Die Anfänge der Reformation und die Ketzerschulen" in *Vorträge und Aufsätze der Comenius-Gesellschaft* (Berlin: R. Gaertner, n.d.), vol. 4, 1-2; p. 7.

[33] The Pilgrim Fathers started with a short communitarian experiment, a *kibbutz* or *kolkhoz*, one would be tempted to say. Yet after the starvation period in 1623 Governor Bradford ordered them to abandon the unholy experiment, "That they should set corne every man for his owne particular, and in that regarde trust to themselves."

[34] Max Weber's work is *now* known in America and Britain. (The first

translations came with World War II.) Still fairly unknown are the writings of Alfred Müller-Armack, professor at the University of Cologne and formerly state secretary of the German Federal Republic's Ministry of Economics. Most important is his *Religion und Wirtschaft* (Stuttgart: Kohlhammer, 1959), a work of over 600 pages in the Max Weber tradition.

[35] *Cf.* the essay of Paul Kecskeméti in J. P. Mayer, *Political Thought: The European Tradition* (London: J. M. Dent, 1939).

Chapter VI

[1] Even in 1776 a correspondent of Samuel Adams informed him that, with independence gained, America could now choose a monarch from another nation. *Cf.* William S. Carpenter, *The Development of American Political Thought* (Princeton: Princeton University Press, 1930) p. 35.

[2] Let us have a look at the career and the connections of Leopold of Saxe-Coburg-Gotha, first King of the Belgians. Born as the youngest son of the ruling Duke of Saxe-Coburg-Gotha, he entered the Russian army at the age of fifteen, but managed the affairs of the Duchy during the absence of his brother. He accompanied Emperor Alexander I on many campaigns, to the Congress of Vienna, and on his visit to London. In 1816 he married the daughter of George IV of England, expecting to become Prince-Consort, and received British citizenship. His young wife, however, died the following year. He also became a British field marshal. Early in 1830 he was offered the crown of Greece which he rejected. In 1831, however, he accepted the crown of Belgium and married the daughter of Louis-Philippe, King of the French. He was the uncle of Queen Victoria and the father-in-law of the Emperor of Mexico, Maximilian I, brother of Franz Joseph.

[3] *Cf.* Chapter IV, Note 7. It is worth remembering that George VI of Britain hardly had a drop of English blood and was almost purely German. But the same is true of Philip, Duke of Edinburgh, who was born a Greek prince without any Greek ancestry (just as King Constantine II). His real family name is not Mountbatten either, but Sonderburg-Glücksburg-Augustenburg. Theoretically, after the death or abdication of Queen Elizabeth II, the Sonderburg-Glücksburgs would be ruling (though under different dynastic names) in Britain, Norway, Denmark, and perhaps Greece. In 1900 the Saxe-Coburg-Gothas ruled in Saxe-Coburg, Britain, Belgium, Bulgaria and Portugal.

[4] *Cf.* Chester V. Easum, *Prince Henry of Prussia, Brother of Frederick the Great* (Madison: University of Wisconsin Press, 1942), p. 339.

[5] *Cf.* F. Loraine Petre, *Simon Bolivar, "El Libertador"* (London: John Lane, The Bodley Head, 1910), pp. 300-303, 408-409. The same is borne out by Salvador de Madariaga, *Bolívar* (Buenos Aires: Editorial Sudamericana, n.d.) The tragedy of decolonialization took place in Africa and Asia at a time

even more unfavorable to the monarchical idea than the earlier part of the nineteenth century. Hence the adoption of demo-republican forms of government. Hence the alternation of chaos and dictatorship.

[6] *Cf.* John C. Miller, *Origins of the American Revolution* (Boston: Little, Brown, 1943) p. 499.

[7] *Cf.* Martin Van Buren, *Inquiry into the Origin and Sources of Political Parties in the United States*, edit. by his son (New York: Hurd and Houghton, 1867), p. 28.

[8] *Cf. The Works of Alexander Hamilton*, H. Cabot Lodge, ed. (New York-London: Putnam, 1885), vol. 1, pp. 353ff., 372, 390, 431.

[9] *Cf.* Francis Lieber, *On Civil Liberty and Self-Government* (Philadelphia: Lippincott, 1874), p. 257.

[10] *Cf.* p. 73, and Chapter VII, Note 123.

[11] *Cf. The Writings of Thomas Jefferson*, Paul Lester Ford, ed. (New York: Putnam, 1896), vol. 7, p. 24.

[12] *Cf.* Wyndham Lewis, *America and Cosmic Man* (London: Nicholson and Watson, 1948), p. 133.

[13] *Cf.* Edmund Burke, "Observations on a Late Publication Entitled 'The Present State of the Nation' " in *Burke's Politics*, Ross J. S. Hoffman and Paul Levack, eds. (New York: Alfred Knopf, 1949), pp. 71-72.

[14] De Kalb was, no doubt, of humble origin. The titles of nobility in France are spurious to an incredible degree. They have never been duly registered in the past and there exists in France nothing like the *Gothaische Genealogische Taschenbücher, Debrett's or Burke's*. Many French titles have been faked and arbitrarily assumed but used and accepted for centuries. Especially in the 18th century a wave of "self-nobilitations" took place, often on the basis of the purchase of castles and other properties. *Cf.* Wilhelm Weigand, *Der Abbé Galiani* (Bonn: Röhrscheid, 1948) pp. 199-201.

[15] *Cf.* John C. Miller, *op. cit.* pp. 190-191, 373-374.

[16] *Cf.* Ray Allen Billington, *The Protestant Crusade 1800-1860* (New York: Macmillan, 1938), *passim*, also quoting Daniel Barber, *History of My Own Times* (Washington, 1827).

[17] Many Americans have observed this. *Cf.* Dean Willard L. Sperry, *Religion in America* (Cambridge, England: University Press, 1945), pp. 218-219. and also foreigners, as for instance Evelyn Waugh in his article "The American Epoch in the Catholic Church" (*Life*, International Edition, Vol. 7, No. 8, October 10, 1949, p. 63) or the unnamed author of "Problèmes et aspects du catholicisme américain" in *La Semaine Religieuse de Paris*, vol. 97, No. 5025, September 2, 1950, p. 797.

[18] In American Catholic colleges one particularly likes to represent St. Robert Bellarmine as a sturdy democrat, but James Brodrick S. J. in *The Life and Work of Blessed Robert Francis Cardinal Bellarmine S. J.*, 1572-1621 (London: Burns, Oates and Washbourne, 1928), vol. 1, p. 230 tells a different story: "Like his masters, the scholastics, he is a convinced monarchist, and

goes out of his way to justify and exalt the monarchical regime." The relevant passages show St. Robert a true patriarchalist—especially so *De Romano Pontifice*, lib. 1. c.2. As a matter of fact, the Cardinal was convinced that majority decisions in large communities are bad, because the wicked and the stupid are more numerous than the good and the wise. (*De clericis*, VII). The basis of the Bellarmine legend in Catholic America is the assumption that Jefferson in writing the Declaration was profoundly influenced by Sir Robert Filmer's summing up of Bellarmine's stand in his *Patriacha*. (There was a pencil mark of uncertain origin in Jefferson's copy of that book.) This thesis is untenable if we read Jefferson's letter to Madison dated August 30, 1823, his letter to Henry Lee dated May 8, 1825, and his letter to Dr. James Mease, dated September 26, 1825. (These are to be found in the Monticello Edition of his *Works*, vol. 15, p. 426 and vol. 16, pp. 118-119 and 123x) *Cf.* also J. C. Rager, *The Political Philosophy of Blessed Cardinal Bellarmine* (Washington D.C.: Catholic University of America, 1926).

Yet the stand taken by the other great late Scholastic, Suárez, was of a rather different character. It has rightly been said that "in the Suárezian doctrine any form of government other than direct democracy becomes substitutional—a consequence palpably opposed to the whole political doctrine of Aristotle and St. Thomas. *Cf.* Charles N. R. McCoy, "Note on the Origin of Political Authority," *The Thomist*, vol. 16, No. 1 (January 1953), pp. 80-81. Compare also with Gabriel Browe O. P. *The Origin of Political Authority* (Dublin: Clonmore and Reynolds, 1955), p. 94.

Efforts to "monopolize" democracy have been ridiculed by Maritain in his younger years. He called them *"indiscutablement une sanglante absurdité."* *Cf.* his *Trois Réformateurs* (Paris: Plon 1925), p. 198.

[19] Here one has to read the warning sentence of Erik Peterson in connection with the efforts to establish a "political theology." *Cf.* his *Der Monotheismus als politisches Problem, Ein Beitrag zur Geschichte der politischen Theologie im Imperium Romanum* (Leipzig: Jakob Hegner, 1935), pp. 98ff. *Vide* also footnote 5 in James Brodrick, S. J. *p. cit.*, p. 247. A similar warning—mainly to Catholic leftists—has been given by Professor Hans Maier in his essay "Politische Theologie (Einwämde eines Laien)" in *Stimmen der Zeit* (Munich), February 1969, pp. 73-91.

[20] Gouverneur Morris, naturally, knew about America's debt to the Bourbons and so did Alexander Hamilton. *Cf.* the latter's piece in the *Gazette of the United States*, signed "Pacificus," July 13, 1793, in *The Works of Alexander Hamilton*, vol. 4, No. 5.

[21] *Cf.* the letter of George Washington to James McHenry, September 30, 1798: "My opinion is . . . that you would as soon scrub the blackamore white as to change the principle of a profest Democrat, and that he will leave nothing unattempted to overturn the Government of this Country." In *The Washington Papers*, Saul Padover, ed. (New York: Harper and Brothers, 1955), p. 389. On the difficulty to reform a once corrupted democracy *cf.*

Rafael Gambra, *La Monarquía social y representativa* (Madrid: Rialp, 1954), pp. 136-137.

22 *Cf. The Selected Writings of John and John Quincy Adams,* p. 129.

23 *Cf. The Complete Jefferson,* Saul Padover, ed. (New York: Duell, Sloane and Pearce, 1943), p. 1276.

24 *Cf. The Works of John Adams,* Charles Adams, ed. (Boston: Little, Brown, 1851) vol. 6, p. 516.

25 *Ibid.,* p. 520.

26 *Cf.* John Adams, *A Defense of the Constitution of the United States of America,* New Edition, (London, 1794), vol. 3, pp. 493-495.

27 Letter, dated 16 July, 1814, in Jefferson's *Collected Writings.* Monticello Edition (Washington: 1904) vol. 14, p. 152.

28 *Cf. The Works of John Adams,* vol. 6, p. 516.

29 *Cf.* James Madison, *Works,* Jonathan Elliot, ed., vol. 1, p. 501.

30 *Cf.* E. M. Burns, *James Madison, Philosopher of the Constitution* (New Brunswick, N.J.: Rutgers University Press, 1938), p. 63.

31 *Cf.* Madison, *Writings,* Gaillard Hunt, ed., vol. 5, p. 81.

32 *Cf. A Compilation of the Messages and Papers of the Presidents* (Washington, D.C.: Bureau of National Literature, 1897), vol. 3, pp. 493-495.

33 *Cf.* Arthur H. Vandenberg, *If Hamilton Were Alive Today* (New York: Putnam, 1923), pp. xxlv-xxvi; Ralph Adams Cram, *The End of the Democracy* (Boston: Marshall Jones, 1937), p. 20: Charles A. and Mary R. Beard, *America in Mid-Passage* (New York: Macmillan, 1939), vol. 3, pp. 922-923; Andrew Cunningham MacLaughlin, *Democracy and Constitution* (Proceedings of the American Antiquarian Society, New Series, 1922), p. 310; Albert Jay Nock, *Our Enemy the State* (New York: Morrow, 1935), p. 141n.

34 Where did Hamilton, staunchest conservative among the Founding Fathers, stand "metaphysically?" Were there any religious foundations to his views? His will shows him to be a convinced Christian. *Cf. The Basic Ideas of Alexander Hamilton,* Richard B. Morris, ed., (New York: Pocket Library, 1957), pp. 449-451.

35 *Cf.* Mortimer Adler in *Philosophy of the State.* Fifteenth Annual Proceedings of the American Catholic Philosophical Association, Charles Hart, ed. (Washington, 1939), p. 163. The same view is manifested by James N. Wood in *Democracy and the Will to Power* (New York: Knopf, 1921), pp. 48-51.

36 *Cf.* Thomas Jefferson, *Writings,* P. J. Fort, ed., vol. 10, p. 22 (Letter to DuPont de Nemours, written in 1816): "We in the United States are constitutionally and conscientiously Democrats." On the other hand, Dr. Benjamin Rush, friend of the Founding Fathers, confessed in a letter to John Adams (July 1789) that he saw in democracy "the Tivil's (devil's) government." *Cf. The Letters of Benjamin Rush,* L. H. Butterfield, ed. (Princeton: Princeton University Press, 1951), vol. 1, p. 523.

37 *Cf.* Jefferson's letter dated February 14, 1815, mentioned by Sainte-Beuve in *Premiers Lundis,* vol. 2, p. 147, (February 25, 1833).

³⁸ *Cf.* Thomas Jefferson, *Writings*, vol. 2, p. 249.

³⁹ Cited by Russell Kirk, *The Conservative Mind* (Chicago: Regnery, 1953), p. 130. Compare this with the declaration of one of the great Swiss, J. J. Bachofen, "Because I love liberty, I loathe democracy." *Cf.* his "Autobiographische Aufzeichnungen," *Basler Jahrbuch* (1917), p. 329.

⁴⁰ *Cf.* Thomas Jefferson, *Writings*, P. L. Ford, ed., vol. 2. p. 249.

⁴¹ *Cf.* Thomas Jefferson, Letter to Madison, December 20, 1787 in *Works*, H. A. Washington, ed. (New York: Derby and Jackson, 1859), vol. 2, p. 332.

⁴² *Cf. The Writings of Thomas Jefferson*, Lipscomb and Bergh, eds. (Washington D.C., 1903), vol. 5, p. 94. (Letter to John Jay, August, 23, 1785.)

⁴³ *Cf. Ibid.*

⁴⁴ *Cf. The Writings of Thomas Jefferson* (Washington D.C.: 1904), vol. 13, pp. 401-402.

⁴⁵ *Ibid.*, p. 396.

⁴⁶ *Cf.* Albert J. Nock, *Our Enemy, The State* (New York: Morrow, 1935), p. 141n.

⁴⁷ These confusions—in part at least--have already been exposed by Madison in the Federalist Paper No. 14.

Chapter VII

¹ *Cf. The Discovery of Europe* Philip Rahv, ed. (Boston: Houghton, Mifflin, 1947).

² *Cf. The Basic Ideas of Alexander Hamilton*, p. 324.

³ *Cf. The Works of Alexander Hamilton*, vol. 8, p. 259, Letter to Colonel Edward Carrington, dated May 26, 1792.

⁴ *Cf. Diaries and Letters of Gouverneur Morris*, Anne Cary Morris, ed. (New York: Scribner's, 1888), vol. 1, p. 104.

⁵ *Ibid.*, vol. 1. p. 443 and Jared Sparks, *The Life of Gouverneur Morris with Selections of His Correspondence* (Boston: Gray and Bowen, 1832), vol. 3, p. 263.

⁶ *Cf.* Wyndham Lewis, *op. cit.* p. 135.

⁷ *Cf.* Theodore Roosevelt, *Gouverneur Morris* (Boston: Houghton, Mifflin, 1898), pp. 240-241.

⁸ *Cf.* Elizabeth Brett White, *American Opinion of France* (New York: Knopf, 1932), p. 24.

⁹ The first phase of the French Revolution, its preparatory and its initial stage, put the emphasis on liberty rather than on equality. Hence the nobility strongly participated—because of its anarchical temperament and its memories of the Fronde. Excessive sobriety and self-control are bourgeois-puritanical rather than typically aristocratic virtues, spread by English nannies in the households of the nobility on the Continent. This, at least is the opinion of

Ida Friederike Görres (née Countess Coudenhove-Kalergi) in *op. cit*. pp. 33-35.

[10] Maximilien de Robespierre belonged to a family of the lower nobility of relatively ancient vintage. But, as Albert Mathiez remarked in his *La Révolution Française* (Paris: Armand Colin, 1946), vol. 1, p. 3, there existed also an animosity of the lesser nobility toward the big, wealthy families usually centered around the Court. American and British readers are reminded that the *de* in France—as in the case of Charles de Gaulle—has, as *particule*, almost always the character of a title. This is also true of the *von* in Germany, Austria and Switzerland, but not of the *van* in the Netherlands nor the *de* or *di* in Italy and Spain.

[11] The eminent role played by the entire nobility in the French Revolution is also underlined by Alexis de Tocqueville in his "L'Ancien Régime et la Révolution" in *Oeuvres complètes*, J. P. Mayer, ed. (Paris: Gallimard 1952), vol. 2, pp. 68-69, 72. Count Philippe Paul Ségur also commented on this suicidal tendency of the French nobility. *Cf.* his *Mémoires ou souvenirs et anecdotes* (Paris: Eymery, 1824), vol. 1, pp. 292, 295. Against masochism in the political sphere, which not only characterized the French nobility prior to 1789 (or a certain part of the American upper crust today) Georges Bernanos spoke in ringing terms. *Cf.* his *La liberté pour quoi faire?* (Paris: Gallimard, 1953), p. 129. Albert Mathiez, in *op. cit.* p. 15, says correctly that "the Revolution could not have come but from above." See also Louis Villat, *La Révolution et l'Empire* (Paris: Presses Universitaires de France, 1940), vol. 1, pp. ix, 3. Pierre Gaxotte in *La Révolution Française* (Paris: Fayard, 1947), puts the emphasis very strongly on the ideological character of the French Revolution and discounts all economic aspects. A. de Tocqueville in his "L'Ancien Régime" insists that the mounting wealth of France prepared the Revolution and that the most revolutionary regions were the richest. (*Cf. Oeuvres complètes*, vol. 2, pp. 218ff., 222-223).

Nor was it true that the countryside lived in misery. Serfdom survived only in a few isolated spots in the Bourbonnais and in the Jura. The last remnants of serfdom had been abolished by the King in his domains in 1779. About half of the area of France was in the possession of smallholders. (*Cf.* P. Gaxotte, *op. cit.* pp. 37-38.) Foreign trade, four times greater than in 1700, reached a value of over a billion francs in 1786, a record until 1848 (*Ibid.*, pp. 32-33). De Tocqueville comments on this in "L'Ancien Régime" (*Oeuvres complètes*, vol. 2, p. 223).

[12] One ought to remember the battlecry of the Polish noblemen:

Cudzych królow gromić a grozić swojemu!

Menace foreign kings, but resist your own!

[13] *Cf.* Henry Thomas Buckle, *History of Civilisation in England* (New York: Appleton, 1880), vol. 2, p. 614; Augustin Gazier, *Histoire générale du Mouvement Janséniste* (Paris: Honoré Champion, 1923), vol. 2, p. 137,

citing also Siccard, *L'Ancien clergé de France*; (Sir) Denis W. Brogan, *French Personalities and Problems* (London: Hamish Hamilton, 1946), p. 70.

[14] *Cf.* Edmund Burke, "Remarks on the Policy of the Allies," in *Works* (Boston: Little, Brown, 1869), vol. 4, p. 452.

[15] *Cf.* André Siegfried, "Le Protestantisme cévénol," in Marc Boegner, André Siegfried *et al. Protestantisme Français* (Paris: Plon, 1945), p. 43.

[16] *Cf.* G. de Félice, *Histoire des Protestants de France* (Paris: Cherbuliez, 1856), pp. 577, 603-604.

[17] Anglomania on the Continent had and still has all sorts of versions —an aristocratic, a bourgeois, a proletarian-socialist, a Catholic, a "Protestant," a Jewish one. There exists an Anglophile sportsman and businessman, a feminist and an educationist, a technologist and a male fashion designer, a navy man and a tourist manager. Anglophobia always appeared as a dissenting opinion, as a "heresy," as a manifestation of bad taste, as a wanton opposition against a prevailing ideal.

[18] *Cf.* Metternich, *op. cit.* vol. 8, p. 531.

[19] *Ibid.*, p. 407.

[20] *Cf.* Alfred Müller-Armack, *Das Jahrhundert ohne Gott* (Münster: Regensberg, 1948), pp. 57-58.

[21] *Cf.* Charles Seignobos, *Histoire sincère de la nation française*, (Paris: Presses Universitaires, 1946), p. 291.

[22] Even in the year 1896 the per capita income of the Swiss was way below that of Britain and France and only slightly above the European average. (*Cf. Handbuch der Staatswissenschaften*, 1923, p. 767). Hard work and wise investments plus good organization are responsible for the Swiss economic miracle. Tourism, on the other hand, provides Switzerland only with 8 percent of her national income while in 1966 not less than 33 percent of the budget was spent on military expenditures.

[23] *Cf. Mémoires, correspondance et manuscrits du général Lafayette*, publiés par sa famille (Brussels: Société Belge de Librairie, 1837), vol. 1, pp. 193, 268, 416; vol. 2, pp. 139-140.

[24] *Cf.* Philippe Paul Comte de Ségur, *op. cit.*, vol. 1, p. 321.

[25] *Cf.* la baronne de Staël, *Considérations sur les principaux événements de la Révolution Francaise* (London: Baldwin, Craddock, Joy, 1818), vol. 1, p. 88.

[26] *Cf.* Madame de Campan, *Mémoires sur la vie privée de Marie Antoinette* (Paris: Baudouin Frères, 1823), vol. 1, p. 234.

[27] *Cf.* Alphonse Marie Louis de Lamartine, *Histoire des Girondins* (Paris: Furne et Cie, 1847), vol. 1, p. 62.

[28] *Cf.* H. Taine, *Les origines de la France contemporaine* (Paris: Hachette, n.d.). vol. 2, p. 66. Taine admits the "infection," but denies the introduction of an American political pattern in the ideology of the French

Revolution. On erroneous European judgments concerning the United States *cf.* Russell Kirk, *op. cit.*, pp. 425-426 and 427-428. "The European thinks that what Americans brag, they practice," Kirk concludes wisely (p. 428).

²⁹ *Cf.* Chateaubriand, *Mémoires d'outre tombe*, M. Levaillant, ed. (Paris: Flammarion, 1948), vol. 1, p. 274.

³⁰ *Cf.* G. E. Fasnacht, *Acton's Political Philosophy* (London: Hollis and Carter, 1952), p. 79.

³¹*Cf.* Alexis de Tocqueville, *"L'Ancien régime et la révolution,"* in *Oeuvres complètes*, (Paris: Gallimard, 1952), vol. 2, t. 2, p. 157: "The worst imitators were those who had adopted the abstract principles of the United States Constitution without having felt the necessity to apply them in a conservative way as it was done in America."

³² *Cf.* Philippe Sagnac, *La fin de l'Ancien Régime et la Révolution Americaine* (Paris: Presses Universitaires, 1941), pp. 241, 286-300.

³³ *Cf.* his letter "Réponse de M. Jellinek à M. Boutmy: La Déclaration des Droits de l'homme et du Citoyen," in *Revue du Droit publique et de la Science Politique en France et à l'Entranger.* vol. 18, p. 385sq.

³⁴ *Cf.* Felix Somary, *Krise und Zukunft der Demokratie* (Zürich-Vienna: Europa Verlag, 1952), pp. 28-30.

³⁵ *Cf. Selected writings of John and John Quincy Adams*, pp. 159-160.

³⁶ *Cf. The Works of John Adams*, p. 485.

³⁷ Hanns Johst even became President of the *Reichsschrifttumkammer*, the supreme Nazi organ for controlling and "guiding" the writers of the Third Reich. Josef Nadler in his *Literaturgeschichte des Deutschen Volkes* (Berlin: Propyläen-Verlag, 1941), p. 347 calls *Thomas Paine* "the first political play of the new Germany."

³⁸ *Cf.* Dr. Friedrich Schönemann, *Amerika und der Nationalsozialismus* (Berlin: Junker and Dünnhaupt, 1934), pp. 28-29. On p. 31 this author says pointedly, referring to National Socialism, "For our new popular form of government, for this entire system of popular community, there is no better and more beautiful word than 'democracy'."

³⁹ *Cf.* Cornélis de Witt, *Jefferson and the American Democracy*, trsl. R. S. H. Church (London: Longmans, 1862), originally published in the *Revue des Deux Mondes*: Johann Georg Hülsemann, *Geschichte der Demokratie in den Vereinigten Staaten von Nordamerika* (Göttingen: Vandenhoeck und Ruprecht, 1832) p. xi. This author wrote, "The supremacy of the Democratic Party which started earlier in this century and is daily receiving momentum is for us not only of a sad interest because the hopes which Washington and Alexander Hamilton raised for the future of that country have been dashed. Far more catastrophic is this evolution to us for the reason that the Party of Revolution has thus acquired a sure base from which to operate." Alexis de Tocqueville commented in his "L'Ancien Régime et la Révolution" that the

"worst imitators were those who had copied abstract principles from the Constitution of the United States without ever having felt the necessity of adding certain conservative provisions which were applied in America." *(Oeuvres complètes*, vol. 2, p. 157.)

[40] *Cf.* Le chevalier Félix de Bonjour, *Aperçu des Etats-Unis au commencement du XIXe siècle* (Paris: Michaud et Delaunay, 1814), p. 164.

[41] Abel Bonnard, *op. cit.*, p. 218 tells us about Lafayette's letter to the Princesse d'Hénin in which he mentions the "delicious sensation caused by the smile of the masses." *Cf.* also Harold Wade Streeter, "Sainte-Beuve's Estimate of Lafayette," *The French-American Review* (Washington: 1950), vol. 3, no. 2-3, pp. 164-186. In a letter addressed to Madison on January 30, 1787, Jefferson mentioned Lafayette's "canine appetite for popularity and fame." *Cf.* Th. Jefferson, *Works*, H. A. Washington, ed., vol. 2.

[42] *Cf.* Pierre Gaxotte, *op. cit.*, p. 392, who depicts de Robespierre as a frustrated nobleman.

[43] Maurice Heine was a prolific writer. One of his most ghoulish essays was his well-illustrated description of burnt corpses. *Cf.* his "L'enfer anthropoclasique," *Minotaure* (Paris), No. 6.

[44] *Cf.* Gilbert Lely, *Vie du Marquis de Sade* (Paris: Gallimard-NRF, 1952 and 1957), 2 vols.

[45] *Cf.* Gilbert Lely, *op. cit.*, p. 273.

[46] *Cf.* Paul Boudin, *Correspondance inédite du Marquis de Sade, de ses proches et de ses familiers* (Paris: Librairie de France, 1929) p. 269.

[47] *Cf.* G. Lely, *op. cit.*, pp. 452-453, letter from Picpus to the *Sûreté Générale*, December 19, 1793.

[48] *Cf.* G. Lely, *op. cit.*, vol. 2, pp. 677-685.

[49] *Cf.* Dr. Eugen Dühren (Iwan Bloch), *Le Marquis de Sade et son temps* (Paris: Michalon, 1901), pp. 392-393.

[50] *Cf.* Paul Eluard, in *La Révolution Surréaliste* (Paris) vol. 2, No. 8 p. 8.

[51] *Cf.* Bertrand d'Astorg, *Introduction au monde de la terreur* (Paris: Editions de Seuil, 1945), p. 32.

[52] *Ibid.*, p. 33.

[53] *Cf.* Geoffrey Gorer, *The Revolutionary Ideas of the Marquis de Sade* (London: Wisehart, 1934), p. 188.

[54] *Cf.* Dr. Eugen Dühren, *op. cit.*, p. 391.

[55] *Cf.* *L'Oeuvre du Marquis de Sade*, Guillaume Apollinaire, ed., (Paris: Bibliothèque des Curieux, 1909), p. 227.

[56] *Ibid.*, pp. 236ff.

[57] *Cf.* Oswald Spengler, *Jahre der Entscheidung* (Münich: C. H. Beck, 1933 and 1953), p. 144.

[58] These destructive left-of-centrists without well-grounded convictions

were the special object of horror of one of the greatest German-American novelists, the late Hermann Borchardt. *Cf.* his *The Conspiracy of the Carpenters*, trsl. Barrows Mussey (New York: Simon and Schuster, 1943).

[59] *Cf.* Louis Althusser, "Despote et monarque," in *Esprit*, vol. 26, No. 267, November 1958, pp. 213-214.

[60] *Cf.* Alexander Rüstow, *Das Versagen des Wirtschaftsliberalismus* (Düsseldorf: Küpper, 1950), p. 82.

[61] *Cf.* Hugo Lang, O.S.B., *Der Historiker als Prophet* (Nuremberg: Sebaldus-Verlag, 1947), p. 124.

[62] *Cf.* Voltaire, *Oeuvres Complètes*.

[63] *Cf.* *Dictionnaire de philosophie par Voltaire* (Paris: Lebigre Frères, 1834), vol. 3, p. 196.

[64] *Cf.* Franz Schnabel, *op.cit.*, vol. 2, p. 186.

[65] Montesquieu too was of the same opinion. *Cf. Esprit des Lois*, Book 8, c. 16. Rousseau repeated these views in the *Contrat Social*, Book 3, c. 3.

[66] *Cf.* Pierre Gaxotte, *op.cit.*, p. 406.

[67] *Cf.* George D. Herron, *Germanism and the American Crusade* (New York: Mitchell Kennerley, 1918), p. 21.

[68] *Cf.* Jacques Maritain, *Principes d'une politique humaniste* (Paris: Paul Hartmann, 1945), p. 39.

[69] *Cf.* Walter Lippmann, *The Public Philosophy* (Boston: Little, Brown, 1955), p. 73: "In America and in most of the newer liberal democracies of the Western World, the Jacobin heresy is, though not unchallenged and not universal, the popular and dominant theory in the schools." On the inherent totalitarian dangers in democracy see also, Friedrich A. v. Hayek, "Die Anschauungen der Mehrheit und die zeitgenössische Demokratie," *Ordo*, vol. 15-16 (1965), pp. 19-41.

[70] *Cf.* Walter Lippmann, *op. cit.*, p. 75.

[71] *Cf.* Chapter VII, Note 23.

[72] *Cf.* Dr. A. J. M. Cornelissen, *Calvijn en Rousseau* (Nijmegen-Utrecht: H. V. Dekker, 1931), pp. 229-230.

[73] *Cf.* Calvin, *Institutiones*, I, vii, 5.

[74] *Cf.* Corrado E. Eggers-Lecour, "Calvino y Rousseau o la ambivalencia ginebrina" in *Razon y Fé* (Madrid), vol. 165, no. 772 (May 1963), pp. 481-496.

[75] The Swiss indeed have done more than invent the cuckoo clock —which, by the way, is a product of the German Black Forest. Take away a city such as Geneva and all Western history, *all world history is utterly different*.

[76] *Cf.* Georg Jellinek, *op. cit.*, vol. 2, p. 13.

[77] *Cf.* (Baron) Ernest Seillière, *Le peril mystique dans l'inspiration des démocraties contemporaines, Rousseau visionnaire et révélateur* (Paris: Renaissance de Livre, 1918).

[78] *Cf.* Werner Kägi, "Rechtsstaat und Demokratie" in *Demokratie und Rechtsstaat, Festgabe für Zaccaria Giacometti* (Zürich: Polygraphischer Verlag, 1953), p. 110. A brilliant essay by the most outstanding Swiss political scientist. On the *Rechtsstaat* (constitutional state of law and order) see also Francisco Elias de Tejada, *Las doctrinas políticas en la Cataluña medieval* (Barcelona: Aymà, 1950), pp. 196-198.

[79] *Cf.* Irving Babbitt, *Rousseau and Romanticism* (Boston-New York: Houghton, Mifflin, 1919), p. 345.

[80] *Ibid.*, p. 436.

[81] *Ibid.*, p. 367.

[82] *Cf.* Werner Kägi, *loc. cit.*, p. 117.

[83] *Ibid.*, p. 120.

[84] *Ibid.*, pp. 115-116.

[85] *Ibid.*, p. 114.

[86] *Cf.* J. J. Rousseau, *Contrat Social*, Book 1, ch. 7.

[87] *Ibid.*, Book. 4, ch. 2.

[88] *Cf.* J. J. Rousseau, "Traité de l'économie politique," in *Oeuvres complètes* (Paris: Hachette, n.d.), vol. 2, p. 553.

[89] *Cf.* J. J. Rousseau, *Contrat Social*, Book 3, ch. 16.

[90] *Cf. The Living Thoughts of Thomas Jefferson*, John Dewey, ed. (New York: Longmans, Green, 1940), p. 62: "The first principle of republicanism . . . to consider the will of the society announced by the majority of the single vote, as sacred as if unanimous, is the first of all lessons in importance, yet the last, which is thoroughly learned." Jefferson thought that the alternative leads to despotism, yet precisely the sticking to such principles leads almost inevitably to totalitarianism. *Cf.* Angel López-Amo, *El podér político y la libertad* (Madrid: Rialp, 1952), p. 152, and Bertrand de Jouvenel, *Du Pouvoir. Histoire naturelle de sa croissance* (Geneva: Cheval Ailé, 1945), pp. 25-26.

[91] At the sight of a newborn babe one is not particularly struck by the thought that it is exceedingly "free." Freedom rather seems to be the fruit of constant personal struggles. In medieval parlance freedoms (the "freedom of a city," for instance) were as much as privileges.

[92] *Cf.* J. J. Rousseau, *Contrat Social*, Book 7.

[93] *Cf.* Louis Rougier, *La France à la recherche d'une constitution* (Paris: Sirey, 1952), p. 127.

[94] *Cf.* Note 77. Also: T. E. Utley, "Mandatory Democracy," *Confluence*, (Cambridge, Mass.) vol. 1, No. 2. (June 1952), pp. 29-30.

[95] *Cf.* Louis Rougier, *op. cit.*, p. 132.

[96] *Cf.* Georges Vedel, *Manuel élémentaire de droit constitutionnel* (Paris: Sirey, 1949), p. 196.

[97] *Ibid.*

[98] The de Broglie ducal family is one of the most gifted in France. In the last generation there were two brothers (one a prince, the other one *the* Duke) who were famous physicists (one a Nobel Prize winner), while the

sister (Comtesse de Pange) is famous as a writer and historian. These are great-grandchildren of Madame de Staël whose daughter Hortense married a de Broglie. Originally this family comes from the Piedmont side of the Matterhorn region.

⁹⁹ Reforms carried out with a strong hand were those of Peter the Great, Frederick William III (through von Stein and Hardenberg), and the Council of Trent.

¹⁰⁰ Certainly the recent reforms in the Catholic Church were "mismanaged" insofar as they got out of hand. Hilaire Belloc might have said, "What do you expect from a bunch of clerics in Rome?" (*Vide* Diana Cooper, *Trumpets from the Steps*, 1960, p. 268). Actually, misrepresentations were made and thus many confusions were caused by disappointed theologians and, above all, by overidealistic, ambitious Catholic journalists. A short outline of the roots of the present confusion in the Catholic Church can be found in my essay, "The Church in Crisis" special to *Pro Ecclesia*, vol. 3, no. 6, June 1972.

¹⁰¹ *Cf. Athenäumsfragmente*, I, 2.

¹⁰² In *L'Ile des pengouins*.

¹⁰³ He can get them in Dr. A. Cabanès and L. Nass, *La névrose révolutionnaire* (Paris: Albin Michel, 1924), pp. 88ff., and Gilbert Lely, *op. cit.*, vol. 2, p. 405, n.6.

¹⁰⁴ *Cf.* D. W. Brogan *The Free State* (New York: Knopf, 1945), p. 2.

¹⁰⁵ *Cf.* Gérard Walter, *La guerre de Vendée* (Paris: Plon, 1953), pp. 339-341. Louis-Marie Turreau, a monstrous sadist, became a baron under Napoleon. He was French Minister to the United States from 1803 to 1811. One can imagine that he was lionized by "progressives" in the United States as Soviet diplomats would be during the honeymoon of World War II. One can also admire this criminal's likeness on the east side of the Arc de Triomphe in Paris—not really a fitting decoration for the tomb of the Unknown Soldier.

¹⁰⁶ *Ibid.*

¹⁰⁷ *Ibid.*, p. 311. "The big army of useless mouths." The same noble motive can be found in the Nazi extermination of the insane.

¹⁰⁸ *Cf.* Otto Flake, *Marquis de Sade* (Stuttgart: Deutscher Taschenbuch-verlag, 1966), p. 89.

¹⁰⁹ *Cf.* Pierre Gaxotte, *op. cit.*, p. 380.

¹¹⁰ "The Republic needs no scientists." According to another version Coffinhal said, "The Republic needs neither scientists nor chemists."

¹¹¹ This has also been deplored by John U. Nef in an essay "On the Future of American Civilization," *The Review of Politics*, vol. 2, no. 3. *Cf.* also the unsigned editorial "Untragic America" in *Life*, December 2, 1946.

¹¹² *Cf.* Pierre Gaxotte, *op. cit.*, p. 33. In the docks of Nantes seven ships were under construction in 1738, but thirty-three in 1784.

¹¹³ Obviously a mounting wealth creates an enthusiasm for a *race* for

riches. In a race, however, there are losers and winners, and it is the bitterness of those left behind which creates part of the unrest.

[114] *Cf.* Chapter VI, Note 14. Actually André Maurois tells us in his *Histoire de France* that precisely those provinces were most attached to the *Ancien Régime* where the feudal traditions were strongest. This reminds one of Victor Hugo's outcry: "Equality, political translation of the word envy!" *Cf.* his *Journal 1830-1848*, Henri Guillemin, ed. (Paris: Gallimard, 1954), p. 346. Ida F. Görres, *op. cit.*, pp. 53-54, speaks about the mixture of fury and envy which could be observed in the old German Youth Movement when it became evident that somebody had acquired wealth without too much effort. A hundred years earlier a great Lutheran theologian of the conservative school, A. F. C. Vilmar made a similar observation about the younger generation in his time. *Cf.* his *Schulreden über Fragen der Zeit* (Marburg: Elswerthsche Universitätsbuchhandlung, 1846), pp. 133ff.

[115] *Cf.* Pierre Gaxotte quoting Le Trosne, *op. cit.*, pp. 41-42.

[116] *Cf. Burke's Politics*, p. 332, or *Works of the Right Honorable Edmund Burke* (Boston: Little, Brown, 1865-1867), vol. 3, pp. 102-121. (Letter of Edmund Burke to M. Dupont.)

[117] *Cf. Ibid.* This is corroborated by James F. Cooper in *The American Democrat* (New York: Knopf, 1931), p. 83 (originally published 1838 in Cooperstown, N.Y.).

[118] *Cf.* Gérard Walter, *Histoire des Jacobins* (Paris: Aimery Somogy, 1946), p. 306.

[119] *Ibid.*, p. 268.

[120] Oswald Spengler, in his *Jahre der Entscheidung* (Munich, C. H. Beck, 1933), p. 90, remarked: "In such times we find a certain clerical scum which drags the faith and the dignity of the Church into the dirt of party politics, which allies itself with the powers of destruction and while mouthing the phrases of altruism and protection of the poor helps the underworld to destroy the social order—the order on which the Church irrevocably and fatally rests." The revolutionary and socialistic character of a large sector of the Russian clergy and especially of the seminaries has been well described by Ernst Benz in *Geist und Leben der Ostkirche.* (Hamburg: Rowohlt, 1957), p. 128. The assassinating "guerrilla-priests" of Latin America were clearly foreseen by Georges Bernanos, who wrote in November 1926: "I believe that our children will see the main body of the troops of the Church on the side of the forces of death. I can see myself being executed by bolshevik priests who carry the *Social Contract* in their pocket but have a cross dangling from their neck." *Cf.* his *Correspondance inédite 1904-1934* (Paris: Uöon, 1971), p. 278. Yet Camillo Torres Restrepo was imitated (though less murderously) by Father Nicholas Riddell in St. Louis. *Cf. St. Louis Globe-Democrat*, October 19, 1971; October 20, 1971; March 9, 1972.

[121] *Ibid.*, p. 31.

[122] *Cf. Encyclopaedia Britannica*, 11th-12th edition, vol. 17, p. 487.

A "definite" work on Malesherbes is Pierre Grosclaude, *Malesherbes, témoin et interprète de son temps* (Paris: Fischbacher, 1961). The death of Malesherbes was nevertheless inspiring. *Ibid.*, pp. 747-748. He seems to have returned to the faith of his childhood.

Cf. Pierre Gaxotte, *op. cit.*, p. 84. "The perfect type of a liberal who is always afraid to be taken to be a reactionary." The suicidal tendency of certain aristocrats is well illustrated by the common action of Count Michael Károlyi and (Lord Bertrand) Russell to get the Hungarian Communist Rákosi released from jail (February 1935). He was actually exchanged in 1940. After World War II Rákosi established in Hungary the grimmest Communist tyranny. Cf. *The Autobiography of Bertrand Russell, 1914-1944* (Boston: Little, Brown, 1968), pp. 314-315.

[123] A collège in France is a high-school including college (ages ten to eighteen) run by priests or a religious order. College in Britain is the equivalent of a preparatory school in America. Prep schools in Britain are schools for boys eight to twelve.

[124] One of the church spires was actually demolished—in Besseen-Chandesse. (The present spire is new.) The town council of Strasbourg already had decided to tackle the world famous cathedral when Robespierre, luckily, was overthrown.

[125] *Cf.* Clarence Crane Brinton, *The Jacobins* (New York: Macmillan, 1930), p. 149.

[126] *Ibid.* The author quotes A. Philippe, *La Révolution dans les Vosges*, vol. 4, p. 133.

[127] *Ibid.*, p. 150. The author quotes F. Heitz, *Les sociétés politiques de Strasbourg pendant les années 1790-1795* (Strasbourg, 1863).

[128] *Ibid.*

[129] My conviction rests on investigations I made in 1947 among Austrian and German relatives and friends. *Cf.* p. 312.

[130] Did the United States Government, with excellent channels of information, know about the fate of the Jews, without doing anything about it? Arthur D. Morse, author of the book *Why Six Millions Died* (New York: Random House, 1967) thinks it knew about it.

[131] *Cf.* Louis Blanc and Jacques Crétineau Joly, *Les guerres de Vendée*, Armel de Wismes, ed. (Paris: Hachette, n.d.), pp. 284-285.

[132] *Ibid.*, p. 277.

[133] *Ibid.*, p. 275.

[134] *Ibid.*, p. 225.

Chapter VIII

[1] *Cf.* Chapter V, Note 16 and Dr. Eduard Zeller, *Das theologische System Zwinglis* (Tübingen: Fues, 1853), pp. 163-164.

² *Cf.* Martin Luther, "Tischreden," *Kritische Gesamtausgabe* (Weimar: Böhlau, 1921), vol. 6, p. 143, no. 6718: *Ladem*, "Predigten über etzliche Kapitel des Evangelisten Matthäi," *Gesammelte Werke* (Erlangen, 1850), vol. 44, pp. 156-157. Here also lies a disagreement between Catholic and Calvinistic theological thinking. *Cf.* Herman Doyeweerd, *In the Twilight of Western Thought, Studies in the Pretended Autonomy of Philosophical Thought* (Philadelphia: Presbyterian and Reformed Publishing Company, 1960), pp. 192-194.

³ *Cf.* Herbert Schöffler, *Die Reformation* (Frankfurt-am-Main: Klostermann, n.d.), particularly pp. 42-60.

⁴ *Cf.* Luther's outcry: "I do not concede that my teaching can be judged by anyone, not even by the angels." In *Gesammelte Werke* (Erlangen Edition), vol. 28, p. 144. Luther went on to say that he who does not accept his doctrine cannot be saved, because his doctrine is God's and God's is his: "Enough with all this silly humility!"

⁵ One of the first authors in modern times to deride the concept of Luther as an "early liberal" was Johann Friedrich Böhmer. *Cf.* his *Briefe und kleinere Schriften* (Freiburg i. Br.: Herder, 1868), vol. 2, p. 427. How the whole picture of Luther from a stern disciplinarian to a mild liberal spirit with subjectivist-relativist leanings has been changed and forged through the centuries is well shown by Ernst Walter Zeeden in his *Martin Luther und die Reformation im Urteil des deutschen Luthertums* (Freiburg i. Br.: Herder, 1950), 2 vols. The research covers the period from Luther's death (1546) to Goethe, but unfortunately does not go beyond 1832. *Cf.* also Etienne Gilson, *Les idées et les lettres* (Paris: Vrin, 1932), p. 174, and Alexander Rüstow, *Ortsbestimmung der Gegenwart*, vol. 2, p. 288, where Rüstow insists that Luther's *interpretatio liberalis* is long dead among scholars, but survives in the deeper layers of public opinion. Luther's real stand is the reason for the inherent severity of civilizations fashioned by the Reformation. *Cf.* Erich Fromm, *Die Furcht vor der Freiheit* (Zürich: Steinberg, 1945), *passim*.

⁶ Hence a country such as Lutheran Prussia is infinitely more disciplinarian than Catholic Austria or Bavaria. Still in the Austro-Prussian struggle over the soul and mind of Germany the "progressive" thinkers of the West sided with Prussia—not only William James but also H. F. Amiel. *Cf.* his *Journal intime de l'annee 1866*, Léon Bopp, ed. (Paris: Gallimard-N. R. F. 1959), pp. 328, 376-377.

⁷ Here I refer the interested reader to my *Liberty or Equality*, pp. 223-229 or to *Freiheit oder Gleichheit?* pp. 342-348.

⁸ Luther's essay *De servo arbitrio*, showing quite distinctly his Augustinian heritage, can be found in vol. 18 of the Weimar *Kritische Gesamtausgabe*.

⁹ Was Luther a "Lutheran"? He certainly went to confession every week of his life until his death, and we know that once when, in his old age, he spilled a few drops of the consecrated wine, he knelt down and licked up

every drop from the floor. Whereupon, as the chronicler tells us, the congregation wept at the sight of such piety in this holy man. And in the preface of his translation of the Mass, the *Deutsche Messe* (1525) he expressed his conviction that only the Latin Mass could be the uniting bond of all Christians the world over. (Auricular Confession was revived in the German Evangelical Church in 1956. Luther always considered it as a possible sacrament and as such it figures in the *Confessio Augustana*.) Those who want to know something about the real Luther should read his "Etliche Artikel von den Papisten jetz neulich verfälschet und böslich wider uns Lutherischen gerühmt," written in 1534 in *Sämtliche Werke* (Erlangen Edition, 1855), vol. 65, no. 57. Here (p. 96) Luther says: "The Confession is necessary in the churches, and the priest should give Absolution, because in this way the Christians will be consoled, and the simple-minded as well as the ignorant will be taught and instructed in Confession." In the same essay Luther admits that good works serve as an ornament to faith (p. 97) and that "the intercession of the Saints could not be completely laid aside." (p. 98)

[10] We find a scholarly description of Geneva under Calvin in F. W. Kampschulte's *Johann Calvin, Seine Kirche und sein Staat in Genf* (Leipzig: Duncker und Himblot, 1869 and 1899), 2 vols. As to Calvin's political views *cf.* Hans Baron, *Calvins Staatsanschauung und das konfessionelle Zeitalter* (Munich-Berlin: Oldenbourg, 1924).

[11] The contrary was the case. The antagonisms between Church and State produced a certain strife; now Church and State formed an organic whole. The sovereigns became heads of the Church—even if they were of another faith. Thus, theoretically, Emperor Franz Joseph was the head of the Evangelical Church of Austria, etc. (William II as the head of the Evangelical Church in Prussia even *conducted* divine services.)

Nor, to be sure, were the Puritans in America true apostles of liberty. They wanted their own freedom but granted none to others. They executed Quakers repeatedly and established a political-social-ecclesiastical monolith reminiscent of the Genevan order. Catholic Maryland and Pennsylvania and not Massachusetts spearheaded religious liberty in North America.

[12] On the disciplinary influence of the Irish monks on the Continent *cf.* Alfred Mirgeler, *Rückblick auf das abendländische Christentum* (Mainz: Matthias Grünewald Verlag, 1961), pp. 79ff.

[13] *Cf.* Alexander Rüstow, *Ortsbestimmung der Gegenwart*, vol. 2. p. 291.

[14] Klaus J. Heinisch in his commentary to *Der utopische Staat, Morus: Utopia, Campanella: Sonnenstaat, Bacon: Neu-Atlantis* (Hamburg: Rowohlt, 1960), p. 226, insists that Campanella died in the "Jacobin" monastery of the Rue St. Honoré, where the Jacobin Club later was located. (So does the *Encyclopedia Italiana*, 1930, vol. 8, p. 568). In this book we also find a full text of the *Civitas Solis*. *Cf.* also J. Kvačala, *Thomas Campanella, ein Reformer der ausgehenden Renaissance* (Berlin: Trowitzsch, 1909), especially

pp. xi, 144ff. and 150. Kvačala rightly discounts Campanella's influence on the Jesuit *reducciones* in Paraguay.

On "Monasticism" *cf.* also my essay "El monasticismo," *Revista de Occidente* (Madrid), vol. 3 (2nd series), no. 32, pp. 178-201 and "Der Monastizismus," *Civitas* (Lucerne), vol. 2, no. 6, pp. 321-335. Actually, as Monsignor Otto Mauer said, today the Counsels of Perfection are imposed on the majority of the population. (Ida F. Görres, *op. cit.*, p. 152) Yet the real danger of all "monasticisms" lies in the fact that especially in the realm of economics all efforts to expect a moral level, substantially higher than the one actually existing, must provoke a wave of coercions and lies. *Cf.* Wilhelm Röpke, *Jenseits von Angebot und Nachfrage*, (Erlenback-Zürich: Eugen Rentsch, 1958), p. 165.

[15] *Cf.* Morelly, *Code de la Nature*, introduction by V. P. Volguine (Paris: Editions Sociales, 1953). On pp. 127ff. we find the blueprint for the ideal state and society, the "Model of legislation in conformity with the intentions of nature." There is in Morelly's work a tendency to guess a "natural order" and then to impose it by force. The analogy with Rousseau is obvious.

[16] In Brazil Comte's Positivism became the "official theology" of the nascent republic in 1888. Actually the overthrow of the monarchy and the establishment of the republic was the result of a conspiracy of bitterly disappointed slaveholders who had not forgiven Pedro II for having abolished slavery. They were joined by Comtean Positivists (all leftists) in the army and in the administration. The slogan on the Brazilian flag: *"Ordem e Progresso"* is taken from Comte.

The pioneer of Positivism in Brazil was Benjamin Constant Botelho de Magalhaes. About him *cf.* João Camillo de Oliveira Tôrres, *O Positivismo no Brasil* (Petrópolis: Editôra Vozes Limitada, 1943). Also *passim* in the magistral work of this Brazilian monarchist scholar *A Democracia Coroada, Teoria Política do Império do Brazil* (Petrópolis: Editora Vozes Limitada, 1965).

[17] As a matter of fact, most manufacturers lived rather spartan lives. The lavish spenders in the large cities were rather the visiting big landowners, not the factory owners or the managers. Even the bankers were thrifty. Thomas Mann lets one of his heroes (in *The Buddenbrooks*) remark critically that a certain burgher family of Lübeck was living from the interest on their capital and not from the interest on interest. The drive for investments was enormous and laid the foundations for free Europe's present wealth—and high living standards for everybody.

[18] Metternich wrote to Emperor Francis I about the general moral, intellectual and social decay of the Paris proletariat in 1825. He also described the flood of immoral publications sold at half price to young men and women. Metternich remarked: "Here missions as among savages ought to start their work." (*Cf.* Metternich, *op. cit.*, vol. 4, pp. 164-165.)

[19] The Comte de Saint-Simon was a collateral descendant of the Duc de Saint-Simon, famous for his rather frivolous autobiography describing court

life in the late seventeenth and early eighteenth century. The Socialist Comte de Saint-Simon revolted in a very concrete sense against his class and the traditions of his family.

[20] Brissot in his younger years was deeply interested in the emancipation of the Negroes (particularly in the West Indies), became later an ardent Girondist, and was guillotined on October 31, 1793 with a number of other supporters of his faction.

[21] Scenes of the downfall of the high and mighty could be seen in most medieval churches over the west entrance. Popes, emperors, kings, friars, bishops, priests, nuns and noblemen went to Hell—yet representatives of these groups could also be found among the saved.

[22] This is contradicted by the enormous amount of crime in the Soviet Union. (The crime syndicates of the USSR, far larger than anything of this sort in the United States, extend from coast to coast.) Individual crimes can be mentioned by the press only in exceptional cases. Divorces, suicides and accidents also are taboo. There are no crime statistics available for the Soviet Union and there is good reason to believe that they are not even compiled.

[23] *Vide* Chapter III, Note 7.

[24] I am partly repeating here the views of Professor Paul Gaechter, S. J., Professor emeritus of New Testament exegesis at Innsbruck University, author of *Maria im Erdenleben* (Innsbruck: Tyrolia, 1954) and *Das Matthäus-Evangelium* (Innsbruck: Tyrolia 1962). Yet it frequently seems profitable to "church strategists" or Christian "democratists" to maintain that Christianity in its origins was a movement of the poor, the humble and the ignorant. Gioberti obviously liked this thesis. *Cf.* Vincenzo Gioberti, *Del rinnovamento civile d'Italia*, Fausto Nicolini, ed. (Bari: Laterza, 1912), vol. 3, p. 7. And Montalembert with great irony described the sudden discovery of French ecclesiastics in 1848 that republicanism took its origin at Golgotha, *Cf. Montalembert, Textes choisis*, Emmanuel Mounier, ed. (Paris: Egloff, 1945), p. 94. Friedrich Engels had the same notion (i.e. the early Church being formed by proletarian outcasts) and his view is clearly reflected by the *Bolshaya Sovyetskaya Entsiklopediya* (Moscow 1957), vol. 46, p. 352 sq. For a corrective view cf. Philip Hughes, *The History of the Church* (New York: Sheed and Ward, 1949), vol. 1, pp. 162-169.

[25] *Cf.* Chapter V, Note 13.

[26] *Cf.* Louis Dupré, "Marx and Religion: An Impossible Marriage." *Commonweal*, vol. 88, no. 6, April 26, 1968, pp. 171-176.

[27] The dialogue between Christians and Marxists has largely foundered, for external reasons among others, one of them being the fact that up to August 1969, Czechoslovakia largely served as a bridge. The cringing attitude of some of the Christian debaters did not last too long when they became aware of the fact that they were expected to make all the concessions. On the other hand, the more enthusiastic Communists soon were anathematized by their party and expelled, as shown in the case of the French "Communist Humanist" Roger Garaudy.

[28] There is most obviously a real contradiction between democracy and socialism; socialism stands for a planned, centralized economy; democracy rests on perpetual change. Socialism could theoretically be combined with absolute monarchy, but not with a political system which carefully registers the "fermentation of the masses" or easily yields to the cry "let's throw the rascals out." Still, socialism, including the dictatorship of the proletariat, can be brought about by highly democratic methods, just as suicide (resulting in inaction) can be achieved by action. The connection, however, between political democracy and the desire for equality in all other domains was evident already to Aristotle. *Cf.* his *Politics*, V, i, 2. And when Lenin was accused by his enemies that his doctrines contained as integral part the Jacobinism of the "bourgeois" French Revolution, he replied, "What is Marxism if not Jacobinism fused with the working class movement?" *Cf.* Bertram D. Wolfe, *One Hundred Years in the Life of a Doctrine* (New York: Dial Press, 1965), p. 164. Yet in the realm of ideas filiation is no safeguard against contradiction. As a matter of fact, without a growing contradiction filiation will hardly take place.

[29] *Cf.* Willmoore Kendall, "John Locke and the Doctrine of Majority Rule," Illinois Studies in the Social Sciences (1941), vol. 26, no. 2, p. 132.

[30] Jan Czyński, a Polish Socialist, in his preface to Fourier's *Théorie de l'Unité Universelle*, compared him to Christ.

[31] The Socialist-republican equation was not even known to Saint-Simon. Of course the labels attached to forms of government do not always disclose their real character. Professor Adolf Merkl says that an aristocratic republic with limited franchise can be a *Rechtsstaat*, a constitutional state of law and order, while a parliamentary monarchy with radically democratic franchise may not be. *Cf.* his essay "Idee und Gestalt der politischen Freiheit," in *Demokratie und Rechtsstaat. Festgabe für Zaccaria Giacometti*, p. 176, quoting also Fritz Fleiner. Merkl also insists that the German Third Reich and the USSR are formally and constitutionally *republics*. (p. 177)

[32] *Cf.* Charles Fourier, *Textes choisis*, Félix Armand, ed. (Paris: Editions Sociales, 1953), p. 150. ("Theorie de l'unité universelle," in *Oeuvres complètes*, vol. 4. p. 419.)

[33] *Ibid.*, p. 148 (*Oeuvres complètes*, vol. 3. p. 254).

[34] *Ibid.*, p. 149 (*Oeuvres complètes*, vol. 3. p. 494).

[35] *Ibid.*, p. 137 (*Oeuvres complètes*, vol. 3. p. 464).

[36] Louis Napoléon himself wrote a book in 1844 entitled *L'extinction du pauperisme* in which the emperor-to-be attacked capitalism as a source of poverty. *Cf.* Félix Armand, *Les Fourieristes et les luttes révolutionnaires de 1848 à 1851* (Paris: Presses Universitaires, 1948).

[37] Not far from San Antonio, Texas is the town of New Braunfels, founded by a Prince Solms-Braunfels, a colorful, romantic man who wanted to establish a haven for the European nobility in America, for aristocrats wanting to escape the rising tide of democracy in their homelands.

[38] Orestes A. Brownson was also loosely connected with Brook Farm.

Like Isaac Hecker he became a Catholic but remained a layman and can be considered one of the most brilliant minds on the Catholic scene in nineteenth-century America. An outstanding conservative, he is now largely ignored by friend and foe. *Cf.* Doran Whalen, *Granite for God's House* (New York: Sheed and Ward, 1941); Theodore Maynard, *Orestes Brownson, Yankee, Radical, Catholic* (New York: Macmillan, 1943); H. I. Brownson, *Orestes Brownson, The Middle Life* (Detroit, 1899); Lawrence Roemer, *Brownson on Democracy and the Trend Towards Socialism* (New York: Philosophical Library, 1953). This volume gives us a good synthesis of Brownson's political thought. His collected works were published toward the end of the nineteenth century in Detroit but have not been reissued since.

[39] At the turn of the century Arthur Brisbane was one of the best-known American journalists. He worked for the Hearst press and, even more than Charles A. Dana and James G. Bennett Jr., drove his country into the sterile Cuban adventure. Hudson Strode in his *Pageant of Cuba* gave a good description of the journalist drive leading to American armed intervention.

[40] *Cf.* Th. G. Masaryk, *Zur russischen Geschichts und Religionsphilosophie* (Düsseldorf-Cologne: Eugen Diederichs, 1965. A photographic reproduction of the 1913 edition), p. 315.

[41] *Ibidem*, pp. 335n., 362.

[42] The importance of this novel cannot be overestimated. *Cf.* N. G. Chernyshevski, *Shto dyelat'*? (Moscow-Leningrad: Dyetgiz, 1950). The preface by N. Bogoslovski keeps close to the party line. Lenin called one of his most important pamphlets also *Shto dyelat'*? ("What to do?")

[43] The basic inhumanity of leftist thought, of the entire leftist mind, comes from and leads to madness. To view man as a merely gradually differing relative of termites, bedbugs, and earwigs, and to blueprint something as (virtually) dynamic as a society in the form of an arithmetic-geometric pattern inevitably leads to a nightmarish mentality, to insanity. On the pathology of egalitarianism *cf.* Sigmund Freud, *Gesammelte Werke* (London 1940), vol. 13, p. 134sq.

Chapter IX

[1] *Cf.* Chapter VII, Note 129.

[2] The Catholic *Staatslexikon* of the "Görres-Gesellschaft" (Freiburg i.Br.: Herder, 1931), vol. 4, col. 476 says of him: "His broad intellectual interests, his untiring compassion, his life spent in purity and poverty all manifest the nobility of Proudhon's character."

[3] *Cf.* J. P. Proudhon, *Les confessions d'un révolutionnaire* (Paris, 1849), p. 61. Again and again Proudhon dealt with the problem of God's existence and hotly defended the Catholic position against Feuerbach. *Cf.* Daniel Halévy, "Proudhon d'après ses carnets inédits (1843-1847)," *Hier et Demain* (Paris: Sequana, 1944), no. 9, pp. 26-27.

[4] *Cf.* Henri de Lubac, *Proudhon et le christianisme* (Paris: Editions du Seuil, 1945).

[5] *Cf.* Constantin Frantz, *Das neue Deutschland* (Leipzig: Rossberg'sche Buchhandlung, 1871), p. 375.

[6] *Cf.* J. P. Proudhon, "Confessions d'un révolutionnaire," in *Oeuvres complètes* (Paris: Marcel Rivière, 1929), p. 353.

[7] Voting by classes on the basis of educational levels, taxes or incomes continued in Europe right into the early twentieth century. Austria, for instance, introduced the one-man-one-vote system only in 1907, but still, earlier than Britain. Independent Rhodesia, timocratic rather than democratic, has two "classes" ("rolls"). *Cf.* State of Rhodesia, *Democracy and the Constitution* (Salisbury: Fact Papers, 1966), no. 8. (The new Constitution of 1970 is not basically different). George Bernard Shaw, a Fabian with very bright moments, said, "I do not see any way out of this difficulty as long as our democrats persist in assuming that Mr. Everyman is omniscient as well as ubiquitous, and refuse to consider the suffrage in the light of facts and common sense. How much control of the Government does Mr. Everyman need to protect himself against tyranny? How much is he capable of exercising without ruining himself and wrecking civilization? I think not. . . ." "It is a matter of simple natural history that humans vary widely in political competence. They vary not only from individual to individual but from age to age in the same individual. In the face of this flat fact it is silly to go on pretending that the voice of the people is the voice of God. When Voltaire said that Mr. Everybody was wiser than Mr. Anybody he had never seen adult suffrage at work. It takes all sorts to make a world, and to maintain civilization some of these sorts have to be killed like mad dogs whilst others have to be put in command of the State. Until the differences are classified we cannot have a scientific suffrage, and without a scientific suffrage every attempt at democracy will defeat itself as it has always done." (*Cf.* his *Everybody's Political What's What*, London, 1944, pp. 45-46.) While these lines are being written, British socialism, at the behest of African potentates, is still trying to rein Rhodesia economically in order to enforce the one-man-one-vote system. Little it matters that those who will suffer most from the blockade (in which the totalitarian assassins of several continents participate) are precisely the people for whose benefit Rhodesia is being persecuted, the economically weaker element of Rhodesia, the Africans. Leftists almost always are pitiless and will sacrifice everything and everybody to their fixed notions.

[8] *Cf.* Proudhon's letter dated April 2, 1852.

[9] *Cf.* Proudhon, "La solution du problème social," *Oeuvres complètes* (Paris: Marpon et Flammarion, n.d.), vol. 6, p. 86.

[10] *Ibid.*, p. 75.

[11] *Ibid.*, p. 75.

[12] *Ibid.*, p. 56.

[13] *Ibid.*, p. 59

[14] *Ibid.*, p. 64.

¹⁵ *Cf.* P. J. Proudhon, "Du princip fédératif," *Oeuvres complètes* (Paris: Marcel Rivière, 1959), pp. 34-35. Compare with Denis de Rougemont, "Gedanken über den Föderalismus," *Mass und Wert* (Zürich), March-April 1940.

¹⁶ *Cf.* Proudhon, "Du principe fédératif," p. 375.

¹⁷ *Ibid.*, p. 334.

¹⁸ *Ibid.*, pp. 302-303.

¹⁹ *Cf.* Proudhon, cited by Henri de Lubac, *op. cit.*, p. 58.

²⁰ *Cf.* letter to Robin, October 12, 1851, cited in Henri de Lubac, *op. cit.* p. 61n.

²¹ *Cf.* letter to A. Marc Dufraisse, cited by Emmanuel Mounier, *Liberté sous conditions* (Paris: Editions du Seuil, 1946) p. 213.

²² *Ibid.*, p. 214.

²³ *Cf.* Proudhon, "Du principe fédératif," pp. 355-356.

²⁴ *Cf.* P. J. Proudhon, *De la pornocratie ou Les femmes dans les temps modernes* (Paris: A. Lacroix, 1875).

²⁵ As an ill man he went into exile to Belgium in 1858 and returned broken in 1862 to die three years later. He was befriended by Prince Joseph Bonaparte who, intellectually very active, was interested in "advanced ideas."

²⁶ *Cf.* Daniel Halévy, *op. cit.*, p. 52.

²⁷ *Cf.* Werner Blumenberg, *Karl Marx in Selbstzeugnissen und Bilddokumenten* (Hamburg: Rowohlts Monographiem, 1962), p. 29.

²⁸ *Cf.* Ernst Kux, *Karl Marx—Die Revolutionäre Konfession* (Erlenbach-Zürich: Eugen Rentsch, 1967), p. 15. The study of this St. Gallen professor is most valuable for the understanding of Marx. "His practice remains theoretical," Kux adds, "He destroys only realms of ideas, of the spirit, of thought—not in order to replace them with superior constructions, but only for the sake of destruction." (p. 25)

²⁹ *Cf.* Heinrich Heine, "Geständnisse" in *Sämtliche Werke* (Leipzig: Insel-Verlag), vol. 10, p. 180.

In this connection it should be noted that Marx' criticism of the Hegelian philosophy (from which he borrowed liberally, if one-sidedly) is to a large extent based on the "romanticized" version of Heine's Hegelian concepts. *Cf.* Ernst Kux, *op. cit.*, p. 32.

³⁰ *Cf.* Karl Marx and Friedrich Engels, *Historisch-Kritische Gesamtausgabe*, D. Ryazanov, ed. (Marx-Engels Institute: Moscow, 1930), vol. 3, p. 120.

³¹ *Ibid.*, vol. 5, p. 22. "Everybody in whom dwells a Raphael should have a chance to develop" his art. *Ibid.*, p. 372.

³² *Ibid.*, vol. 1, part 1, p. 607. ("Zur Kritik der Hegelschen Rechtsphilosophie.") The term *Entfremdung* ("alienation"), on the other hand, has first been used by Adam von Müller. Nietzsche might have been inspired by Marx' "Superman" notion, while he copied the "God is dead" formula from Hegel.

[33] *Cf.* Ernst Kux, *op. cit.*, p. 127, note 181.

[34] This attitude is dictated by an absolute belief in an automation of the historic process which the helpless individual cannot change. "Communism, for us, is not a situation which has to be created, an ideal, which reality will have to take into account. We call Communism a genuine motion which cancels the present state of affairs." (Marx-Engels, *Gesamtausgabe*, vol. 5, p. 25.)

[35] *Ibid.*, vol. 5, p. 227. *Vide* also the preface to *Das Kapital* (Hamburg: Otto Meissner, 1909) p. viii, on which the person's lacking responsibility within the pattern of society is strongly emphasized.

[36] *Cf.* Ernst Kux, *op. cit.*, p. 85.

[37] *Cf.* Polina Vinogradskaya, "Zhenni Marks," in *Novy Mir* (Moscow), vol. 40, no. 3, March 1964, pp. 179ff.

[38] *Cf.* Arnold Ruge *Briefwechsel und Tagebuchblätter*, Paul Nerrlich, ed. (Berlin: Weidmann, 1886), p. 381.

[39] *Cf.* Carl Schurz, Lebenserinnerungen (Bis sum Jahre 1852) (Berlin: Georg Reimer, 1906), pp. 142-143. Yet this mixture of spite and arrogance is due to a *ressentiment*, as Eugène Ionesco rightly guessed when he wrote in his *Journal en miettes* (Paris: Mercure de France, 1967), p. 60. "Marx must have suffered from a secret wound to his pride, as did all those who wanted revolutions. It is this secret wound which he hides, consciously or not."

[40] *Vide* his essay "Zur Judenfrage" in Karl Marx, *Die Frühschriften* Siegfried Landshut, ed. (Stuttgart: Alfred Kröner, 1953), p. 171sq.

[41] *Cf.* Karl Marx and Friedrich Engels, *Das kommunistische Manifest*, Rosa Luxemberg, ed. (Vienna: Verlag der Arbeiterbuchhandlung, 1921).

[42] The German for it is *Gespenst* which means "ghost," "spook." *Specter* is a much milder expression. The word "bourgeois" in Continental language implies rather the propertied, upper part of the middle class with a somewhat stuffy character. This subtle meaning of the term developed only gradually in the last two hundred years.

[43] One ought to remember that Marx believed the proletariat to form the *majority* of most nations. If this were the case the rule, even the dictatorship, of the proletariat could be considered democratic. Democracy *is* majority rule.

[44] To Marx, especially to the younger Marx, economics serve as an intellectual explanation, his aims and motives, however, always remain emotional. Gustave Thibon remarked rightly that "One should not forget that the totalitarian tyranny is a child of the humanitarian and democratic *mystique*. The former is not opposed to the latter as the illnesses to their remedies: We are dealing here rather with two successive but basically identical manifestations of the corruption of *homo politicus*." *Cf.* G. Thibon, "Le risque au service de la prudence," *Etudes Carmélitaines*, 24 year, vol. 1 (Spring 1939), p. 52n.

[45] President Roosevelt said that "In the hands of a people's government this power is wholesome and proper. But in the hands of political puppets of an economic autocracy such power would provide shackles for the liberties of the people." Cited by Garet Garrett, *The Revolution That Was* (Caldwell: Caxton Printers, 1945), p. 35. One really wonders about this logic. As if the American worker does not enjoy a far greater liberty than the "toiler" in the USSR.

If we look for a more extreme but still just formulation of the difference between free enterprise and socialism-communism, then we can say with Wilhelm Röpke that the final sanction in the former is the bailiff and in the latter the hangman. *Cf.* his *Die Gesellschaftskrisis der Gegenwart* (Erlenbach-Zürich: Eugen Rentsch, 1948), p. 147. This brilliant book of the late neo-Liberal thinker is still as timely as when it came out for the first time in 1942.

[46] However, even "right-wing" countries show a rather obsolete tendency to "carve up" large estates, although it is by now an established fact that the future farming lies in large-scale farms; small ones, unless they are truck farms, are becoming increasingly uneconomic. Under Marshal Costa e Silva Brazil enacted an agrarian reform although no less than 5.5 million square kilometers are Federal Property, an area the size of Europe without the prewar Soviet Union.

[47] *Cf.* Alexander Pauper (pseudonym for a high Austrian government official), "Was ist ein 'Reicher' ?" *Die Industrie* (Vienna), December 23, 1960. This author mentions here the statement of a budget committee of the United States Congress in 1957 to the effect that all income tax in excess of 50 percent yields only 2 percent of the income tax revenue or 1 percent of the total revenue of the United States. The situation in Sweden is not very different. We can read in a pamphlet entitled *"The Role of Taxation in the Redistribution of Income in Sweden"* (Edited by the Swedish Taxpayer Association, Stockholm, 1963) that only 6 percent of the tax revenue comes from progressivity (p. 5). A maximum rate of 25 percent would yield 80 percent of the present revenues (p. 6.) and only 1 percent of all income is redistributed by progressivity (p. 9). In 1962 the total income of the Swedish state from private persons in all forms was 16 billion crowns (one crown is about twenty U. S. cents): out of this the income tax accounts for 3.45 billion crowns. Less than 10 percent of this sum (315 million crowns) comes from those who are taxed at a rate of 25 to 45 percent, and only 1.5 percent (or 45 million crowns) from those in the top bracket, i.e., 45 to 65 percent (p. 7).

The nature of most tax systems in the Western world is demagogical rather than economical: there is the pressure exercised by the Socialist parties and the general belief that a radical redistribution of wealth would not only remove objects of *envy* (which it would), but also would improve the living standards of the lower classes (which it would not). Questions of this sort can only be answered by studying all-round statistics with paper and pencil. Were we

480

(taking Alexander Pauper's statistics into consideration) to confiscate the total income of every Austrian earning more than 1,000 dollars a month after taxation and hand to every Austrian every day his equal share of this, he could get 1.7 U. S. cents a day. Were we to have made in 1956 a somewhat similar regulation in Germany by confiscating everybody's income above $250.00 a month, every German would have gotten from that jackpot a nickel a day! *Cf.* Ludwig Reiners *Verdienen wir zu wenig?* (Baden-Baden: Lutzey, 1957), p. 4. Reviewing the income structure of the United States we see that in 1960 the gross national income was about 100 billion dollars; of this wages and salaries account for about 65 billion, other payments for 10 billion, benefits for 5 billion, self-employed incomes for almost 12 billion (farms for 3.1 billion), the *total unearned income* moved around 6 percent and Americans of all walks of life shared in this. *Cf.* The National Industrial Conference, *The Economic Almanack 1962* (New York), p. 115. Roughly the same picture emerges from Italy when we study the full page advertisement of the "Confederazione Generale dell'Industria Italiana," Communication no. 2. in *Gente*, vol. 8, no. 48. (November 26, 1964). It shows the balance sheets of the thirteen biggest Italian companies. In 1963 these companies paid 44.5 billion lire in dividends but 526 billion lire for labor. Other sums went for taxes and reinvestments. These companies employ 258,000 people but have just over half-a-million shareholders. (Two of the companies paid no dividends.) If, for instance, there are really 5,000 millionaires in Mexico (in pesos of 8 cents, well understood) then the total egalitarian distribution of their wealth would give each Mexican the sum of eighteen U. S. dollars once and for all. Yet Mexico is one of the richest nations in the Latin-American community. Radical "social reforms" further south would have an even lesser effect. It is worthwhile to note that Europe's leading Catholic sociologist, Father O.von Nell-Breuning, S.J., not at all noted for rightist leanings, has strongly denounced the idea that the masses can be made wealthier by expropriating the rich. (This, he insists, is equally true of the "underdeveloped nations.") Cf. his "Kritischer Rückblick auf Quadragesimo Anno," *Zur Debatte* (Munich, April 1972), vol. 2, no. 4, p. 3.

[48] People with larger incomes are thus discouraged from engaging in additional enterprises and, under these circumstances, additional jobs and additional production are thwarted. Progressive taxation, in this way, is opposed to the common good.

[49] The needless crisis of the American railroads is largely the result of the impossible labor situation with its excessive featherbedding. In Europe the railroads, *in spite* of government ownership, are constantly improved.

[50] *Cf. Karl Marx*, Franz Borkenau, ed. (Frankfurt-am-Main: Fisher Bücherei, 1956), p. 118. (Point 17 of the "Demands of the Communist Party in German," published in the *Neue Rheinische Zeitung*.)

[51] *Cf.* Louis Dupré, *The Philosophical Foundations of Marxism* (New York: Harcourt, Brace and World, 1966), p. ix, "Marx's early works represent

one long struggle to detach Hegel's dialectic method from his idealistic system; without a solid knowledge of both, Marx cannot be understood."

⁵² A technological system of mass production will always go through a difficult period in its early stages, but in the world of free enterprise eventually the general levels will be raised. It is interesting to note that while every excuse was made by leftist intellectuals for the terrible sacrifices in connection with the Soviet Five-Year Plans, no such concessions were made for early capitalist enterprises in other parts of the world. "Getting ahead" always demand sacrifices and the question is only this: Are the sacrifices worth it or are they senseless? Will they or won't they help to establish a way of production which assures a dignified way of life and a modicum of prosperity to all?

⁵³ Curiously enough all big state combines and monopolies in the Soviet Union are officially called *trusts* (*trēst*) which, of course, is part of the Soviets' morbid American fixation. When I told Soviet citizens that trusts in the United States are subject to prosecution, they could hardly believe me.

⁵⁴ *Cf. Aus dem literarischen Nachlass von Karl Marx* (Stuttgart, 1902), Vol. 1, pp. 405ff.; S. M. Dubnow, *Die neueste Geschichte des jüdischen Volkes* (Berlin: Jüdischer Verlag, 1920), vol. 2. pp. 508. Engels' letter addressed to Marx on March 7, 1856 can be found in *Karl Marx, Friedrich Engels, Kritische Gesamtausgabe*, Third Series, Vol. 2, p. 122. Other anti-Jewish remarks of Engels can be found in Vol. 3, p. 192 and of Marx (all in connection with the hated Lassalle) in Vol. 2, pp. 365, 366, 371, in vol. 3, pp. 82, 84, 90, 91. (Lassalle was to Marx a "Jewish nigger.") See also Arnold Künzli's monumental *Karl Marx: Eine Psychographie* (Vienna-Frankfort-Zürich: Europa Verlag, 1966).

⁵⁵ *Cf.* Erik v. Kuehnelt-Leddihn, "Do Jews tend towards Communism?" *The Catholic World*, November 1946, pp. 107-113. A certain trait in the Jewish character perhaps directs the attention of Jews towards all ideas pointing to the future. Ida F. Görres also remarks that Jews are frequently fascinated by the "shape of things to come." *Cf.* her *Zwischen den Zeiten. Aus meinen Tagebüchern 1951-1959* (Olten: Walter, 1961), p. 439.

⁵⁶ *Cf.* Franz Werfel, *Between Heaven and Earth*, trsl. Maxim Newark (New York: Philosophical Library, 1944), p. 202, no. 21.

⁵⁷ *Cf.* Nathaniel Weyl, *The Jew in American Politics* (New Rochelle: Arlington House, 1968), *passim*.

⁵⁸ *Cf.* Edmund Silberner, *Sozialisten zur Judenfrage*, trsl. A. Mandel (Berlin: Colloquim, 1962). This richly documented book is largely a translation of *Western European Socialism and the Jewish Problem (1800-1918): A Selective Biography*. (Jerusalem, 1955).

⁵⁹ *Cf.* Solomon N. Schwarz, "Anti-Semitism in the Soviet Union," in *Commentary* (New York), June 1949. See also Samuel Gringauz, "Anti-Semitism in Socialism," *Commentary*, (New York), April 1950. It is obvious, however, that the percentage of Jews in Marxist parties will be higher in areas where they are materially or socially depressed or oppressed. In the leadership

of the French or Italian Communist Parties Jews were and are exceedingly rare. The same is true of Scandinavia. One ought to remember the fact that Western Europe's refugee camps after 1945 were crammed with East-European Jews. Nazism was defeated—so why? Because these Jews (who wanted to go to Palestine) dreaded the return to Soviet-dominated areas! While America still enjoyed the Red honeymoon, *they knew*. It is their refusal to return where they came from (and by no means the specter of a dead Nazism) which "made" the state of Israel.

[60] *Cf.* Max Nomad, *Apostles of Revolution* (Boston: Little, Brown, 1939), p. 423, where that author mentions a dispatch of Walter Duranty, dated October 10, 1938, to the effect that Stalin up to that time had killed more Jews than Hitler. The North American Newspaper Alliance distributed this news, but the *New York Times* on October 11, 1938, omitted these lines about the murdered Jews.

[61] Two stories are current about Jewish support for the Bolshevik Revolution. One deals with the "financing" of the Soviets by Kuhn, Loeb, and Schiff from New York. Yet why should a "capitalist" Jewish banking house be interested in the overthrow of a democratic republic? *Cf.* Walter Laqueur, *Deutschland und Russland* (Berlin: Propyläen Verlag, 1965), pp. 105-106. An earlier *canard* was a forged report, the so-called Sisson-Papers, according to which the German-Jewish banking house Warburg had financed the overthrow of the Kerensky Regime. *Cf.* George F. Kennan, *Russia Leaves the War* (Princeton: Princeton University Press, 1956), pp. 441sq.

[62] *Cf.* Antonio Machado, *Obras completas* (México: Edición Seneca, 1940), p. 702.

[63] *Cf.* Karl Marx, *Die Frühschriften*, p. 201. He sums up his thesis with the words: "The *social* emancipation of the Jews is the *emancipation of society from Jewry*." (Marx' emphasis,) p. 209.

[64] *Cf.* Dr. J. Goebbels, *Der Nazi-Sozi, Fragen und Antworten für den Nationalsocialisten* (Munich: Eher, 1932), p. 12. Alfred Rosenberg in one of his purple passages insisted that he who wants to be a National Socialist has indeed to be a Socialist in order to paralyze "international capitalism" and to overcome the narrow concept of private property. *Cf.* his *Der Mythus des 20. Jahrhunderte* (München: Hoheneichen Verlag, 1943), p. 538. Hitler considered himself the "executor of Marxism" and repeatedly expressed his admiration for German Socialism whose methods he was ready to copy. *Cf.* Hermann Rauschning, *Gespräche mit Hitler* (Zürich-New York: Europa Verlag, 1940), pp. 174ff.

[65] *Cf.* Waldemar Gurian, *Der Bolschewismus, Einführunglund Lehre* (Freiburg i.Br.: Herder, 1931), p. 187sq.

[66] *Cf.* Ben Hecht, *Erik Dorn* (New York: Putnam, 1921), p. 381.

[67] *Cf.* E. F. W. Tomlinson, *Criterion* (London), no. 46.

[68] Nicholas I, Russian Emperor, was profoundly interested in this experiment. The reader is reminded that "social" and "socialistic" are by no means the same. Socialism rests primarily on the ownership of the means

of production by "society," i.e., to all practical purposes by *the State*. Sir Stafford Cripps, defending the Socialist viewpoint has said correctly in his book *Towards Christian Democracy* that the injustices men create for themselves can only be removed by the State, which is "in fact, accepted as the nearest we can get to an impartial judge in any matter." *Cf.* John Jewkes, *Ordeal by Planning* (London: Macmillan, 1948), p. 210. This, naturally, is an honestly naive statement by a naive man. The often badly misused term "social" has very aptly been analyzed by Friedrich A. v. Hayek in brilliant and biting essay entitled: "Was ist und was heisst 'sozial?' " in *Masse und Demokratie* (Erlenback-Zürich: Eugen Rentsch, 1957), pp. 71-84. He quotes approvingly Charles Curran in *The Spectator* (July 6, 1956, p. 8) who said: "Social Justice is a semantic fraud from the same stable as People's Democracy." Yet one must read this essay in its entirety to understand an argument which, at first sight, might shock pious hypocrites.

[69] Bakunin's position was severely shaken by his association with Sergey Nyechayev who had committed murder only to make himself more interesting and important. Since his crime had no strictly political character, he was arrested by the Swiss and extradited to Russia where he received a life sentence. The Nyechayev case was used as a theme by Dostoyevski in *The Possessed* (*Byessy*, also called *The Demons*). On Bakunin and Nyechayev *cf.* also Edward Hallett Carr, *The Romantic Exiles* (Harmondsworth: Penguin Books, 1949).

[70] According to certain rumors there exists in the vaults of the Marx-Engels Institute in Moscow an unpublished very anti-Russian manuscript from the pen of Karl Marx. On account of the purges in the 1930s many editors of the *Gesamtausgabe* have been jailed and killed and thus this still unfinished edition of the *Karl Marx-Friedrich Engels Gesamtausgabe* underwent considerable difficulties. In Marx' articles published by the *New York (Daily) Tribune* (1853-1856) his anti-Russian stand comes out clearly and prophetically.

[71] *Vide* G. K. Chesterton's outcry: "Aristocrats are always anarchists." *Cf.* his *Man Who Was Thursday* (New York: Dodd, Mead, 1908), p. 190. There is, one should always bear in mind, a certain "anarchical" undercurrent in all genuine "rightist" thought. The French essayist Charles-Albert Cingria, flatly rejecting democracy, called himself "an anarchist of the extreme right." *Cf.* Marcel Bisiaux, "C. A. Cingria," in *Arts* (Paris), No. 419 (July 10-16, 1953), p. 5. To the Reformers, who were temperamentally disciplinarians and rigorists, the nobility was always a rather odd and unreliable estate. *Cf.* Luther in his "Table Talks," *Sämtliche Werke* (Erlangen Edition), vol. 62, pp. 209-214. (No. 2751-2761). On Calvin and the aristocracy *cf.* Karl Holl, *Gesammelte Aufsätze zur Kirchengeschichte* (Tübingen: J. C. B. Mohr, 1928), vol. 3, pp. 279-280.

[72] It was perhaps the real misery conditioned by financial circumstances that caused the death of his only legitimate son, Edward (whom he did not particularly like), at the age of eight.

[73] *Cf.* Werner Blumenberg, *op. cit.*, pp. 115-117.

[74] *Cf.* Hans Freyer, *Theorie des gegenwärtigen Zeitalters* (Stuttgart: Deutsche Verlagsanstalt, 1955), p. 119. Freyer points out that clever ideologies usually anticipate most criticisms and counter them with preventive arguments.

[75] *Cf.* Otto Fürst Bismarck, *Die gesammelten Werke* Petersdorff, ed. (Stuttgart: Deutsche Verlagsgesellschaft, 1923-1935), vol. 15, p. 485, and Prinz Philipp zu Eulenburg, *Aus fünfzig Jahren* (Berlin: Paetel, 1923), p. 225. When William II once called the German Social Democrats *"vaterlandslose Gessellen"* (fellows without a fatherland), the outcry was great and the protestations vehement, but the rather undiplomatic words of the Emperor were merely a repetition of Marx' statement in the "Communist Manifesto." *Cf.* p. 132 of this book.

[76] The picture of Winston S. Churchill as a leftist radical eager for nationalizations and the introduction of the Provider State in Britain is well drawn by Peter de Mendelssohn in his biography *The Age of Churchill, 1874-1911* (London: Thames and Hudson, 1961), *passim.*

[77] Professor Mark de Wolfe Howe, editing the *Holmes-Laski Letters 1916-1935* (Cambridge: Harvard University Press, 1941) was forced to admit that Mr. Laski had not always stuck to the factual truth and had engaged in interesting inventions.

[78] Hobson makes rather amusing reading. Thus he tells us in his *Imperialism* (1938 edition, p. 57): "Does anyone seriously suppose that a great war could be undertaken by any European State, or a great State loan subscribed, if the house of Rothschild and its connections set their face against it?" Similar nonsense can be found in Nazi textbooks. The economic explanation of history is a facile "false but clear" idea.

Chapter X

[1] *Cf.* Edward Crankshaw, "Russia in Europe: The Conflict of Values," *International Affairs* (Toronto), vol. 22, no. 4, October 1946, p. 509. A similar observation was made by Bruno Bauer, the ex-friend of Karl Marx in his *Russland und das Germanenthum* (Charlottenburg: Egbert Bauer, 1835), p. 12, and by Joseph de Maistre in his famous *Quatre chapitres inédits sur la Russie*, published by his son.

Analogous observations had been made about the Spaniards. Elie Faure thought that the Inquisition for them must have been a necessary evil, an "iron belt for this undisciplined people." (*Cf.* his essay "L'âme espagnole," *La Grande Revue*, vol. 33, no. 12, December 1929, p. 195.) It has been my thesis for a long time that the anarchical and "absolutistic" drives of the Catholic and of the Eastern Church nations make parliamentary democracy in the long run impossible because the latter must rest on a *basic conformity*. Ideally the various political parties (everywhere) should only be ins and outs.

Vide the chapter "The Political Temper of Catholic Nations" in *Liberty or Equality*, pp. 179ff., *Freiheit oder Gleichheit?* pp. 285ff. The individualism and absolutism of the non-post-Reformatory nations results automatically in a variety of ideologically incompatible parties and factions without a common denominator. This speedily ruins a democratic republic while it is still bearable in a (constitutional) monarchy where the monarch has definitely the last word and acts as a unifying force. Hence the abortive effort of America and Britain (with their great uniformity and readiness to compromise in the field of political thought) to make the countries of the "Old Church" safe for democracy. This George Washington and Alexander Hamilton knew very well indeed, witness the passage of Washington's Farewell Address, drafted by Hamilton, in which the great President spoke about the dangers of a strong and violent party spirit leading finally to "the absolute power of an Individual" who, as "the chief of some prevailing faction," will turn "his disposition to the purpose of his own elevation, on the ruins of Public Liberty." Washington concluded this passage with the words, "There is an opinion that parties in free countries are useful checks upon the Administration of the Government and serve to keep alive the Spirit of Liberty. . . . This within certain limits is probably true—and in Governments of a Monarchical cast, Patriotism may look with indulgence, if not with favor, upon the spirit of party. But in those of a popular character, in Governments purely elective, it is a spirit not to be encouraged." *Cf. The Washington Papers*, Saul K. Padover, ed. (New York: Harper, 1955), p. 317. For Hamilton's draft *cf. The Basic Ideas of Alexander Hamilton*, R. B. Morris, ed., pp. 387-388.

[2] *Cf.* N. S. Timasheff, "On the Russian Revolution," *The Review of Politics*, Vol. 4, No. 3, July 1942, also citing Sir Bernard Pares, *The Fall of the Russian Monarchy*, London, 1939. Writes Timasheff, "The Russian peasants had received at the time of the liberation of the serfs more than half of the arable soil of Russia, namely 148 million hectares (versus 89 million which remained the property of the landlords and 8 million which were the property of the State). Half a century later, on the eve of World War I, the situation was quite different. Only 44 million hectares were still the property of the landlords, the rest, as well as about 6 million hectares of State land had been bought by the peasants." (p. 295) It should be mentioned here that one hectare equals about 2.5 acres. The agrarian situation of Russia before the Revolution can also be gleaned from the article on "Russia, the Agrarian Question," in *Encyclopaedia Britannica*, 13th edition, vol. 31, pp. 402-403.

If we compare the agrarian situation of Russia with that of Britain we see that in the 1870s 5207 proprietors of more than 1000 acres owned over 18 million acres or 55 percent of the surface of Britain. *Cf. Brockhaus Lexikon*, 14th edition, 1898, Vol. 8, p. 493.

The history of the agrarian problem in Southern Italy is characterized by *repeated* agrarian reforms—under the Bourbons, under Joseph Bonaparte and Murat, under the Bourbon restoration and under the Fascists—and by a renewed concentration after redistribution. Absentee landlords became more numerous when a new urban class started to buy up land. *Cf.* Vincenzo Ricchioni, *Le leggi eversive della feudalità e la storia delle quotizzazioni demaniali nel mezzogiorono* (Istituto editoriale del mezzogiorno, n.p.n.d.), pp. 3-4: Romualdo Trifone, *Feudi e Demani nell' Italia meridionale* (same publishing house), pp. 12-13.

[3] *Cf.* Manya Gordon, *Workers Before and After Lenin* (New York: Dutton, 1941), pp. 428-430, and D. M. Odinetz and Paul Novgorodtzev, *Russian Schools and Universities in the World War* (New Haven: Yale University Press, 1929). Of special interest are the statistics on the class structure of the *gymnasia* (high school-colleges) on pp. 33ff.

[4] This is true of the Russian classics of the nineteenth century. A Hungarian Communist who emigrated to Russia in the 1930s was told by a longtime German resident, referring to the Imperial Regime, "There was beastly brutality on the part of the working class, indeed, beastly brutality, but no haughtiness." *Cf.* Erwin Sinkó, *Roman eines Romans, Moskauer Tagebuch* (Cologne: Verlag Wissenschaft und Politik, 1969), p. 122. *Cf.* Anatole Leroy-Beaulieu, *L'Empire des Tsars et les Russes* (Paris: Hachette, 1889), Vol. 1, Chapter VI, 1-4. Ivan Sergeyevitch Aksakov wrote quite rightly that "to the Russian national feeling the contemptuous concept of the Greek *demos* or of the Latin *plebs* is entirely alien." (*Cf.* the daily *Moskva*, February 10, 1867.)

[5] *Cf.* Manya Gordon, *op. cit.* p. 17, mentioning Nisselovitch, *Istoriya zavodno-fabritchnego zakonodatel'stva v Rossii* (St. Petersburg, 1883). Eugene Lyons, *Workers' Paradise Lost* (New York: Paperback Library, 1967), p. 86, rightly points out the fact that the annual rates of Russian industrial output between 1885 and 1889 and again between 1907 and 1914 substantially exceeded the corresponding rate of growth during the same period in the United States, Britain, and Germany. Rapid development was a characteristic feature of the whole period from 1861 to 1914. This fact was also stressed by Lenin in his book *Capitalism in Russia* written in 1899. As to the agricultural domain, peasants owned 82 percent of all cattle and 86 percent of all horses. (p. 89)

[6] *Cf.* Ilya E[h]renburg, "Lyudi, gody, zhizn'," *Novy Mir*, Vol. 41, No. 4, April 1965, p. 74.

[7] In the years 1945-1946 sugar was still a great rarity in the USSR and people begged the prisoners-of-war for a piece of sugar. The P.O.W.s in many parts of Russia were better fed than the population: they were, after all, potential propagandists for communism in their homelands.

[8] *Cf.* William H. Chamberlin, in *Confessions of an Individualist* (London, 1940), p. 102, "I have outlived a good many early enthusiasms, but my respect and admiration for the prewar Russian intelligensia grew steadily while I lived in Moscow." Yet this Russian *Intelligentsiya* (to which Lenin also belonged) had a truly ascetic, nay, monastic character, which is a good breeding ground for the leftist outlook. *Cf.* S. I. Frank, "Etika nigilisma" in *Vyekhi*, 1909, reprinted by Possev Publishers, Frankfurt, 1967.

[9] The abbreviation of their party was until a decade ago WKP[b]—All-

Union Communist party (bolsheviks). They have dropped the "b" in brackets.

[10] The lower nobility (*dvoryane*) had no formal titles but could be wealthy or poor. Vladimir Nabokov, for instance, is descended from a family of rich *dvoryane*. *Cf.* his *Conclusive Evidence* (New York: Putnam, 1967). On the revolutionary tendencies of the nobility, old or new, poor or affluent, *cf.* Anatole Leroy-Beaulieu, *op. cit.* Vol. 1, VI, 2 and VI, 4.

[11] *Cf.* Comte Joseph de Maistre, *Quartre chapitres inédits sur la Russie*, Comte Rudolphe de Maistre, ed. (Paris: Vaton Frères, 1859), p. 27.

[12] Lenin was the son of a high school-college inspector who had received the hereditary title of nobility. In Moscow's Lenin Museum we find his passport issued by the Police Prefect of Pskov, dated February 28, 1900, in which Vladimir Ilyitch Ulyanov is described as "hereditary nobleman." According to Louis Fischer ("Die ungleichen Brüder," *Der Monat*, Berlin, Vol. 17, No. 203, August 1965, p. 5). Lenin's father's mother was an illiterate Kalmyk. His paternal grandfather, according to Fischer, was a "Great Russian" from Astrakhan, but I think that the name Ulyanov is probably of Mongol-Kalmyk (not of Tartar) origin. According to C. J. Renstedt's Kalmyk Dictionary (*Kalmückisches Wörterbuch*) published by the Finnish-Ugrian Society in Helsingfors, 1935, p. 454, *ula, ulu* means mountain, hill. (In Mongolian *ulan* means "red"!) The Russian ending for Asian names is quite frequent. Robert Payne in his *The Life and Death of Lenin* (London: Pan Books, 1967), p. 39, makes the case that the name Ulyanov is frequent among the Chuvash tribe. "He was German, Swedish and Chuvash and there was not a drop of Russian blood in him" (p. 47).

Lenin's mother was a Lutheran German-Russian, daughter of a Dr. Blank, a physician and fairly wealthy landowner. According to Stefan Possony, *Lenin, The Compulsory Revolutionary* (Chicago: Regnery, 1964), p. 3, Alexander Dimitriyevitch Blank also belonged to the nobility. From childhood on, Lenin spoke German very fluently with his mother and aunt. Interestingly enough, the *Bolshaya Sovyetskaya Entsiklopediya* (1956), Vol. 44, p. 216, has half a column about Lenin's mother but does not give her maiden name. She died in 1916 and it is admitted even in Communist circles that this very distinguished-looking lady did not share her sons' political views.

Alexander, the eldest, a member of the terroristic *Narodnaya Volya*, had been executed because of his participation in an abortive attempt to assassinate Alexander III, but Vladimir Ilyitch was a prize pupil in an academy for young noblemen and earned a gold medal. His wife, by the way, was the Socialist daughter of an officer also belonging to the nobility, and he married her in an Orthodox church. Yet while many Soviet artists painted moving scenes from Lenin's life (as, for instance, his dramatic parting from his "unconverted" mother), nobody so far portrayed his wedding with crowns held over the heads of bride and groom.

Vladimir Ilyitch Ulyanov, who used the pen name Lenin (but never called himself "Nikolai"), was born in Simbirsk, today called Ulyanovsk. This was also the birthplace of Gontcharov who in his novels described the inane life of the Russian gentry, and of Kerensky who went to the *gimnaziya* where Lenin's father was principal. Lenin, born in 1870, died in 1924, while Kerensky, born in 1881, died in the early 1970s in the United States.

[13] *Cf.* Robert K. Massie, *Nicholas and Alexandra* (New York: Dell, 1969), p. 514ff. Here we find a description of the ghastly and ghoulish death of the Emperor and his wife. Michael the first Romanov was elected Czar while staying with his mother at the Ipatiev Monastery near Kostroma. The house in Yekaterinburg (Sverdlovsk) where the imperial family was slaughtered belonged to a merchant by the name of Ipatiev.

[14] *Ibid.*, p. 457.

[15] On Pyotr Arkadyevitch Stolypin *cf.* M. P. Bok, *Vospominaniya o moyem ottsye P. A. Stolypinye* (New York: Chekhov Publishers, 1953).

[16] *Cf.* Fëdor Stepun, *Vergangenes und Unvergängliches aus meinem Leben 1884-1914* (Munich: Josef Kösel, 1947), pp. 228-229.

[17] In Britain (or in America) the phrase "an ambitious young man" is rather laudatory. *Un jeune ambitieux* in French (or in any Continental language) is devastating.

[18] *Cf.* Fëdor Stepun, *op. cit.* p. 73. There Stepun asks the pointed question, "How could a liberal regime have any permanence if a man like Maxim Gorki, after a political banquet in 1905, could succeed in making the representatives of the business world and industry donate over a million rubles for the continuation of the Revolution and thereby for their own expropriation?" We, however, know of similar stupidities committed in the Western world by people whom Lenin liked to call "useful idiots." Such "useful idiots" were very frequent in the Russian clergy and today are to be found in the West as well.

[19] Witness the complaint of Styepan Trophimovitch in Chapter 1, 6 about the evolution and change of his original ideas and ideals. This particular novel is unobtainable in the USSR—except as a volume in his collected works. And this is part of the reason why people will wait in line for days to buy the rather limited edition of his collected works, issued once every ten or fifteen years.

[20] Dostoyevski, too, belonged to the (newer) hereditary nobility. He was deprived of his rank after receiving his death sentence (and the subsequent jail term), but was reinstated after his return from Siberia. There exists in Moscow's Dostoyevski Museum a copy of his passport where he figures in a German version as "von Dostoyevski." *The Recollections of a Death House*, Dostoyevski's great classic, depicts a terrible state of affairs, but a book such as Anatoli R. Marchenko's *My Testimony* gives with its description of torture and cannibalism an infinitely more frightening picture of post-Stalin prison camps in European Russia. More impressive because on a higher literary level is Alexander Solzhenytsin's *The First Circle* in which a comparison is drawn between Soviet and old Russian jails where (with reference to the *Recollections*

of Dostoyevski) the latter are made to appear idyllic. Ilya Ehrenburg told me very interestingly about his experiences in a Russian jail when at the age of 17 he was imprisoned for conspiratorial activities in his *gimnazia*. "Was it very uncomfortable?" I inquired. "No, not particularly. We all only suffered from a lack of sleep." "Endless interrogations?" "By no means," he replied. "But the director was interested in political and philosophical questions, so he brought the samovar to the 'politicals' and among endless cups of tea we had interminable discussions until the small hours of the morning." Leon Trotsky, if we give credence to his memoirs, had an equally charming recollection of his jailers. About the comforts and amenities of Lenin's exile in Shushenskoye see also Bertram D. Wolfe's truly excellent *Three Who Made a Revolution* (New York: Penguin Books, 1966), p. 155-157.

[21] *Cf.* Dmitri Myerezhkovski, *Tsarstvo Antikhrista* (Munich: Drei-Masken Verlag, 1919), p. 231.

[22] *Cf.* V. Rozanov, "Apokalipsis nashego vremeni," *Vyersty* (Paris, 1927), No. 2.

[23] Communism—where everybody gets goods "according to his needs"—is a state of society so unimaginable that we can safely discard this utopian vision from our speculations. Either needs are desires, or they are "fixed" by our fellowmen who thus become our superiors. This again is the "secularized monastery." Yet the Communists still have sympathy and admiration for "utopian socialism," as witness the articles on Campanella and Morelly in the *Bol'shaya Sovyetskaya Entsiklopediya*, (1954) Vol. 19, pp. 545-546, and Vol. 28, p. 297.

[24] Men such as Lenin, Chicherin, Lunacharsky, Dzerzyński, Tukhachevski, Mayakovski, Plyekhanov, Alexei Tolstoy, Alexandra Kollontay, to name just a few. Without the collaboration of the lesser nobility in the bureaucracy the Communists would hardly have survived their first decade. *Cf.* Galina Berkenkopf, "Russische Elite als Wegbereiter und Opfer des Oktober" in *Ostprobleme*, 19 Year, No. 22-23 (Nov. 17, 1967), pp. 609-613.

[25] In Finland the "Red General" Antikainen reportedly boiled in a kettle all students serving in the White army who fell into his hands. He had a special dislike for them. The female Red regiments in Finland, operating in the Tammerfors (Tampere) region, were also dreaded for their abysmal cruelty to male prisoners.

[26] The Jewish student Kannegiesser murdered the founder of the Tshe-Ka, Moses Uritzki, because he considered him a blot on the Jewish name. The Tshe-Ka was then taken over by the Polish nobleman (*szlachcic*) Feliks Edmundowicz Dzerzyński, son of a landowner, who later became the head of the Railroad Commissariat. The Tshe-Ka was then renamed G.P.U. ("Governmental Political Administration").

Fanya Kaplan, who tried to assassinate Lenin, was also Jewish. So was Judas Mironovitch Stern, who tried to kill the German diplomat von Twardowski in Moscow. Stern considered German aid to the Bolsheviks as fatal for Russia. On Fanya Kaplan *cf*. Stefan Possony, *op. cit.* p. 289, and Louis Fischer, *The Life of Lenin* (New York: Harper and Row, 1964), p. 599.

[27] Stalin also complied with Hitler's request to hand over a number of leading German Communists who had fled to the Soviet Union. One of them, Heinz Neumann, had been murdered in an earlier purge by the wily Georgian. His widow, Margarete Buber-Neumann, was extradited in early 1940 to the Nazis after she had spent years in Soviet concentration camps. She then landed in Ravensbrück, a Nazi "K.Z" for women (and, to give the Devil his due, far more luxurious than its Eastern counterparts). The account of her sufferings under Red and Brown beasts is one of the great books of our time. *Cf*. Margarete Buber-Neumann, *Als Gefangene by Stalin und Hitler* (Munich: Deutscher Taschenbuchverlag, 1962), originally Stuttgart: Deutsche Verlags-Anstalt, 1958.

[28] We discount the rather widespread thesis that communism is just another form of "eternal Russian imperialism." Nor, to be sure, were the Nazis just "successors of Frederick the Great." Of course, Russian nationalist feelings may not be entirely alien to a Russian Communist, and officers of the Imperial army (Tukhachevski, Shaposhnikov, Brussilov) have fought in the Red Army against "foreign interventionists."

Chapter XI

[1] *Cf*. Benito Mussolini, *Il Trentino veduto da un socialista* (Florence: Casa Editrice Italiana, Quaderni della Voce, 1911).

[2] Mussolini, aged 21, translated *Les paroles d'une révolté* of the Anarchist Prince Pyotr Kropotkin. He wrote (as *Duce*), "Twenty years have passed by, but the *Paroles* seem quite recent, so alive are they with present-day interests. . . . They overflow with a great love for oppressed mankind." *Cf*. *Opera omnia di Benito Mussolini*, (Florence: La Nuova Italia, 1951), Vol. 1. p. 50.

[3] The most radical of the whole lot—so radical that they were persecuted even by Žižka and his Taborites—were the Adamites who practiced nudism, the community of women and property. Žižka massacred them wholesale in 1421. *Cf*. also K. V. Adámek, "Adamité na Hlinecku v XIX věku," *Casopis Ceského Musea* (Prague, 1897), part 48. Adámek describes here the revival of the Adamites as a result of the Toleration Law of Emperor Joseph II in the eighteenth century, documenting the tenacity of this weird sect. *Cf*. also Josef Dobrowsky, "Geschichte der böhmischen" *Akademie der Wissenschaften* (Prague, 1788). The main source for the entire period is Magister Laurentius de Březina (or Březowa). *De gestis et variis accidentibus regnis Boemiae 1414-1422* which can be found, edited by Dr. Karl Höfler, in the

series "Geschichts-schreiber der hussitischen Bewegung," Part I in *Fontes rerum Austriacarum* (Vienna, 1856).

4 *Cf.* Willy Lorenz, *Monolog über Böhmen* (Vienna: Herold, 1964), p. 30.

5 *Cf.* Andreas de Broda, "Tractatus de origine Hussitarum," *Fontes rerum Austriacarum* (Vienna), Vol. 6, pp. 343-344.

6 *Cf.* Louis Leger, *Nouvelles Etudes Slaves* (Paris: Ernest Lerouex, 1886), p. 159.

7 *Cf.* Dr. Paul Tóth-Szabó, *A cseh-huszita mozgalmak és uralom története Magyarországon* (Budapest: Hornyánszky, 1917), p. 50.

8 While the influence of Marsiglio of Padua on Wyclif was considerable. *Cf.* Note 43.

9 *Cf.* E. v. Kuehnelt-Leddihn, *Freiheit oder Gleichheit?* p. 328ff.

10 *Cf.* Josef Pekař, *Žižka a jého doba* (Prague: Vesmir, 1927), 2 vols. Also Kamil Krofta, *Žižka a husitská revoluce* (Prague: Laichter, 1936); Th. G. Masaryk, *Jan Hus, Naše obrozeni a naše reformáce* (Prague: Laichter, 1925); Alois Hajn, *Jan Hus a jého vyznam v době přitomně* (Prague: Svaz Národniho Osvobozeni, 1925); František Palacký, *Dějiny národu českého w Cachach a w Morawě* (Prague: Tempský, 1877), Vol. 3.

11 The *Los-von-Rom-Bewegung* ("Away from Rome Movement") was a concentrated effort by the Austrian Evangelicals to convert Catholic German-Austrians to the Lutheran faith. This allegedly religious action had a strongly nationalistic flavor and enjoyed the financial support of the "Gustav Adolf Verein" centered in Germany. Georg von Schönerer, Hitler's mentor, had been intimately connected with the movement, which scored its greatest successes (roughly in the 1895-1910 period) among the Germans of Bohemia and Moravia.

12 *Cf.* J. Evola, *Gli uomini e le rovine* (Rome: Edizioni dell' Ascia, 1953), pp. 106ff. The same view has been expressed by Guglielmo Ferrero in *Pouvoir. Les génies invisibles de la cité* (New York: Brentano, 1942), p. 297.

13 *Cf.* Massimo Rocca (Libero Tancredi). *Come il fascismo divenne una dittatura* (Milan: Edizioni Libraria Italiana, 1952), p. 329. Rocca insists that Mussolini, upon higher orders, was never sent to the front lines, whereas the King always courageously visited the trenches.

14 *Cf.* Jean-Jacques Chevalier, *Les grandes oeuvres politiques de Machiavel à nos jours* (Paris: Armand Colin, 1949), p. 331.

15 *Cf.* Giulio Evola, *Il fascismo* (Rome: Volpe, 1964), pp. 53-54. Most important for a knowledge of fascism and Mussolini's mind is the Duce's personal contribution to the *Enciclopedia Italiana*, i.e., the article "*Fascismo.*" (*Cf. Enciclopedia Italiana de scienze, lettere ed art*, 1932, Vol. 14, Part II. Mussolini invokes as "ancestors" of fascism Sorel, Péguy, and Lagardelle, but rejects de Maistre, (pp. 848, 850). Péguy was the great patron saint of the *résistance* during World War II, but one of his sons publicly adhered to

the Pétain regime which shows how arbitrary the interpretation of an original thinker can be.

[16] Fascist Italy's privilege (the diarchy of King and Leader) which Nazi Germany tragically lacked was strongly underlined by Pietro Silva in his *Io difendo la monarchia* (Rome: Fonseca, 1946), pp. xii ff.

[17] Cf. Hannah Arendt, *The Origins of Totalitarianism* (New York: Harcourt, Brace, 1951), p. 303.

[18] In V. Dudintsev's novel *Nye Khlyebom yedinym* ("Not by Bread Alone"), published in *Novy Mir* (Moscow, 1956), Vol. 32, No. 8, 9, 10, the bureaucratic villain, factory director Drozdov, refuses to lead a private life. He has no time. "We have to overtake capitalist America," is his constant excuse. Posters all over the Soviet Union show the comparative strength and progress of both countries, the USSR and the U.S.A.

[19] We find the best description of the tenuous relationship between the Catholic Church and Italian Fascism in Daniel A. Binchy's *Church and State in Fascist Italy* (London-New York: Oxford University Press, 1941).

[20] As a young man, Mussolini confessed to his wife that he had been an atheist, yet he affirmed in his last letter to her that he now believed in God. Cf. Gino de Sanctis, "La vedova dell'impero," *L'Europeo*, November 30, 1947, p. 9. The Duce also seemed to have a curious respect for the Papacy. To the French journalist Lucien Corpechot, a *Maurassien*, Mussolini shouted in reference to the headline "Non Possumus" in the *Action Française*: "Who dares to say *non possumus* to the Pope? One just does not say *non possumus* to the Pope!" Cf. Adrien Dansette, *Histoire religieuse de la France contemporaine* (Paris: Flammarion, 1951), Vol. 2, p. 595.

[21] On the Spanish Falange, cf. Bernd Nellesen, *José Antonio Primo de Rivera, der Troubadour der spanischen Falange* (Stuttgart: Deutsche Verlagsanstalt, Schriftenreihe der Vierteljahrshefte für Zeitgeschichte, 1965). Important, however, are not only the writings of Primo de Rivera (*Obras completas*, Madrid, 1942) but also those of the Falange's cofounder Alfonso Garcia Valdecasas. The Rumanian Iron Guard, on the other side, had an essentially religious basis. Its strong anti-Judaism had no racist foundation. An authoritative work on this interesting, partly even fantastic movement, has not yet been written. (Most of the sources could be found only east of the Iron Curtain, though much has been destroyed.) Due to its strongly religious (Eastern Church) outlook, the strain of idealism was stronger than in the other totalitarian movements. Sternly repressed by Carol II, it had many martyrs, but it also produced a brutality all its own.

[22] Cf. Victor Serge, "Pages de Journal, 1945-1947," *Les Temps Modernes*, Vol. 4, No. 45, July 1949, pp. 78, 79. Ernst Nolte in his *Der Faschismus in seiner Epoche* (Munich: Pieper, 1963), p. 300 shows very clearly how the aging Mussolini's *Repúbblica Sociale Italiana* returned to his old ideals—Mazzini, Garibaldi, republicanism, and socialism.

[23] Cf. Massimo Rocca, *op. cit.* p. 359.

[24] *Ibid.*, p. 360.

[25] *Cf.* "Le confessioni di Vittorio Mussolini," *Il Tempo* (Rome), Vol. 5. February 23, 1948, p. 2.

[26] *Cf.* Giulio Evola, *Il Fascismo*, p. 32. The formula used by Abraham Lincoln in terminating the Gettysburg Address is supposedly taken from Wyclif. Carefully going through Wyclif's writings, I could not find it, though these words somewhat reflect the spirit of Wyclif's political thinking during a certain phase of his life. They are definitely Marsiglian.

[27] *Cf.* Jules Romains, "Le tapis magique," Vol. 25 of *Les hommes de bonne volonté* (Paris: Flammarion, 1946), p. 151. Unfortunately Americans were taught by the press that fascism and Nazism were "aristocratic." Take, for instance, Harold Rugg in *Democracy and the Curriculum* (New York: Appleton Century, 1939), p. 524, "Thus the word *fascism* as currently used is really only a name for the characteristic method of government by the 'best people' . . . the leading citizens." As to the anti-Nazi novels manufactured in Britain and, above all, in the United States, they rarely lack a leading noble Nazi. The names of authors such as Sir Philip Gibbs, Ethel Vance, Louis Bromfield, Kressman Taylor, Ellin Berlin, and Nina Galen come to one's mind. Lillian Hellman even invented a Nazi Rumanian *count*(!)—all a hangover from World War I. Professor Helmut Kuhn (Munich) is only too right when he speaks about four groups of victims—the Jews, the Rich, the Nobles, the Priests. *Cf. Der Staat* (Kösel, Munich, 1967), p. 443. (It was worse for those who belonged into more than one of these categories.) Nazism, F. Reck-Malleczewen, wrote, *op.cit.* p. 180, was indeed the revolt of postmen and elementary school teachers.

Chapter XII

[1] *Cf.* Ceskoslovenská Vlastivěda, Part 5, "Stat," Emil Capek, ed. (Prague: Sfinx, 1931), p. 479. Here we read that the National Socialist Czechoslovak Party rests on the religious and social traditions of Hussitism.

[2] *Cf.* Masarykův Ottův Naučný (Prague, 1925), Vol. 1. p. 1129: See also the article of Karel Slavíček in *Ottův slovník naučný nové doby* (Prague: 1936), Vol. 4, p. 437 as well as the earlier edition of the same work, *Ottův slovník naučný* (Prague, 1909), Vol. 28, pp. 984-985. Further consult *Slovník národnohospodářsky, sociálni a politický* (Prague, 1933), Part iii, pp. 515-516.

[3] *Czechoslovak Sources and Documents* (Prague: Orbis, 1936), No. 9.

[4] *Cf.* Th. G. Masaryk, *The Making of a State*, Wickham Steed, ed. (London: Allen and Unwin, 1927), p. 439, and Wickham Steed, "A Programme for Peace," in *Edinburgh Review*, 1916, (separate reprint).

The anti-Jewish Czech riots in Prague are mentioned by Hermann Münch in *Böhmische Tragödie* (Braunschweig: Westermann, 1950); and H. Münch, "Panslawismus und Alldeutschtum" *Neues Abendland* (Munich, July 1950),

Vol. 5. No. 7, p. 278. German-speaking Jews in 1945 were forced by the Czechs to exchange their Star of David (enforced by the Nazis) for a Swastika which now became de rigeur for the Sudeten-Germans. Yet while these Jews were "racially Semites" in Nazi eyes, they were now "ethnically German" from a Czech viewpoint—the tragicomedies of an identitarian age!

[5] Cf. A. Ciller, *Vorläufer des Nationalsozialismus* (Vienna: Ertl, 1932), p. 135.

[6] Cf. Karel Engliš, "Le 'socialisme allemand': Programme du parti allemand des Sudètes," in *Sources et Documents Czechoslovaques* (Prague: Orbis, 1938), No. 46, p. 59. Further references to that period: Ingenieur Rudolf Jung, *Der nationale Sozialismus. Seine Grundlagen, sein Wedegang, sein Ziele* (Munich; Deutscher Volksverlag, 1922); Dr. Karl Siegmar Baron von Galéra, *Sudetendeutschlands Heimkehr ins Reich* (Leipzig: Nationale Verlagsanstalt, 1939); Hans Krebs, *Kampf in Böhmen* (Berlin: Volk und Reich Verlag, 1936); Hans Krebs, *Wir Sudetendeutsche* (Berlin: Runge, 1937); Hans Knirsch, *Aus der Geschichte der nationalsozialistischen Arbeiterbewegung Altösterreichs und der Tschechoslowakei* (Aussig, 1931).

Vide also Andrew Gladding Whiteside's analysis of early National Socialism: "Austrian National Socialism was in essence a radical democratic movement: its official programs and propaganda emphasized social and economic equality, popular sovereignty, opposition to traditional authority, and radical changes in the existing order. Its appeal was to the poor, to the workers in ill-paid jobs, to the underdogs. National Socialism's first political program had been based on the Linz program, whose principles had by 1900 been accepted by all Austrian German democratic parties" (The Linz program refers to the Social Democratic program). Cf. A. G. Whiteside, *Austrian National Socialism* (The Hague: Martinus Nijhoff, 1962), p. 112.

[7] Cf. A. Ciller, *op. cit.* p. 141. Of interest in this connection are also the revealing memoirs of Franz Langoth, *Kampf um Osterreich, Erinnerungen eines Politikers* (Wels: Welsermühl, 1951). Langoth was an old Pan-German, republican, anticlerical fighter in the tradition of 1848 who died in his nineties in 1952. In his book we can clearly see the interconnection between nascent National Socialism and the "black-red-gold" heritage of the "forty-eighters" who fought the internationalism of the Hapsburgs, the aristocracy, and the Catholic Church. Langoth became an ardent Nazi in a perfectly logical evolution of his ideas. As Aristotle has pointed out (*Politics*, III, viii, pp. 2-4) equality and hatred for the extraordinary man, the privileged person is the main postulate of democracy and, therefore, of all leftist thought.

[8] Count Richard Coudenhove-Kalergi, founder of the Pan-Europe Movement, frequently pointed out in the 1920s that the Jews were rapidly becoming Europe's new aristocracy, a view not without foundation at that time. Yet at the same time the Jewry of Western Europe was rapidly dwindling owing to the triple losses through conversions, mixed marriages, and low birth rates. Without further immigration from the East the German Jews would have practi-

cally disappeared by the end of this century. The Jewish population of Germany in 1930 was only 0.9 percent. Juan Comas in his *Racial Myths* (Paris: UNESCO, 1951), p. 31, informs us that in Germany between 1921 and 1925 out of every 100 Jewish marriages, 42 had one gentile partner. In 1925 851 all-Jewish and 554 mixed marriages took place in Berlin. The Nazi mass-murders of Jews took place abroad.

9 This speech was published in the form of a leaflet.

10 In the *op. cit.* of Hans Krebs (*Kampf in Böhmen*) we find a reproduction of this proclamation. Another facsimile shows a swastika for the first time in the history of National Socialism. Yet the Nazi swastika is the reverse of the Hindu original and thus does not imply luck or success but certain doom. Baron Wilhelm Ketteler, Papen's secretary in Vienna, pointed this out at a social gathering. (He was promptly murdered after the *Anschluss*.)

11 *Cf.* Josef Pfitzner, *Das Sudetendeutschtum* (Cologne: Scharffstein, 1938), pp. 23-24. Jules Monnerot in his *Sociologie du communisme* (Paris: Gallimard-N.R.F., 1949) pp. 395-396 affirms that modern tyranny must always combine the social (or socialistic) with the national appeal. Analogies between socialism and nationalism were already fully realized by Nietzsche. He considered both to be "dominated by envy and laziness," the laziness of the head characterizing the nationalists, the laziness of the hands the socialists. *Cf.* his "Menschliches, Allzumenschliches," Vol. 1, No. 6, p. 480.

Joseph Pfitzner was executed in Prague after World War II; Rudolf Jung, who played such a fatal role in the origins of National Socialism, died of starvation in Prague's Pankrac prison. *Cf. Dokuments zur Austreibung der Sudeten-deutschen*, Dr. Wilhelm Turnwald, ed, published by the "Arbeitsgemeinschaft zur Wahrung sudetendeutscher Interessen," 1951, p. 50. (Document No. 15) Goebbels called Jung "a fine head. With him one can collaborate." *Cf. Das Tagebuch von Joseph Goebbels, 1925-1926*, Helmut Heiber, ed. (Stuttgart: Deutscher Verlagsanstalt, 1960) p. 64.

12 *Cf.* Konrad Heiden, *Geschichte des Nationalsozialismus* (Berlin: Rowohlt, 1933), p. 19.

13 Aussig (in Czech: Usti-nad-Labem) was the center of early National Socialism in Bohemia. *Cf. Bei unseren deutschen Brüder in der Tschecho-slowakei* (Tübingen, 1921), pp. 38-39. (This is the collective report by a group of Tübingen students.)

In Aussig, after the retreat of the German armies, there took place the biggest spontaneous massacre of Germans in history. At least four times as many Germans were killed here by a Czech mob as Czechs by the SS in Lidice. *Cf. Londynské Listy* (London), Vol. 2, No. 14, July 15, 1948. Decent Czechs (like the publishers and editors of the aforementioned paper) condemned such beastly horrors.

14 About Streicher's earlier career, *cf.* R. Billing. *N.S.D.A.P. Geschichte eine Bewegung* (Munich: Funk, 1931), p. 112.

15 *Cf.* Professor Dr. Fanz Jetzinger, *Hitlers Jugend* (Vienna: Europa-

Verlag, 1956), pp. 25-35; Hans Frank, *Im Angesicht des Galgens* (Neuhaus bei Schliersee: Brigitte Frank, 1955), pp. 320-321. Frank was the Nazi governor of Poland. He was executed after the Nuremberg Trial. Hitler's illegitimate birth, however, was openly admitted in the Third Reich. *Cf. Die ahnentafel des Führers. Ahnentafeln berühmter Deutscher*, III (Leipzig, 1937), p. 39. In the most recent, so far "definitive" biography of Hitler by Werner Maser—*cf.* his *Adolf Hitler* (Munich: Bechtle, 1971)—the Führer's Jewish ancestry is denied without, however, solving the riddle. The grandfather remains unknown and Hitler's *suspicion* of his own "non-Aryan" ancestry not really challenged.

[16] Hitler's house of birth, a rather sinister building, now has on its ground floor the very symbol of half-education, a *Volksbücherei*, a popular library. The largest single professional group in the Nazi party, the elementary school teachers, were the real protagonists of this type of education. In France, however, the teachers traditionally veered towards the "laicist," "radical socialist," or Socialistic outlook; on the village level they were the sworn enemies of the priest. This development could clearly be seen in the earlier part of the nineteenth century. Carl Ernst Jarcke foresaw graphically this development. *Cf.* his *op. cit.*, Vol. 4, p. 229.

[17] Chancellor Brüning knew quite well (as he told me) the circumstances of the birth of Hitler's father, but some other people "in the know" were murdered on and after June 30, 1934 in Bavaria. Of course, besides the reasons given us for Hitler's hatred for his father there must have been a number of others: *Hatred* always stems from a feeling of inferiority and/or helplessness. The aged official (who was much older than Adolf and also considerably older than Adolf's mother, his second wife) must have treated his dreamy, introverted, and odd son not only in a stern way, but must have criticized him frequently and, probably, very much to the point. Yet this is precisely what a person, tortured by an inferiority complex, cannot stand. It is always the truth which really hurts. Hitler fled his father, as he later fled Austria. When Hitler's Minister Albert Speer saw a house with a memorial tablet in the village of Spital (Lower Austria) where Hitler's father had been born, Hitler completely lost his balance and furiously demanded the immediate removal of the plaque. "Obviously, there was a reason," Speer wrote, "why he wanted to eliminate a part of his youth. Today one knows about the lack of clarity concerning his family background which gets lost in the Austrian forest." *Cf.* A. Speer, *Erinnerungen* (Berlin: Propyläen, 1969), p. 12. Hitler died with the conviction that the Germans were "no good" (as Mussolini came to consider the Italians) and he suspected that the English were really superior to them.

[18] *Cf.* August Kubizek, *Adolf Hitler, mein Jugendfreund* (Graz: Stocker, 1953). For the true understanding of Hitler this book is invaluable. Not uninteresting are the memoirs of Hitler's commanding officer in World War I, Captain Fritz Wiedemann's *Der Mann, der Feldherr werden wollte* (Velbert und Kettwig: Blick und Bild Verlag, 1964). Wiedemann writes that

Hitler was not promoted (he remained a private first class), "because we could not detect in him qualities necessary for a leader." (p. 26). A misjudgment? Not in the least, because military and political leadership are of an entirely different order. A general does not need to have rhetorical gifts, while demagogues often suffer from neurotic disorders. Masses are often swayed more by hysterical orators than by calm thinkers or soberly calculating managers. Hitler, moreover, as a nonstop talker, was decidedly unpopular with the other soldiers. Still, there are certain legends about Hitler which, thanks to the research of Werner Maser, we have to consider exploded. Hitler suffered material hardships only during a very short period of his life, he was very much a ladies' man, he was a voracious (though unmethodical) reader, he had a very modest but steady income from his pictures, and never was a corporal, but only a private first class (*Gefreiter*). Not truly educated, he was nevertheless gifted in many ways. The mutual dislike between him and the General Staff grew even more after the outbreak of the war when he became increasingly a very sick man.

[19] On the Continent four to five years of elementary school (the age group is five, six or seven to ten) are followed either by a dead-end school lasting three or four years *or* by a high school-college lasting eight to nine years and terminating in a bachelor's degree. This school requires an entrance and a final examination. The universities have no colleges of the American pattern; they are graduate schools and impart no general instruction. The rather common belief that the junior and senior years of American colleges are the equivalent of the first two years of Continental universities is therefore quite erroneous. The Continental high school-colleges (*liceo, lycée, Gymnasium, gimnazia,* etc.) are of the classic, semiclassic, or scientific type. Hitler tried the scientific type and failed. (Hitler was always "scientific" and "antimetaphysical" in his outlook which reminds one of Morelly's precept that only the experimental sciences should enjoy freedom in Utopia. *Cf.* Morelly, *op. cit.* p. 151, and chapters 4 and 5 of the *Lois des Etudes*.) It would be interesting to know whether the trend in favor of the Nazi ideology was more marked among those who had a classic rather than a scientific education. The American reeducators considered a classic education as breeding totalitarianism yet all indications point in the opposite direction. Nazism was a "biologism" and the tenor of Nazism distinctly "antimediterranean," romantic rather than classic.

[20] Up to the end of the monarchy there was no "German army." Bavarians gave an oath of allegiance to the King of Bavaria, Hamburgers to the Senate of the Republic of Hamburg, etc. Some German states had their own postage stamps, and prior to the Third Reich there was no German citizenship except for the natives in the colonies. Diplomatic representatives were exchanged between Bavaria, Saxony, and Prussia until 1933.

[21] Foreigners accepted by the civil service of a German state automatically received its citizenship. This is also true of university professors, even today. A Brazilian, for instance, receiving a chair at a German university

immediately becomes a German citizen. In Europe multiple citizenship is not uncommon.

[22] Hitler's other fixation was for people whose names began with the letter "H" or one near to it in the alphabet, to wit, G, I, J, or K. Hitler also blindly believed in astrology, a fact known to the Allies. Thus, during the war, they were able to foretell some of his decisions based on the classic rules of astrology. (We are told this by Louis de Wohl who worked in London along these lines.) Hitler and other Nazi leaders surrounded themselves with clairvoyants and soothsayers. One of these, Erik Jan Hanussen, who foretold their victories as well as their final defeat, had to pay with his life for this forecast.

[23] *Cf.* Carl J. Burckhardt, *Meine Danziger Mission 1937-1939* (Munich: Deutscher Taschenbuch Verlag, 1962), p. 265, (originally Munich: Callwey, 1960).

[24] This role of the demotic-democratic *Führer* has been stressed by Gottfried Neesse, *Die Deutsche Nationalsozialistische Arbeiterpartei. Versuch einer Rechtseutung* (Stuttgart: Kohlhammer, 1935), p. 145, and Max Irlinger, *Die Rechte des Führers und Reichskanzlers als Staatsoberhaupt des Deutschen Reichen* (Dissertation at Innsbruck University, 1939), p. 71. *Cf.* also Rodolphe Laun, *La démocratie* (Paris: Delgrave, 1933); Gerhard Leibholz, "La nature et les formes de la démocratie," *Archives de philosophie du droit et de sociologie juridique*, (Vol. 6, (1936), No. 3-4, p. 135; Alfred Weber, *Die Krise des moderne Staatsgedankens in Europa* (Stuttgart: Deutsche Verlagsanstalt, 1925), pp. 139, 151; Gustave Le Bon, *Psychologie des foules* (Paris: Alcan-Presses Universitaires, 1939), pp. 93 ff.; Giulio Evola, *Il fascismo*, pp. 53-54 (on the incompatibility between *ducismo, Führertum*, and the ideals of the rightist outlook); Karl Thieme, *Lixikon der religiösen Zeitaufgaben* (Freiburg i. br.: Herderol, 1952) citing Baldur v. Schirach's poem "Hitler" which sums up quite nicely the concept of the *Führer:*

> You are many thousand people behind me,
> And you are I and I am You.
> I have never lived a thought
> Which has not trembled in your hearts.
> And if I form words, I do not know a single one
> Which is not fused with your will.

There we have the *volonté générale* of Rousseau embodied in a single person—identity made flesh.

(German text)

> Ihr seid viel tausend hinter mir
> und ihr seid ich und ich bin ihr.
> Ich habe keinen Gedanken gelebt,

Der nicht in euren Herzen gebebt.
Und forme ich Worte, so weiss ich keine,
die nicht mit euren Wollen eins.

[25] Careful research seems to indicate, however, that the *Lebensborne* combined mating and parturition institutes, did not really exist in the narrow sense of the term. There were, to be true, *Lebensborne* in the form of maternity homes in which especially unwed mothers producing "purely Aryan" babies were most welcome. Yet the idea of *Mutterhöfe*, real mating and maternal institutions, really did come up and was proposed to Heinrich Himmler. *Cf. Reichsführer! Briefe an und von Himmler*, Helmut Heiber, ed. (München: Deutscher Taschenbuch Verlag, 1970), pp. 346-347. What equally existed were stupid, idealistic girls who "donated a child" to the *Führer*. This nice phrase was also used under other circumstances. A Viennese Nazi in a relatively high position had a neurotic daughter in a private home. She was scheduled to be "liquidated" and the desperate father literally went on his knees before a top Nazi in Berlin to save his daughter. *"Nanu,"* the ogre exclaimed, "Don't you want to donate your child to the *Führer*?"

[26] *Cf.* Dr. Henry Picker, *Hitlers Tischgespräche im Führerhauptquartier 1941-1942*, Pery Schramm, ed. (Stuttgart: Seewald, 1963).

[27] *Cf.* Wilfried Daim, *Der Mann, der Hitler die Ideen gab* (Munich: Isar Verlag, 1958). This book by a well-known Viennese psychologist is richly documented.

[28] On the *Vertretertagungen* in Salzburg, *cf.* Erich F. Berendt, *Soldaten der Freiheit* (Berlin, Etthofer, 1936), especially pp. 181-210.

[29] *Cf. Deutsche Arbeiter-Presse* (Vienna), August 14, 1920.

[30] After the Armistice (1918) General Ludendorff fled to Sweden wearing blue spectacles and with papers made out to "Herr Lindström." Following his return he quarreled violently with Field Marshal von Hindenburg and joined Hitler's Nazi party. After the abortive *Putsch* in Munich (November 1923) he fell out with Hitler and with his new wife, a physician, founded a semireligious, semipolitical league, the *Tannenbergbund*, based on the "cognition of God through the voice of the blood." In his weekly, *Ludendorffs Volkswarte*, which saw conspiracies and secret societies everywhere, he accused Nazism of being Christianity in disguise, the swastika a mere mask of the Cross. This paper was suppressed in 1934 and Ludendorff died in 1937. With a mental horizon not transcending Germany he certainly was, if we remember his collaboration with Lenin, one of the gravediggers of Europe.

The Bavarian Prime Minister in November 1923, August von Kahr, was murdered in the *Reichsmordwoche* (1934), a pure act of revenge against an old man who opposed Hitler as much as Cardinal von Faulhaber did. Men such as Prime Minister von Kahr and General von Lossow are indirectly referred to in the lines of the party hymn, the *Horst Wessel Lied*: "Comrades who have been killed by the Red Front and Reaction are marching invisibly in our ranks."

[31] In Central Europe political delinquents (just like duelists) were jailed under the older dispensation in fortresses or so-called "state prisons." There they had to be treated as gentlemen, addressed by their full titles, etc. They had the right to receive visitors at any time and their mail was not censored. In a fortress they were supervised by the army, not the police. The food came from the officers' mess. The famous cartoonist Th. Th. Heine, who lived in Bavaria and published caricatures of William II, the "King of Prussia," was arrested while making a trip through Prussia and received a six-month sentence for lampooning the Kaiser. He confessed afterward that he had never had such a wonderful opportunity for work. This form of detention naturally no longer exists in a democratic age averse to most forms of privilege. Political offenders now are treated as common criminals. "All criminals are equal."

[32] Cf. E. v. Kuehnelt-Leddihn, *Liberty or Equality*, after p. 224, German edition after p. 336. The areas least Nazi were Upper Bavaria (with Munich!) and the Cologne-Aachen district. The areas most Nazi were Southern East Prussia, whose population is Polish but Lutheran. These maps are based on the elections of July 31, 1932. They feature the maximum of votes the Nazis received in truly free elections. The elections and plebiscites after Hitler's ascent to power have little value for our purpose. The results were often "doctored." Cf. Fritz Reck-Malleczewen, *Tagebuch eines Verzweifelten* (Stuttgart: Goverts, 1966), p. 183.

[33] From this particular map, however, it also becomes evident that the demarcation line between the Soviet Zone and Western Germany was drawn carefully by the Soviets according to the local strength of the Communists in Germany's last free elections. The Americans and the British, naturally, were not aware of this interesting circumstance.

[34] Among non-Catholics regarding Luther as an important spiritual ancestor of National Socialism we find men such as Karl Barth, Reinhold Niebuhr, Dean Inge, G. P. Gooch, Erich Fromm, Werner Hegemann, Franz Neumann, Karl Otten, et al. Cf. also *Critique* (Paris), No. 66, November 1952, containing an interesting review of a series of books dealing with the relationship between the Evangelical Church of Germany and National Socialism (pp. 981-996). The resistance of the Church against National Socialism, the dilemmas Christians had to face (in Germany much more so than in the occupied countries) are, in a way, not open to "historical research." They can only be understood existentially and experimentally. For this very reason the books written by "fact finders" who did not live through this agony are almost worthless. Knowing the anatomy of a human being does not mean in the least knowing his person.

[35] Cf. Martin Luther, *Kritische Gesamtausgabe* (Weimar Edition), Vol. 53, pp. 523 ff.

[36] Cf. *Philadelphia Record*, April 30, 1946. Some German Evangelicals, confused by the issues and quite ignorant of the basic tenets of their faith, tried to work out an Evangelical-Nazi synthesis. Typical of these efforts is a book which exists in an English translation, Wilhelm Kraft, *Christ versus*

Hitler? (New York: The Lutheran Press, 1937), particularly pp. 32 and 75. The confusion was even greater in Austria where the Lutherans felt by-passed and ignored by Dollfuss' Christian-Corporate State of a distinctly Catholic nature and were hostile to the Hapsburg traditions. They often wanted the *Anschluss* because they preferred the status of a majority to that of a minority. And since they constituted in Austria a progressive (nonconservative), nationalistic, democratic, scientifically minded, "enlightened" element, they fell for Nazism much more easily than their Catholic fellow citizens. They were proud of this evolution as can be seen from two books, *Die evangelische Kirche in Osterreich*, Dr. Hans Eder, ed. (Berlin: Verlag des Evangelischen Bundes, 1940), and Pfarrer Endesfelder, *Evangelische Pfarrer im völkischen Freiheitskampf der Ostmark und des Sudetenlandes* (Berlin: Verlag des Evangelischen Bundes, 1939). Interestingly enough, an Italian Fascist, Giuseppe Gangale, in a book entitled *Revoluzione Protestante* (Turin, 1925) has made the case that fascism could only fruitfully cooperate with "Protestants," but not with Catholics.

Yet in all fairness it must be said that there were German Lutherans and Calvinists who not only sentimentally, but also "theologically" opposed Nazism, and organized in the *Bekenntniskirche* ("Professing Church") opposed the Brown creed no less than the "German Christians," the traitors within the Evangelical Church. It is important to note, however, that these resisters had almost always a "neo-orthodox," a conservative or fundamentalist background. The betrayal of Christian values and tenets was rife in the ranks of the modernists and relativists.

Catholics have supported the Fascists, the Pétain regime, Chancellor Dollfuss, or General Franco. There were and there still are Catholic Socialists. There were also Catholics who thought that they could "square" their religion with the milder forms of National Socialism, but there exists no Catholic-Nazi "literature" on this subject.

[37] The reader is reminded of the fact that the Weimar Edition of Luther's *Collected Works* comprises well over eighty volumes of at least 250,000 words each. I am proud that I have read more than one-fourth of this colossal work.

[38] The Low German dialects are spoken north of a line stretching from the Belgian border to Silesia. South of it are the High German dialects. High and Low refer to altitudes above sea level, not to classes. Thanks to Luther's choosing the idiom used in the Thuringian-Upper Saxon area for his translation of the Bible, this High German dialect became the basis of literary German. Dutch is essentially Low German, English ("Saxon") is also derived from Low German, and Low German is taught in certain North German schools twice a week. There are also literary works published in Low German.

[39] Thus my own record according to the broadcast. The official text, as so often with Hitler's speeches, shows minor deviations.

[40] *Cf.* John Wheeler-Bennett, *Hindenburg, the Wooden Titan* (London:

Macmillan, 1936), pp. 353-368. Dr. Brüning confirmed to me the veracity of this account. Churchill too lamented the fall of the Hohenzollerns and the Hapsburgs which resulted in the rise of the Nazis. *Cf.* Winston S. Churchill *The Second World War* (London: Cassell, 1948), Vol. 1. pp. 21, 49-50.

[41] During the War a Hungarian refugee in America wrote a book on Papen called *The Devil in Top Hat*. Actually, the intellectual acumen of Papen was so minute that people took his lack of intelligence as a ruse, as a guise for shrewdness. His own family considered *das Fränzchen* their least gifted member to put it mildly. They had indeed no illusions. On the other hand, there is no doubt that Papen's so-called "intrigue" was entirely in keeping with the Constitution. Giselher Wirsing in "Der Herrenreiter in Morast," *Christ und Welt*, Vol. 5, No. 45, November 6, 1952, p. 4, could write without danger of refutation, "It was the irony of history that Hitler's ascent to power was perfectly legal and that every effort to prevent it, would have been illegal as, for instance, a coup of the army. Had such a move taken place no more than 100 out of 584 deputies would have backed General von Schleicher, and in any case, certainly not the Social Democrats."

Papen in his own memoirs—*Der Wahrheit eine Gasse* (Munich: Paul List, 1952)—tries to whitewash himself but the account of the events leading to the fateful January 30, 1933 is basically correct.

Leopold Schwarzschild, a German liberal refugee, warned Americans during the last war about their misconceptions relating to Nazism: "The master-race idea did not originate in the ruling class but was wedded to the democratic tendencies of the period . . . readiness to accept such ideas showed up first in the "people" . . . . It is wrong also to ascribe the growth of the Nazi movement preponderately to the money of the wealthy Hitlerites . . . . The democratic process was not falsified. It actually worked in Hitler's favor." *Cf.* his "Six Delusions about Germany," *New York Times Magazine*, October 1, 1944. And socialism worked in the same direction, engendering "semifascist" views. It was socialism, not "Prussianism" that Germany had in common with Russia and Italy. This was strongly emphasized by Friedrich A. von Hayek in his *The Road to Serfdom* (Chicago: University of Chicago Press, 1944), pp. 8-9.

[42] As to the helplessness of the German army vis-à-vis a strongly Nazified working class. See Chapter XVII, note 23.

[43] *Cf.* A. Hitler, *Offener Brief an Herrn von Papen*, dated Coburg, October 16, 1932, which was published in pamphlet form (Berlin, 1932). The phrase "workers of the forehead and the fist" is typical Nazi jargon. One has to remember the full name of the party. "National Socialist German *Workers'* party." The archetype in the Jungian sense was the worker. Only the misfortunes of the war alienated the worker from *his* party.

[44] *Cf.* Hermann Rauschning, *Gespräche mit Hitler* (Vienna; Zürich: Europa-Verlag, 1940), pp. 119-120.

[45] *Ibid.*, p. 85. The Austrian Socialists inherited this anti-Hapsburg

frenzy from the Nazis. But also in other domains they have loyally continued Nazi traditions—in the (German) marriage laws, the prohibition of Austrian titles of nobility, etc. Already in the pre-Anschluss period it was evident that they preferred Hitler to the Hapsburgs, the Anschluss to a Restoration. *Cf.* Victor Reimann, Innitzer, *Kardinal zwischen Hitler und Rom* (Vienna: Molden, 1967), pp. 80-81. The tenor of the Socialist leaflets was anticlerical and antimonarchist as those of the Nazis (pp. 46-47). Both parties were suppressed by the Dollfuss regime.

[46] *Ibid.*, p. 190.

[47] *Ibid.*, p. 174.

[48] *Ibid.* Not only the anti-Hapsburg but also the anti-Catholic bias tied Hitler to the Marxists. Victor Reimann writes about the demonstration on Vienna's Heldenplatz after the Anschluss where 200,000 people congregated —"Vienna's anticlerical army consisting of National Socialists, Social Democrats, and Communists" who "celebrated the greatest triumph in their history. Into this mass of fanaticized priest-haters Reichskommissar Bürckel thundered the worst demogogical speech ever uttered on this square." (V. Reimann, *op. cit.* p. 194).

[49] *Cf.* Wilhelm Röpke, *Civitas Humana* (Erlenbach-Zürich: Rentsch, 1946), p. 268. On the inner connection between socialism and nationalism in Austria prior to 1914, *cf.* Dr. Paul Molisch, *Die deutschen Hochschulen in Osterreich und die politischnationale Entwicklung nach dem Jahre 1948* (Munich: Drei-Masken Verlag, 1922), pp. 143-144. It is important to remember that the great Austrian Socialist leader Viktor Adler started out as a German nationalist, while Dr. Walter Riehl, cofounder of the D.N.S.A.P., was originally a Social Democrat. A biography whose purpose was to extol the merits of Dr. Riehl for the earliest Nazi cause is Alexander Schilling-Schletter's *Dr. Walter Riehl und die Geschichte des Nationalsozialismus* (Leipzig: Forum Verlag, 1933). Here we can read, "Dr. Walter Riehl came to National Socialism over the detour of Social Democracy as so many of our leaders. The two sources of our idea chronologically following each other can be traced in crystal clearness until they flow together and constitute today one big turbulent river destroying everything rotten and decadent." (p. 9.) Riehl's program was a socialism free of Romish and Jewish influences. He was the great-grandson of a smith and the grandson of a student who in 1848 had fought on Vienna's barricades for national democracy. His father was a lawyer like himself and a close friend of another leading Austrian Social Democrat, Engelbert Pernerstorfer, whom he called "uncle." In November 1918, Riehl became director of the "Interstate National Socialist Chancellery of the German-speaking Territories." From the Munich leader, Herr Drexler, he received a letter dated March 1, 1920, informing him that "a Herr Adolf Hitler" has been appointed propaganda manager (*Webeobmann*). Riehl and Hitler were on intimate terms and the leading German Nazi, Hermann Esser, called him even in 1933 a "Saint John of Hitlerism." Yet Riehl resigned in

504

Salzburg in August 1923, was expelled from the party in 1933 and was incarcerated by the Gestapo for some time after the *Anschluss* in spring 1938—another piece of jealousy and disloyalty so frequent in the history of leftist movements. *Cf.* Adam Wandruszka, "Osterreichs politische Struktur" in *Geschichte der Republik Osterreich*, Dr. Heinrich Benedikt, ed. (Munich: R. Oldenbourg, 1954), pp. 406-408.

The famous Nazi slogan *Blut und Boden* (blood and soil) stems from the German Social Democrat August Winnig. *Cf.* his *Das Reich als Republik 1918-1928* (Stuttgart and Berlin: Cottao, 1928), p. 3. Here one should not forget that both Marx and Engels were highly enthusiastic about Bismarck, convinced that he really was doing their work. *Cf. Marx-Engels Kritische Gesamtausgabe*, Series III, Vol. 4, p. 358.

[50] *Cf.* Hermann Rauschning, *op. cit.* p. 177.

[51] *Ibid.*, p. 124. Jacques Ellul, *op. cit.* p. 290 writes, "Nazism, however, far from being opposed to Marxism, completes it and confirms it. It gives the solution to numerous problems of adaptation. Hitler's methods stem directly from Lenin's precepts, and conversely, Stalinism learned certain lessons about technique from the Nazis." While Erwin Sinkó (*op. cit.*, p. 200), until his death an unregenerated Communist, admits that there is a mutual infection of fascism, Nazism, and Stalinism, John Lukács, though opposed to the term "Brown Communism" and "Red Fascism" insists that Hitler, Stalin, Mussolini, Nasser, Tito, Perón, Sukarno, Mao Tse-tung, etc. were all national socialists. The influence of the national factor on socialism has always been undervalued. *Cf.* his *Historic Consciousness and the Remembered Past*. (New York: Harper and Row, 1968), p. 188.

[52] *Ibid.*, p. 265.

[53] *Cf.* (Sir) Herbert Read, *To Hell with Culture*, No. 4 of the series "The Democratic Order" (London: Routledge and Kegan Paul, 1941), p. 49. Sir Herbert, born in 1893, was director of a London publishing company and had been professor of Fine Arts.

[54] *Cf.* (Sir) Herbert Read, *Politics of an Unpolitical* (London: Routledge, and Kegan Paul 1943), p. 4.

[55] Speech on December 10, 1940, *cf. Völkischer Beobachter*, December 11, 1940.

[56] Speech on November 8, 1938, *cf. Völkischer Beobachter*, November 10, 1938.

[57] Speech on January 30, 1937, *cf. Völkischer Beobachter*, January 31, 1937.

[58] Speech on May 21, 1935, *cf. Völkischer Beobachter*, May 22, 1935.

[59] *Cf.* A. Hitler, *Mein Kampf* (Munich: Eher, n.d.), p. 99.

[60] Dr. Paul Goebbels, speech on March 19, 1934, *Cf. Völkischer Beobachter*, March 20, 1934.

[61] Dr. Paul Goebbels as quoted by *Der Völkischer Beobachter*, April 25, 1933.

62 *Cf.* Gottfried Neesse, *op. cit.* p. 187.

63 *Cf.* Michael Oakeshott, *The Social and Political Doctrines of Contemporary Europe* (New York: Macmillan, 1944), p. xvii. The notion that democracy is a form of government favoring only the poor and ignorant is old. St. Thomas Aquinas expressed it in his commentary of Aristotle. *Cf.* his *Politicorum seu de rebus civilibus*, Liber 3, Lectio 6. Also: Aristotle, *Politics*, V, viii, 6-7 and V, ix, 4 where Aristotle deals with the "low-class" character of tyranny and its democratic background.

64 *Cf.* interview in the *Petit Journal* (Paris), No. 25729, June 26, 1933.

65 *Cf.* Dr. Josef Goebbels, *Der Nazi-Sozi. Fragen und Antworten für den Nationalsozialisten* (Munich: Eher, 1932), p. 10. Goebbels wrote very candidly in his diary on October 23, 1925, "After everything is said and done, I would rather perish with bolshevism than live in the eternal slavery of capitalism." *Cf. Das Tagebuch von Josef Goebbels*, p. 10. Not much later he confessed, "The destruction of Russia means that the dream of a National Socialist Germany would have to be buried once and forever." *Cf. Nationalsozialistische Monatshefte*, (Munich, January 15, 1926.

66 *Cf. Der Hochverratsprozess gegen Dr. Guido Schmidt vor dem Volksgericht, Die gerichtlichen Protokolle*, (Vienna: Osterreichische Stattsdruckerei, 1947), p. 356.

67 For a background study, *cf.* Hedwig Conrad-Martius, *Utopien der Menschenzüchtung, Der Sozialdarwinismus und seine Folgen* (Munich: Kösel, 1955).

68 Sometimes Hitler chanced to adopt this pessimistic view, as we can see in his reply to Speer's memorandum of March 18, 1945. General Guderian quotes Hitler to the effect that he expected that the best men, not the worst, would be killed in battle. *Cf. Der Nationalsozialismus, Dokumente 1933-1945*, Walther Hofer, ed. (Frankfurt-am-Main: Fischer-Bücherei, 1957), p. 260.

69 One of my friends who got into the German Foreign Office during the War belonged to a group of officials trying to persuade the *Reichskanzlei* to give the Ukraine some autonomy. There was in Berlin ever since 1923 a Ukrainian national committee which considered itself the rightful candidate for a government in the Ukraine. The Foreign Office kept asking that these men be sent to the Ukraine so that they could establish the foundations of a local government. More than a year elapsed without any reaction from Hitler's Chancellery. At long last the reply came—over the phone. My friend took the call. An unpleasant voice at the other end of the wire, said "We have to nix your plans about those Ukrainians. The *Führer* on the last roundtrip through the Ukraine was racially not impressed by these people. So the answer is 'no dice'!" To this one can only add that those whom the gods want to destroy they first deprive of their wits.

70 *Cf.* Martin Bormann's strictly confidential circular letter partly reported in *Der Nationalsozialismus, Dokumente 1933-1945*, pp. 180-181 and in *The Tablet* (London), (February 28, 1942), Vol. 179, p. 110. Here we see

National Socialism clearly as a nineteenth-century synthesis. *Cf.* also Alfred Müller-Armack, *Das Jahrhundert ohn Gott, Zur Kultursoziologie unserer Zeit* (Münster: Regensberg, 1948), p. 140.

[71] *Cf.* Gustav Stolper, *This Age of Fable* (New York: Reynal and Hitchcock, 1942), p. 328. For more about the fairy tale of the "financing" of the NSDAP by German big industry and finance, *cf.* among others Otto Kopp, ed. *Widerstand und Erneuerung* (Stuttgart: Seewald, 1966), Louis P. Lochner, *Tycoons and Tyrants* (Chicago: Regnery, 1954), and Konrad Heiden, *Das Zeitalter der Verantwortungslosigkeit* (Zürich, 1936), p. 312. The thesis that victories in free elections depend upon cash investments is highly "undemocratic" and confirms the Nazi view that democracy is plutocracy.

[72] *Cf.* Felix von Papen, *Ein von Papen spricht* (Nijmwegen, 1939), p. 14. We hear the same from Eugen Kogon in *Der-SS-Staat* (München: Karl Alber, 1946), p. 209. Yet the Communist-Nazi interplay and cooperation prepared the fall of the Weimar Republic which was keenly felt by such sharp observers as the American journalist H. R. Knickerbocker and the German novelist, essayist and historian Frank Thiess. *Cf.* his *Freiheit bis Mitternacht* (Vienna; Hamburg: Zsolnay, 1965), pp. 509-510. Yet one should never forget that Hitler always preferred the Communists to the "decadent West" and efforts to establish a closer Brown-Red collaboration were made right until June 1941. *Cf.* Walter Laqueur, *op. cit.*, pp. 68-77: Otto-Ernst Schüddekopf, *Linke Leute von rechts* (Stuttgart: Kohlhammer, 1960), pp. 199, 264, 364, 374-376. No wonder that after Hitler's takeover many Communists tried to enroll in the Storm Trooper formations. *Cf.* Rudolf Diels, *Lucifer anti portas. Zwischen Severing und Heydrich.* (Zürich, n.d.), p. 127 sq. We have to ask ourselves whether, after 1945, the opposite process did not take place in East Germany.

[73] *Cf.* Graf E. Reventlow, *Völkisch-kommunistische Einigung?* (Leipzig: Graphische Werke, 1924), pp. 17-38. On Hitler's anticapitalist outlook, *cf.* Dr. Henry Picker, *op. cit.* p. 203. Hitler wanted to "nationalize" all stockholding companies.

[74] *Cf.* Baron Friedrich von Hügel, "The German Soul and the Great War," *The Quest*, Vol. 6, No. 3, April 1915, pp. 6-7.

[75] *Cf.* Ernst Jünger, *Strahlungen* (Tübingen: Heliopolis Verlag, 1949), p. 562.

[76] One of the most destructive leftist reviews published in Paris, totally pro-Communist, but by no means tolerated in the Soviet Union—a real product of Luciferism. Yet not only the "Divine Marquis" was a forerunner of this attitude but also Saint-Just, the alter ego of Robespierre who wrote sexual poetry, made blueprints of totalitarian utopias reminiscent of Morelly's plans and declared that "a nation regenerated itself only on mountains of corpses. *Cf.* Albert Ollivier, *Saint-Just et la force des choses* (Paris: N.R.F. Gallimard, 1954), p. 257.

[77] *Cf.* Nicolas Calas, *Foyers d'incendie* (Paris: Denoel, 1939).

78 *Cf*. Translation of extracts in the *Partisan Review*, Vol. 17, No. 1. January-February 1940, p. 45.

79 *Ibid*., p. 46.

80 *Ibid*., pp. 46-47. Calas reminds one of Franz Werfel's self-accusing outcry, "I have experienced many varieties of arrogance, in myself and in others. But since I myself shared these varieties for a time in my youth, I must confess from personal experience that there is no more consuming, more insolent, more sneering, more diabolical arrogance than that of the artistic advance guard and radical intellectuals who are bursting with a vain mania to be deep and dark and subtle and to inflict pain. Amid the amused and indignant laughter of a few philistines we were the insignificant stokers who preheated the hell in which mankind is now roasting." *Cf*. Franz Werfel, p. 250 *Between Heaven and Earth*, M. Newmark, translator (New York: Philosophical Library, 1944), ("Theologoumena," No. 126).

81 *Cf*. *The Pollock-Holmes Letters, Correspondence of Sir Frederick Pollock and Mr. Justice Holmes 1874-1932*, Mark DeWolfe Howe, ed. (Cambridge, England: Cambridge University Press, 1942), Vol. 2, p. 36.

Chapter XIII

1 The late Alexander Rüstow remained curiously unknown in the English-speaking world. *Cf*. p. 198 and Chapter XI, note 15.

We are referring here to an important minor work of this brilliant scholar, "Das Versagen des Wirtshaftsliberalismus als religionsgeschichtliches Problem," in *Istanbuler Schriften (Istanbul Yazilari)*, p. 12.

2 Achille Charles Léonce Victor Duc de Broglie, French statesman, married to the daughter of Madame de Staël, had his career destroyed by the imperial dictatorship of Napoleon III. He characterized this regime as a government which the "poorer classes desired and the rich deserved." One might have extended this analysis to the Nazis if one added "and which leftist intellectuals unwittingly had prepared." Before his death de Broglie said, "I shall die a penitent Christian and an impenitent liberal." More pronouncedly Catholic and Christian was that other great liberal aristocrat, Montalembert, who could write in retrospect before his death, "People should know that there was at least one old soldier of the Catholic faith and of liberty who, before 1830, has clearly distinguished the Catholic from the royalist cause: who under the July regime has pleaded the cause of the Church's independence from civilian control: who in 1848 has fought with all his energies against the alleged identity of Christianity and democracy, and who in 1852 has protested the surrender of freedom to brute power under the pretext of religion." *Cf*. *Montalembert*, Emmanuel Mounier, ed. (Paris: Egloff, 1945), pp. 98-99.

3 *Cf*. Thomas Aquinas, *De Regimine Principum*, Book II, Ch. 3.

4 Frau Heddy Neumeister is economics editor of the *Frankfurter*

Allgemeine Zeitung, visits Mont-Pèlerin Society Meetings, and is the author of *Organisierte Menschlichkeit?* (Herder-Bücherei, No. 116).

[5] *Cf. Correspondance du R. P. Lacordaire et de Madame Swetchine*, Comte de Falloux, ed. (Paris: Didier, 1880). As to Lacordaire's political views, he had gone through a demo-republican phase. See *Lacordaire, Sa vie par lui-même* (Marseilles: Publiroc, 1931), pp. 225-229. His speech upon taking the *fauteuil* of de Tocqueville in the Academy, *cf. ibid.* p. 306 ff. About his life in general in a concise form, *cf.* Marc Escholier, *Lacordaire ou Dieu et la liberté* (Paris: Fleurus, 1959).

[6] *Cf.* Antoine Redier, *Comme disait M. de Tocqueville* (Paris: Perrin, 1925), pp. 47-48 (letter in facsimile). See also his letter to Count Leo Thun, dated February 26, 1844, quoted by Christoph Thienen-Adlerflycht, *Graf Leo Thun im Vormärz* (Graz: Böhlau, 1967), p. 177, in which he deplores all disestablishment of the aristocratic order.

[7] As to Alexis de Tocqueville, *cf.* my Introduction to his *Democracy in America* (New Rochelle, N. Y.: Arlington House, n.d.) pp. v-xxii. De Tocqueville was also convinced that pre-Revolutionary France was much freer than in the mid-nineteenth century and that in this old freedom the freest and most independent minds could develop. *Cf.* his "L'Ancien regime," *Oeuvres complétes*, J. P. Mayer, ed., Vol. 2. pp. 176-177.

[8] *Cf.* Nicholas Berdyaev, *The End of Our Time*, D. Atwater, translator (New York: Sheed and Ward, 1933), pp. 174-175. Russian original: *Novoye srednovyekovye* (Paris: S.P.C.K., 1928).

[9] One can see the change in Maritain's political thinking from his *Primauté du spirituel* to *Christianisme et la démocratie* in which he praises the "atheistic Communists of Russia" for having "abolished the profit motive." Yet it is not likely that the author of *Le paysan de la Garonne* would subscribe to these ideas today. (All the more so as desperate but sterile efforts are now being made in Eastern Europe to install the profit motive in a socialistic economy.)

[10] *Cf.* Henri Bergson, *Les deux sources de la morale et de la religion* (Paris: Félix Alcan, 1933), pp. 304-305.

[11] In World War I Thomas Mann wrote a most bellicose, extremely nationalistic book of essays, *Betrachtungen eines Unpolitischen*. Asked after World War II whether he did not want to disavow it, he answered with a flat "no," which surprised everybody.

[12] *Cf.* Alexis de Tocqueville, "De la démocratie en Amérique," in *Oeuvres* (Paris, 1864), Vol. 3, pp. 516-523. In English: Arlington House edition, Vol. 2, pp. 335 sq.

[13] *Cf.* letter of A. de Tocqueville to Count Gobineau, November 17, 1853, in *Revue des Deux Mondes* (Paris, 1907), Vol. 40, pp. 62 ff.

[14] A scholarly work covering the whole of National Socialist radical thinking and its actual racist policy has yet to be written. The *op. cit.* of Hedwig Conrad-Martius provides us merely with a historic background. So does

Ernst Nolte in his *op. cit.* (pp. 345-355). The American influence on Nazi thought in this respect was not inconsiderable (Madison Grant, Lothrop Stoddard). Compare also with Albert Jay Nock, "The Jewish Problem in America," *The Atlantic Monthly*, June 1941.

[15] Staunch Lutherans, like Ernst Ludwig von Gerlach, opposed Bismarck and his National Liberals violently. So did the arch-conservative Prussian *Kreuz-Zeitung*. Gerlach later joined, out of sheer protest, the "Catholic" Center party. *Cf.* Hans Joachim Schoeps, *Das andere Preussen*, (Stuttgart: Friedrich Vorwerk, 1952), *passim*.

[16] This was already noted by the English volunteer officer C. F. Henningsen in his *Campaña de doce meses en Navarra y las provincias vascongadas con el general Zumalacárregui*, R. Oyarzun, translator (San Sebastián: Editorial Española, 1939), originally published in 1836. It was largely the gentry which was Carlist and conservative.

[17] The Bavarian aristocracy turned toward the conservative (and royalist) *Bayrische Volkspartei* (Bavarian People's party, forerunner of the present C.S.U., the *Christlichsoziale Union*) only after 1918. In Bavaria, before World War I, a "gentleman" was liberal, not "clerical"!

[18] Guglielmo Ferrero rightly considered the House of Savoy to be the "quasilegitimate" rulers of Italy. In Spain and Portugal the liberal branches of the royal families ruled until 1931 and 1910 respectively: in Spain the descendants of Isabel II, in Portugal those of Maria da Gloria. The Carlists and Miguelinos represented the conservative (and truly legitimate) pretenders who in civil wars had vainly tried to make tradition and legality prevail. Britain gave full aid to the liberals and British volunteers had fought in both wars on the side of the liberal lines. Today—in the 1970s—the Carlist line (but not the Carlist tradition) has died out in Spain while true Braganças survive in Portugal, claiming the throne. (The descendants of Maria da Gloria—Maria II—were Saxe-Coburgs.)

[19] It was amazing to see even *young* people disgusted by the word "liberty." And this was precisely the situation in large parts of Europe prior to World War II. The explanation is the visual impression made by the liberal camp—an agglomeration of petty, frightened mice without *positive* beliefs. European youth, on the other hand, naively thought that it was strong enough to bear even very heavy chains.

[20] When Mussolini fell into the hands of the largely Communist partisans they shouted, "Why have you betrayed Socialism?" The Italian left had never forgotten that Mussolini belonged basically to them. *Cf.* Paolo Monelli, *Mussolini piccolo borghese* (Milan: Garzanti, 1959), p. 347. Yet there were, needless to say, many Fascists who after 1944 turned Socialist or Communist as, for instance, Curzio Malaparte (whose real name was Suckert). His last book was on Red China. On his deathbed, however, this erstwhile Lutheran of German extraction became a Catholic.

Among the former Socialists and Communists serving Mussolini we also have to mention Nicola Bombacci, Robert Farinacci, Cesare Rossi, Massimo Rocca, Leandro Arpinati.

[21] *Cf.* Eduard Heimann, "The Rediscovery of Liberalism," *Social Research*, Vol. 8. No. 4. (November 1941).

[22] *Cf.* Heinrich Denzinger, *Enchiridion Symbolorum*, Karl Rahner, ed. (Freiburg i. Br.-Barcelona: Herder, 1955), p. 450. The *Syllabus* can be fully understood only if the individual propositions are read in their full context (Allocutions, Breves, Encyclicals, etc.) and the full context studied in relation with the historic occasion which provoked them. Without such double control the *Syllabus* (a hasty and misleading compilation in any case) makes no sense at all. When the *Syllabus* was published, the French public protested violently, but the famous liberal Bishop Dupanloup wrote a very necessary commentary which became a best-seller and earned the author a highly laudatory Breve of Pius IX. *Cf.* R. P. Lecanuet, *Montalembert* (Paris: Poussielgue, 1902), pp. 386-389.

[23] See the passionate plea of Wilhelm Röpke for Christianity as the last defense against totalitarianism in *Civitas Humana*, pp. 224-225. (*Cf.* also pp. 194-198).

[24] Walter Eucken was the son of the famous German philosopher Richard Eucken (Nobel prize winner for literature in 1908) and the economics teacher of Dr. Ludwig Erhard, Finance Minister and later Chancellor of the German Federal Republic.

[25] See the spirited defense of Christianity by Rüstow and his insistence that Western civilization stands and falls with it, in *Ortsbestimmung der Gegenwart*, (First Edition), Vol. 2, pp. 235-236.

His grandfather's generation consisted of three brothers, all Prussian generals. They were Alexander and Cesar, both killed in Austria in 1866, both military writers of renown, and the very colorful Wilhelm Friedrich, also an officer who wrote a pamphlet against militarism. He was arrested but fled to Switzerland before his trial in 1850. There he lectured on military affairs at the University of Zürich and became a major in the Swiss Army. In 1860 he joined Garibaldi in Sicily where he was made a colonel on the general staff. He was the actual victor of the Volturno battle. After the Italian campaign he returned to Switzerland and in 1870 was elected colonel of the Swiss Army—in peacetime the highest rank. He was the author of numerous military works. Here was a Prussian officer, intellectually and internally active, liberal and adventurous, an antimilitarist and yet a war enthusiast.

[26] A large group of German conspirators entrusted the American journalist Louis P. Lochner to inform President Roosevelt of their plan to restore the monarchy under Prince Louis Ferdinand, second son of the former Crown Prince who had spent some time in the United States working in Detroit. Lochner reached the United States only in July 1942 and then failed to be received by President Roosevelt who would not even hear about the German resistance. The President considered such information "highly embarrassing."

Cf. Hans Rothfels, *Die deutsche Opposition gegen Hitler* (Krefeld, Scherpe, 1949), pp. 166 ff.

Austrian monarchists in 1945, some fresh out of Nazi concentration camps, were often arrested by "His Majesty's officers" and again thrown into jail. In the State Treaty of 1955, Britain, the United States, France, and the Soviet Union obliged Austria not to restore the Hapsburgs (and, much more amusing, not to possess submarines—in a landlocked Alpine state!). It cannot be doubted that Communism has a vested interest in keeping the Hapsburgs out of Austria. But in what way have America and Britain?

[27] In 1955 an enterprising young American, Patrick M. Boarman, director of the Bureau for Cultural Relations of the N.C.W.C. in Germany, organized a meeting between neoliberal and Christian thinkers in Gauting near Munich. The papers read on this occasion can be found in *Der Christ und die soziale Marktwirtschaft*, P. M. Boarman, ed. (Stuttgart: W. Kohlhammer, 1955). *Cf.* also Roland Nitsche, *Mehr als Soll und Haben* (Vienna: Herder, 1962). Nitsche too is a Catholic economic neoliberal. So is Baron Georg Bernhard Kripp who wrote an excellent thesis: *Wirtschaftsfreiheit und katholische Soziallehre* (Zürich: Polygraphischer Verlag, 1967). Practically valueless is the work of the Dominican E. E. Nawroth (O.P.) *Die Sozial und Wirtschaftphilosophie des Neoliberalismus* (Heidelberg-Loẅen, 1961). The author, unfortunately, mistook a membership list of the Mont-Pèlerin Society for a catalog of neoliberals, yet the society contained old as well as new liberals. As a result half of the "authorities" cited are totally irrelevant. Therefore, so is his effort to identify neoliberalism with medieval nominalism.

For a further clarification of the neoliberal ethical stand in the field of economics, *cf.* particularly Dr. Berthold Kunze "Wirtschaftsethik und Wirtschaftsordnung" in Boarman, *op. cit.* and Alexander Rüstow, *op. cit.* See also Alexander Rüstow, "Soziale Marktwirtschaft als Gegenprogramm" in *Wirtschaft ohne Wunder*, A. Hunold, ed. (Erlenbach-Zürich, 1953), and Alfred Müller-Armack, *Diagnose unserer Gegenwart* (Gütersloh: Bertelsmann, 1949), pp. 293. sq., and Müller-Armack, "Die Wirtschaftsordnung sozial gesehen," in *Ordo*, Vol. 1. (1948).

[28] *Cf.* F. A. v. Hayek, *The Constitution of Liberty* (London: Routledge and Kegan Paul, 1960), pp. 397 ff. Here Hayek expresses his opinion that, contrary to H. Hallam (*Constitutional History*, 1827), the origin of the political sense of the term "liberal" is not Spanish. Hayek quotes Adam Smith (*Wealth of Nations*, II, 41) on the "liberal plan of equality, liberty and justice," but I think that the term here is still used in the old sense of the *liberalitas*.

Chapter XIV

[1] *Cf.* Benjamin Disraeli, *Endymion* (London: Longmans, Green, 1920), p. 7. "They are trying to introduce here the continental Liberalism," said the

great personage. "Now we know what Liberalism means on the continent. It means the abolition of property and religion. Those ideas would not suit this country." These remarks were exaggerated, but not without substance when we remember how palaeoliberalism had replaced early liberalism. See the critical letter of Bishop Ketteler, "Reply to Professor Bluntschli in Heidelberg," in *Briefe von und an Wilhelm Emmanuel Freihern von Ketteler, Bishop von Mainz*, J. M. Raich, ed. (Mainz: Kirchheim, 1879), pp. 439-440. Harsh is also the judgment of Arthur Moeller van den Bruck, frequently but falsely accused of being a Nazi precursor, when he writes that "liberalism is the freedom to have no convictions and, at the same time, to maintain that this precisely is a conviction." *Cf.* his *Das dritte Reich* (Hamburg: Hanseatische Verlagsanstalt, 1941), p. 84. The book was originally published in 1924. The old liberals were obviously too optimistic about human nature. Ludwig von Mises, the great old liberal, wrote in *Human Action* (New Haven: Yale University Press, 1949), p. 861: "After having nullified the fable of the anointed kings, the liberals fell prey to no less illusory doctrines, to the irresistible power of reason, to the infallibility of the *volonté générale,* and to the divine inspiration of majorities."

[2] The expression "sectarian liberals" for narrow-minded, anticlerical old liberals was used by Professor Carlton J. H. Hayes in *A Generation of Materialism* (New York: Harper, 1941), p. 49. The derivation of the term "liberal" from Spanish sources is vouchsafed by *The Oxford English Dictionary*, B I, Vol. 6, Part 1, p. 238, and by Román Oyarzún, *Historia del carlismo* (Bilbao: Ediciones Fe, 1939), p. 12 n.

[3] The reactionary truly *reacts* in a hostile way against the existing order. He is not, in other words, a "sovereign thinker," but an emotional protester.

[4] *Cf.* Eugene Lyons, *The Red Decade* (Indianapolis; Bobbs-Merrill, 1941). On the American pilgrims visiting the USSR see pp. 92-95.

[5] This goes hand in hand with pedolatry, the worship of youth.

[6] So is welfarism and, naturally, so is socialism. Harold Laski, who preached this all the time, made himself rather unpopular among good American democrats without Socialist inclinations—but he was right. (Only an intense tradition of freedom, as we have it in Switzerland, will upset this trend.) *Cf.* also Harold Laski, *Reflections of the Revolution of Our Time* (London: Allen and Unwin, 1943), pp. 128 ff. Yet the realization that democracy leads naturally to socialism is fairly widespread. *Cf.* Ralph Henry Gabriel, *op. cit.* p. 378: Gonzague de Reynold, *La demócratie et la Suisse* (Bern: Editions de Chandelier, 1929), p. 298; *Joseph Conrad, Life and Letters*, G. J. Aubrey, ed. (London, 1927), Vol. 1. p. 84.

[7] *Cf.* Oliver Wendell Holmes, Jr., *The American Law Review*, Vol. 5 (1871), p. 534.

[8] *Cf. The Pollock-Holmes Letters, Correspondence of Sir Frederick Pollock and Mr. Justice Holmes 1874-1932*, Mark de Wolfe Howe, ed. (Cambridge, England: Cambridge University Press, 1942), Vol. 2., p. 36.

[9] *Cf.* Richard Hertz, *Chance and Symbol* (Chicago: University of Chicago Press, 1948), p. 107.

[10] *Cf.* Oliver Wendell Holmes, Jr. in Harry C. Shriver, *Book Notices, Uncollected Letters and Papers* (New York: Central Book Co., 1936), p. 202.

[11] *Cf.* Felix Morley, in *Barron's Magazine*, June 18, 1951.

[12] *Cf.* *The Pollock-Holmes Letters*, Vol. 2, pp. 238-239. Letter of Holmes to Sir Frederick Pollock, February 5, 1929.

[13] *Cf.* Eduard May, *Am Abgrund des Relativismus* (Berlin: Lüttke-Verlag, 1941), pp. 136-138.

[14] *Cf.* Hans Kelsen, *Reine Rechtslehre* (Leipzig and Vienna: Deuticke, 1934), pp. 15-16.

[15] *Cf.* Lord Percy of Newcastle, *The Heresy of Democracy* (London: Eyre and Spottiswoode, 1954), pp. 32, 61. Also: Reinhard Steiger, "Christliche Politik und die Versuchung zur Gewalttätigkeit," *Hochland*, Vol. 52, No. 4. (April 1960), pp. 360-367. Relativism, as these two authors insist, is an essential element in Western democracy. Orestes Brownson believed that democracy was "political atheism." *Cf.* Lawrence Roemer, *op. cit.* p. 44.

[16] *Cf.* Fëdor Stepun, "Die Kirche zwischen Ost und West," *Schweizer Rundschau*, Vol. 52, No. 11-12 (February-March 1953), p. 701.

[17] *Cf.* Graf Hermann Keyserling, *Das Reisetagebuch eines Philosophen*, (Darmstadt: Otto Reichl, 1923), Vol. 1, p. 43.

[18] *Cf.* F. S. Campbell (E.v.Kuehnelt-Leddihn), "The Whiff from an Empty Bottle," in *The Catholic World*, October 1945, pp. 20-27. This short story tries to dramatize my thesis.

[19] *Cf.* *The New York Times*, June 28, 1939, cited by Thomas F. Woodlock in his column "Thinking it Over," *The Wall Street Journal*, December 22, 1939.

[20] *Cf.* *Teachers College Record*, vol. 27, No. 6. (February 1926).

[21] *Cf.* p. 102. Ernst Walter Zeeden in *Martin Luther und die Reformation im Urteil des deutschen Luthertums* (Freiburg i. Br.: Herder, 1950), vol. 1, p. 379 speaks rightly about the "Protestant bipolarity" by which he means the evolution of the ideas of the Reformation into their opposite.

[22] *Cf.* Chapter V, note 25. And here we would like to add that the term "Catholicism" *(Katholizismus, Catholicisme)* neither figures in the old *Catholic Encyclopedia*, nor in the *Dictionnaire apologétique de la foi catholique*, the *Dictionnaire de théologie catholique*, or the *Lexikon für Theologie und Kirche*.

The new *Der Grosse Herder*, vol. 5, p. 286 says clearly: "Catholicism, a term coined in imitation of the word Protestantism, rather describes the social phenomena of the Catholic Church . . . than her inner life." Pope Pius XII called the term "Catholicism" "neither customary, nor fully adequate" for the Catholic Church. (Allocution at the 10th International Congress of Historical Sciences, reported by *The Tablet* (London), vol. 206, no. 6018, September 24, 1955, p. 293.)

[23] *Cf.* Chapter VIII, note 4. Josef Lortz in his *Einheit her Christenheit, Unfehlbarkeit und lebendige Aussage* (Trier: Paulinus Verlag, 1959), p. 43 says that in Reformation theology "not even a hint of relativistic attitude [toward truth] can be found." W. H. van de Pol in *Das reformatorische Christentum in phänomenologischer Betrachtung* (Einsiedeln-Cologne: Benziger, 1956), p. 66 berates very severely all those who accuse the Reformation of fostering "private interpretation" or the "free exploration of Scriptures"—among whom he mentions Jaime Balmes *(El protestantismo comparado con el catolicismo)* and Henry Newman *(Lectures on the prophetical office of the Church)*. Yet José Luís L. Aranguren in his *Catolicismo y Protestantismo como formas de existencia* (Madrid: Revista de Occidente, 1957), pp. 44-48 has seen more clearly that Luther's "subjectivism" is really an existentialism.

[24] *Cf.* Chapter VIII, note 9. The introduction of the vernacular—the second such move in the Latin Rite (after the Vulgate, translation of the Liturgy from Greek to Latin, etc)—was in view of the internationalization of the world, a rather "reactionary" decision. It was a late triumph of nationalism which, in view of the progressive "shrinking" of the globe, will some day have to be revised.

[25] *Cf.* Milton Friedman, *Capitalism and Freedom* (Chicago: University of Chicago Press, 1962), p. 6.

[26] The term "left-of-center" seems to have been invented—characteristically enough—by President Franklin D. Roosevelt.

[27] Typical was the reaction of Oliver Wendell Holmes, Jr. to Spengler's *The Decline of the West*. He wrote to Sir Frederick Pollock on July 18, 1924, "It is long since I have got so much from a book as this, and if I heard that the swine were dead, I should thank God." In April 1932 he referred to Spengler as "an odious animal which must be read" and on May 15, 1932 he said, "The beast has ideas, many of which I don't know enough to criticize. I wish he were dead. On the other side that dear delightful Wodehouse whom I read and even reread with guffaws." *(Cf. The Pollock-Holmes Letters,* vol. 3, pp. 139, 307, and 309.)

[28] W. H. Auden asked me once why I would not like to live permanently in Britain. "It's the British horror for the absolute," I said. "How right you are!" he replied. *Cf.* also (Sir) Compton Mackenzie's preface to Jane Lane's *King James the Last* (London: Dakers, 1942) pp. vii-viii. The rejection of compromise and the *juste milieu* we find, however, also in the thought of the German religious philosopher Franz von Baader. *Cf.* his *Grundzüge der Societätsphilosophie* (Würzenburg: Stähel, 1832), p. 39, where Baader speaks about the "double lie of the *juste milieu.*"

[29] *Cf.* p. 207 and Chapter XIV, note 12. Interesting is Newman's reaction to the problem; he thought that the gentleman falls short in many respects of the Christian ideal of a complete man. (*Cf.* his *The Idea of a University*. Discourse VIII, chapters 9 and 10.) Karl Löwith in his essay, "Can There Be a Christian Gentleman?" (*Theology Today*, vol. 5, no. 1, April, 1948,

pp. 58-67) also gives a negative reply. Yet the reasoning of Newman and of Löwith are of an entirely different order.

[30] *Cf.* James Burnham, *Suicide of the West* (New York: John Day, 1964), pp. 40-42.

[31] The excuse of the *moderate* leftist for this inequality is that progressive taxation serves to equalize living standards and wealth to a considerable degree: the *radical* leftists will say that such an inequality ought to be eliminated by equal incomes. In either case ambition is penalized and laziness amply rewarded. Hence also the backwardness of Socialist countries. Christian sentimentalists might believe that such tamperings with incomes will eliminate the "proletariat." They should read, however, the address of Pius XII of September 14, 1952, to the Austrian Catholic Congress in Vienna. The Pope insisted that the proletariat in the Western World survives only in isolated instances. Real welfare lies in the cooperation between various social layers. Now the main task of the Church is the "protection of the individual and the family from an all-embracing socialization, a process in whose terminal stage the terrifying vision of the Leviathan State would become a gruesome reality. The Church is going to fight this battle without a letup because the issue here is concerned with final values, the dignity of man and the salvation of souls." I cannot remember having seen parts of this highly important address in Catholic American papers.

[32] Naturally, every state exists for the welfare, the "commonweal" of its citizens. Unfortunately, the term "welfare state" stands today largely for what Hilaire Belloc called the "servile state," and in German, if we want to be exact, the *Versorgungsstaat*, the "provider state." Yet the "provider state" is not inevitably socialistic even if it clearly has totalitarian features. Sweden, for instance, is a provider state—and not a Socialist state since 90 percent of the means of production are privately owned.

[33] On American misogyny *cf.* David L. Cohn, *Love in America* (New York: Simon and Schuster, 1943). *Cf.* also Edith Wharton, *The Custom of the Country* (New York: Scribner's, 1913) and Francis J. Grund, *Aristocracy in America*, George E. Probst, ed. (New York: The Academy Library-Harper Torchbook, 1959), pp. 39-40. (This book was published originally in London in 1839.) When Dr. Benjamin Rush visited France he was amazed about the mixing of sexes and the high educational and cultural level of French women—quite a variance with the English or American tradition. *Cf. The Selected Writings by Benjamin Rush*, by D. D. Runes, ed. (New York: Philosophical Library, 1947), pp. 379-385. Yet American misogyny is clearly inherited from British patterns. Johanna Schopenhauer, mother of the German philosopher, became aware of it on her trip through the British Isles in 1805. *Cf.* Johanna Schopenhauer, *Reise durch England und Schottland*, L. Plakolb, ed. (Stuttgart: Steingrüben-Verlag, 1965), pp. 186-187. The Anglo-American institution of the club is certainly a means to escape women.

[34] A proto-Nazi German author was Hans Blüher, who in an early book,

Die deutsche Wandervogelbewegung als erotisches Phänomen, Preface by Dr. Magnus Hirschfeld (Berlin, 1912), proudly attributed a homosexual character to the *Wandervogel* movement which in many ways had prepared the Nazi rebellion against the "father." (We have emphasized the strongly identitarian, egalitarian, homosexual, and "fraternal" character of the leftist movements at the beginning of this book.)

Blüher's Nazoid views became more distinct in a later book, *Die Erhebung Israels gegen die christlichen Güter* (Hamburg: Hanseatische Verlagsbuchhandlung, 1931), in which he accused the Jews of deriding the homosexual tendencies in non-Jews—tendencies which are essential for the foundation of political units since they rest on *Männerbünde*, male leagues. The high priest of Nazi doctrine, Alfred Rosenberg, repeated this argument in *op. cit*, p. 485.

Homosexuality was strong in the early history of Nazism, especially among the S. A. (A high Vienna police official told me in the late 1920s that youthful homosexuals frequently banded together in paramilitary Nazi formations.) The accusations against S. A. Chief Roehm and his friends were well founded.

[35] The main reason why the Soviets persecute homosexuals is their tendency to establish small private worlds, little enchanted circles which totalitarianism automatically dislikes. For very similar reasons it dislikes the family, sex, and Eros, an attitude which finds its literary reflection in Orwell's "Anti-Sex League" in his novel *1984*. *Vide* the revolt of Soviet writers such as Olga Berggolts, Dovzhenko, and Vagarshanian against the official opposition to the literary representation of all forms of love—sexual, erotic, familistic, etc. *Cf.* E. v. Kuehnelt-Leddihn, "Contemporary Soviet Literature," *The Critic*, vol. 19, No. 1. (August-September 1960), pp. 18, 21.

[36] Dr. Benjamin Rush in a letter to Jeremy Belknap (October 13, 1789) expressed his disappointment that capital punishment had been abolished in the Duchy of Tuscany (ruled by a Hapsburg who later became Emperor Leopold II). "How disgraceful for our republics," he wrote, "that the monarchs of Europe should take the lead of us in extending the empire of reason and humanity in this interesting part of government!" *Cf. Letters of Benjamin Rush*, L. H. Butterfield, ed. (Princeton: Princeton University Press, 1951), vol. 1, p. 526.

[37] Yet the murder of the Archduke and the Duchess of Hohenberg received, after the end of World War I, a monument from the Karagjorgjević dynasty to perpetuate the gloriously foul deed in Sarajevo. We do not know whether representatives of Britain, France, and the United States were invited to participate in the unveiling. The cult of the assassins continued until the collapse of Yugoslavia in 1941 when the statue was destroyed by the Croats, who had to suffer Serb rule for twenty-three years. After World War II the murderer was honored by Tito with a museum. (Again we wonder about the presence of Western diplomats at the opening ceremonies.)

There are still people in the West who believe that Austria-Hungary in 1914 delivered a totally unjustified ultimatum to Serbia which was in fact organizing and praising murder. (We should ask ourselves how Teddy Roosevelt would have reacted against the assassination of an American Vice President by an organization whose head was the Vice President, let us say, of Nicaragua. Would he not have demanded at least the admission of plainclothes detectives to investigate the background of the murder?) Yet the first six "political" demands of Austria were not fulfilled and it is significant that, when the Serb answer to the Austrian ultimatum arrived, not a single soldier of the imperial royal army was mobilized. *Cf.* Freiherr von Musulin, *Das Haus am Ballhausplatz* (Munich: Verlag für Kulturpolitik, 1924), pp. 225-226, 241-245.

[38] In the twentieth century, the historical period when most monarchies fell and were transformed into republics, *not one monarchy* went down fighting. Not one monarch ordered the slaughter of his subjects. (And this precisely because monarchy at long last had reached its maturity.) On this subject *cf.* Louis Rougier, *La France à la recherche d'une constitution* (Paris: Recueil Sirey, 1952), p. 124.

[39] I deduct the *moral* superiority of the monarchy from the fact that it rests far more than the republic on the theological virtues of faith and charity. It rests on trust and affection. It is, in a wider sense, "erotic" government. Republics, however, rest on suspicion, democracy on envy. *Cf.* (Lord) Bertrand Russell, *The Conquest of Happiness* (New York: Liveright, 1930), pp. 83-84. Montesquieu thought that the monarchy's outstanding characteristic is *clemency*, the republic's *virtue*. (Nevertheless, it is significant that the expression "the republican virtues" has been dropped from the dictionary of the French Academy.) Louis Philippe said, in exile, when he heard about General Cavaignac's brutal slaughter of the French workers, "Only democratic regimes can fire at the people because they do it in the name of the people and, in a way, by order of the people." *Cf.* René Gillouin, *Trois études politiques* (Paris: Ecrits de Paris, 1951), p. 30, and Gaetano Mosca, *Ciò che la storia potrebbe insegnare* (Milan: Giuffrè, 1958), p. 529, note 132.

[40] Having been brought up in Europe, I haven't the slightest personal aversion against African Negroes or American mulattoes. (The latter regularly fail to take roots in Africa. *Cf.* Harold R. Isaacs, "Back to Africa," *The New Yorker*, May 13, 1961, pp. 105-143.) A Negro could be not only his "brother" but also his brother-in-law. And he does not accept the argument that if the population of Europe were 10 percent black, the same problems would arise as in the United States. (Brazil has more than 20 percent people of mixed blood and its color problem—which I have studied—is only a shadow of what it is in the United States.) Yet he is certain that a solution to this painful issue by legislation and laws is as impossible as one by *thoughtless* social action. The first step in the right direction would be the gradual decrease of the *mutual* inferiority complexes (they exist on both sides!) and a subsequent meeting of the "races" at the top—not at the bottom. The idea of solving the "Negro problem" by "busing" or by inviting an elevator man to sit down in one's parlor and offering him a martini is perfectly childish. All real meet-

ings of nations have always been a meeting of elites, not of the masses who tend to be strongly identitarian in sentiment and to hate all manifestations of otherness.

[41] Yet during the Spanish Civil War leftists tried to rouse popular passions against the *Franquistas* by reminding Americans that the wicked Generalissimo fought with the help of evil blackamoors against lily-white democrats.

[42] On the guilt as to the outbreak of aerial warfare *cf*. pp. 297-298. Pilots of the Polish Army in exile played an important part in the Battle of Britain.

[43] Originally Lithuania should have fallen under German "influence," but the too rapid advance of the German Army into Polish territory resulted in a swap by the two aggressors: the Germans got some lands east of the Vistula and the Soviets occupied Lithuania.

[44] This aid was military (Poland), economic and moral. The German war news was featured prominently in the Soviet press: that of the Allies got second place.

[45] *Cf. The City of Man: A Declaration of World Democracy* (New York: The Viking Press, 1940), p. 113.

[46] I have a letter from Professor Reinhold Niebuhr in which he sincerely regrets the signing of the declaration under circumstances somewhat beyond his control.

[47] *Cf.* the final phrasing of his review of the book in *The Thomist*, October 1941.

[48] *Cf. The City of Man*, p. 33.

[49] *Cf.* Ralph Henry Gabriel, *The Course of American Democratic Thought* (New York: The Ronald Press, 1940), p. 382, "The persistence of the democratic faith in an age of science is a phenomenon of significance. Not one of its doctrines can be proved by any scientific sense." Also Crane Brinton, *Ideas and Men: The Story of Western Thought* (New York: Prentice-Hall, 1950), p. 549:

Democracy, in short, is *in part* a system of judgments inconsistent with what scientists hold to be true. This inconsistency would not create difficulties—or at least would not create some of the difficulties it now creates—were the democratic able to say that his kingdom is not of this world, able to say that his truth is not the kind that is in the least tested by the scientist, any more than the truth of the Catholic doctrine of the Eucharist is tested by the chemical analysis of the bread and wine. Such a solution of the democrat's intellectual quandary is not a happy one, but it is not altogether inconceivable. Democracy may become a genuinely transcendental faith, in which belief is not weakened by lack of correspondence between the propositions it lays down and the facts of life on this earth. . . . In short, democracy may be able to take its promised heaven out of this world, and put it in the world of ritual performed, of transcendental belief, or vicarious satisfactions of human wants, may keep it an ideal not too much sullied by the contrast with the spotted reality.

The opinions of H. B. Mayo on democracy are not very different: "So we can say that acts of faith may be demanded . . . but perhaps not in a religious sense, we come in the end to a justification by faith or, as it is sometimes put, to those ultimate beliefs and ideals which we cannot wholly validate by rational means." *Cf.* his "How Can We Justify Democracy?" *The American Political Science Review*, (September 1962), p. 566. Orestes Brownson took a simpler approach and referred merely to the "idiocy of talking about 'self-government.' " *Cf.* Lawrence Roemer, *op. cit.*, pp. 147-148.

[50] *Cf. The City of Man*, pp. 40, 45.

[51] See the condescending and menacing formulations in the proposal.

[52] *Ibid.*, pp. 45-46.

[53] *Ibid.*, pp. 34-35, 36. All this is quite in keeping with Morelly who in the *Code de la Nature* provided lifelong imprisonment for all those who conspired against the sacred fundamental laws of his ideal state. *Cf.* his Legislation, (12, I) in Morelly, *op. cit.* p. 152.

[54] *Ibid.*, p. 36. The total lack of understanding of Christianity's and Judaism's nature is simply startling.

[55] *Ibid.*, p. 37.

[56] *Ibid.*, p. 43.

[57] *Ibid.*, p. 46.

[58] *Ibid.*, p. 84.

[59] *Ibid.*, pp. 81-82.

[60] *Ibid.*, p. 85.

[61] Since none of the German Catholic bishops followed the Reformation, the apostolic succession was interrupted and the German Lutherans remained without bishops. The situation was different in Scandinavia where the Reformation was largely introduced by collaboration between the rulers and the bishops. *Cf.* also Georg Schwaiger, *Die Reformation in den nordischen Ländern*. (Munich: Kösel, 1962).

[62] The *Bekennende Kirche* was formed in Barmen to prevent the perversion of Lutheranism and Calvinism through Nazi ideas. The *Deutsche Christen*, especially, stood for a "dejudaized" Christianity, a trend theologically not entirely new as it had been promoted (in a very different form) by the school of Evangelical liberal theology—exemplified to a certain extent by Adolf von Harnack's *Marcion*. (The translation of *Bekennende Kirche* as "Confessional Church" can be quite misleading: "Professing Church" would be less equivocal.) Gerhard Ritter in *op. cit.*, p. 116 is quite emphatic on the fact that Evangelical resistance was led by the orthodox wing of the Reformation

churches. Obviously, one is far more ready to die for absolutes than for mere guesses or for polite doubt shrouded in a religious cloak.

[63] *Cf. The City of Man*, p. 58. Here we see the old democratic-totalitarian rejection of close family ties and all forms of "familism."

[64] *Ibid.*, p. 72.

[65] *Ibid.*, p. 27.

[66] *Ibid.*, pp. 30-32.

[67] *Ibid.*, p. 33.

[68] *Ibid.*, p. 34.

[69] Bernard Wall, the editor of *Colosseum*, a pre-World War II British and Catholic conservative review, once issued a number with the words "Utopias are Opium for the People" printed repetitiously all over the cover.

[70] *Cf. The City of Man*, p. 89. Planning is not at all "implicit" in democracy and this for two reasons: (1) planning requires permanence, a virtual certainty about conditions in the future, whereas democracy rests on change and unpredictability; (2) planning requires expertise; democracy, however, rests not on reason but on volition and subjective preferences.

[71] It would be interesting to investigate the rise and the determining role of the concepts "majority" and "minority" in Western thinking, feeling and arguing—and the subtly pejorative meaning attached to "minority." ("Rhodesia has a minority government.")

[72] Separation of State and Church has been used as a means to weaken the Church more often than to the contrary, but the idea of destroying the Church through excessive cooperation is not too rare either. It is the system in force at present in Czechoslovakia.

[73] In leftist systems the state school becomes the standard avenue of attack against the hated "closed family." As early as 1537 Capito of Hagenau (Köpphel von Hagenau) in his book, *Responsio de missa, matrimonio et iure magistratus in religionem* (Strasbourg) demanded state education for children, who "belong rather to the state than to the parents." Dr. Benjamin Rush had rather totalitarian ideas about education in order to make the Americans a homogeneous people, and in 1791 Robert Coram published a plan for national public schools in which foreign or dead languages as well as religion would be strictly outlawed. *Cf.* Hans Kohn, *The Idea of Nationalism* (New York: Macmillan, 1944), p. 304. Frances Wright, in the first half of the nineteenth century, propagated state education for all children in the two to sixteen age group, all in uniform and with identical food. *Cf.* Theodore Maynard, *op. cit.*, pp. 36-37. De Sade made almost identical remarks. *Cf.* Guillaume Apollinaire, *op. cit.*, p. 228. Hitler raved about the boarding schools, orphanages, and foundling hospitals as ideal means for a nationalistic education. *Cf.* Dr. Henry Picker, *op. cit.*, p. 293.

Krushchev hoped that by 1980 no less than 90 percent of all youngsters between the ages of six and sixteen would be in state boarding schools. (Today an estimated 9 percent of all Soviet children are educated collectively in boarding schools.)

⁷⁴ *Cf. The City of Man*, p. 58.

⁷⁵ *Cf.* Friedrich Heer, *Grundlagen der europaischen Demokratie der Neuzeit:* (Vienna: Frick-Unesco Schriften-Reihe, 1953), pp. 86-87.

⁷⁶ Democracy as substitute for religion manifests itself often in rather interesting ways. A play *Saint of Democracy* was printed by Samuel French, a New York theatrical publisher, during World War II. And how totalitarian the concept of democracy can become is shown by a book, *Dogs for Democracy* (New York: Ackerman, 1944). Here we can read the beautiful sentence on page 32: "It is a story of thousands of sensitive nostrils and straining ears that pierce the night's darkness to guard unceasingly and untiringly the ramparts of American democracy."

⁷⁷ *Cf.* Chapter I, note 6.

Chapter XV

¹ Melville's political ideas can be found in a number of his novels and epics (especially in *Clarel): on Orestes Brownson cf.* Lawrence Roemer, *op. cit.*; on William Graham Sumner *cf.* W. G. Sumner, *Challenge of Facts and Other Essays*, A. G. Keller, ed. (New Haven: Yale University Press, 1914), pp. 264, 271, 286.

² *Cf.* Thomas Mann, *Von Deutscher Republik* (Berlin: S. Fischer, 1923), p. 399. On the intrinsic connection between homosexuality and democratic (as well as leftist) trends *vide* also Donald Webster Cory, *The Homosexual in America* (New York: Greenberg, 1953), pp. 152, 163, 164. On homosexuality and Nazism *cf.* Chapter XIV, note 34.

³ *Cf.* Walt Whitman, *Democratic Vistas* (London: Walter Scott, 1888), p. 58.

⁴ *Cf.* Reinhold Niebuhr, *The Irony of American History* (New York: Scribner's, 1952), pp. 24-25. In conjunction with this read also the brilliant book of Thomas Molnar, *The Two Faces of American Foreign Policy* (Indianapolis-New York: Bobbs-Merrill, 1962), pp. 51ff. Compare also with Felix Somary, *Krise und Zukunft der Demokratie* (Zürich-Wien: Europa Verlag, 1952), p. 66. (Published in America as *Democracy at Bay*.)

⁵ *Cf.* in this connection Vianna Moog, *Bandeirantes and Pioneers*, trsl. L. I. Barnett (New York: G. Braziller, 1964), p. 263. At the International Conference of Christians and Jews in August, 1948, in Fribourg, Switzerland, the American delegation showed short films to demonstrate how they combated racism in the United States. The tenor of these films shocked the Europeans as they debunked racist prejudices in favor of a flamboyant nationalism under the "We're Americans All!" slogan. It was nationalism which, more than anything else, even more than racism, had ruined Europe.

[6] This is sweetly and very directly expressed in Edgar A. Guest's poem: "The Best Land" which starts out with the ringing lines:

If I knew a better land on this glorious world of ours,
Where a man gets bigger money and is working shorter hours;
If the Briton or the Frenchman had an easier life than mine,
I'd pack my goods this minute and I'd sail across the brine. . . .

[7] This attitude created in the mid-nineteenth century an anti-American literature in Europe. Anti-American utterances were not rare in the works of Heinrich Heine, Gustave de Beaumont, Ferdinand Kürnberger, Nikolaus Lenau, etc.

[8] The *leyenda negra*, the "Black Legend" about Spain always had numerous American devotees, *Cf.* Julián Juderías, *La leyenda negra* (Barcelona: Casa Editorial Araluce, n.d.), pp. 315ff. Salvador de Madariaga informs us that the Hispano-American Inquisition, having dealt with over 3,000 cases during centuries of its activities, had passed not more than thirty death sentences and among these fifteen implied the stake. This means that less than one percent were punished with death. English courts dealing with sorcery generally condemned 19 percent of those accused and in the first four years of the rule of James I 41 percent had to face the supreme penalty. During the Hopkins campaign in 1645, nineteen of twenty-nine indicted women were executed. The Scotch courts were far more severe and the last witch in Scotland paid with her life in 1780! *Cf.* de Madariaga's *El auge del imperio español en América* (Buenos Aires: Editorial Sudamericana, 1959), pp. 220-221.

[9] There is a good account of the American press propaganda against Spain at the time of the Cuban crisis in Hudson Strode's *Pageant of Cuba*. Little it mattered that the Spaniards were far more tolerant toward Cuba's colored population than the American "liberators" towards their own. In 1965-1966 we again see the American leftist press rant against Rhodesia, a newly independent country with—in spite of its nearness to the Republic of South Africa—a much more marked "color blindness" than one often finds nearer home. Yet Britain's Labour government obviously can do no wrong, nor the "progressive" new African nations from Zambia to Ghana, from Nigeria to the Negro-slaughterers from Khartoum. Ideological blindness is certainly the worst of all.

[10] It would be worth an investigation to find out why in Germany during World War I the hatred for Britain was far more intensive than any other one. Was it, perhaps, the hatred of disillusioned Anglomaniacs which the Germans decidedly were—and, in a sense, still are?

[11] Russia even released war prisoners who were skilled workers: they sometimes made minor fortunes until the Red Revolution broke out. During these years I was a boy, living in Baden bei Wien, the headquarters of A. O. K., the Austro-Hungarian Army. My "Sunday best" was a British sailor

suit with a cap bearing the inscription "H. M. S. Renown." I had, needless to say, a French governess. National hatred was for the mob. The feelings for the Italians were harsher: They had been members of the Triple Alliance but, having unsuccessfully tried to blackmail their Austrian ally in a desperate situation, they had gone over to the enemy. This was, in a sense, unforgivable.

[12] Almost without parallel were the cartoons of Louis Raemakers, a Dutchman, famous for his painting of the naked crucified French girl near Suippes. These organized lies, unmasked after World War I, made the accounts of *real* Nazi atrocities during World War II so unbelievable.

[13] The Napoleonic Wars were still highly civilized. When Baron Wintzingerode, a Hanoverian in Russian services, was arrested near Smolensk as a spy, the French officers restrained Napoleon who lost his temper at the insolence of the German. The latter finally ate in the officers' mess and Napoleon sulked alone in his tent. *Cf. Mémoires du Général de Caulaincourt*, Jean Hanoteau, ed. (Paris: Plon, 1933), Vol. 2, pp. 100-108. Baron Haugwitz, political advisor to the King of Prussia, told the Abbé Sièyes, French Ambassador to Berlin, confidentially, "Our real interests are those of the monarchy against the republican system . . . between monarchies one will always wage a few wars but one is not going to destroy each other." *Cf.* René Gillouin, *Aristarchie ou Recherche d'un gouvernement* (Geneva: Cheval Ailé, 1946), p. 305. Yet how brutal and stupid was the war propaganda waged in France during World War I we can see from Georges Bernanos, *La Grande Peur des Bien-Pensants* (Paris: Grasset, 1949), pp. 414-418.

[14] Soon after World War I the historians in the United States became divided in their opinion as to the guilt for this horrendous blunder. The spectrum reached all the way from Bernadotte Schmitt (condemning the Germans almost unilaterally) to Harry Elmer Barnes. Charles Callan Tansill leaned toward Barnes and so did Sidney B. Fay, who in his *Origins of the World War* (New York: Macmillan, 1928), expressed the opinion that a further investigation of Serb documents would tend to strengthen the case for Serbia's initial guilt. (In this field of research, no doubt, the real weakness of most Western historians lies in their lacking knowledge of Slav languages.)

Fay also warned (*Current Events*, vol. 6, No. 34, October 1939, p. 241) not to confuse the origins of World War I with those of World War II. As could be expected, a leftist school trying to exonerate Hitler arose in our days. Its most prominent representative in Britain is Professor A. J. P. Taylor, who, significantly enough, has strong leftist inclinations and has been known for his dislike for the Hapsburg Monarchy. *Cf.* his *The Origins of the Second World War* (Greenwich, Conn.: Fawcett Publications, 1963). Yet even in World War II the war guilt was not uniform in the Axis camp. Hungary and Bulgaria had genuine grievances. The outbreak of the war itself, no doubt, is unimaginable without Soviet connivance—just as fascism and Nazism are unthinkable without the Communist inspiration *and* challenge.

[15] Count Bernstorff's nephew, Count Albrecht Bernstorff, who during

World War II served in the German Foreign Office, was a staunch anti-Nazi and was executed in 1944. Franz von Papen's intelligence is well highlighted by the account of his collaborator in the United States, Rintelen, who gives a glaring description of Papen's more comic than tragic "underground" activities. *Cf. The Dark Invader* (Penguin Books).

[16] George D. Herron insisted that Wilson's reelection "was not only opposed by all Germans between Potsdam and San Francisco but also by the Roman Catholic Hierarch." (La *Semaine Littéraire*, Geneva, December 19, 1916.)

[17] *Cf.* Harry Elmer Barnes, *Perpetual War for Perpetual Peace* (Caldwell, Idaho: Caxton Printers, 1953), p. 35: "The columnist Jay Franklin gave us a good picture of the fruits of interventionism. Since 1900 under five Republican Presidents *no* casualties, under three Democratic Presidents (Theodore Roosevelt, Taft, Harding, Coolidge, Hoover, versus Wilson, Roosevelt, and Truman) '0' versus 1,628,480 casualties." (Here the casualties under J. F. Kennedy and L. B. Johnson obviously are not yet included.) Naturally, Americans are *by nature* isolationists—and so are the Russians, *if* they are not driven by specific ideologies. Felix Somary in his *op. cit.* discusses this in a brilliant passage and adds the remark, "Americans like to be judges of the world, not its rulers, but do not realize that the former position cannot be achieved without the latter" (p. 101). Viewed from this angle the Republican party is "naturally" the more American party.

[18] Ben Hecht in his *Erik Dorn* referred to Wilson in Paris as a "long-faced virgin trapped in a bawdy house and calling in valiant tones for a glass of lemonade." *Cf.* Oscar Cargill, *Intellectual America: Ideas on the March*, (New York: Macmillan, 1941), p. 504. In summing up the three main actors at the Paris Peace Conference, John Maynard Keynes described: "Clemenceau, aesthetically the noblest; the President, morally the most admirable; Lloyd George, intellectually the subtlest. Out of their disparities and weaknesses the Treaty was born, child of the least worthy attributes of its parents, without nobility, without morality, without intellect." *Cf.* J. M. Keynes, "David Lloyd George" in *Essays and Sketches in Biography* (New York: Meridian Books, 1956), p. 180.

[19] Woodrow Wilson, to be true, had not only been professor, but even professor of government at a leading American university. A defender of democratic amateurism and a critic of expertise could point this out triumphantly and use it as an argument. Wilson knew neither geography, history, neither sociology nor theology. The humanities (and perhaps not only the humanities) can never be properly understood outside of their wider context. In these domains specialization has always been fatal. On the American professor *vide* also C. Wright Mills, *White Collar: The American Middle Classes* (New York: Oxford University Press, 1951), pp. 129ff.

[20] Whatever the faults and shortcomings of William II, (and there were indeed many) he never actively prepared World War I. We have this on the

authority of several historians, among them G. P. Gooch and Arthur Rosenberg who in 1919 had been charged by the German Social Democratic party to make an investigation of the primary responsibility of the German Emperor for the holocaust. His negative conclusions can be found in his *Die Entstehung der deutschen Republic, 1871-1918* (Berlin: Rowohlt, 1930), pp. 66-67. Yet in the American folklore "Kaiser Bill" was the villain, the good boys were the forty-eighters. Hence one should not be surprised that Mr. Walt W. Rostow, one of the professional planners in the State Department, declared on September 9, 1963, that the Federal Republic is the fulfilment of the dream of the men who produced in 1848 the liberal Frankfurt Parliament, though the Revolution was then crushed by the Prussians and the German nationalists. Statements like these are screamingly funny because the liberal Frankfurt Parliament offered a (hitherto inexistent) German crown to the King of Prussia whereas the forty-eighters *were* the nationalists working for a German *national* state excluding nationally pluralistic Austria.

[21] *Cf.* Gladstone's election speech at Edinburgh, March 17, 1880, quoted by Carlton J. H. Hayes, *op. cit.*, p. 38.

[22] *Cf.* Introduction, note 3. Wilson's misunderstanding of Russia was only part and parcel of his misreading of the European mind. For a Continental Russia is more comprehensible than the United States (even if he prefers the latter to the former). *Cf.* the admission of Ida F. Görres in *Zwischen den Zeiten* (Olten and Freiburg i. Br.: Walter, 1961), pp. 429-430.

[23] Quoted by Carlos Pereyra, *El crimen de Woodrow Wilson*, Madrid, 1917.

[24] *Cf.* Burton J. Hendrick, *The Life and Letters of Walter H. Page* (Garden City, N. Y.: Doubleday, Page and Co., 1925), vol. 1, p. 188. Page's most interesting views on Europe ("In all the humanities, we are a thousand years ahead of any people here, etc.") can be found in a long letter to Frank N. Doubleday, dated Bournemouth, May 29, 1916.

[25] *Cf. The Intimate Papers of Colonel House*, Charles Seymour, ed. (Boston: Houghton, Mifflin, 1928), vol. 4, pp. 13-14.

[26] *Cf.* Walter H. Peters, *The Life of Benedict XV* (Milwaukee, Bruce, 1959), pp. 149-151.

[27] Fénélon said the "peace treaties are meaningless if you are the stronger one and if you force your neighbor to sign a treaty to avoid greater evil; then he signs in the same way as a person who surrenders his purse to a brigand who points his pistol at his throat." *Cf.* Fénélon, "Direction pour la conscience d'un roi," in *Oeuvres* (Paris, 1787), vol. 25, t. 3, p. 489.

[28] *Cf.* Charles A. Beard and Mary R. Beard, *The Rise of American Civilization* (New York: Macmillan, 1948), vol. 4. ("The American Spirit"), p. 357.

[29] The "far south Tyrol," the *Trentino*, is Italian by language, but the vast majority of the Trentinese did not want to join Italy. Cf. Chapter XI,

note 6. When in 1915 the Italians demanded territories from their embattled Austrian (former) allies, Vienna reluctantly promised them the *Trentino* after the war. This so embittered a young Italian *Reichsrat*-deputy hitherto loyal to Austria, that he embraced the Italian cause. He felt betrayed. His name was Alcide de Gasperi. *Cf.* Dr. Friedrich Funder, *Von Gestern ins Heute* (Vienna: Herold, 1953), pp. 527-528. In this book de Gasperi is not mentioned by name. The late Dr. Funder informed me about the identity of the deputy who had opened his heart to him.

[30] *Cf.* Thomas A. Bailey, *Woodrow Wilson and the Lost Peace* (New York: Macmillan 1944), p. 252.

[31] *Cf.* S. Miles Bouton, Robert Dell and Charles H. Herford, *English and American Voices about the German South Tyrol* (New York: C. J. Bernard, 1925).

[32] *Cf.* J. M. Keynes, *The Economic Consequences of the Peace* (1919) (New York: Harcourt, Brace, 1920), p. 43.

[33] *Ibid.*, p. 31n.

[34] *Cf.* George F. Kennan, *American Diplomacy 1900-1950* (Chicago: University of Chicago Press, 1951), p. 56.

[35] *Ibid.*, pp. 55-56.

[36] Lord Lansdowne's letter was published in the (London) *Daily Telegraph* on November 29, 1917. Its publication had been refused by the *Times*. A year earlier it had been sent to the Prime Minister. For the passage cited in the text, *cf.* Lord Newton, *Lord Lansdowne* (London: Macmillan, 1929), pp. 482-483. Walter Lippmann has well described the situation in 1917 prior to American intervention: "The existing governments had exhausted their imperium—their authority to bind and their power to command. With their traditional means they were no longer able to carry on their hyperbolic war, yet they were unable to negotiate peace. They had, therefore, to turn to the people. They had to ask still greater exertions and sacrifices. They obtained them by 'democratising' the conduct and the aims of the war, by pursuing total victory and by promising total peace." *Cf. op. cit.*, p. 12. Hence the "Holy War." André Malraux saw clearly that the French Revolution with its republicanism for export had to end in a bellicose "Islamic" expansion. (*La Nouvelle Revue Française*, vol. 3, no. 25, p. 18)

[37] Wilson was born, to be sure, on the Day of the Innocents, on Childermass. As could be expected, he was hailed by the Calvinists all over Europe as their Savior. *Cf.* Emile Doumergue, "Calvin et l'entente de Wilson à Calvin." *Revue de Métaphysique et de Morale*, vol. 25 (September-December, 1918), especially p. 825.

[38] *Cf. Letters of Franklin Lane*, A. W. Lane and L. H. Hall, eds. (Boston: Houghton, Mifflin, 1922), p. 297. Professor F. A. Hermens in his book *Democracy or Anarchy* (Notre Dame: University Press, 1941) claims that *Anschluss* after the war would have prevented (numerically) the Nazi electoral

victories. If, in all-German elections, the Austrians would have voted much like their Bavarian neighbors with whom they are linked by ethnic, racial, religious and cultural ties, the thesis of Professor Hermens seems correct.

[39] *Cf.* Stanley A. Hunter, *The Religious Ideals of the President* (Allahabad: Mission Press, 1914), p. 8.

[40] *Cf.* E. I. Woodward, *Three Studies in European Conservatism* (London: Constable, 1929), p. 228: *"Je suis leur chef: il faut hien que je les suive."* Naturally we like to see in the statesman that *rara avis*, the scholarly trained practitioner—or a practically trained scholar. Neither the pure scholar not the uneducated pragmatist will do . . . which is equally true of the great medical men. *Cf.* the views of the Arab sage, Ibn Khaldun, quoted in Chapter 3 of his "Prolegomena," in *Arab Philosophy*, Charles Issawi, ed. (London, 1950), pp. 64-66.

[41] *Cf.* Hugo Münsterberg, *American Patriotism and Other Social Studies* (New York: Moffat, Yard and Co., 1913) p. 3.

[42] *Ibid.*, pp. 15-16. Also *cf.* Denis W. Brogan, *The American Character* (New York: Knopf, 1944), p. 146.

[43] *Cf.* Ernst Bruncken, *Die amerikanische Volksseele*, quoted by Elias Hurwicz, *Die Seelen der Völker, Ihre Eigenarten und Bedeutung im Völkerleben*. (Gotha: Andreas Perthes, 1920), pp. 91-92. Joseph de Maistre said that "the prejudices of the nations are like boils, one has to touch them gently so as not to break the tissue." *Cf.* Sainte-Beuve, *Causeries de lundi*, (Paris: Garnier Frères, 1927), vol. 15, p. 80.

[44] *Cf.* Richard M. Weaver, *Ideas Have Consequences* (Chicago: University of Chicago Press, 1948), p. 76. On the medieval concept of the "Divine Rights of Kings" see particularly Fritz Kern, *op. cit.*, pp. 10-11, 283-284.

[45] Absolutism, including monarchical absolutism, is certainly a political aberration which was always rejected by European "conservatives." C. L. von Haller, to name only one typical representative of Romantic conservatism, (no less than Ludwig von Gerlach) equated royal absolutism with Jacobinism. *Cf.* Franz von Schnabel, *op. cit.*, vol. 4, p. 175.

[46] *Cf.* Reinhold Niebuhr, *op. cit.*, pp. 77-78. For the rational defense of monarchy *cf.* also C. Northcote Parkinson, *The Evolution of Political Thought* (London: University of London Press, 1958) with pertinent quotes from Simón Bolívar (p. 253), Alberdi (p. 259), and others. The arguments of this famous inventor of "Parkinson's Law" are on pp. 315-316.

[47] According to a letter from Walter Lippmann (who knew Herron) addressed to this writer, dated Washington D. C., May 17, 1956.

[48] The term "post-Protestant era" figures (as a possibility, not as a certainty) in Paul Tillich's theological thinking. *Cf.* his *The Protestant Era*, trsl. and edit. J. L. Adams (Chicago: University of Chicago Press 1948). "Post-Protestant" defines a mentality and outlook containing essential characteristics from the Reformation and the post-Reformation period in a secularized

form. All great religions have such a "version" wherever they have (or had) great cultural force or cohesion. Yet this is rarely the case with religious bodies in the dispersion where they often try to combine their own "factual" theology with mind patterns of the majority. A Spanish Presbyterian—however fervent —is in a certain way a "Catholic," and a Danish Catholic a "Lutheran." And let us also bear in mind that the only Church which *officially* calls itself Protestant is the Protestant Episcopal Church of America (and it is not too happy about this either). Neither Luther nor Calvin, neither Zwingli nor Melanchthon would have tolerated this label, a term of insult and contempt coined by the Catholic Counter-Reformers. (In Europe the term "Protestant" is officially employed only in the Anglican Coronation Service, but in *none* of the Continental rituals.)

[49] Compton MacKenzie called the League of Nations quite aptly a "typist's dream of the Holy Roman Empire, for politicians a new hypocrisy, for diplomats a sitting on addled eggs." *Cf. My Religion* (New York: Appleton, 1926), p. 52.

[50] *Cf.* Document VII a, of Volume 12 of the *Herron Papers*. (In Manuscript, Hoover Institute, Stanford, California.) Letter of Herron to Wilson, dated Geneva, March 20, 1919. Calvin, Herron insisted, not Luther, is the father of the Scottish Covenanters and the English Puritans.

[51] Reply of Wilson to Herron, Document XIII, *Ibid.* Letter dated Paris, April 17, 1919. Wilson was delighted with this proposition.

[52] *Ibid.*, Document XXVII, vol. 12. Letter dated Geneva, April 17, 1920. There are thirteen larger cardboard boxes with the *Herron Papers*, most of them retyped. To read them all over the years was a major effort for me.

[53] *Cf. The Letters of William James*, Henry James, ed. (Boston: Atlantic Monthly Press, 1920), Vol. 1, p. 139. Sir Charles Petrie, very much to the contrary, called the major tragedy of Central Europe the fact that German unity was not accomplished under the leadership of Austria rather than of Prussia. *Cf.* his *Twenty Years Armistice and After* (London: Eyre and Spottiswoode, 1940), p. 126.

[54] *Cf.* Th. G. Masaryk, *The Making of a State*, Henry Wickham Steed, ed. (New York: Stokes and Co., 1927), pp. 308-309.

[55] *Ibid.*, p. 375.

[56] *Cf.* Raymond Aron, *Les guerres en chaîne* (Paris: Gallimard, 1951), p. 34. Th. G. Masaryk's son, Jan Masaryk (the later, ill-fated foreign minister murdered by "defenestration") was captain in an Imperial Royal Regiment until the collapse of the Danubian Monarchy. He had nothing but praise for the old regime. *Cf.* Indro Montanelli, "La sua insomnia si chiama Gottwald," *Il Nuovo Corriere della Sera*, March 11, 1948, p. 1. A very good summing up of the anti-Hapsburg sentiments, disastrous for everybody in their final consequences, has been given by Carl J. Burckhardt in a letter to Hugo von Hoffmansthal. *Cf.* H. v. Hofmannsthal, Carl J. Burckhardt, *Briefwechsel* (Frankfurt: S. Fischer, 1956) p. 75 (letter dated November, 1921).

[57] *Cf.* Th. G. Masaryk, *op. cit.*, p. 309.

[58] *Cf.* Mitchell Pirie Briggs, *George Herron and the European Settlement* (Palo Alto: Stanford University Press, 1932), p. 29.

[59] The United States first declared war on Germany, then on Austria-Hungary and finally on Turkey. *Bulgaria was left out.* The Bulgar minister in Washington during World War I tried to make himself as inconspicuous as possible. (In World War II the United States refused to declare war on Finland, etc.)

Still, George D. Herron in a letter to Hugh R. Wilson, American *chargé d'affaires* in Berne, urged a declaration of war against Bulgaria, "the worst enemy, after Prussia, of Americanism in Europe." (Dateline, Geneva, May 25, 1918). *Cf. Herron Papers*, vol. 9, document I. One truly wonders why "Americanism" was so uniquely incompatible with "Bulgarianism" . . . and how Herron could realize this by "long distance."

[60] Actually, Maximilian of Mexico, who sympathized with every "progressive" cause in Europe, was an extreme liberal. Thus he had "ideological differences" with his brother Franz Joseph who was a moderate liberal. (It is quite possible that Maximilian was a Freemason.) Benito Juárez, on the other hand, played up by the present Mexican regime as a fierce nationalist, was really an agent of the hated *Gringos* and enjoyed full American support. Popular historiography is at least as confused as politics.

[61] The Inquisition, naturally, never operated in Austria. As a matter of fact, a Lutheran in the eighteenth century was much freer in Austria than a Catholic in England.

[62] *Cf. Dictionary of American Biography* (New York: Scribner's, 1932), vol. 8, pp. 594-595.

[63] Iowa College was founded by Congregationalists in 1847. The town of Grinnell in which the college was located had been named after Josiah Grinnell (1821-1891), a Congregationalist minister who had been a close friend of John Brown of Harper's Ferry fame.

[64] The *Rand School of Social Science* in New York, which always had a strong socialistic flavor, was founded by this wealthy family.

[65] *Cf. A Socialist Wedding, Being an Account of a Marriage of George D. Herron and Carrie Rand* (New York: Knickerbocker Press, n.d.).

[66] *Cf.* George D. Herron, *Ot revolyutsii k revolyutsii, Uroki parizhskoy kommuny 1871 g.* (St. Petersburg, O. N. Rutenberg, 1906).

[67] *Cf.* George D. Herron, *The Day of Judgment* (Chicago: Kerr and Co., 1906), p. 29.

[68] *Cf.* Thomas A. Bailey, *op. cit.*, p. 330. Two days after the German declaration of limitless submarine warfare on February 2, 1917, Wilson declared, "in response to a question as to which side he 'wished to win,' that 'he didn't wish either side to win.' " But was he sincere? Mr. Laughlin who was attaché to the American Embassy to London in 1914 told this writer in 1937 about Wilson's precipitated offers to aid Britain, offers which Ambas-

sador Page refused to pass on, informing the President that his messages were incompatible with diplomatic usage.

[69] Pressure of time prevented me from fully using my research material. In the meantime the Austrian historian, Professor Heinrich Benedikt (Vienna) published salient parts of Herron's dealings in *Die Friedensaktion der Meinl-Gruppe 1917-1918* (Graz-Cologne: Hermann Böhlau, 1962). His book also contains a portrait of Herron, who looks exactly as one would expect him to look.

[70] *Cf*. Herron's cable to the President after the first news of his illness reached Europe: "Multitudes beyond number rejoice with me in the supreme news of your recovery. You are still the hope of the world. You are the living barrier against universal reaction and dark ages. For the sake of all mankind you must and will get well and fight on." (*Herron Papers*, vol. 5, document XXII).

[71] *Cf*. George D. Herron, *Germanism and the American Crusade* (New York: Kennerley, 1918), *Woodrow Wilson and the World's Peace* (New York: Kennerley, 1917): *The Menace of Peace* (London: Allen and Unwin, 1917).

[72] *Cf*. Wilson's letter, dated October 1, 1917, in *Herron Papers*, Vol. 12, Document I.

[73] We want here merely to cite a letter of Herron to Hugh R. Wilson, dated July 11, 1918. (*Herron Papers*, vol. 2. document XXVIII). It deals with Admiral von Hintze whom he had met before the war:

> I regard Admiral von Hintze as one of the most sinister figures in the political world of today. Indeed, I am convinced there is no other such dangerous character in any place of great power. He is unqualifiedly a cynic, and his mind is clearly medieval in its constitution and methods; his conception of world politics differs not from the conception that prevailed in the courts of Borgia and Sforza. . . . He is clever to the last degree; and not only Machiavellian, but positively diabolical in both his thinking and acting: and his mental and tactical diabolism are clothed with medieval refinement.

All of which clearly sheds a new light on the Middle Ages and the Devil.

[74] According to Walter Lippmann, the main drafter of the Fourteen Points, the original plan of the President foresaw merely a federalization of Austria-Hungary, not its destruction—precisely the plan of Emperor Charles. (Personal information.) Influences and events changed his original plan and thus the foundations of World War II were carefully laid.

[75] *Cf*. Stefan Osuský, *George D. Herron, Dôvernik Wilsonov počas vojny* (Pressburg: Naklad "Prudov," 1925), p. 52. This is an invaluable and indispensable book written by the former Czechoslovak minister in Paris. Osuský, a Slovak student at the University of Chicago, knew Herron intimately. Much of the book is dedicated to Herron's political philosophy.

[76] Even stronger were the reactions of Clemenceau and Ribot, the French Foreign Minister, to the Austrian peace action aided by Prince Sixtus of Parma, the brother of Empress Zita. Lansing decried Clemenceau's action as "a piece of the most outstanding stupidity . . . an unpardonable blunder." Cf. *The War Memoirs of Robert Lansing* (Indianapolis-New York: Bobbs Merrill, 1935), p. 265.

[77] Cf. *Herron Papers,* vol. 1. document XXVI, letter to Hugh R. Wilson.

[78] Cf. Heinrich Lammasch, *Seine Aufzeichnungen, sein Wirken und seine Politik,* Marga Lammasch and Hans Sperl, eds. (Vienna: Deuticke, 1922), pp. 99-102.

[79] Cf. George D. Herron, *Defeat in Victory* (Boston: Christopher Publishing House, 1924), p. 53.

[80] Cf. *Herron Papers,* vol. 12, document XXVII, letter to William A. White, dated April 17, 1920.

[81] Cf. letter of G. D. Herron to Stewart E. Bruce, dated November 1, 1923, published in *Fight for Light Leaflet* (Hamburg: Antikriegsschuldlügenliga, R. I. Orchelle, ed.).

[82] Cf. James Kerney, *The Political Education of Woodrow Wilson* (New York: The Century Company, 1925), p. 476.

[83] That so many Jews accept democracy and believe in it with almost religious fervor can only be explained by the fact that they become fascinated with its egalitarian aspect while forgetting democracy's majoritarian nature . . . and except in Israel they always will be in a minority. An eminent German sociologist, Winfried Martini, has commented upon this paradox in his crucially important work *Das Ende aller Sicherheit, Eine Kritik des Westens* (Stuttgart: Deutsche Verlagsanstalt, 1954), pp. 16-19.

[84] Cf. *Herron Papers,* vol. 13, document IX. Letter to Leo Ragaz, dated April 1, 1919. Naturally, it was Herron's argument (at that time), that "International Finance" with its center in Paris was dominated by German Jews who acted on Germany's behalf. Hitler's argument was that international Jewry was intrinsically and congenitally anti-German.

[85] Cf. *Herron Papers,* vol. 13, documents IX and VII, and vol. 11, document 11. In typical Nazi fashion Herron thought that international Jewish finance was collaborating with the Vatican and that the emissaries of these dark forces met in Fribourg.

[86] *Ibid.,* vol. 11, document XVII. Letter dated Geneva, October 15, 1919, addressed to the Socialist leader George Strobell, on the early Socialist contacts of Herron and his second marriage. Cf. also Philip M. Crane, *The Democrat's Dilemma* (Chicago: Regnery, 1964), pp. 75-78.

[87] Cf. George D. Herron, *Umsturz und Aufbau. Der Pariser Friede und die Jugend Europas* (Berlin: Rowohlt, 1920). No translator mentioned.

[88] Cf. George D. Herron, *The Greater War*, p. 27.

[89] Cf. George D. Herron, *Umsturz und Aufbau*, p. 7.

[90] *Ibid.*, pp. 16-17.

[91] *Cf.* Le Capitaine De Gaulle, *La discorde chez l'ennemi* (Paris: Berger-Levrault, 1924), particularly p. vi. The (London) *Times* in October 1918 also admitted in an editorial that the impending end of the war was in part caused by the effectiveness of Allied propaganda.

[92] *Cf.* Thomas A. Bailey, *op. cit.*, p. 49.

[93] *Cf.* Max Weber in the *Frankfurter Zeitung*, October 27, 1918.

[94] *Cf. Herron Papers*, vol. 10, document XXV. Letter to Norman Thomas, dated Geneva, April 27, 1920.

[95] *Cf. Herron Papers*, vol. 11, document XVII. Letter to George Strobell, dated Geneva, October 15, 1919.

[96] Robert (Roberto) Michels, born in Cologne in 1876, was a German Social Democrat who had migrated finally to Italy where he received a professorship. Together with Gaetano Mosca and Marchese Vilfredo Pareto he became the father of the thesis that every democracy is, in fact, a party oligarchy. Later, like so many other Socialists, he supported fascism. Curiously enough, the original (Fascist) *Encyclopedia Italiana* omits his name, but he is mentioned in the "Third Supplement" (1961). He died in Rome in 1936. His main work was *Zur Soziologie des Parteienwesens in der modernen Demokratie* (Leipzig: Kröner, 1925). *Cf.* also his "Studii sulla democrazia e sull'autorità" in *Collana di Studi Fascisti* (Florence: La Nuova Italia, 1923). No. 24-25, and *Sozialismus und Faschismus in Italien* (Munich-Karlsruhe: G. Braun, 1925), 2 vols. (The informations on Robert Michels in *Chi è ? Dizionario degli Italiani d'oggi*, Rome: Formiggini, 1931, pp. 495-496 are not too revealing.)

[97] *Cf.* George D. Herron, *The Revival of Italy* (London: Allen and Unwin, 1922), pp. 76-87.

[98] *Cf.* Herron's letter to Mrs. Charles Berry, dated Geneva, November 10, 1922. To be found in the Hoover Institute, Near East Department, H. 567, pp. 5-6.

Chapter XVI

[1] The crucial point of accusation was the "Potsdam Crown Council" on July 5, 1914, in which allegedly the decision was taken to start a world war. This meeting, however, never took place. It figures in Article 231, but it was the merit of G. P. Gooch to have destroyed this evil legend. Yet Lloyd George was at least honest when he declared in all candor on March 3, 1921 that the entire Versailles Treaty rested squarely on the German war guilt. "We want to make it clear," he said, "that the German responsibility for the war has to be treated by the Allies as a *cause jugée*."

[2] *Cf.* Algernon Cecil, *Facing Hard Facts in Foreign Policy* (London: Eyre and Spottiswoode, 1941), p. 59: "For the scene of their labour the peace-

makers fixed upon Paris, which was of all places the least likely to countenance a dispassionate peace, and as a result secured for their chairman an old tiger of a man whose lack of religious opinions assured the absence of any spiritual quality in the settlement. They dictated instead of negotiating peace, which was a blunder if the goodwill of all parties was desired, and they failed to occupy the Rhine frontier, which was a crime if in the alternative they hoped to keep the enemy in permanent subjection. They assumed that a hard peace would produce hard cash, which it never did, and that a confession of guilt extorted by pressure would provoke repentance, which it never has.''

[3] Mr. J. O. B. Bland, Herron's contact man in the British Foreign Office, wrote to Herron on September 10, 1918: "If they want any suggestion what to do with the Germans after the war, they are welcome to my idea, which is that for five years they should only be admitted in civilized countries on taking out a dog license. And that is rough on the dogs." (*Herron Papers*, vol. 11, document XVIII.)

[4] *Cf. The Memoirs of Raymond Poincaré*, trsl. Sir George Arthur (London: Heinemann, 1929), vol. 3, pp. 11-12.

[5] When I lived in England in 1935-1936 I wrote the Rt. Hon. David Lloyd George a letter to the effect that he was widely quoted as saying that Germany could not be carved up since it was a "Protestant country," while there could be no such qualms about Catholic Austria-Hungary. I asked him to confirm or to deny this rumor. He replied through his secretary (whom he subsequently married) that he was unfortunately too busy to answer my query. This letter, to my regret, was destroyed as a result of the Allied air raids preparing the Russian occupation of Vienna in March 1945. On the general ignorance of Lloyd George see also *World Within World; The Autobiography of Stephen Spender* (London: Hamish Hamilton, 1951), pp. 79-80.

[6] *Cf.* Ernst Kornemann, "Von antiken Staat," *Breslauer Universitätsreden* (Breslau: Ferdinand Hirt, 1927), no. 1, p. 35.

[7] *Cf.* H. A. Macartney, *Problems of the Danube Basin* (Cambridge, England: Cambridge University Press, 1942), p. 98.

[8] *Ibid.*, p. 71.

[9] In 1918 Czech exile politicians concluded in Pittsburgh a treaty with Slovak representatives (some of them American citizens) stipulating that the two ethnic units should form a common state for ten years. When the Slovak professor Vojtěch Tuka in 1928 declared in a newspaper article that there now existed a *vacuum iuris*, he was promptly tried for high treason and condemned by the Czech authorities. (This was not the end of Tuka's political career: nearly blind, he left jail when Slovakia became almost independent, was hailed as a national martyr, became prime minister of the Slovak Republic and was executed by the then half-Communist Prague government as a "traitor" in 1947. His tragedy mirrors the calamitous emergency in which an ill-conceived and ill-constructed Central Europe found itself ever since 1918.)

[10] The Czech Atlas, *Atlas Republiky Ceskoslovenské*, Jaroslav Pantof-

líček, ed. (Prague: Nakladatelstvo Orbis, 1935), refused to distinguish between Czechs and Slovaks. The official language of Czechoslovakia was (and is) "Czechoslovak"—a truly nonexisting language.

[11] The official Yugoslav atlases showed no difference between Slovenes, Croats, Serbs, and Macedo-Bulgars either. Only Germans, Magyars, Albanians, Rumanians, and Italians figured separately on the ethnic maps—yet even Roosevelt knew better. Robert E. Sherwood tells us that "the President expressed his often repeated opinion that the Croats and Serbs had nothing in common and that it is ridiculous to try to force such antagonistic peoples to live together under one government. *Cf.* his *Roosevelt and Hopkins* (New York: Harper Brothers, 1948), p. 711.

[12] Here we have the tragic realization of Mazzini's dreams who declared that "the indisputable tendency of our epoch is towards the reconstitution of Europe into a certain number of homogeneous states as nearly as possible equal in population and in extent." *Cf.* Graham Wallas, *Human Nature in Politics* (New York: Crofts, 1921), p. 290. This led, unfortunately, to the artificial coalescence of related, but hostile nations in order to make it possible for them to stand up to their bigger neighbors. These artificial combinations, however, were bound to fail.

[13] *Cf.* William Flavelle Monypenny and George Earle Buckle, *The Life of Benjamin Disraeli, Earl of Beaconsfield* (London: John Murray, 1929), vol. 1, pp. 998-999.

[14] *Cf.* Winston S. Churchill, *The Second World War*, (London: Cassell, 1948), vol. 1, pp. 9, 21-50.

[15] *Ibid.*, p. 8.

[16] *Cf.* Winston S. Churchill, *op. cit.*, (1954), vol. 6, p. 640.

[17] *Cf.* H. A. Macartney, *Hungary and Her Successors* (London: Oxford University Press, 1937).

[18] The Croats then had a very substantial amount of autonomy: they ruled over a Serb and a (very small) Italian minority.

[19] To my knowledge this is the only monument in honor of a political assassin in Europe—with the exception of statues commemorating Wilhelm Oberdank (Guillermo Oberdan), a neurotic who tried to murder Emperor Franz Joseph but was caught before he could strike. He figures as an Italian national hero.

[20] Nothing in history is entirely new. As a precedent we had the French folly, all through the sixteenth, seventeenth and even during the first half of the eighteenth century, to strengthen the power of Brandenburg-Prussia. After 1766 Prussia became politically and morally a British protectorate and also fully enjoyed American sympathies. (*Cf.* Chapter XV, Note 53). When the news of the Franco-Prussian War reached the House of Representatives in Washington, a spontaneous applause broke out. *Cf.* Othon Guerlac, "Le suicide de Prévost-Paradol à Washington et l' opinion américaine," *Revue de littérature comparée* vol. 8, no. 1. (January-March 1928), p. 116.

[21] Today the Austrian payment balance is in the black because industrialization and agrarian improvements have made great strides in the last thirty years, and the rather substantial tourist trade acts as an equalizing factor, thus making up for the imports, being still larger than the exports.

[22] The *Anschluss*, the union of Austria with Germany, had not merely identitarian-ethnic motives. Vienna had been the capital of the Holy Roman Empire, the "First Reich," whose insignia remained in Vienna's Imperial treasury. The Hapsburgs, not the Hohenzollerns were the old German dynasty. When Madame de Staël came to Vienna, she commented that, at least, she had arrived at the *capitale de l'Allemagne*. Even Franz Joseph called himself in 1908 "a German prince." Most Austrians today have an independent feeling of statehood but not necessarily of what we over here call "nationality." Still the best people in Austria opposed the *Anschluss* in 1938, just as decent people in West Germany oppose reunion with the "German Democratic Republic" under the conditions laid down by the Red Pankow regime.

[23] No country called Czechoslovakia, Yugoslavia, or Rumania existed before 1850. "Rumania" was founded in 1857 (without historic precedence) through the union of Wallachia and Moldavia: Czechoslovakia was established in 1918. "Yugoslavia" was the new official name (1929) for the "Kingdom of Serbs, Croats and Slovenes" founded in 1918. (Hungary, Poland, Lithuania, and Bulgaria, on the other hand, were ancient historic realms.)

[24] There was a "Czech Legion," consisting of ex-prisoners-of-war, in Russia. They fought in the beginning against Austro-Hungarian armies, but later against the Communists. Placed finally in a tight spot in Siberia they "bought" their free passage to Vladivostok by surrendering to the Red Army their foe, the "white" Admiral Koltshak, who was shot. *Cf.* Generalleutnant Konstantin W. Sakharov, *Die verratene Armee* (Berlin: Reichel, 1939), pp. 358-361. Another "Czech Legion" was established in Italy, where it was commanded by Colonel Graziani who played such a big (and fatal) role in the Fascist movement, in the Ethiopian War and in Mussolini's "Italian Social Republic." The officers taken over from the Austro-Hungarian army were not overly trusted and played secondary roles. (The Austro-Hungarian army, on the other hand, had little ethnic or religious prejudice. The last generalissimo of the Imperial-Royal army was a Transylvanian Lutheran, the last Chief Admiral a Hungarian Calvinist, and the Commander on the Italian front a Greek-Orthodox Serb.)

[25] *Cf.* Professor Caroline Robbins (Bryn Mawr), "The Teaching of European History in the United States," *Bulletin of the Polish Institute of Arts and Sciences in America*, vol. 2. no. 4 (July, 1944), pp. 1110-1111.

[26] I remember that of America's leading universities in 1937 only Harvard had a minor geography department. (The only university with a reputation in geography was Clark University in Worcester, Mass.) Geography at best eked out a humble existence as a poorly endowed chair in the Department of Geology. On the Continent, however, two hours a week are dedicated to

536

geography, (an obligatory subject) in every high school-college. The same is true of history.

[27] Here Jefferson insists that Americans are better than anybody else. "If all the sovereigns of Europe were to set themselves to work to emancipate the minds of their subjects from their present ignorance and prejudice and that as zealously as now they attempt the contrary, a thousand years could not place them on the high ground on which our people are now setting out." This reminds one sharply of the thousand-year backwardness accredited to Europeans by Walter H. Page. Did Jefferson conceive of a *racial* superiority of Americans? At least our great demócrat advocated harems for the elite to spread their superior qualities. *Cf.* Lester J. Cappon, *The Adams-Jefferson Letters* (Chapel Hill: University of North Carolina Press, 1959), vol. 2. pp. 387ff. American nationalism, we should not forget, was stronger in the past than it is today. Clara von Gerstner heard over 120 years ago an orator in Charleston affirming that Americans "possess an intelligence not exceeded by any portion of the world." *Cf.* her *Beschreibung einer Reise durch dei Vereinigten Staaten in den Jahren 1838 bis 1840* (Leipzig: J. C. Hinrich, 1842), p. 295. Lincoln in an address to the New Jersey State Senate in 1861 referred to Americans as the "almost chosen people of God." *Cf. Collected Works of Abraham Lincoln* (New Brunswick, N. J.: Rutgers University Press, 1953), vol. 4, p. 236. Today the left (and near left) preach an American masochism, criticizing and denigrating all American values and traditions.

[28] *Cf.* Richard Hofstadter, *Anti-Intellectualism in American Life* (London: Jonathan Cape, 1964), pp. 50-51.

[29] An American aristocracy? The expression might not be popular but Grund wrote in 1839, "I have heard more talk about aristocracy and family in the United States than during my whole previous life in Europe." (*op. cit.*, p. 145)

[30] "Post-Protestant" civilizations instinctively reject extremes, but the "radical," as the word implies, wants to "go to the roots." As I have pointed out in *Liberty or Equality?* "radicalism" disappears in Europe's *Orbis Reformatus* by the eighteenth century—except in denominationally mixed Germany. Yet, significantly enough, one spoke in Germany in jest about *Radikalinskis*, as if they were Slavs. The Catholic and Eastern Church world never had the cult of the *juste milieu* (as Herzen and Leontyev remarked). *Cf.* Chapter XIV, Note 28.

[31] An anarchical tendency is not *per se* a leftist one. Henry Adams called himself quite aptly a "Christian Conservative Anarchist" and I would not be reluctant to use this term for myself. *Cf.* the letter of Henry Adams to Elizabeth Cameron, in *Letters of Henry Adams (1892-1918)*, W. C. Ford, ed. (Boston: Houghton Mifflin, 1938), p. 364. Anarchism pure and simple, after all, is nothing but extreme liberalism and individualism. Political anarchism of the nineteenth and twentieth century, however, had strong leftist implications.

³² There are, as a matter of fact, occasionally women of real genius. I have known three of them in my life.

³³ The views and ideas of William E. Dodd will be discussed on pp. 278-280.

³⁴ Ambassador Joseph E. Davies thought that the purge trials in the 1930s were absolutely genuine. *Cf.* his *Mission to Moscow* (New York: Simon and Schuster, 1941), pp. 155sq. This book was also filmed. As to Stalin, this was Mr. Davies' opinion: "A child would like to sit in his lap and a dog would sidle up to him." *Cf.* Foster Rhea Dulles, *op. cit.*, p. 4.

³⁵ A curiously antihistoric feeling pervades the leftist creeds. Gerrard Winstanley in *The Laws of Freedom* (1952) not only insisted that science (and not metaphysics) alone should be taught, but also that history should be kept out of the curricula of schools, because history looked "backward" and not "forward." *Cf.* Friedrich Heer, *op. cit.*, pp. 46-47. On the other hand, Yves Simon correctly pointed out that there is no proper and fruitful understanding of history without theology. ("Philosophie chrétienne, Notes complémentaires," *Etudes Carmélitaines*, XIX, vol. 1. pp. 114-115.) And Duff Cooper is right when he says, "Perhaps one of the reasons why so little is learned from experience is that the men who conduct the affairs of the nations are always changing and that too few of them read history. This is particularly true of democracy." *Cf. Old Men Forget* (London: Hart, Davis, 1953), pp. 193-194.

History irks leftists because, if they do not ignore it altogether, they have to "rewrite" it, which means that they have to forge it. This they have to do since they have a concrete concept of the future and the (artificially adapted) past must appear to be an organic and logical preparation of the "shape of things to come." Leftists (and this includes the radical democrats) have to be suspicious of history because on their program is the "end of history"—at least of history as we understand the term. Even the perfect global democracy of the convinced "democratist" is utopia, is paradise on earth. As far as history generally is taught in "programmatic democracies," it assumes the character of an evolution (interspread with revolutions) toward a specific goal: beatitude for the millions. This view is also quite deeply imbedded in American popular feelings. Writes Professor Eugene N. Anderson, "European history in the hundred years after Napoleon has been regarded in the United States as the story of the slow, but certain victory of liberalism over the *ancien régime*. In writing this history the episodes emphasized have been those in which liberalism clashed with the old order and either overcame it or, unfortunately, was temporarily defeated by it. American historians have assumed that the goal of the century was to establish the ascendancy of the American social and political ideals: they have interpreted European history according to their own wishes, and they have been abetted in this work by the memoirs and biographies of liberal exiles from the Continent and the tendency to translate these works about Continental history which fitted their own theories." (*Social Edu-*

cation, May 1938.) All this optimism, needless to say, is equally applicable to the Asian scene. Today democratism and socialism have replaced the old liberal outlook.

[36] Representative Sol Bloom of the Democratic party, to quote an instance, was a warm admirer of Mussolini.

[37] William II knew about Dreyfus' innocence but could not publicly intervene. Had he done it, he would only have aggravated Dreyfus' position. However, he informed Queen Victoria of the truth. H. B. von Bülow, the German chargé d'affaires in Paris wrote to Chancellor Hohenlohe that the verdict against Dreyfus was a "mixture of vulgarity and cowardice, the surest sign of barbarism," and that France "has therewith excluded herself from the family of civilized nations." *Cf.* Wilhelm Herzog, *Der Kampf einer Republik* (Zürich, 1933), cited by Hannah Arendt, *The Origins of Totalitarianism* (New York: Harcourt, Brace, 1951), p. 91, n. 6.

[38] The Russian philosopher Vladimir Solovyov demanded that after the assassination of Emperor Alexander II the murderer be handed over to the Holy Synod for religious instruction and spiritual regeneration. Yet this sensible proposal was rejected and the law carried out: for a successful or unsuccessful attempt to murder a member of the Imperial Family Russia had a statutory death sentence (and sometimes for this crime only). *Cf.* Fëdor Stepun, "Poet—providyets, K stolyetiyu so dnya rozhdyeniay Vladimira Solovyova," *Za Svobodu*, 1953, no. 7, p. 7. The highly strung Irish lady who wounded Mussolini was returned for medical attention to the British Isles. Drčil, who failed to kill Dollfuss, got a slight jail sentence, so did Jawurek who gravely wounded the Austrian Chancellor, Monsignor Ignaz Seipel (and thus eventually caused his death). The assassin of Empress Elizabeth was imprisoned for life. Friedrich Adler, who murdered Prime Minister Count Stügkh during World War I, was formally condemned to death but was released from jail a year later. The French, to be true, were more spiteful: Gorgulov, the mentally deranged Russian assassin of President Doumer, was actually executed. Anatole Leroy-Beaulieu in *op. cit.*, vol. 2, iv. 7, tells us that during the rule of Alexander II from 1855 to the first months of 1879 only one execution took place in Russia, that of Karakosov, would-be assassin of the Emperor (1866). Nor had the number of murders increased since the days of Nicolas I. Percentagewise they were fewer than either in France or Prussia.

Were Sacco and Vanzetti guilty or not? The best book on this issue is Francis Russell, *Tragedy at Dedham*, (New York: McGraw-Hill, 1962). That author is convinced that Sacco either fired the fatal shot or knew who the assassin was, but Vanzetti was probably innocent (p. 466). The book by this leading American conservative writer is based on serious research.

[39] This I experienced in connection with the Chessman case, when I wrote for a Catholic American monthly a column merely *explaining* the psychological reasons for the European reaction. I even carefully avoided taking sides. As a result the editorial staff (mostly female) threatened to walk

out if the editor-in-chief were to publish the column. (Chessman had been indicted for rape, not for murder, and received the death sentence for a technicality: he had *dragged* his victim a few yards from the car. Cases like these highlight, above all, the fact that "East is East and West is West, and never the twain shall meet.")

[40] One wonders whether much-heralded experiments like those of the humane reformatory camp (in Bolshevo, for instance) did not serve as a smokescreen for less humanitarian "experiments"—further east and further north.

[41] One ought to say: something the Communists considered to be "new," nay, to be "American." The fascination which the long-distance (and thoroughly distorted) picture of America exercised on Russian communism has so far never been made the subject of serious research. In the writings of Lenin and Stalin we repeatedly encounter expressions of boundless admiration for America and of the sub-conscious feeling that all the United States needed was the elimination of wicked Wall Street—and everything would be all right. To Stalin the "style" of communism consisted in "Russian Revolutionary Dynamism" and in "American Pragmatism" (*Dyelovitost'* is best translated this way, but it also might mean sobriety, work-readiness, industriousness). *Cf.* I. Stalin, *Ob osnovakh Lyeninizma, K voprosam lyeninizma* (Moscow: Partizdat, WKP-b, 1935), pp. 75-76. Immediately after the Russian Revolution a new artistic and architectural style sprang up, called *Chicagizm*, and based on the notion of a new city in a new world without a past. Needless to say that *Chicagism* had no connection with the reality of Chicago.

Yet the Soviets knew how to impress their American visitors with the label "new," and this in spite of the fact, as I hinted, that the American is not truly a friend of the radically new, but rather of familiar things in a "bigger and better" edition. Nor was or is the USSR anything genuinely modern. It breathes the spirit of nineteenth-century bourgeois culture, *vide* the Moscow subway stations reminding one of great-grandmother's drawing room. Or look at the railroad station of Sotchi which resembles an oversexed Munich beer-brewer's dream of an Oriental harem. Still there is a certain type of American or British leftist whose heart beats faster when he sees travel folders inviting him to come to the "New Czechoslovakia," the "New Egypt," or the "New Algeria" where he can admire uniformed girls marching with broad smiles and shouldered submachine guns.

[42] I was told in Moscow in 1930 by an American woman that never-ever could I see in the United States such fine, modern, clean and streamlined streetcars as in the USSR. I could not prove the contrary as I had not yet been in America, but, I could show her a metal plate in one of the trolley cars indicating that it had been built prior to 1917. Was the good lady a Socialist or a Communist? Probably not. But she suffered from the modern malady of accepting unthinkingly the "axiom" of Socialist inevitability. This has been castigated by Gaetano Mosca in his *Elementi di scienza politica* (Turin: Fratelli

Boccao 1923), p. 319. After all, it seems better to rejoice in the shape of things to come than to deplore them.

[43] *Cf.* Chapter XV, Note 5.

[44] In the United States higher female education, public or private, is more markedly leftist than its male counterpart. "Conservative Clubs" in women's colleges are more frowned upon by the administrations than in men's colleges. This is not only due to the leftist *ressentiment* as delineated by Werner Sombart, but to the close links between leftism and militant feminism which are particularly strong in the English-speaking world. There feminism is not unrelated to the misogyny so strongly entrenched in America and Britain. It is naturally impossible to evaluate the position of women in a country by studying its laws. If this were the "key," one would have to think that women in English-speaking countries have a higher position than in old Russia or in France which is by no means the case. *Cf.* Randolph Bourne's letter published in *Twice a Year* (New York), no. 2 (Spring-Summer 1939), and no. 5-6 (Spring-Summer 1941). *Cf.* also chapter XIV Note 33.

[45] I heard the President's French only once. It was a unique experience. Still he was certain that he could "charm Stalin." Without a means of direct communication?

[46] According to Frances Perkins, Secretary of Labor, Roosevelt relied on mere hunches and he rarely read serious books. *Cf.* her *The Roosevelt I Knew* (New York: Viking, 1946), pp. 34, 352. To William C. Bullitt the President also confessed that he relied primarily on hunches, intuitions. *Cf.* W. C. Bullitt, "How We Won the War and Lost the Peace," *Life*, International Edition, vol. 5, no. 7 (September 27, 1948), p. 48. Here we read how Roosevelt insisted that Woodrow Wilson's decisions were also prompted by mere feelings. But "intuitivism" is a worldwide disease particularly frequent in democracies and personal dictatorships, where people without previous training, study or experience achieve dominant positions. Not only FDR and Wilson, but also Beneš and Hitler (with his *traumwandlerische Sicherheit*, the "inner security of a sleepwalker") boasted of it—and all failed fatally. There is no substitute for knowledge *and* experience. In the male sheer intuitivism is always coupled with mediocrity. And this observation is so pertinent for Napoleon, whose intellectual mediocrity startled Léon Bloy. *Cf.* his *Le mendiant ingrat (Journal de l'auteur 1892-1895)* (Paris: Mercure de France, 1946), p. 127.

[47] He was actually what psychiatrists call a mythomaniac. Without aiming at personal profit he invented stories, made statements and promises which had no basis in fact.

[48] This Nazi enthusiasm for the populist American tradition (the Jeffersonian-Jacksonian trend) has deeper psychological and theological roots which became apparent when one reads Soren Kierkegaard's violent strictures on democracy and his praise for monarchy, to be found in his diaries. *Cf. Die Tagebücher*, Hayo Gerdes, trsl. and ed. (Düsseldorf-Köln: Eugen

Diederichs, 1963), vol. 2, pp. 218, 220, 245-247, and *Christentum und Christenheit*, Eva Schlechta, ed. (Munich: Kösel, 1957), pp. 87, 286. *Cf.* also Chapter VII, Note 30.

[49] The Spanish character is aristocratic only in the sense that people are proud and have a sense of spiritual relativity. The beggar might address the passer-by with *hermanito*, "little brother." Upper-class arrogance is rare in Spain. *Cf.* also Salvador de Madariaga, *Hernán Cortés* (New York: Macmillan, 1941), pp. 40-41, H. F. Brownson, *Equality and Democracy* (Detroit: H. F. Brownson, 1897), p. 22, or Havelock Ellis, *The Soul of Spain* (New York: Houghton, Mifflin, 1909), pp. 12-13.

[50] *Cf.* Miguel de Unamuno y Jugo, *Vida de Don Quijote y Sanco* (Madrid: Renacimiento, 1914), pp. 213-214.

[51] Salvador de Madariaga in his *Spain* (New York: Creative Age Press, 1943), p. 332 after describing the 1934 rising, added: "I shall not dwell on atrocities. Both sides flooded Spain and even foreign countries with harrowing tales, both unfortunately true though both possibly exaggerated." (I knew reliable eye witnesses who had seen carved up priests in the windows of butcheries.) And then Madariaga adds: "The revolt of 1934 is unpardonable. . . . As for the Asturian miners, their revolt was entirely due to doctrinarian and theoretical prepossessions. Had the hungry Andalusian peasants risen in revolt, what could one do but sympathize with their despair? But the Asturian miners were well paid and, in fact, the whole industry, by a collusion between employers and workers, was kept working at an artificial level by state subsidies." (Here again I want to warn the reader not to put too much sense and reason into history but to remember man's fallen and irrational nature. He is always a sinner and usually a half-wit. I am amazed about historians, above all Christian historians, who overlook this fact. Who are the staunchest Communists in Sweden? The best-paid workers in all of Europe, the steel workers in Lapland.) *Cf.* Winfried Martini, *Freiheit auf Abruf, Die Lebenserwartung der Bundesrepublik* (Cologne-Berlin: Kiepenheuer und Witsch, 1960), p. 114. *Vide* also Fredrick B. Pike, "The Modernized Church in Peru: Two Aspects." *The Review of Politics*, vol. 26, no. 3 (July 1964), p. 316, where he speaks about the strong Communist domination of the Peruvian stevedores' trade union, of men who earn between $400.00 and $600.00 a month, a royal wage for Latin America. "Throughout Latin America," he adds, "it is those members of the middle class who have grown indifferent or hostile to spiritual forces that furnish the most recruits to communism. The Communist promise to bring about the fall of the upper class feeds the envy of the spiritually adrift but often economically securely anchored middle class." There is nothing more ridiculous than the naive cause-effect school in history which, above all, refuses to consider Grace and Evil.

[52] The spirit of the *Tercio* had been admirably portrayed by the French novelist Pierre MacOrlan in his novel *La Bandera*, made into a highly successful film in 1935. During the Spanish Civil War I had an opportunity to talk

542

to its founder, General Millan Astray, a real soldier with a hawk face who had only one arm and one eye.

[53] The pilot, Juan Antonio Ansaldo, finally wrote a book of recollections, *Mémoires d'un monarchiste espagnol, 1931-1952*, trsl. J. Viet (Monaco: Editions du Rocher, 1953). The memoirs are as violently antirepublican as they are anti-Franco.

[54] Louis Bolín, who was half-British, became after World War II the organizer of modern Spanish tourism attracting millions, which eventually made Spanish economic reconstruction possible in the late fifties. Without Bolín's groundwork the Neo-Liberals (mostly *Opus Dei* members) could never have effected the economic transformation of Spain.

[55] The vast majority of Spanish "Protestants" sided with the Republic, the Jews (who knew something about communism elsewhere) supported Franco, whom Hitler considered "a Freemason." *Cf*. Dr. Henry Picker, *op. cit*., p. 49. During the Civil War I had occasion to talk in Seville with Pastor Santos y Molina (today Evangelical Bishop in Madrid) who told me in the presence of a Press and Propaganda official very frankly about the grievances he had against the Nationalist government. About Franco and the Jews *cf*. pp. 331-332.

[56] To the Carlists (and to the serious historian) the monarchy ever since the days of Isabel II belonged to the Liberal order. The Spanish monarchy which fell in 1931 and the Portuguese monarchy which collapsed in 1910, in the eyes of the conservative Iberian, had been usurped by nonlegitimate, leftist-liberal monarchs. While in Portugal the liberal branch had died out with Dom Manuel, the Carlist branch in Spain had come to an end with the accidental death of Don Alfonso de Borbón in Vienna late in 1936.

[57] There is a symbolic value in the killing of a Carlist wearing a badge with the Sacred Heart of Jesus by the confused American hero in Hemingway's (historically valuable) novel *For Whom the Bell Tolls*.

[58] Franco had a brilliant record in the Rif-War. He was known to be extremely courageous. *Vide* the thumbnail sketch of Franco in Arturo Barea's *The Forging of a Rebel*, trsl. Ilse Barea (New York: Reynal and Hitchcock, 1946). Barea fought in that war with the *Tercio* and had a chance to see Franco in action. "I've seen murderers go white in the face because Franco had looked at them out of the corner of his eye." (p. 365). Franco's relationship with the Nazis appears partly in Dr. Picker's *Tischgespräche*, partly in the *Akten zur deutschen auswärtigen Politik 1918-1945* (Baden-Baden: Imprimerie Nationale, 1951), series D, vol. 3. From these documents it appears that there was no Nazi support of Franco prior to the rebellion (p. 3), that Franco was furious about Italian aerial attacks on Barcelona (p. 552), and that the German Ambassador in Paris (January 8, 1937) was certain that the Spanish Government would show no gratitude for the aid accorded it during the Civil War (pp. 181-182). From the *Tischgespräche* we learn about Hitler's contempt for Franco and for Catholic Spain.

[59] There is a beautiful Picasso-Museum in Barcelona, right in "Francospain." Military dictatorship is rarely ideology-ridden.

[60] The old influential liberal monthly, *Revista de Occidente*, founded by José Ortega y Gasset, has been revived three years ago. Its editor-in-chief is Ortega's son, José Ortega Spottorno.

[61] The persecution and massacre of nonorthodox Communists and other leftists is well described by George Orwell in his *Homage to Catalonia* (London: Secker and Warburg, 1938—Penguin, 1962).

[62] Most of the organizers of these "inner-leftist" massacres, men like Vladimir Antonov-Ovseyenko, were later killed in the Stalinist purges. Executions, like those of Nin, were part of the *Yezhovshtshina*, the bloody rule of Nikolay Ivanovitch Yezhov, who later also perished. (He was substituted by Beriya.) At least half of the men Ilya Ehrenburg knew in Spain became Stalin's victims—as he later admitted. Others who survived played subsequently infamous roles, like Ernst Gerö, the bloodhound of Budapest. The man, however, who played the role of Stalin's chief prosecutor (and who knew the truth all the time) was the renegade Pole Andrzej Wyszýnski, who for years represented the USSR at the United Nations in New York. The UN provided no disinfectant to those who, in the line of duty, had to shake hands with him.

[63] *Cf.* Madariaga, *op. cit.*, p. 397. Nin was a relative of Anais Nin, noted American writer.

[64] In spite of his violent condemnation of the warfare of the "Nationalists," Bernanos remained until his death a confirmed right-winger. One of his sons stayed until the very end as a volunteer in the Spanish National Army.

[65] Hugh Thomas, a British Labourite, in his *The Spanish Civil War* (London: Eyre and Spottiswoode, 1961) part II, ch. 19, reflects on the many assassinations and executions carried out by the Franco forces, but he tells us nothing about elaborate cruelties committed by the "Nationalists." The delirious atrocities perpetrated by the forces of enlightenment, progress, and democracy are, however, honestly dealt with in the following chapter and they make very gruesome reading. Ilya Ehrenburg in his mémoirs, "Lyudi, gody, zhinz,' " published in the summer 1962 in *Novy Mir* (Moscow), gives a less detailed picture of the atrocities and attributes them almost exclusively to the Anarchists. But Hugh Thomas is emphatic on the horrors committed by the "Tshekas."

[66] Which reminds one of the desecrations in St. Denis, where the graves of the French Kings can be found. In 1793 a revolutionary mob performed ghoulish acts on the remains of the "sons of St. Louis" . . . a real throwback to the practice of past ages. Hatred always comes from helplessness mixed with envy. Of course, to "punish the dead" is a time-honored pastime, but in the last 200 years it has become a privilege of the left—including the Nazis, who desecrated Jewish cemeteries.

[67] I possess a Red Spanish poster celebrating the "Revolution of the 18th of July."

[68] Unfortunately these horrors are not purely Spanish—or German, or Russian. One has to remember Dan Davis of Waco, Texas, a mulatto, shouting from the stake in 1916, "I wish some of you gentlemen would be Christian enough to cut my throat." (It may well be that some of these gentlemen were already dreaming of hanging Kaiser Bill and of making the world safe for democracy.) One also has to remember the attorney of Colorado County (Texas) who protested against the lynchers being called a mob: "I consider their act an expression of the will of the people." (But the truth might have been on both sides: the lynchers *were* a mob who *did* express majority views.) *Cf.* Frank Shay, *Judge Lynch, His First 100 Years*, p. 118. The inhumanities in Spain too, were perpetrated more often than not by large crowds, a fact our Roussellians do not like to face. Here we must recall Reinhold Niebuhr's statement that it is far more difficult for a group to be ethical than for an individual. *Cf.* his *Moral Man and Immoral Society* (New York: Scribner's, 1941), p. xi. (Rivarol put this into simple words: "Le prince absolu peut être un Néron, mais il est quelquefois Titus ou Marc-Aurèle, le people est souvent Néron, et jamais Marc-Aurèle." Hence the masses are psychologically invited to be against excellence.) Half a century before the discovery of America, revolutionary German peasants congregating in Worms in 1428 voted for a program which they entitled "Postulates of the Common Man." The most salient points were the abolition of all private property and the exiling or killing of all Jews. These demands were raised again in our progressive century. *Cf.* Felix Somary, *op. cit.*, p. 80.

[69] The United States at least showed gratitude in the *beginning*. Ségur tells us that after his arrival in the United States during the War of Independence "at all solemn occasions, during all festivities, in all toasts one never forgets to mention the names of Louis XVI and of France." He adds, "America indeed has always avoided ingratitude of which history has charged almost all republican governments." *Cf.* Monsieur le Comte de Ségur, *op. cit.*, vol. 1, pp. 446-447.

[70] The Spanish Socialists, unlike their Northern brethren, were very orthodox in their Marxism: they were really Bolsheviks rather than Mensheviks. Margarita Nelken, a leading Socialist, said, "We want the Revolution, but the Russian Revolution to us is insufficient. There must be enormous flames which can be seen in the entire world and rivers of blood have to color the seas." Largo Caballero, another Socialist leader, announced: "If the Popular Front collapses, which we expect, the victory of the proletariat is certain. Then we will establish the dictatorship of the proletariat." *Cf.* Hugh Thomas, *op. cit.*, Book. 1, ch. 11.

[71] *Cf.* Alfonso García Valdecasas, "Los Estados totalitarios y el Estado Español," in *La Revista de Estudios Políticos* (January 1942), pp. 5sq. In this article the cofounder of the Falange (and recently Rector of the University of Barcelona) declared (p. 9) that Spain refuses to follow the general political trend in Europe (in 1942!), that the new movements are totalitarian in nature (pp. 20-21), that Spain always believed in immutable moral principles and that

the State is to be merely in the service of these values: "These are, for us, as an example, the liberty, the dignity and the integrity of man, and it is the strict duty of the State to respect them and to make them respected." (p. 27). A more outspoken rejection of Nazi and Fascist ideas can hardly be imagined—and yet these words were written at the height of Nazi victories. Such views, of course, are typically Spanish; hence the leftist dislike for traditional Spain. No wonder Alfred Rosenberg, the Nazi "ideologist" chief, told us that "nowhere else in Europe could one find such psychological and intellectual backwardness as in Spain before April 1931." (*Cf. op. cit.*, p. 186) Such views were shared by most "progressive" people in the West!

[72] *Cf.* Salvador de Madariaga, *op. cit.*, p. 368: "During the Eighth Congress of the Communist International which took place in Moscow in 1935, the 'Trojan Horse' policy to be adopted by the Comintern from then on was formulated and expounded by Comrade Dimitrov. This was the policy which led Russia to Geneva, to the International Peace Campaign, and to the Popular Front. The chief agent for the policy in Spain was to be Señor Alvarez del Vayo, the stronger and more efficient for his remaining officially a Socialist. His trips to Moscow had begun in 1930, a year before the fall of the Spanish Monarchy. In April 1936 a party of over a hundred Spaniards and pseudo-Spaniards who had been living in Moscow passed through Paris and were forwarded to Spain with every possible care and attention by the Spanish Embassy." It is important to note that Señor Alvarez del Vayo for years handled a foreign policy column in *The Nation*, a respected "liberal" paper. *Cf.* also Hugh Thomas, *op. cit.*, book. I, ch. 11, note 18.

[73] *Cf.* Salvador de Madariaga, *op. cit.*, p. 402, note 1, "I believe the first time a Spanish airplane bombed a Spanish town was on July 20th at Toledo, where Don Francisco Caballero had the city bombed at regular intervals for three days in the hope of regaining it from the Rebels." Guernica still poses a problem to the historian. Was it bombed by the Germans or not? Hugh Thomas is convinced of it, but newer research points in the opposite direction. *Cf.* Helene Schreiber, "Guernica—Mythos von Malerhand," *Rheinischer Merkur*, January 17, 1969, no. 3, p. 32. Harold G. Cardozo, correspondent of the London *Times* denied the bombardment in the May 5, 1937 issue. Today the Spanish government tries to persuade Picasso to "reclaim" his famous painting *Guernica* still on loan at the Museum of Modern Art in New York. They would like to show it in Madrid's new Modern Art Museum.

[74] Again, was the Church so bad that one had to expect such a dreadful reaction? *Again* we have to warn—even at the risk of sounding repetitious—against the simple theory that where there is smoke there is fire. Big fires are known to have produced little smoke and vice versa. Among priests the best ones (since they were a major "provocation") usually suffered more than the bad, lazy, or stupid ones—because, from a Red point of view, they were harmless if they lowered the prestige of the Church. Some people in the West will insist that all these "troubles" could have been avoided if

there had been separation between State and Church. Yet strict separation, taking the intrinsic character of the Church and of the modern State into consideration, is not really feasible—something Reinhold Niebuhr well realized. *Cf.* Jerome G. Kerwin, "The Church and the State," *Commonweal*, vol. 62, no. 14, pp. 342-344.

[75] Franco tried vainly to embody the synthesis by sporting the blue shirt of the Falangists with the *boina roja*, the red beret of the Carlists. The synthesis did not work. Today Franco appears either in civilian clothes or in a strictly military uniform.

[76] This much he told to his friend the famous Italian journalist Indro Montanelli who published it in January 1948 in the *Corriere della Sera*. Yet some of the Falangists later drifted into violent opposition against the Franco Government: among them Dionisto Ridruejo, author of the Falangist Hymn *Cara al sol*. Others, such as García Valdecasas, broke with the Falange whose political importance today is almost nil. Whatever remains of the Falange (especially as far as newspapers go) is in a vague sense republican and leftist. On the (undoubtedly very idealistic) founder of the Falange, *cf.* Bernd Nellessen, *José Antonio Primo de Rivera—der Troubadour der spanischen Falange* (Stuttgart: Deutsche Verlagsanstalt, Schriftenreihe der Vierteljahrshefte für Zeitgeschichte, 1966).

[77] Among them we find Don Gregorio Marañón, medical expert, historian, politician, and writer who took a hand in the abdication of Alfonso XIII, and José Ortega y Gasset. Salvador de Madariaga held out to this day, though his works can again be published in Spain. Pablo Casals also refuses to return, but he is said to have a Spanish passport. Yet what is today the prevailing sentiment in Spain? There has been a general liberalization in the intellectual and artistic domain and an "economic miracle" to boot—but only since the neo-liberals of the *Opus Dei* liberalized the economy. Careful demoscopic investigations reveal the fact that about two thirds of the population are in favor of the present government. *Le Monde,* the excellent, but very leftist Paris daily admits that most Spaniards (on the right or on the left) dread democracy far more than "Francoism" since they see the danger of a total anarchy. *Cf.* Charles Vanhecke, "L'Espagne et la peur du vide," *Le Monde*, May 5, 1972.

[78] *Cf.* Salvador de Madariaga, *Spain*, pp. 376-377, "The fact that the Church was being ruthlessly persecuted by the Revolutionists can only be disputed or contested by ignorant or prejudiced critics. Whether the priests murdered were 16,000 or 1,600 time will tell. But that for months, years perhaps, the mere fact of being a priest was tantamount to a capital sentence, and the fact that no Catholic worship was allowed at all till the end of the War or very nearly, and that churches and cathedrals were used as markets and thoroughfares for animal-driven vehicles cannot be disputed." (The Basque nationalist attitude Madariaga considered a case of schizophrenia.) A group of non-Catholic clergymen visiting Spain in the winter of 1937 reportedly

laconically about the Spanish priests: "Many certainly have been killed . . . unless the parish priest was actively unpopular, he was not killed by his own people." *Cf. Report of a Group of Anglican and Free Churchmen who Visited Spain, January 29 to February 9, 1937* cited by E. Allison Peers, *Spain, the Church and the Orders* (London: Burns, Oates and Washbourne, 1945), p. 254.

[79] In large parts of the Basque Provinces the population wanted autonomy and since the Cortes of the Republic voted the Basque Statute, the Basques, led by their priests and ignorant of the persecution of the Church in the rest of Republican Spain, sided with the Republic. Territorially they were cut off from the main area and thus took the stories of the persecution of their Church further south as mere propaganda of the Burgos Government. Yet Basque exiles, later on, fanatically spread the anti-Franco gospel in Catholic circles abroad—and successfully so. It cannot be doubted, however, that the Basques did have a just grievance, and still have it today, against the perennial centralism of the various governments seated in Castile. This is a rather perverse situation as it is normally leftism which stands for centralism and centralization. The *fueros* (ancient local privileges) of Navarra were not seriously impaired, but in case of a Spanish reform, one can only wish for a restoration of the time-hallowed *fueros* of the three Basque provinces. It is true, however, that the state as such (and the modern state even more so) is essentially "annexationist" and decentralizes only with the greatest reluctance (and with a minimum of sincerity). *Cf.* Rafael Gambra, *La monarquía social y representativa* (Madrid: Rialp, 1954), p. 204. Our democratic age is basically opposed to minorities. Says Winfried Martini, "From the concentration camps and later from the gas chambers which—though unawares—the will of the people had brought on, the frightening yelling screams of our century could be heard: 'Woe to the minorities!' " *Cf. Das Ende aller Sicherheit*, p. 118.

[80] Leon Trotsky was a Freemason, but neither Lenin nor Stalin nor Khrushchev belong to the Brothers. *Any* organization not "of the State" is forbidden in the USSR, and thus the religious communities are an anomaly scheduled for liquidation. (Hence also the pressure on Zionism.) For this reason alone any true "liberalization" of genuine communism is unthinkable.

[81] Harold Laski wrote to Oliver Wendell Holmes on August 6, 1933 that he had spoken to Azaña and that this politician's "resonant anticlericalism" went to his heart. *Cf. Holmes-Laski Letters, 1916-1935*, p. 1446. The joint letter of Stalin, Molotov and Voroshilov to Largo Caballero, dated December 21, 1936, advising him to use democracy, republicanism and Azaña as a convenient camouflage against the accusation of Communist takeover, can be found in S. de Madariaga, *Spain*, pp. 472-474.

[82] Numerically the Communists in Spain were then relatively not more numerous than the Communists in Russia in 1917, but in Spain, unlike Russia, the Socialists were hardly distinguishable from the Communists. The Russian *bolsheviki* totally disregarded democratic procedure, whereas the *mensheviki*

548

still clung to the time-honored notion of legality. On January 23, 1936, Largo Caballero said in Madrid, "When things change, the Right need not ask for our benevolence. We will not respect the lives of our enemies as we did on April 4, 1931, when the Republic came in. If the Right is not defeated at the Polls, we will find other means to beat them: means to obtain the total triumph of the Red flag, because, and I emphasize this, if the Right wins, we shall be forced to turn to civil war." *Cf.* Richard Pattee, *This is Spain* (Milwaukee: Bruce, 1951), p. 177. The chapters of this book dealing with the events leading to the Civil War, are well documented.

[83] As we have said before, this was largely due to Basque influences, particularly to the friendship which bound Señor José Antonio Aguirre y Lecube, the former President of the Basque Republic, to Jacques Maritain. And yet an English observer could state unequivocally, "The attack on religion has been more radical in loyalist Spain than anywhere else in the world, even Mexico and Russia. All Roman Catholic churches had been closed down as places of worship and nearly all have been completely destroyed. . . . In loyalist Spain there is nothing left to persecute." *Cf.* Arthur Loveday, *Spain 1923-1948* (London: Boswell, 1949), p. 119, quoting the liberal *Manchester Guardian*. Of course some readers might think that the Church in Spain created a boundless envy due to its wealth amidst poverty. Yet prior to the outbreak of the Civil War priests received about eight dollars a month (!), bishops about $1,500 a year. Granted that the purchasing power of these sums ought to be doubled or tripled, the vast majority of the clergy was living evidently on a proletarian level. The situation, in this respect, is not so very much better today.

[84] Curiously enough there is no equivalent to the term with this particular meaning in Continental idioms.

[85] *The Protestant*, edited by Kenneth Leslie and published during World War II in New York was an amazing publication. On its editorial board were a number of communists and fellow travelers, among them Mr. Pierre van Paassen. It fought a valiant battle against the Nazis and the Catholic Church (considering them nearly identical) and declared (vol. 5, no. 6, June-July 1942, p. 3) that the two most hated men of our time were not Hitler and Mussolini, but—Franco and Pétain. On the last page of that number an appeal was printed for additional readers because "the Fascists, whichever side wins, plan to win the peace. If the Fascists or the Falangists win the peace, the war will have been fought in vain. Their victory would mean the renewed and intensified persecution of the Jews and of all those who have become in any way identified with the age-old struggle for democracy." One of the editors of this delightful periodical, Heinz Pol, in a letter published in the *New York Times* demanded a mass slaughter of "German militarists and junkers," a demand reiterated by Stalin during the Teheran conference. Yet the main target of the attack of *The Protestant* was never National Socialism, but "Franco Spain" and Pétain's régime which was also considered "clerico-Fascist."

[86] There was also a Spanish Catholic who was used by the Republic

as an alibi: Angel Ossorio y Gallardo, who served as a representative of Republican Spain in Paris. One of the archbishops opposed Franco more and more in the years to come, Cardinal Segura of Seville. He attacked Franco, the Americans, "Protestants," the Falangists, modern dances (beginning with the waltz and polka) and, finally, Pius XII. His case was really *unique*. Luckily he died before he had a chance to hear about the bikinis on the Costa del Sol. He was, however, no danger to the Church. Far more dangerous is the fascination of certain ideologies for the Church—and today, as Bernanos foresaw it clearly, the trap is no longer the throne-and-altar-complex but Leftism. *Cf.* his *Le Chemin de la Croix des Ames* (Paris: Gallimard-NRF, 1948), p. 452.

[87] In the Germanic and Slavic countries the Socialist parties called themselves "social democratic," but they were originally pledged to the Marxist program. The Russian Social Democrats were split into Mensheviks and Bolsheviks. Until 1917 Lenin figures, naturally, as a Social Democrat, a term which sounds harmless to Anglo-American ears. In the Latin countries these parties called themselves always plainly "Socialists." (Yet the French *Radicaux Socialistes* were never Socialists, but radical liberals claiming a social outlook: they were very bourgeois, anticlerical middle-of-the-roaders and, in a way, the ideological backbone of the III Republic.) In Austria, after World War II, the Social Democrats reconstituted themselves as "Socialists," probably in order to emphasize their Marxian heritage *vis-à-vis* the heavily Soviet-supported Communists. This Marxist heritage can be found even deep down in the heart of the Labour party. We have seen a picture of the late Lord Attlee where his Lordship in "Loyalist Spain" gives the Communist salute with the clenched fist.

[88] There is a good and impartial description of these events in the book by Hellmut Andics, *Der Staat, den keiner wollte* (Vienna: Herder, 1962), pp. 431ff.

[89] British journalists on the Continent, needless to say, have similar mental-intellectual handicaps. *The abyss, as always, is the Channel, not the Atlantic.* Of course, journalism *per se* has many pitfalls. Michael Clark, a one-time *New York Times* correspondent, wrote that according to the advice given by a "most experienced" American reporter young journalists should always write what the folks "back home" would like to hear and that their bias should be fully taken into account. In Clark's particular area (Northwest Africa) these items were scandals involving American air bases and the bad treatment of natives by the French colonialists. *Cf.* Thomas Molnár, *The Decline of the Intellectual* (Cleveland and New York: Meridian Books. 1961), p. 226n.

[90] After the war he was tried in Boston and received a stiff jail sentence.

[91] *Cf.* Heinrich Benedikt, ed. *Geschichte der Republik Osterreich* (Munich: R. Oldenbourg, 1954), pp. 10-11: "The First Austrian Republic had been a sovereign state, yet it was so in name only. Subjected to the control

550

of the League of Nations—the typical example of power politics in disguise—Austria's self-government was only another name for the administration of the country by the Allies. In the Tripartite Conference from March 14 to 17, 1934, and in the Protocols of Rome, Italy took over the role of a tacit agent of the League of Nations and deputy of the Great Powers." And Benedikt adds, "The Abyssinian venture resulted in the surrendering of Austria to Hitler." (p. 11). Compare also with Kurt von Schuschnigg, "Neuösterreichische Geschichts-schreibung," *Wissenschaft und Weltbild*, vol. 4 (1951).

[92] He repeatedly made such and similar declarations. I also have oral informations from Professor von Schuschnigg. Yet in his doctoral thesis published in Paris in 1908 (for the University of Dijon) entitled *Le problème autrichien et la question tchèque, Etude sur les luttes politiques des nationalités slaves en Autriche*, Beneš had demanded merely a "federalization" and by no means a destruction of Austria-Hungary. His growing anti-Catholic and anti-Hapsburg bias drove him finally into the arms of Hitler and Stalin at the same time and thus into political suicide. His fanatical anti-Hapsburg stand, preferring the Anschluss to restoration, is also testified to by his admirers. *Cf.* Jaroslav Papoušek, *Eduard Beneš, Třicet let práce v boje pro národ a stát* (Prague: Orbis, 1934), and Louis Eisenmann, *Un grand Européen: Edouard Beneš* (Paris: Hartmann, 1934), pp. 111-114. *Cf.* also Sisley Huddleston, *The Tragic Years, 1939-1947* (New York: Devin Adair, 1955), p. 12; Jean de Pange, *Les meules de Dieu* (Paris: Alsatia, 1951), p. 182, *Der Hochverratsprozess gegen Dr. Guido Schmidt* (Vienna: Osterreichische Staatsdruckerei, 1947), p. 361; Comte de Sainte-Aulaire, *François-Joseph* (Paris: Fayard, 1945), p. 583. Beneš, unlike Masaryk, was a Freemason, belonging to the lodge *Pravda Vítěži* in Prague, whose ideology might have colored his political thinking. *Cf.* Eugen Lennhoff and Oskar Posner, *Internationales Freimaurerlexikon* (Vienna: Amalthea, 1932), col. 164-165. (These authors are Masons.) *Pravda Vítěži* (as I imagine) would have been connected with the Grand Orient much rather than with the *Grande Loge Nationale Indépendante et Regulière pour la France*.

In dealing with the political effects of Freemasonry on the Continent one has to be beware of three pitfalls: to underrate them, to overrate them, to fail to distinguish between the various trends, lodges, organizations. The book by Roger Peyrefitte, *Les fils de la lumière* (Paris: Flammarion, 1961) though not exactly of a scholarly character, gives at least an inkling as to the large variety of Masonic dogmatic positions. On Freemasonry in French politics, *cf.* also D. W. Brogan, *French Personalities and Problems* (London: Hamish Hamilton, 1946), pp. 37-40.

One has to take care not to see in history nothing but a chain of conspiracies. Count Prokesch-Osten remarked that in "Metternich's heart there lived the ineradicable mania (Gentz called it the *Urlüge*, the original lie), that all revolutions are the work of secret societies and that Lafayette could have organized the revolt in Poland no less than in Paris." *Cf. Aus den Tagebüchern des Grafen Prokesch von Osten* (Vienna: Christoph Reisser, 1909), p. 68, (entry of December 7, 1830).

[93] *Cf.* Edvard Beneš, *"The Organization of Post-War Europe," Foreign Affairs*, vol. 20, no. 2 (January 1942), p. 231.

[94] *Cf. Der Hochverratsprozess gegen Dr. Guido Schmidt*, pp. 367, 393, 397, 399. Franz von Papen, as we see, fought valiantly on the side of the Little Entente. Professor von Schuschnigg (the former Chancellor) told me of his encounter with the Yugoslav Foreign Minister Boško Jevtić in Geneva, where Jevtić informed him in all candor that Belgrade could never consent to a Hapsburg restoration in Austria because such a change would render the already very difficult Croats totally recalcitrant. A restoration would be a *casus belli* since it would be a life-and-death question for Yugoslavia.

[95] In the mid-1930s Paris considered a Hapsburg restoration as a minor evil, but Britain seemed totally opposed. *Cf. Der Hochverratsprozess gegen Dr. Guido Schmidt*, pp. 397-399. Edward VIII might have been personally in favor of a restoration, but his reign was short-lived.

[96] *Cf.* Elizabeth Wiskemann, *The Rome-Berlin Axis* (London: Oxford University Press, 1949), p. 52, "The remarkable and admirable reaction of the British against the Hoare-Laval plan was all the greater, the Stresa front was dissolved and Hitler unshackled, let loose to advance step by step, from the militarization of the Rhineland to the invasion of Poland. History has perhaps never played a stranger trick upon Man than to allow British indignation against international lawlessness and imperialist and racialist bullying to have smoothed the path of Adolf Hitler. Out of this misconception was born that deformity, the Italo-German alliance, of which Hitler has so long dreamed."

It was not at all a "strange trick," but the inability of the well-meaning masses to assay an immensely complex political situation from the Somali Desert to the Bavarian border. Starry-eyed idealism in history has often played a more disastrous role than diabolical malice. For the same good reason that St. Thomas considers the intellectual virtues to be higher than the moral ones, Fouché (though hardly a reader of the *Summa*) exclaimed when Napoleon ordered the execution of the Duc d'Enghien, "This is worse than a crime, it's a blunder!"

[97] To this day Abyssinia is one of the most "backward" countries in Africa. (One among six Rhodesians is in school, one out of eight Ghanaians, but only one out of 108 Ethiopians.) The advantage Abyssinia has over the ex-colonies of Africa is a far more *stable* government.

[98] *Cf.* Herbert L. Matthews, *Eyewitness in Abyssinia* (London: Secker and Warburg, 1937), p. 319. "Yesterday I wrote an article about the resources of the country, and what the Italians hope to get out of it. I wish them luck. They have earned the place." Later Mr. Matthews became an apologist of Republican Spain and, quite naturally, of Castro's Cuba.

[99] According to a reliable estimate the Hoare-Laval Agreement would have left to Ethiopia 200,000 out of 350,000 square miles—the higher, wetter, and better lands.

[100] Elizabeth Wiskemann thinks that it was Pertinax and Madame Tabouis "who learnt of the Hoare-Laval Plan from Herriot, but Laval afterwards told Cerutti (the Italian Ambassador in Berlin) that Herriot did not know, and that he (Laval) suspected a Quai d'Orsay official: naturally he himself disclaimed all responsibility for betraying Hoare to the press." (*op. cit.*, p. 52n.) And the same author tells us later in all candor, "It has often been supposed—and to this the present writer pleads guilty—that Abyssinia, the Rhineland and Spain formed a chain of Nazi-Fascist connivance. This is not true—how untrue in the case of Ethiopia has already been seen. But from the moment the Hoare-Laval Plan existed Ethiopia became a trump card for Hitler, because it had split the Stresa front and freed him from 'encirclements'." (p. 53)

Duff Cooper, so strongly anti-German, was convinced that: ". . . . The half-hearted sanctions that we imposed served only to infuriate Mussolini and drive him into the arms of Hitler. Doing a minimum of harm we incurred a maximum of ill-will." (Duff Cooper, *op. cit.*, p. 193.) And later he remarks, "I was unhappy about Anthony Eden's departure. I wrote him to tell him so and to say that I had always found myself in agreement with him, except on this one question of Italy." There was a true personal enmity between Eden and Mussolini which grew as time went on. Eden himself in his memoirs—The Rt. Hon. Earl of Avon, *The Eden Memoirs*, (London: Cassell, 1965), vol. 3, "The Reckoning"—is singularly reticent about his blunder but regrets the *Anschluss* in several passages. Neville Chamberlain, on the other hand, thought that Halifax (in Eden's place) could have saved Austria by cooperating with Mussolini more closely. Cf. Keith Feiling, *The Life of Neville Chamberlain*, (London: Macmillan, 1946).

[101] *Cf.* Erich Kordt, *Wahn und Wirklichkeit* (Stuttgart: Union Deutsche Verlagsgesellschaft, 1948), p. 102, n 2.

[102] *Cf.* Gordon Brook-Shephard, *Der Anschluss*, trsl. G. Coudenhove (Graz: Styria, 1963). This author strongly criticizes the German feelings of the anti-Nazi leaders of independent Austria. Anybody conversant with the history of Austria could hardly expect this to be different. After 1945 an effort was made by the Allied occupation authorities to eradicate all German sentiments. In the school report cards the word "German" could not be mentioned and thus the subject was called *Unterrichtssprache*, "language of instruction." Antimilitarism too was written with capital letters, and Austrian public libraries were not even permitted to handle books pertaining to the history of World War I.

[103] It was precisely this role of Austria as the "other German State" which created in German Nazi circles the feeling of an "intolerable provocation." It ran counter to the formula, "One people, one realm, one leader":

Peter F. Drucker in *The End of Economic Man* (New York: John Day, 1939) well analyzed the value of pre-Anschluss Austria as a "psychological alternative" to many a German.

[104] Dr. Karl Renner, A Socialist and first President of the Austrian Republic after World War II, had stated on April 3, 1938, three weeks after the *Anschluss*, in an interview (*Tagblatt*, Vienna) that he would vote "yes" for Austria's inclusion into Germany. Having been Austria's State Chancellor in 1919 he admitted to feeling a real satisfaction for the humiliations of 1918 and 1919 as well as for the Treaties of Versailles and St. Germain-en-Laye. Cardinal Innitzer (in spite of his courageous protest in November 1938) was "morally dead" after his unfortunate declaration at the plebiscite, while Renner (who also had written to Stalin in 1945 a letter addressing him as "dear comrade") became President of Austria with the blessing of the Allies. *Cf.* Hellmut Andics, in *Die Presse* (Vienna), July 4, 1962, no. 4231, p. 8.

[105] *Cf.* G. E. R. Gedye, *Fallen Bastions* (London: Gollancz, 1939), p. 235: "Except for the Jews, the aristocracy which remained loyal to the old ruling House met perhaps with the worst treatment of any class from Hitler, Bürckel, and Globočnik: there was not even the brief attempt to flatter and cajole them which the Reds 'enjoyed.' "

This policy was supported by Hitler's ingrained antimonarchism. He was always grateful to the Social Democrats for having destroyed the German Monarchy. He said verbally about the Republic: "It was a big step ahead. She, above all, prepared our way." *Cf.* Hans Frank, *op. cit.*, p. 288, and Albert Speer, *op. cit.*, p. 67. On the other hand he really feared the survival of monarchist feelings in Austria which had been very strong up to November, 1918. *Cf.* Ludwig A. Windisch-Graetz, *Der Kaiser kämpft für die Freiheit* (Vienna: Herold, 1957), pp. 86-105.

[106] Cordell Hull was born in a hamlet in Tennessee. His higher education consisted of one year in the National Normal University, Lebanon, Ohio—all traces have now been lost of this famous educational institution—and of one year in the Cumberland University Law School in Lebanon, Tennessee. (One could really speak here of a "Lebanese fixation!") In the same year in which he finished his extensive studies, he was admitted to the bar of Tennessee. This worthy man who, to say the very least, passively contributed to laying the foundations of World War II, received the Nobel Peace Prize in 1945.

[107] *Cf. Documents on German Foreign Relations, 1918-1945*, series D. I, pp. 604-605.

[108] *Cf. Ambassador Dodd's Diary*, William E. Dodd Jr. and Martha Dodd, eds. (New York: Harcourt, Brace, 1941), Introd. Charles A. Beard.

[109] Martha Dodd, years later, fled to Prague to escape arrest by the FBI. She had become an active Communist.

[110] *Cf. Ambassador Dodd's Diary*, p. 101.

[111] *Ibid.*, pp. 309 and 396. Lord Lothian became wartime British

Ambassador to Washington. According to Dodd Lothian was thoroughly pro-Nazi (p. 406).

[112] *Ibid.*, p. 119.

[113] *Ibid.*, p. 360.

[114] Talking to a professor of a big American university, a specialist in modern German history, I once passed the remark that Hitler was a demagogue like Cleon. "Cleon?" "Yes, Cleon of Athens." "Ah, that's antiquity. It's none of my business." This phenomenon of specialization is by no means restricted to the United States; it is beginning to be worldwide and now invades *all* areas of study and knowledge as a new form of *docta ignorantia.*

[115] *Cf. Ambassador Dodd's Diary*, p. 413.

[116] *Cf.* his *The Black Record* (London, 1940).

[117] The geographical-historical confusions created by journalists would be worth a separate study. Remember the Near East which in World War II mysteriously became the Middle East. (The Far East, some time earlier, had become the "Orient.") Hitler's "West Wall" suddenly was named the Siegfried Line by a reporter who remembered the *Siegfried-Linie* ("Victorious Peace Line") of mere trenches across Northern France in World War I. Thus a new mixup took place. The *Blitz* ("*Blitzkrieg*") refers to the rapid advance of the (German) motorized units. The term had nothing to do with air attacks on more or less defenseless cities. (The German word *Blitz*, lightning, metaphorically refers to speed, not to a blow from the skies.) And Hitler never was a corporal, only a private first class, called in England "lance corporal." Hence another confusion.

[118] William E. Dodd tells (*op. cit.*, p. 422) about a conversation between the British Ambassador in Berlin, Henderson, and a high Austrian official. "The British Ambassador said Austria, being Nazi, must be annexed to Germany. This was at once reported to Schuschnigg, the Chancellor of Austria, and that led to immediate telegraphic inquiries in London. Schuschnigg was satisfied by denials from Eden." There can be little doubt that Henderson profoundly sympathized with the Nazi incorporation plans. *Cf. The Eden Memoirs*, vol. 3. p. 8.

About the desperate efforts of the Austrian Foreign Minister, Dr. Guido Schmidt, to get British (and French) aid to save Austrian independence, or even to move Sir Robert Vansittart, *cf.* Hellmut Andics, *op. cit.*, pp. 537-538.

[119] Jacques Bainville had already ridiculed in 1918 (*Action Française*, February 14) the idea that the disappearance of the Austro-Hungarian monarchy would mean "any progress." It rather would result in endless German ethnic revindications. And in his *Conséquences politiques de la paix* (Paris: Nouvelle Librairie Nationale, 1920), pp. 119-120 he said about the successor states: "They are not at all disposed to make themselves instruments of the too simple and really naive system imagined by the designers of the peace. These people wake up and reexamine the situation. They feel, they know that their States

are fragile, that they are, in a way, amorphous, that they will immediately be shattered if they clash with a power stronger than themselves. They will assume a prudent neutrality and will take great pains to avoid a conflict with Germany.'' Only Yugoslavia was imprudent and paid dearly for it (though it saved Moscow by delaying the German attack against Russia). And, as Bainville clearly foresaw, none of the successor states lifted a little finger for France in her hour of distress. The poor French taxpayers had again been gypped in vain.

[120] Cf. Roger Peyrefitte, *Les Ambassades* (Paris: Flammarion), pp. 237-238.

About Beneš' secret negotiations with the Nazis, *cf.* the letter of Dr. Stefan Osuský in the *New York Times*, October 20, 1958. Beneš was ready to accede the Friedland, Rumburg, and Eger districts to Germany.

[121] An Austrian Socialist deputy, Dr. Robert Danneberg, who tried to flee the Nazis after the *Anschluss*, was extradited to the German authorities who first brought him to Dachau and then to the gas chambers in Poland. *Cf. Neue Volkszeitung*, New York, April 10, 1943. Naturally, there were many other similar cases as a result of Dr. Beneš's efforts to ingratiate himself with the Nazis.

[122] *Cf.* Beneš's speech before the foreign affairs committee of the Czechoslovak Parliament. *Vide Sources et documents tchecoslovaques*, no. 24, pp. 49, 51. See also Louis Eisenmann, *op. cit.*, p. 111. In early 1932, while working for an influential Hungarian newspaper, I tried through the aid of the Czech Minister in Vienna, Hugo Vavrečka, to get an interview from Dr. Beneš for my paper with the purpose to achieve a *détente* between the two countries. The Nazi danger in Germany, at that time, was mounting. The answer from Prague was negative, and Vavrečka told me frankly that it was the policy of his country to bring Hungary economically down to her knees: the "democratic" Hungarian peasant should march on Budapest and destroy the "feudal government" which aimed at the revision of the revision of the iniquitous peace treaty. Vavrečka at the same time acknowledged the Nazi danger, but fully defended the stubbornness and ideological blindness of his country. Even at the ripe old age of twenty-three years I was aghast at the sight of so much stupidity and hatred.

[123] *Cf.* Dr. Edvard Beneš, *My War Memoires*, trsl. P. Selver (London: Allen and Unwin, 1928), p. 258.

[124] A certain Czech propaganda in the West always urged that the Czechs (who had the relatively largest Communist party in free Europe prior to 1930) were "born democrats" because they had no aristocracy. Their old nobility allegedly had all been exterminated after the Battle of the White Mountain. *This is totally untrue*. A large part of the Bohemia-Moravian nobility was either Czech in origin or sentiment. Families of German extraction had powerfully aided the revival of the Czech language. A Czech "Almanack de Gotha" was published by Z. R. Kinský, *U nás*, Leopold Novák, ed. (Chlumec:

Knihtiskarna V. Klemens, 1933). As a matter of fact, the Bohemian-Moravian nobility was always much richer and more influential than the more indigent aristocracy of Alpine Austria. (The old Slovak upper crust, on the other hand, really had become magyarized.) The concept of the "nonaristocratic Czechs" is an integral part of the twentieth-century mythology.

[125] *Cf.* László V. Taubinger, "Beneschs Vermächtnis," *Neues Abendland* (Munich), vol. 9, 11 (February 1954), p. 91 quoting Count Carlo Sforza's *The Totalitarian War and After* (London; Allen and Unnin, 1942).

[126] *Cf.* Fritz Weil, *Das Werden eines Volkes und der Weg eines Mannes: Eduard Beneš* (Dresden: Reissner, 1930), p. 132.

[127] *Cf.* Kurt von Schuschnigg, *Austrian Requiem*, trsl. Franz v. Hildebrand (New York: Putnam, 1946), pp. 153, 195.

[128] He was also the clever man who apparently passed on the Gestapo-fabricated documents "proving" the treason of Tukhachevski to Stalin. (*Cf.* Winston S. Churchill, *The Second World War*, vol. 1, p. 225n.) Yet to get a real grasp of the man's ignorance one has to read his *Democracy Today and Tomorrow* (New York: Macmillan, 1939). On p. 8 we read that Alexander Hamilton and John Adams were "pioneers of democracy"—and so forth.

[129] *Cf.* Louis P. Lochner, *What about Germany?* (New York, 1942), pp. 48-49. (This happened in March 1938.) Compare this with the account of Beneš's stubbornness and unpopularity in John de Courcy's *Behind the Battle* (London: Eyre and Spottiswoode, 1942), p. 241.

[130] *Cf.* Edvard Beneš, "The Organization of Post-War Europe," p. 242.

[131] *Cf.* Edvard Beneš, *Democracy Today and Tomorrow*, p. 182.

[132] *Cf.* Edvard Beneš, "The Organization of Post-War Europe," pp. 237-238.

[133] *Cf.* Edvard Beneš, "Toward Peace in Central and Eastern Europe," in *The Annals of the American Academy of Political and Social Science* (Philadelphia), March 1944, pp. 165-166. Here we see how one National Socialism was learning from another one.

[134] Jan Masaryk told Halifax on May 2, 1938, that his father had not wanted to include the Sudeten Germans in the new republic, but Lloyd George insisted on it. *Cf. Documents on British Foreign Policy*, III, 1, p. 237.

[135] *Cf.* Francis Deák, *Hungary at the Paris Peace Conference* (New York: Columbia University Press, 1942), p. 531. The murder of German-speaking Bohemians and Moravians in armed attacks during the transition period (1918-1919) shook world opinion as little as the large-scale massacres in 1945.

[136] The late Wenzel Jaksch, former leader of the Social Democratic Party of the German minority in Czechoslovakia, wrote that during the mobilization in 1921 only 30 percent of the *Czech* population followed the call to arms when an invasion of Hungary was planned to foil the attempted restoration of Emperor-King Charles. He was an ocular witness of this failure of a brand-

new "loyalty." *Cf.* his *Europas Weg nach Postdam* (Cologne: Verlag für Wissenschaft und Politik, n.d.), p. 528.

[137] *Cf.* Daniel Seligman, "The Collapse of Czech Democracy," *The American Mercury,* March 1948, p. 313.

[138] Yet Beneš's popularity was great only in Western leftist circles; at home he was unpopular and he knew it: "Don't you realize that I am the most unpopular man in Czechoslovakia?" he asked a Swiss journalist. *Cf.* Robert de Traz, "M. Masaryk et M. Beneš," *La Revue de Paris,* vol. 37, no. 5. (March 1, 1930), p. 58.

[139] Douglas Woodruff tells in his column in *The Tablet* (London, December 20, 1947, p. 394) about Stanley Baldwin: "He was, it must be admitted, intensely insular: I recall this, for instance: 'That was the first thing, I said on packing up my traps and leaving Downing Street, now I never need speak to another foreigner again!' " And about the nomination of Eden, Baldwin had remarked, "Nobody else knew all the foreigners about whom it was necessary to be informed, and there was no time for anyone else to get to know them." Churchill also spoke about the "marked ignorance of Europe and aversions from its problems in Mr. Baldwin." (*The Second World War,* vol. 1. p. 69).

[140] *Cf.* A. P. report, dated London, September 21, 1936, in the *New York Herald Tribune,* September 22, 1936. When Lloyd George returned to his hotel in Berchtesgaden, his daughter greeted him facetiously with "Heil Hitler!" The old gentleman became very serious and replied earnestly and with gravity, "Yes, indeed, Heil Hitler, this is what I say myself, because he is, in fact, a great man." *Cf.* Dr. Paul Schmidt, *Statist auf diplomatischer Bühne, 1923-1945.* (Vienna: Ullstein Verlag, 1953), p. 346.

[141] *Cf.* Chapter XVI, Note 23.

[142] Viscount Templewood (Sir Samuel Hoare) informed us that in October 1938 the British air force had 100 fighter planes against 1,000 German bombers, *Cf.* his *Nine Troubled Years,* (London: Collins, 1954), p. 333, Ian McLeod says that in October 1938 Britain only had two, in September 1939 five fully armed divisions. *Cf.* his *Neville Chamberlain,* (London: Atheneum, 1962), p. 264. In October 1938 Britain had only one-tenth of the necessary antiaircraft guns and only 1,430 searchlights; in London there were only sixty fire engines. (*Ibid.,* p. 266.) These were the bitter fruits of the pacifism of the preceding Labourite government eager to antagonize Hitler but not to rearm.

[143] On the "democratic," mass-character of the dictatorships born in the first half of this century *cf.* Emil Lederer, *State of the Masses: The Threat of the Classless Society.* (New York: W. W. Norton, 1940), pp. 98, 110, and Gyula Szekfü, *Három nemzedék és ami utana következik* (Budapest: Egyetemi nyomda, 1934), p. 497. Also Frank Thiess, *Freiheit bis Mitternacht* (Zsolnay: Vienna-Hamburg, 1965), p. 474sq.

[144] *Cf.* end of note 117 of this chapter. *"Der böhmische Gefreite"* is the German version.

[145] The Nazis had tried to frame General von Fritsch with a homosexual agent provocateur, an effort which failed. Baron Fritsch was killed during the seige of Warsaw in September 1939. Fritsch's removal was necessary in order to eliminate a generalissimo (*Oberbefehlshaber der Wehrmacht*) opposing armed German intervention in Austria. At this juncture the German General Staff should have acted—and did not. If only Germany had had a "political army" as most Latin American republics have, ready to intervene if things go from bad to worse!

This expression of regret I voice in all sincerity, if for no other reason than to remind the British or American reader that what is sensible in one part of the world becomes pointless in another or vice-versa.

[146] After the abortive attempt to assassinate Hitler in July 1944 three German army regulations were changed: instead of saluting the military way, soldiers and officers had to use the *deutscher Gruss*, i.e., to say *Heil Hitler*; it became permissible that non-Christians (*Gottgläubige*, mere theists) be made commissioned officers; soldiers in the *Wehrmacht* no longer had to deposit their party membership card with the NSDAP before entering military service. In other words, no active party member, before July 1944, could be a soldier in the German army. This dualism Army-Party has to be understood in the light of the anti-Nazi sentiment of the bulk of the officers' corps, of the so-called "Junkers and Militarists."

[147] *Cf.* Eberhard Zeller, *Geist der Freiheit. Der Zwanzigste Juli* (Munich: Hermann Rinn, 1954), p. 37; Gerhard Ritter, *Carl Goerdeler und die deutsche Widerstandsbewegung* (Munich: Deutscher Taschenbuchverlag, 1964), pp. 195-196; Franklin L. Ford, "The Twentieth of July in the History of the German Resistance," *The American Historical Review*, vol. 51, July 1946, pp. 616-617; Allen Welsh Dulles, "Le complot qui eu fait échouer Munich," *France-Illustration*, no. 110 (November 8, 1947), pp. 415-419. Ewald von Kleist (later executed) had too gone to London and at that time Mr. Churchill showed himself still very cooperative. Kleist informed Churchill that the aim of the conspiracy was peace and the restoration of the monarchy. (G. Ritter, *op. cit.*, p. 188.) By now the literature about this tragic chapter in the history of the German resistance is colossal. What we have cited is only a small fraction.

[148] (Sir) Ivone Kirkpatrick told me in July 1939 about the Godesberg meeting at which he had been present in his capacity as a British diplomat accredited in Berlin. Hitler ranted and shouted, spoke about the German spirit embodied in Marienburg Castle in Prussia, invoked philosophers, theologians, kings and generals. Dr. Paul Schmidt, official German interpreter, questioned Kirkpatrick with his eyes, asking whether he should translate this rot. All the time Neville Chamberlain looked like a little boy expecting to be given a nasty medicine. There was not the slightest meeting of minds. (Sir Ivone Kirkpatrick became British High Commissioner in Germany after the war.)

At the same time it was true that the Sudeten Germans had a real case. H. N. Brailsford, famous British leftist journalist, already in 1920 pointed out the fact that the more than three million Sudeten Germans, put under Czech rule, against their will, were a serious handicap to world peace. Arnold J. Toynbee in a large article published on July 10, 1937 in *The Economist* had to admit that "in Czechoslovakia today the methods by which the Czech are keeping the upper hand over the Sudetendeutsch are not democratic." The Dean of St. Paul's Cathedral (W. R. Matthews), in a letter to the *Times* on June 2, 1938, advocated "Self-Determination" for the Sudeten Germans and protested against the possibility of Britain fighting a war preventing self-determination. The same ideas were expressed by Lord Noel Buxton, a true liberal, in a letter to the *Times* on March 22, 1938. These facts have to be viewed in relation with Göring's boast to Sir Neville Henderson that "London had only fourteen antiaircraft guns and nothing to prevent Germany from dropping 1,000 to 2,000 bombs a day on London." (*The Times*, November 25, 1940).

[149] To get some of the more sinister or ironical aspects of the peace treaties of 1919 the reader should turn to Harold Nicolson, *Peacemaking 1919* (Boston: Houghton Mifflin, 1933) H. W. V. Temperley, *A History of the Peace Conference of Paris* (London: H. Frowde, 1920-1924, 6 vols.), André P. Tardieu, *La Paix* (Paris: Payot, 1933), Francesco Notti, *La Pace* (Turin: P. Gobetti, 1925), and Henri Pozzi, *Les coupables* (Paris: Editions Européennes, 1935) (not always reliable, but with valuable details) and *La guerre revient* (Paris: P. Berger, 1933). Hatred, prejudice, and ignorance found here a new synthesis. Often the Peace Treaty of Brest-Litovsk (1918) is mentioned as a proof that the Central Powers, had they won the war, would not have been more lenient and prudent. John Wheeler-Bennett (*The Forgotten Peace*, New York, 1948) had made this point. But one forgets that the Central Powers in 1918 were not prepared to hand over a maximum of territory to Red tyranny and that in 1920 Lenin had offered *additional* territory to Poland. The Treaty of Brest-Litovsk left to Soviet Russia and to the Ukraine (*unjustly*, to be sure) *more* than the Russian share of all three partitions of Poland.

[150] Almost all of these Americans of Slovak origin belonged to the (pro-Czech) Lutheran minority. Of course, Czechoslovaks exist no more than "Bulgaroserbs." Henri Pozzi tells that Wilson, not so surprisingly, confused the Slovaks with the Slovenes (and Silesia with Cilicia). Not only do Slovaks and Slovenes exist, but also Slovyaks, Slavs, Slavonians, and Slovintsians. Also there is Old Slavonic, a dead, liturgical language (which has nothing to do with Slavonia).

[151] Cf. *Franklin D. Roosevelt: His Personal Letters, 1928-1945*, Elliott Roosevelt, ed. (New York: Duell, Sloane, Pearce, 1950), vol. 2. p. 818. Letter of the President to Ambassador William Phillips in Rome, dated October 17, 1938. The President expressed his satisfaction in letters to the Canadian Prime Minister. *Cf. Ibid.*, p. 816. Sumner Welles was also in favor of the Munich Agreement. *Cf.* the *New York Times*, October 4, 1938. (The *New York Times* itself in an editorial on September 30, 1938 made a few reservations but, by and large, accepted the pact.)

[152] *Cf.* Harold Nicolson, *Curzon: The Last Phase* (London: Constable 1934), p. 204. Mr. Bevin, later Foreign Minister (1945), then a TUC leader, went so far as to threaten a general strike were the British Government to assist Poland "directly or indirectly."

[153] Of Churchill's political meandering in his earlier years *cf.* Peter de Mendelssohn, *The Age of Churchill 1874-1911* (London: Thames and Hudson, 1961), *passim.* Churchill's religious practice was unnoticeable. *Cf.* Randolph S. Churchill, *Winston Spencer Churchill* (London: Heinemann, 1966), Vol. 1, pp. 157-158.

[154] If one remembers that Churchill demonstrated to Stalin, with the help of three matches, how Poland could easily be "moved" westward at the expense of Germany (vol. 5 of his *Second World War*) one wonders about his words in the famous Fulton speech (March 5, 1946), "I have a strong admiration and regard for the valiant Russian people and for my wartime comrade Marshal Stalin. . . . The Russian-dominated Polish Government has been encouraged to make enormous and wrongful inroads upon Germany, and mass expulsions of Germans on a scale grievous and undreamed of are taking place." (The mass deportations, however, had been agreed upon in Potsdam!)

[155] *Cf.* Winston S. Churchill, "The Truth about Hitler," *Strand Magazine* (London), November 1935, pp. 19-20.

[156] *Cf.* Winston S. Churchill, *Step by Step* (New York, 1939), pp. 143-144. This was written in 1937.

Chapter XVII

[1] One should not entirely forget that in the fourteenth and sixteenth centuries Prague had been repeatedly the capital of the first German *Reich*, where the Holy Roman Emperors (of the Luxemburg and Hapsburg dynasties) resided. Prague had a Germanic character and, before Luther's translation of the Bible, standard German was the language used by the Imperial Chancellery in Prague (*Prager Kanzleisprache*). Czech history is an integral part of German history—Polish, Hungarian, Croat history is not.

[2] *Cf.* Winston S. Churchill, *The Second World War*, Vol. 1, p. 252. Czechoslovakia, created only in 1918, (and without historic precedent) had been considered by Hungary and Poland a merely temporary arrangement. The Teschen region occupied by Poland in October 1938 had a clear Polish majority (Polish deputies in Vienna and later in the Prague parliaments!) and had been adjudicated to Czechoslovakia by the conference of the ambassadors on July 28, 1920 when the Red army was marching on Warsaw. Poland protested in vain. The Hungarians reoccupied Magyar-inhabited areas which had belonged to Hungary for over 1,000 years until 1920 (Treaty of Trianon). Not to occupy these areas would have meant leaving them to the Nazis. If the French had annexed Kent and Sussex at the time of the Congress of Vienna, would it

have been immoral for Britain to invade these undoubtedly British areas in 1871 from a "prostrate France"?

We now know from Lord Moran how gravely ill Churchill was during and after World War II and should view his actions and words with a certain leniency. *Cf.* his *Churchill* (London: Constable, 1966). The fact that in the Great Emergency there was nobody else around endowed with manliness, authority, and courage is merely one more proof that the qualities of the pre-World War I generation had not been in our times. Around 1960 we still saw in Europe the rule of septuagenarians and octagenarians. They are now all being succeeded by "small fry."

As to the Teschen (Cieszyn) area, *cf.* the letter of Ignacy Jan Paderewski, addressed on July 28, 1920 to the President of the Council of Ambassadors, A. Miller, and quoted by W. Kulski and M. Potulicki in *Recueil de textes de droit international* (Warsaw, 1939) pp. 278ff.

[3] Polish Jews did not live in ghettos prior to World War II: there were, quite naturally, Jewish quarters or rather neighborhoods predominantly populated by Jews, a phenomenon one also can witness in Western Europe and in North America—just as there are in Dutch cities predominantly Catholic or in New York predominantly German quarters. Nor was the medieval Jewish quarter in its origin an institution imposed by the Christian authorities. Jews, according to their religion, were not permitted to live in *trefen*, gentile houses. *Cf.* Guido Kisch, *The Jews in Medieval Germany* (Chicago: The University of Chicago Press, 1949) p. 292: "There can no longer be any doubt that the separation of the Jewish from the general settlements in medieval cities had its origin in the free will of the early Jewish settlers and by no means in compulsory measures imposed on them. Such measures would be absolutely contradictory to the alluring conditions of settlement offered at times to Jewish immigrants, such as those included in the old Rhenish Jewry privileges. . . . Inclosure within walls or behind a gate was at first considered a particular favor by the Jews."

[4] The Polish "Fascist aristocratic landowner" (with monarchist, clerical, and plutocratic innuendos) is a bugbear in the Western world. Yet large landownership in Poland prior to 1939 was by no means substantial. Before the agrarian reform, enacted by the old "reactionary" government, 73 percent of the arable land belonged to the peasants, rich or poor, i.e., to persons holding less than 100 hectares or 247 acres. After the land reform which divided just over eight million acres or 47 percent of the bigger holdings, more than 87 percent of the arable territory belonged to small and middle-size holders of not more than the aforementioned 247 acres. These data do not include forests. *Cf.* R. Krygier, "Poland's Agrarian Policy," *The Polish Review* (New York), vol. 3, no. 38 (October 18, 1943), p. 11.

[5] This is the real Prussia. (West Prussia was a nonhistorical name given to the lands which had been Polish between 1446 and 1776.) East Prussia is a much maligned area of Germany. *Cf.* the nice sentence, "In view of East

Prussia's long history of leadership in German militarism its complete euthanasia is, on the whole, justifiable." Where do we find this bright remark? In John Kenneth Galbraith's *Reconstruction in Europe*, (Washington, D. C.: The National Planning Association, 1947), p. 21. What about Kant, Herder, Simson, Hamann, and Wiechert? Were these militarists? The so highly humanitarian wisdom of Mr. Galbraith, an economist of note, has its counterpart in the representation of East Prussia in the *New Yorker*'s "Our Own Baedeker" (vol. 20, no. 23, July 22, 1944, p. 12). These facetious irresponsibilities often have disastrous effects in the long run.

[6] On Anglomania *cf.* Chapter VII, note 20. Hitler's anglomania knew no bounds. This much emerges clearly from his "Table Talks." *Cf.* Dr. Henry Picker, *op. cit.*, *passim*. Take, for instance, p. 145 (September 8-10, 1941) when Hitler spoke about the glorious day he probably would not live to see, when the British and the Germans, shoulder to shoulder, would be fighting against the United States. Needless to say he knew neither England nor America.

[7] *Cf.* Dr. Paul Schmidt, *op. cit.*, pp. 473-474. Ribbentrop despised England and was deeply impressed by Russia. He was desperate when Hitler declared war upon the USSR. *Cf.* Henry Picker, *op. cit.*, pp. 238-239, and Valentin Byerezhkov, "Na rubyezhe mira i voyny (S diplomaticheskoy missiyey v Berlinye 1940-1941)." *Novy Mir*, vol. 41, no. 7 (July 1965), pp. 143-184.

[8] *Cf.* Joseph C. Harsch, *Germany at War* (New York: Foreign Policy Association, 1942), pp. 7-8, and Albert Speer, *op. cit.*, pp. 180-181. Since I spent the first three days of World War II in Germany and saw the general despair (comparing it with the genuine enthusiasm and the clear conscience in 1914) I told everybody upon my return to the United States that such a melancholy nation could not possibly win a war. I was *basically* right. Yet while it is relatively easy to foretell events, it is most difficult to forecast their timing. I could not guess that defeat would come as late as 1945 (nor could I guess its main cause-to-be: unconditional surrender).

The lack of enthusiasm was especially strong in the army. Harsch (*op. cit.*, pp. 46-47) said rightly, "Thinking back over a year and a half in wartime Germany, I am impressed by the fact that the most intelligent, the most interesting, the most fair-minded—in fact, in all respects the most honorable—men I met were in the army, serving people they despised to an end in which they did not believe, but welcoming the opportunity to forget their feelings about these men and those ends in what seemed to them a last means of serving their country." This frightening dichotomy under which the army suffered is highlighted by a conversation which Ernst Jünger had in Russia with Colonel Ravenstein, a man he knew from World War I. "I asked him about the mass-murder caves and how he could square their evidence with the honor of arms and the wearing of military decorations. Without entering into the matter he gave me a reply which to me came unexpectedly: 'For this, perhaps, my youngest daughter will have to pay some day in a Negro brothel.' " *Cf.* his *Strahlungen*, p. 330.

[9] Another American observer was convinced that the generals were more bitter enemies of Hitler than the Communists: *Cf.* Howard K. Smith, *Last Train from Berlin* (New York: Knopf, 1942), p. 280. Hitler suspected quite rightly that nobody among the *bourgeoisie* or the Marxists would dare to assassinate him. (Dr. Henry Picker, *op. cit.*, p. 307, May 3, 1942). Actually the man who came nearest to killing him was a Catholic Officer, Count Klaus Schenk von Stauffenberg, indeed neither a bourgeois nor a Marxist.

Another good account of Germany during the war was given by the Swedish journalist Arvid Fredborg in his book *Bakom Stålvallen*, American edition: *Behind the Steel Wall (A Swedish Journalist in Berlin 1941-1943)* (New York: The Viking Press, 1944), especially pp. 74-75, 239, 241, 248, 275.

[10] The diaries of Ulrich von Hassell, a German diplomat executed by the Nazis, make the most melancholy reading. Every victory of Hitler, every success of his country ("My country wrong, not right!") plunged him into a new fit of depression. *Cf.* his *Vom anderen Deutschland. Aus den nachgelassenen Tagebüchern 1938-1944* (Zürich: Atlantis, 1946).

[11] By far the best biography of Canaris is K. H. Abshagen, *Canaris, Patriot und Weltbürger* (Stuttgart: Union Deutsche Verlagsgesellschaft, 1949). This splendid book not only brings out the facts, but also presents the man's character. It sounds incredible, but I heard about Canaris' role in New York in 1943, while the Admiral was still active. His widow was invited by Franco to come to Spain where she was given a pension.

[12] See his book, *Die Zweite Revolution* (München-Zwickau: Franz Ehek, 1927), p. 47, where he writes, "We are looking to Russia because she is most likely to march with us in the direction of socialism—because Russia is for us the natural ally against the diabolic infection and corruption coming from the West."

[13] Hitler repeatedly boasted about the speed with which the opinion of his press on political matters could "make a 180 degree turn." He cited the case of his attack on Russia, *Cf.* Henry Picker, *op. cit.*, p. 344. Yet one should not forget that the press can change public opinion so swiftly only because the masses are so fickle, their loyalties ephemeral, their convictions not grounded. The people of Milan had wildly cheered Mussolini only in January 1945. A few months later they spat at his corpse. *Cf.* Luigi Barzini, *The Italians* (London: Hamish Hamilton, 1964), p. 155

[14] Joachim Ribbentrop was adopted by a titled aunt and used the name "von Ribbentrop." He figures in the *Genealogisches Handbuch der adeligen Häuser* (Limburg: Starke, 1961), vol. 5, p. 306 as "nonnoble user of the name." This means that in the defunct monarchy he would have been prosecuted for using a title without the monarch's patent or permission.

[15] *Cf.* Paul Schmidt, *op. cit.*, p. 481.

[16] While the western border of Poland was fixed at Versailles, the east-

ern one was the result of the Treaty of Riga (1921) between Poland and Soviet Russia. The Versailles Treaty, American and British readers (and news editors) should bear in mind, dealt only with *Germany*—and with no other country. Many other treaties were made in the 1919-1923 period: St. Germain-en-Laye (Austria), Neuilly (Bulgaria), Sèvres (first treaty with Turkey), Trianon (Hungary), Lausanne (second treaty with Turkey).

[17] Molotov's speech was made before the Ts.I.K. (Central Executive Committee of the USSR) on October 31, 1939. It was reprinted in *Soviet Russia Today* (New York), November 1939.

[18] Not only Portuguese and Spanish volunteers went to fight with the Finns, but even Britishers. (One of my English friends lost a leg in Karelia.) Actually London and Paris were preparing an expeditionary corps to come to the aid of Finland, when the armistice was declared.

[19] The *relatively* largest organized Communist parties west of the Iron Curtain are those of Iceland and Finland. Iceland is a very prosperous country with high living standards and so is Finland, which even "enjoys" the immediate neighborhood of Russia. Yet ideology is blind to experience. It is autonomous. And Nordic communism (as in Swedish Lapland) is based on convictions, not, as in Italy, on mere grudges or some sort of collective blackmail—believing that a big Red vote means better wages and salaries.

Without the German army assisting Baron Mannerheim's "White Guard" in 1917-1918, Finnish communism would have won out in the Civil War. The Finnish Communists were famous for their unparalleled cruelty—especially, however, the Red women's regiments from Tampere (Tammerfors) who tortured their prisoners to death. The Red "General" Antikainen, who had a special dislike for students, apparently had them boiled in large kettles. These delirious horrors of Europe's *most literate nation* just show that the beast is always right in us—which should give little comfort to our "humanist" Roussellians.

[20] Terijoki is a resort about halfway between Viborg (Viipuri) and Leningrad on the Karelian Isthmus. It now belongs to the USSR. Here was established the first "People's Democratic Republic," a delightful pleonasm coined by an illiterate. The next step would be a "Popular People's Democratic Republic"—with no rights for the people whatsoever.

[21] Sir Owen O'Malley, British minister to Hungary, was also evacuated through Vladivostok, making the trip from Hungary through the Soviet Union eastward. He and his party were treated like criminals in early 1941 whereas the Germans trying to reach their fatherland were practically guests of honor.

[22] *Cf.* Georgi Dimitroff, *Der Kampf gegen den imperialistischen Krieg*, (Stockholm: Weltbibliothek, 1940), p. 14. On Georgi M. Dimitrov *cf. The Fate of East Central Europe* (Notre Dame: The University of Notre Dame Press, 1956), pp. 275-276. The late Georgi Dimitrov, like all the Communists of the older generation, had been a Social Democrat in his earlier years.

[23] An anonymous German author wrote in 1949, *Cf.* "La responsabilité

des officiers,'' in *Temps Modernes*, 5. year, no. 46-47, August-September 1949, pp. 495-496.

National Socialism could have been overcome from inside, by a revolution only if a very important opposition had existed among the lower layers, prepared to sacrifice everything to the revolution, to follow the officers, flag-bearers of the revolt. Any other attempt at rebellion would have been considered reactionary by the masses and passionately resisted. . . . There is no revolution of leaders without the people. Yet, for the fact that an ideology favoring an uprising was lacking among the people, the very men should feel responsible who today think they must put the entire blame on the German officer: Also one must assume that they believe it would have been possible for a new revolutionary uprising to mature only then, years after the events of 1933.

[24] If one reads about the plans of Himmler for the time after victory—these included periodic shooting parties with human victims in the Eastern Marches of the great German Reich—one has to come reluctantly to such a conclusion. I admittedly reason as a Christian that the liquidation of Christianity was a definite Nazi plan. On February 2, 1942 Hitler declared he would exterminate Christianity—just as the superstition of witchcraft had effectively been wiped out. He called Christianity *eine Kulturschande*, a ''cultural scandal.'' *Cf*. Henry Picker, *op. cit*., p. 176.

[25] *Cf*. letter in *The Commonweal*, March 12, 1965, p. 751. *Cf. The Journals of Soren Kierkegaard*, A selection of Alexander Dru, ed. (London-New York: Oxford University Press, 1938), no. 1210 (April 1951).

[26] A complete English translation of *Mein Kampf* did not exist before 1941. Of course, the *modern* statesman cannot (or hardly could be) a scholar or at least a real *student* of world affairs: vote-getting consumes half of his time. Nor, we must confess, were all leading Nazis avid readers of *Mein Kampf*. Fritz Wiedemann says that many people in Hitler's entourage had never perused this fateful book. (*op. cit*., p. 56). Göring also admitted this in 1946 during the Nuremberg trial. We obviously are going through an interesting period of semiliteracy, where everybody can write, but few people will or can read.

[27] *Cf*. Chapter XVI, Note 107. And, as Robert Murphy pointed out, ''Hull was often depicted as the most anti-Soviet member of the Roosevelt cabinet, whereas he was virtually cocreator with the President of the 'Grand Design' for the postwar world, a plan which assumed that the United States and Soviet Russia could become partners in peace because circumstances had made them partners in war.'' Murphy quotes Hull's address to Congress after his return from the Foreign Ministers' Conference in Algiers during which the Secretary of State said, ''There will no longer be need for spheres of influence, for alliances, for balance of power, or any other of the special arrangements through which, in the unhappy past, the nations strove to safeguard their security or to promote their interests.'' *Cf*. Robert Murphy, *Diplomat Among War-*

riors (London: Collins, 1964), p. 259. For such a brilliant mind the Nobel Peace Prize was indeed a shabby reward.

[28] *Cf.* Jan Ciechanowski, *Defeat in Victory* (Garden City, N.Y.: Doubleday, 1947), p. 223.

[29] *Cf.* Graf Hermann Keyserling, *Das Spektrum Europas* (Heidelberg: Niels Kampmann, 1928), pp. 23-33.

[30] *Cf.* Jan Ciechanowski, *op. cit.*, pp. 330-331.

[31] *Vide*, for instance, *The Stilwell Papers* (New York: William Sloane, 1948), pp. 251-254.

[32] *Cf. The Economist* (London), vol. 152, no. 5393 (January 4, 1947), pp. 20-21.

[33] *Cf.* Robert I. Gannon, S. J. *The Cardinal Spellman Story.* (New York: Doubleday, 1962), pp. 222-225. See also Note 66 of this Chapter.

[34] *Cf.* Elliott Roosevelt, *As Father Saw It* (New York: Duell, Sloane and Pearce, 1946), p. 117. On Churchill and unconditional surrender *cf.* also Emry Hughes, *Winston Churchill in War and Peace* (Glasgow: Unity Publishing, 1950), pp. 206ff. The formula, of which Roosevelt thought that it had terminated the War between the States, was actually used by U. S. Grant in February 1862 during the siege of Port Donelson in Tennessee. One would think, quite naturally, that the unconditional surrender formula today would hardly find a defender in the West, but as late as 1955 an American scholar could write (and publish) an essay about this calamity, terminating with the words, "On all counts and contemporary criticisms notwithstanding, it was one of the most effective achievements of American statesmanship of the entire war period." *Cf.* John L. Chase, "Unconditional Surrender," *The Political Science Quarterly*, Summer 1955, p. 279. No wonder that, reacting to such academic wisdom, we also have an anti-intellectualism of the right!

[35] *Cf.* General Albert C. Wedemeyer, *Wedemeyer Reports!* (New York: Henry Holt, 1958), pp. 90-91. Churchill's quoted remark was made on February 27, 1945, in the House of Commons. (*Cf.* also his speech on September 31, 1943).

[36] *Cf.* David Irving, *The Destruction of Dresden* (London: William Kimber, 1963) pp. 20-25. Irving points out that under the terms of Article 25 of the 1907 Hague Convention Rotterdam could be attacked because it was not an undefended city. (The same could be said of Warsaw.) Only forty of the 100 attacking planes heard the signal cancelling the attack. The number of people killed according to the American press was 40,000. The rectified data were supplied to David Irving by Rotterdam authorities in 1962.

[37] *Cf.* Winston S. Churchill, *The Second World War*, vol. 2. p. 567.

[38] *Cf.* Chapter XVI, Note 118.

[39] *Cf.* J. M. Spaight, *The Battle of Britain 1940* (London: Geoffrey Bles, 1941), pp. 22-24, 30, 34, 217, 220.

[40] *Cf.* J. M. Spaight, *Bombing Vindicated*, (London: Geoffrey Bles, 1944), p. 74.

⁴¹ *Cf.* Basil Liddell-Hart, "War Limited," *Harper's*, March 1946, pp. 198-199.

⁴² *Cf.* J. C. F. Fuller, *The Second World War, 1935-1945* (New York: Duell, Sloane and Pearce, 1949), pp. 222-223.

⁴³ In Buchenwald concentration camp Princess Mafalda, daughter of King Victor Emmanuel III and wife of Prince Philip of Hesse, was severely wounded and died a few days later. In an Allied attack on the Hague 800 Dutchmen were killed (almost as many as by the Germans in Rotterdam!) and 20,000 were left homeless. *Cf. The New York Times*, March 25, 1945. The Easter Sunday Massacre of Belgrade in 1943 turned many Serbs against the Western Allies. Only one-half of the Allied bombs were dropped on Germany, one-eighth on Italy, *one-fifth on France*. More Frenchmen were killed by the Allies than by German bombs. According to a semiofficial statistic, no less than 67,078 Frenchmen were killed and 75,660 wounded by the Allied air warfare between 1941 and 1944. *Cf.* Robert Aron, *Histoire de Vichy 1940-1944* (Paris: Fayard, 1954) p. 604.

⁴⁴ *Cf.* Bernard Iddings Bell, *Crowd Culture* (New York: Harper, 1952), pp. 25-26.

⁴⁵ Even Sir Compton MacKenzie did. This great Conservative, Scottish Nationalist, and Catholic convert suddenly developed pro-Soviet sympathies, as can be seen in the last volume of his *Winds of Love*. The fascination undoubtedly transcended the leftist camp.

⁴⁶ As quoted by Oswald Garrison Villard in the *Christian Century*, March 14, 1945, p. 334. (Speech of December 5, 1939.)

⁴⁷ This is the reason why the Socialist (Social Democratic) parties are always susceptible to the "Call of the Wild." (The term Social Democrat has been coined by the near-anarchist Bakunin.) It is true that the East German, Hungarian, Czech, Polish, Rumanian, Socialists have often fled the dominions of Moscow, but the Communists have forced Socialists (Social Democrats) into the camp of "Socialist Unity"—not other parties. Among the run of the mill Socialists there are two kinds: those who really have watered the Marxist wine, and those who have remained Marxists but want to achieve the Great Goal democratically by parliamentary majorities. In an emergency, i.e., in case of a Communist takeover, the former usually emigrate and the latter collaborate. Yet Socialists who want to establish a collective state and society by persuasion (i.e., by "cerebral conquest") are just as much enemies of the right order as the revolutionaries who want to achieve an evil social system by the "dictatorship of the proletariat." The ends always remain reprehensible, only the means differ morally. And, in a deeper sense, popular feelings notwithstanding, the seducer is more diabolic and destructive than the rapist.

⁴⁸ Eugene Lyons called this film the intellectual abdication of America. It probably was the grossest piece of propaganda ever projected on the American screen.

⁴⁹ Miss Lillian Hellman also helped to direct a film with idyllic scenes of Russian collective farms.

⁵⁰ *Cf.* Quentin Reynolds, *Only the Stars Are Neutral* (New York: Random House, 1942).

⁵¹ *Ibid.*, p. 284.

⁵² *Ibid.*, p. 207.

⁵³ *Ibid.*, p. 98. If one knows the highly critical public utterances of Father Braun after his return, one really wonders what he told or did not tell Mr. Reynolds. As to religion in the USSR, the recent authoritative books of Walter Kolarz, *(Religion in the Soviet Union*, London: Macmillan, 1962) and Nikita Struve (*Les chrétiens en USSR*, Paris: Seuil, 1964) paint a depressing and frightful picture.

⁵⁴ Only Rhode Island among the original States had no establishment or religious tests for office. Disestablishment in Massachusetts came only in 1833. In New Hampshire until 1877 only "Protestants" could be elected for Congress, in New Jersey until 1844 nobody but a "Protestant" could hold political office. Congress also continued to vote public funds for "Protestant" missions among Indians. Here again is a potent myth! *Cf.* also Joseph McSorley CSP, *Father Hecker and His Friends* (St. Louis: B. Herder Book Co., 1952), p. 69. See also the letter by Mr. H. J. Freeman in *The Commonweal*, vol. 76, no. 20, September 7, 1962, pp. 495-496 full of specific data and referring to a recent decision of the Supreme Court proving its irrational stand on the First Amendment. "If the Black-Rutledge interpretation of the amendment was correct," he wrote, "then Congress had been acting unconstitutionally for 160 years during which it passed law after law concerning religion or religious institutions, and Madison did not know the meaning of the amendment he himself had drafted."

⁵⁵ Those who read Alexander Solzhenytsin's splendid novel *The First Circle* about a "swank" concentration camp (for technological specialists) in 1949 should also delve into the even more terrifying account of Anatoli Marchenko, *My Testimony*, which deals with concentration camps *today*. Only the very naive think that they have disappeared with Stalin's death.

⁵⁶ *Cf.* the terrible statistics of Nikita Struve's *op. cit.*, Annex IV, dealing with the martyred bishops of the USSR.

⁵⁷ *Cf.* Quentin Reynolds, *op. cit.*, p. 173.

⁵⁸ *Ibid.*, p. 110.

⁵⁹ *Cf.* Erik von Kuehnelt-Leddihn, *Black Banners* (Caldwell, Idaho: Caxton Printers, 1954), pp. 279-280. The brazen lies, needless to say, are usually the most successful ones, especially if they are stupid and most obviously contradict truth. Take for instance, the review of Abel Plenn's *Wind in Olive Trees* by W. E. Garrison in the *Christian Century*, June 1946, p. 781. There we find the statement that "most Spanish liberal leaders, including 30,000 Protestants, had been exterminated" (i.e., by the Franco regime). Mr.

W. E. Garrison was literary editor of the *Christian Century* and I immediately hastened to write a letter to the editor of this left-of-center weekly, inquiring why nobody had previously reported the biggest "sectarian massacre" in all history. I never got a reply and my letter, naturally, never appeared in the worthy paper.

[60] In 1914 people in England stoned dachshunds and burnt German pianos, a Russian mob stormed the German embassy in St. Petersburg, in Paris German-owned shops were destroyed, in Germany patriots greeted each other with *"Gott strafe England!"* and in the United States *sauerkraut* was re-named "liberty cabbage"—phenomena unthinkable in the earlier eighteenth century.

[61] Miss Lisa Sergio was probably one of the most fanatical "anti-Fascist" and leftist radio commentators, yet in a book which she had published a few years earlier in Italy—*From Intervention to Empire* (Rome: Novissima, 1937)—she wrote, "Notwithstanding the many deficiencies in this first book of Fascist Dates I dedicate it to the memory of all the Black Shirts who, within Italy and abroad, have written in their blood the glorious dates of the Fascist Era." This historic calendar is not uninteresting. Thus we read on page 177 under the heading July 25, 1934: "Herr Dollfuss, Austrian Chancellor, is assassinated by the Reds in Vienna." That these Reds were Nazis is a piece of newspeak.

[62] When I asked a Hungarian refugee and noted Iranian scholar of whom I heard that he was working in the O.W.I. (Office of War Information), whether he was in the German department, he answered sombrely, "Je ne suis pas encore tombé si bas"—"I have not fallen as low yet."

[63] *Cf.* Gustav Stolper, *This Age of Fable* (New York: Reynal and Hitchcock, 1942), p. 328, "The position of Hitlerism in public discussions has been largely fixed by the fact that the bulk of anti-Hitler literature . . . was written by Marxist authors of various denominations. As their political thinking was tied down to the Procrustean bed of primitive social philosophy, all they had to do was to fit the phenomenon of Hitlerism into their ready-made scheme. Since Hitler was anti-Marxist—whatever that meant—he must be the puppet of Capitalists. Once that was taken for granted, the details of the story were freely invented." Here again one has to bear in mind that the connection between class and ideology or financial interest is most flimsy. The three "Angels" of the New York *Daily Worker* were wealthy ladies: Susan Homans Woodruff, a D.A.R.; Anne Whitaker Pennypacker, daughter of Samuel Pennypacker, Governor of Pennsylvania; and Mrs. Fernanda W. Reed, daughter of a Cambridge physician.

[64] In the earlier 1940s General Electric published in leading American periodicals a full page ad featuring a miserable crowd of women and children dragging a plow. The text said that this was a common sight in Central Europe. A poster showing American schoolchildren, two of them barefoot, drew violent protests. And I know of American teachers who tried to bolster the patriotism of their pupils by telling them that their ancestors in Europe ate *black* bread! As indeed they did; but it is now sold in America as a delicacy.

[65] Ribbentrop had been neither a nobleman nor a noble man. *Cf.* Note 14 of this Chapter. Two of the accused were acquitted, the silly reactionary and the shrewd financier—Franz von Papen and Hjalmar Greeley Schacht (born in Brooklyn). But Papen, after all, had been nearly killed by the Nazis and Schacht had been liberated from a concentration camp in 1945.

[66] *Cf.* Note 33 of this Chapter. We also get some nice tidbits about Roosevelt's near-insanity from the *Eden Memoirs*, vol. 3, p. 464 (the Mikolaj-czyk wild goose chase), and p. 373. We hear about the president's plan to carve out a new state to be called "Wallonia" consisting of Southern Belgium, Luxembourg, Alsace-Lorraine, and parts of Northern France. Eden "politely poured water on it."

[67] *Cf.* Walter Lippmann, *op. cit.*, p. 21: "The masses have first to be frightened . . . the enemy has to be portrayed as evil incarnate, as absolute and congenital wickedness. The people wanted to be told that when this particular enemy had been forced to unconditional surrender, they would reenter the golden age. This unique war would end all wars. This last war would make the world safe for democracy. This crusade would make the whole world a democracy." Let us remember Lord Bryce who warned against the idea that democracy is "here to stay." *Cf.* Viscount Bryce, *Modern Democracy* (London: Macmillan, 1921), vol. 1, p. 47.

[68] *Cf.* his *Time for Decision* (New York: Harper, 1944). The following year another volume came out, a sort of guide to the postwar world, written more or less by two confirmed leftists and merely "edited" by the old gentleman. It was Muscovite propaganda pure and simple. (*An Intelligent Man's Guide to the Peace*, Sumner Welles, ed, New York: Dryden, 1945).

[69] *Cf.* Henry Morgenthau, *Germany Is Our Problem* (New York: Harper, 1945). In his book we find a map showing a partitioned Germany. Yet Morgenthau's propositions from a purely territorial viewpoint were *far less harsh* than the reality: Morgenthau gave only Upper Silesia and East Prussia to Poland. Typical is the remark (p. 57) that the Junkers were "backward in their social outlook."

[70] *Cf.* Theodore N. Kaufman, *Germany Must Perish!* (Newark: Argyle Press, 1941), particularly pp. 97-98. This book was a "godsend" to Goebbels. But in a preface written for *Men at War*, an anthology, Ernest Hemingway also proposed the sterilization of all Germans.

[71] By 1939 the *New Leader* was, to be true, a socially-minded rather than a Socialist paper. It had shed its original Marxism.

[72] *Cf.* William H. Chamberlin, "The Tragic Case of Finland," *The American Mercury*, vol. 59, no. 247, July 1941, pp. 7-15.

Here is the record in the *New York Times*: Monday, June 23, 1941, p. 2, Finnish Communiqué; Soviet flyers start bombing, A.P.; Clashes not yet recorded, U.P.; Russians violate Finnish territory. P. 3: Finland declared not to be at war. U.P. relates interview of Soviet Minister Orlov in Helsinki: "We are convinced that neither side wants to fight." Tuesday, June 24, 1941: Gripenberg, Finnish Minister in London, enlightens Eden as to Russian attacks.

P. 5: Finland professes neutrality in war. Wednesday, June 25, 1941: p. 2: Continuous aerial bombardments in the entire south of Finland. (Informations of the *New York Times* correspondent.) Thursday, June 26, 1941, pp. 1 and 2: Associated Press describes the big damages caused by Soviet bombardments. Friday, June 27, 1941: *Five days after German attack* Finland declared war (on June 26). The declaration is decided upon after a plenary session of the *Eduskunta* (parliament). Soviets protest against Finnish "Fascist militarism."

[73] *Cf.* Fitzroy How MacLean, *Escape to Adventure: Eastern Approaches* (Boston: Little, Brown and Co., 1951), pp. 309-312. Another observer, the American Leigh White, wrote, "Surely the Serbs were as precious as the lives of Britons and Americans—or were they? Let us face it: they were not. We fought the war according to a double standard of human values. In Western Europe we afforded the *guerrilleros* to husband their resources, human lives included, until the eve of victory. In Eastern Europe we demanded increasingly suicidal adventures in the unexpressed conviction that Slavic and Balkan blood was less valuable than the blood of Saxons, Latins, and Scandinavians." *Cf. Balkan Caesar* (New York: Scribner's, 1951).

[74] On Mussolini's authoritative views on the collectivist and leftist nature of fascism *cf.* Hans Sennholz, "Who Is the Fascist?" *Human Events*, December 25, 1965. This essay is carefully documented.

[75] *Cf.* Harold Nicolson, *Curzon: The Last Phase*, pp. 205-207: H. W. V. Temperley, *op. cit.*, vol. 6, pp. 267, 275; Ferdinand Lot, *Les invasions barbares et le peuplement de l'Europe* (Paris: Payot, 1937), p. 191n. Leszek Kirkien, *Russia, Poland and the Curzon Line* (London: Caldra House, n.d.); Stanislaw Grabski, *The Polish-Soviet Frontier* (London: 1943, no publisher mentioned); Hans Roos, *Geschichte der polnischen Nation 1916-1960* (Stuttgart: W. Kohlhammer, 1961), pp. 78-79.

There seems to exist, however, an old British-Polish incompatibility of character and outlook also affecting the political scene. This mutual incomprehension is partly the result of the confrontation of the Catholic thirst for the Absolute and the post-Protestant delight in *justemilieu* and compromise. Already Disraeli disliked the Polish refugees and resented their activities. *Cf.* W. F. Monypenny and G. E. Buckle, *op. cit.*, vol. 2, p. 71. Yet the great "professional" hater of the Poles was Lloyd George, the friend of Hitler, great Franco-baiter and erstwhile protector of Winston Churchill. In all Polish border questions Lloyd George opposed them violently and in the Polish-Soviet war of 1919-1920 the Premier stood solidly on the side of Bolshevism. *Cf. Lord Riddell's Intimate Diary of the Paris Peace Conference 1918-1923* (New York: Reynal and Hitchcock, 1934), pp. 221-224. When the Poles defeated the Red army Lloyd George (who had danced with joy when he heard in Chequers that the Reds were in the suburbs of Warsaw), was deeply disappointed. (*Ibid.*, p. 233). To him the Poles were mad and arrogant, they were hopeless, they were a menace to the peace of Europe. (*Ibid.*, pp. 191, 227, 198). His hatred for the Poles never abated, Count Kessler heard him (March 24, 1925) rant against the Poles in the House of Commons and was disgusted by the "grotesque sight of an old ham actor demagogically attacking his own work." *Cf.* Graf Harry Kessler, *Tagebücher 1918-1937* (Frankfurt: Insel-Verlag, 1961), p. 427. The (London) *Sunday Express* published on September 24, 1939 (!) an article by Lloyd George entitled "What is Stalin up to?" in which the former Premier reviled the "class-ridden" Polish government and "Polish Imperialism" and praised the Soviets for "liberating their kinsmen from the Polish yoke." *Cf.* Count Edward Raczyński, *In Allied London* (London: Weidenfeld and Nicolson, 1962), p. 37. Worse still, on September 27 Lloyd George attacked prostrate Poland in the House of Commons as the "worst feudal system in Europe," a line which his friend Adolf Hitler took up on October 7 in the *Reichstag* calling Poland a country "ruled by aristocrats since 1919." *Cf.* the *New York Times*, September 28, 1939, p. 5:6 and October 7, 1939, p. 8:3. The root of this attitude is to be found elsewhere. When Virginia Cowles asked him why he was so anti-Franco while approving of Hitler, he replied with a twinkle, "I always line up on the side against the priests." *Cf.* Virginia Cowles, *Looking for Trouble* (London: Hamish Hamilton, 1941), p. 107.

[76] *Cf.* Sumner Welles, *op. cit.*, p. 310. Malcolm Muggeridge, one of the wittiest of contemporary British writers, wrote a brilliant parody on Winston Churchill's attitude towards Poland in *Punch* (1953), *Cf.* Burling and Lowrey, eds. *Twentieth Century Parody: American and British Anthology* (New York: Harcourt, Brace, 1960), pp. 133-135.

[77] Once a member republic of the USSR has its artificially boosted Russian majority, it is regularly disestablished. Thus the Karelo-Finnish Soviet Socialist Republic was first deprived of Eastern Karelia and the rest then placed under the RSFSR, the Russian Soviet Federal Socialist Republic. One wonders what will happen (in the near future!) once Kazakhstan will have a Russian majority. In the years 1945 to 1948 the area in Europe incorporated into the USSR or occupied by it was about 700,000 square miles (1,757,500 square kilometers) which is about the size of New England, the Middle Atlantic States, the South Atlantic States down to Key West, Michigan, Indiana, Kentucky, Ohio, Tennessee, and West Virginia. Subsequently only Eastern Austria was lost and, in a way, Yugoslavia.

[78] *Cf. Concise Statistical Year Book of Poland* (London, 1941), p. 9, F. A. Doubek, "Die Ostgrenze der polnischen Volkstumsmehrheit," *Jomburg* (Leipzig), vol. 2. no. 1. Among eminent Poles born west of the Hitler-Stalin Line we shall mention a few: King Jan III Sobieski who saved Vienna and Europe in 1683; the painter Henryk Siemiradzki; the two national heroes Kościuszko and Pulaski; the pianist and statesman Paderewski; Poland's two greatest poets Mickiewicz and Slowacki; the writer Joseph Conrad (Korzeniowski); the philosopher Cieszkowski; and General Pilsudski. We can say without

exaggeration that very few of the Poles known to educated Americans or Britishers are born *west* of the Hitler-Stalin line. (Sienkiewicz and Sikorski were the exceptions proving the rule.)

[79] Indeed the great liberal, Franz Grillparzer, was right when he wrote in 1849 under the impact of the Revolution:

> The way of civilization goes
> For humanitarianism
> Over nationalism
> To beastliness.

[80] Peoples speaking an identical (or very similar) language often fought bitterly wars among themselves: the Irish and the English, the Americans and the British, the Union Forces and the Confederates, the Austrians and the Prussians, the Chileans and the Peruvians, etc.

[81] On the natural borders of Poland with Russia *Cf.* Albrecht Penck, "Die natürliche Grenze Russlands," *Meereskunde* (Berlin, 1917), vol. 12, no. 1.

[82] *Cf.* Viscount d'Abernon, *The Eighteenth Decisive Battle of the World, Warsaw, 1920* (London: Hodder and Stoughton, 1931), p. 81; Harold Nicolson, *Curzon: The Last Phase*, p. 205; H. W. V. Temperley, *op. cit.*, vol. 6. p. 320; Stanislaw Grabski, *op. cit.*, pp. 21-25; Hans Roos, *op. cit.*, pp. 79-80.

[83] Hetman Simon Petlyura was assassinated years later in Paris by a Jewish emigrant in revenge for the pogroms carried out by Ukrainian troops during the war. The Ukrainian troops were certainly not innocent in the sacking of Jewish quarters, yet also the Polish army was guilty of about thirty, the Red army of no less than 106 *pogromy*. (*Cf. The Jewish Encyclopedia*, New York, 1943, vol. 8, p. 562). Did the Jews in these borderlands prefer Red Freedom to Polish "Military Facism"? Between November 11, 1918 and June 30, 1924 no less than 33,000 "ethnical" Jews fled from the East to the West. This number excludes Jews considering themselves Poles, Ukrainians, Russians, etc. *Cf. Maly Rocznik Statystyczny*, Warsaw, 1939, p. 52. (There were also 122,000 Ukrainians, 492,000 White Ruthenians, and 121,000 Russians fleeing in the same direction.)

[84] *Cf.* Note 75 of this Chapter. Also Frank H. Simonds, in the (London) *Times*, April 25, 1919.

[85] *Cf.* Viscount d'Abernon, *op. cit.*, pp. 20-21.

[86] General Weygand always disclaimed a share in the victory. *Cf.* Winston S. Churchill, *The World Crisis* (London: Thornton Butterworth, 1929), vol. 5, pp. 271-272; Ferdinand Lot, *op. cit.*, p. 194; Général Camoin, *La Maneuvre libératrice du maréchal Pilsudski contre les bolchéviks en août 1920* (Paris: 1929); Hans Roos, *op. cit.*, pp. 88-89. Roos says that the idea of Weygand's exclusive merits came from the Polish National Democrats who

hated Pilsudski. De Gaulle, who accompanied Weygand on his mission, was deeply impressed by the strategic genius of Pilsudski, and General Hans von Seeckt, the reorganizer of the German army, saw in him a "Polish Frederick the Great."

[87] *Cf. Bolshaya Sovyetskaya Entsiklopediya* (Moscow: Gossudarstvenny Institut, 1940), vol. 46, p. 247.

[88] *Cf.* Note 83 of this Chapter.

[89] *Cf. Vnyeshnaya politika sovyetskogo soyuza v periodye otyechestvennoy voiny* (Moscow: Ogiz, 1944), vol. 1, p. 121.

[90] Typical was an editorial in the *New Republic* on February 20, 1943 dealing with the Soviet claims on the Baltic States: "Yet, however forceful or dubious the Russian legal claims, the crux of the problem must be sought not in legal genealogies, but in the need of an enduring friendship between Russia and America." Today the United States is being asked by our leftists to make other human sacrifices on the altar of an enduring friendship between Washington and Peking.

[91] The Ukrainians in Poland had just grievances, such as a university of their own. They wanted a university in Lwów (Lviv, Lemberg), but the Polish government offered one elsewhere. Still the Ukrainian language was even taught in certain ethnically Polish schools. The literary life of the Ukrainians in Southeast Poland was flourishing. Take only the number of Ukrainian periodicals: sixty-four in 1932, seventy-two in 1934, 116 in 1936. *Cf.* Bochénski, Loś, and Baczkowski, *Problem polsko-ukraínski w Zemiej Czerwieńskiej* (Warsaw, 1938). On the schools *cf.* Stanislaw Sobiński, *L'enseignement public en Petite Pologne orientale au point de vue national* (Lwów, 1923), especially p. 12 and Tables 1, 2, 3. These two books represent a Polish viewpoint. Still Professor Chubatyj was right when he said in 1944 that no more than 5 percent of the population of East Poland would freely vote for the USSR. *Cf.* "The Ukraine and the Polish-Russian Boundary Dispute," *The Ukraine Quarterly*, vol. 1 (October 1944), p. 70.

[92] Here we must not forget that the Ukrainians (Ruthenians) from Polish-dominated Eastern Galicia were in many ways different from the Ukrainians who had been for a long time under Russian rule. (Those from Eastern Galicia were predominantly Catholics of the Eastern Rite, those from the "Russian" Ukraine were "orthodox." The Russian *Entsiklopeditcheski Slovar* (St. Petersburg, 1892), vol. 7-A, p. 907 insisted that these differences were marked. It added that many Jews in that area considered themselves to be Poles (p. 908). The Ukrainian Encyclopedia *Ukrainska Zagalna Entsiklopediya* (Lviv), vol. 2, p. 567, dealing with Lwów, provides the following statistics: 50 percent Poles, 35 percent Jews, and 15 percent Ukrainians.

[93] From being a minority in Poland these people would merely have become minorities in the USSR. Today, due to the Soviet demographic policies, the Ukrainians are a minority even in Kiev, their own capital.

[94] As a matter of fact, none of the more respectable American papers

expressed positive belief in Soviet innocence. At the Nuremberg trial, the accusation that the Nazis had perpetrated the crime was quietly dropped. In view of the Katyn crime Ernst Jünger could write about the Nuremberg trial: "The worst thing of all is to put yourself into the wrong *vis-à-vis* a scoundrel. He will talk to you of morals and there is no more pitiless judge than one who is in the right, and a scoundrel to boot. Shylock gives us a pale notion of such a person.

"In this respect the non-plus-ultra is a court consisting of murderers and puritans. Then the slaughter knife is given a moral handle." *Cf.* his *Strahlungen III* (Munich: Deutscher Taschenbuchverlag, 1966), p. 254.

[95] The Katyn crime was discovered at a rather early date by the German occupants. The janitor of the GPU-NKVD building in Smolensk, where the German staff was quartered, babbled about it once when he was drunk. Only upon an order from Berlin to make an inquiry into Soviet atrocities was a regular investigation started. Actually nobody had originally believed the janitor's story, but now he furnished the details. First the German authorities tried to determine the date of the mass murder by analyzing the decomposed brains of the victims, but the age of the trees planted over the huge mass graves gave a more exact clue. (Information was given to the author by the late Prince Erich Waldburg zu Zeil.) When the Poles demanded an impartial inquiry through the International Red Cross, the Soviets broke off with the Polish Government in Exile. The number of the murdered officers, the cream of the Polish Army, was between 9,000 and 12,000—a piece of genuine class genocide. The discussion between Sikorski, Anders, Stalin, and Molotov about the fate of the missing officers a year earlier (as reported by Anders) must have been amazing. Stalin maintained that these officers must have fled somewhere, perhaps to Manchuria. The older lie, that the boats carrying them to Solovki had been torpedoed in the White Sea, had then already' been dropped. *Cf.* Général W. Anders, *Mémoires* (Paris: La Jeune Parque, 1948), trsl. I. Rzewuska, pp. 119-120. Anders' book cannot be read but with an intense feeling of moral nausea.

[96] There is no reason to assume that Andrzej Wyszyński, the Soviet prosecutor and delegate at the United Nations, one of the vilest creatures in modern history, is in any way related to Cardinal Wyszyński. Andrzej Wyszyński, also of Polish extraction, was a Menshevik and joined the Bolsheviks only in 1920. Thus he had to make extraordinary efforts to prove his loyalty—to the Soviet Union and to communism.

[97] *Cf. The Case of Henryk Erlich and Victor Alter,* foreword by Camille Huysmans (New York: General Jewish Workers' Union of Poland, 1943).

[98] One of the most moving documents on these efforts to escape from the huge Soviet dungeon is Slawomir Rawicz's book, *The Long Walk,* (New York: Harper and Row, 1956) describing the flight of three Poles, two men and one girl, from Siberia over Mongolia and Tibet to India.

[99] A big mass rally of the "Congress of American Soviet Friendship"

was held in New York's Madison Square Garden on November 7, 1942, to celebrate the 25th birthday of the Soviet Union. Congratulations came in from President Roosevelt and General Eisenhower. There were 20,000 delegates. Thomas W. Lamont (of J. P. Morgan) spoke for greater tolerance, William Green of the A.F. of L. gave a speech and Senator Pepper explained that "It behooved the United States to be worthy of such a friend as Russia." Professor Ralph Barton Perry of Harvard "warned against a policy of first trying to destroy the Soviets, then ignoring them and, finally, treating them as poor relations." *Cf.* Foster Rhea Dulles, *The Road to Teheran*, p. 245.

[100] In a letter to Eden (dated December 3, 1944) Churchill had called Stalin a "great and good man"—fully realizing that man's crimes. *Cf.* Winston S. Churchill, *The Second World War*, vol. 6, p. 616.

[101] David Irving in *op. cit.*, p. 112, talking about the high degree of saturation bombing: "Every time it had been employed before, it had caused a fire-storm of some degree. Previously the fire-storm had been merely an unfortunate result of the attack: In the double-blow on Dresden the fire-storm was to be an integral part of the strategy." And let nobody believe that Mr. Churchill was innocent about the A-Bomb on Hiroshima. He agreed upon its dropping. *Cf.* The Earl of Avon, *The Eden Memoirs*, vol. 3, p. 547. However, he knew nothing about Harry S. Truman's additional designs on the cradle of Christianity in Japan, about the impending devastation of Nagasaki.

[102] *Cf.* Albert C. Wedemeyer, *op. cit.*, pp. 416-418.

[103] On these efforts *cf.* Allen Welsh Dulles, Gerhart Ritter, Eberhard Zeller, *op. cit.*

[104] *Cf.* B. H. Liddell-Hart, *The German Generals Talk* (New York: Morrow 1948), pp. 292-293, referring to Germans and the German troops during the war; " 'black-listening' to the Allied radio service was widespread. But the Allied propaganda never said anything positive about the peace conditions in the way of encouraging them to give up the struggle. Its silence on the subject was so marked that it tended to confirm what Nazi propaganda told them as to the dire fate in store for them if they surrendered. So it greatly helped the Nazis to keep the German troops and people to continue fighting —long after they were ready to give up." Thus Roosevelt's "originality" *cost the lives of countless Americans*. Government-by-brainwaves sometimes is murder.

The U. S. army was anything but enthusiastic about the unconditional surrender formula as it had to pay its price in blood. *Cf.* Captain Harry C. Butcher, *My Three Years with Eisenhower* (New York: Simon and Schuster, 1946), Entry of August 12, 1943. The real beneficiaries were the Nazis and the USSR.

[105] The efforts of Louis P. Lochner, an American journalist (Associated Press) to inform President Roosevelt in 1942 about the German conspiracy against Hitler proved totally abortive. The President refused to receive him because such a meeting would have been "highly embarrassing." *Cf.* H. Rothfels, *Die deutsche Oposition gegen Hitler* (Krefeld: Scherpe, 1949), p.

166sq. One might add almost cynically the well-known adage, "Don't confuse me with facts, I have already made up my mind." This, however, was an *indoctrinated* leftist mind.

[106] *Cf.* Allen Welsh Dulles, *op. cit.*, p. 42; George A. Bell, Bishop of Chichester, in the *Contemporary Review* (London), October, 1945. Eden's reply to the Bishop can be found in *20. Juli 1944* (Freiburg i. Br.: Herder, 1961) "Herder-Bücherei," vol. 96, p. 52. Regrettably we do not find it in the *Eden Memoirs*.

[107] Churchill, in his speech to the Commons on August 2, 1944, declared that the only point of interest in the July Conspiracy was the spectacle of "Nazis" murdering each other. (Gerhard Ritter, *op. cit.*, pp. 333-334.) Yet Churchill was ceaselessly informed about the German opposition by Dr. Bell, Anglican Bishop of Chichester, Dr. Bell in turn was in permanent contact with the now famous German theologian, Pastor Dietrich Bonhoeffer, via the latter's brother-in-law, Dr. Leibholz, a refugee in Britain. (Bonhoeffer, now erroneously claimed by God-is-dead theologians abroad, was an intimate friend of the conspirators and was executed in Flossenbürg.) The Bishop of Chichester wrote to Leibholz on August 8, 1944: "I heard Churchill . . . but he is living in a world of battles only, and seeing time with the mind of a child with regard to deep policy—for Home affairs as well as the far graver matters. And disaster gets nearer and nearer. One feels so powerless. . . ." *Cf.* Eberhard Bethge, *Dietrich Bonhoeffer, Theologe, Christ, Zeitgenosse* (Munich: Chr. Kaiser-Verlag, 1967), p. 1004.

[108] I spoke with Cardinal Count von Preysing in Berlin a few weeks before his death. He assured me that neither he nor Cardinal von Galen had known concrete facts about the extermination camps in the East. They had information about the extermination of the insane and thus they protested against this kind of leftist-humanitarian atrocity which sails under the label of "euthanasia" in the West. Had they known about genocide in Polish camps, they would have done the same. The German philosopher Karl Jaspers and Herr Rudolf Augstein, editor-in-chief of the leftist *Der Spiegel* were similarly ignorant. They only had vague notions of the horrors and knew the truth only in 1945. *Cf.* Karl Jaspers, *Wohin treibt die Bundesrepublik?* (Munich: R. Piper and Co., 1966), p. 36. Albert Speer admitted to have heard rumors but failed to have them confirmed or denied—for which he feels guilty. *Cf. op. cit.*, pp. 385-386.

Cf. also George N. Shuster (former President of Hunter College and U. S. Commissioner of Bavaria), "Catholic Resistance in Nazi Germany," in *Thought*, vol. 22, no. 84 (March 1947), p. 13, talking about Msgr. Johann Neuhäusler's book *Kreuz und Hakenkreuz*: "He goes on to conclude that if the bishops were not afraid to attack euthanasia as a means for disposing of the mentally sick, they most assuredly would have spoken out against the gas ovens of Auschwitz had they known of their existence. With this I am in agreement. The Cardinal of Cologne as well as the late Cardinal of Münster, whose courage none will doubt, assured me that they were without an inkling of the nefarious acts committed during the final years of the Third Reich."

[109] *Cf.* Léon Blum, in the *New Leader* (New York:) July 21, 1946. Constantin Silens in *Irrweg und Umkehr. Betrachtung über das Schicksal Deutschlands* (Basel: Birkhäuser, 1946), p. 216, thinks that Niemoeller's assumption of one in 100,000 Germans knowing about the extermination camps is an overstatement. There were fewer. The *bulk* of the personnel in the extermination camps was undoubtedly East European.

[110] The "Gerstein Report" (a German translation from the French, the German original having been lost) had been published for the first time by the *Vierteljahrshefte für Zeitgeschichte,* vol. 1, (Stuttgart, 1953). Gerstein was a former SS man who before the war had left this organization, became a devout Lutheran and was redrafted after the outbreak of the war. Arrested by the French, he gave a full description of the horrors of the extermination camps. Brought to Paris he perhaps committed suicide by hanging, but there is a distinct possibility that he was murdered by other Nazis in the jail.

[111] *Cf.* the letter by William N. Harrigan in *Commonweal*, April 3, 1964, p. 48. In this letter the official publication *Foreign Relations 1942* (Washington, D.C.: United States Government Printing Office, 1961), vol. 3, pp. 772-778 is cited. Cardinal Maglione insisted that the Vatican had no detailed or certain knowledge about large-scale Nazi atrocities. Cardinal Tisserand insisted that the Vatican knew nothing about the mass slaughters and mass cremation of Jews until the advancing Allied Armies began to reach Rome. *Cf.* N. C. "Cardinal Says He Criticized Curia, Not Pius, on Hitler," in *The Catholic Universe Bulletin,* April 3, 1964, (vol. 90, no. 51), pp. 1-2. It is perhaps necessary to bring up this matter because a German playwright, Rolf Hochhuth, has fabricated a drama which rather conveniently makes Pius XII morally the most responsible man in that terrible slaughter. It is significant for the radical ignorance of the period in which we live, that a play such as *Der Stellvertreter* ("The Deputy") can be staged all over the world without the public seeing immediately the total ignorance, the silliness, and the inanity of the text. *Cf.* my review of this play in *The Timeless Christian* (Chicago: Franciscan Herald Press, 1969), pp. 184-194. (German original: *Hirn, Herz and Rückgrat*, Osnabrück, Fromm, 1968, pp. 221-233.) Yet the audience of a modern theater in our age of affluence and illiteracy is made up of people unable to judge history, past or contemporary.

Pius XII had done his level best to save Jewish lives: he had no concrete knowledge about the extermination camps, but even had he been informed, what could he have done? One has to remember the protest of the Dutch Catholic bishops against the deportation of Jews to an unknown destination. The Nazis retaliated by rounding up Catholics of Jewish descent—and sending them to Auschwitz. In this group the Carmelite nun and philosopher Edith Stein (a disciple of Husserl) perished. The Church (in the words of St. Augustine) is always *pauper et inops*, poor and helpless . . . and this certainly includes the Middle Ages when the "power" of the Church was also an optical illusion, like the light of the moon which is nothing but reflected sunlight. Not Canossa is the end of the struggle between Henry IV and the Church, but the bitter end of Gregory VII in exile, who, when dying, repeated the words of the Psalm: *"Dilexi iustitiam et odi iniquitatem propterea morior in exilio."*

[112] I was present when one of my Jewish friends debated this issue in New York with a Red Cross delegate who had come out of Germany in late 1943. The Red Cross official, a man of unquestionable anti-Nazi conviction, poo-poohed the idea that extermination camps existed. Euthanasian measures such as death in a gas chamber he considered more humane than slow death by beatings and attrition in a concentration camp, but he warned my friend not to spread false information which would merely aid the Nazis.

[113] *Cf.* Chapter VII, Note 136. At the same time one wonders what was known—and duly noted—about the Soviet concentration camps by the USSR's Western Allies. *Vide* the rather comprehensive picture in Robert Conquest's account *The Great Terror: Stalin's Purge of the Thirties* (New York: Macmillan, 1968). And that horror still continues.

[114] Even today these wounds are far from healed. The old hatreds, as I could find out during a recent trip through Yugoslavia, still have lost nothing of their hideous strength. As a matter of fact, the resistance against the Communist regime is paralyzed by the subconscious (and sometimes conscious) fear that with the collapse of the Red dictatorship the various artificially united nationalities and nations of Yugoslavia would again be at each other's throats. Thus the foundation of Yugoslavia in 1918 actively fosters the survival of communism today.

The worst mutual massacres, however, did not take place between Serbs and Croats, but between Albanians and Serbs in the Kossovo Region which had been annexed by Serbia in 1912-1913, but got a "breathing spell" under German occupation. Then the Albanian minority saw the fine opportunity for revenge. In 1944 the Serb Communists took their revenge and slaughtered about 40,000 to 50,000 Albanians, and another massacre took place (this time methodical and organized) in the winter 1955-1956 under the "Stalinist" Minister of the Interior, Ranković. The details of these crimes were only revealed at the session of the *Savez Komunista* (League of Communists) in 1966 in Priština.

[115] This does not mean that situations do not arise in which a man of integrity and knowledge is incapable of finding a way out. Count Paul Teleki, a great scholar and statesman, my former teacher and personal friend, was forced by the Nazis, while he was Hungarian Prime Minister in 1941, to choose between dishonor and the ruin of his country. In a fit of depression this devout Catholic committed suicide.

[116] Though I was not a political refugee in the United States, (having left Austria for Hungary in 1929, I had gone there from Britain in 1937, before

the *Anschluss*), I still regret that I did not stay in Europe—whatever the cost —to resist the evil on the spot.

[117] I think of authors such as Frank Thiess (*Das Reich der Dämonen*), Ernst Wiechert, Werner Bergengruen (*Im Himmel und auf Erden*), Reinhold Schneider, Ernst Jünger (*Auf den Marmorklippen*), Friedrich Georg Jünger *(Der Mohn)*, and above all, Fritz Reck-Malleczewen who wrote a bit too obviously. His *Bockelsohn: Geschichte eines Massenwahns* is a description of Hitler under the mask of Jan van Leiden. He perished heroically in a concentration camp.

[118] When Baron Leonrod, a member of the July 20 conspiracy, admitted that he had asked a priest whether tyrannicide was morally permissible, the Nazi authorities were able to trace the priest. Leonrod as well as the priest were hanged. *Cf.* Allen Welsh Dulles, *op. cit.*, pp. 115-116. Tyrannicide has been part of traditional (but never "officially accepted") Jesuit moral theology. *Cf. Documents historiques, critiques, apologétiques concernant la Compagnie de Jésus* (Paris: Carié, 1828), vol. 2, pp. 83ff. Naturally, the originator of this theory is Juan de Mariana S.J. who dealt with it in *De Rege et Regis Institutione*. St. Thomas opposed tyrannicide, but permitted rebellion—and the killing of the tyrant in a rebellion. *Cf.* Fernando d'Antonio, "Il tirannicidio nel pensiero dell'acquinate," *Annali di Scienze Politiche* (University of Pavia, 1939), vol. 12, fasc. 1-2. John of Salisbury took a positive attitude towards tyrannicide. *Cf.* his "Policraticus sive de nugis curialium et vestigiis philosophorum," book 3, ch. 4 in Migne, *Patrologia Latina*, vol. 199, col. 512. The same opinion was defended by Joannes Parvus. *Cf. Ionnis Gersonis Opera Omnia* (Antwerp, 1706), vol. 5, p. 27. Luther naturally opposed it. *Cf.* his "Ermahnungen zum Frieden." *Krit. Gesamtausgabe* (Weimar), vol. 18, p. 303. So also did Calvin, who called a tyrant *un ire de Dieu* who should not be resisted. (*Institutions*, IV, xx, 25)

The views of the South American political theorists in the colonial period were also directly or indirectly favorable to tyrannicide. *Cf.* Agustín de Assís, *Ideas sociopolíticas de Alonso Polo (el Tostado)* in the series "Estudios Hispano-Americanos", (Seville, 1955), vol. 94, pp. 57-61.

[119] Robert Green Ingersoll (1833-1899) was that professional atheist, author, and lecturer who, as proof for the nonexistence of God, placed his watch on a lectern and gave his Creator three minutes to strike him dead. God failed to comply with this somewhat peremptory demand.

[120] "I am afraid of liberalism," Samuel Butler wrote in 1893, "or, at any rate, of the people who call themselves liberal: They flirt with radicals who flirt with socialists who flirt with anarchists who do something a deal more than flirt with dynamite."

[121] Mrs. Roosevelt participated in the United Nations' Commission for Human Rights. She obviously had all the intellectual and ideological qualifications to cooperate in important ventures of this august body.

[122] Nobody asked what they were fleeing from. Obviously not from Nazism which had been defeated. Many of them were Jews who knew that

581

they had no chance of a decent life under communism. Without this highly justified fear Israel as we know it today would hardly exist.

[123] Mrs. Roosevelt might have received this idea from one of her good leftist friends, Louis Adamič, a Slovene immigrant and a White House habitué who wrote, "Stalin is apt to insist on outright Sovietization of all Eastern Europe and the chances are he will achieve this end. The majority of the Slavic peoples in the region would be for it. Under those circumstances so would I." Cf. his *My Native Country* (New York: Harper, 1943), p. 483. He spoke in a similar vein in his *The Native's Return*: "America will have to go Left. . . . She will go Left, too, because Americans, like Slavs, are essentially constructive—people of the future. I guess my job in the next few years, perhaps for the rest of my life, will be to harp on that idea." He had not much opportunity to do a lot of harping because soon after the war—in a fit of complete disillusionment, one could assume—he took his own life. Yet it was certainly tragic that there was nobody else to interpret Southeastern Europe to Americans but Mr. Adamič, author of *Dinner at the White House*.

[124] Separation of State and Church (which certainly was *not* the issue over which Cardinal Mindszenty was tortured) can assume all sorts of forms —peaceful—neutral or hostile. In a totalitarian state it makes little difference (if any) whether Church and State are separated or not, just as it makes no difference to a man in a straitjacket whether its fabric is glued to his body or not. ("Largest landowner?" Well, obviously no single landowner had more acreage than the Church which had big obligations—buildings, salaries, schools, hospitals, cemeteries, etc.)

It is interesting to note, however, that Red tyrants in persecuting the Church have repeatedly and hypocritically invoked the example of the United States.

[125] When I returned to Austria in 1947 an American friend said mournfully to me, "I suppose you go back where the two One Worlds meet."

[126] How did Mr. Willkie know? He should have read Manya Gordon's *Workers Before and After Lenin* to learn the contrary. Mr. Willkie's bestseller—a dollar apiece—was filled with one delightful boner after the other. In the chapter dealing with Egypt he inquires into the reason for Egypt's cultural sterility. Why, for instance, were there no outstanding Egyptian painters? Obviously because Egypt lacked a sound middle class! It never dawned upon Mr. Willkie that Moslems (unless they are Shiites) are traditionally forbidden by their religion to depict the human or animal figure.

[127] The meaning of an oath in the case of a theist is clear to me. But why should an agnostic not commit perjury in good faith since he is skeptical about the human attainability of truth? And whom does he invoke as a witness? Mr. Alger Hiss, moreover, had been secretary to Justice Oliver Wendell Holmes, Jr. (1929-1930) and taking Holmes' *Weltanschauung* into consideration we have no reason to believe that Mr. Hiss—if he followed his late employer's argumentation—could have condemned perjury. Still, a society liv-

ing from the "Whiff of an empty bottle" (of Christianity, that is) for a long time refused to believe in Hiss' guilt. *Cf.* E. Digby Baltzell, *The Protestant Establishment: Aristocracy and Caste in America* (New York: Random House, 1964), pp. 282-283.

[128] The term "National Socialist" was inadmissible to the Soviets. In official parlance there were only Germans, Hitlerites (*gitlerovtsi*), or "Fascists," but never National Socialists or Nazis. Is it now not perhaps the "German Democratic Republic," the Soviet satellite, which represents "real National Socialism"?

[129] *Cf. The Memoirs of Cordell Hull* (New York: Macmillan, 1948), vol. 2, p. 1297. In his memoirs, Hull stated (p. 1293) that Eden was the driving force in the "Austrian Declaration." And James F. Byrnes in his *Speaking Frankly* (New York: Harper, 1947), p. 161, could not refrain from remarking, "It is not unfair to describe this policy now as one that seems to punish the Austrians for their association with the Germans during the Nazi occupation, and one that tries to make Austria an economic if not political dependency of the Soviet Union." The Austrian resistance, coming mainly from Monarchists and Catholics, was very substantial and, in the meantime, a number of books have been published on that subject. The first coherent account was given by Wilhelm Schmidt SVD in *Gegenwart und Zukunft des Abendlandes* (Luzern: Stocker, 1949), pp. 214-322. More detailed: Otto Molden, *Der Ruf des Gewissens* (Vienna: Herold, 1959). The weakest resistance came from the Social Democrats, (p. 226). Cordell Hull excused the recognition of Nazi Germany's grab with the fact that the United States wanted to collect the Austrian debts from Germany, the "incorporator." (*The Memoirs*, pp. 575-576). Naturally, the main culprit in the *Anschluss* (after the Nazis themselves) were the Western Powers, mainly England. *Cf.* also L. v. Tončić Sorinj (the present Chairman of the Council of Europe in Strasbourg), "Die Kollaboration Europas. Die unteilbare Schuld der Mächte am Aufstieg Hitlers," *Berichte und Informationen*, vol. 2 (1947), no. 59.

When I protested after the "Declaration" in a letter to the *New York Times* (signed by my pen-name F. S. Campbell), I was contradicted by the editor of the pro-Communist *Austro-American Tribune* who pointed out that Austrian ammunition plants worked for the Germans. (And what about the Skoda Works in Czechoslovakia, Schneider-Creuzot in France, and so forth?) These and other criticisms infuriated Cordell Hull to the extent that he became violently anti-Austrian. On this subject matter George Creel had an acrimonious discussion with him. (Verbal communication of the late G. Creel.) Eden was right when he wrote about Hull: "Yet it was impossible to forget the beak and the claws. I could never watch him without recalling the song of his native Tennessee about the Martins and the Coys. I felt that he too could pursue a vendetta to the end." (*The Eden Memoirs*, vol. 3. p. 380). His vindictiveness fully centered on Austria.

[130] The involuntary French contribution to the German war effort was

considerable. Not only did a French Legion fight in Russia, but the French war industry was working full blast for Germany.

[131] One of the last public acts of Mr. Hull was to remind the Austrians that they had to rebel openly against Germany, as an active contribution to their liberation, because the final judgment of the Allies would depend upon whether Austria in some way atoned for "having participated in the war on Hitler's side." He ended by remarking, "I want to say that the time for Austria to make that contribution is almost up." (*Cf.* the *New York Times*, September 12, 1944, p. 6:1). One really wonders whether the inertia of the Austrians dreading the Soviet steamroller more than anything else, could have resulted in a continuation of the *Anschluss*. "You won't knife German soldiers? All right, then you'll keep your present status." Anything was possible on this leftist-dominated globe! General Eisenhower was boiling mad about this political interference which was contrary to his plans. He sent a blistering note to Washington and a spokesman for the General exhorted the Austrians over the radio to dissociate themselves from their Nazi masters, to form clandestine committees, to gather food in order to help later the Allied administration—but not to revolt. (*Cf.* the *New York Times*, October 2, 1944, p. 3). A few days later Cordell Hull resigned and was replaced by Edward R. Stettinius, Jr.

[132] There is a good psychological thumbnail sketch of the Potsdam Conference in Robert Murphy, *Diplomat Among Warriors* (London: Collins, 1964), pp. 326-343.

[133] Soon after he became President, Mr. Truman pardoned his former associates in the Pendergast administration of Kansas City (Mo.) who thus were released from jail. Yet reading Jack Lait's and Lee Mortimer's *U. S. A. Confidential* (New York: Crown, 1952), pp. 232-241, one should think that Mr. Truman would have had the right training to deal with a man like Stalin.

[134] *Cf.* Winston S. Churchill, *The Second World War*, vol. 5, p. 320.

[135] *Ibid.*, p. 351.

[136] *Cf.* Jan Ciechanowski, *op. cit.*, pp. 332-335.

[137] *Cf.* Note 35 of this Chapter. When General Anders, the admirable Polish leader who with his valiant men had fought on the Italian front for the greater glory of the Western democracies, pointed out to Churchill that the mass migrations would be inhuman to the Germans as well, Churchill remarked cynically that six million Germans already had perished and some more would soon be biting into the grass. *Cf.* Wladyslaw Anders, *op. cit.*, p. 308.

[138] *Cf.* Jan Ciechanowski, *op. cit.*, p. 249.

[139] *Cf.* William L. Neumann, "How American Policy Toward Japan Contributed to War in the Pacific," in *Perpetual War for Perpetual Peace*, H. E. Barnes, ed., p. 306: "Hull was hell-bent for War. The constant needling by Chiang Kai-shek had gotten under his skin and President Roosevelt felt pressured from his administrative assistant, Lauchlin Currie, also a warm admirer of Soviet Russia. At this point Owen Lattimore, American adviser

584

to Chiang Kai-shek sent a strongly worded cablegram against any modus vivendi or truce with Japan." (This cable was received on November 26, 1941.) The next day Cordell Hull handed to the Japanese diplomats, Kurusu and Nomura, the ultimatum which—in the words of Albert Jay Nock—would have been a deadly insult even to a state such as Luxembourg.

Also *Cf.* Harold L. Ickes, "The Lowering Cloud, 1939-1941," vol. II of *The Secret Diaries of Harold L. Ickes* (New York: Simon and Schuster, 1954), p. 630: "For a long time I have believed that our best entrance into the war would be by way of Japan. . . . And, of course, if we go to war against Japan, it will inevitably lead to a war against Germany." The *sequitur*, however, was provided by Hitler who arbitrarily and with no cogent reason declared war against the United States. There might have been, at the same time, two separate wars going on. Actually the Germans hoped that Japan would attack the USSR.

[140] This is the thesis in the well-reasoned article of Gar Alperovitz "Why We Dropped the Bomb," *The Progressive*, August 1965, pp. 11-14. On page 12 Alperovitz cites Admiral William D. Leahy, Admiral Ernest J. King as well as Generals Henry A. Arnold, Dwight D. Eisenhower, and Curtis E. LeMay as convinced that the actual dropping of the bomb on an inhabited center was perfectly superfluous. Einstein himself was opposed to the Atomic Board in 1945 and declared: "We can only hope that we have not put dynamite into the hands of children." He was a religious man, believed in God, and was profoundly afraid of the technological development. *Cf.* Antonina Vallentin, *Das Drama Albert Einsteins* (Stuttgart: Günther Verlag, 1955), pp. 259, 261, 149-150, 163, and Graf Harry Kessler, *op. cit.*, p. 242.

[141] *Cf.* Walter Lippmann, *op. cit.*, p. 24.

[142] There were more than 100,000 cases of rape in Vienna and surroundings. Females between the ages of three and ninety were the victims.

[143] If only the Elbe had been the demarcation line up to the Czech border! But it is actually a boundary only for thirty-nine miles—then the Soviet controlled area extends way west and comes within 180 miles of the Netherlands.

[144] General Eisenhower, by refusing to advance on Berlin and, later, by evacuating Thuringia and parts of Saxony, not only did great disservice to his country, but also struck a mighty blow against the Free West. It will be argued that he did not do anything but obey a Commander-in-Chief. Another one gave an analogous order to General MacArthur a few years later in the Korean War. Did General Eisenhower have to obey the President? If so, then what about the German generals who were tried in Nuremberg because they obeyed Hitler?

[145] Robert Murphy told us how the Czechs implored the Americans to advance even further, when they were within sight of Prague. But Eisenhower, knowing that the commander of the Russian troops had demanded that the American Army be halted, declared at a staff meeting, "Why should we endan-

ger the life of a single American or Briton to capture areas we shall soon be handing over to the Russians?'' (R. Murphy, *op. cit.*, pp. 312-313). The matter, unfortunately had been settled by the politicians in Yalta with Mr. Alger Hiss advising the President.

¹⁴⁶ Robert Murphy informs us how he brought up the subject of a formal definition of the Western Allies' rights to their communication routes to Berlin. Whereupon Ambassador John Winant exclaimed vehemently that the Russians were ''inclined to suspect our motives, and if we insisted on this technicality, we should intensify their distrust.'' Thus this crucial matter could not be settled. Not much later Ambassador Winant committed suicide. (*Cf.* R. Murphy, *op. cit.*, pp. 285-286.)

¹⁴⁷ *Cf.* Winston S. Churchill who (*The Second World War*, vol. 5, p. 359) insisted that the Allies envisioned the Eastern Neisse, not the Western Neisse as a boundary line, and ''This is still our position.'' The evil might have been lessened (the main bulk of the city of Breslau would have been retained by Germany), but rivers—as geographers know only too well—never are ideal boundaries. Rivers not only sometimes change their course, but they are means of communications and thus they *unite*: they do *not* divide. With the exception of a longer stretch of the Lower Danube between Bulgaria and Rumania, no river ever separated language groups. (Thus the boundary between the German and the French idioms are the Vosges mountains, not the Rhine.)

¹⁴⁸ If the reader thinks that this, at least, was some sort of punishment for the Germans who, after all, ''had turned Nazi en bloc,'' he is very much mistaken. Let us consider East Prussia, whose center was German, Catholic, and (as the last free election proves) anti-Nazi. The highest Nazi percentages in the Wiemar Republic could be found in Southern East Prussia where the people are Lutheran by religion, but Polish by language. Yet while the anti-Nazi Germans were expelled, the pro-Nazi Masurian Poles could stay in their ancestral homes.

¹⁴⁹ It is difficult to verify whether cannibalism was actually practiced during these terrible months. *Cf.* also the authentic report ''Germania Deserta'' in *The Catholic World* (New York), April 1947, pp. 17-25. About this tragedy Bishop (later Cardinal) Muench of Fargo, Papal Co-ordinator of Catholic Affairs and later Nuncio to Germany wrote, ''The one thing which is perhaps even a greater atrocity than the Allied looting and expulsion of twelve million people is the conspiracy of silence about it.'' (*Cf. The Catholic Action News*, Fargo, N.D., November 1946).

¹⁵⁰ We put the world ''reasonably'' in quotation marks. Politics is the art of the possible, Christianity the art of the impossible.

¹⁵¹ *Cf.* Friedrich Engels, *Der Ursprung der Familie, des Privateigentums des Staates* (Stuttgart: Dietz, 1894), p. 181. The idea, however, that democracy is in an evolutionary and/or revolutionary way the matrix, the preparatory school of tyranny was already expressed by Plato, Aristotle, and Polybius. In our time the fear of a natural metamorphosis has been expressed

by a host of writers, concretely dealt with in my *Freiheit oder Gleichheit?* To their number I would like to add: Gustav Gundlach, "Von Wesen der Demokratie," *Gregorianum,* vol. 28 (1947), pp. 572-573; Werner Kägi, *op. cit.,* pp. 119-120; Winfried Martini, *Das Ende aller Sicherheit,* pp. 79-82; Thomas Gilby O. P., *Between Community and Society: A Philosophy and Theology of the State* (London: Longmans, Green, 1953), pp. 171ff.; Angel López-Amo, *op. cit.,* pp. 89, 152; Jürgen Rausch, *In einer Stunde wie dieser* (Stuttgart: Deutsche Verlagsanstalt, 1955), p. 424, and of the last century two rather divergent thinkers with acute observations; Bismarck in his *Gedanken und Erinnerungen* (Stuttgart: Cotta, 1898), vol. 2, p. 60; and Rosmini-Serbati, *La società e il suo fine* (Milan: Edizioni di Uomo, 1945), p. 102.

[152] David J. Dallin wrote in *Russia and Post-War Europe* (New Haven: Yale University Press, 1943) that the USSR wants a democratic order outside of its borders because "democracy provides special ways and opportunities for an unhampered building up of a Communist party—for its propaganda activity, its press, and its congresses. Not until there is formed a firm party framework will it be possible to proceed with the major task of the Communist program." This is the reason why the Communists everywhere want a full, and unhampered democracy and prefer a republican to an authoritarian or even a constitutional monarchy. In this respect their desires only too often met and still meet with popular trends and desires in America—if not in Britain. In 1946 not only the Communists but even influential American circles fostered the cause of republicanism in the Italian referendum; and in the Austrian State Treaty of 1955 the insistence that Austria should have a republican form of government came not only from the Soviet delegation. *Cf.* also Walter Lippmann, *op. cit.,* pp. 56-57. Maritain, naturally, is quite right when he says that the normal form of expression for democracy is the republic. *Cf.* J. Maritain, *Christianisme et démocratie* (Paris: Paul Hartmann, 1947), p. 65.

[153] *Cf.* Dorothy Thompson, *Listen Hans* (New York: 1942), p. 117.

[154] See Chapter XI, Note 27. This policy of leftist administration was evident all over American-occupied Germany. Thus Baron Franckenstein with a fine anti-Nazi record who had been elected mayor of a Bavarian village was immediately deposed by the horrified American *Gauleiter* who nominated (by nondemocratic *fiat*) a Social Democrat. However, the poor man abdicated quickly, yielding to the *vox populi,* and the baron with the truly monstrous name finally won out.

[155] The interminable questionnaire can be looked up in Ernst von Solomon's *Der Fragebogen,* published in a Ro-Ro-Ro pocket edition.

[156] It is a little known fact that the British also nearly arrested Cardinal Count Galen, Bishop of Münster, probably the most outstanding anti-Nazi in the defeated country. The manly protest of a higher British officer prevented this enormous *gaffe.* Still, Labourite leftism had a field day in the British zone of occupied Germany.

[157] Former Judge Leibowitz, interested in the reasons for the low rate

of juvenile delinquency in Italy, made a personal investigation in the Appenine Peninsula. He found the surviving paternal authority a major reason for this state of affairs. The accusation that German paternal authority carried a major responsibility also was made by Bertram Schaffner in his Columbia University Press: *Fatherland, a Study of Authoritarianism in the German Family* (New York: 1948). We have to face it squarely: certain American influences and impacts are detrimental to Europe. (And the reverse is possible too.) A Russian proverb says, "What is healthy to the Russian is deadly to the German." (*Shto russkomu zdorovo, to nyemtsomu smert'*.) Values, concepts, institutions cannot always be exchanged without detriment between Nations. An early German critic of American influences on Europe was Wilhelm von Schütze. *Cf.* his *Russland und Deutschland oder über den Sinn des Memoirs von Aachen* (Leipzig: Gerhard Fleischer, 1819), pp. 161-163.

[158] Mr. Robert Hutchins, after World War II was asked in Frankfurt by American "reeducationists" to address German teachers and professors. He shocked the organizers by imploring the Germans to stick to their old, traditional ideals and not to yield to their reeducators. (Especially the classic high school-colleges, the *Humanistische Gymnasien*, were strongly criticized by the occupants—for strengthening "class-consciousness.")

By far the best book on the American efforts to cast the German mind into a leftist pattern is Caspar Schrenck-Notzing's *Die Charakterwäsche* (Stuttgart: Seewald, 1965). Here we find a brilliant description of the work of American leftism, partly paralyzed in their home activities by the late Truman and Eisenhower administration but all the more active in the highly malleable German postwar world. The most amusing parts of the book deal with the psychological-ideological tests used by the reeducators, the historically most valuable ones are concerned with the American-sponsored establishment of a leftist German Press which is still highly active. In 1945 and 1946 the American "reeducators" still insisted that Communist journalists be included in the editorial boards of the newly licensed newspapers. It took some time until this delightful regulation was recalled.

[159] *Cf.* pp. 376-380.

[160] President Wilson was rather eager to have William II tried. On July 1, 1919, Pope Benedict XV wrote to the President a letter and added a clipping form the *Osservatore Romano* of June 2, 1919. The extract from the Vatican daily reproduced the views of a professor of Bologna University who spoke about the legality of bringing the German emperor to trial. Point One of his observations was "that the accusers themselves should constitute the Tribunal of Justice is unprecedented in the history of criminal law."

[161] I know personally the man who conceived the idea of the Nuremberg trials. I am quite sure that the notion of mere revenge hardly entered his mind. He thought that a "precedent" should be set, a common law notion which has no meaning in the non-English-speaking world since most of Europe is wedded to the Roman principle of codified law and the *nullum crimen sine*

lege concept. He stated to a mutual friend that he realized the gamble involved, but that the risk ought to be taken: he admitted that the thing could misfire. It did. Caspar Schrenck-Notzing remarks that since the amnesty of 1951 by McCloy the "Nuremberg Law, just like the Potsdam Agreement is a 'Sleeping Beauty' waiting for the day when a Red Prince will kiss it awake." (*Op. cit.*, p. 195.)

[162] *Cf.* Winston S. Churchill, *The Second World War*, vol. 1, pp. 456-458.

[163] The widow of one of the leading German chemical industrialists informed me that the judge told her at Nuremberg after her husband's acquittal: "I can assure you, Madam, your husband is a most perfect gentleman." But the aged gentleman spent four years in a very strict jail waiting for the verdict while his wife worked as a laundress. Still, she replied to the judge as a lady would—and not as a laundress. In the "little Nuremberg trials" one indeed could see the popular (folkloric and unsystematic) Marxist mind at work.

[164] The Krupps died out in the male line. Bertha Krupp married a Herr von Bohlen und Halbach: the oldest son (or male heir) uses the name "Krupp von Bohlen und Halbach" while all other males are Herren von Bohlen und Halbach.

[165] *Cf.* Thilo Freiherr von Wilmowsky, *Warum wurde Krupp verurteilt?* (Stuttgart: Vorwerk, 1950). This book is very informative on the ideological background of the process. Amusing is the comparison between the attorney's "anticapitalistic" writ in the Flick trial and Andrzej Wyszyński's tirades on pp. 37-38. Wars—who dared to doubt it?—are made by wicked capitalists.

[166] *Cf.* Thilo von Wilmowsky, *op. cit.*, p. 9.

[167] The supporters of this theory forget that in modern wars the sons and brothers of the "war-mongering" manufacturers are drafted into the armies like everybody else—and face death. (Old Krupp von Bohlen had four sons: one had to stay behind and faced death from the skies, but three were at the front. One of them was killed, another one was a prisoner of war in the USSR for eleven years.) What is really the use of another cool million if you lose your sons . . . and other relatives? The egregious nonsense of looking for purely (or predominantly) economic reasons for wars and, particularly for the present age of continuous wars has been well dealt with by Felix Somary, *op. cit.*, pp. 33-34; Morris Ginsberg, *Reason and Unreason in Society*, (London: Longmans, Green, 1947), pp. 184-185; Wilhelm Röpke, *Internationale Ordnung* (Erlenbach-Zürich: Rentsch, 1945), pp. 73ff; 2nd edition, 1954, pp. 101ff. Here Röpke says: "The statement that Imperialism is an unavoidable consequence of capitalism would only be convincing if an empirical proof in two directions could be offered to us: (1) that imperialism without capitalism and (2) that capitalism without imperialism never existed. One only has to ask for these proofs to know in advance that they never could be produced." (p. 116)

[168] Since I knew Yamashita personally I wrote an article about him

for a "liberal" Catholic publication usually very eager to come to the aid of the innocently persecuted. The article was turned down.

[169] *Cf.* A. Frank Reel, *The Case of General Yamashita* (Chicago: University of Chicago Press, 1949). The author terminates his book with the following words: "We have been unjust, hypocritical and vindictive. We have defeated our enemies on the battlefield, but we have let their spirit triumph in our hearts." (p. 247)

[170] Mr. Bevin, who in this case was one of the most important decision makers, had a fine ultraleftist record. (*Cf.* Chapter XVI, Note 153.) He was not too encumbered by knowledge and preliminary studies as can be gleaned from Joseph Frayman's sketch: "Careers of Bevin and Morrison Reveal Background Similarities," *New York Times*, March 10, 1951, p. 5. Yet the decline in the quality of parliamentarians is unavoidable. *Cf.* René Gillouin, *op. cit.*, pp. 142-143.

[171] Even Winston Churchill protested against the renewed enslavement of the South Tyrol in a speech held before the House of Commons. *Cf. New York Times*, June 6, 1946.

[172] Another Nazi hangover are the anti-Hapsburg stipulations in the Austrian State Treaty of 1955—interesting in the light of the democratic principle of self-determination. Yet, as we said before, the Western Powers gladly acceded to this Brown-Red demand. American antimonarchism always was a live, popular force. This attitude is well represented by Dr. Benjamin Rush, *Cf. op. cit.*, pp. 264, 265. Yet Rush, who wanted to frighten naughty children with the specter of a king, saw the future in a rather different light. In a letter to John Adams (July 21, 1789) he admitted that "a hundred years hence, absolute monarchy will probably be rendered necessary in our country by the corruption of our people. But why should we precipitate an event for which we are not yet prepared?" (p. 522)

[173] Needless to say, most of the victims were women, adolescents, and small children of the lower classes: most of them were Social Democrats who had boasted of their "proletarian status," but this did not protect them in the least. "You want to be proletarians, but you live like bourgeoisie!" they were told in a mixture of surprise and indignation.

In the Napoleonic Wars the Russian armies fought all over Europe. At that time the majority of these soldiers were Christians and illiterate. In 1944 they were largely literate and probably without a religious faith. Friz Reck-Malleczewen speaks about the Christian spirit of Russian soldiers in World War I in his *Tagebuch eines Verzweifelten* (Stuttgart: Henry Goverts, 1966), pp. 80-81.

[174] They were buried by Austrian peasants. *Cf.* pp. 328-332.

[175] A description of the events near Lienz can be found in Nikolay Nikolayevitch Krasnov, *The Hidden Russia* (New York: Henry Holt, 1960).

[176] *Cf. New York Times*, January 20, 1946.

[177] When the British entered (Austrian) Carinthia from the South, Sir Harold Alexander issued a declaration to the local population starting with the

words, "We have come as conquerors, not as liberators." But "conqueror" (*Eroberer*) in German merely implies lasting territorial conquests. To make it worse, the soldiers and officers were forbidden to extend "common courtesy" to the inhabitants, i.e., to greet them, to say "thank you," etc. A few weeks later it dawned upon the British that all this was nonsense, that such treatment of the Austrians was not at all in their interest, that they should distinguish between Austrians, Nazis, and Germans. Everything was now reversed. Austrians were told that *all* the Allies were their good friends and that they should not believe the nonsense told to them by the Nazis about communism in Russia and Yugoslavia. Communism was just the last stage of development in democracy.

Thus the Austrians, who as neighbors of the Communist world knew much better what communism was, finally woke up from the Nazi hell and found themselves in an insane asylum.

[178] France *eventually* lost most of her colonial possessions but gained a few square kilometers along the Italian frontier in the Alps.

[179] *Cf.* Louis Rougier, *Les Accords Pétain-Churchill, Histoire d'une mission* (Montreal: Beauchemin, 1945). As was to be expected, nobody from Britain's Foreign Office dared testify at the Pétain trial that, behind De Gaulle's back, Britain had made secret agreements with the Marshal.

[180] There were, of course, noncommunist and even rightist groups in the *résistance*. One of these groups on the right was led by the ex-Maurassian Guillain de Bénouville. *Cf.* his *Le sacrifice du matin* (Paris: Laffont, 1946), especially pp. 65-69. Bénouville became a close associate of De Gaulle in the late 1940s.

Nor were the members of the House of Bourbon spared by the Nazis in their leftist furor. Prince Xavier de Bourbon-Parma was nearly beaten to pulp in the Struthof (Alsace) concentration camp. The notion that the right collaborated while the left resisted is simply not true. Laval, a Radical Socialist, for instance, came distinctly from the left.

[181] *Cf.* Louis Rougier, *La France Jacobine* (Paris and Brussels: Diffusion di Livre, 1947), pp. 169-171, and Donald B. Robinson, "Blood Bath in France," *The American Mercury*, April 1946.

[182] *Cf.* Gilles Perrault, "Fallait-il sacrifier ces résistants?" *Historia*, June 1965, pp. 765ff.

[183] *Cf.* Gallicus, "Terror in the Air," *Politics* (New York), vol. 2, no. 11 (November 1945).

[184] *Cf.* Thilo. v. Wilmowsky, *op. cit.*, pp. 182-183.

[185] *Cf.* Winston S. Churchill, *The Second World War*, vol. 1, p. 482. Churchill gave the following instructions to Major General Macksey, selected on April 5, 1940 to command an expedition to Narvik: "It is clearly illegal to bombard a populated area in the hope of hitting a legitimate target which is known to be in the area but which cannot be precisely located and identified." This injunction was later blissfully overlooked.

[186] After prisoners of war were repeatedly killed in Germany by Allied

raids, Brigadier General B. M. Bryan declared that these incidents were regrettable, but "the pilots' instructions are to disrupt transportation and strafe every German vehicle they can see on the road," *Cf. New York Times*, April 8, 1945. A.P. Dispatch.

[187] The destruction of Le Havre *after* the evacuation of the city by the Germans which cost the lives of 3,500 Frenchman was described by Anne O'Hare McCormick in the *New York Times*, October 9, 1944. De Gaulle was present at the mass burial. When he protested against this misdeed, he was informed that one *thought* that the Germans were still in the town and that merely their absence made the French holocaust so regrettably senseless. De Gaulle almost hit the ceiling. In acts like these one finds part of the explanation for his attitude. (And some of Couve de Murville's actions might be explained by the treatment he received in North Africa by Messrs. Roosevelt and Morgenthau, accompanied and advised by the Soviet spy Harry Dexter White. *Cf.* Robert Murphy, *op. cit.*, pp. 188-189.)

[188] The wanton destruction of a French village (in Alsace) was mentioned *passim* in an article in the *New York Times*.

The villagers did not seem to have been particularly enthusiastic about their American liberators. They were on the whole "unconcerned," but some boys were "spitting in the tracks of the Army trucks" and "there were those three blond, husky women strolling down arm in arm, singing and laughing and mocking everyone else." When the Nazi counterpush came, the inhabitants kissed the German soldiers and removed the American and French flags. "Somehow a few soldiers got back and told the story to the colonel. The colonel suddenly remembered that there were a lot of enemy tanks in the village and told the artillery to pound it to rubble. And so they did." Killing how many French citizens? Or only the three husky blondes? *Cf.* Ralph G. Martin, "What Kind of Peace? The Soldiers' Viewpoint," *New York Times Magazine*, March 11, 1945, pp. 43-44.

[189] This frightening confusion was not restricted to the United States. I heard a famous French Catholic philosopher with leftist leanings speak about the "Fascist" Polish Army in Italy.

[190] There were millions of "displaced persons"—an expression which marks a record in the realm of understatements, just like "relocation center" (for concentration camp).

[191] It was significant that the Jewish refugees, less than anybody else, wanted to go back to the Red paradise. There were a variety of reasons for this. When the regime broke down in Odessa and Kiev, history's most terrible spontaneous slaughter of Jews took place. Most of the Jews in the Ukraine, however, had not fled because they did not believe the Soviet tales about the Nazi anti-Semitism and considered them sheer propaganda. Tragically enough, quite a number of Jewish soldiers in the Red Army were even *eager* to surrender to the Germans. The pro-German sympathies of the Russian Jews had always been very marked.

[192] *Cf.* Chapter XVI, Note 59. Also Henry Picker, *op. cit.*, pp. 390, 394-395, 447-449.

[193] An official publication of Spain on its Jews can be found in the series *Temas Españoles*, no. 252, "Los Sefardíes" by Jesús Cantera Ortiz de Urbina (Madrid, 1958).

[194] In Sweden the Jews were admitted only at the end of the eighteenth century (in Norway only by the end of the nineteenth century). Until the end of the nineteenth century Jews became Swedish citizens only in isolated cases. Jesuits were admitted to Norway only a few years ago. A greater liberalization of the civic laws pertaining to non-Lutherans in Sweden took place only in 1952. *Cf.* Peter Hornung, "Das schwedische Gesetz über Religionsfreiheit," *Stimmen der Zeit*, vol. 150, no. 8 (May 1952), pp. 122-133.

[195] The year 1924 symbolizes the expiation—with rearranged numbers —of the year of expulsion 1492. This act was an imitation of the forced exodus of English Jews in 1290. Actually only two Jewish communities had never been moved nor ransacked in past centuries, those of Rome and Avignon.

[196] Sephardic descent could easily be proved by the family name. Proof of an (unbroken) genealogical tree was never required by the Spanish authorities. The cofounder of the Falange was A. García Valdescasas, until recently Rector of the University of Barcelona. *Cf.* Chapter XVI, Note 15. Yet he was not alone in rejecting totalitarianism and the deification of the State. The main founder, José-Antonio Primo de Rivera, had the same attitude. *Cf.* his speech in answering Gil Robles, held before the Cortes on December 19, 1933 in "Discursos Parlamentarios," vol. 2. p.9. of José-Antonio Primo de Rivera, Marqués de Estrellas, *Obras Completas* (Barcelona: Ediciones Fé, 1939).

[197] Let us admit that the camp of Miranda de Ebro, where many of the Jewish (and non-Jewish) refugees were temporarily located was anything but a swank resort. The food was miserable. But at that time much of Spain was actually starving.

[198] I wrote a larger paper on the effects of the "Fascist" Spanish Government to save Jewish lives during World War II. For about half a year I "negotiated" with a leading American-Jewish "Liberal" monthly to get it accepted. Exception was taken once on this, then on that statement. I wanted to get the facts across and made compromises in style and in wording. Yet, finally, the answer was "No." It could not be done. Spain was "Fascist" after all, and nothing more could be said about it. Thus I published the essay in France, "L'Espagne et les Juifs," Etudes (Paris), vol. 289, no. 4 (April 1956), and in the *Catholic World* (N. Y.). Needless to say, I was thoroughly disgusted by the petty and, in a deeper sense, dishonest American "liberal" publication. This bit of truth nevertheless was communicated to the American public at large in 1970 when Rabbi Chaim Lipschitz divulged the facts to *Newsweek* magazine.

[199] The French Sephardic community, about 3,000 families, thanked

Franco in a letter (October, 1941) for his effective aid. The Spanish government saw to it that these Sephardic Jews with their property were placed under the protection of the Spanish consulate. They were also exempt from wearing the Star of David.

[200] Which resembles a statement about another republic: *"Hominum confusione et divina providentia regnatur Helvetia."* Yet Switzerland no less than the United States exercised in the eighteenth century an immense political-social fascination on romantic minds—a fascination mobilized by Jean-Jacques Rousseau who appeared as spokesman of *la libre Helvétie. Cf.* Gonzague de Reynold, *La démocratie et la Suisse* (Bern, Editions du Chandelier, 1929), pp. 191-192.

[201] Mr. Owen Lattimore propagated assiduously the transformation of Japan into a democratic republic, but it was Mr. Joseph C. Grew, former United States Ambassador in Tokyo, who succeeded in preventing the worst. The trouble with Japan in the remote past was the weakness of the monarch, which resulted in an oligarchic military dictatorship (*bakufu*, literally: "rule of the tent") headed by the Shôgun. The Restoration of 1868 meant the return of the emperor to full power, after his abeyance for many centuries. In the 1920s-1930s a new *bakufu* arose casting the emperor into the role of a sacred cow, remote and ineffective, and emasculating the parliament. At present the role of the emperor is dangerously weakened, the army is reduced to a minimum and the country is in permanent danger of being taken over by the extremist parties. Due to the nature of American intervention not only the balance of power is lost in East Asia, but also the internal balance of Japan which needs a sound imperial authority. The warnings of Gaetano Mosca in his *Ciò che la storia potrebbe insegnare*, pp. 289-290, 308 have not been heeded. Still the evolution (through constitutional reform) of a stronger imperial center is still possible. On Owen Lattimore's ideological and political background *cf.* also the summarized Senate Report's short section in M. Stanton Evans, A. H. Ryskind, William Schulz, *The Fringe on Top*, (New York: American Features Book, 1962), p. 111-112.

[202] I am so frequently reminded of a conversation in F. Scott Fitzgerald's *The Beautiful and the Damned* (Garden City, N. Y.: Perma-Books, 1951, p. 239):

MAURY: I imagined you were broad-minded.
PARAMORE: I am.
MURIEL: Me, too. I believe one religion's as good as another and everything.
PARAMORE: There's some good in all religions.
MURIEL: I'm a Catholic but, as I always say, I'm not working at it.
PARAMORE (with a tremendous burst of tolerance): The Catholic religion is a very—a very powerful religion.

Luckily (or unluckily) this is a very widespread illusion—an illusion related to the belief that the Church is a purely dogmatic monolith. Writes a Lutheran theologian: "There is probably no other Church which has the capacity for harboring so many widely divergent theological points of view as the Roman Church. . . . There is a fixed dogmatic limit, but within this limit there is room for divergent and often contradictory opinions." *Cf.* F. E. Mayer, *The Religious Bodies of America* (St. Louis: Concordia Publishing House, n.d. 2nd ed.), pp. 32, 38.

[203] The writer of this volume had been to Vietnam four times in the last fifteen years (twice during the Ngo Dinh Diem régime) and emphatically rejects the story of the "suppression of the Buddhists." The United Nations sent a commission to Vietnam after the violent death of the Ngo brothers: this commission reported that there was not a shred of evidence as to a persecution of Buddhists in the past or present. An American reporter who "substantiated" the myth received the Pulitzer Prize for his great journalistic achievement. To a considerable part of the American public the idea to place the main burden of the war effort squarely on the shoulders of the "Buddhist majority" (instead of a Catholic minority) made sense. Yet the Buddhists do not form a majority in Vietnam—the anti-Christian Mahayana-Buddhists even plus the far more spiritual Hinayana (Teravada) Buddhists. The estimates are: 35 to 40 percent Mahayana and Hinayana-Buddhists, 12 to 18 percent Catholics, the rest Caodaists, Hao-Hoa supporters and, above all, Animists. At the present moment the Mahayana Buddhists are politically even more divided among themselves than ever before. *Cf.* also Piero Gheddo, *Cattolici e Buddisti nel Vietnam* (Florence: Vallecchi, 1968).

[204] The weakness of the countries bordering on Vietnam, Cambodia and Laos, is due precisely to their intensive Buddhist character—which involved peacefulness, vagueness of mind, indifference and lacking "aggressiveness." Prince Norodom Sihanouk, the Hamlet of Cambodia, very well represents the local character of these very kind and attractive people. (Merchants and entrepreneurs in these two delightful countries are almost exclusively Chinese, Viets, Indians, or Europeans.)

[205] Formosa now has a population well over fifteen million on an area 15 percent smaller than Switzerland and with a not unsimilar distribution of high mountains and lowlands. (The highest mountains in Switzerland are over 15,000, in Formosa over 12,000 feet). The Formosans have the third highest living standards in all of Asia, lower only than those of Israel and Japan.

[206] Again we want to sound the warning note not to confuse the Welfare State *(Wohlfahrtsstaat)* with the Provider State *(Versorgungsstaat)*. It is the latter which has common traits with the Socialist State, without being one. Sweden (and even New Zealand) are Provider States, not Socialist States in the narrow sense of the term. Yet the Provider State, no less so than the Socialist State, is a Servile State in the sense Hilaire Belloc used this term. In the final paragraph of his famous book he wrote: "The internal strains which have threatened society during its Capitalist phase will be relaxed and eliminated,

and the community will settle down upon that Servile basis which has its foundation before the advent of the Christian faith, from which that faith slowly weaned it, and to which in the decay of faith it naturally returns.'' (H. Belloc, *The Servile State*, London, 1912, p. 183). Yet under the spell of "monasticism" this process is even possible under Christian auspices.

[207] *Cf.* Le Capitaine Charles De Gaulle, *La discorde chez l'ennemi* (Paris: Berger-Levrault, 1924).

[208] *Cf. Economic Council Letter,* (New York), no. 271, September 15, 1951, p. 1.

[209] Antoine de Rivarol, who died in 1801 in his Berlin exile, was a French Royalist, the son of an innkeeper and bearer of one of the many fake French titles. He was unexcelled in his witty and profound remarks, many of a political or social nature. Ernst Jünger has written a profound book about him.

Chapter XVIII

[1] Walter Sulzbach in *Afrika und seine Probleme*, A. Hunold, ed. (Erlenbach-Zürich: Rentsch, 1965), pp. 16-17 informs us that according to J. R. McCullock England's trade with India around 1811 was not greater than with Jersey or the Isle of Man. Exports to the Thirteen Colonies just before 1776 amounted to around 15 million dollars, but had reached 61 million dollars to the United States in 1806. (*Ibid.*, p. 21) Bismarck in a letter to War Minister von Roon expressed his conviction that economic gains from colonies would remain illusory. *Cf.* Alfred Zimmerman, *Geschichte der deutschen Kolonialpolitik* (Berlin: Mittler and Sohn 1913), p. 6. The profit desired by France from trading with and investing in her colonies amounts according to the most liberal estimate, to not more than one-fourth of her original investment. *Cf.* letter of Constant Southworth in the *New York Times*, July 13, 1960.

[2] In a discussion following a lecture I gave in an American university I was asked whether I sincerely believed in my statement to the effect that the European colonies in their majority were not profitable. That there could be other than commerical reasons for the acquisition of colonies seemed incredible to these young (subconscious) Marxists. Naturally, in the past Conservatives as well as Liberals opposed "colonialism." In 1852 Disraeli spoke about the "miserable colonies" and Richard Cobden (who thought strongly in economic terms) asked: "Where is the enemy who will do us the favor to steal these possessions?"

[3] *Cf.* Chapter V, Note 14.

[4] On the abuse of the United States development aid read Helmut Schoeck's brilliant essay "Die USA und die Entwicklungsländer—Geschichte einer Ernüchterung," in *Afrika und seine Probleme*, A. Hunold, ed.

[5] The overseas aid given by the United States worked in many cases

as an inducement to "prove" the receiver's independence from the Big Friend. Curiously enough, it is always far easier to give than to receive . . . from a psychological, not from a material point of view, to be sure. The trouble with the "underdeveloped" (or "emerging") nations also lies partly in their prelogical mentality. See, for instance, a piece of news in the *Times of India*, February 4, 1962 (dateline: Trivandrum, February 3): "The Government of Kerala delayed the filing of the defamation case against the Communists on account of Ashtagrahi, i.e., bad constellation of planets which has caused all over India a real hysteria." The reason for "backwardness" lies partly in the squandering of public monies for purely representative purposes. The marble palace for President Houphouet-Boigny of the Ivory Coast gobbled up ten million dollars. Pieces of marble had to be brought from Italy by airlift. A few years ago no less than 50 percent of the budget of the Central Africa Republic was still paid by France, which now puts more money up for its former colonies than in the darkest days of "colonialism." Things were not brighter in Ghana during the N'krumah regime. His Minister of Industry, Krobo Edusei, had built for himself a luxurious villa for 180,000 dollars and his wife bought herself in London a golden bed for 9,000 dollars. Mr. Edusei was made to resign. (*Cf. Frankfurter Allgemeine Zeitung*, August 21, 1962, p. 17.) The trouble is partly also a lacking readiness for systematic hard work. In Guatemala City there are 10,000 licensed (and how many unlicensed?) lottery ticket vendors among a population of over 300,000 people. *Cf.* Carlo Coccioli, "Come i cittadini di Guatemala vengono distratti dai loro guai," *Corriere della Sera* (Milan), March 28, 1962, p. 3. In the same city bingo parties are held with as much as eight thousand participants. Whoever thinks that the problem is merely a matter of "Social Reforms," of re-distribution of wealth, is very much mistaken. Especially in the Catholic Church such is the prevailing view as regards Latin America. See, however, the excellent essay of Professor Fredrick B. Pike, "The Modernized Church in Peru: Two Aspects," *The Review of Politics*, vol. 26, no. 3. (July 1964), pp. 307-308. Richard F. Behrendt is very right when he says that our material superiority engendered in the backward nations envy and the urge to imitate only the most superficial elements of our civilization. Solidarity with or friendship for the West is very rare among them. (*Cf.* his compendium *Soziale Strategie der Entwicklungsländer* (Frankfurt: S. Fischer, 1965), p. 33. Hence the immense difficulty of getting recognition in return for the aid given.

[6] One *Bharat*, two Pakistans separated by the *Bharat*, and Burma.

[7] *Cf.* E. v. Kuehnelt-Leddihn, "Christentum, Technik, 'Kolonialismus' und die Entwicklungsländer," *Ordo*, XIII (1962), pp. 41-85. *Vide* also Denis de Rougemont, *L'Aventure occidentale de l'homme* (Paris: Albin Michel, 1957), p. 186sq.

[8] Yet Labourites and, naturally, Communists, made concerted efforts in British universities to convert them to their own ideologies.

[9] There was only one racial "by-law" in the Lovanium: all ball teams

had to be "racially mixed." Africans could not play against Europeans. This, however, might have been changed since I was there in early 1960.

[10] Yet even the new investments did not always pay off. (Sir) Denis W. Brogan in *The Price of Revolution* (New York: The Universal Library, 1966), p. 147-148, has pointed out that colonial investments never bring an early return to the private investor. Of all Belgian exports only 3 percent went to the Congo, of the imports 5.5 percent went to the Congo, of the whole national income 5 percent were derived from the Congo. (*Cf. New York Times*, August 7, 1960). During the entire colonial period the Belgians invested 280,000,000 gold francs in the Congo and earned 25 million gold francs. *Cf.* William L. Langer, "Farewell to Empire," *Foreign Affairs*, October 1962. See also William Woodruff, *Impact of Western Man* (New York: St. Martin's Press, 1966), especially pp. 51-52, 293-294.

[11] A note like this can merely hint at the enormity of the problem which turns on the question of work ethics in the underdeveloped countries. The inclination of free man for hard and systematic work is to be found only in a large part of Euramerican and East Asian civilization—and even there only in relatively recent times. (In Euramerica since the Reformation, in Japan since the Tokugawa regime, etc.) In Africa, to make matters worse, physical labor is considered to be a woman's domain. René Dumont in *L'Afrique noire est mal partie* (Paris: Seuil, 1966), p. 188 tells about agricultural labor in a part of the Congo where men work on the average of fifteen hours a week in the fields. Since they were forced to pay equal wages by their own law, the Belgians imported bricklayers from the homeland. The average African laid 750 bricks daily, and the Belgian laborer 2,400 and more.

In Latin America people (as Keyserling had already remarked in his *Südamerikanische Meditationen*) are pushed by *Lust*, (inclination, fancy), by *gana*, and not by a sense of duty or ambition. *Cf.* also José Gutierrez, *De la pseudo-aristocracia a la autenticidad* (Bogotá, Tercer Mundo, 1966), p. 85. Compare also with Fredrick B. Pike, *The Modern History of Peru* (London: Weidenfeld and Nicholson, 1967), p. 122. The Argentine proverb: "*El vivo vive del tonto, el tonto vive del trabajo*—The intelligent man lives from the stupid man, the stupid man from work," is not uncharacteristic. The same phenomenon can be found in India. *Cf.* Jean Gebser, *Asienfibel* (Ulsteinbuch, No. 650, n.d.), pp. 21-22. There the lack of sense of time renders the situation even more difficult. Dr. J. S. Kanwar from the Indian Council for Agrarian Research in New Delhi has stated that if only two of India's 16 states were to exploit the soil with intelligence and diligence, all of India could be fed: if, however, this were done in all of India, two-thirds of the agricultural products could be exported. *Cf. Kontinente*, 3 year, no. 4, August 1968. On the same problem in Russia *vide* Erwin Sinkó, *op. cit.*, p. 143. Of course, in the USSR the lack of "Protestant work ethics" is made more keenly felt through collectivism, socialism, and the dearth of consumer goods.

[12] I take this idea from the title of Léon Ferrero's wise book, *Amérique*,

mirroir grossissant de l'Europe (Paris: Rieder, 1939). (This son of Guglielmo Ferrero died young in an automobile accident in New Mexico.)

[13] In Francis Móra's beautiful novel *Enek a búzamezökröl*, a leftist propagates the republic in a Hungarian village inn towards the end of World War I. He explains that there should be and that there would be no king. An old peasant shakes his head: "But then," he cries out, "if there is no king, whose head would one see on the coins?" "There would be no head on the coins." "But that's impossible, such a coin would be no good," the old man retorted, and everybody agreed. The agitator was licked. The possibility, nay, the likelihood of a return to monarchy lies in the human heart's rejection of anonymity: monarchy, therefore, often comes back in republican guise to satisfy cerebral postulates. *Cf.* Ernst Jünger, *Der Waldgang* (Frankfurt: Klostermann, 1951), p. 135, and Otto Seeck, *Geschichte des Untergangs der antiken Welt* (Berlin: Siemenroth und Tröschel, 1897), vol, 1. pp. 11-12.

[14] Hence the long drawn out article is as typical for the Continental press as the short, cabled report is for the American or British one. Today (for the same reason) many Continental papers subscribe to the services of American press agencies.

[15] This term has been coined by Alexis de Tocqueville. *Cf. De la démocratie en Amérique*, vol. 1, p. 277: "Une idée fausse, mais claire et précise, aura toujours plus de puissance dans le monde qu'une idée vraie, mais complexe."

[16] The American Indian has not only a grave educational, but also a moral problem. Only 5 percent of the population of Utah are Indians, but among the inmates of the penitentiaries 34 percent, of the boy reformatories 25 percent, and of the girls' reform schools 50 percent are Indian. *Cf.* Lawrence E. Barry, "The Indian in a Cultural Trap," *America*, vol. 112, April 10, 1965, pp. 482-484.

[17] The worst and most sadistic crimes were committed by the Simbas of Gbenye and Mulele in the Stanleyville and Kivu regions. Further south we had the case of the Italian Red Cross volunteers eaten by cannibals. Unfortunately such happenings are not only confined to darkest Africa. Even in Ghana young men often live in fear of being buried with deceased chieftains, so they go into hiding. Highly "advanced" Nigeria has seen delirious horrors in the last ten years—not only in the civil war, but also in the various revolutions. There was the Mau-Mau movement in Kenya whose nauseating details I would like to spare my readers. They might gather them from Robert Ruark's outstanding novel, *Something of Value*. Yet it is interesting to see how the frightfulness of that large-scale conspiracy is played down in the Socialist Albert Meister's *L'Afrique noire peut-elle partir?* (Paris: Seuil, 1966), pp. 172-173. Better is F. D. Corfield, *The Origins of Mau-Mau* (Nairobi: Colony and Protectorate of Kenya, 1960), p. 163sq. One can understand the nervousness of South Africans (and Rhodesians) about the possibility of "full democracy" in their country. In 1960 they took care of the wounded and the maimed

shipped down from the Congo. And in 1952 a Catholic medical sister, Dr. Elsie Quinlan, was not only murdered in East London (South Africa) but even partly eaten by members of the African National Congress Youth League. Her car was stopped, she was knifed to death, the vehicle was set afire. (*Cf.* the two Capetown papers, *The Argus* and *Die Burger* on November 10, 1952.) Yet it would be erroneous to draw "racist" conclusions from such events. Man is a predatory animal and only ideas will limit his beastliness. If these ideas (like Christianity) fail, then the return to savagery is close at hand.

[18] A girls' convent school of the lycée level which I visited in Brazzaville had never had an African graduate. In the Lovanium there was not a single African female student in 1960, though there were a number of (very popular) European girls.

[19] Professor Robert Maistriaux of the "Institute St. Louis le Grand" in Brussels, who worked for years in Elizabethville, told me of fairly numerous cases of Belgian civil servants adopting black babies in the Congo. If they grow up from earliest infancy in a European milieu (in the Congo or in Belgium) their intelligence is vastly superior to that of Africans. Of importance is his analysis of the African intelligence in "La sous-évolution des Noirs d'Afrique. Sa nature, Ses causes, Ses remèdes," published in *Revue de Psychologie des Peuples*, vol. 10 (1955), no. 2 and 4, vol. 11 (1956), nos. 1. and 2. Of political importance is the African's difficulty in abstracting with which Maistriaux dealt principally in the last instalment of his essay.

[20] This qualification has been dropped in the United States so that (certain) Americans can with "good conscience" condemn the Rhodesians for not giving the vote to illiterates. To the democratist (who, indeed, is a leftist), voting assumes a quasi-religious character. The American polling booth with its well-oiled machinery and ritualistic curtain shown at the U. S. Exhibition in Moscow was half-tabernacle, half-confessional, and had pseudoreligious significance. Thus the modern leftist, opposed to all hierarchies, no longer laughs about naked natives voting for animal symbols. In the nihilism of perfect equality reason comes to an end and superstition takes over. It is evident that the "native" intelligence of persons is not always the same. *Cf.* Prof. Arthur J. Jensen, "Nature and Nurture," *The Harvard Educational Review*, Winter 1969. Then shall we be surprised if there are such differences also between races? At least Pierre Teilhard de Chardin thought so, emphasizing that he was a "universalist," but not a democrat. *Cf.* Robert Speaight, *Teilhard de Chardin* (London: Collins, 1967), p. 220.

[21] If on a map of Europe we would paint red the regions which knew the institution of serfdom, we would not get a large area, merely a slowly broadening belt from Central France to Central Russia. And what was really the *iniquity* of serfdom? Not so much that the serf was *glebae adstrictus* (tied to the soil). The lacking communication system made it easy to run away, to take abode in a city, and to acquire the freedom of the city, i.e., "citizenship" after a year and a day. The drawback of serfdom was the obliga-

tion to work one or two days a week for the manorial lord (the monastery, etc). But what does the modern American city dweller do in many cases? He works on Mondays and half of Tuesday for his land*lord*; and on Tuesday afternoon and half of Wednesday for a mythological figure called Uncle Sam. (According to an estimate the *average* American citizen starts to work for himself on April 16th!) And if he does not comply, he will be in much deeper water than the serf who could never be *dispossessed*. Yet political propaganda has misrepresented the European past even in Europe. Modern man is "unhistorical" and therefore he can be told every imaginable nonsense which he readily will believe. How many Hungarians, for instance, are convinced that their country went through a period of feudalism? It never did. *Cf.* Károly Eszláry, "Propaganda és valóság," *Unio*, (Munich) vol. 6, no. 3 (March, 1955), pp. 1-3.

[22] Mussolini insisted that *per il fascismo lo stato è un assoluto*, "for Fascism the state is an absolute." (*Cf. Enciclopedia Italiana*, vol. 14, p. 850). Fascism was to him a democracy—*una democrazia organizzata, centralizzata, autoritaria* (p. 849). The Jacobins would have made an analogous claim: they also believed in superorganization, centralization, authoritarianism. Of course, both Jacobinism and fascism took their inspiration from the Roman Republic—the *fasces* (i.e., the beating rods of the lictors) with the axe was their common symbol. The inner relationship between "national democracy" with its distinctly Jacobin roots and the modern totalitarian state is best analyzed in Heinz O. Ziegler, *Autoritärer oder totaler Staat* (Tübinger: J. C. B. Mohr, 1932), another brilliant book which has never been translated into English.

[23] Witchcraft is by no means based purely on superstition. In the nineteenth century, at the time of our grandparents who were exceedingly "enlightened," black magic was relegated to the realm of fairy tales. Modern ethnologists and anthropologists of the first order accept it. *Cf.* for instance Hans Findeisen, *Schamanentum* (Stuttgart: Kohlhammer, 1957), pp. 13-14. The cases of Navaho witchcraft which I have told or alluded to in *Die Gottlosen* (Salzburg: Berglandbuch, 1962), are also authentic. Compare also with André Dupeyrat, *Savage Papua*, trsl. E. and D. Demauny (New York: Dutton, 1954), pp. 145ff. At the same time we should not close our eyes to the fact that genuine superstition might live side on side with the truly supernatural. The partly ludicrous, partly tragic "Cargo-Cult" in New Guinea is a point in question. *Cf.* Joseph Höltker SVD, "Der Cargo-Kult" in Neuguineas lebt noch," *Neue Zeitshrift für Missionswissenschaft*, vol. 18, no. 3, pp. 223-226. The same: "Die Mambu-Bewegung in Neuguineas. Zum Prophetentum in Melanesia," *Annali Lateranensi*, vol. 5, (1941), pp. 181-219.

[24] *Cf.* André Dupeyrat, *op. cit.*, pp. 217ff. and 246ff.

[25] For this very reason an honest man such as President Tubman of Liberia admitted that many of Liberia's ills stem from the fact that his country never had "the benefits of colonialism." (*Time*, January 17, 1969, p. 28). Emperor Haile Selassie expressed himself in a similar way.

²⁶ *Cf.* Sigrid Undset, *Selvportretter og Landskapsbilleder*, (Oslo: H. Aschehoug, 1938), pp. 195-196.

²⁷ *Cf.* Jacob Burckhardt, *Briefe an seinen Freund Friedrich von Preen 1864-1893* (Stuttgart: Deutsche Verlagsanstalt, 1922), p. 248 (letter dated Baden, July 24, 1889).

²⁸ Big *Apartheid* stands for the territorial separation of Negroes and non-Negroes in South Africa. One can question—and very much so—its practicality, but it is not so easy to attack it on moral grounds. It is different with the Little *Apartheid* which regulates the "coexistence" between the various racial groups, involving separate schools, buses, elevators, postoffice windows, etc. This is a costly setup and involves real discrimination which is to be rejected. Yet for a full understanding of the Afrikaaner (Boer) mentality one has to take all sorts of psychological factors into consideration.

²⁹ As Senator, John F. Kennedy delivered a blistering speech in early 1957 against the continued French presence in Algeria. One wonders what specific knowledge he had of the Algerian situation. The result? An increase of anti-American feelings in France and no gratitude whatsoever from a "New Algeria" which still follows a strongly anti-American foreign policy. In order to assure the survival of French cultural influence (above all the French language), France is still paying enormous subsidies to her ex-colonies, i.e., between 1 and 2 percent of its GNP. Algeria, for instance, is wholly dependent upon France. If, in the case of a serious economic crisis, France were to send home her Algerian workers, Algeria would quietly collapse. *Cf.* Germaine Tillion, *L'Algérie en 1957* (Paris: Minuit, 1957), p. 99.

³⁰ The Swiss diplomat and scholar Jacques Albert Cuttat, a man with the greatest knowledge and affection for Asia, in his lecture "Die geistige B. deutung Asiens und es Abendlandes für einander," in *Münchner Universitätsreden*, (Munich: Max Hueber, 1961), pp. 26-27, pointed out the danger of a sterile guilt complex on the part of the West. Having studied conditions in Southern Italy with the aid of the *Cassa per i mezzogiorno* and knowing Nigeria, I can sympathize with Naomi Mitchison who said that living standards in Eastern Nigeria (the ill-fated Biafra) were higher than in Southern Italy. *Cf.* her *Other Peoples' Worlds: Impressions of Ghana and Nigeria* (London: Secker and Warburg, 1958), p. 94.

³¹ Original text: "Estamos pobres porque un estado *traidor* entrega los bienes del pueblo argentino como un tributo colonial a su majestad británica!" Hardly had Perón nationalized British-owned railroads when they went into a decline from which they have not recovered to this day.

³² This remark might be extended to the United States. Although Americans of part-African ancestry are emphatically not Negroes, Peter F. Drucker is right when he says that "Black Harlem is one of the world's wealthiest communities—fifth or so in per capita income of all communities outside of North America and Europe, and easily the richest of all Negro communities in the world." *Cf.* his *The Age of Discontinuity* (New York: Harper and Row, 1968), p. 123.

602

[33] But what happens if one person is very industrious and the other one "takes it easy"? The ambitious man automatically creates an "undemocratic" situation. In Austria at present the law foresees the 40-hour week for the working class after 1971. I work 80 hours a week. A statistic compiled in 1969 revealed that the self-employed in Austria work an average of sixty two-and-a-half hours a week. To remedy the consequently almost unavoidable increasing financial inequality one has to punish the ambitious worker through progressive taxation, thus rendering intensive or extensive work materially unattractive.

[34] The Soviets, one need hardly emphasize, do not suffer from the widespread modern evil of Western masochism. *Cf.* Helmut Schoeck, "Der Masochismus des Abendlands" in *Europa—Besinnung und Hoffnung*, A. Hunold, ed. (Erlenbach-Zürich: Rentsch, 1957), pp. 221-256. These brilliant pages require a supplementary reading of H. Fortmann's book on "cultures of shame" and "cultures of guilt." (*Cf.* H. Fortmann, *Schuldcultuuren en Schaamtecultuuren*, Hertogenbosch, 1962). Ours obviously is a culture of guilt, and our "friends" and enemies know very well how to exploit this.

[35] *Cf.* Chapter XVII, Note 208.

[36] To embassies (representing the heads of states) as well as legations (representing merely the heads of governments). Before World War I only world powers (including the Vatican and Turkey) had *mutual* representations with embassy rank. (Thus the United States had an embassy in Paris, but only a legation in Brussels or Monrovia.) During and after World War II the megalomania of newly created nations changed the order. There are very few legations left. It is delightful to see an Embassy of Trinidad and Tobago in Addis Ababa, but one sincerely wonders what enormous sums are squandered by the new small nations for their diplomatic service—and where these monies originally came from.

[37] This little word "they" (*oni*) is the one constantly heard in all political conversations with Moscow's "man in the street."

[38] Almost immediately after the Six-Day War in the Near East, Mrs. Indira Gandhi handed a check of 50 million U. S. Dollars to the Government of the United Arab Republic. It is surprising to see an emerging nation, plagued by bitter poverty, and clamoring for aid being able to give such generous handouts.

[39] I am referring to the already once mentioned novel, *Die Gottlosen*. (A Dutch translation was published in 1965.) Hemingway, of course, was careful. His main hero in European background novels was always an American.

[40] One of the most priceless books of this sort is Dmitri Sergeyevitch *Na golubom Dunaye* (Odessa: Oblastnoye Izdatelstvo, 1955), a novel about postwar Vienna concocted with the help of encyclopedias. It is even funnier than Hochhuth's *The Deputy*. It is certainly a book which ought to be published in English with the help of a foundation. Even to those not knowing Austria it would be an exhilarating experience. Americans might be more amused by the play of an Esthonian Communist, Jacobson, *Shakaly*, trsl. into Russian

by L. Toom (Moscow: Iskusstvo, 1953) because it represents the South of the United States. The villain is an American general with the name of McKennedy and he is assisted by an evil college professor who with his wealth and power dominates a whole city. Phrases like "Now they go to the lynchings in their smart sports cars while their ancestors went with covered wagon" add flavor to the play. (And so do the "Imperialist War Hymns" in praise of the A-bomb sung by the Salvation Army.) A Western reader could also derive the most devastating fun from Ivan Kurchavov's *Moskovskoye Vremya* (Tallin: Estonskoye Gosudarstvennoye Izdatelstvo, 1956) which describes an Estonian ne'er-do-well being trained in the Vatican to disrupt labor organizations. He becomes a friend of the Pope, learns to use poison, pistols and false signatures, studies the history of the Inquisition and makes himself very popular by shouting: "We have to burn them all on the stake—from the Communists to the Metropolit of Moscow" (p. 293). Yet all this is not so very surprising if one looks at the sources. The article "Jesuits" in the *Bolshaya Sovyetskaya Entsiklopediya* (Moscow, 1952), vol. 27, pp. 341-342 is also a priceless piece—it could have been printed in any Nazi magazine.

[41] Before his death the liberator Simón Bolívar fell into utter despair and admitted that Spanish rule had been superior to the "freedom" he brought about. *Cf.* also Chapter XIX, Note 6.

Chapter XIX

[1] As to the Old World aspects of this phenomenon, *cf.* my essay "Student Revolts—European Version" in *Seeds of Anarchy: A Study of Campus Revolution*, F. Wilhelmsen, ed. (Dallas: Argus Academic Press, 1969), pp. 91-105.

[2] *Cf.* Wilfred van Oven, *Argentinien, Paraguay, Uruguay* (Nuremberg: Glock und Lutz, 1969), p. 98.

[3] *Cf.* Fredrick B. Pike, *The Modern History of Peru* (London: Weidenfeld and Nicolson, 1967), pp. 211, 223. From the beginning on the *cogobernación* was fought by the great conservative educator and thinker, José de la Riva-Agüero. *Cf.* his *Afirmación del Perú* (Lima: Pontificia Universidad, 1960), vol. II, pp. 164-166.

[4] On the "anarchical" character of the Catholic (and Greek-Orthodox) nations *cf.* my *Freiheit oder Gleichheit?*, pp. 285-321. It is worthwhile to keep in mind that the New Left is better anchored in the Catholic countries (and in those with large Catholic minorities), while hippieism pure and simple finds a greater echo in the world of the Reformation. The New Left and hippieism are naturally not identical but they do overlap.

[5] *Cf.* Graf Hermann Keyserling, *Südamerikanische Meditationen* (Berlin-Stuttgart: Deutsche Verlagsanstalt, 1932), *passim.*

[6] Here are the two famous exclamations of Bolívar shortly before his

death: "There is no good faith in America, whether between individuals or between nations. Treaties are mere papers, constitutions nothing but books, elections are combats, liberty is anarchy, and life a torment." The other one is not less depressing: "America is ungovernable. Those who have served the Revolution have ploughed the sea. The only thing to be done in America is to emigrate. These countries will inevitably fall into the hands of an uncurbed multitude, to pass later into those of petty tyrants of all colors and races. Devoured by every crime and extinguished by ferocity, they will not be worthy of conquest by Europeans. Were it possible that a part of the world should lapse into primeval chaos, that would be the last state of America." *Cf.* F. Loraine Petre, *op. cit.*, pp. 422-423. That these negative factors are not due to "Indian blood" is proved by the deep state of anarchy now prevailing in Uruguay, once Latin America's Exhibit A for "sound democratic government." Yet today chaos and terror have also affected many young Catholics including priests who are lustily greasing their rifles in the service of "Social Justice." Besides the famous Camilo Torres of Columbia we have in Uruguay the murderous Father de Silva. The result are such ghastly murders as those of the German Ambassador in Guatemala, Count Karl Spreti—and many more.

[7] Lykourgos once said to a man: "You want democracy? Then organize it first in your family." This is being done today—though not too successfully.

[8] See Chapter IX, Note 65.

[9] *Cf.* Herbert Marcuse, *One-Dimensional Man: Studies in the Ideology of Advanced Industrial Society* (Boston: Beacon Paperback, 1966), pp. xii-xiii, 19-25.

[10] I have purposely not dealt with Marxian economics. Having been proved empirically wrong, they do not merit more than a footnote. (Nor is to the New Left disciple a *homo economicus* pure and simple.)

[11] *Cf.* Herbert Marcuse, *op. cit.*, pp. 256-257, where the author appeals to "the substratum behind the conservative popular base," the outcasts and outsiders, the exploited and persecuted of other races and other colors, the unemployed and the unemployable. . . . Their force is behind every political demonstration for the victims of law and order. The fact that they start refusing to play the game may be the fact which marks the beginning of the end of a period." A very good summing up of Marcuse's "Critique of Society" can be found in Gerd-Klaus Kaltenbrunner's essay "Vorbild oder Verführer?" in *Wort und Wahrheit*, vol. 25, 1 (January-February 1970):

1. The late capitalist society succeeded, contrary to the prognostications of Marx and Engels, in gaining stability under the conditions of increasing technological perfection.

2. Coexistence with the Communist camp fosters the stabilization of Western society under the banner of forced rearmament.

3. Thanks to their increasing access to consumer goods, the working class, once an enemy of the capitalist system, has today become one of its pillars and has lost all revolutionary potentialities.

4. Without being conscious of it and without rebellion on the part of the victims, a manipulation and instrumentalization of man has taken the place of proletarian misery, brutal terror and sexual repression in a universe without any dialectic opposition.

5. This society is characterized by a one-dimensional conscience, a non-dialectic thinking lacking utopia or transcendence, a positivistic philosophy which is the very negation of philosophy.

6. Since the discontinuation of social change is the most salient feature of modern industrial society, only those individuals, groups, and layers can be agents of fundamental change who are outside of the democratic process: the unemployed and the unemployable, the inmates of jails and lunatic asylums, etc. Obviously all the leftist movements have a purely intellectual leadership and never start from the "grassroots." This Lenin knew only too well. *Cf.* his famous pamphlet *Shto dyelat'?* (Moscow: Izdatel'stvo politicheskoy lityeratury, 1970), p. 34.

[12] The democratic age has, above all politically, no inbuilt "futurism." One lives from one election to the other. The monarchs think about their grandchildren—and remember their grandfathers. Leftism is "antifamilistic."

[13] *Cf.* Theodor W. Adorno, *Minima Moralia* (Frankfurt a.M.: Suhrkamp, 1969), p. 243. It would be most erroneous to think that Marcuse has any love left for Sovietism. *Cf.* his *Soviet Marxism: A Critical Analysis* (New York: Vintage Books, 1961).

[14] *Cf. Der Spiegel*, January 5, 1969, p. 79sq. The "shock," however, was surprising, because in a number of publications Horkheimer had previously advertised his change of heart, thus, for instance, in Horkheimer, Rahner, von Weizsäcker, *Uber die Freiheit* (Stuttgart: Kreuz-Verkag, 1965).

[15] On "revolutionary conservatism" *cf.* Armin Mohler, *Die konservative Revolution in Deutschland* (Stuttgart: Vorwerk, 1950.) Interesting materials also can be found in Otto-Ernst Schüddekopf, *Linke Leute von rechts* (Stuttgart: Kohlhammer, 1960).

[16] In this pagan and youth-worshipping age any criticism of the young seems to be taboo. Most refreshing therefore is the clever book by Robert Poulet, *Contre la jeunesse* (Paris: Denoël, 1963). In this connection, however, we have to bear in mind that the rebellious "kids" are rarely the offsprings of staid conservatives, but of moderately left parents (New Dealers, for instance), children who *think and act consistently.* This is well brought out by the novel of J. Anthony Lukas, *Don't Shoot—We Are Your Children* (New York: Random House, 1971).

[17] *Cf.* Armin Mohler, *Was die Deutschen fürchten* (Stuttgart: Seewald, 1965), pp. 129sq.

[18] Sadistic drives against inanimate objects do exist. Vandalism directed against schools (including universities) seems to be a good preparation for the New Left way of life. At the same time it is a blow against authority. In the United States the damage done annually to schools is estimated to be

between 15 and 20 million dollars. (Neither, we must add, should one force adolescents without any talents or intellectual curiosity to attend school until the age of eighteen.)

[19] Of the many scandalous New Left "performances" one of the worst took place in the aula of Vienna's university. The theme was "Art and Revolution." Four "artists" undressed and showed—to use a circumlocution—all the varieties of their physical secretions. In a German university the *rector magnificus* was bound and gagged in his office and a young couple cohabited before him: "We're begetting a little revolutionary." These tales could be repeated literally *ad nauseam*. On the profound reasons for the present "sexual revolution" *cf.* Professor Viktor Frankl cited by C. Härlin, "Sexualität und Sinnenentleering" in *Rheinischer Merkur*, March 27, 1970, pp. 18-19. Frankl believes in the frequent existence of a "noögenous neurosis," a neurosis rooted in the failure to make sense out of life. A morbid sex-centeredness is often the result. Frankl says: "As opposed to the beasts, instincts do tell man what he *must* do; traditions no longer tell him what he *ought* to do; often he therefore no longer knows what he really *wants* to do. As a result he merely wills what the others do, or does what the others want. This leads either to conformism or totalitarianism."

[20] New Left art is opposed to the beautiful. It represents all creation in hateful distortion, and especially so the human figure . . . an indirect form of atheism.

In its artistic aspects we see a decided connection between Dadaism (of the 1918-1922 period) and the New Left. Dadaism, however, was not only an artistic movement but also had deep political and social implications. It was at the same time libertine and antitheistic. *Cf.* Richard Huelsenbeck, *En avant Dada* (Hanover, 1920). Here we hear that Dadaism is an international, revolutionary league of all creative persons on the basis of a radical communism, that progressive unemployment should be introduced, that dadaist poems (of a "brutist nature") ought to be read in churches, that all sexual relations ought to be organized by a sex center, etc. Dadaism, finally, influenced surrealism, and former dadaists acted in that movement (Aragon, Breton, Eluard). A pamphlet of that group issued in May 1931 applauded the burning of churches in Spain and made an appeal to the French to do likewise: "Only the proletariat has the power to sweep God from the surface of the earth." (Aragon later become a leading Communist.)

[21] On Satan and Non-Being, *cf.* my *The Timeless Christian*, pp. 173-174.

[22] One of the accusations leveled by the antiauthoritarian school against "conservatives" is to the effect that they are overly clean and dress too neatly. *Cf.* Theodor W. Adorno, *The Authoritarian Personality* (New York: Harper & Row, 1950), p. 448.

[23] There is obviously a sizeable amount of money which can be made by pornography. "Permissiveness" has its own vested interests.

²⁴ On the Paris revolt *cf.* Patrick Seale and Maureen McConville, *French Revolution, 1968* (A Penguin Special, 1968). This book is amusing to read because it is written by young Catholic leftists. Well observed is Raymond Aron's *La révolution introuvable* (Paris: A. Fayard, 1968). Marcuse cited the Communist daily *Humanité* (Paris) on the riots which wrote: "Every barricade, every car burned gave tens of thousands of votes to the De Gaullist party." Then Marcuse added: "This is perfectly correct—yet this risk of defeat must be taken." *Cf.* H. Marcuse, *An Essay of Liberation* (Boston: Beacon Press, 1969), p. 68.

²⁵ German students pay roughly forty dollars for a semester, Austrian students about twelve dollars. In other words, the universities in Europe exist almost wholly on public support. There are Sorbonne professors who think that the evil of rebellion could be alleviated by organizing private universities with very high tuition fees (while letting the public universities go to the dogs). This, I am afraid, might be another miscalculation. Columbia University with a tuition fee of roughly $2,200 per annum had just as bad riots as many a nearly gratuitous state university. As one can easily imagine, the leftist guerilleros and leading Communists in Latin America are mostly the sons and daughters of the upper-bourgeoisie and the oligarchs of those nations. *Cf.* Alphons Max, *Guerillas in Lateinamerika* (Zürich: Schweizerische Handelszeitung, 1971), also my *Amerika-Leitbild im Zwielicht* (Einsiedeln: Johannes Verlag, 1971), pp. 107, 143.

²⁶ *Cf.* F. R. Allemann, "Adolf und die Bengel," in *Die Weltwoche*, February 28, 1969, p. 5. It is, however, not wholly correct to call the National Democratic Party "neo-Nazi." Obviously there are many ex-Nazis in it, but this is equally true of the other German parties. Adolf von Thadden has no Nazi record and he comes from a notoriously anti-Nazi family. (His aunt Elisabeth was beheaded.)

²⁷ I heard similar talks in Spain by a high government official. In one or two years, he insinuated, workers' brigades could be sent against rioting students. A "fascist reaction," however, coming precisely from the working class, figures as a distinct possibility in the thought of Marcuse. *Cf.* his *Psychoanalyse und Politik* (Frankfurt: Europäische Verlagsanstalt, 1968), p. 66. As a matter of fact, this fear of a technological world dominated by an industrial society is quite characteristic of the New Left. (There is also a suspicion that technology implies a great deal of discipline and order.) Mohler is right when he says that the enthusiasm for technology has switched from the left to the right. *Cf.* his "Konservativ 1969" in *Formeln deutscher Politik* (Munich: Bechtle, 1969), pp. 110-111.

²⁸ This long poem "Il PC ai giovani" was published 1969 in the Italian weekly *Il Tempo* and immediately created a big controversy. (There is, needless to say, the fear of the various Communist parties that they will lose the young generation to the New Left as Raymond Aron has stated in his *Révolution introuvable.*) It is obvious that the leaders and most of the rank and file of

the New Left in Latin America are the negating, protesting sons of the rich and the well-to-do. A brilliant analysis of that particular state of affairs can be found in Alphonse Max' "El comunismo latinoamericano como fenomeno tridimensional" in *Correo de la Tarde* (suplemento 3), August 26, 1969. The New Left indeed is, in the words of Herbert Marcuse, "the Great Refusal." Cf. *One-Dimensional Man*, p. 257: "The critical theory of society posesses no concepts which could bridge the gap between the present and its future; holding no promise and showing no success, it remains negative. Thus it wants to remain loyal to those who, without hope, have given and give their life to the Great Refusal." This Great Refusal has been lived by the female Weatherman, Diana Oughton, whose frightening life has well been described by Thomas Powers in *Diana, The Making of a Terrorist* (Boston: Houghton Mifflin, 1971). The illustrations are even more eloquent than the text.

[29] It is evident that however bright these young men of the New Left be, they do lack the experience, the very groundwork of knowledge which alone gives the possibility for real insights. A revealing experience for me was a trip to Huancayo, a provincial town in Peru with two universities and eleven bookstores. The latter were fully stocked with books of all sorts, but mostly "timely" publications of a political, sociological and psychological order. *Missing were the great classics, basic works of lasting value.* The counterpart to these books were the grafitti of the students of the National and the Catholic universities. They could be found everywhere, in every nook and corner. The wild battles between Apra-supporters, Maoists, Guevarists, Castroists, Muscovites, Trotskyists, and other leftists received literary and pictorial expression here.

[30] JUSPAO, the American information office in Saigon, has mountains of Viet Cong horror photos, but these are often so obscene that they are just not fit for publication. American troops seeing such nauseating scenes might often lose their balance and not keep the rules of war. But surely they would not disembowel people, make them watch how pigs eat their entrails, bury them alive (as it happened to the Benedictine Father David Urbain) or only half-bury them so they were eaten alive by ants (as it happened to Father Jean de Compiegne). The Tet offensive and its gory details should have been an eye-opener to the most fanatical peacenik, denying that premature American withdrawal would involve the martyrdom of *millions*.

[31] A former rector of San Marcos, the oldest university of the Americas, declared to me more than ten years ago that he had resigned his exalted office because either the students or the professors were on strike. Regular teaching had become well-nigh impossible. Student Comanagement destroyed whatever standards there were left. The military government now tries to effect a change.

[32] In certain ways the German universities (especially in the North) are worse than their American counterparts. The picture painted by Baron Caspar Schrenck-Notzing in his *Zukunftsmacher. Die neue Linke in Deutschland und ihre Herkunft* (Stuttgart: Seewald, 1968) provides us with a terrible picture.

Professor Helmut Kuhn of Munich University stated unequivocally: "Whether the Republic will survive the student rebellion in the universities *as republic*—this is the alarming question." *Cf.* his essay "Die Studentenschaft in der Demokratie" in *Stimmen der Zeit*, vol. 183, June 1969, p. 371. As for the American scene *vide* the excellent article by Arthur H. Hobbs, "The SDS Trip: From Vision to Ego Shrieks," in *The Intercollegiate Review*, Vol. 5 (Spring 1969), pp. 147-157. Significantly enough, the German university rebels also called themselves *SDS*—"Socialist German Students" (but not "Students for a Democratic Society"). Still, the German high school students (age group ten to nineteen) also have started to organize and have demanded a democratization of the schools *and the parental homes*. Their organization is the AUSS. (*Cf.* IDW. *Informations-und Dokumentationszentrum West*, February 23, 1968.) Such news would have gladdened the hearts of the American (leftist) reeducators in the immediate postwar years. They have left Germany in the meantime but are now reaping a rich harvest.

[33] As one can see, so many of these new heroes come from the "Third World." They indeed are "outlandish" and underline the existence of a "Masochism of the West," a general phenomenon, but dominant in the ranks of the New Left.

Chapter XX

[1] There is, to be true, in the Western Hemisphere a Conservative party in Colombia and the remnant of one in Chile.

[2] The *Freisinnige* in Switzerland are most emphatically not "liberals" in the contemporary American sense. As a matter of fact, apart from its subtly hidden anticlericalism, a *fresinnig* daily with a worldwide prestige such as the *Neue Züricher Zeitung* would be called "conservative" in America.

[3] In Central Europe Joseph II became a legendary figure surrounded with an endless number of anecdotes—many of them invented. Yet in Belgium (the "Austrian Netherlands") his liberal reforms were furiously opposed by the people and led to serious rebellion. They wanted none of his "enlightened" ideas.

[4] Unless we give credence to Alfred Noyes who presented him as an "irregular Catholic," Voltaire was a preliberal deist. He was violently opposed to Rousseau, a genuine totalitarian democrat. About Voltaire's reaction to Rousseau, *cf.* his *Oeuvres complètes* (Paris: Société littéraire-typographique, 1785), vol. 68-69 which contain Voltaire's correspondence with d'Alembert.

[5] The feeling of the masses was that the immensely brutal giant with bulging eyes, six feet eight inches tall, was Antichrist. These sentiments were well dramatized in Dmitri Myerezhkovski's *Pyotr y Alexey* (St. Petersburg: Pirozhkov, 1905). Yet he is almost worshiped by the Soviets who also named a big Black Sea steamer after him. (*Pyotr Vyeliki.*) His picture hung in Stalin's

study and one can admire his terrifying effigy in Leningrad's Winter Palace.

[6] The concept of man as the measure was first used by Protagoras, but the great Nicholas Cusanus employs it also in his treatise *De beryllo*, ch. 5. *Cf.* Louis Martinez Gomez S.J. "El hombre 'mensura rerum' en Nicholas de Cusa," *Pensamiento* (Madrid), vol. 21, no. 81, pp. 41-64.

[7] *Cf.* Paul Dabin S.J. *Le sacerdoce royal des fidèles dans la tradition ancienne et moderne* (Brussels: Edition universelle, n.d.); F. X. Arnold, *Mann und Frau in Welt und Kirche* (Nürnberg: Glock und Lutz, 1959), pp. 81-82, 91-92. In other words, according to Catholic doctrine and traditions there exists a general priesthood of all those baptized, based on St. Peter's concept of the *basileion hieráteuma*, the "royal priesthood" of all Christians. In the narrowest sense the priesthood finds its embodiment in the bishops only. *Cf.* also Rosmini-Serbati, "Diritto derivato, II, Diritto sociale," *Opere edite e inedite* (Milan: Libreria Pogliani, 1883), vol. 17, pp. 264-266.

[8] Henry Kissinger (differently from Peter Viereck) sees in Metternich an eighteenth century rationalist whose roots lie perhaps not in the spirit, but in the thinking grooves of the Enlightenment.

[9] The struggle for a synthesis between heart and mind has always been very marked among Spanish and Russian thinkers. *Cf.* Miguel de Unamuno, *Del Sentimiento trágico de la vida* (Buenos Aires: Espasa Calpe, 1945), p. 152, and D. S. Myerezhkovski, *Gryadushtshiy Kham i Tshekhov i Gorki* (St. Petersburg: Pirozhkov, 1906), p. 33.

[10] *Cf.* also E. I. Watkin, *The Catholic Centre* (New York: Sheed and Ward, 1945), pp. 101ff.

[11] Luther's antirationalism was extremely radical: he was convinced that faith and reason are real opposites. *Cf.* his "Tischreden," *Krit. Gesamtausgabe* (Weimar), vol. 6, no. 6718 or Erlangen Edition, vol. 44, pp. 156-159. The basically irrational attitude of Calvin can be seen exemplified in passages such as *Institutiones*, I, vii, 5, *Cf.* Edgar Sheffield Brightman, *A Philosophy of Religion* (New York: Prentice-Hall, 1940), p. 6. Also W. H. van de Pol, *Das reformatorische Christentum* (Zürich, Benziger, 1955), p. 218 and Leroy Nixon, *John Calvin's Teaching on Human Reason* (New York: Exposition Press, 1963), particularly pp. 31, 32, 51, 52, 59. Reinhold Niebuhr considers Calvin's attitudes toward reason to be halfway between Luther and the Catholic viewpoint. *Cf.* his *The Nature and Destiny of Man* (New York: Scribner's, 1941), p. 285n.

[12] *Cf.* I. M. Bocheński, O.P., *Der sowjetrussische dialektische Materialismus (Diamat)* (Bern: Francke, 1956), p. 14.

[13] I still remember, almost nostalgically, the fire my strictures against Thomism drew when I published an article on democracy in *New Scholasticism* (vol. 20, no. 3, July 1946). Today the dangers are coming from the opposite quarter.

[14] The Russians have also another word for it: *mirosozertsaniye*. The difference is very subtle. Yet more and more the word *ideologiya* is adopted.

[15] *Cf.* Unamuno, *Del sentimiento trágico de la vida*, p. 31.

[16] *Cf.* Joseph de Maistre, *Oeuvres complètes* (Lyons, 1884-1887), pp. 155-156.

[17] The "source book" on the concept of the English gentlemen is, according to Sir Ernest Barker, the translation of Castiglione's *Il Cortegiano* by Sir Thomas Hoby, published in 1528. *Cf.* Sir Ernest Barker, *Traditions of Civility* (Cambridge, England: University Press, 1948), pp. 141-148. Reading Baldassare Castiglione's *Il Libro del Cortegiano* (Milan: Ulrico Hoepli, 1928) one is struck by the description of the *cortegiano* (the "pregentleman") as an amateur *and* intellectual—the term "amateur" taken in its original sense. The differences between the *cortegiano* and the gentlemen are thus not inconsiderable.

[18] The "ideologue" of the Prussian Conservatives was the Jewish convert Friedrich Julius Stahl, a university professor, the "ideologue" of the Dutch conservatives the historian Guilleaume Groen van Prinsterer. Agrarian societies usually get their political ideas in a systematized form from "outside sources."

[19] The word *"socialism"* was first used by Robert Owen, the term *social democracy* (for socialism organized in a party) by Bakunin. *Cf.* Th. G. Masaryk, *Zur russischen Geschichts und Religionsphilosophie*, vol. 2, p. 32.

[20] On this reaction, to be found particularly in Central Europe (Germany, Austria, etc.) see the letters written by A. de Tocqueville to Baron Herbert de Tocqueville on February 24, 1854 and to N. W. Senior on September 19, 1855. *Cf. Oeuvres complètes*, vol. 7, pp. 325 and 372.

[21] How bitter these memories of the French Revolution were is proved by the custom of letting the sons and daughters of those guillotined—the *jeunesse dorée*—wear silk red ribbons around their necks at the balls given by French nobility after the end of the terror.

[22] Here one must regretfully remember that many of the old diets were not revived in the nineteenth century. In the Tyrol, for instance, where I live, the beginnings of popular representation go back to the fourteenth, its full development to the fifteenth century when in the Tyrolean *Landtag* four Estates were represented: Nobility, Clergy, Burghers, and Peasantry. They were equal. Serfdom was unknown in the Tyrol. The right to bear arms was abolished by the Nazis only in 1938.

[23] The Republic of Cracow existed only between 1815 and 1946 in which year it was annexed by Austria.

[24] The "Dutch" Netherlands had been separated from the Spanish (later, Austrian) Netherlands by the end of the 16th century. They were united in 1815 but again broke asunder in 1830.

[25] Apart from Pilsudski we find names like Jodko-Narkiewicz, Limanowski, Niedzialkowski, and many others, Pilsudski's victory in 1926—nearly a thousand people were killed in street fighting—was made possible by the P.P.S., the Polish Socialist party which proclaimed a general strike

and thus prevented the transport of loyal troops to Warsaw. Yet Pilsudski figured in the American press as a "Rightist War Lord"! *Cf.* Hans Roos, *op. cit.*, p. 114.

[26] The murder of August von Kotzebue gave to central European conservatism a reactionary twist. This brilliant German playwright with an adventurous mind went to Russia, became a Russian citizen, but then returned to Germany where he combatted leftist-nationalist ideas. His assassin, Karl Ludwig Sand, was an idealistic though neurotic national democrat. Kotzebue's second son, Otto, was a famous navigator and explorer in Russian services. The town of Kotzebue in Alaska has been named after him.

[27] One of Sand's closest friends, Karl Follen, was professor of civil law at the universities of Giessen and Jena. Following the assassination of Kotzebue he took refuge in France where he became suspect after the murder of the Duc de Berry in 1820. He fled to Switzerland and from there in 1824 to the United States. Here he became professor of German at Harvard College in 1825, but resigned in 1835, his radical abolitionist stand having made him unpopular with the authorities. A year later he was ordained a Unitarian minister in Lexington, Mass. He died on a steamer between New York and Boston in 1840.

Sand and Follen were typical representatives of early German national liberalism (and not only of national democracy). The National Liberal (*Nationalliberale*), the protagonists of Bismarck's *Kulturkampf*, as Karl Buchheim has pointed out, were in so many ways the precursors of National Socialism. *Cf.* K. Buchheim, *"Der Ursprung der deutschen Weltanschauungsparteien," Hochland*, vol. 43, no. 6 (August 1951), p. 550.

[28] *Cf.* Karl Euler, *Friedrich Ludwig Jahn, Sein Leben und sein Wirken* (Stuttgart: Krabbel, 1881), pp. 483-484. "Oddballs" such as Jahn were the precursors of twentieth-century German "democracy" and were hailed as such. (But, later, they were equally praised and worshiped by the Nazis.)

[29] Jarcke saw only too clearly the danger of "national democracy" for the Germans. He considered this sort of national egoism to be French, in its more brutal form British, in its most nauseating edition—"westernized Russian." He was sure that it would eventually spell the ruin of the German people. *Cf.* Carl Ernst Jarcke, *Vermischte Schriften* (Paderborn: Schöningh, 1854), vol. 4, pp. 448-450, 452-453. *Cf.* also letters of Jarcke to C. L. v. Haller, 1836-1842 in *Historisch-Politische Blätter*, vol. 154 (1914), pp. 402ff. C. E. Jarcke was a North German convert and a typical representative of early nineteenth-century *genuine* conservatism, very similar in his outlook to Gerlach and to George Phillips, son of an English merchant, born in Königsberg (East Prussia) and also a convert. *Cf. Staatslexikon* (Herder, 5th ed.), vol. 2, col. 1396-1400 and vol. 4, col. 189-190. For a more general outline of the conservative outlook (though in a nutshell) *cf.* Russell Kirk, *The Conservative Mind from Burke to Santayana* (Chicago: Regnery, 1953), pp. 7-8, alluding to Professor Hearnshaw's *Conservatism in England*.

[30] *Cf.* Alexander Graf Razumowsky, "Turnfest der Superlative (Im-

pressionen von der Spartakiade in Prag)," *Frankfurter Allgemeine Zeitung*, July 6, 1965, pp. 7-8.

[31] We all remember the outcry of the leftist press when Moise Tshombé, first in the Katanga region, then for the Central Government of the Congo, hired mercenaries—i.e., *volunteers* who of their own free will were ready to fight as professionals for a cause which we know was a just one. For the typical leftist, wedded to the ideals of the French Revolutionary Democracy, the soldier apparently ought to be a conscript and an amateur too who, in order to get the right fighting spirit, is "indoctrinated," i.e., incited to group hatred.

[32] Among those who regretted the transition from the professional military system based on the mercenaries to the modern "democratic" mass army of conscripts we find not only authors such as Raymond Aron and General J. C. F. Fuller, but also an American military writer of renown, the late Hoffman Nickerson. *Cf.* his *The Armed Horde, 1793-1939* (New York: Putnam, 1940 and 1942). De Gaulle also preferred the professional army. He expressed his view in a book entitled *Vers l'armée du metier*. Léon Blum, the Socialist leader, naturally opposed this idea because he thought that it would endanger the republic (and or socialism?). De Gaulle refers to this in his *Mémoires de Guerre* (Paris 1955), vol. 1, p. 15.

[33] Men such as Friedrich Julius Stahl, Guillaume Groen van Prinsterer, Benjamin Disraeli (Lord Beaconsfield), Juan Donoso Cortés Marqués de Valdegamas, Carl Ernst Jarcke, George P. Phillips, Carl Ludwig v. Haller, Constantin Frantz, Konstantin Leontyev, Louis Veuillot, Aleksey Khomyakov, Philipp v. Segesser, Ludwig v. Gerlach, F. M. Dostoyevski. By 1890 almost all of these men had died. A new crop of conservative thinkers matured in Europe (and in North America) only after World War I.

[34] The Dreyfus affair in France brought about a wave of strong anti-Jewish feelings and thus we encounter anti-Jewish conservatives such as Albert de Mun. A man such as Baron C. v. Vogelsang, however, was convinced that any "Jewish rule" would only assert itself if and when Christianity abdicated. Then the Church makes way for the Synagogue and the Jews are again the "first born" for which the Christians have to blame themselves. *Cf.* his article "Die Judenverfolgungen in Russland," *Das Vaterland*, April 26, 1882, also in Freiherr C. v. Vogelsang, *Gesammelte Aufsätze über socialpolitische und verwandte Themata* (Augsburg: Max Huttler, 1886), vol. 1, pp. 133-134.

[35] So was the murdered Walter Rathenau for a while, but then he became reconverted to the idea of a monarchy in Germany. *Cf.* Winfried Martini, *Freiheit auf Abruf*, pp. 240, 433. Also Graf Harry Kessler, *op. cit.*, pp. 553-554.

[36] *Cf.* Chapter XVII, Note 5.

[37] And this for two reasons: (1) monarchy itself is an interethnic, interracial institution, and (2) ethnic nationalism is "identitarian." The President of the United States must be "American born."

[38] One cardinal protested against the outlawing of the *Action Française*—the Jesuit Cardinal Louis Billot. Pope Pius XI forced his resignation and Billot spent the rest of his life in an Italian monastery. *Cf.* Adrien Dansette, *op. cit.*, vol. 2, pp. 583-610.

[39] *Cf.* Armin Mohler, *op. cit.*, pp. 106ff.

[40] There has been in Japan a Shintoist revival in the eighteenth century (Motoori Norinaga gave expression to it) and Shintoist feelings there have repeatedly resulted in minor persecutions of Buddhism which, after all, is for Japan an alien, Indian religion imported via China and Korea. Efforts toward a political Shinto-revival were made in the early 1960s by Professor Chikuo Fujisawa of the Nippon University (Tokyo). *Cf.* his essay *"Der shintoistische Grundbegriff des Politischen und die existenzphilosophische Eigenschaft des japanischen Kaisers"* (Tokyo: Research Institute of the New Teaching, 1957). This essay is dedicated to Martin Heidegger. I knew the late Professor Fujisawa, but was unable to find out whether he really "believed" in Shintoism. I would say, not in any Western sense.

[41] We purposely do not say, "Western Civilization." Yet Western Civilization has an essentially Christian foundation. Hilaire Belloc formulated: "Europe is the Faith and the Faith is Europe." The first half of this statement is definitely true, even if the cultural limits of Europe are by no means its geographical boundaries. The second part can only be accepted with a number of reservations and corrections. Should Christianity conquer the world, it will still always retain qualities from its European "phase," just as a Lithuanian or a Swede will only know it with (never without) its Jewish, Greek, and Roman elements. Christianity is not a mathematical abstraction hanging in midair, nor is the Church a chemically pure theorem. It is in space and time, in geography and history.

[42] *Cf.* Erik von Kuehnelt-Leddihn, "Neukonservatismus und Neu-liberalismus," *Neues Abendland* (Munich, 1956), no. 2, p. 124. To what extent genuine conservatism is allied to the demand for personal liberty can be seen from the fact that as a young man Georges Bernanos was put into jail for his monarchist convictions and actions. (He "sat" in the cell No. 13 of the 6th division in the *Santé*.) At the same time he was a member of the "Cercle Proudhon" and wrote articles (his first ones!) for *Soyons Libres*, a periodical claiming to support "Integral Liberalism" (in the Continental sense, that is). *Cf. Bernanos par lui-même*, Albert Béguin, ed. (Paris: Editions du Seuil, 1954), p. 89.

[43] Disraeli said in 1836: "The native tendency of the Jewish race, who are justly proud of their blood, is against the doctrine of the equality of man. They have also another characteristic, the faculty of acquisition. . . . Thus it will be seen that all the tendencies of the Jewish race are conservative. Their bias is to religion, property, and natural aristocracy, and it should be the interest of statesmen that the bias of a great race should be encouraged and their energies and creative powers enlisted in the cause of the existing society." *Cf.* W. F. Monypenny and George E. Flavelle, *op. cit*, vol. 1, p. 880. It

is, of course, true that Lev Bronstein-Trotsky became a Communist, but Baron Ginsburg was a personal friend of Nicholas II, Albert Ballin of William II, Ignacio Bauer y Landau of Alphons XIII—and Disraeli—Lord Beaconsfield —of Queen Victoria.

[44] We could oblige here also with an American list: Ralph de Toledano, Frank S. Meyer, Victor Lasky, Allan H. Ryskind, Max Geltman, Will Herberg, William S. Schlamm, Nathaniel Weyl. To these names could be added a list of *genuine* liberals who figure in America frequently as "conservatives."

[45] When the writings of Maurras (including his paper, the *Action Française*) were put on the index, it was argued that the Church was "playing politics" and trying to gain the favors of "official France." We cannot go into this complex and perplexing argument here, but it is certain that in the eyes of the Church Maurras committed the unpardonable crime, i.e., to take personally an agnostic viewpoint and to declare the Catholic faith to be "useful to France." Against such a patronizing, nationalistic pat on the back Rome would react nervously and energetically. During the war the fanatically anti-German Maurras collaborated with the Germans and narrowly escaped the death sentence after Liberation. Still, he died "in the Church." About his death *cf.* Chanoine A. Cormier, *Mes entretiens de prêtre avec Charles Maurras, mars-novembre 1952* (Paris: Plon, 1953). The canon kissed the hands of the dying man. *Vide* also Chanoine Aristide Cormier, *La vie intérieure de Charles Maurras* (Paris: Plon, 1956). Paul Claudel, a man on the extreme right, a monarchist and Catholic, was strongly anti-Maurras. *Cf.* André Saurès et Paul Claudel, *Correspondance 1904-1938*, Robert Mallet, ed. (Paris: NRF-Gallimard, 1951), pp. 159-160. (Letter of Claudel, dated February 10, 1911).

[46] Significantly enough the Calvinist conservative party of the Netherlands (fathered ideologically by Groen van Prinsterer) calls itself "Anti-Revolutionary." We encounter all through the nineteenth century the term "*the* Revolution," *la revolution*, in political writings, always referring to the French Revolution as if it were a permanent specter, an invisible, *continued* threat. In its derivations it indeed still is.

[47] The Central and East European definition of culture and civilization has not largely entered English semantics on both sides of the Atlantic—civilization being classified as the practical-material, culture as the spiritual-intellectual order. Law and manners belong to both. Spengler was emphatic on the difference between the two but, actually, since they are "situated" in man, they are interconnected. Technology, for instance, belongs to civilization, yet it rests on philosophical-psychological and even on theological premises and foundations.

[48] Unfortunately the entire sentence is rarely quoted: *Enrichissez vous par le travail et l'epargne*—"enrich yourselves by working and saving," which is a very different matter. Guirot was really both, an early liberal and a conservative.

[49] There really is no "First" and "Second" Estate—only a Third Estate

616

so-called after the burghers became politically represented. There was no "hierarchy" of the Estates either. In the old French Diet the majority of the Estates decided. Today we have the concept of upper and lower *classes*: there were politically no "upper" or "lower" Estates.

[50] *Cf.* Prinz Philipp zu Eulenburg, *Aus fünfzig Jahren* (Berlin: Paetel, 1923), p. 225; Otto von Bismarck, *Gesammelte Werke*, Petersdorff, ed. (Berlin: Deutsche Verlagsgesellschaft, 1923-1935). Vol. 15, p. 485.

[51] Agrarian paternalism often prompted the Swedish Conservatives to vote with the Social Democrats against the Liberals, the party of the industrialists and bankers.

[52] *Cf.* Joseph A. Schumpeter, *Capitalism, Socialism and Democracy* (New York: Harper, 1942), p. 341. *Vide* also Schumpeter's remark on the quarrel between William II and Bismarck—siding unequivocally with the emperor. *Cf. op. cit.*, pp. 342-343 and note 20.

[53] The last Bourbon of the main line, the Comte de Chambord ("Henri V") who in his exile refused the French crown because he would have had to accept the despised tricolor, and therefore figures as an arch-reactionary, was nevertheless profoundly interested in the labor question. His "Letter to the Workers" in 1865 created quite a sensation. *Cf.* Adrien Dansette, *op. cit.*, vol. 2, pp. 186-187. The head of the Orléans branch of the family, the Comte de Paris (Louis Philippe Albert d'Orléans) had almost identical views. *Cf.* his *Les associations ouvrières en Angleterre* (Paris: Félix Alcan, 1884). This volume was also strongly prolabor. Of course, one can also state that the equidistance of all subjects increases and becomes more marked with the absolute power of the monarch. Hollywood notions notwithstanding, the social hierarchies, let us say in 1900, were infinitely more developed in Britain than in Russia, more so in Sweden than in Turkey.

[54] Of great importance were the nobilitations of outstanding men— plutocrats, officers, civil servants, artists, scholars—because new titles *fostered* social mobility. It was one of the roles of the monarchs to *facilitate* social rise and to aid the formation of fresh elites. The social fabric becomes more easily static in a republican-aristocratic framework, *vide* the case of Venice and Genoa. Therefore one should not be surprised at William Dean Howells' declaration that "Inequality is as dear to the American heart as liberty itself." (Quoted by Cleveland Amory, *Who Killed Society?* New York: Harper, 1960.) F. J. Grund, who insisted that American institutions are "English, improved or mutilated," quoted a Bostonian who complained that a "ridiculous equality pervades all classes of French society." (*Op. cit*, pp. 50 and 51.) C. Wright Mills was correct when he maintained that the American upper crust becomes more and more self-perpetuating, and more and more a closed caste. *Cf.* his *The Power Elite* (New York: Oxford University Press, 1956), pp. 104-105. Naturally, American class feelings from time to time can assume curious forms (as in other places) and they will be more marked in a female than in a male ambiance. This is specifically true of American sororities. (*Cf.* "The Trouble

with the Greeks'' *Time*, Atlantic Edition, February 2, 1953, pp. 36-37.) Yet, on the other hand, it is equally true that the liberal, freedom-loving outlook of Americans has an aristocratic foundation. *Cf.* Peter Viereck, ''The Aristocratic Origin of American Freedom,'' *Southwest Review*, vol. 37, no. 4 (Autumn 1959), pp. 331-334.

[55] *Cf.* Manya Gordon, *op. cit.*, pp. 17, 64. Yet especially in view of the sufferings resulting from the transition from one system of production to another, one has to remember Cicero's remark (2. Catilina) to the effect that great iniquities are frequently caused by circumstances over which governments have no control.

[56] And this in spite of the fact that absolute monarchies at the end of the eighteenth century had been the pioneers of humanitarian penal legislation. (*Cf.* Chapter XIV, Note 36.) The guiding spirit of this change was Marchese Cesare Beccaria Bonesana (1738-1794), a native of Milan, pupil of the Jesuits, professor of law, who as an Austrian civil servant enjoyed the support of Empress Maria Theresa and of Emperor Joseph II.

[57] *Cf.* Note 41 of this Chapter. It is precisely the waning of theistic religion which is responsible not only for the increasing criminality of our age and day, but also for most of the political horrors of our generation. In spite of all the atrocities and brutalities of religious wars in the past, we had to wait for this century to experience Auschwitz, Katyn, Dresden, Hiroshima, the illimited bestialities of the Red Chinese ''purges'' and the calculated fiendishness of the Viet Cong. Gaetano Mosca tells us about the hair-raising plan of an Italian anarchist to exterminate all the bourgeoisie, their women folk and children down to the age of two or three. (*Elementi di Scienza Politica, p. 297.*) Another anarchist published in Australia a delightful book in which he described in gory details a tremendous massacre in whose memory a huge column was erected, made of skulls and bones carrying an inscription warning all posterity not to fall back into the ''old corruption, iniquity, and lies'' of the bourgeois way of life. *Cf.* Edmund Boisgilbert, *Caesar's Column* (Melbourne: Cole, 1892). Bakunin's visions were not very different. He went on record saying that: ''We see in the Revolution precisely the unleashing of what one calls today the 'evil passions' and the destruction of what is called in the same language 'the public order.' '' Arnold Ruge wrote to Feuerbach from Paris on May 15, 1844 that ''everybody speaks here with hope and determination about the collapse of bourgeois rule as a result of sanguinary catastrophes and the beginning of a millennium of liberty and equality.'' Engels too dreamed of a happy, sacred last war preceding thousand years of a *Reich* of freedom. *Cf.* Werner Sombart, *Der proletarische Sozialismus* (Jena: Gustav Fischer, 1924), vol. 1, pp. 165 and 322. We see here clearly from whom the National Socialists received the idea of a *tausendjähriges Reich*—from the Socialists rather than from the Nationalists.

These horrors were all ''logical,'' thanks to the grim philosophic determination of Sade, the grandfather of all leftist currents. Robert Owen who started "formal socialism" was certain that there was no liberty of volition or feeling. There would be no criminals in the new society and those who attacked it would not be treated as criminals, but as "mentally deranged," a system now quite popular in the USSR. *Cf.* Thilo Ramm, *Die grossen Sozialisten als Rechts und Sozialphilosophen* (Stuttgart: Gustav Fischer, 1955), vol. 1. pp. 446, 449.

[58] The question has not yet been fully answered whether the hardships of the Industrial Revolution were avoidable or not. In many cases they were exaggerated and the fantastic illusions about profits "especially in French Catholic leftist circles" have clearly nineteenth century origins. *Cf.* Goetz Briefs, *Das Gewerkschaftsdchaftsproblem gestern und heute* (Frankfurt a. M.: F. Knapp, 1955), p. 98. Transitions *always* create sufferings and the leftists everywhere offered this truism as an excuse for the sacrifices demanded by the "Soviet Experiment." Today, however, the Red experimental stage has lasted half a century and has produced very little. The idea to live well through the agency of the State is by no means new. Frédéric Bastiat told us in the *Journal des Débats* (September 25, 1848) that the "State is a great fiction through which everybody is trying to live at everybody else's expense." Which reminds one of the dictum of V. Muthesius that "Politics is the art to get the money of the rich and, at the same time, the votes of the poor under the pretext to protect one from the other." *Cf.* S. G. Fudalla, *Die Gegenwart als Patient* (Bern-Stuttgart: A. Scherz, 1960), p. 243. To avoid this type of demagoguery in a democracy the panacea of a Socialist system is offered, but Wilhelm Röpke was only too right when he said, "Every attempt to establish an economic system on ethics which are substantially higher than those of the average man, has to resort to force and the intoxication of the masses through lies and propaganda." *Cf.* Wilhelm Röpke, *Jenseits von Angebot and Nachfrage* (Erlenbach-Zürich: Eugen Rentsch, 1958) p. 165. "Angelism" is a bloodbrother of "Monasticism."

[59] Karl Otten, a German author investigating the psychological roots of the brown tyranny, bluntly gave a crude list of the "demands by the masses to be fulfilled here and now":

(1) Ample work,
(2) Ample wages,
(3) Stable prices,
(4) Recreation and pleasure:
    (a) Stimulants and tobacco, ample and cheap.
    (b) Ample and cheap films,
    (c) Sports and opportunities for betting,
    (d) Sexual pleasures, great variety, prior to and
        during marriage with no restrictions by judges,
        priests, or any other authority.

Cf. his *A Combine of Aggression, Elite and Dictatorship* (London: Allen and

Unwin, 1942), p. 299. Franz Zweig's *Labour, Life and Poverty*, (London: Gollancz, 1948) which contains seventy-five interviews with members of Britain's laboring class, is a confirmation of Otten's views. The rule and prevalence of materialistic mediocrity, however, is always fostered by the democratic prelude to totalitarian tyranny. John Stuart Mill emphasized this in his *Representative Government*, (London: Dent, Everyman's Library, 1926), pp. 265-266: "The natural tendency of representative government, as of modern civilization, is toward collective mediocrity, and this tendency is increased by all reductions and extensions of the franchise." On one hand this might foster the rise of a wealthy party oligarchy with little education and taste. According to a West German statistic, among the Bundestag deputies in Bonn there are twenty-one millionaires, eight belonging to the CDU, seven to the Free Democratic Party and *six Socialists*. *Cf. Die Krone*, vol. 12, no. 18 (September 15, 1964). On the other hand we see that materialistic masses are voting for extreme leftist parties without believing in their program or aims—just as means to "frighten" and to blackmail the entrepreneurs. This is the situation in Italy where the Communist vote in the last fifteen years has been rising steadily but party membership and the sale of Communist papers had continuously decreased. In 1954 the PCI had 2,145,000 members and about six million voters; in 1963 there were 1,615,000 members and 7.8 million voters. *Cf. Süddeutsche Zeitung*, March 14-15, 1964, p. 2. Physical wellbeing, not ideology seems to be increasingly the determining factor. Yet it matters very little whether Communist majorities are due to confused minds or of mere cupidity. The results are equally disastrous.

[60] The only safeguards against the megalomania of rulers are (1) their conviction that they owe their exalted position to mere accidentals and (2) a burning theistic belief.

[61] Geheimrat Alfred Hugenberg, a wealthy entrepreneur, was the chairman of the somewhat pseudoconservative *Deutschnationale Volkspartei* which allied itself fatally with the Nazis. Hugenberg, even more so than Brooklyn-born Hjalmar Greeley Schacht, looked like the very caricature of the German *bourgeois* and came to regret bitterly his policy twenty-four hours after Hitler had become Chancellor. At that time he admitted to Carl Goerdeler, the martyred resistance fighter, "I committed yesterday the greatest stupidity of my life, I have allied myself with the world's greatest demagogue." *Cf.* Gerhard Ritter, *op. cit.*, pp. 65-66. The silly *Geheimrat* was indeed a worthy counterpart to the stupid Captain Franz von Papen.

[62] Düsterberg, one of the leaders of the *Stahlhelm*, was made to quit before the death knell was dealt to this league: the Nazis had found out that he had a Jewish great-grandfather (who, by the way, had been a soldier in the War of Liberation, 1812-1815).

[63] Such was the case not only in Germany (the *Harzburg Front*), but also in Japan, though in a much milder form. Another analogy can be found in the twentieth-century history of Indochina where conservative forces, hostile

to the foreign colonizers and aiding (in some sort of national fervor) "national socialism" and "national communism," were completely eclipsed and suppressed. For the sake of appearances the Viet Cong, rejecting fiercely this label, hypocritically still calls itself the Viet Minh (*Front de Liberation Nationale*).

[64] Often we encounter medieval representations of the "Synagogue" as a blindfolded female figure whereas the "Church" clearly can see. (Bamberg Cathedral is a good example.) Yet in beauty and nobility they are equal. And, as a matter of fact, in countries with a *very* ancient Christian tradition Jews were actively aided in this century of persecution. This is especially true of the Western Mediterranean. *Cf.* Dino Buzzati, "Perchè una foresta in Israele ha il nome di un Italiano non Ebreo," *Il Nuovo Corriere della Sera*, vol. 80, no. 91, April 17, 1955, p. 3.

[65] There are a variety of reasons for this state of affairs, which are of a religious, sociological, historical, "statistical," and racial nature. Nor should the fact be overlooked that the Jews originally are a Mediterranean people.

[66] This mistake is often made in the United States, more rarely in the Argentine where anti-Jewish feelings have not only been increased by Nazi immigrants, but also by the forcible abduction of Eichmann from Argentine territory, an insult to a nation extremely sensitive about its sovereignty. The Eichmann trial did not resuscitate a single murdered Jew: it gave, on the other hand, a powerful impulse to anti-Jewish feelings in a rather large and important country. As far as one can see today, it did more harm than good.

[67] One cannot help but quote here Georges Bernanos, the Kierkegaard of our age: "I have dreamt about the saints and the heroes, neglecting the intermediary forms of our species, and I am aware of the fact that these hardly exist in reality and that only the saints and the heroes count. The intermediary forms are a paste, a mash: he who takes a handful of it, knows all the rest and this jelly would not even deserve a name if the saints and heroes would not provide it with one, with the name 'man.' In other words: it is the saints and the heroes who have in the past peopled my dreams and have preserved me from illusions." *Cf.* Georges Bernanos, *Les enfants humiliés* (Paris: Gallimard, 1949), pp. 199-200. All this contradicts the egalitarian mania prevalent in Western civilization, but C. G. Jung was right when he said that egalitarianism is always the result of a naive, primitive, and childish mind. *Cf.* his *Wirklichkeit der Seele* (Zürich: Rascher, 1947), p. 35. Hence "simple" conditions favor democracy; emergencies, however, demanding greater maturity soon prove detrimental to it. Hence also the extraordinary importance of prosperity for the democratic system. *Cf.* Carl L. Becker, *Modern Democracy* (New Haven: Yale University Press, 1941), pp. 13-14. For the same reason *optimism* becomes the life-blood of democracy—in a collective as well as in a personal form. Horatio Alger and Mickey Mouse symbolize thus the "little man's" typical chance in a democratic society. *Cf.* C. Wright Mills, *White Collar:*

The American Middle Classes (New York: Oxford University Press, 1951), p. 337. A different idea has been expressed by Vianna Moog in his *Bandeirantes e Pioneiros*. He thinks that the minor tragedies of Donald Duck are more "realistically American" than Mickey Mouse.

[68] Klemens von Klemperer insists that in the nineteenth century conservatives and liberals had not been brothers, but still cousins. They had gentlemen's agreements and did not represent *systèmes absolus*. (*Op. cit.*, p. 11.)

[69] *Cf.* Note 39 of this Chapter. It seems that the term has been used before Mohler by Hugo von Hofmansthal, Austrian poet and playwright (1874-1929). See also p. 373 on Horkheimer.

[70] Nor can the Pope be treated that way, and yet he is officially the *servus servorum Dei*, "servant of God's servants." Permanence, however, helps to breed power. Power in its legitimate place obviously is as Jarcke said, a "necessary evil." And he added, "Power which cannot possibly be abused just is not power." (*Op. cit.*, vol. 4, no. 28, p. 156.)

[71] Hence the curious but well explainable fact that many Europeans collect gold, hoard gold coins, hide them in their homes, or even bury them. Interestingly enough this is forbidden in the United States, as it is in the USSR. Man should face the state without reserves to fall back on and the value of his money (bankbills) should be under the control of the State. Here democratic totalitarianism and democratic envy meet halfway. The democratic tendency to expropriate the rich was as strong in antiquity as it is today. *Cf.* Aristotle, *Politics*, VI, 1, 12.

[72] Friedrich Engels, who believed that the democratic republic was the ideal starting point for a Socialist-Communist state, nevertheless poked fun at its principle: "The idea that somebody's liberty consists in voting and saying, 'Look, now I control the twenty-thousandth part of a speaker in our National Blathering Institution' . . . this sort of notion I consider one of the best jokes in the world." *Cf.* Marx-Engels, *Kritische Gesamtausgabe*, vol. 1, p. 536. Dr. Johnson was right when he spoke with contempt about the vote and insisted that all that mattered to him was habeas corpus.

[73] Herr Fischer-Karwin organized in Vienna a most devastating general quiz for the Austrian Radio Network a few years ago. (Even the university students showed an appalling ignorance.) The Germans are by no means better to judge by the quiz organized by the "Allensbach Institute" in the spring of 1953. *Cf. Der Rheinische Merkur*, May 1, 1953. On October 28, 1952, the *Süddeutsche Zeitung* (Munich) published the result of a question put to fifty people about the meaning of the then hotly debated European Defense Community. Only eight out of the fifty people knew the answer. Of the sixteen women and girls questioned only one seemed informed. In December 1952 another German demoscopic organization, E.M.N.I.D., asked 2,100 Germans about the *Bundestag,* the equivalent of the House of Commons or the American House of Representatives. Less than half were able to provide a correct answer (61 percent of the men, 25 percent of the women). Among the public officials

21 percent proved to be ignorant. *Cf. Das ganze Deutschland*, May 24, 1952. Elmo Roper's Public Opinion Research Institute declared that among the American citizenry 10.3 percent can be called "politically very active" as far as their information and interests go, 16.8 percent "active," 34.6 percent "rather indifferent," and 38.3 percent "very indifferent." Asked which Senator they considered most praiseworthy, 33 percent of the "very active" failed to name one. When invited to point out the one most negative member of the Senate, 51 percent were "speechless." The Gallup Poll in 1951 offered six questions to a large variety of citizens: Where lies Manchuria? Where Formosa? What is the meaning of the 38th parallel? What is the Atlantic Pact? Who is Chiang Kai-shek? Who is Tito? All those questioned read newspapers daily and listened to the radio, and the questions asked pertained to problems dealt with in the headlines. Only 12 percent could answer all questions, 19 percent were not able to produce a single correct answer. (To one full third the Marshall Plan was unknown, and 34 percent had no idea who was then Secretary of State—Dean Acheson.) Under these circumstances one can easily imagine what the general political knowledge of the Cambodians, Vietnamese, Tanzanians, and Cameroonians is like. *Cf.* Winfried Martini, *Das Ende aller Sicherheit*, pp. 119ff. One of the men demonstrating against President Nixon in Salzburg told the Austrian radio when asked why he was "marching" (May 19, 1972): "Everybody knows that America is an imperialist nation which exploits the workers and peasants of Vietnam." Wall Street will be happy to know this. Under primitive conditions democracy might therefore be perfectly natural, i.e., in a state and society where the problems are simple. The very primitive societies are usually democratic. *Cf.* my *Freiheit oder Gleichheit?* note 526. Also Bronislaw Malinowski, *Kultur und Freiheit*, trsl. E. Heinze (Vienna-Stuttgart: Humboldt Verlarg, 1951), pp. 212-229.

[74] This, of course, raises the question why one denies the vote to the seventeen-year-old ones, to those of sixteen, ten years or even less. If knowledge, experience, and character are not imponderabilia for the vote, why an arbitrarily set age limit? Yet the one-man-one-vote dogma is so sacred today that a great many idealists propagated a crusade against Rhodesia requiring everybody to have at least six years of elementary schooling and an income of 28 dollars a month in order to be eligible for the vote. On the voting mania *cf.* also Eugenio Vegas Latapie, *Escritos Políticos* (Madrid: Cultura Espanola, 1940), pp. 183-185; Gaetano Mosca, *Teorica dei governi e governe parlamentare* (Turin: Loescher, 1887).

[75] Unemployment, then rampant in Germany, has often been used as an "explanation" for the political radicalism of the dying Weimar Republic. Yet unemployment was also rampant in the United States in 1932 and it resulted merely, a year later, in the election of Franklin D. Roosevelt who emerged as a victor on a very moderate platform. The *New Deal* came later. There is an innate extremism in the Continental character (Particularly in the South and East European character) which the English-speaking nations do not

share. Halifax, in his *Character of a Trimmer*, wrote almost 300 years ago: "Fundamentals are dangerous. There are some issues in life which are better left sleeping: we will raise only the issues on which we may disagree without imperiling our country, and even on them we will disagree with buttons in the foils." *Cf. The Character of England*, Sir Ernest Barker, ed. (Oxford: Clarendon Press, 1947), pp. 558-559.

[76] Presidential or parliamentary elections with photogenic candidates have a strongly erotic (rather than sexual) aspect in this age f television. Here comes into action what Ernst Jünger calls *der flüchtige Eros*, "fleeting Eros." The attraction of a male candidate for the ladies and of his wife for the men might be of crucial importance in a narrow vote. A deep, melodious voice or a pair of good legs might be worth 100,000 votes. (Just as a poor show on the television screen might be catastrophic even to one of the few good men entering a political career today.)

[77] *Cf.* Pascal, *Pensées*, part 1, art. 10, no. 13.

[78] *Cf.* Eliseo Vivas, "On the Conservative Demonology," *Modern Age*, vol. 8, no. 2 (Spring 1964), pp. 119-133. These errors, however, make tradition not superfluous. On the necessity of tradition *cf.* Eugenio Vegas Latapie, *Romantic ismo y Democracia* (Santander: Cultura Española, 1938), p. 147; Vázquez Mella, speech of May 17, 1903, in *Vázquez Mella*, Rafael Gambra, ed. (Madrid: Publicaciones Españolas, 1953), pp. 65-69; Josef Pieper, "Bemerkungen über den Begriff der Tradition," *Hochland*, vol. 49, June 1957, pp. 401-413, and J. Pieper, *Tradition als Herausforderung* (Munich: Kösel, 1963), pp. 11-35.

[79] *Cf.* Eliseo Vivas, *loc. cit.*, p. 121. Armin Mohler in "Konservativ 1969," p. 97, similarly insists that the crucial question for all conservatives is this: "What is there to keep? What to drop?"

[80] Interestingly enough, relativism not only colors the intellectual scene of the English-speaking countries, but also of India—to be more precise, of India since roughly the sixteenth-seventeenth century. Today the visiting philosophy professor from the United States or Britain is often highly welcome in India (and other parts of Asia)—and this not merely because he speaks the only idiom understood by educated people in all parts of the country but because he is a relativist. *Cf.* also *Hinduismus und Christentum*, J. Neuner, ed. (Vienna: Herder, 1962), pp. 235ff. Also Raimundo Panikkar, "Zur Einführung in die indische Weltanschauung," *Stimmen der Zeit*, vol. 170, no. 9 (June 1962), pp. 177-185, and Jacques Albert Cuttat, *op. cit.*, pp. 30-31.

[81] *Cf.* Chapter XIV, Note 12 and p. 385. Compare with Kierkegaard's outcry: "Personality is aristocratic—the system a plebeian invention: with the help of the system [that omnibus] everybody can get about." *Cf. The Journals of Soren Kierkegaard*, no. 29, p. 519. Excellent on this matter is the Hungarian exiled philosopher Tibor Hanák in his *Ideológiák és korunk* (London: Szepsi Csombor Kör, 1969), especially pp. 7-26. He points out that even anti-ideologism is an ideology. Marx himself furiously ranted against ideologies, but his disciples know much better.

[82] As a matter of fact, the enemy could prepare the great attack on the United States precisely on the day of a presidential election, thus *also* creating a very involved Constitutional problem. Remember the Hungarian Revolution and the Suez War exploding—on October 26 and 31, 1956—just a few days before the presidential election in November. The confusion was indescribable, and it might have been even worse (though this is difficult to visualize) had President Eisenhower not been reelected and if another man (Adlai Stevenson) had been scheduled to take over in the near future.

[83] John Adams reports that William V of Orange, Stadhouder of the Dutch Republic, after studying the American Constitution in 1788 told him bluntly: *"Monsieur, vous allez avoir un roi sous le titre de président—*Sir, you are going to have a king with the title 'president.' " Cf. *The Works of John Adams*, Charles F. Adams, ed. (Boston: Little, Brown, 1851), vol. 6, p. 470. Here it must be realized that deep into the nineteenth century the leading minds in political science were in favor of monarchical government (or mixed government with a monarchical head.) This was also the opinion of theological minds—Catholic, Lutheran, Calvinist, Anglican. Jaime Balmes defended monarchy in eloquent words. *(Obras completas,* vol. 30, pp. 153-154), but so did the luminaries of the Reformed faith which he had attacked so strongly (and not always too wisely).

[84] *Vide* Herbert Hoover's speech at the American University, reported in the *Chicago Sunday Tribune*, March 25, 1951, p. 11ff; Ralph Adams Cram, *The End of Democracy* (Boston: Marshall Jones, 1937), pp. 216-217. Albert Jay Nock too turned sharply against political amateurism. *Cf.* his *Our Enemy the State* (New York: Morrow, 1935) p. 136. The antiexpert stand of American conservatives is predominantly (but not solely) the result of the conquest of the American administrative machinery by leftist parochialists who *pose* as an intellectual elite. Of course, formal ignorance plus common sense is still better than half an education with intellectual blindness. On the necessity of placing these intellectually more qualified in commanding positions (*praeeminentia intellectus)* in the thought of St. Thomas, *cf. Summa contra gentiles,* lib. 3, c. 79; *Ibid.*, lib. 3, c. 81; St. Thomas, *Summa Theologica*, II, II, 10, art 1. Resp. St. Thomas was convinced that the four worst sufferings of man are: to lie in sickness, to live in great poverty, to be in prison and to be subjected to a stupid master. *Cf.* his *Opusculum*, 64, c. 6. *Cf.* also Jacques Zeiller, *L'idée de l'état dans saint Thomas d'Aquin* (Paris: Félix Alcan, 1910) especially pp. 19-20.

[85] *Cf.* Eduard von Hartmann, *Zur Zeitgeschichte: neue Tagesfragen,* Alma von Hartmann, ed. (Leipzig: Kröner, n.d.), pp. 14-15. This problem, admittedly, is not as simple, democracy having greater and lesser *local* affinities. In this domain American and British influence on the Continent were fatal, (though based on pure motives). A good analysis of the nature of this influence we find in the work of the French Calvinist René Gillouin—*Aristarchie ou Recherche d'un Gouvernement* (Geneva: Cheval Ailé, 1946), pp. 201-202.

⁸⁶ Proudhon, father of socialism but truly independent in his thinking, has warned us that "those we call 'the people' are always necessarily the least advanced which means the most ignorant, the most cowardly, the most ungrateful part of society." (*Correspondence*, V, 3, letter dated December 2, 1852, addressed to Madier-Monjau). In another letter he insisted that it is the greatest crime to idolize and to flatter this ignorance. If democracy really were reasonable it would have to be preceded by "demopedy." *Cf.* Emmanuel Mounier, *Liberté sous conditions* (Paris: Seuil, 1946), pp. 213-214. Mounier added that democracy can easily become *cratie du nombre*, power of numbers, which is the opposite of a republic (p. 217). Yet how could one prevent it?

⁸⁷ The Nazis and the Soviets, for purely ideological reasons, have again and again fired, expelled or murdered first rate experts because they did not "fit in" ideologically. (If the Nazis, like the Fascists until 1938, had had no anti-Jewish bias, history might have taken a very different turn.) Yet democratism—as an ism—was near fatal to the Western Powers, especially so to the United States. When back in 1945 the Soviets invited German technologists to a life in luxury, all the Americans offered them at first was work behind barbed wire in the United States, apart from their families, at a straight six dollars a day. Yet even this step was protested by the "League for the Prevention of World War III" through open letters in American dailies, and one still sincerely wonders who the men behind this spurious association really were. They certainly served the interests of the Soviet Union.

⁸⁸ A startling display of ignorance happened at the interrogation of Mr. Maxwell H. Gluck who was nominated United States ambassador in Ceylon. This president of a chain store had valiantly contributed to the funds of the Republican Party. Cross-questioned by a Senate committee, he had to confess that he did not know the name of the president of either Ceylon or neighboring India. *Cf. New York Times*, August 1, 1957, cited by Richard Hofstadter, *op. cit.*, pp. 10-11.

Sir Ernest Barker is right when he insists that "when the service of the state had been made a science elsewhere, Professor Pollard had remarked, Englishmen still preferred to consider it a task for intelligent amateurs." *Cf.* his *Traditions of Civility* (Cambridge, England: University Press, 1948), p. 149. Sir Ernest thinks that this is a piece of Renaissance inheritance, and even in this he is right. The crisis of amateurism came when the *scienda* so brutally overtook the *scita* and when the Renaissance notion of the amateur (who is a "lover") was replaced with Roussellian optimism and democratic indifference toward truth and knowledge. *The amateur also was a student*, though not necessarily a systematic one and he was not beset by "beastly earnestness" (*tierischer Ernest*), the besetting vice of "little men." The amateur is an aristocrat according to the definition of Michel de St.-Pierre: "Un aristocrate est d'abord celui qui parle avec légèreté des sujets graves." *Cf. Les aristocrates* (Paris: La Table Ronde, 1954), p. 202.

American films and comic strips love to feature the successful amateur—the man who never sat in a plane, jumps into the cockpit, almost kills himself but finally gets the Silver Cup and the girl. This sort of hero of the preindustrial and prescientific civilization is really obsolete. His time, *most unfortunately*, is past.

[89] Richard Hofstadter, in *op. cit.*, p. 46, cites a passage of B. R. Hall's *The New Purchase or Seven-and-a-Half Years in the Far West* (originally published in 1843) in which that author tells how, in frontier life, smartness and wickedness, incompetence and goodness were equated. Cotton Mather in his *Pouring Out of the Seven Vials* (London, 1642) recounts that "the more learned and witty you be, the more fit to act for Satan," and that intellectuality leads to the "learning of the Jesuits." This strong identification of evil and intelligence belongs integrally to American folklore, and it appears often in the comics where we see "crazy professors" diabolically torturing innocent maidens on weirdly wired operating tables. I am convinced, however, that this democratic opposition against *knowledge* (which is intrinsically esoteric-aristocratic) does have a "Protestant" root or, rather, a "Low Church" origin. The notion that there are religious truths and insights, theological verities, and cognitions accessible only to the serious student, the scholar, is unacceptable to a *certain* post-Reformation "Protestant" outlook—hence the notion that everybody can understand Holy Scripture unaided. Yet the understanding of large parts of Holy Scripture is immensely difficult. And nobody knows this better than, paradoxically enough, the Bible scholars of the Reformation faiths who were the pioneers of modern Biblical studies.

On the other hand, it is untrue that Luther believed in "private interpretation," a myth believed widely in Britain and in America. How this myth arose we can read in Albert Hartmann S.J., *Toleranz und christlicher Glaube* (Frankfurt: J. Knecht, 1955), pp. 11-12, and in W. E. Zeeden, *op. cit.*, vol. 1, p. 20. Luther felt to be inspired and filled with a divine light; however, he did not concede these properties easily to others. His religious outlook was basically authoritarian.

[90] The Twenty-Second Amendment, limiting the President to two terms, was favored by American conservatives because: (1) they are tradition conscious, and (2) because this particular tradition had been broken by the rather leftist Franklin D. Roosevelt. Yet it makes no sense to remove an amateur after, at long last, he has mastered his job. The removal of Adenauer was quite a calamity for Germany and in spite of our severe criticism of Churchill we would have preferred to see him in office after mid-1945. Yet there is also the question whether the masses really prefer the expert to the dilettante. Renan said that "placed between the quack and the serious physician the people will always go to the quack." *Cf.* Ernest Renan, *Oeuvres complètes*, Henriette Psicharia, ed. (Paris: Calmann-Lévy, 1949), vol. 3, p. 1109. Still there also exists a yearning for mediocrity in politics. A British author in 1929 wrote the fallacious but soothing words terminating his treatise on democracy: "But the ice-age is passing: For not only by new laws or new institutions, but also

by the acts of Nobodies the democratic ideal becomes daily more operative and the minds of men are freed from fear. In the hands of the Nobodies is the hope of the future." *Cf.* C. Delisle Burns, *Democracy, Its Defects and Advantages* (London: Allen and Unwin, 1929), p. 212. This reminds me of a conservative friend who once argued that he would prefer to be ruled by the first 500 people in the telephone book rather than by "intellectuals" like the faculty members of the University of X. Viewed superficially, this seems a counsel of despair. However, professors nowadays are by no means in their vast majority intellectuals but rather educators, compilers, examiners, and administrators.

[91] A very typical case was that of Felix Somary's book *Democracy at Bay* published 1952 by A. Knopf in New York. This is a translation of his *Krise und Zukunft der Demokratie* which originally came out in Switzerland. Somary was a financial expert and banker of Jewish (Austro-Hungarian) extraction, married to a Countess Demblin, a Swiss citizen of great political acumen and benefiting from his international connections. His book is not deep or scholarly, but wise, brilliant, and witty. Its message is frankly "libertarian" and—antidemocratic. I was most interested to see how this excellent book fared in the United States. It seems to have been reviewed only by one paper—*The Nation*—with a very few negative remarks. Not even the backing of such an important publisher such as Knopf could save the book in face of the Establishment. Friedrich Heer in his *Grundlagen der europäischen Demokratie der Neuzeit* (Vienna: Frick, Unesco, Schriftreihe, 1953) pp. 86-87, could write about the "Inner Inquisition" of European Paleoliberalism in the nineteenth century which "no longer was manipulated by Kings, Popes, or Orders," but by society itself, which excluded all "outsiders," all nonconformists, condemning all those who do not subscribe to its formulas, judgments, and tabus. *The life history of many artists and great writers, even of a few scholars and inventors of the nineteenth century is the history of heroic efforts to resist this "Inner Inquisition" and its silent, but fast-working tribunals.* (Herr's emphasis.) This "Inner Inquisition" is very often conducted by writers and critics who always play important parts in revolutions. (Here one ought to remember the crucial role of *literati* in the preparation of the Russian Revolution: "Bolshevism" really begins with Chernyshevski.) Alexis de Tocqueville saw this menace in his "L'Ancien régime et la Révolution" where he said: "We will see a new and terrible thing in this world, an immense revolution in which the most illiterate and brutal classes will play a tough role and whose leaders will be *gens de lettres.*" *Cf. Oeuvres complètes*, J. P. Mayer, ed., vol. 2, p. 336. There are obvious psychological reasons for this state of affairs.

[92] Which they do not always do. Conservatives in so many domains of American life still adopt clichés as if they were inverted leftists. Since the non-Marxist American leftist often raves about modern art (which, as every art, can be beautiful, mediocre, a terrible failure, or even downright diabolic), the American "conservative" occasionally falls for the line that modern art

is "leftist." Thus Representative George Dondero of Michigan repeatedly attacked modern art as "communistic." But, first of all, it is outlawed in the Soviet Union and, second, it is highly undemocratic, highly esoteric, which is not only true of modern painting and sculpture but also of modern poetry. The fine arts are actually, even if subconsciously, revolting against the "dear people." This does not mean that we do not have a "modern art" (as, for instance, the nonobjective school) which at best is merely "decorative art" or such pseudoart which cleverly takes advantage of the ignorant snob. Modern art, indeed, is an affirmation of the private or semiprivate world. In its perfection it is an extremely difficult achievement. Those who insist that a five-year-old boy could practice it, should take brush and colors and get going. Yet, as all higher art, it admittedly gives splendid opportunities to the phony and the faker.

[93] *Cf.* Carey MacWilliams, "Moving the West-Coast Japanese," *Harper's*, September 1942, particularly pp. 363, 366.

[94] *Cf.* my *Amerika-Leitbild im Zwielicht*, pp. 53-79.

[95] This is true if we compare the European countries: the more "progressive" they are, the more race-conscious they will be. (What seems to be race-consciousness in Eastern Europe are actually religious or ethnic prejudices. In Imperial Russia the converted Jew immediately became a full citizen and Pushkin figured as a *dvoryanin*, a nobleman, not as a "nigger.") "Progress" in the Moslem World was accompanied by a frightening rise of intolerance of all sorts. To be a Greek, an Armenian, a Copt, a Kurd, a Jew, or an "Assyrian" 200 years ago was much better than it is today. In this area too our blessed twentieth century has seen the most fiendish massacres. The first genocidal crime was carried out in this century in Armenia by the young Turks, the "Turkish Committee of Union and Progress" of leftist character.

The percentage of persons belonging to another race has little to do with the degree of racism. There are at least twice as many people of part African origin in Brazil than in the United States, yet racist feelings are stronger there than among the Brazilians. (And maybe they are *really* stronger in Chicago and Detroit than in Charleston and New Orleans.) "Eurasians," very scarce in China, had a most miserable time, particularly in the universities where their fellow students often persecuted them mercilessly. Moslem racial tolerance is not greater or lesser than that of Christians (where the different denominations have different records). In this age more Negroes have been slaughtered by Arabs (in the Sudan) than by any lily-white group elsewhere. (But Moslem Arabs have been murdered *en masse* by Negroes in Zanzibar.) Yet "African solidarity" prevents this information from being appropriately dealt with in the press of "emerging" African states. All this should help to dispel the notion of anything like automatic progress. *Cf.* Juan Valera's essay "La doctrina del progreso" written in 1859. *Cf. Obras Completas de Juan Valera* (Madrid: Enrique Prieto, 1913), pp. 63-177.

[96] Professor Donald Pierson thinks that racial intolerance is Catholic

rather than "Protestant," but his explanatory arguments to the effect that Catholics are more "communitarian" and the adherents of the Reformed faiths more "individualistic" is totally erroneous. The truth is the other way round —apart from the fact that an individualist is relatively unconcerned about his qualities, physical or otherwise, of his neighbor. *Cf.* Donald Pierson, *Negroes in Brazil, A Study of Race Contact at Bahia* (Chicago: University of Chicago Press, 1942), pp. 193-194.

[97] In theory the USSR is a federation of states; in practice Russification is pushed everywhere.

[98] Not such a long time ago an attempt was made to extinguish the local privileges of Navarra, but energetic demonstrations made the Madrid government change its mind. In Italy the Communists favor regionalism because, being very strong in specific areas, they hope thus to entrench themselves locally and to defy the non-Communist central power. For the same reason Spanish leftism has long supported autonomy for Catalonia. Yet nationalism (as we know from the French Revolution) will always favor centralization. It is only patriotism which delights in diversity. *Cf.* Maurice Blondel, *Patrie et humanité* (Paris: Chronique Sociale de France, 1928); Rafael Gambra, *op. cit.*, pp. 174-181.

[99] Thanks to the lacking unity of Germany and the plurality of German local dynasties, small republics and leading universities, German cultural life assumed a variety unknown in France. Whereas today French publishing is almost solely concentrated in Paris, German publishing houses of note existed in 1930 in Berlin, Jena, Leipzig, Dresden, Weimar, Frankfurt, Stuttgart, Münster, Mainz, Freiburg, Munich, and Ratisbon—today also in Nuremberg, Cologne, Hamburg, Osnabrück, Heidelberg, Würzburg, and Düsseldorf. (There are also German publishing houses in Austria, Switzerland, and Alsace.)

[100] Professor Wilhelm Röpke warned before his death against the specter of an overcentralized "United States of Europe." His fears were firmly rooted in his neo-Liberal convictions. On February 20, 1946, Pius XII addressing the diplomats accredited at the Holy See praised variety among the nations and warned against "merging them all in a grey uniformity." *Cf. Acta Apostolicae Sedis*, (vol. 38, 1946), pp. 146-147.

[101] *Cf.* Hermann Borchardt, *The Conspiracy of the Carpenters,* trsl. Barrows Mussey (New York: Simon and Schuster, 1943), p. 371. This book, though not easy to read, is the work of a genius, a Jewish convert who had suffered under the Communists and the Nazis. Unfortunately it is hardly known by "conservatives" anywhere.

Chapter XXI

[1] As to the "dialogue" so warmly recommended by the Second Vatican Council, one has to distinguish between dialogues which might really enrich

both sides and help to bring the partners nearer to each other in mind and heart, and dialogues which have merely an explorative character and serve "research." The genuine dialogue is possible only on the basis of a common denominator. A dialogue between an atheistic nihilist and a theist can produce valuable psychological insights, not a *rapprochement*. Or could they finally agree that there exists only "half a God"? (Nobody has yet proposed a fruitful dialogue between Nazi extermination camp commanders and members of the World Council of Churches.)

[2] The only monument to democracy I have ever seen I found in Bangkok. This, however, does not mean that Thailand is Exhibit "A" of formal democracy. On the other hand, this is also a piece of lip-service in stone to the ideological American export drive to the "imperialism" inherent in American political thinking. *Cf.* David C. Williams, "The New American Revolution," *The Twentieth Century*, August 1951, pp. 119-127. The force of this drive lies in the expectation that the *material* living standards of the United States might be the natural reward for accepting American political ideals. This superstition is quite common.

[3] The régime of "Papa Doc" Duvalier, leaning heavily on Voodoo, engaged in the most delirious atrocities. Fort Dimanche (near Port-au-Prince) was its Auschwitz and the Tontons-Macoutes its SS. This government based on superstition and terror had been established (with some U.S. aid because Papa Doc is after all an American-trained physician) in the Western Hemisphere's second nation to achieve independence and to throw off its "colonial yoke." Involuntarily we have to ask ourselves whether Haiti is not perhaps a prefiguration of African rule 150 years hence. Certainly the naked body of a murdered political antagonist, tied to a chair in the main square of Port-au-Prince and falling apart under the tropical sun, is not a reassuring symbol for "progress in freedom."

[4] This "permissiveness" in sensual matters is not uniformly strong everywhere in the leftist world. In the Soviet orbit it plays the role of a (limited) "outlet." The Old Left is by and large puritanical, the New Left hedonistic. The free use of drugs is a postulate of the New Left. The Nazis persecuted homosexuals, but they busily undermined the stability of marriage and instituted brothels not only for the armed forces but even for many concentration camps.

[5] In the vast majority of historical works published in the United States he figures as General Erich *von* Ludendorff, probably because it seems inconceivable that a commoner had such a high rank in the old Prussian Army. (Contrary to general belief the high aristocracy played a minor role in the various German Armies after 1900 and an even lesser one in the Austro-Hungarian Army.)

[6] *Cf. Die Gottlosen*, p. 303.

[7] In Spanish: *Toda ciencia es locura, si bueno seso no la cura.*

[8] The great Prussian patriot and conservative thinker Ernst Ludwig von

Gerlach, who became a severe critic of Bismarck, always carefully distinguished between the positive and negative traditions and historic achievements of his country. Thus he always refused to call Frederick II of Prussia "Frederick the Great." *Cf.* Hans Joachim Schoeps, *Das andere Preussen* (Stuttgart: Friedrich Vorwerk, 1952), p. 36. This book—*The Other Prussia*—should serve foreign as well as German readers as a healthy corrective for the cliché concept of Prussia.

[9] There are, needless to say, situations where common sense demands a break with tradition, particularly if they are destructive to basic moral and spiritual principles which have a primacy. Constitutions, for instance, are here merely to *serve* a higher purpose. They are not ends in themselves. They can always be perverted, particularly by literal applications of their articles, laws, and by-laws ignoring their spirit. To an intelligent conservative only the sacred should be sacred, quite in keeping with the dictum: *Nihil nihi sacrum nisi sacrum.* It is perfectly legitimate for any good American (conservative or otherwise) to visualize the future of his country with a radically different Constitution. Not even the most patriotic American, while of sound mind, can conceive that his country will have the same Constitution in 2970 as in 1970. And even today there is hardly a thinking person in the United States who does not desire to change this or that aspect of the Constitution by adding something new or eliminating something old. There are relatively few monarchies in this world which have not been republics; there are even fewer republics that have not been monarchies. Reinhold Niebuhr says that "the final test of a free culture is its ability to re-examine its own presuppositions." (*Cf.* "The Unity and Depth of Our Culture, *Sewanee Review*, vol. 52, Spring 1944, p. 198.) Yet even without considering the reflective qualities of the human mind one has to maintain: *Stat Crux dum volvitur orbis*, the Cross stands while the Earth rotates.

[10] One of the oddest scenes in modern history—and certainly a symbol of the decline of our Western civilization—was that acrimonious verbal exchange between Mr. Richard Nixon, Vice President of the United States, and Comrade Nikita Khrushchev, at the American Exhibition in Moscow. They were leaning over washing machines and were wildly debating household gadgets in the light of mutually hostile ideologies.

[11] Dmitri Ivanovitch Mendeleyev, the world-famous chemical theorist, was not only violently opposed to socialism but also had no use for the introduction of parliamentarism. *Cf.* Th. G. Masaryk, *op. cit.*, vol. 2, p. 394n. The question whether democracy is able to cope with the emergencies of modern life is rarely posed. A leading German sociologist and political scientist, Eberhard Welty O.P., considers this problem "which goes to the nerve of our existence" as not yet solved. *Cf.* his "Freiheit und Ordnung in Staat und Gesellschaft," *Die neue Ordnung*, vol. 9, no. 6 (1955), p. 326. On incompatibility between science, technology and democracy *Cf.* Hans Freyer (editor) in *Technik im technischen Zeitalter* (Düsseldorf: Schilling, 1965), p. 211.

(Essay by Ernst Forsthóff). A slight sensation was caused in Germany when *Der Spiegel* (May 22, 1972), pp. 128-129, published an article by Emilio Daddario ("Demokratie und Fortschritt") in the same negative vein. The crisis no longer is a secret.

[12] There is a pertinent analysis of this problem in St. Thomas Aquinas, *Summa contra Gentiles*, book I, ch. 4.

[13] Walt Whitman felt outraged when Americans were not jubilant about the fall of the monarchy in Brazil. Certainly in this case the popular reactions were saner than those of the *"divine literatus."* Whitman obviously did not foresee the still continuing political agony of the Brazilian republic built on the principles of Auguste Comte. On the character of the old Brazilian monarchy *cf.* Joã Camillo de Oliveira Tôrres, *A Democracia Coroada, Teoria Política do Império do Brasil* (Petrópolis: Editora Vozes Limitada, 1964).

[14] The possible evil was clearly seen by Louis Veuillot in a prophetic passage written in 1859 where he talked about a German "popular emperor," elected by the people and not anointed by Christ, who would cause untold misery. *Cf.* his "Parfum de Rome" in *Oeuvres complètes* (Paris: P. Lethielleux, 1926), vol. 9. p. 357. Jacques Bainville, another French conservative, was no less perspicacious. *Vide* his article in *Action Française*, September 29, 1914, and his *Les conséquences politiques de la paix* (Paris: Nouvelle Librairie Nationale, 1920). But poor old Masaryk had typical nineteenth-century illusions. "By the war," he wrote, "Germany had actually gained. She has become a republic, she is racially homogeneous and is consequently able to pursue pacific, democratic aims." *Cf.* his *Making of a State*, H. Wickham Steed, ed. (London: Allen and Unwin, 1927), p. 376. The word "consequently" makes us really shake our heads. One has to take German extremism into account, i.e., the potentiality for either good or evil already signaled by Wilhelm von Schütze in *op. cit.*, pp. 302-303. A hundred years later D. H. Lawrence saw it. *Cf.* his "A Letter from Germany," written February 19, 1924, and reprinted in *Selected Essays* (London: Penguin Books, 1950), pp. 178-179. All the more dangerous is the present German vacuum. The Allied occupants have destroyed the few chances democracy had in Germany—obviously against their own intentions and without the majority of the Germans realizing it. Yet the vacuum is right there. *Cf.* H. C. Wallich, "The German Miracle," *The Yale Review*, vol. 44, no. 4, (Summer 1955), especially pp. 518-519.

A reaction has probably already set in. That of the New Left with its terrorists (a German edition of the *Weathermen*, the Baader-Meinhof-Gang) has received much publicity. Yet there also seems to be a rightist groundswell in the youngest generation. Cf. *Der Spiegel*, May 24, 1971, p. 177 and *National Review*, July 13, 1971, p. 758.

[15] *Cf.* Romano Guardini, *Das Ende der Neuzeit* (Würzburg: Werkbund, 1950), p. 99, and Josef Pieper, *Tradition als Herausforderung* (Munich: Kösel, 1963), pp. 332-333.

¹⁶ The same thought has been expressed by John Lukacs, *Historical Consciousness and the Remembered Past* (New York: Harper and Row, 1968), pp. 304-315.

¹⁷ Leon Samson in *The American Mind* (New York: J. Cape and H. Smith, 1932), p. 77 spoke some time ago about the intellectual estrangement from political theory in America.

¹⁸ "The lesson we are to draw from a whole is that where a majority are united by a common sentiment and have an opportunity, the rights of the minority become insecure." *Cf. Documents Illustrative of the Formation of the Union of the American States* (Washington, D. C.: Government Printing Office, 1927), p. 163.

¹⁹ *Cf.* Helmut Kuhn, *op. cit.*, p. 428, and E. v. Kuehnelt-Leddihn, *The Timeless Christian*, pp. 72-82.

²⁰ *Cf.* Paul Tillich, "Die gegenwärtige Weltsituation" in *Gesammelte Werke*, R. Albrecht, ed. (Stuttgart: Evangelisches Verlagswerk, 1959), vol. 10, p. 124.

²¹ We never get around the problem of Plato's Philosopher-King. Pius XII in his Christmas Allocution on Democracy (1944) made it clear that parliaments have to consist of an *elite (una eletta)* of "high moral character, practical experience and intellectual capacity." This, he insisted, is in a democracy a "question of life or death." *Cf. Acta Apostolicae Sedis*, vol. 27 (1945), pp. 15-16.

As to the end of democracy due to the increasing ignorance of the voters, *cf.* Denis de Rougemont, *op. cit.*, p. 249sq. Also my *Luftschlösser, Lügen und Legenden* (Vienna: Herold 1972), pp. 69-86.

²² The German trade unions, once very enthusiastic about the *Mitbestimmungsrecht* (Codetermination), now would like to see a radical reform with delegates of the national trade unions, i.e., with complete outsiders, participating in board meetings. This, of course, is inadmissible in a free market economy because competition demands secrecy in internal planning. Codetermination in Germany has helped to make the labor management-conscious and has reduced the atmosphere of egotistic collective irresponsibility so characteristic of the labor movement in many a country.

²³ The *asesores* of General Onganía, whom the dictator of Argentina called "my little parliament," consisted of ten young men between the ages of twenty-five and thirty-five. They not only acted as an advisory body but also as channels of public opinion leading to the top of the government. From such admittedly modest beginnings new constitutional forms could be developed in time. A pity that the fall of Ongania terminated this experiment. None of the military men has ever succeeded in rousing mass emotions as had Perón, who with his first wife Evita provided a true monarchical father-mother image.

²⁴ I wish that there were an English language edition of Rodrigo Fernandez-Carvajal, *La Constitución Española* (Madrid: Editoria Nacional,

634

1969), a very clear, critical, and by no means servile book of a Murcia University professor.

²⁵ *Cf.* Peter F. Drucker, *op. cit.*, pp. 241-242.

²⁶ *Cf.* Herbert Marcuse, *Psychoanalyse und Politik*, p. 47.

²⁷ *Cf.* Alexander Mitscherlich, *op. cit.*, pp. 447-448.

²⁸ Typical for these publications is a German women's magazine *Frau im Spiegel*, appealing to a lowbrow readership. The no. 9 of vol. 24 (March 1, 1969) features stories and informations on twenty members of royalty, two belonging to the aristocracy and one untitled couple. I had the privilege to watch the funeral of President J. F. Kennedy on television. This was psychologically and phenomenologically a "monarchical" event. Before their misfortunes, the Kennedys had probably come nearer than any other family to becoming an analogy to the Medicis, drugstore people whom it took 200 years to become Grand Dukes of Tuscany. Originally they also were the leaders of the populist, antiaristocratic, "democratic" party. (This is equally true of Caesar who was the nephew of Marius.)

²⁹ To be more precise 63.7 percent of the men and 67.6 percent of the women. The poll was taken by "Doxa." *Cf. Rheinische Merkur*, April 17, 1970, p. 6.

³⁰ *Cf.* Romano Guardini, *op. cit.*, p. 96.

³¹ *Der Vater Staat* is a current German expression. The implication, however, is not patriarchal—it denotes the *provider*.

³² It is the thesis of Karl Bednarik's *Die Krise des Mannes* that there is a constantly decreasing scope for male aggressiveness while woman has been (biologically) emancipated by the Pill. At the same time the number of self-employed is constantly decreasing. Real decisions are made only on the political top, in sports and in tourism. And "heroes," we would like to add, are most exclusively imported from the Third World. Still, Karl Bednarik (*op. cit.*, p. 218) believes that much of the usual hate against the father (who, today, is powerless) is now directed against the state.

³³ *Cf.* Adrien Dansette, *Histoire religieuse de la France contemporaine* (Paris: Flammarion, 1951), vol. 2, p. 643 on Ferry and Viviani, vol. 1, p. 475, and 473 on Ferry and Clemenceau; on Jaurés *cf. Dictionnaire apologétique de la foi catholique* (Paris: Beauchesne, 1911), vol. 2, col. 1781-2. The speech of Jaurés was held in the Chambre des Députés on February 11, 1895.

³⁴ The expression *un christianisme du chien battu* comes from Cardinal Jean Daniélou in his *Tests* (Paris: Beauchesne, 1968), p. 7. "The greatest danger for the future of the faith does not come today from outside attacks," he writes, "but from inside resignation." (p. 5.) This attitude is aided by a Christian masochism exaggerating the faults of the past. Yet the crimes of Christianity have been deviations and aberrations from its basic tenets; they did not belong to the *program* as in the case of the Jacobins, Nazis, and Communists.

[35] Cf. Hans Urs von Balthasar, *Spiritus Creator* (Einsiedeln: Johannes-Verlag, 1967), p. 262.

[36] Cf. Louis Bouyner, *La décomposition du catholicisme* (Paris: Aubier-Montaigne, 1968), p. 26: "To serve the world signifies nothing else, but to flatter it, as one flattered yesterday the vicar in his parish, the bishop in his diocese or as one idolized the pope on the throne of Saint Peter."

[37] Max Horkheimer said flatly: "The modern liberalization of religion, in my opinion, will lead to its end." Interview to *Der Spiegel*, p. 81. The same thing could be said about the notion of a "democratization" of the Church. Dr. Heinrich Drimmel, former Minister of Instruction in Austria pointed out the fatal error of such a plan, an error all the more so because democracy is in a grave crisis, so grave that it has to be protected with taboos. Cf. "Proteste, Revolten, Reformen" in *Die Furche*, February 8, 1969, p. 11.

[38] The danger of reducing Christianity to the level of the mere "social" (or the "collective") has clearly been seen by Simone Weil, Cf. her *L'Attente de Dieu* (Paris: Vieux Colombier, 1950), p. 197 and *Cahiers* (Paris: Plon 1953), vol. 2, p. 239 as well as *La connaissance surnaturel* (Paris: Gallimard, 1950), p. 272. She considered such evolution as practically "satanic." And surely Simone Weil was anything but "antisocial." Here we would like to remind pious Catholics who exclaim: "But what do you do then with the Social Teaching of the Church?" that a thing called *the* Social Teaching does not exist. Cf. P. Bartolomeo Sorge S.J. "E superato il concetto tradizionale di dottrina sociale della Chiesa?" in *Civiltà Cattolica*, 119 year, vol. 1, pp. 423-436. (March 1968). This author insists rightly (p. 436) that we merely should talk about "models of society with a Christian inspiration."

[39] According to the notes of an attentive listener. Such views, implying that God is nearer to Katyn and Vorkuta than to Wall Street and Detroit, were uttered by a man who had more than just a hand in writing social encyclicals. They betray the influence of leftist thought right in one of the centers of Christendom. In this connection it is worth remembering that Dr. Boris Talantov, a Russian religious leader who died (January 1971) in Kirov Jail, said in his famous manifesto that economic socialism is intrinsically bad and inferior to free enterprise. This needs emphasizing at a time when so many Christian ecclesiastics in the free world cast longing glances in the direction of socialism if not communism. Cf. Cornelia I. Gerstemmaier, *Die Stimme der Stummen* (Stuttgart: Seewald, 1971), pp. 347-348.

[40] H. U. von Balthasar has described the confrontation of a "progressive" Christian with a commissar in a brilliant and most hilarious sketch. Cf. his *Cordula oder der Ernstfall* (Einsiedeln: Johannes Verlag, 1966), pp. 111-113.

[41] Cf. Helmut Kuhn, *op. cit.*, p. 392: "To endure in skepticism is not proper to [entire] nations, and the determination to believe in nothing can only produce new heresies."

[42] Here lies the deeper meaning of Schiller's lines in "Wallenstein's Camp":

Und setzet ihr nicht das Leben ein,
Nie wird euch das Leben gewonnen sein.

[43] *Cf.* Georges Bernanos, *La liberté pour quoi faire?* (Paris: Gallimard, 1953), p. 129.

[44] *Cf.* Rousas John Rushdoony, *The Messianic Character of American Education* (Nutley, N. J.: Craig Press, 1963), p. 339: "A realistic appraisal of our time requires recognition of this grim fact: chaos is the goal of contemporary human endeavor. Chaos is thus not a threat but an objective."

Appendix

[1] *Cf.* Madame de Campan, *Mémoires sur la vie privée de Marie Antoinette* (Paris: Baudouin Frères, 1823), vol. 1, p. 234.

[2] Tuffin de la Rouërie is occasionally mentioned in the writings of the Founding Fathers. He appears, for instance, as Rouverie in Jefferson's letter to John Jay, dated August 3, 1788. *Cf. Works*, Washington Edition, vol. 2, p. 451.

[3] The purpose of the Order of the Cincinnati to whom only Americans and Europeans who had actively fought in the War of Independence could belong was "an incessant attention to preserve inviolate those exalted rights and liberties of human nature for which they have fought and bled and without which the high rank of a nation is a curse instead of a blessing." Among the European members were two princes, five dukes, two *grandees* of Spain, forty-one marquesses, eighty-two counts, twenty-three viscounts, fourteen barons. The Order became immediately suspect in the eyes of nascent American leftism. *Cf.* Philippe Sagnac, *La formation de la société moderne franderne* (Paris: Presses Universitaires, 1946), vol. 2, p. 289.

[4] *Cf.* Pierre Gaxotte, *op. cit.*, 106-107: "There reigned in the aristocracy of these two provinces [Brittany and Vendée] a curious revolutionary spirit, a mixture of love for the new and an attachment to the old institutions, a local fanaticism and an exaltation of philosophy. In Brittany . . . the humiliation of the *parlement* was felt as a violation of the contract of Duchess Anne and an attack against the independence of the Breton nation."

[5] Other letters to Washington were dispatched on October 17, 1789, January 1, 1790, and March 22, 1791.

[6] Pasteur asked why, as such a great scientist, he was so pious, replied: "Since I know as much as I know, I am as firm in my beliefs as a Breton peasant; would I know more, I would have the faith of a Breton peasant woman."

[7] *Cf.* Louis Blanc, Jacques Crétineau-Joly, *op. cit.*, p. 20. According to this text de la Rouërie was an aristocratic forerunner of the Chouannerie. The peasants, however, really started it.

[8] *Chouan* is the French word for screech-owl. The imitation of its cry was used by the counterrevolutionaries of the Vendée and of Brittany to make

contact with each other at night. The resistance movement was therefore called *La Chouannerie*.

[9] Armand Tuffin, Marquis de la Rouërie is also mentioned by Chateaubriand in his *Mémoires d'outre-tombe*, Maurice Levaillant, ed. (Paris: Flammarion, 1948), vol. 1, p. 242. The most exhaustive treatise on de la Rouërie is G. Lenôtre, *Le Marquis de la Rouërie et la conjuration bretonne* (Paris: Perrin, 1899 and 1905). Other works of value are A. Botrel, *La conspiration de Tuffin de la Rouërie* (St. Brieuc: F. Guyon, 1879): P. A. Delarue, *Une famille bretonne du douzième au dix-neuvième siècle, Charles-Armand, marquis de la Rouërie, chef de la conjuration bretonne* (Rennes: Pliton et Hervé, 1899).

Index

Lisle, Rouget de, 88
Lithuanians, 308
Lloyd George, David, 142, 149, 164, 177, 183, 203, 232, 235, 236, 237, 249, 278, 283, 284, 287, 308
Lochner, Louis P., 507n71, 557n129
Locke, John, 114
L'Oeuvre, 330
Lope de Vega, 340
López-Amo, Angel, 587n151
Lorenz, Willy, 492n4
Lortz, Josef, 515n23
Lossow, General von, 168
Lot, Ferdinand, 572n75, 574n86
Lothian, Lord (Philip Kerr), 278
Louis XIV, 34, 94, 438
Louis XVI, 88, 94, 267, 415, 437
Louis XVIII, 110
Louis-Philippe, 127, 128
Loveday, Arthur, 549n83
Low, David, 354
Lowell, James Russell, 119
Löwith, Karl, 515n29
Lubac, Henri de, S.J., 122, 124, 477n4, 478n20
Ludendorff, General Erich, 137, 150, 168, 335, 415, 631n5
Ludwig I, Emperor, 51
Lueger, Dr. Karl, 305
Lukács, John, 505n51, 634n16
Lukas, J. Anthony, 606n16
Lumumba, Patrice, 343, 352, 357, 369
Luther, Martin; Lutheranism, 51, 55, 89, 93, 102-103, 155, 169-170, 176, 186, 193, 209, 217, 218, 239, 256, 279, 382, 455n25, 471n2,4,8,9; 484n71, 501n35, 581n118, 611n11
Lyons, Eugene, 202, 205, 259, 260, 487n5, 513n4

MacArthur, Gen. Douglas, 335
Macartney, H. A., 250, 534n7,8; 535n17
MacDonald, Ramsey, 246
Machado, Antonio, 137, 266, 483n62
Machiavelli, Niccolò, 106, 159
MacKenzie, Sir Compton, 515n28, 529n49, 568n45
MacLaughlin, Andrew Cunningham, 460n33
MacLean, Fitzroy H., 307, 572n73
MacOrlan, Pierre, 542n52
MacWilliams, Carey, 629n93
Madariaga, Salvador de, 48, 266, 457n5, 523n8, 542n49,51; 544n63, 546n72,73; 547n78, 548n81
Madeiros, Celestino, 259
Madison, James, letter to Jared Sparks 68; letter to Edmund Randolph 69, 420, 460n29,31; 461n47
Maier, Hans, 459n19
Maier, Heinrich, 452n1
Maine, Sir Henry, 447n3
Maistre, Joseph Comte de, 148, 256, 384, 485n1, 488n11, 612n16
Maistriaux, Robert, 600n19
Majority rule, 29-30, 68, 221, 325, 402
Malesherbes, Chrétien de, 88, 95, 96
Malby, 88
Malinowski, Bronislaw, 623n73
Malraux, André, 527n36
Maly Rocznik Statystyczny, 574n83
Manchester Guardian, 549n83
Manchester School, 185, 192, 193, 405
Mann, Thomas, 83, 189, 215-216, 229, 473n17, 509n11, 522n1
Mao Tse-tung, 151, 247, 380, 417
Marañón, Gregorio, 266
Marat, Jean Paul, 319, 439
Marceau-Desgraviers, 99
Marcel, Gabriel, 447n3
Marchenko, Anatoli R., 489n20
Marconi, Guglielmo Marchese, 359
Marcuse, Herbert, 373-374, 376, 421, 446n3,

605n9,11; 606n13, 608n24,27; 609n28, 635n26
Maria Theresa, 305
Mariana, Juan de, S.J., 581n118
Marie Antoinette, 436
Marinetti, Emilio, 204
Maritain, Jacques, 84, 189, 270, 459n18, 466n68, 509n9, 587n152
Marmontel, Jean François, 96
Marshall, Ray, 447n1
Marsilius of Padua, 51, 55, 453n10
Martin, Everett Dean, 451n13
Martin, Ralph G., 592n188
Martinez Gomez, Louis, S.J., 611n6
Martini, Winfried, 450n13, 532n83, 542n51, 548n79, 587n151, 614n35, 623n73
Marx, Karl; Marxism, 93, 112, 121, 123, 124-141, 163, 173, 209, 220, 257, 258, 272, 274, 284, 302, 304, 324, 327, 347, 360, 374, 375, 376, 380, 392, 397, 398, 405, 420, 478n30,31,32; 479n34,35,40,41; 481n50, 482n54, 483n63
Masaryk, Jan, 283
Masaryk, Thomas G., 156, 162, 163, 164, 240, 287, 308, 476n40,41; 492n10, 494n4, 529n54,55; 530n57, 612n19, 632n11, 633n14
Maser, Werner, 497n15
Massie, Robert K., 489n13
Mather, Cotton, 627n89
Mathiez, Albert, 74, 462n10
Matthews, Herbert L., 262, 270, 276, 552n98
Matthews, W. R., 560n148
Matthys, Jan, 56
Maurois, André, 469n114
Maurras, Charles, 42, 113, 159, 256, 393, 395, 616n45
May, Eduard, 514n13
Mayer, F. E., 595n202
Maynard, Theodore, 476n38, 521n73
Mayo, H. B., 520n49
Max, Alphons, 608n25, 609n28
Maximilian, Emperor, 153, 194
Maxwell, Clerk, 359
Mazzini, Giuseppe, 240, 393, 411
McCall's, 318
McCarthy, Sen. Joseph, 316
McConville, Maureen, 608n24
McCormick, Anne O'Hare, 304, 592n187
McCoy, Charles N., 459n18
McLeod, Ian, 558n142
McSorley, Joseph, CSP, 569n54
Mein Kampf, 168, 174, 295
Meinecke, Friedrich, 106
Meissinger, Karl August, 455n25
Meister, Albert, 599n17
Melanchthon, Philipp, 103
Mellah of Tetuan, 265
Melville, Herman, 30, 230, 449n6
Mencken, H. L., 204
Mendeleyev, Dmitri Ivanovich, 417
Mendelssohn, Peter de, 485n76, 561n153
Menéndez Pidal, Ramón, 266
Mensheviks, Menshevism, 148
Merkl, Adolph, 475n31
Metchnikov, Iliya, 417
Metternich, Prince Klemens von, 38, 42, 75, 91, 186, 234, 240, 382, 388, 389, 390, 453n4, 464n18,19; 473n18
Meyer, Frank S., 447n1
Michels, Roberto, 28, 247, 448n1, 453n7, 533n96
Migne, J. P., 447n7, 454n14, 581n118
Mihajlović, Draža, 307, 313
Mikolajczyk, Premier Stanislaw, 296, 321
Mikoyan, Anastas Ivanovich, 90
Mill, John Stuart, 387, 447n3, 620n59
Miller, John C., 65, 458n6, 458n15
Mills, C. Wright, 525n19, 617n54, 621n67
Milton, John, 217

Pyetrashevskı conspiracy, 150

Quakers, 64
Queipo de Llano y Serra, 265

Rabaut Saint-Etienne, Jean Paul, 75
Racine, Jean, 340
Racism, 166, 167, 176, 294, 325, 409, 419
Raczyński, Count Edward, 573n75
Radbruch, Gustav, 450n13
Radić, Stiepan, 252
Rager, J. C., 459n18
Raggland, 327
Rahv, Philip, *Discovery of Europe*, 73, 461n1
Ramm, Thilo, 619n57
Ranconnet de Noyan, 438, 439
Rand, Mrs., 241-242, Carrie, 242
Randolph, John, 69
Rapp, Georg; Rappites, 138
Rappard, William F., 448n2, 449n3
Rausch, Jürgen, 587n151
Rauschning, Hermann, 173, 483n64, 503n44, 45; 505n50,51
Ravachol, Franz August, 379
Rawicz, Slawomir, 576n98
Raynal, Guillaume, abbé, 88
Razumowsky, Alexander, Count, 613n30
Read, Herbert, 174, 505n53,54
Reck-Malleczewen, Fritz, 494n27, 501n32, 581n117, 590n173
Redier, Antoine, 509n6
Reel, Frank A., 327, 590n169
Reformation, 50, 55, 186, 209, 255, 256, 270, 383
Reformed Churches (Evangelical), 186, 187, 209
Reichstag, 37
Reimann, Victor, 504n45,46,47,48
Reiners, Ludwig, 481n47
Renan, Ernest, 100, 627n90
Renner, Dr. Karl, 554n104
Renstedt, C. J., 488n12
Republic, republicanism, 27, 28, 29, 61, 63, 66, 70, 157, 259, 329, 389
Republican Defense League, 271
Reuchlin, Johann, 103
Reventlow, Count E., 507n73
Reventlow-Radek negotiations, 177
Reynold, Gonzague de, 270, 513n6, 594n200
Reynolds, Quentin, 299-303, 569n50,51,52,53,57,58
Rheinische Merkur, 622n73, 635n29
Rheinische Zeitung, 126
Ribbentrop, Joachim, 289, 292, 564n14
Ribot, Alexandre, 232
Ricardo, David, 134
Ricchioni, Vincenzo, 487n2
Richelieu, Cardinal, 106
Riddell, Lord, 572n75
Riehl, Dr. Walter, 163, 165, 168
Riezler, Sigmund, 449n6
Right (political), 36, 39, 40, 41, 42, 266, 273, 377, 420, rightist concepts, 426-433, 445n1
Rimsky-Korsakov, Nicolai A., 417
Ripley, George, 119
Ritter, Gerhard, 559n147, 577n103, 578n107, 620n61
Riva-Agüero, 604n3
Rivarol, Antoine de, 335, 596n209
Robbins, Caroline, 536n25
Roberto, Holden, 94, 343
Roberts, Kenneth, *Oliver Wiswell*, 63
Robespierre, Maximilien de, 74, 78, 81, 87, 88, 93, 95, 97, 99, 100, 219, 220, 316
Robinson, Donald B., 591n181
Rocca, Massimo, 160, 492n13, 493n23, 494n24
Rochambeau, Comte Jean-Baptiste de V. de, 64
Rodriguez Casado, Vicente, 455n25
Roemer, Lawrence, 449n6, 476n38, 514n15, 520n49, 522n1

Röhm, Ernst, 175
Rolland, Romain, 241
Romains, Jules, 160, 494n27
Romanov (dynasty), 232
Rome, Roman Empire, 49, 61, 411-412
Rommel, General Erwin, 178
Roos, Hans, 572n75, 574n82, 574n86, 613n25
Roosevelt, Elliot, 450n11, 567n34
Roosevelt, Eleanor (Mrs. F.D.R.), 215, 261, 316-317, 318
Roosevelt, Franklin D., 32, 261, 262, 279, 280, 287, 294, 295, 296, 307, 310, 321, 331, 333, 365, 560n151
Roosevelt, Theodore, 233
Röpke, Wilhelm, 173, 198-199, 201, 208, 324, 450n13, 473n14, 480n45, 504n49, 511n23, 589n167, 619n58
Rosebery, Archibald Philip Primrose, 203
Rosenberg, Alfred, 176, 483n64, 517n34, 546n71
Rosenberg, Arthur, 526n20
Rosenberg, Julius and Ethel, 260, 318
Rosmini-Serbati, Antonio, 447n3, 587n151, 611n7
Ross, Colin, 262
Rothfels, Hans, 512n26, 577n105
Rouërie, Marquis de la (Charles-Armand Tuffin), 64, 77, 435-443, 637n2, 638n9
Rougemont, Denis de, 451n13, 597n7, 634n21
Rougier, Louis, 467n93,95; 518n38, 591n179,181
Roundheads, 63, 64, 183, 184, 185, 202, 386, 388
Rousseau, Jean-Jacques, 60, 84-88, 89, 111, 116, 191, 208, 214, 220, 239, 343, 466n65, 467n92
Roux, Jacques, 92, 93
Royer, Claude, 95
Royer-Collard, 186, 189, 402
Rozanov, V., 151, 490n22
Ruark, Robert, 599n17
Rudolf, Crown Prince, 194
Ruge, Arnold, 125, 126, 127, 479n38
Rugg, Harold, 494n27
Ruggiero, Guido de, 450n13, 451
Rush, Dr. Benjamin, 214, 460n36, 516n33, 517n36, 590n172
Rushdoony, Rousas John, 637n44
Russell, Bertrand, 470n122, 518n39
Russell, Dean James E., 208
Russell, Francis, 539n38
Russia, 388, 396, 417
Rusticucci, Luigi, 260
Rüstow, Alexander, 185, 198-199, 201, 455n25, 466n60, 471n5, 472n13, 508n1, 511n25, 512n27
Ruthenians (Ukrainians), 283, 308
Ryskind, A. H., 594n201

Sacco, Nicola, 259, 260
Sade, Marquis de, 21, 60, 78-83, 88, 178, 179-180, 191, 209, 213, 266, 456n55,56
Sagnac, Philippe, 76, 464n32, 637n3
Saguard, Francois M., 451n1
Saint-Brice, Marquis de, 437
Saint-Pierre, Jacques Henri de, 440, 441
Saint-Just, Louis Antoine Léon de, 87, 88, 92
Saint-Simon, Comte Henri de, 108, 109, 110, 114, 115, 116, 128
Saint-Aulaire, Comte de, 551n92
Sainte-Beuve, C. A., 460n37, 528n43
Sakharov, Konstantin W., 536n24
Salazar, Antonio de Oliveira, 260
Salvemini, Gaetano, 215
Samson, Leon, 634n17
Sanctis, Gino de, 493n20
Sand, Karl Ludwig, 390
Sandburg, Carl, 230
Sanjurjo Sacanell, General José, 264-265
San Martin, General, 62
Sartori, Giovanni, 451n13
Savoy, House of, 156, 393

652